Human Resource Management in Context

Strategies, insights and solutions

3 Edition

David Farnham

Professor David Farnham is Professor Emeritus at the University of Portsmouth, a visiting professor at the University of Greenwich and has been visiting professor at the University of East London, visiting senior research professor at the University of Glamorgan, and visiting senior research fellow at the Catholic University Leuven. David is Chief Examiner for the CIPD and member of the advisory board of the Personnel Policies Study Group of the European Group of Public Administration, Brussels. He is a board member of a housing association, commissioner of a trust port, trustee of a social enterprise, and works with colleagues locally, nationally and globally on a variety of academic and applied projects. David is a Chartered Fellow of the CIPD.

The Chartered Institute of Personnel and Development is the leading publisher of books and reports for personnel and training professionals, students, and all those concerned with the effective management and development of people at work. For details of all our titles, please contact the publishing department:

tel: 020 8612 6204

email: publish@cipd.co.uk

The catalogue of all CIPD titles can be viewed on the CIPD website:

www.cipd.co.uk/bookstore

Human Resource Management in Context

Strategies, insights and solutions

3rd edition

David Farnham

Chartered Institute of Personnel and Development

Published by the Chartered Institute of Personnel and Development,
151, The Broadway, London, SW19 1JQ

This edition first published 2010
First published 1999
Reprinted 1999, 2001, 2002, 2003 (twice), 2004
Second edition published 2005
Reprinted 2006, 2007, 2009, 2011

Typeset by Fakenham Photosetting Ltd, Norfolk

Printed in Great Britain by Pureprint Group

British Library Cataloguing in Publication Data
A catalogue of this publication is available from the British Library

ISBN 978 1 84398 259 3

cipd

Chartered Institute of Personnel and Development, CIPD House,
151 The Broadway, London, SW19 1JQ
Tel: 020 8612 6200
Email: cipd@cipd.co.uk
Website: www.cipd.co.uk
Incorporated by Royal Charter
Registered Charity No. 1079797

Contents

Contents

Figures

Tables

Preface

This text on human resource management (HRM) differs significantly from others in the field. It is not about HRM 'toolkits', which are covered in other parts of the CIPD's new professional framework and other texts. This book explores why and how the *contexts*, both external and internal, within which HR professionals operate are key drivers of HR strategies and practices in organisations and the rules and structures within which they work. Its overall aim is to provide in one source a comprehensive description, analysis and review of the concepts and theories relevant to studying these external and internal contexts and the issues they raise for the HR function. Five themes impacting upon the HR function recur throughout the text: globalisation; the competition, choice and change agenda; the search for improved performance in organisations; the ambiguities and tensions within the HR profession; and the importance of 'historical path dependency'. Path dependency explains how institutions, social structures or patterns of behaviour in the present, including the HR function, are influenced by what has happened in the past, even though past circumstances may no longer apply.

The content of the book is drawn from the 'strategy, insights and solutions' professional area of the CIPD's Human Resources (HR) Profession Map. The learning module covering this professional area is *Human Resources Management in Context* (HRMC) and the unit – 7HRC – corresponds to level 7 in England and Wales, 9 in Scotland and 1 in Ireland. It is one of four compulsory modules in the CIPD scheme at advanced postgraduate level. HRMC has links with the 'Managing in a Strategic Business Context' and 'People Management and Development' standards of the former Professional Development Scheme. The chapters of this book follow the purpose and aim, learning outcomes and indicative content of module 7HRC. The text is aimed at CIPD students and lecturers teaching in centres offering the national examination and internally assessed centres, as a resource to be used jointly. It is also aimed at students studying independently or by flexible learning and seeks to be a demanding and challenging work to its readers.

Within the HR Profession Map, the professional area of strategy, insights and solutions covers a wide-ranging field of underpinning knowledge and professional behaviours. It is concerned with understanding business activities, strategies and plans, and the underlying drivers of and barriers to sustainable organisational performance. It is also concerned with the needs of customers and employees in organisations, as well as providing unique insights for driving business performance, through creating and delivering appropriate HR strategies and solutions in organisations (CIPD 2009).

In practice, of course, the boundaries between the 'external' and 'internal' contexts of organisations are fluid and osmotic but they are helpful tools of analysis. An organisation's external and internal contexts, in turn, interact with an organisation's business and managerial contexts. These incorporate the managerial roles, organisational rules and corporate structures which facilitate organisational direction and enable managerial responses to be made to external contextual drivers.

The drivers identified here are described as 'contexts' rather than 'environments' because, with increasing concern being shown in the global eco-system and biosphere, the word 'environment' today tends to have a specific, technical meaning, rather than a business one. The term 'environment' in other words relates to the world's natural resources and not specifically to the business world. However, the concept of 'environmental scanning' continues to be used in this text wherever a series of contexts are examined analytically to determine their collective potential impacts on organisations, their activities or HR practices. The starting point of this text therefore is the recognition that HR professionals and line managers work today within complex and changing organisational contexts, whether in the market, public or 'third' sectors. This is the case whatever the size of an organisation, the types of goods or services it produces, or the customers and clients it serves. Clearly, levels of complexity and rates of change differ widely amongst individual organisations but both are realities, to varying degrees, in contemporary organisational life.

To summarise the argument so far, for analytical and heuristic purposes, a basic if elementary distinction is made in this text between the principal *external, internal* and *business and managerial* contexts of organisations, as indicated in figure P.1 below. This framework classifies these organisational contexts into three layers or clusters. A nominally outer layer identifies seven external contexts, described, in no order of priority, as socio-cultural, technological, economic, environmental, political, legal and ethical contexts (known by the acronym STEEPLE). A second, intermediate layer identifies five internal contexts, again in no order of priority. These are: the culture; layout; innovation; power, conflict and control; and social components of an organisation (identified by the acronym CLIPS). A third, central core layer identifies the business and managerial contexts of organisations. These comprise: management; managerial functions; 'modern' managerial functions; managerial power, authority and influence; managerial politics; and models of HR and relationships with employees (specified here as the '6Ms' framework).

The purpose and aim of HRMC is, first, to provide learners with an understanding of the principal external, internal and business and managerial contexts of contemporary organisations within which HR professionals, managers and workers are employed in conditions of change and uncertainty. Second, the module examines how those leading organisations respond to these dynamic contexts. Third, the module indicates how leaders in organisations, those in the HR function and line managers with HR responsibilities, need to recognise and acknowledge that corporate decisions and HR choices are not always shaped by managers alone. They are also shaped by external and internal forces beyond their immediate control. Having studied this module, learners will be aware

Figure P.1 The external, internal and business and management contexts of organisations: a framework for analysis and learning

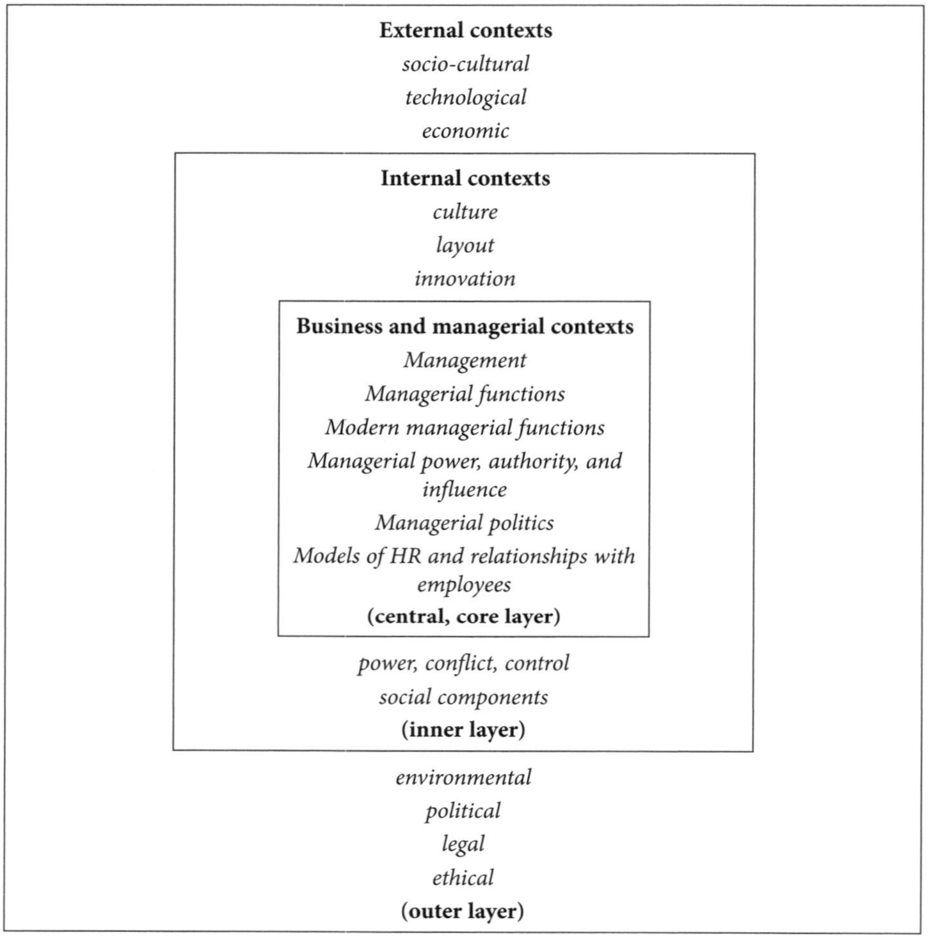

External contexts

socio-cultural
technological
economic

Internal contexts

culture
layout
innovation

Business and managerial contexts

Management
Managerial functions
Modern managerial functions
Managerial power, authority, and
influence
Managerial politics
Models of HR and relationships with
employees
(central, core layer)

power, conflict, control
social components
(inner layer)

environmental
political
legal
ethical
(outer layer)

that HR professionals and managers, in different types of organisations (large, small, national, global), in responding to their external, internal and business contexts, not only have opportunities and choices when taking organisational and HR decisions but also face constraints on their autonomy in determining their futures. This module and text also explore the implications of these contexts for professional practice and provide opportunities for applied learning and continuing professional development. It is a wide-ranging module, requiring a text that covers a lot of substantive knowledge, concepts and theories which are sometimes contradictory and contested.

The HRMC module is suitable for persons who:

- have responsibility for HR decision making within organisations at operational, tactical or strategic level

- are HR professionals in a team or HR functional management role who are seeking to enhance and develop their careers

- have specialist responsibilities for the HR function and activities within an organisation

- are independent or employed consultants who support organisations in meeting their goals

- have career and CIPD professional membership aspirations.

The learning outcomes of HRMC are to enable learners, on completion of this module, to be able to understand, analyse and critically evaluate:

- contemporary organisations and their principal, external and internal contexts

- the managerial and business contexts within which HR professionals work

- how organisational and HR strategies are developed in response to external and internal contextual factors

- the market and competitive contexts of organisations and how organisational leaders and the HR function respond to them

- globalisation and international forces, and how they shape and impact on organisational and HR strategies and HR practices

- demographic, social and technological trends, and how they shape and impact on organisational and HR strategies and HR practices

- government policy and legal regulation, and how these shape and impact on organisational and HR strategies and HR practices.

Having completed this module, those studying HRMC will be able:

- to identify, understand and analyse the major external and internal contexts within which HR professionals operate in the market, public and third sectors

- to review and critically evaluate these contexts

- to generate effective, reasoned responses to these contexts from an organisational and HR perspective

- to provide insights into the creation and delivery of effective HR strategies, practices and solutions in different national and global organisational contexts

- to reflect on their continuous personal and professional development.

The indicative content of HRMC, covered in the 10 chapters of this text, is taught and assessed at M-level standard. This means that HRMC is a conceptually demanding and intellectually stretching module. It requires postgraduate HR students to demonstrate on completion of their programme of study the following M-level performance descriptors:

- a systematic understanding of knowledge and critical awareness of current problems and/or new insights in HRM, much of which is at the forefront of this field of study

- a comprehensive understanding of the techniques applicable to their own research or advanced scholarship

- originality in the application of professional knowledge, together with practical understanding of how established research techniques are used to create and interpret knowledge

- conceptual understanding enabling students to evaluate critically both current research and advanced scholarship

- conceptual understanding enabling students to evaluate methodologies and develop critiques of them and, where appropriate, propose new hypotheses.

Typically, successful students of HRM at M-level can also:

- deal with complex HR issues both systematically and creatively, make sound judgements in the absence of complete data, and communicate their conclusions clearly to specialist and non-specialist audiences

- demonstrate self-direction and originality in tackling and solving problems and act autonomously in planning and implementing tasks at professional level

- continue to advance their knowledge and understanding, and develop new skills to a high level.

M-level students also have the qualities and transferable skills for employment requiring:

- the exercise of initiative and personal responsibility

- decision making in complex and unpredictable situations

- the independent learning ability required for continuing professional development.

This text therefore seeks to be intellectually demanding, academically robust and professionally relevant. It draws upon a wide range of literature and provides keen insights into the complex external and internal contexts of contemporary organisations within which HR practitioners and line managers operate. It is recommended that readers use it as a source of knowledge and ideas and as a stimulus to wider reading. In this way, they can make their own judgements about the subject matter and commentary within it. To complement this text, students are strongly advised to keep up to date with current strategic and contextual issues, by regularly reading the quality press and accessing the websites of relevant national, international and public organisations. Major newspapers to be examined include the *Financial Times*, *Guardian*, *Independent*, *Times* and *Daily Telegraph* and Sunday papers such as the *Observer*, *Sunday Times* and *Independent on Sunday*. Readers should also make use of *The Economist* and some key websites listed in this text.

Another feature of this text is its variety of pedagogic features. These include, in each chapter, figures (or tables) summarising key concepts or providing data sets, activities seeking understanding or application of knowledge of specific topics, questions for review, and an integrative case study. These are aimed at engaging readers, enhancing their understanding of complex issues and stimulating their learning and thinking.

Because it is written for an M-level audience, a major underpinning objective of this text is to help its readers meet this advanced level of understanding and analysis. There is considerable emphasis within it on knowledge and understanding rather than on skills and competencies, which are addressed more fully in module 7SBL, *Developing Skills for Business Leadership.*

As indicated in figure P.2, the book is divided into three parts, each linked with the professional area strategy, insights and solutions. Part 1 sets the background to the text by introducing HRM, organisations and management and providing insights into some of the contexts of the HR function. It has three chapters: HRM and its external contexts, Contemporary organisations and their internal contexts, and The managerial and business contexts of organisations. Part 2 examines strategy, reviewing it in terms of strategy formulation and implementation. It consists of two chapters: Developing corporate strategies and Developing HR strategies. Part 3 provides further insights into the contexts within which HR strategies and decisions are determined. It does this by describing and analysing the external contexts of HRM in some depth. This part of the book consists of five chapters: Markets and the competitive context, Globalisation and international factors, Demographic and social trends, The technological context, and Government policy and legal regulation.

Figure P.2 HRM in context: strategy, insights, solutions

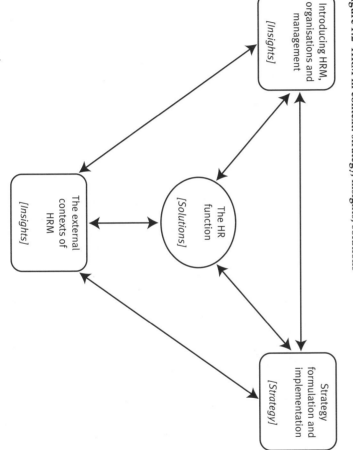

Chapter 1 provides the theoretical and practical backgrounds to the rest of the book, by giving an outline description, analysis and overview of contemporary HRM within the United Kingdom (UK) and the external contexts driving it. These contexts are identified within the framework of the strategy, insights and solutions professional area of the CIPD's HR Profession Map. The chapter starts by examining the factors influencing these developments and considers the changing nature of HRM and how it has developed historically. The key issues explored are how the HR function is organised, HR and performance, line managers and HR, outsourcing HR, HRM and ethics, and HR strategy. The chapter also summarises the major institutional, external contexts impacting on the HR function which influence HR strategy and practices. It then puts these developments into a global context by discussing trends in international HRM.

Chapter 2 explores and analyses the complex nature of contemporary organisations and the internal contexts affecting them. It starts with an examination of some theories of organisations. This is followed by a review of the types, objectives and internal contexts of organisations. The internal contexts considered are: culture; layout; innovation; power, conflict and control; and social components. The chapter also examines some current issues in organisation: old and new organisation forms, including networking and strategic alliances; integration, control and HRM; performance, profit and efficiency; and continuity and change in organisations. Finally, the chapter considers the major stakeholders in organisations and issues of corporate governance and accountability.

Chapter 3 examines the managerial and business contexts of organisations. It starts by analysing the nature of the management function and the basis of managerial power and authority in organisations, especially in relation to the search for managerial legitimacy and how managerial power is exercised. The chapter goes on to outline and review the traditional functions of management, such as finance, marketing, operations and strategy. This is followed by descriptions of risk management, quality management and customer care, and performance management. The chapter concludes by outlining some models and roles of the HR function.

Chapter 4 considers some basic ideas about strategy, strategy making and the strategic management process. With organisations operating in increasingly complex, unstable external contexts, those leading them – in the private, public and third sectors – are using techniques of strategic management. The *deterministic* view of strategy is rationalist and is concerned with assessing where an organisation is at the moment, how it got there, analysing the directions in which it might go in order to survive and prosper, determining how it can get there, and evaluating whether it has achieved its objectives. The *emergent* view is that strategy can be 'shaped', without any predetermined objectives, and that it 'emerges' over time in response to changing organisational needs. Other issues discussed are the tools and techniques of environmental analysis and factors shaping the external contexts.

Chapter 5 is a core chapter in the text, since it examines the origins of HR strategy and its links with business strategy. It analyses the development of

HR strategy in term of pre-personnel management, traditional personnel management, a development strategy for employee flexibility, and a partnership strategy of employee commitment. Another framework identifies three stages of strategic HR: the person–job fit, systemic and value creation stages. In examining contemporary HR strategy, best practice HR, best fit HR and the resource-based view of the firm, models are analysed and critically reviewed. Best practice considers which bundles of HR practices are conducive to improved performance. Best fit examines links between HR and business strategy and the external contexts of firms. The resource-based view of the firm examines strategy creation around the internal competencies and strategic capabilities of firms. The chapter concludes by exploring debates about strategic leadership.

Chapter 6 outlines some of the key issues in the UK market economy arising out of problems of economic scarcity, competition and choice. With the economic demands of people virtually unlimited, and the supply of economic resources to satisfy those demands fixed in the short term, economic choices have to be made to determine economic priorities. For the purposes of analysis, the traditional distinction between micro-economics (the economics of markets, prices, supply and demand) and macro-economics (the economy as a whole) is made. In this broad overview of economic activity, the chapter provides the setting for the other parts of the book, by touching on related issues, such as economic policy, corporate strategy and key labour market trends. The chapter concludes by analysing sources of competitive advantage.

Chapter 7 reviews the phenomenon of contemporary globalisation, the responses of market economies to globalisation, the role of multinational corporations in the global economy, major international organisations and the European Union (EU). Globalisation, which incorporates the internationalisation of economic activity as well as social, cultural and political dimensions, has implications for all organisations. It also impacts on those managing them, their workers, other stakeholders, governments, state agencies and regional supra-national bodies such as the EU. Contemporary globalisation is linked with the international spread of production systems, promoted by changing patterns of trade. Its key features are expansion of cross-border trade, growth of ICT systems, internationalisation of finance and production and the downsizing of governments and the public sector.

Chapter 8 explores the interrelated themes of demographic changes and some major social trends, mainly within the UK but including some comparative, international data. Changes in demography are important because they have implications for markets, organisations, management, the HR function and government. The demographic indicators used in this chapter are descriptive and selective, since the aim is to indicate general trends and some future projections rather than detailed and sophisticated statistical analyses. The topics focus on demographic structures, the determinants of population growth, the changing working population and immigration. The social trends explored are also selective in coverage, concentrating on changing family structures, diversity in society and organisations, and social stratification. Wider issues such as public services, changing social values and the increased secularisation of UK society are also examined.

Chapter 9 analyses some of the main technological developments taking place in the digital age and outlines their impacts on people, organisations and society. These new technologies are important because flexibility, teamwork, teleworking, networks, and distributed and virtual organisations point to radical new ways of working and organising work, based on new technological possibilities. In the era of the 'automation of automation', sometimes called cybernation, the totality of an organisation's automated operations are electronically integrated and linked together. In the past, technology transformed processes rather than producing goods or services. Today information and communication technologies (ICTs) are not only transforming processes but also producing information as an output, so that information itself is a commodity. ICTs are pervasive and are fundamentally changing the social, cultural and political spheres of society.

Chapter 10 discusses the role of government in the UK, EU social and economic policy, and the 'new' regulatory state. It discusses some major policy initiatives and those of the main opposition parties, in their historical contexts. It also considers the evolution of EU economic and social policies and their impact on the UK. The chapter explains how, in recent years, neo-liberal policies under the Conservatives, and modified neo-liberal ones under Labour governments, have dominated macro- and micro-economic management. Emphasis has been on low inflation, fiscal responsibility, low direct taxation, support for free trade and using the market rather than the state to provide goods and services. This chapter discusses the role of regulation in the contemporary state, which provides the interface between the state and the market. In the regulatory state, the law is expected to play a crucial role in mitigating the worst effects of unregulated, free markets.

In writing this book, a lot of people have helped me but I would particularly like to acknowledge the following for their support: Ruth Anderson, the CIPD's senior commissioning editor, for guiding me so helpfully along the high-speed journey towards completing this text on time; the production team at the CIPD for getting the final product out so speedily; the anonymous reviewers of chapters, who helped me rethink some issues and enabled me to make some adjustments to the drafts; my colleagues Stephen Taylor, Manchester Metropolitan University, Dr Mike Asteris, University of Portsmouth, and staff in the University and CIPD libraries for providing academic support in my crafting of this work; and my immediate family and friends who must have wondered what I was doing for several months, while this work was being written. Any errors or fact, judgement or opinion remain mine alone.

David Farnham
University of Portsmouth
July 2010

Human resource management in context: strategies, insights and solutions

The content of this CIPD module is covered as follows:

Human resource management in context learning outcomes	*Human resource management in context* chapters covering learning outcomes
Understand, analyse and critically evaluate:	
1. Contemporary organisations and their principal environments	Chapter 1 Human resource management and its external contexts Chapter 2 Contemporary organisations and their internal contexts
2. The managerial and business environment within which HR professionals work	Chapter 3 The managerial and business contexts of organisations
3. How organisational and HR strategies are shaped by and developed in response to internal and external environmental factors	Chapter 4 Developing corporate strategies Chapter 5 Developing human resource strategies
4. The market and competitive environments of organisations and how organisational leaders and the HR function respond to them	Chapter 6 The competitive environment Chapter 10 Government policy and legal regulation
5. Globalisation and international forces and how they shape and impact on organisational and HR strategies and HR practices	Chapter 7 Globalisation and international factors
6. Demographic, social and technological trends and how they shape and impact on organisational and HR strategies and HR practices	Chapter 8 Demographic and social trends Chapter 9 The technological context
7. Government policy and legal regulation and how these shape and impact on organisational and HR strategies and HR practices	Chapter 10 Government policy and legal regulation

Walkthrough of textbook features and online resources

LEARNING OUTCOMES

By the end of this chapter, readers should be able to understand, explain and critically evaluate:

- the main theoretical approaches to organisations
- types, objectives and internal contexts of contemporary organisations
- current issues in organisations
- the major stakeholders in organisations
- the principles of corporate governance, accountability and corporate social responsibility
- how these contexts impact on HR strategy and HR practices.

In addition, readers should also be able to:

- evaluate current trends and issues in organisation theory and management practice
- identify actual and potential constraints on organisational autonomy
- undertake effective analyses of contemporary organisations.

LEARNING OUTCOMES

At the beginning of each chapter a bulleted set of learning outcomes summarises what you can expect to learn from the chapter, helping you to track your learning.

ACTIVITY 2.4

Examine your organisation in terms of *either* a symbolic perspective *or* a postmodern perspective, drawing upon the sub-headings: the focus of organisation theory, the theory of knowledge and the nature of organisations. What do you infer about your organisation from these observations, compared with Activity 2.3 above?

ACTIVITIES

Questions and activities throughout the text encourage you to reflect on what you have learnt and to apply your knowledge and skills in practice.

KEY LEARNING POINTS

1. Management has a variety of meanings. Basically it is a power resource in organisations, comprising a hierarchy of those people, managers, who have responsibility, both collectively and individually, for enabling organisations to achieve their objectives and making them work. Managerial work is often organised by function and is fragmented, commonly fire-fighting in nature, and involves attending meetings and working with people. The higher managers rise in an organisation the more concerned they are with integrating, co-ordinating and controlling the work of other managers.

2. Whether management is a profession, like other liberal professions, is doubtful. First, despite the growth of management education in the past 30 years, there is little evidence of there being an agreed body of substantive knowledge in the field of management which all managers need to know to be effective. Second, the study, theory and practice of management are not researched and examined by a single professional body claiming to advance standards of managerial performance and managerial practices in organisations, although there are specialist bodies in some areas such as HR and marketing. Third, any semblance of patronage control by managers within organisations

KEY LEARNING POINTS

At the end of each chapter, the key learning points are designed to consolidate your learning.

REVIEW QUESTIONS

1. What are the cases for and against regarding management as a profession?

2. 'Of all the management functions in organisations, financial management is the most important.' Do you agree or not agree, and why?

3. A friend of yours has e-mailed you: 'I've just had a very bad experience with a retailer selling electrical goods. Their customer service standards are a joke and all the talk about "quality" is simply rhetoric.' Draft an e-mail explaining, from your experience and knowledge of quality management, that it is neither a joke nor merely rhetoric but something with a strong theoretical underpinning and practical base.

4. One of your managerial colleagues has said to you: 'The more that I observe managerial behaviour in our organisation, the more I realise that it is about power and control.' Drawing upon research evidence and observation in your organisation, what is your view of this statement and why? What are the implications for the HR function?

REVIEW QUESTIONS

These questions are aimed at reinforcing what you have learnt in the chapter.

EXPLORE FURTHER

BARRY, D. and HANSEN, H. (eds) (2008) *The SAGE handbook of new approaches in management and organization*. London: Sage.

Provides an analysis and review of contemporary approaches to management and organisation, with new chapters allowing readers to stay one step ahead of the latest thinking. Contributors draw on research and practice and introduce ideas that are considered fringe and controversial. Some interesting insights into contemporary management theory and practice.

COLLEY, J., DOYLE, J., HARDIE, R., LOGAN, G. and STETTINIUS, W. (2007) *Principles of general management: the art and science of getting results across organisational boundaries*. New Haven, CT: Darden Graduate School of Business Administration.

Examines the theories and practices of general management, drawing on its origins, steps, analytical concepts, crucial activities of general managers, and the various

EXPLORE FURTHER

Explore further boxes contain suggestions for further reading, encouraging you to delve further into areas of particular interest.

CASE STUDY

CASE STUDY 2.1 ZENOTECH – A NETWORK-BASED ORGANISATION

Background

Zenotech is a high-tech organisation manufacturing quality, innovative micro-electronic products for manufacturers in European and global markets. Founded 10 years ago largely by finance capital from a Norwegian consortium of investors, Zenotech has expanded steadily and successfully over this period, albeit with

difficult period in terms of sales, market penetration and profitability. As a result, it had to undertake a thorough review of its operations to identify what needed to be done to make it more competitive and customer focused, and to find ways of improving its market position. The overall objective was to make the organisation 25 per cent more efficient within three

CASE STUDIES

Each chapter ends with a case study to help you to place the concepts discussed into a real-life context.

ONLINE RESOURCES FOR TUTORS

LECTURER'S GUIDE

Practical advice on teaching the HRM in Context module using this text

- Guidance on chapter activities
- PowerPoint slides – Build and deliver your course around these ready-made lectures, ensuring complete coverage of the module
- Additional case studies – For you to use with students in seminars or lectures

Visit **www.cipd.co.uk/tss**

PART 1

Introducing HRM, organisations and management

CHAPTER 1

Human resource management and its external contexts

INTRODUCTION

This chapter provides the theoretical and practical backgrounds to the rest of the book. It does this by giving an outline description, analysis and overview of contemporary human resource management (HRM) within the United Kingdom (UK) and the external contexts driving it. These contexts are identified within the framework of the strategy, insights and solutions professional area of the CIPD's HR Profession Map (CIPD 2009). HRM, loosely defined as the managing of people at work, has undergone significant changes in its purposes, structures and activities in recent years. This chapter starts by examining the factors influencing these developments and considers the changing nature of HRM and how it has developed historically. The chapter then identifies and discusses some key issues on the HRM agenda. These include: how the human resources (HR) function is organised, HR and performance, line managers and HR, outsourcing HR, HRM and ethics, and HR strategy. Next, the chapter summarises the major institutional, external contexts impacting on the HR function that influence HR strategy and practices; issues that are revisited in greater depth later in the book. Finally, the chapter puts these developments into a global context by discussing some trends in international HRM.

LEARNING OUTCOMES

By the end of this chapter, readers should be able to understand, explain and critically evaluate:

- the changing nature and forms of contemporary HRM and HR practices in the UK
- the principal factors driving these changes
- some key issues in HRM, such as HR strategy and delivery of HR

- the external contexts affecting organisations and the HR function

- developments in international HRM.

In addition, readers should be able to:

- evaluate the impact of these changes on HRM practices in organisations

- review the impact of external contexts on HR work and HR practice

- understand how these changes affect their own organisations

- relate contemporary HR practices to the HR Profession Map.

DEFINING AND UNDERSTANDING CONTEMPORARY HRM

Providing a definitive definition of contemporary HRM is problematic. This is because there is no generally agreed framework for understanding and analysing the HR function; there are only competing models. In practice, the HR function within organisations in the UK (and elsewhere) is infinitely flexible, organisationally contingent over time and driven principally by the external contexts of the age; and these often change within short periods of time. Indeed, the history of HR in the UK and elsewhere shows that it has had to change its priorities and focus its activities by re-inventing itself continuously. This has been largely in response to external socio-economic factors beyond the immediate control of HR practitioners or senior managers. For these reasons a variety of definitions, frameworks and models can be found in any of the basic (or not so basic) texts and in the wide range of articles examining and exploring the functions, roles and antecedents of contemporary HRM in organisations. However, some understanding of the differing frameworks and intellectual underpinnings of HRM is necessary, if readers are to identify, understand and analyse the major external and internal contexts within which HR professionals operate today. It is these dynamic contexts which provide a continuing theme throughout the text.

One major text in the field, Marchington and Wilkinson (2008), defines HRM curtly as the management of employment. Another standard text provides no agreed definition of HRM but distinguishes between 'soft' and 'hard' versions of it. These writers, drawing upon Guest (1987) and Storey (1992), claim soft HRM 'recognises employees as a resource worth investing in, and tends to focus on high commitment/high involvement human resource practices.' Hard HRM 'identifies employees as a cost to be minimised, and tends to focus on "flexibility techniques" and limited investment in learning and development' (Beardwell and Claydon 2007, pp671, 675). Boxall and Purcell (2008) regard HRM in the English-speaking world as all those activities associated with the management of employment relationships in the firm.

FROM PERSONNEL MANAGEMENT TO HRM

For Torrington *et al* (2008, p6), the term HRM is used in two ways. They provide a useful distinction between 'HRM mark 1' and 'HRM mark 2'. The first is a *generic term* used to describe the body of management activities which have been traditionally labelled 'personnel management'. The second is regarded as a *distinctive approach* to HRM and suggests a specific philosophy towards carrying out 'people-oriented organisational activities'. Generic HRM seeks to achieve four key objectives: staffing, performance, change-management and administration. These organisational objectives are delivered primarily by personnel/HR specialists or personnel/HR generalists. HRM as a distinctive approach to managing people delivers organisational objectives by HR professionals in collaboration with line managers.

Guest (1987), in turn, has identified a number of 'stereotypical' features distinguishing the personnel management tradition (HRM mark 1) from the distinctive HR tradition (HRM mark 2). Personnel management is specialist and professionally driven. Its features include: a short-term, ad hoc time perspective; a pluralist, collective approach to managing employment relations; bureaucratic, centralised, organisational structures; and cost minimisation evaluation criteria. The distinctive, 'new' HR tradition (HRM mark 2) is largely integrated with line management. Its features include: a long-term, strategic time perspective; a unitary, individual approach to managing employment relations; more organic, devolved, flexible organisational structures; and maximum utilisation of human resources.

Interestingly, Torrington *et al* identify six main periods or 'themes' in the history of personnel management and its transition into contemporary HRM. Indeed, as Gennard and Kelly (1997, p31) have perceptively observed, delivery of the personnel/HR function has always been flexible and has adjusted its dominant values historically 'as macro circumstances change.' Legge (1995, p xiv) argues, however, that the apparent overshadowing of personnel management by the distinctive HRM tradition lies in its function as 'a rhetoric about how employees should be managed to achieve competitive advantage [rather] than as a coherent new practice.' Keenoy (1990) goes further in his critique of the new HRM, viewing it as 'a wolf in sheep's clothing.' For him, HRM is more rhetoric than reality and simply supports ideological shifts in the employment relationship, driven by market pressures.

Torrington *et al* (2008) describe the first theme in the evolution of personnel management and HRM in the UK as 'social justice.' This originated on a limited scale amongst a few enlightened employers in nineteenth-century Britain. These employers promoted a welfare approach to managing people by attempting to ameliorate working conditions and avoid adversarial industrial relations. Second, in the first half of the twentieth century, 'humane bureaucracy', influenced by managerial practitioners and observers such as Taylor (1911), Fayol (1916) and Mayo (1933) came to the fore in management practices. Taylor's 'scientific management' principles adopted a work study, incentive-based approach to managing people. This was followed by the 'human relations' school, originating in Mayo's works reported in the Hawthorne experiments, and later others, which aimed at fostering good 'human relations', high morale and efficiency at work. Third, in response to strong trade unions in the 1960s, a period of 'negotiated consent' was fostered by personnel and industrial relations managers. This aimed at containing union power and managing workers by representative systems and collective agreements. Fourth, from the late 1960s, the focus was on 'organisation' provided by personnel specialists. They did this by developing career paths, opportunities for personal growth and workforce planning. Fifth, the recent 'HRM' theme, with its focus on performance management, planning, monitoring and control, flexibility and employees as individuals, emerged and grew in the English-speaking world throughout the 1980s, 1990s and 2000s. This was in response to what is loosely described as globalisation and neo-liberal economic policies.

A sixth theme claimed by some observers, such as Bach (2005, pp28–9), is a 'new HR'. Driven by employer demands for competitive advantage, this theme is characterised by a 'new trajectory' in response to significant long-term trends in the business context. These include a global perspective, issues of legal compliance, the emergence of 'multi-employer' networks (or 'permeable organisations'), engagement of individual employees emotionally at work, and a customer-centred focus in business. This trend or theme seems to reflect a shift away from the 'management of jobs' by organisations to the 'management of people' within them (Lepak and Snell 2007).

In their summary review of the HR literature, Beardwell and Clark (2007) identify five comparative models of personnel management and HRM. They describe these as: the planning perspective, people management perspective, employment relations perspective, structure/systems perspective, and role perspective. In each case, practices and theories of managing people within each of the personnel management and HRM traditions differ. In outline, personnel management in the planning perspective is reactive and marginal to corporate plans. In the people management perspective, people are a variable cost, subject to compliance and organisational control. In the employment relations perspective, personnel management accepts that self-interest dominates at work and that conflicts of interests among stakeholders are inevitable. Personnel management in the structure/systems perspective imposes control of staff from the top and control of information flows downwards. In the role perspective, personnel management is specialised, professional and driven by personnel specialists.

Within the HRM tradition, HRM is strategy-focused and central to the corporate plan in the planning perspective. In the people management perspective, HRM views people as social capital capable of being developed and committed at work. In the employment relations perspective, HRM supports coincidence of interests among stakeholders and de-emphasises conflict in the workplace. HRM in the structure/systems perspective promotes employee participation and informed choice by staff, with open channels of communication to management aimed at building employee trust and commitment. In the role perspective, HRM is largely integrated into line management.

Clearly from this brief outline of some of the recent literature in the field, there is no universally agreed definition of contemporary HRM or the practices it incorporates; an issue which is explored more fully in Chapter 5. However, two observations can be made. First, HRM in the UK, as elsewhere, is historically 'path dependent'. This means, and explains how, institutions, social structures or patterns of behaviour in the present are limited by what has happened in the past, even though past circumstances may no longer apply. Second, as Guest (1997, p266) has argued, this lack of consensus about HRM arises from the 'absence of a coherent theoretical basis for classifying HRM policy and practice.' In examining the key literature in the area, Guest identifies three broad categories of general level theory about contemporary HRM. These are: *strategic theories*, such as those of Miles and Snow (1984) and Schuler and Jackson (1987); *descriptive theories*, such as those of Beer *et al* (1985) and Kochan *et al* (1986); and *normative theories*, such as those of Walton (1985) and Pfeffer (1994). Each theoretical category originates in different sets of assumptions about HRM. These are contingency theory, systems theory and motivation theory respectively. What these theoretical schools have in common is that contemporary HRM is deemed to be distinctive in some way or other from traditional personnel management; debates that are revisited later in this book. A summary of the main features of personnel management and HRM is provided in Figure 1.1.

Figure 1.1 From personnel management to HRM: a summary

The personnel management tradition	The human resources management tradition
Driven by employer needs to treat people fairly in organisations	Driven by employer needs for competitive advantage in the marketplace
Operates in relatively stable market conditions	Operates within competitive markets and a change agenda
Is a traditional approach to managing people, with a strong administrative purpose	Is a distinctive approach to managing people, with a strong strategic purpose
Is short term, with an ad hoc perspective	Is long term, with a strategic time perspective
Adopts a pluralist frame of reference to organisation and people management	Adopts a unitary frame of reference to organisation and people management
Negotiates with trade unions where they are recognised	Manages employees individually rather than collectively
Is delivered, monitored and policed by personnel specialists	Is delivered by HR professionals in collaboration with line managers

ACTIVITY 1.1

What do you understand by the 'strategic theories' of HRM, 'descriptive theories' and 'normative theories'? Which approach is the most useful for HR practitioners and why?

THE HR PROFESSION MAP

It is useful to conclude this introductory section by drawing upon the CIPD's HR Profession Map and its commentary on contemporary HR practices (CIPD 2009). The outcomes of the Map are based upon in-depth interviews with senior practitioners across the main economic sectors in the UK in 2008–09. Four issues stand out:

● The Profession Map covers not only the technical elements of professional competence required in the HR profession but also the behaviours.

● The Map describes what HR professionals need to do, what they need to know, and how they need to do it within each of 10 professional areas (outlined below) and eight behaviours, organised into four bands of professional competence.

● Areas of expertise in the Map are organised by professional competence, not by organisation structures, job levels or roles.

● The breadth and depth of the HR profession are covered from small to large organisations, fundamental to 'sophisticated' practices, local to global levels, corporations to consultancies, charities to public services, and traditional to progressive activities.

The CIPD's approach to contemporary HR practice in the Profession Map is a normative, competence-based one. A major conclusion is that a significant shift has taken place in the focus of HR. There has been a move away from a primary focus on supporting line managers and helping them manage people well to one ensuring that 'the organisation has the sustainable capability it needs to deliver its aims both today and in the future.' The Map seeks to do this by examining what HR people do and what they deliver across every aspect and specialism of the HR profession. The professional areas identified within the Map, in addition to 'strategy, insights and solutions', are 'leading and managing the human resources function', 'organisation design', 'organisation development', 'resourcing and talent planning', 'learning and talent development', 'performance and reward', 'employee engagement', 'employee relations' and 'service delivery and information'.

Three observations emerge from the CIPD's analysis. First, the HR Profession Map identifies the underpinning knowledge, skills and behaviours that HR professionals need to have if they are to be successful. Second, it creates a clear and flexible framework for career progression, recognising that both that HR roles and career progression vary. Third, the Map also provides a comprehensive view of how HR adds sustained value to organisations in which it operates, now and in the future (CIPD 2009). The CIPD's HR Profession Map, in short, places HRM at the heart of promoting improved performance, the effective managing of people at work and sustainable capability.

ACTIVITY 1.2

To what extent is your organisation practising HRM or personnel management? Provide indicators justifying your judgement.

SOME KEY ISSUES IN HRM

Given the changing contexts of HRM and HR practices, some key issues in contemporary HRM have emerged out of these developments. These contexts have affected the nature and structure of the HR function, its links with performance, HR and line managers, outsourcing HR, ethics and HRM, and HR strategy.

DEVELOPMENTS IN THE HR FUNCTION

A number of developments have taken place within the HR community and HR work in recent years. First, research by the CIPD (2008) as part of its study on the changing HR function agenda has identified some major changes in the structure of HR in large private and public sector organisations. This reveals that many large organisations are adopting variants of Ulrich's (1997) multi-legged model of HR structures, rather than having centralised HR departments as in the past. This has resulted in HR functions becoming more specialised and being divided between 'shared services', 'business partners', 'centres of expertise' or 'vendor management', overseen by 'corporate HR.' These roles are illustrated in Figure 1.2.

- **Shared services.** Those working in shared services undertake a lot of HR administrative tasks and provide information and advice through intranets and call centres to clients. Staff are often employed for their good interpersonal, customer service and team management skills, which can be prioritised over their HR knowledge.

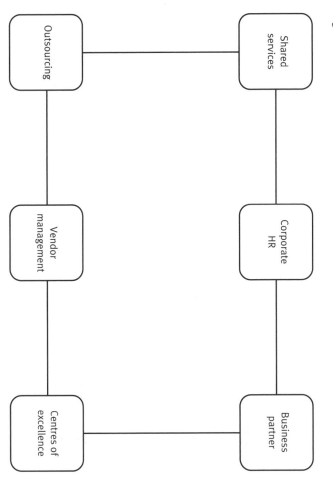

Figure 1.2 Current roles in the HR function

- **Business partners.** This HR role varies widely. Some business partners report to senior HR managers, others to senior line managers. Research shows that business partners are expected to work with business units or line managers on strategic development, organisational design, business performance or change management.

- **Centres of expertise.** Other HR practitioners provide support to business partners, develop detailed policy for corporate HR, and act as reference points for shared services when dealing with complex queries. The most common centres of HR expertise are people resourcing, employment relations, pay and rewards, learning and development, and organisational development.

- **Vendor management.** These staff provide third-party services, such as pension administration, managed through service-level agreements.

- **Corporate HR.** Those working in corporate HR have responsibility for developing HR and people strategy. Corporate HR players increasingly have a governance role, ensuring that organisations uphold corporate values, comply with their legal requirements and follow 'good practice' HR.

According to the CIPD (2008), the separation of transactional, generalist HR roles from transformational specialist ones within large organisations has led to changing skill requirements, and some recruitment problems, within the HR profession. In small and medium-sized enterprises, in contrast, HR is still likely to take on more traditional people management and development activities, based on generalist roles.

As noted below, a second development within HR is continuing delegation of some HR activities to line managers. The HR areas that line managers typically deal with include recruitment and selection, pay and reward, performance management, grievances and discipline, coaching, and learning and development. It is generally accepted that some line managers have skills gaps in people management and development activities and therefore have difficulties implementing HR policies effectively. Devolving HR activities to line managers has implications for HR professionals. who need to be facilitators, help line managers carry out their HR/people management and development activities effectively, and support line managers in getting the most out of the people resources. In designing and developing HR policies and procedures, HR practitioners also need to be aware that these will be delivered by line managers and that line managers need ownership of them; a theme developed further later in this chapter.

A third set of developments is in learning and development (L&D), where the focus is on 'learning' rather than 'training' and where the skills of those working in the field have changed. Today, business awareness and consultancy skills are highly valued among L&D practitioners. They provide solutions to business problems and support organisational change. There has also been a professionalisation of those delivering work-based learning, with staff working in these areas being increasingly certificated and well qualified. E-learning and blended learning have become important as technology develops, in a field where virtual learning environments, podcasts and gaming technology are increasingly popular. Coaching line managers has also been identified as a very effective L&D practice.

HRM AND PERFORMANCE

Since the 1980s and 1990s, there have been fundamental changes in the structures and management processes of organisations in the private and public sectors. Adjustments to the functions, structures and roles of the HR function are partly in response to these changes but also reflect the revolution in information and communication technologies (ICTs) outlined above. Three changes stand out. In this period, first, many large-scale hierarchical organisations have become divisionalised. This has resulted from breaking them up into a number of semi-autonomous operations or quasi-businesses, responsible for all the business activities within their areas of jurisdiction. Examples of divisionalisation include splitting large companies into separate, independent organisations, creating executive agencies and trusts in the public services and, in multinational businesses, setting up international product (or services) divisions with responsibility for individual products on a European or global basis (Hughes 2003, Geppert and Mayer 2006). Second, budgetary devolution is now commonplace. This has resulted in allocating responsibility for managing activities within planned financial resources or targets to the lowest possible levels within organisations. Third, internal markets have been created. This is where services are traded between 'purchasers' and 'providers' to ensure that different groups are responsive to the needs of each other and that such activities are cost-effective. In short, divisionalisation, devolved budgeting and internal markets have resulted in a fundamental shift from the management of tasks in the private and public sectors to management by financial performance (Sisson and Storey 2000).

It follows that the search for improved performance from individuals and groups within organisations is now a crucial managerial goal in most businesses and public enterprises. Customised HR practices and promoting appropriate employee behaviours play critical roles in facilitating this. The framework within which performance is organised, measured and reviewed is established in dedicated, organisational, performance management systems. The underlying aim of these systems is to get the best outcomes and highest efforts from individuals, teams and organisations, in pursuing corporate goals.

A principal feature of performance management is that it connects the objectives of an organisation with the job targets of individuals and focuses on work improvement, learning, development, motivation and reward. A performance management system starts with the induction of new staff when they join an organisation and has four elements: defining performance standards and setting targets, reviewing and appraising performance, reinforcing performance standards, and supporting individuals through counselling and other means to meet performance standards. The review process then identifies the learning and development needs of individuals and allocates rewards for measured outcomes (Armstrong and Baron 2005).

Leading organisations seek therefore to develop, in collaboration with HR professionals, systematic frameworks designed to improve individual and organisational performance in ways that can be measured and reviewed. Analysing claimed links between HRM and performance is now a major area of interest for both researchers and policy-makers. A wide range of studies has attempted to demonstrate the positive relationship or links between certain 'bundles' of HR practices and high organisational performance (Appelbaum *et al* 2000, West *et al* 2002, Godard 2004).

Guest *et al* (2003) provide a useful theoretical framework guiding this analysis, as illustrated in Figure 1.3. In outline, their model suggests possible links between a series of managerial inputs and performance outputs. The inputs are business strategy, HR strategy and HR practices. The HR practices include induction, job design, recruitment and selection, appraisal, pay and reward, training and development, financial flexibility, harmonisation, communication and job security. The outputs are effective HR outcomes, quality of goods and services, productivity and financial performance. Evaluating the effectiveness of these HR activities allows an assessment of how well they are working in practice. In this study, managing directors and HR professionals were asked to assess the effectiveness of each of the above HR practices. There were relatively little differences of opinion between them, with job security deemed to be one of the most effective HR practices and job design and appraisal being the least effective. The more HR practices used, and the more effectively they are used, the better organisational performance is likely to be. From this study at least, HR effectiveness appears to demonstrate the link between HRM and business performance.

There are also critiques of performance management systems. One is that they encourage a short-term view amongst UK managers, which may hamper organisational performance in the longer term. Second, there is growing concern that these systems add unduly to stress in working life for many employees, because of their focus on improving the bottom line. Third, and most importantly, performance management systems do not always deliver what they promise. The main driver of performance management is improving overall organisational effectiveness. However, writers such as Bevan and Thompson (1992) and others have found from surveys of performance management that there was no relationship between high-performing UK companies and performance management systems.

HRM AND LINE MANAGERS

Where HR professionals concentrate on developing strategy, designing performance management systems to match changing business priorities and other high-level business activities, line managers take on an important role in implementing HR strategies, policies and practices. Divisionalisation and devolved budgeting also promote delegation of HR activities. The importance of the line manager role in delivering HR has been highlighted by Hutchinson and Purcell (2003, p ix), amongst others. They found that the behaviour of first-line

Figure 1.3 Possible links between HRM and business performance

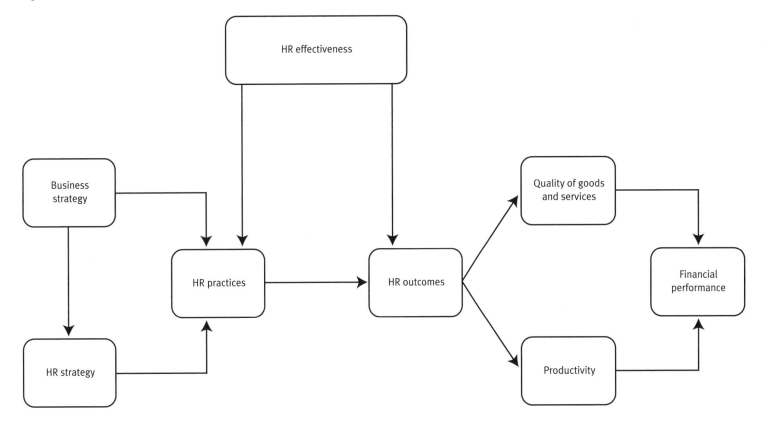

Adapted from Guest *et al* (2003).

managers was the most important factor explaining variations in job satisfaction and job discretion amongst employees. 'It is also one of the most important factors in developing organisational commitment.' It has been noted too that strengthening the relationship between managers and their employees results in a positive approach to employee performance and motivation. Such studies indicate that line managers can make real differences to employee attitudes and behaviour (Purcell *et al* 2003). They also demonstrate the critical role that line managers play in implementing HR policies (Renwick 2003).

To undertake their HR role successfully, line managers need to work closely with HR practitioners to maintain consistency and effectiveness in carrying out their HR activities. A survey by Industrial Relations Services (Industrial Relations Services 2004) asked respondents in 62 organisations about the areas of responsibility typically exercised by line managers. This reported, first, that they had major responsibility in absence management, performance appraisal, team briefing and staff development. Second, line managers and HR professionals had shared responsibility in induction, training and discipline. Third, line managers had little responsibility in recruitment, performance pay, promotions and welfare. Another, later, survey by the CIPD (2007), however, which also examined line management and HR responsibility for HR, found, first, that 39 per cent of line management respondents had main responsibility for recruitment and selection decisions and 10 per cent for training and development. Second, HR was a shared responsibility for 84 per cent of respondents in recruitment and selection, 59 per cent in training and development, 46 per cent in employee relations, and 35 per cent in pay and benefits. In general, successive surveys have highlighted increasing HR responsibilities being devolved to line managers in organisations, normally in conjunction with HR professionals as partners.

Devolving HR activities to line managers, however, is not without its difficulties. As Renwick (2003) points out, there are several problems in doing this. First, line managers do not always have the skills and competencies to manage people effectively. The low technical and educational bases of many UK line managers provide barriers to the effective devolution of HR activities in some organisations. Second, in other cases, line managers are not interested in HR work, believing that competence in the field is gained from a mixture of common sense and experience rather than from training. Line managers think they know how to manage people, motivate them and deal with their problems, but have problems doing this (Cunningham and Hyman 1999). Third, line managers have more pressing priorities than managing and developing the people working for them. HRM is low on their lists of management priorities. Moreover, they need support, recognition and rewards from top managers to become motivated to deal with HR issues effectively (Marchington and Wilkinson 2008). Fourth, the ways in which HR practices are implemented by line managers are often inconsistent and contradictory, resulting in often subjective and discretionary decision-making, unless HR support is provided (Hutchinson and Purcell 2003). Training line managers in their HR responsibilities and working in partnership with HR professionals appear to be key issues here.

OUTSOURCING HR

In addition to delegating HR responsibilities to line managers, organisations commonly outsource some HR activities to outside bodies or agencies. Outsourcing HR is where organisations subcontract HR activities (and in some cases general commercial activities such as catering and maintenance) on grounds of cost savings, the need to draw on specialist external expertise not available internally, and obtaining independent HR advice from outside people with greater knowledge, skills and experience in their fields of competence than insiders have. Cost factors, for example, often cause managers to consider whether support functions can be provided more cheaply externally. Moreover, subcontractors commonly seek to provide a better service by drawing upon expertise unavailable to their client. Other factors increasing the incidence of outsourcing include the argument that firms gain competitive advantage by focusing their efforts on core business activities and distinctive areas of HR competence. There are also benefits associated with flexibility and leanness. Thus where a core activity is outsourced, suppliers can be changed when they perform badly or their prices become uncompetitive.

Outsourcing takes various forms, such as a shared service centre working for a single organisation, a joint venture between organisations combining HR resources or a multi-client call centre providing HR advice to several organisations (Cooke *et al* 2004). The sorts of HR activities typically outsourced include payroll administration, recruitment and selection, learning and development, executive search, and outplacement and redundancy counselling. Research carried out in the United States indicated four main areas of HR covered by outsourcing arrangements: general HR, transactional work, human capital activities, recruitment and selection. This study shows that reliance on outsourcing varied with organisational size and complexity, product market uncertainty and the importance of HR strategy to the business (Klass *et al* 2001).

A number of HR implications arise from outsourcing. There are legal issues to consider when an in-house activity is subcontracted, such as transfer of undertakings regulations. There may be issues associated with control of the subcontracted activities. There are implications regarding the regulation of performance levels. With outsourcing, performance is not regulated through a typical contract of employment, but is managed through commercial contracts and service level agreements. There are also implications for job security and work intensification within outsourced organisations (Taylor 2008).

ETHICS AND HRM

Ethical organisations have always existed although most businesses have traditionally been driven by economic not ethical goals. In the nineteenth century, for example, Quaker companies operated on distinctive ethical principles and firms such as Cadburys incorporated welfare policies into their business philosophies, which benefited their workforces. This was in contrast to most other firms at the time that were driven solely by the profit motive. Today examples of successful businesses noted for the ethical principles they promote include the Co-operative Bank, Scott-Bader and Traidcraft.

Some argue that business organisations cannot have 'ethics' or be 'ethical', as they are not agents of morality and not driven by moral imperatives. However, organisations have sufficient structural complexity to be agents, so they can be called to account for their actions and the consequences of them. If a body can take decisions and implement them, then it must be responsible for those decisions (Kaptein and Wempe 2002). Indeed, as corporate legal entities, business organisations are accountable in law for some of their actions. Therefore part of corporate responsibility stems from legal requirements – such as employment law, health and safety and consumer protection – but part of this responsibility is moral or ethical. Being profitable is a virtue of business organisations but it is not their only virtue. As Kitson and Campbell (1996, p98) argue: 'We can expect organisations to be socially responsible because that is part of the contract out of which they were created.' It is a 'condition of the permission that society granted that they exist in the first place.'

Until recently, there was relatively little mention of ethics in the HRM literature in the UK, although it is growing, stimulated by the growth in ethical investment and ethical consumerism discussed earlier. A different picture emerges in the United States, where ethics and ethical behaviour feature prominently in both HR practice and academic research. Yet almost every HR decision and issue poses ethical questions, since they deal with people issues covering recruitment and selection, managing performance, equal opportunities, learning and development, employee relations, pay and rewards, and termination of employment. Marchington and Wilkinson (2008) argue persuasively that ethical and socially responsible HR practices may become even more elusive as organisations devolve HR activities to line managers, who are required to meet corporate targets that stress production and service targets as their first priorities. However, ethical recruitment and selection, for example, demand properly drafted job descriptions and person specifications, candidates only being invited to interview where they meet the essential requirements and unsuccessful candidates having their applications returned to them, with the selectors' reasons for their decision. Applicants can also be given the results of any assessments made of them. Perhaps the underlying argument for ethical HR practices is that companies adopting them benefit by gaining employee commitment, the trust and loyalty of their workforce and improved organisational performance.

Winstanley et al (1996, p5ff) have written that 'the relationship between ethics and human resource management is emerging as a subject of serious academic enquiry.' They have identified three main issues: ethical concerns, ethical frameworks and putting ethics into practice. They raise concerns about the lowering of employment standards, for example, where several types of undesirable change have been identified. These are, first, job insecurity and risk at work. Second, new forms of work organisation and management control are giving rise to surveillance and control of employees at work. Third, deregulation of management decision-making in firms is leaving little scope for power-based employee participation in the workplace, and this element in contemporary HRM 'is at best unsympathetic to the exercise of democratic rights by employees or to stakeholder models of corporate governance'. Fourth, the rhetoric of HRM, with its themes of commitment and identification, fits poorly with the trend towards less secure employment and evidence of diminished employer commitment to employees, with 'a relentlessly instrumental orientation to the employment relationship on the part of employers'.

Winstanley et al (1996, p9ff) also claim that the prevailing common-sense ethical framework justifying contemporary HRM policies based on their utilitarianism to organisations is a weak principle for ethical action. They identify a number of alternative ethical frameworks lending themselves to analysing HRM. These are:

- **Basic human, civil and employment rights.** This seeks greater job security, openness, and transparency; and aims to avoid making scapegoats at work.

- **Social and organisational justice.** This aims to provide procedural principles for evaluating current employment practices.

- **Universalism.** This emphasises the Kantian principle of treating individuals as ends in themselves and not just means to ends.

- **Community of purpose.** This seeks to adopt a stakeholder and more communitarian view of the firm rather than just a stockholder one.

Another level of engagement with ethics is for HR professionals to utilise appropriate frameworks that help to explain and analyse the nature of changes taking place in the employment relationship and to use the frameworks 'more prescriptively'. In seeking ways of putting ethical principles into practice in HRM, Winstanley et al (1996, p11) propose the use of employment charters, legal regulation, innovation in good practice and challenging 'the inevitability thesis' on the demise of job security. They are unconvinced that the 'ethical stewardship' role of HR professionals in raising awareness of ethical issues is a viable one. 'There is the risk that assuming ownership of the "ethical" issues and conscience in the organisation might yet again serve to decrease their status.' Drawing on Connock and Johns (1995), they conclude that ethical leadership must come from the top of organisations. It must 'not be part of the ghetto of human resource management'. In their view, growing interest in stakeholding, ethical consumerism and international labour standards are some of the most significant developments putting ethics and HRM on the political agenda.

HR STRATEGY

A key feature of HRM mark 2, as indicated above, is its role in and contribution to HR strategy formulation and implementation, which Tyson (1995, p3) describes as the as the intentions of an organisation towards its employees. He defines HR strategy as 'a set of ideas, policies and practices which management adopt in order to achieve a people-management objective'. Rather than consisting of a detailed document, covering all areas of people management, HR strategy is now conceived as an incremental process. It is aimed at influencing key HR practices promoting improved performance and competitive advantage at work, taking account of organisational politics and what is possible in the circumstances. A main characteristic of an effective HR strategy, whatever form it takes, is its integration with business strategy. There are a number of models of HR strategy, which are fully examined in Chapter 5, but each is underpinned by the idea that HR policies and practices need to support the goals of a business, whatever sector it is in, if they are to be effective. HR strategies, in other words, need to have 'external fit' with business strategies and be vertically integrated with them (Fombrun *et al* 1984, Guest 1987, Schuler and Jackson 1987, Pfeffer 1998). Vertical integration thus refers to the links between business strategy, the external contexts and HR policies and practices.

In addition to 'external fit', it is also argued that there needs to be 'internal fit' between different aspects of HR strategy. This 'horizontal integration' of HR means that HR strategy needs to achieve a high level of compatibility of its various elements, not creating policy conflicts between them. One common critique of HR specialists is that they fail to co-ordinate their HR policies and practices to promote consistent and unambiguous messages from management to employees. For example, an HR policy aimed at reducing headcount may be contradictory to another promoting learning at work. Similarly, an incremental pay system without an incentive element, say, may work against a recruitment and selection policy that seeks to attract self-motivated people expecting personal rewards for good performance. A number of studies show that clear benefits accrue from organisations having an appropriate 'mix' of internally consistent HR practices, integrated together and supporting rather than negating one another (Huselid 1995, Wood 1995).

In the managerial literature on HR strategy, then, it is argued that the greater the degree of vertical and horizontal integration within an organisation, the more effective its HR strategy is likely to be. The nature and feasibility of the possible links between business strategy and HR strategy, and the internal consistency of HR strategy, are consistent themes in the strategy literature (Boxall and Purcell 2008).

There is a body of critical literature, however, that challenges these assumptions and questions the links between HRM and its strategic integration with business policy. Legge (1995, p116), for example, argues, first, that the 'matching' approach is based upon a classical, rational approach to strategy that assumes a top-down, unitary planning process which is simplistic and not congruent with reality. She highlights the conceptual problems and 'fuzziness' permeating the major strategy models used to match HR policies with business strategy. Second, this raises doubts 'about their operationalisation in empirical research and the consequent validity of such studies' findings'. She sees these matching models being mainly employed at the normative level, rather than being empirically tested (Golden and Ramanujam 1985). According to one study, an examination of the processes of strategic and HRM change called into question whether managers actually have a genuinely free choice in strategic stance anyway (Storey and Sisson 1993). Third, Legge (1995, p124) questions whether the close matching of strategy and HR policies is desirable anyway. She asks, for example, whether it is possible to have corporate-wide, mutually reinforcing HR strategies, where an organisation operates in highly diversified product markets and, if not, does it matter in terms of organisational effectiveness? Lastly, she questions, in terms of internal integration, whether developing an organisational culture supportive of a particular business strategy stops employees adopting different behaviours in response to changing market demands. In other words, there can be inflexibilities resulting from too close a match between HR strategies and business strategies.

THE EXTERNAL CONTEXTS OF HRM

To summarise the debate so far, contemporary HRM provides a distinctive approach to managing people at work. Although traditional personnel management approaches remain in some organisations, what Torrington *et al* (2008) describe as the 'HRM theme' is the dominant trend in people management in firms and public organisations today. Contemporary HRM by this analysis has a strategic focus, is integrated with line management and is individualistic in its orientation. The work that senior HR professionals commonly undertake, certainly within leading-edge organisations, is scanning their environments in response to external change, working closely with senior managers as business partners, and building HR capability at individual and organisational levels.

HR practitioners also work in complex, changing organisational contexts. In order to address the HR issues arising from these circumstances, HR professionals have to understand these contexts and try to manage them by developing and implementing appropriate HR strategies and practices, in the short, medium and long terms. In this section, what HR professionals 'need to know' to perform effectively in responding to the major *external* contexts impinging on organisations is briefly explored. The external contexts of HRM are important because HR practices, in any country, are socially embedded in their wider, institutional, external contexts. This means that organisations are affected by external forces that require managers to adapt their internal organisational structures and behaviours to deal with them (Berger and Luckman 1967). As Pfeffer and Salancik (1978) argue, organisational activities and outcomes are accounted for by the contexts in which the organisation is embedded. For illustrative purposes, a summary of these external contexts, known by the acronym STEEPLE, and some key drivers within them, is provided in Figure 1.4. The *internal* contexts facing HR practitioners are considered in Chapter 2 and the *business and managerial* contexts in Chapter 3.

Figure 1.4 The external contexts of organisations: some key drivers

Field	Examples of key drivers of strategy
Socio-cultural	Demography by size, age, other social characteristics and geographical distribution, working population, gender, ethnicity, education and training, religion, social values and beliefs
Technological	Information and communication technologies, biotechnology, medical advances, nanotechnology, robotics, technological change, research and development
Economic	Macro-economic policy, markets and prices, price levels, global trends, market structures, size of firms, profits, public spending, taxation, consumption and investment spending, wages and salaries, public services, imports and exports, exchange rates, balance of payments, employment and unemployment, labour and capital markets
Environmental	Global warming, conserving natural resources, sustainable development, pollution, carbon footprints, protecting the eco-environment
Political	Party politics, government, opposition, public administration, public policy, devolved assemblies, local government, pressure groups, public opinion, EU institutions, international organisations
Legal	Contract law, employment law, health and safety, consumer protection law, company law, codes of practice, regulatory bodies, the legal system and the courts, the European Court of Justice
Ethical	Balancing stakeholder interests, ethics in the workplace, ethical business relations, ethical production, ethical consumption, ethical purchasing, promoting employee welfare, human rights, corporate social responsibility

STRATEGY, INSIGHTS AND SOLUTIONS

Drawing upon the HR Profession Map in the professional area of strategy and solutions, a range of prescriptive, underpinning knowledge has been identified that HR practitioners with the highest levels of professional competence 'need to know' to perform effectively. A selection of these are summarised and described below.

First, HR practitioners need an understanding of their own organisation's strategy, its performance goals and drivers, and the sector in which they work. These cover the market factors impacting upon performance, including demography, customers, competitors and globalisation. They need to know, understand and speak the language of the business they work for and the 'full range of human resources levers' driving organisational performance. Second, HR practitioners need a broad understanding and technical capability of all 10 HR professional areas (summarised below), with in-depth knowledge in one or two of them, including strategy, insights and solutions. Third, they need to know or access relevant employment and discrimination law in both their local and international jurisdictions. Fourth, they need to know the external and internal influences, including political and economic ones, impacting on the directions, shape and performance of their organisations and the HR levers that can be applied within them. Fifth, HR practitioners need to be able to shape and lead change programmes and know how to develop organisational strategies and operating plans in response to these forces. Sixth, they need to know how to determine organisational capability and resourcing levels to support the delivery of HR strategy and plans. Finally, HR professionals at the highest levels of professional competence need to know 'what external human resources thought leaders and benchmark companies are doing in a variety of areas'. They also need to consider how these lessons 'may apply to [their] own organisation', which necessitates developing 'fit-for-purpose (though stretching) human resources solutions and anticipation of need' (CIPD 2009, p9).

THE SOCIO-CULTURAL CONTEXT

In the social sphere, population trends are a key driver. There are, however, counter-cyclical shifts in population trends. On the one hand, there is rising population growth in the UK and globally, although this is offset by falling birth rates in west and east Europe generally. Higher immigration into the UK and Europe results in increases in the size of the potential labour force, depending on the ages of the migrant populations and their age distributions. It also affects the supply and demand for goods and services in product markets and public services. On the other hand, a generally ageing population, as is the case in most of west and east Europe, results in not only losses of skills, knowledge and competencies from the labour market but also increased demand for different kinds of goods and services by both younger and older people. It places greater demands on pension funds and social services for the elderly, as opposed to fashionable consumer goods for younger people delivered by leading-edge, hi-tech businesses. Another mega-social trend is increasing socio-economic inequality, with rising affluence for wealthy people and elite groups. This is accompanied by increased relative deprivation for others, rises in asset prices (such as housing stock) and rises in private debt. All these social developments have both strategic and HR implications for organisations in terms of demand for labour, supply of labour and demand for products or services.

At the micro-social level, there are a number of distinctive social trends, all of which impact on organisations, employees, the customers they serve and the HR function. These developments include changing sources of social identity, increased dependency on drugs and alcohol, rising divorce rates, and rising numbers of single-parent households. One social consequence emerging out of these trends is increased solo-living (or single-person households) amongst all age groups. Other social trends include increased self-satisfaction and personal narcissism, with reduced interest in social conformity as well as greater preparedness to take personal responsibility for the self. Underpinning these trends is increased individualism and reduced collectivism at home, at work and in society. The impacts of these developments on working life are wide ranging. These include rising demand for flexible working arrangements and contractual flexibility, more individually oriented HR policies and practices, a lower propensity to unionise and take organised industrial action, and more job mobility within the workforce (Office for National Statistics 2009b).

THE TECHNOLOGICAL CONTEXT

There have been ground-breaking technological innovations in society during the past decades. These have implications for organisations, managers and workers. The most obvious examples are the World-Wide Web, email, intranets, Blackberries, video-conferencing and, in HRM particularly, the introduction of HR databases, electronic payroll systems and electronic record systems, all linked with innovatory ICTs. During the past 10 years or so, ever-newer forms of ICTs have been launched, most of which have implications for how people construct their identities and how they are managed at work. These include Google's search engine; Wikipedia, an online free encylopaedia; Twitter, claimed to be one stage on from Google by applying human intelligence and recommendation to the ordering of information; and, since 2007, the BBC iPlayer. Other technological communication innovations include the iPhone, with its touch screen, rotating screen and zooming screen; Craiglist, the classified advertising database now operating in over 50 countries; and Facebook with over 300 million people active on the website. Developments in medical and health technologies are also extending life expectancies and how long people work and remain in the labour market. Other important technological drivers include improvements in biotechnology, hi-tech medicine and a remarkable range of complex pharmaceutical products.

As Soete (2001) points out, a number of implications arise out of the applications of these new technologies. First, there has been the dramatic reduction in the costs of digital information and communication processing, which is not showing any sign of decreasing returns and is unlikely to do so in the future. Second, there has been the technologically driven 'digital convergence' between communication and computer technology at all levels, which is rendering feasible any combination of communication forms. Third, there has been the rapid growth in international electronic networking, both terrestrial and through satellites. Fourth, these developments affect communication between individuals, within organisations, amongst organisations, and increasingly between individuals and machines. They affect all aspects of society, including work, business and the public sector. Fifth, these technologies render physical space and distance irrelevant in many business, working and human transactions. This effectively makes ICTs the first global, technological transformation process. They radically affect how people work, what they do at work, and how people are managed within organisations.

THE ECONOMIC CONTEXT

In the economic sphere, a number of indicative trends are discernible. One is market uncertainty arising out of recession and slow macro-growth in the 2010s. This, in turn, is likely to be offset eventually by an economic upturn and, most probably, the continued globalisation of business activities. The economy is also affected by government macro-economic policies, such as fiscal policy, monetary policy and its own economic activities, as well as by international economic forces. On the business front, for example, an increased role played by international or multinational companies in national economies, and more intense international competition for goods and services, contributes to falls in demand in domestic markets and a rise in unemployment. These and other economic forces impinge on demand for labour, the types of labour required by firms and public organisations, and labour supply. They determine how people are recruited, trained or retrained. On the other hand, with hyper-competitive conditions in some markets, pressure is put on competing firms to retain labour, reskill it or make it redundant. Firms have to adjust their HR policies and practices accordingly.

In the wider labour market, there continues to be increased demand for higher-skilled workers by UK employers and reduced demand for lower-skilled ones. Certainly in the UK, there appears to be limited growth in skills levels. These create recruitment, training and general HR issues for many organisations. At micro-level, there are indications of greater willingness by some workers to switch jobs and employers, resulting in higher labour turnover, increased transaction costs for employers, and personal disruption for the individuals concerned (Office for National Statistics 2009a). There are also significant changes in the structure of the economy, the manufacturing and extractive sectors being much less important than a generation ago, with increased activity in private and public services today. This has implications for education and training policy generally and for the employment prospects for existing and potential workers particularly, such as graduates in higher education.

Within the European single market, people, goods, services and money move around as freely as they do within one country. People travel across the European Union's (EU) internal frontiers for business and pleasure. Alternatively, they stay at home and enjoy a vast array of products being imported from all over Europe (and beyond). Some argue that the single market is certainly one of the EU's most important political achievements. The single market is certainly at the core of the EU today. Ever since the Single European Act, which established a single market in 1992, the EU has swept away the vast array of technical, regulatory, legal and bureaucratic barriers that formerly stifled free trade and free movement of goods, services and people. In terms of the free movement of goods and services, the single market relies largely on the regulatory authorities to guarantee competition. In terms of the free movement of labour, one consequence is that skilled professional workers can work anywhere in the EU, resulting in firms having to adjust their recruitment and HR policies to this market situation. Thus the UK's economic prosperity, its job creation prospects, and the opportunity for firms and their workforces to benefit from it, are intimately linked with general levels of economic activity in mainland Europe. Indeed, according to the European Commission (2009a), the single market has created several million jobs since its launch and generated more than €800 billion in extra wealth during this time.

THE ENVIRONMENTAL CONTEXT

To protect the ecological environment, there are a number of issues on the business agenda. These include increased interest in sustainable development, sustainable investment and sustainable consumption by producers, investors and consumers respectively. For individuals wanting sustainable production and investment, for example, this means avoiding not only activities likely to cause illness, disease or death, or to destroy and damage the environment, but also those organisations that treat people dishonestly or with disrespect. Second, for firms, it means choosing methods of working and investing that focus primarily on the effects of the company's products or services on the environment, people and communities. Another positive strategy is listing the environmental benefits that producers would like to see their organisations promote. For workers, this can mean good working conditions and for investors the need to articulate what they would like to see their money support. Environmentally-sensitive consumers, in turn, may seek to buy products (or services) which are produced ethically, do not harm the environment and promote the well-being of people at work. From an HR viewpoint, sustainable producers, investors and consumers expect companies to act decently in their dealings with staff. This means acting ethically in their relations with suppliers and local communities and managing their businesses with all their organisational stakeholders.

One outcome of this growing interest in environmental issues has been the emergence of 'green HR policies' by a number of environmentally conscious businesses. These companies are noted as developing strategic environmental management policies, especially in the United States. In one survey of 93 US companies, it was reported that some companies were undertaking common green HR initiatives, whether as part of a strategic business plan or a one-off practice. These included 78 per cent which were using either the World-Wide Web or teleconferencing to reduce travel, 76 per cent promoting reduction of paper use, and 68 per cent implementing wellness programmes fostering employees' proper nutrition, fitness and healthy styles of living (Bucks 2009). Clearly, this trend is likely to continue, given the shift to 'green' the economy by some leading politicians and pressure groups. All these environmental developments have implications for the HR function and the ways in which people are managed at work.

Although green advocacy is limited, employees can have a key role in building a business's reputation for green HR, and contented workers can become 'green' advocates. A number of initiatives are possible. First, 'green' businesses can get the support of their stakeholders in promoting a sustainable business model. Second, a variable pay element can link pay to 'eco-performance', with the concept of eco-performance being an extension of a common HR practice used in environmentally friendly businesses. Third, employees can help customers understand the importance of 'green living', by highlighting the green practices of their own businesses. Fourth, rewards can be provided to employees who follow green practices established within their firms. These include: recycling office paper, turning off lights and appliances when staff are not in a room, and convincing customers they should recycle their packaging. Employees, in short, can be ambassadors for everything good about their company. An important one is advocating sustainability just as naturally as promoting their business over the competition.

THE POLITICAL CONTEXT

In the political context and in a global age, political support for free market economics and centre-right government remains generally strong amongst the electorates of the UK, Europe and internationally. National, European and international policy-makers follow this pathway. Within the UK, there is continuing public support for increased government promotion of a competition-and-choice economic agenda. The main political institutions impacting on HR in the UK are Parliament, devolved assemblies in Scotland, Wales and Northern Ireland, and local authorities, including large bodies such as the Greater London Assembly. In Europe, there are the political institutions of the EU (see Chapter 10).

Organisations in both the private and public sectors have to plan responses to the political pressures emanating from these bodies, using appropriate strategies, policies and practices if they are to prosper or at least survive. They do this by drawing upon the support of organised pressure groups, political lobbying or campaigning publicly. Another ongoing political development is privatisation and marketisation. These are normally offset by increased state and European regulation of private and public businesses on the grounds of accountability and the public good. Both the corporate and public sectors have to address the legal requirements arising out of regulation, such as employment legislation or health and safety law as outlined below. Most importantly in the political sphere, there is increasingly active government involvement in labour markets. This too provides both opportunities and threats to organisations as employers. On the one hand, they have to reward, train and develop existing staff to retain them. On the other, they have to compete with one another for scarce skills and competencies in the open labour market.

THE LEGAL CONTEXT

The legal landscape of employment has expanded exponentially in the last 30 years and there is no sign that this trend will diminish. This is especially the case in regulation of the individual employer–employee relationship, encapsulated in the contract of employment, employment protection, discrimination legislation and health and safety at work. In terms of the contract of employment, unfair dismissal and redundancy laws are the major areas of legal intervention. Discrimination law now ranges across sex, equal pay, ethnicity, disability, religion, age and atypical employment. Health and safety incorporates working time and related working issues. Legislation covering a statutory national minimum wage, statutory sick pay, family friendly policy, human rights and transfer of undertakings are all now recognised fields of employment law. HR departments have to comply with these legal rules, monitor and evaluate them.

In terms of regulatory activity by the UK government, devolved assemblies in Scotland, Wales and Northern Ireland, and local authorities, there is no simple explanation why such an extensive regulatory regime has emerged on a piecemeal basis in the past 20 years. However, a number of factors appear to have influenced the rise of the regulatory state. These include UK membership, first, of the European Common Market and, latterly, of the EU, the decline of trade unionism and collective bargaining, macro-economic policy promoting employment (or at least not increasing unemployment), and political expediency (Taylor and Emir 2009). As Moran (2003, p7) concludes, the private character of the UK's former self-regulatory system has been transformed 'to be replaced by tighter state controls; and the institutions and cultures bequeathed to us by the Victorians have either disappeared or are embattled.' Many HR issues are intrinsically linked with these developments.

THE ETHICAL CONTEXT

Creating, exchanging and distributing wealth in market economies like that of the UK is full of moral ambiguities. In the private sector, for example, businesses exist primarily to make profits. To earn profits, businesses produce goods or services and engage in the buying and selling of goods, services and other factor inputs. If profit making is the first claim on business activities, supporters of stockholder theory (ie that businesses exist primarily for those owning 'stock' or 'shares' within them) argue that there is no need for businesses to act ethically towards their stakeholders, other than shareholders, because the prime responsibility of business is to make money. Others argue, in contrast, that producers should consider the effects of their actions on their wider stakeholders and take their interests into consideration. Producing goods like tobacco and alcohol for profit, for example, is explicitly unethical because of the dangers to the health of people. Some also argue that it is unethical for top business executives to receive excessive reward packages (the 'fat cats' syndrome), when their company's employees are on low wages, non-permanent contracts and are doing what many would perceive as demanding, stressful, low-quality work. Those arguing for social responsibility and ethical responses in business organisations, therefore, say business is not exempt from ethical concerns but must recognise, respond to and manage them appropriately (Mellahi and Wood 2003).

There is, however, no universal model of corporate ethics. Business ethics, or ethical corporate practices, are both subjective and contingent upon those pursuing or evaluating them. Corporate ethics raises questions about how firms should deal with those business issues that have implications for their stakeholders. But firms do not produce universalistic answers to these questions. Chryssides and Kaler (1993, p3) claim that business ethics has two aspects. 'One involves the specific situations in which ethical controversy arises; the other concerns the principles of behaviour by which it is appropriate to abide.' These include: ethics of employment, including pay, unions, workers' rights, equal opportunities and non-discrimination; ethics of accounting, finance, restructuring and investing; and ethics of information technology and whistle-blowing.

Central to the study of corporate ethics is the assumption that 'moral rules' apply to business behaviour, just as they do to individual behaviour and that certain actions are wrong or immoral and others are right or moral. Thus it is generally agreed that employers expect their employees not to steal from them, parties to a contract expect each other to honour it and suppliers expect the businesses dealing with them to pay them promptly. The problem is that there is no universal benchmark of morality. Different people resolve moral dilemmas in business using different approaches and alternative frames of reference; this is the case with HR issues too (Sternberg 2004).

ACTIVITY 1.4

Undertake a STEEPLE analysis of your organisation. Identify the main drivers impacting on HR strategy and HR practices within it. Describe and analyse how any *three* of these drivers impact on your organisation's HR strategies/practices. Give examples of the HR strategies/practices used to respond to them in each case.

DEVELOPMENTS IN INTERNATIONAL HRM

This section addresses briefly the extent to which HRM is a universal model of 'good' HR practice or whether it is culturally and country specific. A second issue is trends in international HRM and whether there is convergence in HRM internationally.

THE ORIGINS AND PROGRESS OF HRM

As noted earlier in this chapter, the origins of HRM as a distinctive way of managing people (HRM mark 2), which has a strategic focus, is integrated with line management and is individualist in orientation, were laid in the United States during the 1980s. By this time, the scientific management, human relations and human capital schools of management theory about managing people had been largely rejected by many management practitioners. Scientific management had been based on effective job design and payment systems; human relations on social and psychological insights promoting harmony in the workplace; and human capital theory on investing in labour as an asset in firms, not viewing it as a cost, to raise labour productivity (Schultz 1971). Interestingly, most of these studies about managing people had also originated in the United States.

The next stage, debated first within the United States, was to move on from the flawed studies of the so-called 'in search of excellence' literature (Tiernan *et al* 2001). The crucial issue was to find a framework through which organisations could link their strategic goals with the people they employed, so as to promote organisational effectiveness in conditions of market competitiveness and technological innovation. In 1984, two seminal works on HRM were published.

One, promoting a 'soft' version of HRM, was developed at Harvard Business School by Beer *et al* (1985). This model of HRM starts with analysing stakeholder interests in the business and the business's situational factors. As indicated in Figure 1.5, the Harvard model provides a 'map' of the determinants of HR policy choices and HR outcomes for developing employee commitment within organisations. HR policy choices include employee influence and rewards. HR outcomes include employee commitment, competence, congruence and cost-effectiveness. Within the model, business strategy is developed in relation to employee needs, with the long-term consequences of HRM being individual, organisational and societal well-being.

The other important work at this time was the Michigan model of HRM promoted by Fombrun *et al* (1984). This is a 'hard' version of HRM, emphasising the importance of having a tight 'fit' between HR strategy and business strategy, which defines and determines the types of employee performance required by organisations. The aim of this model is to improve overall organisational performance, with the underpinning goal of creating a strategically-based value system promoting high employee performance. It is based on an 'HR cycle', as illustrated in Figure 1.6. The focus of this cycle is employee performance. The search for performance is reinforced by adopting HR selection processes that appoint employees with appropriate aptitudes, knowledge and values. Effective selection is supported, in turn, by an appraisal system enabling employee performance to be reviewed regularly and a development system aiming to improve performance shortcomings. Finally, the reward system is designed to distinguish and compensate different levels of performance. The HRM cycle then restarts through an iterative process.

As a result of these path-finding and subsequent studies, the concepts of strategy and strategic HRM were, by the 2000s, firmly incorporated in both the literature and practice of HRM. This was despite problems regarding the nature, significance, consequences and possible applications of the concepts involved.

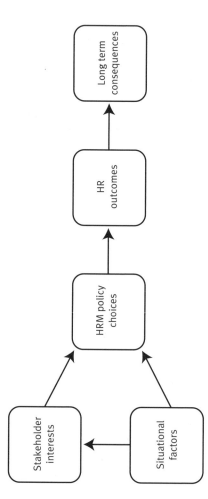

Figure 1.5 The Harvard model of HRM

Adapted from Beer et al (1985)

Figure 1.6 The Michigan HR resource cycle

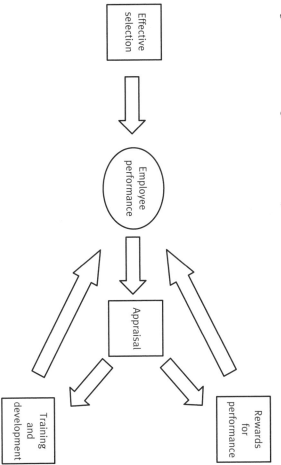

Adapted from Fombrun *et al* (1984)

However, a major debate in the field remains: is the North American HRM paradigm resulting in a convergence of HRM practices universally? Basically, convergence theory or the convergence thesis has a long history (Kerr *et al* 1960). It argues that factors specific to organisations explain HR strategies and policies, with country-specific factors being less important. Thus the US convergence thesis posits that HRM practices are converging internationally as a result of globally driven market and technological forces which affect all firms. Because these forces are universally self-evident, the HR practices associated with them will be transferred around the world (Locke *et al* 1995). In short, the 'market forces model' of convergence posits that market forces generate convergence in HRM within firms towards a US model of HR (Gooderman and Brewster 2003).

The divergence thesis, in contrast, argues that HR systems are determined by national, institutional contexts, not by market and technological forces. This is because national institutions are unique and do not respond readily to market and technological imperatives. Indeed, it is argued, institutional contexts are slow to change, because they derive out of deep-rooted value systems and beliefs. Moreover, change is path dependent and can only be understood in relation to the specific social contexts within which it takes place (Maurice *et al* 1986). Supporters of the divergence thesis argue, because of its North American origins, that HRM is a culturally specific model, largely relevant to Anglo-Saxon business cultures only. The basic assumptions underpinning the Anglo-Saxon approach to HRM are identified with, first, a strong tradition of 'free enterprise' and the 'right to manage'. This means that government intervention in business is expected to be either residual or supportive of it, and that firms are largely autonomous bodies within the market system. Second, the preferred pattern of employment relationships within Anglo-Saxon HRM is individually rather than collectively based; they are not generally subject to trade unionism and collective bargaining. Third, businesses exist primarily to enhance narrow 'shareholder' value, not broader 'stakeholder' interests. The divergence model, in short, suggests that deep-seated differences exist among countries, resulting in continuing divergence in HRM and no convergence in HRM amongst firms.

EUROPEAN AND INTERNATIONAL HRM

Other writers suggest that HRM in places like mainland Europe is essentially different from Anglo-Saxon HRM for a number of cultural, legal and institutional reasons. First, the culture of mainland Europe is far less individualistic than that of North America, the UK and many Commonwealth countries. Above all, the United States is an exceptional case and atypical of the rest of the world (Trompenaars 1985). Second, legislation in Europe protecting individual employment rights, promoting collective employee communication and information channels such as works councils, and providing extensive social security provisions is far more extensive than that found in the United States and elsewhere. Third, the 'Rhineland' model of business enterprise, despite recent reforms within it, contrasts with Anglo-Saxon capitalism by its promotion of the 'stakeholder economy'. Thus whereas the Anglo-Saxon model of 'shareholder' capitalism is characterised by the drive for short-term returns for investors, the Rhineland model is a regulated market economy based on political consensus and comprehensive systems of social security. Fourth, trade union rights are normally incorporated in the Rhineland model but not so strongly within Anglo-Saxon states. Fifth, public ownership is more widespread in mainland European countries than in the United States, whilst in countries like Germany interlocking shareholdings and close management of companies result in less pressure for short-term profits and fewer incentives to drive competitors out of markets (Randlesome 1993).

This analysis gives rise to a corresponding convergence thesis in the European literature, just as in the Anglo-American literature. This is called the 'institutional model of convergence', which suggests that institutional forces generate convergence in HRM amongst European firms towards a common European model of HR. As in the case of the United States, European management and European HRM are claimed to be specific in their nature and common in their culture. This is highlighted by Thurley and Wirdenius (1989), who claim that European management has three main characteristics. First, it is broadly linked to the idea of European integration. Second, it reflects key values such as pluralism and tolerance, although it is not consciously developed out of these values. Third, it is associated with a balanced stakeholder approach and the concept of 'Social Partners' in business.

Katz and Kahn (1978) argue, in turn, that cross-national analyses need to take account of the wider societal variables determining how organisations operate within their external contexts. The national institutional arrangements most affecting national business systems include their employment relations systems, political institutions, the legal framework of corporate governance, education and training systems, the legal system, and product, labour and capital markets. Thus, scope for corporate decision-making on employment issues in countries such as Belgium, France, Germany, the Netherlands and Spain is relatively low, because of the comprehensive labour market legislation in these countries. In the UK, Ireland and the Nordic countries, on the other hand, the state traditionally plays a more limited role in this area, so scope for independent corporate decision-making is greater. In terms of HR practices, the societal contexts of European (and other) countries are likely to explain differences in the extents to which multinational corporations are able to pursue distinctive HR policies within them.

A study by Brewster *et al* (2004, p434) of 23 European countries in the 1990s examined these issues of convergence and divergence, drawing on a large-scale empirical dataset. Figure 1.7 summarises this study's findings in terms of '*directional convergence*' of HR practices amongst countries. This shows that there was strong evidence of directional convergence in four HR areas, considerable evidence in one area and weak evidence in two areas. The authors conclude that: 'From a directional convergence point of view, there seems to be a positive indication of convergence.' In terms of '*final convergence*' of HR practices (ie whether countries are moving towards a common endpoint), however, the answer was not so conclusive. None of the HR practices converged 'at the end of the decade.' There were therefore some signs of HR convergence amongst European countries in the direction of trends. But there were very substantial differences, even continuing divergence, in final convergence. Differences amongst countries, in other words, appeared to be increasing. What this research appears to demonstrate is that whilst some directional convergence in European HRM is apparent, 'there is no unequivocal trend towards final convergence.'

Figure 1.7 Directional convergence in HRM in 23 European countries

Strong evidence	Considerable evidence	Weak evidence
Reduced size of HR departments	Some increases in flexible working practices	Little decentralisation of policy-making; more centralisation
Increased investment in human capital		No general decentralisation of HR responsibilities to line managers; slight centralisation
Increased communication with employees		
Increased use of variable and performance-related pay systems		

Adapted from Brewster *et al* (2004).

MULTINATIONAL CORPORATIONS

A multinational corporation (MNC) is a business organisation with headquarters in one country and operations in a range of others. There are numerous examples of US, UK, European and Asia-Pacific MNCs. These firms, by their very nature, are large organisations and their size means that they often have considerable power and influence globally and locally. The reasons why MNCs expand into different countries vary: reducing transport and distribution costs, avoiding trade barriers, securing supplies of raw materials or markets, and gaining cost advantages such as low labour costs. MNCs also bring benefits to host countries in terms of economic growth and employment opportunities, improvements in production techniques and the quality of human capital, availability of quality goods and services locally, government tax revenues, and improvements in local infrastructures. MNCs also have distinctive HR policies and practices in managing their multinational workforces.

An important characteristic of MNCs and their HR practices is the notion of 'embeddedness'. This suggests, despite the process of globalisation, that economic activity is firmly embedded in distinct national or regional settings or national business systems. The persistence of different national business systems means the contexts in which firms manage their workforces differ markedly. How MNCs manage their workforces across national borders is related to the national business systems of their countries of origin. The evidence relating to MNCs in the United States, for example, indicates that there is a strong 'country of origin' effect in areas such as performance management, diversity and employment relations. However, as MNCs spread geographically, the embeddedness of their original business system declines. Another characteristic of MNCs is that they have scope to tap into the HR practices of their countries of operation, besides their original one. Through the process of 'reverse diffusion' MNCs are able to draw upon HR practices in their foreign subsidiaries and spread these around their international operations subsequently. Since MNCs are embedded in distinct national business contexts, HR practices that are transferred across countries are amended when they are implemented in their new settings.

It is also argued that evidence of convergence across countries is most evident in relation to MNCs and that globalisation is driving a process of convergence of HR practices within them. Ferner and Quintanilla (1998) claim that the internationalisation of French, German and Swiss firms has coincided with them adopting many HR practices common amongst US and UK companies. These include devolved business units and performance-related pay. But other evidence indicates that marked differences amongst MNCs remain. For example, employment regulations differ between countries and there continues to be centralised collective bargaining in some countries but not in others. Thus what is considered normal or accepted practice in HRM continues to vary across national boundaries. One explanation is that while globalisation causes changes in national models of HRM and at firm level, 'these changes are not all occurring at the same pace, nor are they all in the same direction.' Another observation is that pressures of globalisation are not felt evenly across sectors within countries.

So there probably is 'no neat process of convergence.' HRM comes in different national styles but none of these 'is free from pressures to change' (Edwards and Rees 2006, p293).

CONCLUSION: HRM, HR STRATEGY AND HR SOLUTIONS

From the evidence provided in this chapter, to be effective in the business world today HR professionals need to understand the external contexts (STEEPLE) in which their organisation operates and the levers driving change within it. Appropriate and relevant HR strategies, operational HR activities and HR solutions are important factors in meeting organisational needs to promote competitive advantage in the marketplace. The underpinning argument is that people make a difference to organisational performance. Recruiting, selecting, deploying, rewarding, appraising and developing the 'right' people in organisations are necessary conditions for organisational effectiveness, efficiency and business success. Having the 'wrong' people lacking the knowledge, skills, attitudes, and customer-focus to match organisational expectations and requirements is seen to be antithetical to these objectives.

Current good practice indicates that the HR function is critical to formulating and delivering these business and HR objectives and promoting appropriate HR activities. To achieve this purpose, HR specialists have to understand the business they work in, its markets and the forces driving it in the sector where the business operates. They also need to understand their organisation's business strategy, its performance goals and drivers. More specifically, HR practitioners have to draw on insights to lead and influence decisions at strategic, tactical, team, and individual levels across the organisation. They feed these insights and observations to senior managers to influence strategy, as well as developing prioritised HR plans aiming to deliver the needs of the organisation in line with its overall HR strategy. Other roles for HR include: partnering line managers to address sensitive HR issues; advising and coaching managers on the implementation and delivery of HR plans; and, where change is on the agenda, developing project plans to support the implementation of change initiatives, for example during restructuring and mergers.

In carrying out their roles, HR practitioners have to understand the market factors impacting on performance, customers, competitors, globalisation, population change and other factors. Most importantly, in today's competitive business climate, they are expected to speak the 'language of their business' and be able to draw upon the range of HR toolkits available that influence organisational performance.

To be effective, the HR function has to build relationships with internal and external specialists, taking account of current good practice and emerging HR trends, as well as understanding the external HR market. HR is expected to oversee compliance with regulation and corporate policy and to ensure that the organisation has the right people in sufficient numbers, in the right places, with the right experience and capabilities, to deliver the goals of the organisation. HR specialists also need to understand relevant HR technical skills, with in-depth knowledge of some of them. In the HR Profession Map, these are leading and managing the HR function, organisation design, organisation development, resourcing and talent management, learning and talent development, performance and reward, employee engagement, employee relations, and information and service delivery. To support these activities, HR specialists have to access internal and external experts. Finally, HR professionals need to understand the external and internal influences affecting their business or organisation, including political influences impacting on the direction and shape of the organisation and its performance.

In summary, taking account of its contextual circumstances, and to promote appropriate HR solutions, the HR function has to develop critical awareness of what is possible in terms of HR strategy and practices. It also has to recognise what is likely to be acceptable to managers and employees and how strategy and practice can be implemented and reviewed to promote organisational advantage. It does this in the light of the contextual constraints facing it.

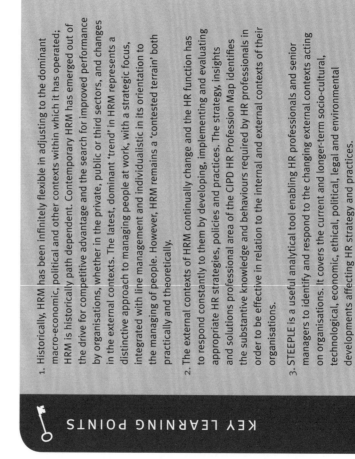

KEY LEARNING POINTS

1. Historically, HRM has been infinitely flexible in adjusting to the dominant macro-economic, political and other contexts within which it has operated; HRM is historically path dependent. Contemporary HRM has emerged out of the drive for competitive advantage and the search for improved performance by organisations, whether in the private, public or third sectors, and changes in the external contexts. The latest, dominant 'trend' in HRM represents a distinctive approach to managing people at work, with a strategic focus, integrated with line management and individualistic in its orientation to the managing of people. However, HRM remains a 'contested terrain' both practically and theoretically.

2. The external contexts of HRM continually change and the HR function has to respond constantly to them by developing, implementing and evaluating appropriate HR strategies, policies and practices. The strategy, insights and solutions professional area of the CIPD HR Profession Map identifies the substantive knowledge and behaviours required by HR professionals in order to be effective in relation to the internal and external contexts of their organisations.

3. STEEPLE is a useful analytical tool enabling HR professionals and senior managers to identify and respond to the changing external contexts acting on organisations. It covers the current and longer-term socio-cultural, technological, economic, ethical, political, legal and environmental developments affecting HR strategy and practices.

4. Major developments in the structure of the HR function are the creation of 'shared services', the 'business partner' role, 'centres of expertise', the 'vendor management' role and 'corporate HR'. Within the new HR paradigm, some HR activities are devolved to line managers. In learning and development, the focus is increasingly on 'learning' rather than on training.

5. With divisionalisation, devolved budgeting, internal markets and increased competition in product and service markets, the search for improved performance is a driving force in most organisations. Linking individual and group performance to the goals and objectives of organisations has been a critical element in the performance management cycle. This involves setting individual targets, finding ways of measuring them, appraising them, reviewing performance, rewarding performance, identifying training needs and setting new targets.

6. Delegation of HR activities to line managers results in them taking on an important role in implementing HR strategies and HR practices. To be effective in this role, line managers need to work with HR professionals and gain their support in managing their staff. Despite the difficulties of this, research shows that line managers play a critical role in motivating staff, promoting job satisfaction and improving performance.

7. Outsourcing of HR activities is another feature of contemporary HRM. It is used to save costs for organisations, draw on external professional expertise, and seek independent HR advice not available in the host organisation. Outsourcing takes various forms. HR activities typically outsourced include payroll administration, recruitment and selection, training and development, executive search, and outplacement and redundancy counselling.

8. Most HR decisions pose ethical questions, since they deal with people issues covering recruitment and selection, managing performance, equal opportunities, learning and development, employee relations, rewards and termination of employment. Also, demands for ethical investment and ethical consumption put further pressure on HR to ensure ethical decision-making in organisations. With the demise of traditional personnel management, and its 'mediatory' and 'welfare' roles between employer and employee, HR practitioners have to be aware of the ethical issues arising from employing people, rewarding them, appraising them, and managing them fairly and consistently.

9. To promote effective HR strategy, the emphasis is on integration. Vertical integration (or 'external fit') refers to the links between business strategy, the external contexts and HR policies and practices. Horizontal integration (or 'internal fit') refers to HR strategy with a high degree of compatibility amongst its various elements.

10. Internationally, a main debate has been the extent to which the Anglo-Saxon, 'new' HRM paradigm is a universal model of practice. On balance, the evidence suggests that HR practices tend to be country-specific, because of powerful institutional and historical path-dependent factors, with HRM diverging among countries rather than generally converging – although some directional convergence is noted in Europe. MNCs exhibit some convergence in HR practices among countries but they also import HR practices from their host countries into local businesses and adapt them.

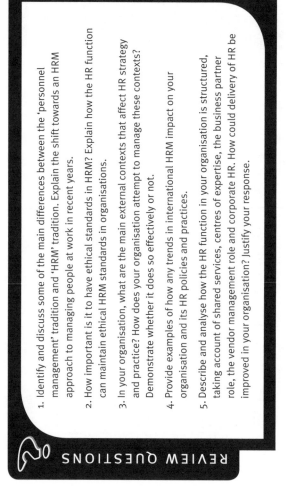

REVIEW QUESTIONS

1. Identify and discuss some of the main differences between the 'personnel management' tradition and 'HRM' tradition. Explain the shift towards an HRM approach to managing people at work in recent years.

2. How important is it to have ethical standards in HRM? Explain how the HR function can maintain ethical HRM standards in organisations.

3. In your organisation, what are the main external contexts that affect HR strategy and practice? How does your organisation attempt to manage these contexts? Demonstrate whether it does so effectively or not.

4. Provide examples of how any trends in international HRM impact on your organisation and its HR policies and practices.

5. Describe and analyse how the HR function in your organisation is structured, taking account of shared services, centres of expertise, the business partner role, the vendor management role and corporate HR. How could delivery of HR be improved in your organisation? Justify your response.

CASE STUDY

CASE STUDY 1.1 DISCRIMINATION ON GROUNDS OF AGE IN EUROPE

Background

In a current analysis of age discrimination in 30 European states, it is reported that public opinion has shifted dramatically since an earlier survey only a year ago. The majority of Europeans now perceive discrimination on grounds of age to be widespread, with opinions about the extent of age discrimination having turned around radically in the course of a single year. Last year, an outright majority of Europeans perceived discrimination on this ground to be rare (52 per cent). This year the balance has shifted, with 58 per cent now perceiving it to be widespread, compared with 37 per cent who believe it is rare. Two per cent think that discrimination on grounds of age is non-existent in their country and a further 3 per cent say they 'don't know'.

When respondents were asked to estimate the extent of age discrimination, they were not asked to differentiate whether it is on the grounds of old age or youth. Thus respondents would have had different ideas in mind when thinking about this question.

Regardless of the above distinction, the majority view in all but six countries is that age discrimination is widespread. In fact, in 22 of the 30 countries surveyed, this opinion is held by an absolute majority. Hungarian respondents top the list, with 79 per cent saying that age discrimination is widespread in their country. This is followed by respondents in the Czech Republic (74 per cent), France (68 per cent), Latvia (67 per cent) and the Netherlands (66 per cent).

Older respondents are more likely to say age discrimination is widespread, although it is uncertain whether respondents associate 'age discrimination' with a specific age group. But on the basis of this survey, respondents aged 40 or over are more likely to say that discrimination on ground of age is widespread. This is in direct contrast to other grounds of discrimination, which are more likely to seen as widespread by the youngest groups of respondents. Women (60 per cent) are more likely to see age discrimination as being widespread than are men (55 per cent).

Changes in perceptions of discrimination on grounds of age

Perception that age discrimination is widespread has increased throughout Europe. Since last year, the perception that age discrimination is widespread has increased from 42 per cent to 58 per cent (+16 points). This trend is noted in all countries surveyed, with the exception of Portugal, where only a minor increase was recorded (+2 points). Further, apart from Italy (+8 points), these shifts are above 10 percentage points in all other countries surveyed. The largest increases were recorded in Cyprus (+27 points), Romania (+25 points), France and the Netherlands (both +22 points).

The economic crisis seems to lie at the core of this shift in opinion: one of the perceived consequences of the crisis is that the jobs of older Europeans are less secure.

In 14 of the 30 countries surveyed, the majority view is that age discrimination is now less widespread. This view is particularly strong in Cyprus (77 per cent) and is next highest in Denmark (64 per cent) and Malta (62 per cent). Conversely, there are also three countries where at least six out of 10 respondents feel the contrary: 73 per cent of Hungarians, 65 per cent of Czech and 60 per cent of Slovaks think age discrimination is more widespread.

Experience of age discrimination

Age is the ground for discrimination that is most frequently experienced by respondents. Whilst public perceptions of age discrimination have shifted in the course of the year, the proportion of respondents reporting that they have been discriminated against has not changed. However, at 6 per cent, 'age' continues to represent the most common ground of self-reported discrimination. Unlike discrimination on ground of ethnicity, there is no significant gap between experienced and witnessed discrimination on grounds of age, with 8 per cent of respondents reporting that they had witnessed this form of discrimination. This comparatively high figure may well be due to the fact that age is a shared attribute relevant to everyone, and young and old may be susceptible to suffer discrimination under various (often differing) circumstances. Age discrimination is 'most' prominent in the Czech Republic, with 11 per cent saying they have experienced it and 17 per cent saying that they have witnessed it. Other countries showing higher than average levels of reported discrimination, for both measures, are Sweden and Slovakia.

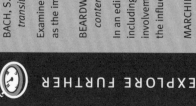

EXPLORE FURTHER

BACH, S. (ed.) (2005) *Managing human resources: personnel management in transition*. Oxford: Blackwell.

Examines and analyses all the contemporary debates about HRM practice, as well as the impacts of environmental change on the ways people are managed in the UK.

BEARDWELL, J. and CLAYDON, T. (eds) (2007) *Human resource management: a contemporary approach*. 5th ed. Harlow: FT/Prentice Hall.

In an edited volume, covers a range of topical HRM themes and debates of today, including HR strategy, gender and diversity, employee rights, and employee involvement and participation. Also examines international HRM issues, as well as the influence of multinational corporations on HR policy and practice.

MARCHINGTON, M. and WILKINSON, A. (2008) *Human resource management at work: people management and development*. 4th ed. London: CIPD.

Undertakes a critical review of current HRM theory and practice and is very strong on up-to-date research evidence. Is comprehensive in coverage and looks outside of the HR box in discussing major topics and includes material on HR research and change management skills.

TORRINGTON, D., HALL, L., TAYLOR, S. and ATKINSON, C. (2009) *Fundamentals of human resource management: managing people at work*. Harlow: Pearson Education.

Offers a comprehensive introduction to contemporary HRM issues affecting HR specialists and line managers, and covers a wide range of both theoretical topics and practical issues.

CHAPTER 2

Contemporary organisations and their internal contexts

INTRODUCTION

Organisations pervade the modern world. They are complex social constructs, with multiple stakeholders and the 'special' interests with which each is associated. Organisations vary in a number of ways. These include size, purpose, structure, technology, ownership, managerial systems, HR practices, types and skills of workforce, geographical location and other factors. Each organisation has its own socially defined contexts or boundaries within which its stakeholders, including management, operate. In Chapter 1, the external contexts of organisations, or those outside the formal boundaries of organisations, were critically examined. Managers have little control over these and respond to them. In this chapter, the internal contexts of organisations, which are more capable of being managed, are examined.

The chapter starts by analysing the complex nature of contemporary organisations through considering some traditional and contemporary theories of organisations. It then reviews the types, objectives and internal contexts of organisations, concentrating on: culture; layout; innovation; power, conflict and control; and social components (CLIPS). The chapter goes on to examine some current issues such as: old and new organisation forms, including networking and strategic alliances; integration, control and HRM; the critical drive for performance, profit and efficiency; and continuity and change. The chapter concludes by examining the major stakeholders in organisations and discussing some issues of corporate governance and accountability.

LEARNING OUTCOMES

By the end of this chapter, readers should be able to understand, explain and critically evaluate:

- the main theoretical approaches to organisations

- types, objectives and internal contexts of contemporary organisations

- current issues in organisations

- the major stakeholders in organisations

- the principles of corporate governance, accountability and corporate social responsibility

- how these contexts impact on HR strategy and HR practices.

In addition, readers should also be able to:

- evaluate current trends and issues in organisation theory and management practice

- identify actual and potential constraints on organisational autonomy

- undertake effective analyses of contemporary organisations.

THEORIES OF ORGANISATIONS

Organisation theory, sometimes described as organisational behaviour or organisation studies, is the interdisciplinary field that systematically examines and applies knowledge of how people act their roles in organisations and the factors influencing this. As a field, organisation theory draws on a range of academic and practical disciplines such as psychology, sociology, economics, politics, philosophy and ethics. This makes it both a demanding and sometimes contradictory field of study. The concept of an organisation is a surprisingly complex and problematic one. But organisations matter in societies if only because just about everything we do occurs within them. Basically, organisations exist for any collective, purposeful activity. They acquire resources or inputs to do this; they then convert them into outputs, as goods or services. The difference between the value of the outputs produced and of the inputs used is added value. This benefits the owners of the organisation, its managers, its workforce, and its customers, as well as contributing to wealth creation and the distribution of wealth in society generally. HR practitioners need to appreciate the underlying principles of organisation theory to enable them to understand the role and functions of management and of the HR function, as well as their limitations.

Organisations do a number of things: producing goods and services which people buy; providing public goods and services to citizens who use them, having paid for them through taxes; satisfying people's religious and political needs; employing people and other resources; creating and distributing wealth; making war; imprisoning criminals; representing workers' interests; and doing other things too. So it is not surprising that people who study the theory and practice of 'management' study organisations and the role of management within them. However, 'organisation' is not synonymous with 'management'. Many mainstream, orthodox approaches to studying organisations are focused through the lens of management alone and are concerned only with managerial interpretations of what organisations are for, or what they *should* be for, and how they can be organised to make them economically successful and managerially effective. This means some organisation studies concentrate largely on the search for efficiency, order and rationality in organisations to enable managers to perform better. But there are also unorthodox schools of organisation theory such as critical organisation theory and radical theory (Parker 2002). These schools ask quite different questions about organisations and provide different answers from the managerial one. There are, then, various approaches to studying and understanding organisations. It is to these 'approaches' to organisation theory that the next section turns. It is important for managers and HR professionals to understand these approaches, as abstract theory influences real-life managerial practices in so many ways.

APPROACHES TO ORGANISATION THEORY

There are three main approaches to studying organisations. In outline, these are: the positivist (or 'modernist') view, the symbolic-interpretive (or 'constructivist') view, and the 'postmodernist' view. Each has its own perspectives, assumptions and interpretations of the field. The underpinning elements within each approach are identified and summarised in Figure 2.1. The differences between them arise, in each case, out of views about the nature of reality, the focus of organisation theory, the theory of knowledge and nature of organisations. Each also has a preferred methodology for researching organisations. Positivists prefer quantitative research, those holding a symbolic viewpoint qualitative research, and postmodernists textual research.

Modernism (or the orthodox) approach to organisation theory is important because it provides models, frameworks and principles for practising managers. This enables managers to design organisations, diagnose organisational problems and try to manage them effectively. The overall objective of positivism is prediction and control within organisations. Its model for human relationships is hierarchy at work and is based on the view that organisational reality is objective, with reality existing independently of organisation theory. For positivists (or modernists), knowledge is universal, developed through facts and data, and recognised through convergence.

The symbolic perspective (or symbolic-interpretivism) argues that organisational reality does not have an objective existence and that people construct organisational realities through giving them their own meanings. Understanding is the overall objective of the symbolic perspective. Its model for human relationships is community and it is based on the view that organisational reality is socially constructed diversity. For supporters of the symbolic perspective,

Figure 2.1 Approaches to the study of organisations

	Modernist	Symbolic interpretivist	Postmodernist
The nature of reality	There is an external, objective reality, independent of knowledge of it	There is no external, independent, objective reality, only subjective awareness of it	Reality appears through language, is situated in discourse, and is a 'text' to be read or performed
Theory of knowledge	Knowledge is 'positivist', based on observation; it is discovered through conceptualisation and reliable measurement; knowledge accumulates	All knowledge is 'interpretivist' and relative to the knower; it is socially constructed; it shifts and changes over time	Knowledge is not 'truth', because its meanings cannot be fixed; there is no independent reality, only interpretations of it; knowledge is a power play
Preferred research methodology	Quantitative	Qualitative	Textual
The nature of organisations	Organisations are objective, real entities in a real world, driven by norms of rationality, efficiency and effectiveness	Organisations are socially constructed entities and are reconstructed by their members, through symbolically mediated interactions	Organisations are texts, produced by and in language; organisations are sites enacting power relations, irrationality and communicative distortion
Focus of organisation theory	Discovering universal laws, techniques of organisation, methods of control, rational structures and procedures	Describing how people give meaning and order to their experiences through interpretive, symbolic acts	Deconstructing organisational texts, challenging managerial ideologies, revealing marginalised viewpoints

knowledge is particular and developed through meaning and interpretation; it is recognised through coherence.

The postmodern approach to organisation theory is that organisations are not characterised by order and unity but by uncertainty, image, complexity and contradiction. The overall objective of the postmodern, unorthodox approach is freedom within organisations. Its model for human relationships is self-determination. It is based on the view that organisational reality is constantly shifting and fluid. For postmodernists, knowledge is provisional, developed through exposure and experience, and is recognised through incoherence, fragmentation and deconstruction.

CLASSICAL STUDIES OF ORGANISATIONS

Classical studies of organisations can be broadly categorised as theories of bureaucracy, scientific management and human relations theory. Originating mostly in the early to mid-twentieth century, these theories, and the principles underpinning them, can still be observed in practice within many organisations today. Central to their purpose is managerial control within organisations, linked with an ideology of progress that is expected to result in more educated, knowledgeable, civilised societies.

Bureaucracy

One of the founding scholars of bureaucratic organisation theory was Max Weber (1947), a German sociologist whose works bridged the late nineteenth and early twentieth centuries. His authoritative study of bureaucracy was published in German in 1924 but not translated into English till 1947. He wanted to understand how industrialisation affected society, especially through its effects on authority structures. He distinguished between three types of authority: traditional, charismatic and rational-legal. Traditional authority is inherited status, defined and maintained by what has happened in the past, such as within religious groups. Charismatic authority emerges out of the personal, magnetic character of some leaders. Charisma justifies their authority without any other reason, and is demonstrated by some political and managerial leaders. Weber argued that industrialisation gave rise to a third form of authority – rational-legal authority. This was based on rules and legally binding procedures. He considered the emergence of bureaucratic authority structures, such as those in large businesses or governments, as being superior to traditional or charismatic authority. Within a framework of rational-legal authority, large societies and big organisations have an endless supply of people to whom authority can be given, because rational choices can be made on the basis of their leadership and technical expertise.

The kinds of organisations emerging from the application of the rational-legal principle, defined by rules and hierarchical relationships, are typical bureaucracies. They became a dominant model of organisation, despite Weber's concerns about them, because they represented the most technically efficient and rational form of organisation. He distinguished, however, between 'formal rationality' and 'substantive rationality'. The first involves the means to achieve a particular end, so that this is done in the most efficient manner for that purpose. The second is concerned with whether the ends themselves are rational. Since bureaucracies are not concerned with ends, only means, Weber warned that formal rationality without substantive (or 'value') rationality leads to an 'iron cage' capable of imprisoning humanity and making humankind into 'cogs' in an ever-moving social mechanism. The basic point is that bureaucracies, in the interests of efficiency, have no underpinning ethical principle, although du Gay (2000) challenges this. His view is that 'pure' bureaucracy incorporates an ethic of 'fairness', although bureaucracies rarely embody this ethic persuasively.

Other studies such as Crozier (1964), Dalton (1959) and Gouldner (1954) demonstrate the dysfunctions of bureaucracy. One implication is that there is commonly a disjuncture between the 'formal' and 'informal' organisation. The formal concerns the rules and procedures that are meant to happen. The informal concerns the personal prejudices, motivations and actions of people in the organisation and gives rise to what actually happens. A second implication is that what is done in organisations has both intended and unintended consequences. The unintended consequences of actions and decisions are perhaps the more important, since they are unforeseen and possibly undesired. This leads Grey (2009, p30) to conclude that the idea of a bureaucratic organisation 'being simply about the establishment of appropriate means to reach given ends is fundamentally, irredeemably and irrevocably flawed'. He identifies human agency, unpredictability and goal displacement within bureaucratic organisations as other factors giving rise to tensions between formal and informal organisation.

Scientific management

By the turn of the twentieth century, big businesses were looking for ever-new ways to make work more efficient and workers more productive. The next big shift in thinking about how work organisation could be improved originated in the iron and steel industry in Pennsylvania in the United States. The person most associated with this was Frederick Winslow Taylor (1911), an industrial engineer who was working in an industry where, at that time, it was normal for workers to organise their own work. To improve efficiency and regain control of the work process, Taylor saw the solution as lying in 'scientific management'. His analysis was based on 'experiments' he had conducted in steel plants. Arising out of this, he identified four principles of scientific management: a science of each element of work, the scientific selection and training of workers, division of labour between managers and workers, and co-operation between managers and workers. His philosophy was that applying scientific methods to working and to labour would maximise the benefits of the factory to society, as well as achieving high levels of co-operation between management and workers. His system was scientific, since he wanted managers to employ research and experimentation to find correct standards, principles and processes. This would result in higher pay for workers and lower production costs for organisations. His system was a managerial one, since he wished to provide managers with practical tools for improving efficiency, raising productivity and improving manager–worker co-operation.

These principles were developed by other observers and later imported into countries around the world including Germany, Japan and Soviet Russia (Merkle 1980). The dominance of some technical aspects of management, such as cost savings, control systems and incentive payments, demonstrates the influence that Taylorism continues to exert in some organisations even today. The scientific management legacy is also embodied in the promotion of rationalisation in contemporary organisations. Scientific management principles, as espoused by Taylor and his acolytes, receded into the background in the late 1930s and 1940s. Subsequent development of operations' research techniques and human engineering methods for organisational problem-solving in the 1940s and 1950s, however, can also be placed in the scientific management category. Each developed a body of technical methods for solving work problems. Both essentially separated the planning of problem-solving processes from the routine acting-out of solutions. What was different from classical scientific management was the nature of the techniques.

Mid-twentieth-century 'Fordism' was an intensification of the Taylorist approach introduced into the Ford Motor Company. Its central feature, the moving assembly line, enabled managers to gain greater control over the effort of workers by speeding up production lines (Beynon 1973). Under Fordism, wages were good, employment relations conflict-ridden, and absenteeism and labour turnover high. Fordism was perhaps the fullest expression of a particular, influential approach to organising work – scientific management. But, like its earlier versions, Fordism failed to motivate the workforce, resulting in alienated workers and dysfunctional industrial conflict.

Human relations theory

The founder of the 'Human Relations School' was Elton Mayo, an Australian who had migrated to the United States in the 1920s. His fundamental model of society, and of organisation, was one of social integration and cohesion rather than conflict. The major contribution that he and his colleagues identified was the importance of the human factor in organisations. Whereas acolytes of scientific management had sought to control working teams by avoiding human relationships in organisations, human relations theorists sought to control them through human relationships. Mayo and his colleagues are associated with the so-called Hawthorne Studies at the Hawthorne plant of the Western Electric organisation, in Chicago, in the late 1920s (Roethlisberger and Dickson 1939). Their studies of the illumination experiment showed that worker productivity changed as a result of group formation. The bank wiring room experiment, in turn, showed how the work group set informal norms around production levels. Despite later criticisms of the Hawthorne data, these studies demonstrated that workers were not simply motivated by economic considerations alone but that the 'informal' side of organisation was just as important (if not more so) as the 'formal' side (ie the organisation's rules and official hierarchy) (Carey 2002).

Mayo's work (1933) emphasised the importance of informal work relations, their role in sustaining formal systems and the necessity of meshing the formal and informal systems together. In the informal system, special attention was focused on what motivates people to maximise their commitment and satisfaction at work. Therapeutic interviews were recommended as a management tool to create better-adjusted workers, with training in counselling and interviewing being viewed as essential management skills. Mayo's later work with academic colleagues at Harvard University contributed to an emergent consensus around the centrality of notions of social order, conformism and the necessity of building rational normative commitments (Clegg *et al* 2008). A central theme of his later work was that rushed implementation of new technologies in organisations gave rise to most of the problems experienced within them. These problems were seen as being essentially psychological. Mayo believed therefore that the technical competencies of managers needed to be complemented by corresponding social competencies.

Three main themes run throughout Mayo's works. First, work is a group rather than an individual activity, where people find a sense of belonging and a need for recognition. These groups have a profound influence on individual workers' disposition and well-being. Second, when workers complain, it indicates underlying psychological issues. Third, management can foster collaboration within informal work groups by creating greater cohesion and unity, resulting in positive organisational benefits.

In the 1960s and 1970s, there was renewed interest in the human factor at work, this time within the 'neo human relations' school. This comprised a disparate group of US scholars who drew largely upon psychological and 'behavioural science' approaches to organisations and their managerial problems. Herzberg (1966), for example, developed a 'motivation–hygiene' model of behaviour. He argued that hygiene factors depend on the context of work and merely prevent job dissatisfaction. Satisfiers or motivators, on the other hand, derive from the job and produce positive effects on productivity. McGregor's (1960) main contribution was to leadership theory and motivation at work, through his 'theory X' and 'theory Y' of management. Theory Y, a participative approach to managing people, was seen as being more effective than the traditional theory X model, which identified people as lazy, disliking work and not wanting responsibility. For him, the intellectual potentialities of people at work were only partially realised. His colleague, Warren Bennis (1966), was a leading theorist in the field of organisation development. Argyris (1960) was concerned with making organisations 'healthy', by using 'intervention theory'. This, he claimed, integrated the needs of individuals and the organisations employing them, thus solving their managerial problems in an in-depth way.

ACTIVITY 2.1

Drawing upon any one or more of the above classical studies of organisations – bureaucracy, scientific management and human relations theory – examine your organisation and explain whether or not it has adopted any of these theoretical perspectives in terms of its organisational structures, processes and methods of managing. If so, what has been their impact on HRM in the organisation?

Recent studies of organisations can be broadly categorised as theories of managing culture, post-bureaucracy, change management and 'fast capitalism.' Each reflects the centrality of people management within contemporary organisation studies. Once again the perspective is strongly positivist and based on instrumental rationality and control within organisations. Many of these theoretical ideas have been incorporated into recent managerial practices, but how effectively is open to debate (Crowther and Green 2004).

MANAGING CULTURE

In the 1980s, a central concern of organisation studies turned to managing corporate culture. This originated in the so-called 'excellence' studies by Peters and Waterman (1982), Deal and Kennedy (1982) and, later, Schein (1997), which propelled 'culture' to the centre stage of corporate analysis and review. There are various definitions of culture but Schein's (1980) is prototypical. He defines it as the pattern of basic assumptions that a given group has invented, discovered or developed. This is done in response to problems of external adaptation and internal integration, which are taught to new members as the correct way to perceive, think, and feel in relation to these problems. The message emerging from these studies was that great (United States) companies have excellent cultures, which deliver outstanding financial success. What makes a culture 'great' are core corporate values that are acted upon and monitored by management. These studies attempted to demonstrate how specific patterns of learned and shared basic assumptions framed the perceptions, thoughts and feelings of organisational members. These works tried to answer questions such as: How are things done in an organisation? What is acceptable behaviour within it? What organisational norms and values are transmitted to new members? What norms are members expected to use to solve organisational problems? And which ones do they use? This theoretical school assumed companies that forged a 'strong,' known culture, incorporating beliefs and commitments shared by organisational members, would achieve good morale, high performance and excellent results.

Later approaches argued that organisational culture tends to be fragmented. There may not be a dominant culture because the nature of culture is dependent upon a range of identities including: occupation, location, social class, gender, ethnicity, age and so on. Thus in a single organisation, several sub-cultures can be embedded and flourish locally in conditions that are highly variable. However, whether organisational culture is largely homogeneous or fragmented, it incorporates important patterns that shape organisational realities. If culture is the pattern of shared meanings and understandings passed down in organisations through language, symbols and artefacts, then, from the cultural perspective, to understand organisations means understanding their cultures.

POST-BUREAUCRACY, CHANGE MANAGEMENT AND 'DISORGANISED CAPITALISM'

Another trend in organisation theory since the 1980s is a reaction against bureaucracy. This led to the search for effective methods of managing organisational change and dealing with the speed of change in contemporary societies. This shift in emphasis of organisation theory is driven by three factors. First, there is the underpinning belief among some observers that the conditions for bureaucracy in organisations no longer persist. Second, there is the claim by others that stability in organisations and societies is no longer the norm and that change is endemic in the contemporary world. Third, there is the observation that both the economy and society are characterised by a preoccupation with the speed of contemporary life.

Thus with globalisation, the emergence of service economies in the Western world and more educated workforces, Taylorist forms of Fordism are viewed as no longer necessary. It is also suggested that people in organisations need to be flexible and innovative, especially in the light of rapid external change. As a result, there has been a development of a range of new organisational forms. Heckscher (1994) has called these 'post-bureaucratic' organisations in contrast to the bureaucratic ideal type. Other descriptions are 'virtual', 'networked' or 'postmodern' organisations. Post-bureaucracy has three main characteristics. First, organisational rules are replaced with consensus and dialogue-based personal influence rather than status, with people being trusted to act on the basis of shared values, not rules. Second, responsibilities are assigned based on competence for tasks done rather than hierarchy and are dealt with personally rather than impersonally. Third, post-bureaucratic organisations have open boundaries, with people coming into and out of organisations in flexible ways, such as through part-time, temporary and consultancy roles.

The origins of this debate can be traced to Burns and Stalker's (1961) seminal study of the management of innovation in the Scottish and English electronics industries in the mid-1950s. They identified two divergent systems of management practice, although neither was fully applied in any of the firms studied. One was the 'mechanistic', which was appropriate to enterprises operating under conditions of relative stability. The other was 'organic' which was appropriate to enterprises operating in conditions of change. These two ideal typologies are summarised in Figure 2.2.

ACTIVITY 2.2

To what extent does your organisation have a mechanistic or organic form? Is it effective or ineffective and why?

Figure 2.2 Mechanistic and organic forms of organisation

Mechanistic form	Organic form
Hierarchical	Horizontal
Predominantly vertical communication	Predominantly lateral communication
Centralised decision-making	Decentralised decision-making
Well-defined specialist roles	Loosely defined, less specialist roles
High reliance on standardised rules and procedures	High reliance on mutual adjustment between co-workers

Adapted from Burns and Stalker (1961).

A number of studies have, however, questioned the extent of post-bureaucratic organisations. Deldridge's (1998, p192) ethnographic study of two British factories, one Japanese-owned and the other European-owned, calls into question the post-bureaucratic transformation. Although the Japanese firm used lean production, just-in-time management, customer focus and HRM techniques, Delbridge concludes that there was considerable similarity between the traditional forms of working in the European firm and new forms of working, such as a flatter hierarchy, participation and trust, in the Japanese firm. In his view, 'there was little to suggest that contemporary manufacturing is best characterised as "postfordist".'

The change agenda has also been an important part of the search for new forms of organisation. Change theorists argue that today's top managers need to keep organisational arrangements under continual review. This means making organisational changes more often than previously, because of changes in their external contexts. It also involves making strategic initiatives of their own choosing. In the last decade, managers and theorists have begun to recognise that the driving force behind change is not always the same. Whereas in the past, changes in the external context were viewed as responsible for innovation, two other considerations have been highlighted recently. These are, first, the roles of different stakeholders, especially customers, in the process and, second, the fact that innovation does not happen in a vacuum. An infrastructure is required to provide a platform for innovation to grow. This includes scientific knowledge, institutional norms, competent human resources, financial investors and informed consumers.

Mumford (1967, p110) observed a generation ago a number of features of contemporary capitalism. These were 'power, speed, motion, standardization, quantification, regimentation, precision, uniformity, astronomical regularity, control, above all control'. The speeding-up of life and working life continues today. The impacts on organisations are many-sided. In the UK, unlike in other states such as France, there has been an internationalisation of corporate ownership, with resultant changes in working practices and HR policies.

Disorganised capitalism, fast capitalism, or 'casino' capitalism depends upon the unleashing of vast amounts of finance capital, following the breakdown of the Bretton Woods agreement in the 1970s. Disorganised capitalism is driven by organisations promulgating 'brands' and pursuing value, with the underlying aim of maximising shareholder value. 'Organised capitalism', in contrast, was mainly concerned with producing useful goods and services for consumers, often based on mass production techniques (Lash and Urry 1994). Today private equity firms especially buy up companies, refinance them and resell them, resulting in redundancies, organisational restructuring and work intensification. As Grey (2009, p115) concludes: 'the idea of speed as necessary, obvious, incontestable and perhaps even desirable becomes insinuated into the very fabric of people's everyday lives and self-understandings.'

Some of the consequences of disorganised, fast capitalism have been noted by Layard (2005), who shows that increases in prosperity in the UK in the post-Second World War period have not resulted in greater happiness. Sennett (1998) records the deleterious effects on working life of this new capitalism, which has destroyed what had been based formerly on solid social relations and 'character' at work. This includes the erosion of stable career structures and long-term organisational stability. James (2007), in turn, identifies the phenomenon of 'affluenza'. This is the ways in which rising prosperity has increased levels of anxiety, selfishness, unsatisfying consumption and mental illness amongst individuals. Fast capitalism also creates winners and losers. For example, it changes the nature of management in organisations. Some managers, especially those with financial skills, are most likely to benefit from the changes outlined above; other, middle managers find their job roles changed and, in some cases, gone as a result of organisational restructuring and continuing, rapid organisational and market changes.

POSTSCRIPT

To sum up, contemporary studies of organisation, as well as classical theory, are rooted in the orthodox managerialist-positivist camp of organisation theory. Managerial writers are interested in organisations from a particular viewpoint: namely how they can be managed more effectively. Their goal is to discover fact-based, reliable organisational predictions which, if realised, will be useful to managers, although, as Grey (2009, p8) and similar scholars argue, they 'have consistently failed to come up with anything of much use to managers or others'. For Hatch and Cunliffe (2006), orthodox studies are important because they provide analytical frameworks, predictive models and principles for organising that managers can use to diagnose organisational problems and design organisational structures. However, orthodox theorists are uncritical about the values they promote, such as order, rationality, structure, progress and efficiency, as well as the practices these values encourage, such as domination and control over individuals and groups within organisations. The orthodox, modern approach, in short, is obsessed with the assumption of organisational manageability.

By contrast, those adopting the symbolic perspective study the role that humankind plays in creating organisational life. They challenge conventional wisdoms about the nature of managerially structured organisations. They argue that there are no 'laws' of organisation to be discovered and, by the very nature of organisational life, prediction is almost impossible. For them, organisational reality is discovered by people in organisations and by organisation theory itself. The symbolic or interpretivist approach, in short, claims that organisational realities are socially produced as members interact, negotiate and make sense of their experiences individually.

Postmodernists, in turn, are associated with narrative approaches to organisation and organisation theory. They stress the importance of organisational 'stories' as small 'narratives' but they do not 'take sides' in determining which are 'reality'. There are, in short, no consensual, all-embracing theories underpinning behaviour, and the understanding of behaviour, within organisations. The postmodernists' greatest preoccupation is with 'change'.

ACTIVITY 2.3

What evidence is there to show that your organisation has adopted any of the above contemporary organisation theories – managing culture, post-bureaucracy and change management – for the purposes of management and control recently? What has been the effect of these interventions on managing people? Have they been effective or ineffective and why?

ACTIVITY 2.4

Examine your organisation in terms of either a symbolic perspective or a postmodern perspective, drawing upon the sub-headings: the focus of organisation theory, the theory of knowledge and the nature of organisations. What do you infer about your organisation from these observations, compared with Activity 2.3 above?

TYPES, OBJECTIVES AND INTERNAL CONTEXTS OF ORGANISATIONS

In terms of concrete forms of organisation, there is a range of methods for classifying them and for examining their objectives and goals. Organisations also have a series of interrelated internal contexts. As explained in the preface, the internal contexts of organisations may be divided into five clusters. These are: culture; layout; innovation; power, conflict and control; and social components (CLIPS). These typical internal contexts of organisations, designed and used by managers, are outlined below.

ORGANISATIONAL TYPOLOGIES

Defining what organisations are is a relatively straightforward task; providing a typology or taxonomy of them is more problematic. An early classification by Blau and Scott (1963) identified the main criterion of an organisation as being its 'prime beneficiaries.' This produced four groupings: mutual benefit concerns (where workers were the main beneficiaries); business concerns (the owners); service organisations (clients or customers); and 'commonweal organisations' (the public at large). Eldridge and Crombie (1974) identified five organisational typologies: functional, technological, regulatory, structural and 'total institutions.' Etzioni's (1975) regulatory typology, for instance, using the concept of 'compliance', is summarised in Figure 2.3 below. He concluded that only three out of his nine possible organisational types were congruent. This was because they were more effective and more frequent than the other six. More recently, Ferguson and Ferguson (2000) produced a six-fold classificatory taxonomy of five economic sectors: the large corporate sector; small and medium-sized private enterprises; the state sector; the 'hidden economy'; and the 'natural economy', such as family, informal networks and community groups. Their typology is based on two main features of organisations: their purpose and degree of institutionalisation.

A key distinction between organisations is whether they are private (market) or public (political) organisations. Yet, in practice, the distinction is blurred, since it is difficult to determine exactly where private organisations end and public ones begin. Dunsire and Hood (1989) suggest that to spend time trying to separate them out is a both a distraction and an irrelevance. Tomkins (1987), in turn, provides a useful spectrum of organisational types, ranging from the fully private to the fully public organisation without competition, as shown in Figure 2.4. He illustrates the interdependence and interrelationships between the market and political spheres.

Another way of classifying organisations is by their 'orientation' and 'ownership.' Orientation relates to the basic goals that organisations seek to achieve; ownership is who legally owns them. The goals of privately owned businesses are to satisfy consumer demand in the market place and to provide profits ('added value') to their shareholders or legal owners. The goals of publicly owned organisations, such as public services, are to satisfy citizens' social demands (or need) for public goods or services. These are paid for by taxes or supported by state subsidies, regardless of citizens' ability to pay for them. Thus privately owned organisations and publicly owned organisations have fundamentally different goals or 'goal orientation'. They are basically distinguishable by the terms 'demand' and 'need' respectively and their derivative objectives (ie making profits and satisfying the 'public good') are characterised differently. The relationship between organisational orientation and organisational ownership is shown in Figure 2.5. Orientation is having either 'profit and added-value goals' or 'welfare, community and budgetary goals'; ownership is either 'private' or 'public'. By this typology, there are four types of organisation: private businesses, public corporations, public services and voluntary bodies or social enterprises.

Figure 2.3 Etzioni's regulatory typology of organisations

Power applied by lower-level participants to the organisation/ *Involvement* by lower-level participants in the organisation	**Coercive power** (application of possible sanctions against lower-level participants)	**Remunerative power** (control of material resources by higher-level participants)	**Normative power** (manipulation of symbolic rewards by higher-level participants)
Alienative involvement (lower-level participants involved against their wishes)	*Congruent*	Not-congruent	Not-congruent
Calculative involvement (lower-level participants attached to extrinsic rewards)	Not-congruent	*Congruent*	Not-congruent
Moral involvement (lower-level participants identified with the values, purposes of the organisation)	Not-congruent	Not-congruent	*Congruent*

Adapted from Etzioni (1975).

advantage. They try to do this because culture is a variable to be manipulated by them to enhance desired levels of organisational performance. These cultural assumptions are a product of both national and internal culture. National cultural differences, as identified by Hofstede (2001), for example, arise out of attitudes to 'power distance' relations, 'uncertainty avoidance', 'individualism versus collectivism' and 'masculine versus feminine' gender roles in different countries.

According to Schein (1997), internal culture is not on the surface of organisations but what lies beneath. It is often covert and unconscious. It is the way that members of an organisation perceive its contexts and the organisation. Schein presents a useful differentiation between three levels of organisational culture. Level 1 is the 'artefacts' of culture. These are the visible features of an organisation such as its architecture, interior design and dress codes. They consist of 'objects', 'narratives' and 'activities' as shown in Figure 2.6. Level 2 is the 'values' of the organisation. These are the invisible features of organisational culture that encompass the norms, beliefs and values that members refer to when discussing internal issues. These include the organisation's mission statement, its commitment to diversity or its attitudes to customers. The third, deepest level is the basic assumptions underpinning the organisation's values and its artefacts. Level 3 is probably the most important level of organisational culture and includes the assumptions that shape the beliefs, norms and views of organisational members. It is these assumptions that guide member behaviour, without being explicitly expressed. Level 3 is the most influential level of organisational culture, because it shapes decision-making almost invisibly. An example of the basic assumptions underpinning public service organisations is 'the seven principles of public life', as illustrated in Figure 2.7.

Figure 2.6 Examples of artefacts of organisational culture

Objects	Narratives	Activities
Architecture	Humour	Ceremonies
Corporate logo	Jargon	Communications
Décor	Metaphors	Customs
Design	Myths	Meetings
Displays	Names	Parties
Dress codes	Nicknames	Rewards
Equipment	Rhetoric	Rituals
Posters	Rumours	Sanctions
Products	Speeches	Social routines
Signs	Stories	Traditions

ACTIVITY 2.6

Identify and explain up to *five* examples of (a) objects, (b) narratives and (c) activities in your organisation that act as artefacts of its culture.

Figure 2.7 The seven principles of public life

Selflessness: Holders of public office should take decisions solely in terms of the public interest. They should not do so in order to gain financial or other material benefits for themselves, their family or their friends.

Integrity: Holders of public office should not place themselves under any financial or other obligation to outside individuals or organisations that might influence them in the performance of their official duties.

Objectivity: In carrying out public business, including making public appointments, awarding contracts or recommending individuals for rewards and benefits, holders of public office should make choices on merit.

Accountability: Holders of public office are accountable for their decisions and actions to the public and must submit themselves to whatever scrutiny is appropriate to their office.

Openness: Holders of public office should be as open as possible about all the decisions and actions that they take. They should give reasons for their decisions and restrict information only when the wider public interest clearly demands such restriction.

Honesty: Holders of public office have a duty to declare any private interests relating to their public duties and to take steps to resolve any conflicts arising in a way that protects the public interest.

Leadership: Holders of public office should promote and support these principles by leadership and example.

Source: Nolan (1997).

LAYOUT

The physical layout of organisations is made up of geographical location, layout of workspaces and equipment, landscaping and internal decor. All have implications for the behaviour of organisational stakeholders, including managers, employees, customers, suppliers, and local communities. For example, physical structure communicates useful clues to the culture of an organisation to all stakeholders. It also has symbolic importance and the impression an organisation gives to others through its buildings, grounds and architecture. Externally, physical structure articulates the relative importance of status symbols, group boundaries and corporate image. Internally, it provides insights into many features of the organisation's social and power structures. These include the relative placement and power of people and groups, the distribution of power in the organisation, the role of technology, the layout of equipment, and organisational workflows.

INNOVATION

Technology as an external context is imported into organisations to be adapted as innovation for specific organisational purposes. Technological innovation consists of the materials and processes used in transforming organisational inputs into organisational outputs, as well as the skills, knowledge and human resources incorporated in this process. It comprises both hardware (materials and operations) and human (knowledge) components. It is the product of human effort, with its operations depending on a degree of human co-operation and involvement. Technological innovation is not therefore 'neutral'; it is also a social product of human creativity and human interactions. Figure 2.8 summarises some major, selected studies of technological innovation and organisation. These classic studies examined a number of issues, including: the social implications of production systems; possible links between technology, structure and size; and technology, interdependence and co-ordination. In the 1980s and 1990s, the conception of technology and organisations as interactive systems was generally recognised. Investment in technology was what managers used to gain competitive advantage and organisations had to adapt to technological change in ways suited to their own circumstances. More recently, managers and theorists have recognised that the driving force behind technological innovation is not always the same. Different stakeholders have different roles and innovation takes place with specific institutional frameworks (Clegg et al 2008).

POWER, CONFLICT AND CONTROL

Organisation implies power, conflict and control. Power in an organisation is the ability of a person or group of people to shape, frame and direct the actions of others, even against their will and where this power is resisted. Conflict whether in organisations or the wider society arises, according to Coser (1956, p8), out of 'a struggle over values and claims to scarce status, power and resources in which the aims of the opponents are to neutralise, injure or eliminate their rivals'. Control in organisations, in turn, is the attempt by managers to subordinate specific sources of personal or group action to some other superordinate preferences. In organisational life, power, conflict and control are intrinsically linked. Classic organisation theorists, such as Weber (1947) and Taylor (1911), sought to deal with internal conflict by making the exercise of power and control in organisations rational and systematic. As Tannenbaum (1966, p3) argues: 'Control processes help circumscribe idiosyncratic behaviors and keep them conformant to the rational plan of the organisation.' Issues and theories of power, conflict and control, then, are not neutral; they are contested. As shown in Figure 2.9, perceptions of power, conflict and control by orthodox organisation theorists and radical political theorists, such as Lukes (1974), differ substantially. Lukes argues that critiques of power should include both subjective interests and those 'real' interests held by those excluded by the political process.

Because of divergent interests within organisations, which can interfere with or deflect organisational goals and strategies, managers have the continual problem of maintaining organisational control. They need mechanisms particularly for controlling employees so that individual or group self-interest is minimised and organisational interests are promoted. Drawing upon the orthodox perspective of control, there are three main theories to be drawn upon for doing this: agency theory; performance evaluation and feedback; and market, bureaucracy or clan control. Two forms of control are used: output control, which focuses on the measurement of work results, and behavioural control, which depends on knowledge of behaviours promoting desired performance levels (see p60).

Figure 2.8 Selected studies of technological innovation, organisation and work structure

Study	Researchers	Summary findings
Socio-technical systems	Trist *et al* (1963), Rice (1963)	Developed the concept of organisations as socio-technical systems, in which inputs and outputs to and from the environment were exchanged. When technical changes are made, managers needed to choose a social structure appropriate to the technical system
The social implications of production systems	Blauner (1964), Goldthorpe *et al* (1968), Gallie (1978)	Suggested strong links between technology, discretion, division of labour, supervision and worker attitudes
Effects of micro-electronic technology on skills and control	Braverman (1974), Noble (1984), Littler and Salaman (1982)	Concluded that automated production systems are inextricably linked with de-skilling, increasing technical and administrative control over the de-skilled workforce, and an increasing polarisation of social divisions under 'monopoly capital'
Links between technology, structure and size	Woodward (1958) (1965), Hage and Aiken (1969), Hickson *et al* (1969)	(1) Argued that there was no best way to manage but it was important to consider the nature of the technical context, before deciding on forms of organisation (2) Developed a four-fold typology of management control systems (3) Later studies provided further support for the technology–organisation structure link (4) Others demonstrated that the smaller an organisation, the more its structure was pervaded by technological effects
Technology, interdependence and co-ordination	Thompson (1967)	Classified production systems, based on the nature of linkages between various parts of an organisation. Different technologies had different interdependencies and different co-ordinating mechanisms – and likely strategies
Effects of technological uncertainty	Perrow (1970)	Argued that technological uncertainty, rather than technological complexity, had the major impact on structure
Management structure and technology	Woodward (1958), Thompson (1967), Perrow (1979)	Concluded that technological characteristics pose uncertainties or create complexities which can be dealt with through appropriate management structures

Figure 2.9 Orthodox and radical perspectives of power, conflict and control in organisations

	Orthodox perspective	Radical perspective
Basis of power	The right to control production	Challenges the owners' right to profit and favours democracy of stakeholder interests
Locus of power	Hierarchy, knowledge and the ability to resolve critical organisational problems	External economic, social and political structures and ideologies
Goal of power	To improve organisational efficiency and effectiveness	To emancipate dominated groups and develop democratic, humanistic forms of communication and decision-making
View of organisations	Rational, political systems	Systems of domination, exploitation, resistance and systematically distorted communication
Frame of reference for managing employees	Unitary, with management the sole focus of organisational loyalty and of authority	Pluralist, with organisations consisting of a variety of interests and power bases, where any conflicts between managers and employees are institutionalised and resolved by compromise, negotiation and agreement
Nature of conflict	Conflict is seen as dysfunctional and counter-productive and requires to be managed by those in power to maximise organisational performance	Conflict is seen as endemic within organisations and in the wider society and is an inevitable consequence of capitalism; conflict is necessary to resolve differences and to challenge those in power and authority
Implications for control	Control is through management, exercised by monitoring employee performance through the market, bureaucracy or organisational culture	Control is exercised through hegemony and systematically distorted communication; employees consent to their own exploitation through 'false consciousness'

- **Agency theory:** aims to get managers to act in the interests of organisational owners, through having contracts between the parties, ensuring agents meet their contractual obligations, and rewarding agents for fulfilling their contracts.

- **Performance evaluation and feedback:** aims to adjust any differences between planned and actual behaviours, through setting organisational goals, setting work targets, monitoring performance, and assessing and correcting performance.

- **Market, bureaucracy or clan control:** aims to achieve co-operation amongst individuals, through comparing economic performance, complying with rules and monitoring with close supervision, and socialising organisational members into the organisation's cultural values and norms.

How does your organisation attempt to control conflict within it? Does it ignore it, does it use an orthodox approach or does it use a radical approach, and why?

SOCIAL COMPONENTS

Every organisation consists of a number of social components. These include people, their positions within the organisation, and the work groups or units to which they belong. Some writers, such as Hatch and Cunliffe (2006), define organisational structure in terms of the hierarchial, division of labour and co-ordination mechanisms within organisations. Others, such as Child (2005), classify them as the 'structural', 'processual' and 'boundary-defining' facets of organisation. Hierarchy of authority defines formal reporting relationships, although these account for only some of the interactions necessary to support an organisation. The division of labour indicates who does what in terms of job tasks, which, in turn, create expectations about who is dependent upon whom in an organisation. An organisation's co-ordination mechanisms range from formal rules, procedures and systems to informal, interpersonal conversations between people (often unrecorded). These further define and support the social structure of the organisation.

Some classic dimensions of organisational structure of interest to both practitioners and organisation theorists include issues of complexity (versus simplicity), centralisation (versus decentralisation) and formality (versus informality). These dimensions offer a means of distinguishing between mechanistic (or bureaucratic) and organic (or flexible) organisations. The important thing is that organisations have choices in determining their structural and other components, each with its implications for HR strategy and practice.

Contingency theory considers the factors or situations that managements have to deal with as part of their normal range of behaviours. It provides a useful means of combining empirical observations with theoretical insights into the multiple dimensions of organisational structure. It demonstrates, first, that small organisations operating in stable contexts are best organised as simple structures, with minimal hierarchy and centralised decision-making. Second, as organisations grow in size in terms of numbers employed, they differentiate internally by increasing the number of hierarchical levels and departments. They add mechanisms such as rules, liaison roles and cross-functional teams to integrate and control them. Formality is the rule and job tasks become more routinised. This is likely to accompany specialisation and greater division of labour in large organisations. Third, unstable contexts and internal differentiation mean that organisational structures require decentralisation as organisations grow. This makes sure that decision-making does not overwhelm the hierarchy. As new contingencies emerge, new webs of relationships develop, further specialisation takes place, and more complex systems of integration and control are created. The basic social components of organisation, and the choices and alternatives within them, drawn from the literature, are summarised in Figure 2.10.

Figure 2.10 Some basic social components of organisation: indicative choices and alternatives

Structural issues	Rules and systems	Co-ordinating mechanisms	Networking
Hierarchy • levels →tall or flat • authority →centralised or decentralised • reporting →single or multiple Division of labour by: • function • process • product • region	Rules • mandatory or discretionary • rule based or relationship based Systems • managing uncertainty or needing to adapt	Integration • vertical or horizontal Control • personal • bureaucratic • target based • cultural • HRM based Rewards • market or performance • individual or group	Outsourcing • core or peripheral Alliances • one partner or more Organising across borders • global or local

Adapted from Child (2005).

ACTIVITY 2.8

Drawing on Figure 2.10, identify the basic social components within your organisation. What changes have taken place in these social components recently? Have they been effective (or not) and why?

SOME CONTEMPORARY ISSUES IN ORGANISATIONS

In this section, four current issues are discussed, all with implications for HRM. These cover: old and new organisational forms, including networking and strategic alliances; integration, control and HR issues; performance, profit and efficiency; and continuity and change in organisations.

OLD AND NEW ORGANISATIONAL FORMS

Some commentators argue, following changes in the external organisational context, that new internal and external organisational forms have emerged in response to these changes. These changes include globalisation, new ICTs, the growth of knowledge-based economies, hyper-competition and rising demands for social accountability. These developments, it is claimed, have resulted in the rejection of bureaucratic forms of organisation and a demand for 'new organisational forms.' The 'new conditions' facing organisations mean, amongst other things, that organisations have to be more flexible, have lean management structures, become more decentralised, promote teamwork, maximise organisational learning, and be more socially accountable. Compared with conventional, 'old' organisational forms, new organisational forms incorporate a number of innovatory features, although not all are represented in every new form organisation. These include:

- **Hierarchy:** authority more widely distributed, leadership through guidance, fewer hierarchic levels, use of teams.

- **Division of labour:** less role specialisation and expanded job roles.

- **Rules and schedules:** more discretionary and relationship based.

- **Systems:** directed towards managing change.

- **Integration:** a strong emphasis on integration, with the mode of integration being through direct contact and ICTs, horizontal integration between smaller units.

- **Control:** decentralisation and target, culture or HRM based.

- **Rewards:** based on group performance.

- **Outsourcing:** non-core activities being outsourced.

- **Alliances:** used between firms to achieve global market penetration.

- **Organising across borders:** complex multidimensional organisations, wanting the benefits of both global co-ordination and local initiative, where integration is vertical and horizontal.

In addition to the emergence of new internal organisation forms – in a period of globalisation, hyper-competition and continuous change – networking, boundary crossing, outsourcing and strategic alliances are being used as novel forms of organisation. Networking is a wide concept and broadly refers to transactions across an organisation's boundaries that are recurrent and involve continuing relationships with a set of external partners. Transactions are co-ordinated and controlled on a mutually agreed basis. This is likely to require common protocols and systems. However, they do not necessarily require direct supervision by the organisation's own staff.

Outsourcing is the contracting out of activities that need to be undertaken on a regular basis. It sometimes refers to activities that were formerly performed in-house and are still performed by organisations in the same sector. It also means activities hived off from one country to another. The advantage of outsourcing is that it enables organisations to concentrate on what they do best and offers cost savings. However, problems arise from outsourcing through weak contracts, inadequate control over the outsourced activity, and difficulties with suppliers and vendors.

Strategic alliances between companies involve sharing ownership and management, in the shape of new joint ventures. They create hybrid forms of organisation which are medium to long-term co-operative arrangements between firms. They are described as strategic, because they are normally formed to help partner firms realise their strategic objectives jointly, rather than individually. They are one of the more important new organisational forms and are regarded as a means of achieving fundamental strategic objectives, including a strong market position, knowledge acquisition and cost reductions.

Organising across borders makes greater demands on a firm's organisation than purely domestic operations. A fundamental issue in MNCs is how to balance and combine the advantages of global integration with the need for sensitivity and responsiveness to the conditions in different localities where they operate. To secure a combination of the flexibility, innovation and integration required, the organisation of MNCs depends significantly on the management of internal networks and support of a well-developed corporate culture. Whatever strategies MNCs adopt for international expansion, each has implications for an organisation's structure and the ways in which it tries to manage organisational processes such as integration. Organising cross-border transactions is one of the greatest challenges facing MNCs today.

Some commentators argue, however, that the claim organisations are becoming 'networks' and are less hierarchic is overstated. Any organisation can be seen as a 'network', since organisations have always been networks. These observers claim that network analysts have shown that hierarchy is a property of a network's structure, not something a network replaces. Within most organisations there is some reliance on informal mechanisms and connections. These are based on principles of co-operation, reciprocity and trust – characteristics that have become most closely associated with the network form. These mechanisms are forged within and outside organisational borders, acting as lubricants to the old bureaucratic tool of administrative fiat (Barley and Kunda 2001). What is new about the network form is the increase in cross-functional project work within organisations and the decomposition of vertically integrated organisations, as activities are outsourced or shared through collaborative arrangements. For Marchington et al (2004, p15), the network is a logic of organising that is diffused within established 'market' and 'hierarchical' governance structures. For these observers, it is more plausible 'to regard "market", "hierarchy", and "network" as concepts that have proved valuable in differentiating elements or dimensions of organizing practices, within and between organizations, rather than as alternative designs of economic organization'.

INTEGRATION, CONTROL AND HR ISSUES

Integration is the co-ordination of various organisational activities to create internal coherence and added value. As organisations have become more complex and are increasingly differentiated, integration becomes more difficult to achieve. Integration is related to organisational control and HR issues and is a vital component of organisation. It is a facet of organisation which is often neglected. Integration is essential to avoid failure in delivering an adequate range of products or services to an organisation's customers. Effective integration is a factor that can drive the people and other resources needed for satisfactory service to customers into a distinctive and dynamic capability. This gives the organisation competitive edge in the marketplace and enables it to adjust successfully to the changing demands facing it. Integration has to be designed into organisational systems.

Different methods of integration exist. One is to rely on a senior manager to provide it, but this has limited application and is only effective in supportive conditions. Another mechanism is to integrate through formal procedures and planning. A third is by using lateral co-ordination, based on integrating the contributions of different people or units in an organisation. However, new forms of organisation are breaking down traditional, functional boundaries. Also with increasing use of project work using teams, teamworking integrates individuals around job tasks. It has been observed that teams normally perform better than individuals working alone, when the tasks to be done require multiple skills, judgement and experience (Mohrman et al 1995). Further, a study of world-class organisations in the United States and other countries demonstrated that teams can work effectively in any sort of organisation (Wellins et al 1994).

Various types of team exist, not only for integration purposes but also to increase employee commitment and involvement. Teams have been found to decrease absenteeism, increase accountability, reduce overheads and speed up communications. Typical examples of teams include:

- top management teams
- cross-functional teams, consisting of middle managers and staff representing departments or functions
- project teams established for the duration of a project
- quality circles for improving quality
- self-managed teams
- affinity groups, composed of professional or knowledge workers.

In traditional organisational structures, work is designed around functions, with no sense of ownership. Jobs tend to be single-skilled, leaders govern teams, managers take organisational decisions and support staff are outside teams. Modern team-design principles organise work around processes. These ensure that teams own a product, service or process for which they are responsible and they contain people with multi-trained or cross-trained jobs and roles. Further, teams govern themselves and are involved in taking organisational decisions.

Control is an elusive concept and two levels of control are generally recognised: strategic control and operational control. Strategic control relates to control over the means and methods upon which the future direction of the organisation depends. It is broadly concerned about effective corporate governance, use and protection of capital assets, and managing the organisation's strategic dispositions. The ability of management to exercise power in organisations derives from control at strategic level. Operational control is about control over the work done within organisations. It is largely concerned with how employees perform their jobs. Operational control requires use of organisational power, although in practice this power may be distributed throughout the organisation, not just centrally. For example, some workers may have strategic power because they possess certain job skills, knowledge and experience that others do not have or that are unavailable in the external labour market such as skilled, trained airline pilots in international airlines. Because of competitive pressures on organisations, managers are now exerting more controls to reduce costs, increase productivity and respond to market forces. Methods of control change as organisations grow in size or if they diversify their activities and locations. Such organisations steadily increase reliance on formal rules, delegation of decisions and personal supervision (Friesen et al 1978).

A range of strategies has been identified for attaining managerial control within organisations. Some are more appropriate to 'new' organisational forms than to 'old' organisational ones. These strategies are:

- **Personal**: this is centralised, involves direct supervision and uses rewards and punishments to reinforce conformity to personal authority.

- **Bureaucratic**: this breaks down tasks into definable elements, uses specified methods, procedures and rules, and draws upon reward and punitive systems that reinforce conformity to these procedures and rules.

- **Target based**: this specifies output standards and targets, and relates reward and punishment to achieving agreed output targets.

- **Culture**: this promotes individual employee identification with managerial goals; it has a strong emphasis on the collective and mutually supportive character of the organisation.

- **HRM based**: this uses selection methods to make sure new recruits fit the organisational profile in terms of attitudes, behaviour and capabilities, and uses assessment procedures and reward systems to encourage conformity.

- **Electronic surveillance**: this assesses speed and quality of work via ICTs, and uses monitoring of performance to reward and discipline employees.

 ACTIVITY 2.9

Which of the above six strategies of control in organisations are more suitable to new organisational forms and which are more suitable to old organisational forms? Justify your responses.

A major HR issue, arising out of the control and integration measures outlined above, is how to reward employees so that they contribute to organisation. An appropriate reward policy is necessary to complement the processes of integration and control. The design of a reward system complements that of organisation to the extent that it is part of organisational policy. Properly conceived, there is interdependence between the organisation and the reward system, although there is no single best way of doing this. Rewards play a critical role in directing people's efforts towards the implementation of organisational strategy. This implies that reward systems require frequent fine tuning to suit individual and organisational contingencies, however difficult this is to achieve in practice. Progress towards the flexibility required of reward policies today is made in terms of both intrinsic and extrinsic rewards.

A number of studies show that intrinsic, intangible rewards are generally more satisfying for employees than are tangible, extrinsic ones such as pay and benefits (Confederation of British Industry 2000). Intrinsic rewards include variety in job content, responsibility, recognition, autonomy, social interaction, and participation in target setting and determining methods of working, with ICTs providing considerable choice over how work is organised (Thompson and McHugh 2002). The shift towards organisational decentralisation, more responsible jobs and teamwork found in new organisational forms represents a policy shift to higher-level intrinsic rewards for organisational members. One way of doing this is giving autonomy to workgroups or teams to organise their own work in consultation with managers. This means arranging work to suit their needs through variety, personal growth and social interaction, but within the constraints required by organisational strategy.

Extrinsic rewards are attached to positions or jobs within organisations, not to actual job content. The principal extrinsic rewards are pay, fringe benefits, security of tenure, promotion, special awards and status symbols. Intrinsic rewards relate to the nature of jobs themselves. The central requirement here is to enable performance criteria to be adjusted as circumstances change. This is ideally carried out through mutual dialogue between managers and employees. Current trends in pay policy favour systems that are compatible with developments in contemporary organisational forms (Pilbeam and Corbridge 2010). These include:

- **Market-driven pay**: provides a flexible approach to pay and benefits, reflecting the worth of employees in the labour market.

- **Performance-related pay (PRP)**: takes the form of either individual PBR systems or team based rewards, as teamwork becomes increasingly used.

- **Broadbanding**: enables increased flexibility in flatter organisations.

- **Competence-based pay**: reflects the growing use of competencies as criteria in managing performance and recognises that competitiveness depends on the quality of these competencies.

- **Flexible benefits**: reflect the needs of a diverse workforce.

- **Harmonisation and consolidation**: eliminates sources of division when management attempts to promote integration and flexible deployment in organisations.

ACTIVITY 2.10

What is the main pay system used in your organisation? To what extent does it match the organisation's integration and control objectives?

In the case of multi-employer networks, a study by Marchington *et al* (2009, p49) shows the complexity of people management within them. Their research on four case study networks indicates that a simple model of people management in networked organisations is not tenable. Relations between the parties within the network depend on processes of trust formation, patterns of dominance between the organisations, and degrees of modularity across the network to examine how co-production systems are designed and implemented. In examining the role of HRM, these observers make use of the concepts of 'alignment, integration and consistency' to see how the HR systems, policies and practices, used by different partners in the network, 'mesh in with each other'. The authors provide a classification of HRM relevant to multi-employer networks: managing the employment contract, building worker identity and engagement, and developing individual and organisational capabilities.

PERFORMANCE, PROFIT AND EFFICIENCY

The driving forces underpinning organisational effectiveness today are performance, profit and efficiency in the private sector, and performance, finance and value for money in the public and third sectors. The reasons for this are clear. With the increasing marketisation of business and public services, and the competition, choice and change agenda, the driving force underpinning business activity is the role of stock markets, banks and other financial institutions in shaping the internal agendas of organisations. Whether in the market, public or third sectors, management attention is increasingly focused on achieving short-term financial targets. Performance, profit and efficiency are the criteria by which contemporary private organisations are measured and evaluated; all three criteria impact critically on how people are managed. Indeed, the distinctive feature of HRM is its assumption that improved performance is achieved through the effective recruitment, deployment and utilisation of people (Guest 1997). The concept of performance covers what has been achieved and how it has been achieved, both collectively and individually. In the private sector, this is done by using key performance indicators such as financial results, profitability or productivity. In the public sector, much attention is paid to achieving measured financial targets and greater efficiency or efficiency savings, following public management reforms. As a result, performance management processes have come to the fore as the means of providing an integrated, continuous approach to managing individual, group and organisational performance compared with the past. Earlier attempts to do this through isolated, inadequate merit rating or performance appraisal schemes were not generally successful. As Armstrong (2009) argues, contemporary performance management is based on the principle of management by agreement or contract rather than by command. It emphasises development and self-managed learning, as well as the integration of individual and corporate objectives in organisations.

Profit and efficiency are closely related, since they are measurable concepts, and are keys to economic performance and efficiency within capitalist market economies. Just as savers expect returns on the financial capital they have invested in companies, firms seek profits for several reasons. First, profits provide firms with the working capital or cash to invest in the firm in expectation of a return on this. Second, profit is used to pay dividends to shareholders. Third, a company showing good returns attracts more investment and, because more people or institutions will want to buy shares, the value of the firm rises. Creditors know they will get their money back with interest; shareholders will know the value of their shares will rise; and the company knows that it has sufficient resources to maintain its capital stock and will invest in new processes and technologies. This re-investment is vital to firms for maintaining quality and improving buildings and equipment. Investment is also needed to continually to improve efficiency, in particular labour productivity.

The driver for efficiency is the profit motive or the need to increase the difference between revenues from sales and the costs associated with capital, labour (or human resources) and material resources. Cost minimisation becomes a core task for any firm. Thus capital investment is needed to achieve cost reductions in labour and material. Reducing capital costs is not an option. In practice, companies invest in technologies that reduce labour costs. For companies, higher labour productivity lowers the costs of products and services. Efficiency literally drives corporate growth forwards. By reducing labour and resource inputs, efficiency brings the costs of goods down over time. Thus the general trend in capitalist economies is to increase labour productivity in the drive for higher output, greater efficiency and higher profits.

The HR implications of the continual search for improved performance, rising profits and increased efficiency are, first, that employees or workers are employed as agents for achieving these objectives or goals. They do this in collaboration with management and by combining with other organisational resources. Second, in periods of corporate growth and expansion, increases in performance or efficiency can be shared with employees in the forms of higher pay, improved benefits and better promotion opportunities. All stakeholders benefit from this: shareholders, employees and customers. Managers are managing growth and expansion. Those who are leading organisations are likely to be involved in consensus building and promoting positive views of the future. This is a positive-sum game, where all parties are beneficiaries and all are winners. Third, when performance, profits and efficiency decline, however, a negative-sum game is played out. This can result in job losses and work intensification for the remaining workforce, with fewer promotion and recruitment opportunities for staff. Managers are managing decline and contraction. Those leading organisations are likely to be involved in fire-fighting and managing conflict with their workforces, whether individually or collectively. Managing performance, profitability and efficiency are critically related to relevant HR practices in organisations, at different stages of the business cycle.

CONTINUITY AND CHANGE IN ORGANISATIONS

The conventional wisdom in much of current management literature, particularly orthodox organisation studies, is that most organisations have become increasingly and inherently unstable and subject to rapid, turbulent change. Evidence of this is cited in the claim that Fordist organisations, based on bureaucratic rules, are being superseded by post-Fordist, post-industrial or post-bureaucratic ones. Another response is that there has been the emergence and development of 'new organisational forms' such as the virtual, networked or postmodern organisations, discussed above, where rules are replaced with consensus and dialogue and personal influence rather than status (Heckscher 1994). What links post-bureaucracy and other contemporary preoccupations of orthodox organisation studies is the centrality placed on the concept of change. However, as Grey (2009, p93) writes: 'Change is like a totem before which we must prostrate ourselves and in the face of which we are powerless.' By this view, this results in an unchallenged consensus about the 'fact' of change and little acceptance of the 'fact' of continuity.

The counter position to this accepted orthodoxy is that both continuity and change are central, and always have been central, in the modern, post-enlightenment world, in organisations, institutions and human society. Sceptics challenge whether today is an especially unprecedented time of change. They argue that the present is not one of any greater change than in the past. Anyway, how can comparisons be made about change over time? This is not to argue that change does not take place. The important thing is how change is apprehended, since it takes place within certain cultural and historical settings (Hirst and Thompson 1996). What matters is how each generation perceives change, and that depends on how it looks at it. Change from a historical perspective is ubiquitous and continuous, not specific to any particular era. Also, although the boundaries between an organisation and its 'contexts' are deemed to be discrete for analytical purposes, in practice, insofar as 'any boundaries can be discerned between an organization and its environment, these are defined by socially and historically specific conventions' (Grey 2009, p97). It follows from the population ecology model of organisations that those adapting to their 'external' contexts survive, whilst those which do not are doomed to failure (Aldrich 1979). By this view, organisational survival is contingent upon adaptation to the contextual environment, because organisations failing to change will lose business to those who do. The counter argument implies that change is better understood as a construction by the interplay of organisations themselves, not because change is 'inevitable'. In other words, organisations, or those leading them, often collectively generate an 'agenda' of change, which is then seen as a problem to be solved and to which an organisational response is needed.

Some unorthodox writers challenge whether change management programmes ever work. This is, first, because change and change management are not fully understood. Second, change management programmes assume that it is possible to systematically control social and organisational relations, which may not be the case. Third, organisational change management programmes are often based on the view that what works in one organisation can be transferred to others. But evidence indicates that they are contingent, not generalisable, programmes. Fourth, today's successful companies are often tomorrow's failed ones. For example, of the 62 'excellent' companies profiled by Peters and Waterman (1982), many had ceased to meet the 'excellent' criteria a few years later, whilst others failed to exist at all.

STAKEHOLDERS IN ORGANISATIONS

It is clear from the above discussions that all organisations have 'stakeholders', each with interests in the activities of the organisation and what it does. This view of organisations is analysed by drawing on 'stakeholder theory'. This argues that every legitimate person or group participating in the activities of a firm or organisation does so to obtain benefits for themselves. However, the priority of the interests of all legitimate stakeholders is not self-evident. The stakeholder theory of the firm differs from the conventional 'input–output model' of business organisations. Donaldson and Preston (1995, p68–9) argue that in the 'input–output model' of the firm, three sets of 'contributors' – investors, employees and suppliers – provide inputs to firms, which the 'black box' of the firm transforms into 'outputs' for the benefit of a fourth party, its customers. Each contributor receives appropriate compensation for its inputs but 'as a result of competition throughout the system, the bulk of the benefits will go to customers.' Stakeholder theorists, in contrast, argue that all persons or groups with legitimate interests participating within an enterprise have economic and moral claims upon it. These include, in addition to management, investors, employees, suppliers, customers, communities, political groups, trade associations and governments. Each of these participates in order 'to obtain benefits and there is no *prima facie* priority of one set of interests and benefits over another'. Donaldson and Preston also stress 'at the outset' that stakeholder theory represents 'a controversial or challenging approach to conventional views' that vary 'greatly among market capitalist economies.'

IDENTIFYING ORGANISATIONAL STAKEHOLDERS

Lynch (2006) defines stakeholders as 'the individuals and groups who have an interest in the organisation, and, therefore, may wish to influence aspects of its mission, objectives and strategies'. He lists the typical stakeholders in large businesses as employees, managers, shareholders, banking institutions, customers, suppliers and government. The concept of stakeholding, then, extends beyond just those working in the organisation. Thus in a limited company, stakeholders with legitimate interests in the ways in which the company conducts its business include shareholders who have invested in it, employees and managers working in it, banks lending it money, governments concerned about employment, investment and trade, and its customers and suppliers. Interests may be informal, as in the case of a football supporters' club and its influence in and on a privately owned football club. In the case of a PLC football club with quoted shares, it may be formal, with supporters owning shares in that company. Unless an organisation's stakeholders remain satisfied with it, or at a minimum 'satisficed' (ie not fully satisfied but not dissatisfied either), then employees and managers are likely to leave, shareholders to sell their shareholdings, banks to stop providing credit, customers to go elsewhere and suppliers to look for other outlets for their products or services.

Cannon (1994) provides another model of stakeholders. He distinguishes between owners, employees, customers, creditors, suppliers, community and government. Each of these, he argues, has 'primary' and 'secondary' expectations about a business. Owners want a financial return on their investment and added value for their investments, achieved by the agency of management. Employees want good pay, followed by good working conditions, job satisfaction and proper training opportunities. For customers, the primary expectation is effective supply of required goods and services and, second, that these are of sufficiently high quality in relation to price. Creditors want creditworthiness and payment on time; suppliers want payment for items received and long-term relationships with the purchasing organisation; and the community wants jobs, a safe environment, and the firms located in their community making a contribution to it. Government, in turn, wants employment for people, compliance with its regulations, laws and taxation rules, and improved competitiveness of firms.

Lawton (1998) uses a different classification of organisational stakeholders in reformed public services. He identifies six sets of key stakeholders: customers, citizens, clients, colleagues, ministers and contractors. Customers are characterised as having 'purchasing power', citizens 'rights and duties', while clients 'lack of power and information'. Ministers, in turn, are characterised by having 'authority', colleagues 'equal status' and contractors 'specifications'. Thus dealing with customers, citizens and clients involves different sets of relationships. Customers are concerned with purchasing power, protected by a legal framework providing consumer protection and rights. The language of citizenship, on the other hand, is that of general rights and solidarity. Clients, in contrast, are interested in ensuring that they receive their entitlements and their interests are protected. Colleagues in public service organisations normally have expectations about being managed 'collegially', which means being involved in the decision-making processes affecting them, being treated equitably by their managers and being promoted on the basis of merit. Ministers and contractors are external stakeholders and they too have interests in the ways in which public organisations are managed. Ministers are concerned with all aspects of public organisations, because these organisations are accountable to Parliament for any matters that arouse public interest. Contractors are concerned with how contracts are specified and monitored and want payments made on time. Managing such diverse stakeholders in public organisations, therefore, means that different interests need to be balanced, while common ones need to be identified and conflicting ones reconciled.

What role stakeholders play in organisations depends partly on their legal status and partly on their power in or over the organisation. The prime legal responsibility of the boards of public companies in the UK, for example, is to their shareholders. But they also have statutory obligations to their employees, customers and suppliers, as well as having to pay their taxes to government and protect the environment. An organisation's system of governance plays a key function here but there are different models of corporate governance internationally and, in the UK, between private and public organisations, with the latter being more likely to have some element of employee involvement imposed on them.

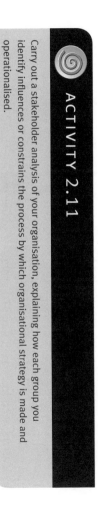

ACTIVITY 2.11

Carry out a stakeholder analysis of your organisation, explaining how each group you identify influences or constrains the process by which organisational strategy is made and operationalised.

TYPOLOGIES OF STAKEHOLDERS

Mitchell *et al* (1997, p854) argue that stakeholder theory has been a popular heuristic device for describing the management context for many years, but that it lacks theoretical status. They produce a comprehensive typology of stakeholders based on the normative assumption that these variables define the field of stakeholders as: 'those entities to whom management *should* pay attention.' In their view, classes of stakeholders can be identified as those possessing one or more of the following attributes:

• the stakeholder's *power* to influence the firm

• the *legitimacy* of the stakeholder's relationship with the firm

• the *urgency* of the stakeholder's claim on the firm.

Power

This attribute is defined as the probability that one actor within a social relationship is in a position to carry out his/her will despite resistance (Weber 1964). It is, in short, the ability of individuals or groups to persuade or coerce others to follow certain courses of action. Sources of power within organisations include formal hierarchical power, informal power (such as charismatic leadership), the control of strategic resources, possession of strategic knowledge and information technology, and negotiating skills. Internal indicators of power are visible signs that internal stakeholders have been able to get their own way. One is the status of the individual or group, such as position in the hierarchy or reputation within and outside the organisation. The second is the individual's or group's claim on organisational resources, as measured by size of budget, number of employees in the group and so on. The third is representation in powerful positions. This might be assessed in terms of the corporate governance arrangements for the organisation, or who is represented on its important committees. The fourth indicator is 'symbols of power', such as size, location and fittings of offices, amount of support services that the group has, and so on. Johnson et al (2009) conclude that no single indicator of power is likely to uncover the structure of power within a company.

Sources of power for external stakeholders are both similar to and different from those for individuals and groups within organisations. The sources of power of external stakeholders are control of strategic resources (such as materials, labour and money), involvement in the organisation (such as distribution outlets and agents) and possession of specialist knowledge (such as that possessed by subcontractors). Another is through internal links and informal influence in the organisation and organised pressure groups.

Few individuals have sufficient personal power to influence either the direction and policies of an organisation or their own interests within it. Even chief executives need to carry influential groups of senior managers and their staff with them. Influence arises because particular individuals share similar expectations with others in the same stakeholder group. Here external stakeholders can be important, such as bankers, customers, suppliers, shareholders and trade unions. These may seek to influence what is happening in the company through their links with internal stakeholders such as managers and people working in the organisation. Thus individuals are more likely to identify themselves with the aims of specific stakeholder groups, such as the corporate board, institutional investors or trade unions with members in the organisation. There have been several examples in the public sector, where internal employee pressure groups, organised and co-ordinated by the trade unions, have produced 'votes of no confidence' in an organisation's chief executive. As a result, the person in question has resigned and been replaced by a new incumbent.

Legitimacy

Power and legitimacy are distinct attributes and they combine to create authority (Weber 1947), as well as existing independently. An entity may have legitimate standing in society, or it may have a legitimate claim on the firm, but unless it has either power to enforce its will in the relationship or a perception that its claim is urgent, it cannot achieve salience with the firm's managers. For this reason, a theory of stakeholder salience requires, first, that separate attention be paid to legitimacy as an attribute of stakeholder–management relations. Suchman (1995, p574) defines the second attribute of legitimacy as 'a generalised perception or assumption that the actions of an entity are desirable, proper, or appropriate within some socially constructed system of norms, values, beliefs, and definitions.' Mitchell et al (1997, p866–7) accept this definition, implying that legitimacy is a desirable social good 'that is something larger and more shared than a mere self-perception' and may be defined and negotiated differently at various levels of social organisation. The most common of these 'are the individual, organizational, and societal'.

Urgency

Mitchell et al's (1997, p867–8) third attribute of classes of stakeholder – the *urgency* of the stakeholder's claim on the firm – is posited as moving their model from a static one to a dynamic one. They define 'urgency' as 'the degree to which stakeholder claims call for immediate attention', arguing that urgency is based on two factors. One is 'time sensitivity', or the degree to which managerial delay in attending to a claim or relationship is unacceptable to the stakeholder. The second is 'criticality', or the importance of the claim or relationship to the stakeholder. In their view, their theory 'captures the resulting multidimensional attribute as *urgency*, juxtaposes it with the attribute of power and legitimacy, and proposes dynamism in the systematic identification of stakeholders'.

Classifying stakeholder classes

Combining these attributes of power, legitimacy and urgency results in three generic groups of stakeholders ('latent', 'expectant' and 'definitive') and a seven-fold typology of stakeholder classes, as shown in Figure 2.11. This recognises that entities with no power, legitimacy or urgency in relation to the firm are not stakeholders and they have no salience with the firm's managers. Mitchell et al (1997, p82) argue stakeholder theorists have only searched for bases of legitimacy in stakeholder–management relationships. They claim that these attributes of stakeholders in a firm's environment 'make a critical difference in managers' ability to meet legitimate claims and protect legitimate interests.' For them, stakeholder theory must account for power and legitimacy and urgency. In their view: 'Power and urgency must be attended to if managers are to serve the legal and moral interests of legitimate stakeholders.'

Figure 2.11 Classes of stakeholder

Latent stakeholders
Low-salience classes, with one of the three attributes
• dormant stakeholders (with power only)
• discretionary stakeholders (with legitimacy only)
• demanding stakeholders (with urgency only)

Expectant stakeholders
Moderate-salience classes, with two of the three attributes
• dominant stakeholders (with both power and legitimacy)
• dangerous stakeholders (with both power and urgency)
• dependent stakeholders (with both legitimacy and urgency)

Definitive stakeholders
Highly-salience classes, possessing all three attributes
• definitive stakeholders

Adapted from Mitchell et al (1997).

ACTIVITY 2.12

Drawing upon Mitchell *et al*'s classification of stakeholder classes, use it to classify the groups of organisational stakeholders you have identified in Activity 2.11.

CORPORATE GOVERNANCE, ACCOUNTABILITY AND CORPORATE SOCIAL RESPONSIBILITY

A central purpose of corporate governance is to ensure the survival, sustainability and good name of the organisation. In this view, effective corporate governance optimises the contribution of stakeholders within organisations to the purposes they are persuaded to share (Monks and Minow 2008).

THE PRIVATE SECTOR

In the private sector, shareholders have traditionally been the key stakeholders in UK companies. But German companies have dual legal accountabilities to both shareholders and employees, with both parties represented on top-tier management boards. Austria and the Netherlands have two-tier board structures too. Historically it is boards of directors that have been agents of shareholders to direct their companies. However, as observed above, customers, employees, suppliers, communities and government are also considered to be stakeholders with interests in modern companies today. In satisfying the demands of the marketplace, those running privately owned organisations (or businesses) are ultimately accountable through their governing bodies for the actions that they take. Organisations and those leading them have a duty to use the resources they employ responsibly, taking account of their obligations to a variety of organisational stakeholders. In practice, a mixture of market, legal, social and moral imperatives enforces the multiple accountabilities within contemporary organisations.

The distinctive feature of private sector businesses is they are market-driven and market-led organisations. This means that the ways in which private businesses are managed reflect the market environment in which they operate. They buy their factor inputs in the marketplace (ie land, labour, capital and other resources), sell their products or services in the market and, if they are to survive, prosper and grow, they are ultimately judged as organisations in the market by their ability to generate profits. 'Unless, over time, private organisations are able to satisfy customer demand in the market, provide a surplus of revenues over costs and ensure capital investment programmes for the future, they cease to trade as viable organisations' (Farnham and Horton 1996, p28). In satisfying the demands of the marketplace, business organisations are ultimately responsible through their governing bodies for the actions they take.

Private businesses are held accountable in a number of ways. Legally, businesses are accountable to their shareholders, who may attend meetings and vote on issues affecting company policy. Shareholders, which are increasingly other companies, also have rights to appoint and remove directors, receive annual reports, examine the accounts and share in corporate profits. To those supporting the 'stockholder' perspective of businesses, this is the norm and is incontestably proper. For them, companies exist solely or primarily to serve the interests of their shareholders. There are certainly interests other than shareholders, whose fortunes are tied up with the company but this is beside the point. These other interests do not own the company. The essential point from the stockholder perspective is that the company is simply a piece of property, no different, in principle, from other property such as land, houses and other artefacts that people own. From the 'stakeholder' perspective, in contrast, corporate status transforms a business into something closer to 'public' property (ie something for which just and fair property ownership rights must be recognised). However, from both the stockholder and stakeholder perspectives, this is nothing to do with being private or public in the legal sense of whether shares are on public sale or not. What is crucial is being incorporated. For stockholder theory, which places organisations less in a moral context, this does not lift a business out of the merely private property category. Stakeholder theory, which places organisations more in a moral context, does.

Private organisations are also legally accountable to their employees, suppliers and consumers in terms of the minimum standards expected of them by the state. Employees, for example, have a series of common law and statutory employment rights, preventing them from being exploited by 'bad' or exploitative employers. Some employees, the low-paid, have a statutory right to a legally enforceable minimum wage. All employees, except those derogated by the law, have statutory rights to maximum working hours per week and paid holiday entitlements. The legal obligations of private businesses to their suppliers are embodied in the law of contract, which provides a legal framework around which business organisations build their mutual commercial activities together. Corporate legal accountability to consumers is largely through consumer protection laws, while the Office of Fair Trading publishes information, proposes new laws and takes action on behalf of consumers who think that their rights have been infringed by offending businesses.

Companies also have legal accountability to the communities where they are located. This incorporates a variety of measures relating to controls over land use, building development, pollution control and noise abatement. The law relating to land use, for example, seeks to achieve a balance between the interests of people within their communities and business organisations. Pollution control is aimed at minimising the potentially hazardous impacts of effluents and noxious substances released into the air, land or waterways. Legislation exists to prevent damage to individuals and households by excessive noise levels from factory machinery, motor vehicles and aircraft.

The social and moral accountabilities of private businesses have become increasingly important in recent years, as businesses have increasingly accepted that they have extra-legal responsibilities. This is in response to pressure group lobbying and changes in public opinion. These have to be taken into account when managements make decisions about issues of production, pricing, resource utilisation and distribution of profits. Businesses are also becoming increasingly customer aware and environmentally conscious. Failing to satisfy these obligations can result in fines, loss of customer loyalty and damage to corporate images or reputations. Ultimately, however, the accountability of business organisations is to the market. If they do not satisfy the marketplace, they go bankrupt and out of business.

PUBLIC ORGANISATIONS

Public organisations, since they are political bodies created by the state, are ultimately accountable to the 'public' whom they serve. In satisfying the demands of their sovereign political 'masters' (ie taxpayers and public clients), public organisations are accountable through their governing bodies, government ministers or public officials for the actions they take. As citizens, taxpayers and consumers, members of the public are interested in the use of public power, the efficiency with which public money is spent, and the quality of public services provided. The public is particularly interested in the performance and behaviour of public organisations for a number of reasons:

- Public bodies are often monopoly providers, leaving the public no choice but to take what they provide.

- Public bodies exercise power to ensure compliance with public laws and can fine people or ultimately deprive them of their liberty if they break the law.

- They provide merit goods or public goods (ie goods that everyone contributes to or benefits from), which directly affect the quality of people's lives.

- They levy compulsory taxation to fund government activities.

- They regulate many areas of social life, including licensing alcohol, providing street lighting and highways, checking building designs and monitoring building plans.

It is this exercise of public power that necessitates public organisations being held accountable in a democratic society. Public officials are expected to act as stewards of the public interest and public purse, as well as being responsible for ensuring that public organisations provide the appropriate goods and services to those entitled to them. The forms that public accountability takes vary according to type of public agency, level of government and its particular functions. Rose and Lawton (1999) argue that it is difficult to generalise about accountability in the public sector, because the mechanics of accountability differ in local authorities, central government, and the National Health Service. It is arguable that there are four main types of public sector accountability: legal, political, customer and 'professional'. All public bodies operate within a strict legal framework. Unlike private businesses, which can do anything that the law does not specifically forbid or prevent them from doing, public ones can do only what the law permits and prescribes for them. This legal rule is known as *ultra vires*. This means that public officials require legal authority for all the actions they perform. If public officials fail to exercise their legal responsibilities or take actions which exceed their legal authority, they can be mandated or restrained by the courts. It is ordinary courts in the UK that hold public organisations to account, both for their actions and the procedures they use. Public officials are required to demonstrate that they have complied with substantive law, procedural law and rules of natural justice.

Political accountability manifests itself in a number of ways. All public officials are accountable directly or indirectly to a political person or body. Civil servants are accountable to a minister, local government officers to elected councillors, and boards of public corporations to appropriate ministers. This model assumes that powers are vested in ministers, who are responsible for what public servants do and who, in turn, are accountable to Parliament for their actions. Similarly, power is vested in elected local authority councils that are responsible to the public for the actions of their officials. The reality of ministerial responsibility has long been disputed, however, and civil servants are now more directly accountable to Parliament, through its specialist committees, than in the past (Drewry 1989). Local officials also deal with the public. In both cases, ultimate accountability to the public, as the electorate, is through periodic elections and the ballot box. Between elections, the press and pressure groups keep public organisations alert and inform the public what is going on inside them.

Professional accountability is particularly pertinent to the public sector, since it employs many professional workers, such as doctors, nurses, teachers, social workers and engineers. Public service professionals seek, where they can, not only to control entry into their occupations but also to determine how they work and how they police their fellow professionals. They claim professional autonomy, clinical freedom or academic freedom, as the case may be. This is because professionals see themselves as being primarily accountable to their professional colleagues and their internal codes of ethics. The Law Society deals with complaints against lawyers and the British Medical Association hears complaints against doctors. However, counter to this, public-service professional workers are increasingly being held accountable to public managers, who may or may not be drawn from among the ranks of the professionals they supervise. This has seriously eroded the autonomy and independence of professional groups in public service organisations. Further, by the early twenty-first century, public service professionals, such as medical practitioners and school teachers, have been the object of increasingly detailed public intervention and regulation in their working practices (Moran 2003).

THE THIRD SECTOR

The so-called third sector is made up of wide range of charities, voluntary organisations, community bodies and social enterprises, all of which exist to create a better 'civil society'. In 2005, the National Hub of Expertise in Governance published a code of governance for the voluntary and community sector. It points out that in this sector it is trustees who take ultimate responsibility for the 'good' governance of their organisations. However, governance is not a role for trustees alone. It is exercised through the way trustees work with chief executives and staff (where appointed), volunteers, service users, and other stakeholders to ensure their organisation is effectively and properly run and meets the needs for which it was set up. All trustees are responsible for ensuring their organisation is run in accordance with its mission, aims and objectives. Trustees are expected to receive copies of all relevant mission statements and strategy documents when they are inducted. It is customary for the strategy to be revisited at least annually and always in the light of changing circumstances. At the very least, the charity's business plan needs annual consideration (National Hub of Expertise in Governance 2005).

The National Hub sets out seven principles of good governance in the third sector, underpinned by the principle of equality. This ensures that equity, diversity and equality of treatment are demonstrated to all sections of the community these bodies serve. The seven principles are:

- **Board leadership**: every organisation should be led and controlled by an effective board of trustees which collectively ensures delivery of its objects, sets its strategic direction and upholds its values.

- **The board in control**: the trustees should collectively be responsible and accountable for ensuring and monitoring that the organisation is performing well, is solvent, and complies with its obligations.

- **The high-performance board**: the board should have clear responsibilities and functions and should compose and organise itself to discharge them effectively.

- **Board review and renewal**: the board should periodically review its own and the organisation's effectiveness and take any necessary steps to ensure that both continue to work well.

- **Board delegation**: the board should set out the functions of subcommittees, officers, the chief executive, other staff and agents in clear delegated authorities and should monitor their performance.

- **Board and trustee integrity**: the board and individual trustees should act according to high ethical standards, and ensure that conflicts of interest are properly dealt with.

- **The open board**: the board should be open, responsive and accountable to its users, beneficiaries, members, partners and others with an interest in its work.

CORPORATE SOCIAL RESPONSIBILITY

Theory and practice in the field of corporate social responsibility (CSR) build upon stakeholder theory. The European Commission defines CSR as being where 'companies integrate social and environmental concerns in their business operations and in their interaction with their stakeholders on a voluntary basis' (European Commission 2001, p7). It is generally accepted in market economies that the main function of business enterprises is to create added value through producing goods and services demanded by people and other organisations in society. This generates profit for their owners and shareholders and provides benefits for society through consumption, investment and job creation. New social and market pressures, however, are leading to changes in the values and horizons of business activities.

There is a growing perception within some members of the business community that sustainable business success and shareholder value cannot be achieved solely through maximising short-term profits. This could be done instead through market-oriented yet responsible corporate behaviour. Companies are therefore becoming aware that they can contribute to sustainable development by managing their operations in ways that enhance economic growth and increase competitiveness, whilst at the same time promoting social responsibility such as consumer interests and environmental protection. With increasing numbers of firms embracing CSR, there is growing consensus on its main features. First, CSR is behaviour by businesses over and above their legal requirements, which is voluntarily adopted because businesses deem it to be in their long-term interests to do so. Second, CSR is linked to the concept of sustainable development, by trying to integrate the economic, social and environmental impacts of their operations. Third, CSR is not an optional 'add-on' to core business activities but is about the ways in which businesses are managed.

Socially responsible business has a long tradition in the UK; examples are Quaker firms and organisations such as Cadburys in Victorian Britain. But the distinguishing feature of CSR today, compared with past initiatives, is in attempts to manage it strategically and develop instruments for doing this. CSR adopts a business approach that puts stakeholder expectations and the principle of continuous improvement and innovation at the heart of business strategies. What constitutes CSR depends on the specific situations of particular organisations and the contexts within which they operate. Whatever forms it takes, however, CSR has found increasing recognition among businesses, policy-makers and other stakeholders as an important element of new and emerging forms of corporate governance (European Commission 2002).

CSR helps organisations respond to some of a number of changes. First, globalisation has created new opportunities for enterprises, but also increased organisational complexity. The increasing extension of business activities internationally has led to new responsibilities taking place on a global scale. Second, considerations of image and reputation play an increasingly important role in the competitive business context. This is because consumers and pressure groups ask for more information about the conditions in which products and services are generated and their impact on sustainability. These parties tend to reward socially and environmentally responsible firms. Third, because of this, financial stakeholders seek disclosure of information about conditions going beyond traditional financial reporting. This allows them to identify the success and risk factors inherent in a company and its responsiveness to public opinion.

Finally, as knowledge and innovation become more important in response to competitiveness, businesses are motivated to retain highly skilled and competent people. Because of the need to respond to international environmental pressure groups, plus impetus from international organisations to reduce hydrocarbon emissions and reduce pollution, organisations have had to develop, implement and evaluate ecological and environmental measures to address these issues.

ACTIVITY 2.13

Evaluate the effectiveness of the board of your organisation (or at some level you have knowledge of) in relation to the organisation's purposes, goals and objectives. What is the board's role in ethical issues?

CONCLUSION: ORGANISATION, HR STRATEGY AND HR SOLUTIONS

The design of appropriate HR strategies and solutions in contemporary organisations is directed towards the purposes of improving organisational performance, efficiency and effectiveness. Those driving the processes associated with these goals have to take account of the features of modern organisational life outlined in this chapter. It has to be recognised, first, that contemporary organisations are highly complex, interactive systems of people and other resources where there is much uncertainty, and where there is no one 'best way' of acting, behaving or doing things. Much of what happens in any organisation is contingent to that organisation alone, so much managerial time is spent 'fire-fighting' and responding to specific issues and problems as they arise. Second, resources, whether human, physical or financial, are always scarce and any actions or decisions taken when managing these resources are likely to have not only benefits for the organisation but also financial implications, social costs and consequences for stakeholders. Competition for these resources, internally and externally, is fierce. Third, organisations are pluralistic bodies, providing arenas for the activities of different interest groups and stakeholders within them, each with different power bases. They are linked together through patterns of consensus, conflict and indifference. This means that people in them have varying opportunities to take possible actions in their own interests, as well as situational, institutional, legal or procedural constraints on them.

Bureaucracy was the starting point in undertaking empirical studies of organisations. Observers studied organisations and analysed them in terms of their degrees of divergence from Weber's ideal type. A range of other models of organisation have superseded this prototype of organisation, although its presence remains well rooted in many cases, even today. Much debate has moved on to new organisational forms, which are seen to be necessary to cope with the demands for flexibility, quick responses to customer needs, and strong control and co-ordination systems. Current concerns with culture and managing culture, for example, are problematic concepts. They are difficult to define, operationalise and legitimise. With the 'in search of excellence' literature having been largely discredited (Peters and Waterman 1982), some observers now see strong cultures as being the problem in organisations, not the solution. Others suggest that some organisations have neither strong nor weak cultures but mixed ones. For postmodernists, representations of culture are complex and difficult to make sense of.

All organisations are systems of power (see Chapter 3), which is normally operationalised through methods of 'soft domination' or 'compliance.' One problem continually facing HR specialists is having the power within organisations to be able to influence decisions that affect the managing of people. It is a major task for HR specialists to gain that power, use it and legitimise it. They have a variety of stratagems for doing this.

Two final points in relation to promoting HR solutions for competitive advantage in organisations need to be made. First, managing change and innovation is a major challenge for those leading organisations. Some claim that change and innovation are normally the result of replacement, merger or acquisition of organisations, rather than re-organisations. HR has a role to play here but change and innovation, rather than being rationally planned processes, are more likely to be incremental and emergent in the way they take place. Second, effective communication between managers and employees, between managers and managers, and between employees and managers, is a vital component of modern organisations. HR specialists have an important role to play in promoting effective intra-organisational dialogues, which are vital parts of change management. Further, employee commitment to organisations is enhanced if they know what the organisation is planning to achieve and how this is being done. Effective communication, especially by top management, can generate trust, as those leading an organisation try to explain to its people what they are trying to do and why.

KEY LEARNING POINTS

1. Organisation theory is the study of organisations and how their stakeholders interact together. There are many types of organisations, with different forms of ownership, control and objectives. Organisations engage in wealth creation, provide job opportunities and supply goods and services to those wanting them. However, organisation theory is not synonymous with management theory. Managers are only one party with an interest in organisations. The search for efficiency, order and rationality to enable managers to perform better is only one perspective of organisation and organisation theory.

2. There are three main approaches to studying organisations: the modernist, symbolic and postmodern views. Each has its own perspectives, assumptions and interpretations of the field of organisation studies. Differences between them arise out of views about the nature of reality, focus of organisation theory, theory of knowledge and nature of organisations. The orthodox approach to organisation theory provides models, frameworks and principles for practising managers to enable them to manage more effectively. The symbolic approach argues that organisational reality does not have an objective existence but that people construct organisational realities through giving them their own meanings. The postmodern approach is that organisations

are not characterised by order and unity but by uncertainty, complexity and contradiction.

3. Classical studies of organisations incorporate theories of bureaucracy, scientific management and human relations theory. These theories, and the principles underpinning them, are still applied in many organisations today. All embody positivist views of organisations. Their central purpose is to legitimise managerial control, linked with an ideology of progress that is expected to produce more educated, knowledgeable, civilised societies.

4. Organisations have a variety of typologies and objectives. Some organisations are market driven and market led, others politically driven and politically led. The organisational typologies used include: prime beneficiaries; functional, technological and structural typologies; regulatory typologies; and sectoral typologies. A useful generic typology is the relationship between an organisation's orientation and its ownership. Orientation is having profit and added-value goals or welfare, community and budgetary goals, and ownership is either private or public. By this typology, there are four basic types of organisation: private businesses, public corporations, public services, and voluntary bodies and social enterprises.

5. The internal contexts of organisations can be divided into five clusters: organisational culture; physical layout; technological innovation; power, conflict and control; and social components. Culture refers to the deep, basic assumptions and beliefs that are shared, to varying degrees, by the members of an organisation. Layout includes geographical location, planning of workspaces and equipment, landscaping and internal decor. Technological innovation consists of the materials and processes used in transforming organisational inputs into outputs, as well as the skills, knowledge and human resources incorporated in this process. Understanding power, conflict and control in organisations is important for managers, including HR, since they have to work within systems where power structures are institutionalised, to mitigate conflict and retain some control over organisational resources. The social components of organisations include people, their positions within the organisation and the work groups or units to which they belong. These provide choices about structure, rules and systems, co-ordinating mechanisms, and networks.

6. Contemporary studies of organisations are categorised as theories of managing culture, post-bureaucracy, managing change and 'fast capitalism'. Each reflects the centrality of effective HRM within organisations. The perspective is again strongly positivist in its analysis and based on instrumental rationality and control within organisations. Many of these ideas have been incorporated into recent managerial practices but they have been challenged by symbolic and postmodern writers. Critical management theory encompasses a wide range of perspectives questioning and challenging traditional theories of organisation and management.

7. Debates about old and new organisational forms, and their implications for HRM, are ongoing. Some writers support new organisational forms; others challenge this new orthodoxy. New organisational forms have implications for internal organisational issues such as: hierarchy, division of labour, rules and schedules, systems, integration, control, rewards, outsourcing, alliances and organising across boundaries. Integration, control and HR are vital issues too.

The emerging orthodoxy is that teamwork increases employee commitment and involvement. Distinctions are made between strategic control and operational control. Some strategies for attaining managerial control are deemed more appropriate to 'old' organisational forms, others to 'new' ones. The strategies used include target-based outputs, individualist culture, electronic surveillance and HRM-based interventions.

8. Two issues are central to understanding contemporary organisations and managerial and employee behaviour within them. First, there is the continuous search for improved performance, profit and efficiency. These are driven by the imperatives of short-term financial returns in a globalised market economy and a cosmopolitan, consumerist market society. These forces promote strong performance management cultures in private, public and third sector organisations. Typically, performance management incorporates a shared vision of an organisation's objectives, connected with goals of customer satisfaction and a drive for continuous improvement, supported by elaborate procedures for identifying, measuring and assessing performance. The HR elements of performance management include individual performance targets, regular performance reviews and performance-related rewards, although they have their critics. Second, there is the question of change management and its function within organisations. Some commentators, however, describe change as an exaggerated process driven by parties, such as senior managers, consultants or academics, who have vested interests in promoting the 'change agenda'.

9. Managers are not the only stakeholders in organisations. Stakeholder theory argues that every legitimate person or group participating in the activities of a firm or an organisation does so to benefit themselves. However, the priority of the interests of all legitimate stakeholders is not self-evident. Typical stakeholders in the private sector include management, employees, shareholders, suppliers, customers, financial institutions, creditors, communities and government. In the public sector, they include civil servants, citizens, clients, colleagues, ministers and contractors. A useful classification of stakeholders distinguishes them as being latent (who may be dormant, discretionary or demanding), expectant (who may be dominant, dangerous or dependent) and definitive, according to their degrees of power, legitimacy and urgency.

10. The purpose of any system of corporate governance is to ensure the survival and sustainability of an organisation. Private organisations have a number of accountabilities including legal accountability to their shareholders, employees, suppliers and consumers in terms of the minimum standards expected of them by the state. However, the social and moral accountabilities of private businesses have become increasingly important in recent years, as businesses have increasingly accepted that they have extra-legal responsibilities. From the stakeholder perspective, the corporate status of businesses transforms them into something closer to being 'public' property and subject to more than just property ownership rights. In the public sector, organisations are accountable through their governing bodies, government ministers or public officials for the actions that they take. In the third sector, it is trustees who take ultimate responsibility for the good governance of organisations. As a result of these developments, CSR is increasingly on the business agenda.

REVIEW QUESTIONS

1. Compare and contrasts the positivist, symbolic-interpretive, and postmodern views of organisations in terms of their perspectives, assumptions and interpretations of the field of organisation studies. Indicate how each perspective provides an insight to understanding behaviour in your organisation.

2. Identify the main organisational typologies for classifying organisations. Which one in your view is the most useful tool of analysis and why?

3. One way of classifying an organisation's main internal contexts is using CLIPS. What are the components of CLIPS? Drawing on CLIPS, rank in order of importance the internal contexts in your organisation. Give reasons for your ranking and justify your response.

4. Explain why performance, profit and efficiency are so critical in understanding behaviour in contemporary organisations within capitalist economies. What are the implications of these drivers for HR strategy, insights and solutions?

5. Explain what is meant by 'stakeholder theory'. What are the main implications of adopting a stakeholder perspective on organisations for managers?

CASE STUDY 2.1 ZENOTECH – A NETWORK-BASED ORGANISATION

Background

Zenotech is a high-tech organisation manufacturing quality innovative micro-electronic products for manufacturers in European and global markets. Founded 10 years ago largely by finance capital from a Norwegian consortium of investors, Zenotech has expanded steadily and successfully over this period, albeit with a very serious blip in its performance and profits about five years ago. It remains a privately owned business but its employees are encouraged to own the company's shares and over 50 per cent of them are now shareholders. With a head office staff of 150, located in Birmingham, Zenotech now employs about 1,000 skilled staff in a number of locations in the UK, Ireland and the Netherlands. Staff turnover is low. Head office deals with new product research, product development, marketing and promotion of existing and new products.

As indicated above, five years ago, the organisation went through a very

difficult period in terms of sales, market penetration and profitability. As a result, it had to undertake a thorough review of its operations to identify what needed to be done to make it more competitive and customer focused, and to find ways of improving its market position. The overall objective was to make the organisation 25 per cent more efficient within three years and to increase profits. A major solution to the problems facing Zenotech at this time was seen to be a new, radical organisational structure, with the aim of making it a flexible, adaptable organisation where individual employees were to be at the core of its business activities.

During this three-year period, the business went through a complete reorganisation. There were changes in its management structure, which is now flat and less hierarchic, and staff reductions took place. This transformation did not take place without some resistance amongst staff, since the restructuring exercise meant a clean break with most of the established routines, systems and co-ordinating mechanisms of the 'old' organisation. However, in planning for the new structure, senior management involved staff fully in the change management process. Employees were kept fully informed of what was going to happen during the three-year period leading to implementation of the new structure. Managers discussed openly the reasons for change and how it was to be done. The possible consequences of these changes for staff were debated too. Most employees were able to participate in planning for and executing the restructuring process. Regular meetings were held with staff, so that all relevant information was passed onto them and any questions they had were dealt with immediately. No one left the company during the first three months following the restructuring, despite some staff still feeling ambivalent and anxious towards the new organisational structure.

The network-based organisational structure

Developments within Zenotech have resulted in a radical, network-based organisational structure. There is no line command, no formal organisational hierarchy, and no specific leaders to whom employees report. Employees no longer work for departments, with the whole organisation being based on projects and project teams. At any one time, employees and project leaders can have varying levels of participation in more than one project. Employees physically move from area to area, working on projects in their locations. People work in 'open plan' areas and no one, including project leaders, has a personal office. Team members relocate themselves in accordance with the projects in which they are involved. All communication is either face to face or by computer. Nevertheless, even using sophisticated technology, there are still a number of routine administrative tasks which have to done to support project

teams. Staff doing these jobs have less freedom and control over their activities than do team members, since their work is much more structured.

The numbers of participants in project teams varies according to the work to be done and the complexity of the tasks involved. For example, a team with the objective of launching a new product typically has two to three members. Larger product development teams may have 10 to 20 members. A product development project with common technology is often linked with other similar projects. The responsibility of the co-ordinating manager is to oversee the marketing of the product, the timing of its introduction to the market and its delivery. Selection of project leaders takes place in some cases by the employee proposing the project leading it. Another method is where senior management suggest the individual they feel is best suited for the job. A range of criteria for selection typically includes technical skills, experience, leadership ability and corporate skills, provided the person has the time available to get involved in the project.

Project managers or team leaders are free to manage their project groups in ways they determine. Thus project teams are run in various ways. Some teams meet all together regularly. Others meet only when necessary. Other groups make all decisions jointly and some leave decision-making to those directly involved with a particular aspect of the project. Project managers are responsible for choosing members of each project. Normally, this means going and asking people to join the project. This results in some employees being in more demand than others. To obtain good project team members, resources and attention from top management, team leaders have to be good at promoting their projects. Project leaders with good track records are more likely to be successful in obtaining resources for their projects than those who are less effective.

Product teams are required to undertake all the tasks connected with a product from its development until its introduction to the market. This means that a project team may exist for some time, with team members covering a range of other job functions in addition to their specialism. Since there are a range of different projects in progress at any one time, different time-scales are attached to each.

Product groups meet with senior management once every three months and present their work and results to them. The criteria for success are that project tasks should be completed within budget and on time. Co-ordination and communication between project teams are not formalised, with connections amongst employees in individual teams being much stronger than those among groups. Employees are responsible for joining product teams themselves and for completing the projects they accept. When a project is completed (or abandoned), employees move on to other projects. All employees are encouraged to suggest new projects and propose new ideas. Because there is no

line of command in Zenotech, ideas can be presented to anyone in the organisation, not just the managing director. However, employees are expected to demonstrate initiative, effort and results. Zenotech, in short, is an umbrella organisation for all the projects going on in the company at any one time, where projects, processes and people are intertwined.

Tasks

1. How did Zenotech manage to minimise resistance to change?

2. Explain the nature and apparent effectiveness of the organisational structure of Zenotech.

3. Identify and explain the advantages and disadvantages of the network organisation structure used at Zenotech.

4. In what ways can Zenotech eliminate the disadvantages of the network organisation for the business?

5. What factors could shift Zenotech away from a network organisation structure to a more bureaucratic, hierarchical one?

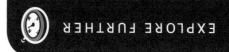

EXPLORE FURTHER

HATCH, M. and CUNLIFFE, A. (2006) *Organization theory: modern, symbolic and postmodern perspectives*. Oxford: Oxford University Press.

Provides a distinctive, clear and comprehensive introduction to the study of organisations and organising processes, drawing on different perspectives; these include the modernist or rational perspective; the symbolic-interpretive perspective sometimes linked with the organisational culture school; and the postmodern perspective with its links to critical organisation and labour process theory.

PARKER, M. (2002) *Against management: organization in the age of managerialism*. Cambridge: Polity.

Argues that there are the beginnings of a cultural shift in the image of management, representing a significant historical change; this is because it opens up the possibility of exploring non-managerial alternatives to contemporary assumptions about organising and organisations.

ROLLINSON, D. (2008) *Organisational behaviour and analysis: an integrated approach*, 4th ed. Harlow: Financial Times/Prentice Hall.

Is a traditional student text and provides a comprehensive introduction to organisational behaviour. It attempts to steer a neutral path through the sociological, psychological and managerial approaches to the discipline. It balances coverage of micro-organisational behaviour with the macro-organisational level of analysis level.

THOMPSON, P. and McHUGH, D. (2009) *Work organisations: a critical approach*, 4th ed. Basingstoke: Palgrave Macmillan

Provides a critical approach to organisations where the authors evaluate the most up-to-date theoretical studies and relevant research findings. They bring together and contrast conventional and critical approaches to organisations from organisation and management studies, labour process theory and social psychology.

CHAPTER 3

The managerial and business contexts of organisations

INTRODUCTION

The theme of this chapter is the managerial and business contexts of organisations. As stated in the preface, these consist of the '6Ms' framework, which are the central, core level of the organisational context. The analysis is largely Anglo-US centred but provides a key to understanding what drives organisational activities and the roles of managers as key actors in organisational life. The chapter starts with an examination of the nature of management and whether management can be considered a profession. The chapter then provides a traditional functional analysis of management and examines each area in turn. More recent or 'modern' managerial functions are described and analysed next, including risk analysis, quality management and performance management. This leads on to a review of managerial power, authority and influence and the search for managerial legitimacy in organisations. A description of the politics of management is also provided, outlining how power is operationalised and used to achieve organisational objectives. Some models of the HR function are identified, followed by an examination of the factors shaping the HR agenda. The chapter concludes by summarising how HR specialists try to integrate or match organisational and employee expectations in the wage–work bargain and the psychological contract so as to gain employee commitment for organisational objectives.

LEARNING OUTCOMES

By the end of this chapter, readers should be able to understand, explain and critically evaluate:

- the traditional roles and functions of management in organisations
- recent developments in managerial practices

- the importance of power, authority and influence in organisations
- the politics of management
- roles and models of the HR function.

In addition, readers should also be able to:

- assess recent developments in management practice
- understand the nature of organisational politics
- advise on external issues affecting the HR agenda
- identify the contribution of HR and people to organisational effectiveness.

MANAGEMENT WITHIN ORGANISATIONS

The first 'M' in the six 'Ms' framework is management. This section examines the complex nature of modern management in terms of what it is, what it does and how the management function is organised. Management represents a division of labour, which is structured into specialist areas within organisations.

MEANINGS OF MANAGEMENT

The term 'management' is a frustratingly difficult one to define. An early definition by Harbison and Myers (1959, p8) sees management as 'the hierarchy of individuals who perform specified critical functions in an organisation. Management thus connotes both people and tasks.' They present a three-fold concept of its development in industrial society: as an economic resource, system of authority and social elite. A later definition by Mant (1979) also provides three (different) meanings of management: the activity of running things, the ideology of management and the people paid to run things. For Clegg *et al* (2008), management is the process of communicating, co-ordinating and accomplishing actions in the pursuit of organisational goals, whilst managing relationships at work. These relationships cover not only organisational stakeholders (including, but not exclusively, employees) but also technology and other artefacts both within and between organisations. For Hales (2001), management has become a complex, differentiated process for planning, allocating, motivating, co-ordinating and controlling work. He identifies three key themes in the literature on management.

- **Separation:** the process of managing work has become separated from the execution of work.
- **Extension:** the function of management is extended by amalgamation with functions flowing from ownership of the inputs and outputs of work.

- **Dispersion:** as a combined function, management has become dispersed through different managerial specialisms and levels.

Hales (2001) sees 'management' and 'organisation' as interdependent, symbiotic concepts and proposes a 'management through organisation' model of the function. This incorporates a variety of organisational arrangements or approaches for attempting the planning, allocation, motivation, co-ordination and control of work. These approaches contain four main elements: the management of operational work, the management of professional and administrative work, the problem of employee commitment and the problem of continuous change. Hales develops a penetrating analysis of what different approaches to work entail, both in theory and in practice. For him, a central focus in 'the management of work' is that it is carried out largely through the institutional mechanisms of organisation.

Perhaps the most illuminating way of understanding and summarising the nature of modern management is by describing and analysing the content of managerial work. Building upon the classical study of Mintzberg (1980), as shown in Figure 3.1, and other writers such as Luthans et al (1976), it is now widely recognised that managers undertake both managerial work and work relating to their professional specialisms. Their managerial roles cover 10 fields of activity:

- acting as figurehead or leader of a work group

- monitoring and disseminating information inside and outside the organisation

- negotiating with subordinates, peers, superordinates and externally

- handling disturbances and solving problems

- allocating resources such as money, materials, space and equipment

- directing, monitoring and controlling the work of staff

- developing, maintaining and activating contacts and liaising with others

- innovating processes, methods and products

- planning and scheduling work

- managing people or human resources.

Other features of managerial work include its fragmented nature, continual interactions with other people, networks of contacts and focus on day-to-day concrete problems. Managers spend relatively little time on strategic issues or reflective planning, tending to react to events rather than initiate them. Finally, managers are subject to constant interruptions, often hold unscheduled, face-to-face, unplanned meetings, and navigate rapidly between meetings and activities (Kotter 1982).

Many studies have shown that there are wide variations in managerial work. These variations reflect the dispersion of management work, the diverse contexts in which the work takes place, and different ways in which the work is organised. They include the balance between different elements of work content (Stewart 1967), patterns or rhythms of work (Stewart 1976) and the degree of choice

Figure 3.1 Mintzberg's analysis of managerial roles

Managerial status and authority

Interpersonal skills	Informational roles	Decisional roles
Figurehead	Monitor	Entrepreneur
Leader	Disseminator	Disturbance handler
Liaison	Spokesperson	Resource allocator
		Negotiator

Adapted from Mintzberg (1980).

available to managers. The variations occur across individuals, jobs, functional specialism, level, organisation and industry, and culture.

Management, then, can be conceptualised, first, as the wide choice of processes used by professional managers to run organisations in ways that promote the objectives set for them. Second, management is the group of people carrying out the managerial functions within organisations, involving wide variations in jobs, functions, levels and contexts. Third, a central concern of management is use of power and the allocation and distribution of resources within organisations.

ACTIVITY 3.1

What are the roles of management in organisations?

THE PROFESSIONALISATION OF MANAGEMENT

Managing organisations or the management of organisations (by managers) is such a central, critical activity in businesses, the public sector and third sector that some commentators see 'management' as a modern profession. This is a controversial view, with some observers supporting it and others opposing it. Trait models of professionalism list the attributes claimed to represent the common core of professional occupations. Millerson (1964), for example, lists 23 elements incorporated within definitions of professions. These include skills based on professional knowledge, provision of training and education, testing the competence of members, altruistic service to clients and adherence to professional codes of conduct. A weakness of trait approaches is that they tend to incorporate the professionals' own definition of what it means to be a professional. Using this checklist, those practising management functions, whether as specialists or generalists, meet only some of these professional criteria.

Functionalist models of professionalism make no attempt to present exhaustive lists of traits. Instead, the components of professionalism are limited to those with functional relevance for society and the 'professional–client' relationship. Barber (1963) claims that professional behaviour may be defined in terms of four essential attributes: a high degree of generalised and systematic knowledge; primary orientation to community rather than personal self-interest; a high degree of control of behaviour through internalised codes of ethics, operated by the professionals themselves; and a system of rewards that are mainly symbols of work achievement. Like the trait model, the functional one excludes from consideration the power dimension of professionalism (ie potential conflicts between professionals and their clients). Judged by these criteria, management is not a *bona fide* profession.

Johnson (1972, p45) has responded to the above by arguing that professionalism can be defined as 'a peculiar form of occupational control rather than an expression of the inherent nature of particular occupations'. For him, a profession is not an occupation 'but a means of controlling an occupation'. He provides a three-fold typology of institutionalised forms of professional control.

- **Collegiate control**: where professionals define the needs of their clients and the manner in which these needs are catered for. Collegiate control is based on either occupational authority or a guild system, as in the medical profession.

- **Mediatory control**: where a third party (either business or the state) mediates the relationship between professionals and their clients (such as between government and professional nurses or schoolteachers).

- **Patronage control**: where professionals define their own needs and how they are to be met. This may be done through either 'oligarchic' patronage (as in the patron–artist relationship) or 'corporate' patronage (such as how some large organisations recruit and promote professional staff). It could be argued that some degree of occupational control for managers is demonstrated through systems of corporate patronage.

Other evidence of the professionalisation of management is demonstrated, first, by the increasing importance of certain professional associations, such as the Chartered Institute of Personnel and Development and the Chartered Institute of Marketing. Bodies such as these examine, regulate and maintain professional standards in their specialisms. Second, there has been a phenomenal rise in the numbers of business schools in the UK over the past 20 years. Originating in the United States, business schools have become repositories of the disciplines of 'business' – which normally offer undergraduate programmes of study – and/or 'management', which normally offer postgraduate programmes, opportunities for doctoral research and consultancy services for private and public organisations. Whether 'management' is perceived as a single, coherent academic discipline or field of study is doubtful, but institutions of higher education offering business and management studies employ a range of specialists in 'soft' and 'hard' areas in these fields. Soft areas include organisational behaviour, HRM, marketing, strategy, operations, and business ethics. Hard areas include business economics, international trade, information systems, finance and accounting, law, and quantitative methods. These academic activities promote knowledge of management, management practice, the training and development of managers, and the legitimacy of management as a field of practice and study.

There are, however, critics of the claimed professionalisation of management. Some come from the academic world; others from practising managers. In the academic community, Parker (2002, p11), whose broader target is 'managerialism', or the generalised ideology of management, argues that 'the market managerial notion of organizing is only one alternative of many.' For him, words like co-ordination, co-operation, barter, participation, collectivity, democracy, community and citizenship have been increasingly erased by managerialism and the professionalisation of management. Grey (2009, p145) makes a similar point when he writes: 'Management education acts to endorse both market relations and managerial dominance as normal, natural and inevitable features of social organization.' He sees the rise of management education in the UK as being closely related to the 'development of a politics which saw management and markets as preferable to unions and public provision.'

Managerial critics of the world of modern management, such as Hopper and Hopper (2009, p133), are similarly dismissive of the professionalism of management, particularly in the form of the 'Cult of the (So-called) Expert,' but for different reasons. They describe this cult as a form of neo-Taylorism, with organisations affected by the 'cult' having five attributes:

- **Measurement:** organisations are administered by people taught to measure, with reliance on quantitative benchmarks, which incentivises manipulation of data. Neo-Taylorism weakens the traditional line of command, which depended primarily on trusting human relationships for transmitting information, most of which was qualitative.

- **Credentialism:** 'experts' are characterised by paper certificates and qualifications which are deemed necessary for professional and other employment.

- **Top-down:** the prime method of operation emphasises management from the top to legitimise 'experts'.

- **Diffusion of responsibility:** neo-Taylorism diffuses responsibility amongst 'experts' (accountants, HR and consultants of all kinds), so that it is difficult to pinpoint responsibility.

- **Appointment of experts:** co-ordinators are appointed as 'experts' to solve particular problems, accompanied by continuous 'initiatives'.

Hopper and Hopper (2009, p xiii) describe and analyse the Puritan legacy on American management from the seventeenth century to the late 1970s, some of which was transmitted to countries like the UK. They describe how America's 'superb managerial culture', originating in seventeenth-century New England, evolved to make the United States the most powerful nation on earth. They argue that the United States subsequently shared the secrets of its economic success with Japan after the Second World War. They diagnose the cause of the recent credit crunch in the United States as the excess of borrowing by government, businesses and individuals. 'In November 2008, it resulted in the near collapse and part-nationalization of the world's largest bank by revenues, Citigroup Inc.' Their basic argument is that in the 'Golden Age of Management' (1920–1970), managerial executives had learned the craft of management on the job, from more senior colleagues. The situation deteriorated in the last third of the century, because management was increasingly regarded as a profession. The new style senior manager, who had not learned management on the job, sought to control organisations through the medium of the finance department, whilst delegating the acquisition and use of 'domain knowledge' to junior managers. The outcome was 'managerial incompetence on a scale inconceivable in earlier generations and extending over much of society'. For these observers, the very notion of professional management is loathsome. Hopper and Hopper set out 25 principles, underpinning good practice management in the period 1920–70, as summarised in Figure 3.2.

ACTIVITY 3.2

Is management a profession? Justify your answer.

ACTIVITY 3.3

Looking at Figure 3.2, how many of the 25 principles of 'good management' listed by the Hoppers do you observe in your organisation? What are the main characteristics of management processes in your organisation?

ACTIVITY 3.4

Hopper and Hopper write (2009, p144) that 'the collegiate style of leadership described so eloquently and accurately by Drucker and Given' has been replaced by the rule of the chief executive officer and collegiality has vanished. The ideal former chief executive 'had been a thoughtful listener and … shared responsibility with his entire top team and was paid only modestly more than they'. What are the pros and cons of a collegiate style of top management?

Figure 3.2 Twenty-five principles underlying good practice management from the 'golden age' of management

SYSTEMS AND ROUTINES
Principle 1: All successful organisations, however simple, consist of systems within systems
Principle 2: All systems are nurtured by routines, which must be regularly reviewed and refreshed
Principle 3: The most important subsystem in any organisation is the managerial hierarchy, which is likely to be based on some form of line and staff relationship
Principle 4: The best hierarchy is 'bottom up'; ie operational responsibility is pushed down to the lowest level capable of accepting it
STRUCTURES AND HIERARCHY
Principle 5: Leadership should be as far as possible collective or collegiate
Principle 6: The middle manager is the keystone in the managerial arch
Principle 7: One person, one manager
DECISION-MAKING
Principle 8: Meetings are the medium of management work
Principle 9: Integrated decision-making leads to the right conclusions
Principle 10: Planning should be for the short term, medium term and long term
Principle 11: You should make a careful study of the mistakes and successes of the pioneers in your field – and learn from them
Principle 12: Excellent internal communications in all directions – but above all upwards – are necessary in any successful organisation
Principle 13: The manager must be a leader in both a practical and moral sense
Principle 14: You should use consultants sparingly – and 'strategic' consultants never
Principle 15: Managers should be aware of their responsibilities to society as a whole, including to the organisation's employees as human beings
Principle 16: If it ain't broke, you should try to make it work better
FINANCE
Principle 17: Avoid debt like the plague – or, if possible, use it sparingly
TRAINING
Principle 18: A manager should possess or acquire what is known as 'domain knowledge', ie a profound understanding of the technology and business of the company, which can normally be gained only through a long apprenticeship in that company or in the same industry
Principle 19: The testing and training of managers should be pragmatic and continuous
Principle 20: Managers who wish to get to the top should start at or near the bottom
Principle 21: Job rotation is desirable to create the 'rounded' executive
EMPLOYMENT
Principle 22: Employment should generally be for the long term – by which is meant at least eight and, if possible, 10 years
Principle 23: Complementarity is one of the keys to making appointments, ie by building teams
Principle 24: The remuneration system should promote and reward group effort
Principle 25: Avoid ostentation like the plague

Adapted from Hopper and Hopper (2009).

MANAGERIAL FUNCTIONS

The second 'M' is management's traditional functions: finance, marketing, operations, strategy and HRM. The role of senior managers is to ensure the integration and co-ordination of these and other managerial functions of an organisation, so as to create internal coherence and added value, as discussed in Chapter 2. For clarity, discussion focuses largely on the private sector, although much of it applies to the public and third sectors too. More detailed and specific accounts of public management are examined in specialist texts (Massey and Pyper 2005, Lynn 2006).

FINANCIAL MANAGEMENT

For a company to be effective and efficient, it is critical to have appropriate financial sources, evaluate capital projects, keep proper accounting records and maintain firm budgetary control. Some basic issues relating to effective financial management, in relation to these four fundamental conditions, are outlined below. Figure 3.3 summarises the main source and flows of finance within private sector businesses.

Sources of finance

Companies need to be properly financed. Both the correct amount and right type of finance have to be available when needed. Even profitable companies, with motivated workforces and innovative products or services, risk their futures if they are not financed properly. This is particularly important when trading conditions are difficult. Companies need financial capital to acquire fixed assets, provide working capital and invest. Fixed assets such as land, buildings and machinery are used to provide the company's products or services. Working capital is needed to finance the day-to-day operation of the business, such as covering the costs of labour and corporate overheads. And, as firms grow, they need additional capital to expand their businesses for investment purposes. Profitable companies generate some additional capital internally. However, insufficient capital is likely to be obtained in this way. Expanding businesses have to get capital from outside the company, with more established businesses needing to expand by strategic acquisitions and external capital (Brearley *et al* 2006).

Permanent capital is normally provided by the company's shareholders, either by buying the company's shares or by not taking profit in the form of dividends. Long-term, medium-term and short-term capital come from external sources in the form of loans. In general, permanent and long-term loans are used to finance the purchase of long-term fixed assets. Medium-term capital is used to give a company additional flexibility. Short-term capital is used to satisfy capital needs of a temporary nature. Other sources of capital include: grants and loans from government and European sources; off-balance sheet financing, where assets are leased from a leasing company; and debtor financing, such as factoring. There can also be hybrid financing in the form of convertible loan stock.

Figure 3.3 The main sources and flows of finance within private sector businesses

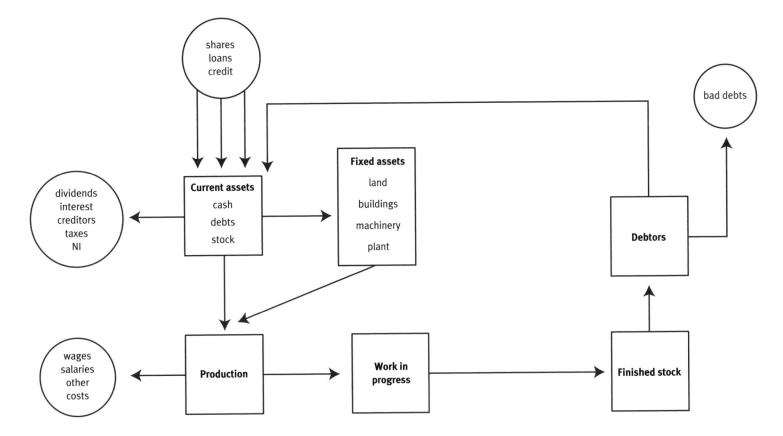

Evaluation of capital projects

Evaluating capital projects involves estimating their future benefits and comparing these with their costs. This analysis is used not only to buy long-lived physical assets but also to anticipate any capital expenditures with impacts on the future, such as sales, mergers and plant closures. The elements necessary for effective capital project planning include:

- access to information
- knowledge of the company's required financial return
- realistic evaluation of project cash inflows and outflows
- analysis of cash flows
- evaluation of strategic implications of large projects
- a well-defined approval procedure
- consistency with strategic objectives
- a review procedure.

The annual accounts

The annual accounts of a company provide the base information for those outside the company wishing to understand its financial standing. Minimum standards are set, principally by legislation, and accounts have to be audited to ensure these standards are met. The information required for statutory accounts has grown enormously in recent years, due to pressures from investors and the general public. The pressures from investors for more financial information have grown with increasing separation of company shareholding from management. Successive governments have responded by enacting new legislation. Further, accounting boards and certain committees, established to examine company practices, have set out standards companies should follow. On a wider front, boards are required to follow formal procedures considered to be 'best practice' in relation to corporate governance and directors' remuneration.

At the core of the annual report are the tables and notes, which collectively offer a massive amount of information and financial data which take time to absorb. The main items are the profit and loss account, profits attributable to shareholders, balance sheet, cash flow adjustment and shareholders' funds, with accompanying notes. In addition to these, a directors' report is required.

The directors' report contains information reviewing the company's affairs for the period of the accounts. Other items include the amount recommended to be paid in dividend, amount of reserves, principal activities of the company, the names of directors, changes in fixed assets, and contracts with the company. Any arrangements between the company and its directors need to be specified, including directors' interests, the authority to issue or purchase shares and any other share interests. Finally, a commentary is made on the company's compliance with the code of practice on corporate governance, the appointment of auditors and company policy on employee involvement (Nobes and Parker 2008).

Budgetary control

A main preoccupation of senior managers is cash. Cash is the starting point and finishing point of a business. Lack of cash is more likely to cause business failure than any other factor. Cash is a 'fact', whereas profit is arbitrary, and cash control by managers is essential for effective financial management. Every cost is a direct cost of the manager incurring it and the principle of matching the principle of accountability with authority is preserved. Budgets are set for the managers of each cost centre, as agreed between themselves and their manager. These are based purely on the expenses incurred within the manager's area of discretion and responsibility. Each month a statement is prepared for each cost centre, showing the actual and budgeted costs analysed under expense headings for the month and cumulatively. Such budgets are reviewed periodically. This results in them being flexible through time but rigid at any point in time. If profit cannot be controlled, cash can (Wood and Sangster 2008).

ACTIVITY 3.5

Examine your organisation's annual accounts. What do they tell you about the organisation?

MARKETING

The marketing function provides the interface between organisations and their customers, with the underpinning aim of assisting buying and selling between them. As a management function, marketing incorporates marketing planning, product pricing, promotion of goods and services, and their distribution. Marketing techniques are now being increasingly used by organisations with welfare, community and budgetary goals. Current views of marketing emphasise its goal of achieving corporate objectives by meeting or exceeding customer needs better than the competition. A key marketing task is understanding customer needs and developing competitive advantage through 'marketing mix' decisions. Figure 3.4 illustrates matching the marketing mix with customer needs. Based on an understanding of its customers, an organisation's marketing mix consists of four major elements: product, price, promotion and place, which are the four key decision areas that marketing staff must manage to satisfy or exceed customer needs (Dwyer and Tanner 2009).

Product

Product decisions decide what goods (or services) are offered to a group of customers. An important issue is new product development. As technology and tastes change, products become out of date and inferior to those of competitors, so companies need to replace them with features that customers value. Product decisions involve choices of brand names, warranties, packaging and the services accompanying the product. A product, distinct from a brand, is anything capable

Figure 3.4 Matching the marketing mix with customer needs

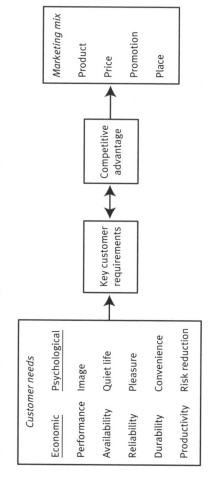

of satisfying customer needs. Brands create individual identities by developing a distinctive name, packaging and design. A product line is a group of brands that are closely related in terms of functions and benefits. A product mix is the total set of brands marketed by a company. Branding augments core products to create differentiation and extra value to customers. There is a variety of specialist methods of brand-building including quality, positioning, repositioning, blended communications, 'being first', taking a long-term perspective and internal markets. With the shift to global and pan-European branding, decisions have to be taken about which parts of a brand can be standardised and which must be varied between customer groups (Heding et al 2009).

Price

Price is a key element of the marketing mix, because it represents on a unit basis what the organisation receives for the product or service being marketed. All other elements represent costs such as expenditure on product design, advertising and salespeople, and transportation and distribution. Marketing people need to be very clear about pricing objectives, methods, and the factors influencing pricing. They also need to take account of discounting and giving allowances in some transactions. These requirements influence the level of the price list chosen, perhaps with an element of negotiation margin built-in. Payment periods and credit terms also affect the real price received in transactions.

Price-setting can be cost oriented, competitor oriented or marketing oriented. Cost-oriented and competitor-oriented methods have drawbacks, and pricing is often based on marketing-oriented considerations. These are marketing strategy, value to the customers, price–quality relationships, product line pricing, explicability, competition, negotiating margins, effects on distributors and retailers, political factors and costs. Techniques such as trade-off analysis, economic value to the customer analysis, and experimentation give estimates of customer value. However, a great deal of management judgement has to enter the equation. It is much more difficult to practise, because of its complexity, than cost-based methods but pay-off in terms of high sales revenue and profits is solid (Gummesson 2008).

Promotion

Decisions have to be made regarding the promotional mix: advertising, personal selling, sales promotion and public relations. By these means, the target audience is made aware of the existence of a product or service and its benefits, both economic and psychological (Doyle 2008).

- Advertising is able to reach wide audiences very quickly. Repetition means a brand-positioning concept can be effectively communicated, with television being a particularly strong medium.

- Personal selling is interactive and questions can be asked and objections overcome.

- Sales promotions with incentives provide a quick boost to sales, although the effects may be only short term.

- Publicity is highly credible, as messages come across from a third party. There is higher readership than for advertisements in trade and technical publications.

Place

Place involves decisions about the distribution channels to be used and their management, location of outlets, methods of transportation and inventory levels to be held. The objective is to ensure that products and services are available in proper qualities at the right time and place. Distribution channels consist of organisations such as retailers or wholesalers, through which goods pass on their way to customers. Producers need to manage their relationships with these organisations well, because they may provide the only cost-effective access to the marketplace.

Distribution channels for services are normally more direct than for many physical goods. Because services are intangible, the services marketer is less concerned with storage, the production and consumption is often simultaneous, and the personal nature of services means that direct contact with the service provider is desirable. Agents are used when the individual service provider cannot provide a sufficiently wide selection for customers. Consequently, agents are often used for marketing travel, insurance and entertainment. Growth for many service firms means opening new facilities in new locations (Dent 2008).

ACTIVITY 3.6

How does the marketing function add value to an organisation?

Operations management

Operations management is concerned with the production of goods and services and seeks to ensure that an organisation's business operations are both efficient and effective in terms of meeting customer requirements. Operations management manages the processes that convert organisational inputs, in the forms of materials, labour and other resources, into outputs in the form of goods and services. Increasingly, the distinction between producing goods and services is difficult to justify. Manufacturers tend to merge product and service systems, while service providers adopt contemporary operation management techniques (Hill and Hill 2009)

Product design

The role of design in business competitiveness is seen by many as a critical determinant in market success. This is because customers are increasingly discriminating, well informed and conscious of what constitutes product quality and product specification. Customers want to buy 'values' as much as the products or services being sold. Consumers demand more of products as they evaluate and select those which conform best to their own value sets and preferences. Concern for the quality of the environment, waste, the adverse effects of possible pollution, energy use, and changes in life style now strongly influence product design and service provision. Design is seen as the formal focus for creativity in businesses. Technological change penetrates businesses through the research and development function and socially oriented change through marketing. Design is seen as the key link between these two sources, with the mix of both technological and social forces being drawn together to solve design problems (Ulrich and Eppinger 2008).

The concept of 'design' is fluid and characterised by modelling. This is where design problems and design solutions are refined jointly. Design problems are changeable. Progress is made by proposing and evaluating alternative solutions and by operations management being solution-focused throughout. Different approaches are used side by side. Thus design activity can be, at one and the same time, analytic and synthetic, divergent and convergent, ad hoc and procedural, and systematic and intuitive. Design is an iterative process, encompassing both the purposes and means of achieving goals.

Design of physical products in manufacturing may be conceptualised as the process leading to the specification of materials, manufacturing methods, control mechanisms, shape, colours, surface finishes and decoration of the objects being produced. A similar process is applied in service provision. The primary decision-making criteria used in establishing these specifications are concerns for appearance, ease of use and maintenance, convenience, reliability, performance in operation, safety, and human factors such as physiological, procedural or task related, and psychological. Other issues include materials and operations processes and utilisation of appropriate technology. Designers need to be aware of how these criteria are influenced by the subtle, complex, changing social values attached to human-made products and their relation to customer needs.

Planning for production

Production management manages the physical resources necessary to create products in sufficient quantities and quality to meet market requirements. In manufacturing, the majority of the workforce and a very high proportion of total capital investment expenditure are devoted to the production function. Efficient production management is critical to the success of such organisations. Although production management is more closely associated with manufacturing, its techniques are increasingly applied in non-manufacturing organisations. Indeed, the problems are very similar in both production and service sectors. Most techniques of manufacturing apply equally to service organisations such as banks, hospitals and public utilities.

Production is divided into two areas. First, there is the design of the production system, which involves deciding performance requirements and desired outputs of the production system. Decisions then need to be made about the number of production facilities required, their location, the methods of production to be used, and the management control procedures to be introduced. Second, there is the task of operating the production system to meet specified performance requirements. This includes production scheduling and control, inventory management and quality control (Slack 2009).

Production control

Production control is concerned with producing goods or services in the right sequence, in optimum time, with the lowest inventory costs. This is a 'balancing' act, involving compromises and what 'fits' and what is theoretically ideal (Russell and Taylor 2008). The main aspects of production control are: provisioning material, parts and production accessories, loading and scheduling work, and monitoring and progressing work. Management information also has to be produced, enabling the system to be controlled.

Every organisation has a different production system, depending on its products, services and operations facilities (Hill and Hill 2009). The main factors include:

- **Complexity of the product**: single operations are easier to control than multiple ones.

- **Length of cycle time**: longer jobs are simpler to re-plan than short ones.

- **Repeatability of work**: regular jobs have predictable cycle times; one-off jobs are not so easy to control.

- **Forward notice available**: jobs that are planned well in advance are easier to manage.

- **Dependence on outside suppliers and subcontractors**: where control is external to a company, more allowance must be made for slippage.

- **Seasonal nature of the workload**: where seasonal peak loads occur, capacity utilisation varies.

- **Availability and quality of information on capacity and workload**:

companies with detailed time standards, process layouts and up-to-date capacities can load to a fuller degree and schedule to tighter time-scales than those relying on estimates.

ACTIVITY 3.7

Review the operations management function in your organisation. Indicate how it might be improved.

STRATEGIC MANAGEMENT

Strategy is a vital part of managing in contemporary organisations and arises because organisations normally face uncertain market conditions. Throughout this text, strategy is considered in relation to the processes and contexts of organisational planning in uncertain times. As a result, those leading and taking strategic decisions normally seek more structured ways of meeting these challenges in a world dominated by skills and resources shortages and by market uncertainties or competition. There are traditionally two elements in strategic management: strategy formulation and strategy implementation. These are covered in greater depth in the next chapter.

The formulation of relevant 'strategic frameworks' by top business leaders is one response to these contextual challenges. However, developing strategic responses is not limited to top people in organisations; it takes place at all organisational levels – corporate, business unit and operational. Indeed, the phrase 'strategic choice' implies that there is no single way in which strategic direction, formulation, implementation and evaluation may be determined and that strategy operates at a multiplicity of levels. This means that the vocabulary of strategy is a linguistic minefield of competing models, paradigms and values, rooted strongly in Anglo-American private sector literature, whereas public sector strategic management literature is more limited (Joyce 1999, Johnson and Scholes 2001). For some observers, the search for an effective strategy is seen more as a pseudo-rational process in which individual, organisational and group attitudes and beliefs play just as important a part in the process as do chosen techniques, logical thinking and sound judgement.

Strategy implementation is crucial to effective strategic management. Most time and efforts of senior managers are directed towards strategy implementation and the planning and control systems which are the main means through which the strategic objectives and policies of an organisation are translated into specific, measurable, attainable goals and plans. However, the importance of people in implementation is not to be underrated, since issues such as motivating employees, communicating with them and facilitating the managing of change all need to be addressed if strategies are to be turned into practical results and actions. Large organisations may decide to use a pilot study or demonstration project as an initial implementation strategy. This becomes an opportunity for organisational learning. Projects are a synthesis of strategy formulation and implementation (Pearce 2009).

ACTIVITY 3.8

Examine the role of the HR function in strategy implementation.

MODERN MANAGERIAL FUNCTIONS

Modern managerial functions are the third 'M' in the six Ms framework – risk, quality, and performance management. These new demands on management have arisen largely out of pressures of competition and regulation in a global economy, externally, and complexity and accountability, internally.

RISK ANALYSIS

Organisations need a certain amount of risk since, in the private sector, it is the prerequisite of profit making. By managing risk effectively, managers can innovate, prevent problems and stick to achieving corporate plans and strategies. There are two methods of managing risk. One is to have systems in place to prevent a business getting out of control – a risk management system. The second is having 'fire-fighting' procedures when disaster strikes. Grouping potential threats and addressing them under the label of risk analysis or risk management gives a business a number of advantages. It encourages the firm to think about its threats, by making managers analyse risks that might otherwise be overlooked. Clarifying risk encourages the firm to be better prepared. In other words, it helps the firm be managed better. Letting the organisation prioritise its investment reduces internal disputes about how money should be spent.

It is useful to distinguish between strategic risk and operational risk (Vose 2008). Strategic risks involve important, high-level issues such as a company's position in the marketplace or threats to its survival as a business. Operational risks involves immediate, obvious threats to its performance and short-term goals. Although organisations need to give equal attention to both strategic and operational risks, strategic risks are clearly more serious and require planned, reasoned responses. Figure 3.5 illustrates some types of strategic risks, the areas they are likely to impact upon, and the sort of factors that provide solutions to them. Clearly, the bigger and more complex the business, the more important it is to have formal risk analysis and risk management processes in place.

Preventing risks

Attempts to prevent risks start by identifying and quantifying the risks relevant to an organisation. The organisation then needs to establish policies for dealing with

Figure 3.5 Some types of strategic risk, impacts and solutions

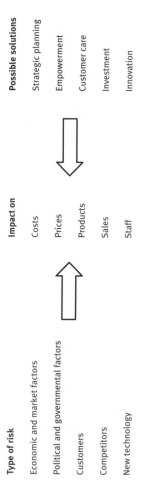

Type of risk	Impact on	Possible solutions
Economic and market factors	Costs	Strategic planning
Political and governmental factors	Prices	Empowerment
Customers	Products	Customer care
Competitors	Sales	Investment
New technology	Staff	Innovation

them, to implement the policies and manage the risks. These need monitoring and assessing regularly. Successful risk management depends heavily on good HRM practices and full involvement of senior management in the process. Some underlying principles of effective risk management include:

- **Encouraging staff to be risk conscious**: this may involve training them to be risk aware and providing training for them which is appropriate to their roles and levels of responsibility.

- **Rewarding success**: honest failure should not be penalised; otherwise staff try to cover up mistakes.

- **Developing a culture of openness**: assist staff to be self-critical and be critical of the business.

- **Encouraging staff to be 'thinkers'**: this means helping them to be forward looking and proactive in their attitudes and sense of planning.

The role of senior management in risk management and risk prevention is pivotal to the whole risk management process. Apart from staff who are risk analysts or risk managers, senior management are best placed to manage risk (Peltier 2009). This necessitates:

- **Thinking strategically**: the chief executive and senior management team are best placed to do this, because other managers are more likely to concentrate on their own functional areas of responsibilities rather than on risk management.

- **Setting policies and procedures**: senior management need to put top-level risk management plans in place. These can be trickled down to line managers and their staff.

- **Allocating roles and responsibilities**: this means typically writing 'risk' into people's job descriptions.

- **Introducing a risk management system**: this is necessary, since people cannot be relied upon to do tasks which are not measured. Without measurement, feedback and review, those leading an organisation are unable to judge how well it is performing.

Most large organisations adopt such principles. They keep records for key risk areas, such as health and safety and disaster avoidance, by carrying out financial or quality audits. A major problem is that senior management normally want a single, reliable 'forecast' upon which staffing, profit plans and shareholder reports can be built. These are, of course, commonly 'political' documents, designed to satisfy company boards, head office or top management that the business is well staffed, solvent and successful in the short and longer terms. Another weakness of forecasts is that they can be wrong and they make companies over-reliant on key assumptions. These two factors suggest that 'scenario planning' is a better solution. It ensures that the company plans for several 'different' futures and possibilities and is a 'what-if?' exercise.

How crises develop

Normally triggered by an outside event or management error, crises include new products by competitors, loss of a major customer contract, or a change in legislation reducing demand for a company's products or increasing costs. Examples of management errors include failures to respond to the sorts of external changes outlined above or faulty decisions, such as excessive investment or clear underinvestment. The organisation might not recognise the problem and many do not. Once senior management recognises the problem, it can remedy it. This leads to improvement and the company often emerges 'fitter' and more responsive than before. In any crisis, an organisation needs an emergency plan, covering all possible eventualities (Peltier 2009).

QUALITY MANAGEMENT AND CUSTOMER CARE

The case for quality management derives out of the demands of customers, in conditions of globalisation and international competition, for high-quality products and services in the marketplace. Continuous improvement, with a focus on customer service and an emphasis on flexibility and quality, is one means by which companies respond to competition. As a result, the quality of products, services and processes has increased considerably during the past two decades. Quality has a variety of interpretations. However, it is normally meant to distinguish one organisation and its products or services from another. Definitions generally refer to either meeting customer requirements and specifications or satisfying and delighting the customer. Figure 3.6 summarises the evolution of quality management systems.

Why quality is important

There are many reasons why quality matters. First, in today's business context the penalties for unsatisfactory product quality or poor service are likely to be punitive. With improvements made by companies in their modes of operation, legislation, deregulation, changes in market share, mergers, takeovers, and collaborative joint ventures, there is much less distinction between companies than in the past. Second, quality increases productivity. Cost, productivity and quality are complementary, not alternative objectives. Another factor is that businesses which know and understand customer priorities for quality improvements can achieve increases in profitability (Roberts 1996). Third, quality

Figure 3.6 The evolution of quality management systems

System	Components
Inspection	Salvage
	Sorting, grading, re-blending
	Corrective actions
	Identifying sources of non-conformity
Quality control	Development of a quality manual
	Process performance data
	Self-inspection
	Product testing
	Basic quality planning
	Use of basic statistics and paperwork controls
Quality assurance	Development of quality systems
	Advanced quality planning
	Use of quality costs
	Failure mode and effects analysis
	Statistical process control
Total quality management	Policy deployment
	Supplier and customer involvement
	All operations involved
	Process management
	Performance measurement
	Teamwork and employee involvement

means improved business performance, and the cost of non-quality is high. The cost of quality has been estimated to be in the range of 5 to 25 per cent of an organisation's annual sales turnover (Dale and Plunkett 1999). Fourth, in today's markets, customer requirements are becoming increasingly more rigorous, and expectations in terms of conformance, performance and environmental friendliness are increasing. Fifth, quality is a way of organisational life and of doing business. An organisation committed to quality requires quality of working life for its people in terms of participation, involvement, development, and the quality of its systems, processes and products.

From inspection to total quality management

As can be seen in Figure 3.6, quality management has evolved, starting with inspection and developing into total quality management (TQM). The starting point of early quality management was compliance to specification and 'allocating blame'. It progressed to involvement, caring for people, empowering people and continuous improvement (Dale *et al* 2007).

- **Inspection**: conformity evaluation by observation and judgement accompanied by measurement, testing or gauging.

- **Quality control**: focuses on fulfilling quality requirements.

- **Quality assurance**: focuses on providing confidence that quality requirements are being fulfilled.

- **TQM**: involves the application of quality management principles to all aspects of an organisation, including customers and suppliers and their integration with key business processes.

TQM is a high level of quality management. It requires that the principles of quality management are applied to every branch and level in an organisation, with an emphasis on integrating it with business practices and balancing technical, managerial and people issues. TQM is an organisation-wide approach to quality, with improvements undertaken on a continuous basis by everyone. It involves the mutual co-operation of everyone, with the aim of producing value-for-money products and services meeting and exceeding the needs and expectations of customers. TQM is both a philosophy and a set of guiding principles for managing an organisation to benefit all its stakeholders. The eight quality management principles defined in ISO 9001, the principal internationally recognised standard of quality management systems, are summarised below (Hoyle 2006), and the key elements in TQM identified by Lal (2008) in Figure 3.7.

- **Customer focus**: organisations depend on their customers and therefore need to understand current and future customer needs, meet customer requirements and exceed customer expectations.

- **Leadership**: leaders establish unity of purpose and direction of the organisation. They need to create and maintain the internal context of an organisation, where people are fully involved in achieving the organisation's objectives.

- **Involvement of people**: people at all levels are the essence of an organisation; their full involvement enables their abilities to be used for the organisation's benefit.

- **Process approach**: a desired result is achieved more efficiently when activities and resources are managed as a process.

- **System approach to management**: identifying, understanding and managing interrelated processes as a system contributes to organisational effectiveness and efficiency.

- **Continual improvement**: continual improvement of the organisation's overall performance should be a permanent objective.

- **Factual approach to decision-making**: effective decisions are based on analysis of data and information.

- **Mutually beneficial supplier relationship**: an organisation and its suppliers are interdependent and a mutually beneficial relationship enhances the ability of both to create value.

Figure 3.7 The key elements of TQM

Leadership of the chief executive	has to take charge and lead the process
Planning and organisation	requires developing the organisation and infrastructure to support improvement activities
Using tools and techniques	gets the process started, and employees using them feel involved
Education and training	needs a formal programme enabling people to cope with increasingly complex organisational problems
Involvement	requires all means of getting employees incorporated in the continuous improvement process; people have to feel empowered to manage and control processes within their sphere of responsibility
Teamwork	is a necessary condition of success, in its various forms
Measurement and feedback	need to be made against a series of key result indicators, developed from external and internal benchmarking, customer surveys and other inputs
Making sure the culture is conducive to continuous improvement	necessitates creating an organisational culture conducive to continuous improvement, in which everyone can participate

Adapted from Lal (2008).

ACTIVITY 3.9

How is quality management organised in your organisation? How effective is it in improving quality and satisfying customer needs?

PERFORMANCE MANAGEMENT

The idea of performance management is not new. However, there are a number of different perspectives on how performance is managed, because performance management is used for different purposes in different organisations. A number of factors have influenced the introduction of performance management since the 1980s. These include increasingly competitive market conditions, public management reforms, management theories of 'excellence' and 'quality', restructuring, technological developments helping to manage performance, and increasing individualisation of the employment relationship. There were also inadequacies in former performance appraisal systems. These included inability to reflect the dynamic nature of jobs and organisational contexts, failure to recognise excellent performance by staff, and failure to build skills through training. Employee grievances often emerged out of these systems, because of subjectivity and bias within them (Spangenberg 1994).

Systems for managing organisational performance

These comprise three main processes: planning, improving and reviewing. They can be applied at whatever level is chosen: organisation, business unit, department, team or individual levels. In this model, performance planning is concerned with activities such as the organisation's vision and strategy, and defining what is meant by performance. Performance improvement takes a 'process' perspective, including business process re-engineering, continuous process improvement, benchmarking and total quality management (Bredrup 1995). Performance review embraces performance measurement and evaluation. Performance management of this type is familiar within strategic and business planning, operations management and so on. The focus of this model is determining the organisation's strategy and implementing that strategy through the organisation's structure, technology, business systems and procedures. Employees are not the primary focus, although they are affected by changes in the business systems and related contexts.

Systems for managing employee performance

There are variants of this model, where performance management is represented as a cycle. It is common within these models that managers and subordinate employees should have a shared view of what is expected of them, with employee involvement and direct participation as the means for arriving at this shared view. Supporting performance is seen as the responsibility of the line manager, who has a particular part to play in performance review. This too is a shared activity between manager and managed, where responsibility rests with the job holder as much as with the manager. Further, review is seen as an ongoing activity rather than something happening once or twice a year. Figure 3.8 illustrates the planning, assessment and feedback aspects of this performance management model.

Figure 3.8 Performance management: the planning, assessment and feedback model

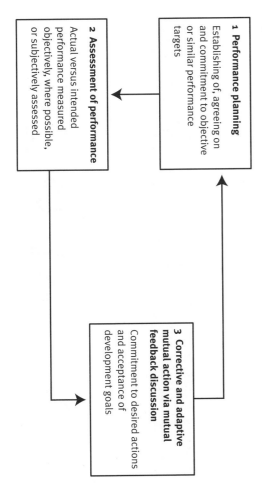

1 Performance planning

Establishing of, agreeing on and commitment to objective or similar performance targets

2 Assessment of performance

Actual versus intended performance measured objectively, where possible, or subjectively assessed

3 Corrective and adaptive mutual action via mutual feedback discussion

Commitment to desired actions and acceptance of development goals

Systems for managing organisational and employee performance

This model combines the two outlined above and is an integrative approach (Dale 2008). According to a number of studies in the field, an integrative approach to performance management incorporates five main elements. First, the organisation has a shared vision of its objectives communicated to all employees. Second, the organisation sets *individual* performance management targets related to *operating unit and organisational* objectives. Third, the organisation conducts regular reviews of progress towards these targets. Fourth, the organisation uses the review process to identify learning, development and reward outcomes. Fifth, the organisation evaluates the effectiveness of the process and its contribution to overall performance to allow improvements to be made.

A number of building blocks are necessary in developing, operating and evaluating such systems. First, there needs to be a process for enhancing communications within the organisation, so that employees are not only aware of the objectives and the business plan but are also able to contribute to their formulation. Second, individual responsibilities need to be defined and the means of measuring individual performance determined, emphasising measurement against one's own objectives, rather than being compared with those of others. Third, appropriate reward strategies need to be implemented and staff developed to further improve performance and their career progression.

Performance management models are not without critics. Winstanley and Stuart-Smith (1996) argue that existing approaches to performance management generally do not succeed in meeting their objectives. They claim such systems are often flawed in implementation, demotivate staff, are perceived as forms of control and are inappropriately used to 'police' performance. They present an alternative methodology for developing performance objectives and managing performance. Drawing upon case study evidence in the British School of Osteopathy, they present a model incorporating ethical concerns over performance management. Using a stakeholder approach, it seeks to engage the parties in a dialogue for designing performance measures and performance improvement. These writers seek to address four ethical principles within performance review: respect for the individual, mutual respect, procedural fairness and transparency of decision-making.

ACTIVITY 3.10

Critically evaluate the performance management system in your organisation. How effective is it in improving (a) organisational performance and (b) individual performance? What criteria are used to measure performance?

ACTIVITY 3.11

How is the management function integrated in your organisation and what mechanisms are used to do this?

MANAGERIAL POWER, AUTHORITY AND INFLUENCE

Managerial power, authority and influence, the fourth 'M', is a central, if not *the* central, aspect of organisational and managerial life. In organisations, power takes several forms but, in descriptive terms, it is the ability of an individual or group of people (normally management) to shape, frame or direct the actions of others, even if they resist this, towards the ends or directions determined by management. Mostly, power is perceived as 'authority', which loosely defined is the legitimate use of power by those having it. Thus power is legitimate when a person in a position does something according to the rules which define what that person can do. Authority attaches to the person in the position, not the person, and is derived from the position itself. Where the person acts in an unauthorised way, s/he may lose the authority she or he has. Influence, in turn, is the attempt to modify the behaviours of others through mobilising power in one's own interests. Thus power, authority and influence are closely linked and are critical to understanding organisational life and how people at all levels act and behave within organisations.

The significance of power, authority and influence is that they are the means by which management (or managers) manage and attempt to control organisations. Beyond this basic level of description, power is a complex concept to analyse. Daft (2008, p5, p490) in his rational, orthodox approach to management defines it as: 'the attainment of organizational goals in an effective and efficient manner through planning, organizing, leading and controlling organizational resources'. His definition of power is descriptive and relatively unsophisticated. For him, power is the 'potential ability to influence the behaviour of others'. He argues that power results from interactions between leaders and followers and that some power comes from an individual's position and some from his/her personal sources. These include an individual's personal interests, goals and values, as well as sources such as access to information or important relationships. He distinguishes, therefore, between 'position power' and 'personal power'. Position power comes from the organisation and takes three forms:

- **Legitimate power or authority**: this comes from a formal management position and the authority granted to it.

- **Reward power**: this stems from the authority to bestow rewards on other people. Managers have access to formal rewards such as pay rises, promotion and other benefits.

- **Coercive power**: this refers to the authority to punish or recommend punishment for actions perceived to be harmful to an organisation.

Personal power comes from 'internal' sources such as the individual's special knowledge or personal characteristics. Daft (2008, p491) identifies two types of personal power, which are the 'primary tool of the leader'. First, expert power results from a person's special knowledge or skill regarding the tasks being performed. Second, referent power comes from an individual's personal characteristics that command the identification, respect and admiration of others, so that they wish to emulate that individual. Referent power is most visible in charismatic leadership. For Daft (2008), influence is the effect a person's actions have on the attitudes, values, beliefs or behaviour of other people.

What is called the 'chain of command' in organisations is the mechanism linking all persons in it and shows who reports to whom. As outlined above, authority is vested in organisational positions. Although authority flows from the top of an organisation downwards, subordinates normally comply with authority because they believe managers have a legitimate right to give orders. The acceptance theory of authority argues that a manager only has authority if subordinates choose to accept his or her commands. If subordinates refuse to obey because the order is outside their zone of acceptance, a manager's authority is lost. Another reason why subordinates obey orders or instructions is the negative consequences of not doing so, such as disciplinary action or even, in some cases, dismissal. In other cases, subordinates may resist instructions, which may put pressure on the manager to modify what they have demanded or requested. So where there is authority in organisations, there is need for managers to legitimise that authority to ensure that the organisation operates within the recognised power and authority structure. But legitimacy, as observed below, can be contested.

At a deeper level, some writers, such as Mintzberg (1983), take the analysis of power further, by arguing that it is a dependency relationship. For them, resources create dependencies because they are unequally distributed. Power resources therefore consist of the means through which the behaviour of others may be influenced and modified. One typology of power resources is provided by French and Raven (1959), for whom power is something exercised and is indistinguishable from influence. They describe the different bases of social power, which are similar to those discussed by Daft (2008) above. In each case, individuals conform to these power resources because of the positive consequences of doing so or the negative consequences of not doing so. These are:

- **Coercive power:** being forced to conform.
- **Reward power:** conforming to obtain benefits.
- **Referent power:** conforming to identify with others.
- **Expert power:** conforming because others have superior knowledge or skill.
- **Legitimate power:** conforming because of the power of others over them.
- **Informational power:** conforming to get desired information.

Hales (2001) goes on to distinguish between four basic kinds of power resources. These are: physical power resources (the capacity to harm others), economic power resources (command over scarce resources), knowledge power resources (having scarce or desired knowledge) and normative power resources (holding desired beliefs and values). In the context of work, Hales subdivides knowledge power resources, in turn, into administrative resources, concerned with how an organisation operates, and technical power resources, concerned with how tasks are performed. Each power resource may be held by individuals as either *personal* possessions, where they are owned by an individual, or *positional*, where they are accessed by holding a particular organisational post.

For each type of power resource, there are corresponding modes of influence, with those in power (and/or authority) positions attempting to modify other people's behaviour by reference to the power resources they control. However, deploying power to influence other people's behaviour is rarely obvious; it is complex and managers use a variety of strategies to do this. Economic resources, for example, may be used by management to influence employee behaviour in a number of ways:

- by providing rewards, such as a pay bonus or pay increase
- by withholding rewards, such as blocking promotion
- by promising rewards, such as a future pay increase
- by threatening withdrawal of rewards, such as a warning of dismissal
- by implying possible rewards, such as through an 'understanding' of pay progression
- by implying possible withholding of rewards, such as an 'understanding' that poor performance will result in dismissal.

There are, therefore, a rich variety of possibilities and ways for seeking to influence other people's behaviour. There are also a range of parties to be influenced: managers to senior managers; managers to peers; managers to subordinate managers; managers to employees; managers to parties outside the organisation; employees to managers; and employees to employees. In influencing others, there are subtle, unobtrusive ways of doing this. In many instances where behaviour is being influenced, there is no visible evidence of power being exercised, only a vague sense of obligation. Indeed, Foucault (1991) distinguishes between 'sovereign power' (the arbitrary, visible exercise of power) and 'disciplinary power' (rational, insidious, invisible power) that people exercise over themselves and which influences their own behaviour. Thus a sense of obligation to behave in certain ways, such as complying with a 'long hours' or a 'presenteeism' culture, is absorbed by individuals where they work. In general, forms of influence deployed by managers may be limited because, first, influence has to correspond to the power resources available. Second, influence is appropriate if it utilises a power resource consistent with its nature, whether based on exchange (or reciprocity), persuasion, reason, feelings or values. Third, modes of influencing must be appropriate to intended outcomes.

ACTIVITY 3.13

Think of examples where your manager has used different forms of influence to impact on your behaviour. What forms of influence were used and what were the outcomes?

THE SEARCH FOR MANAGERIAL LEGITIMACY

Given the complex nature of power, authority and influence in organisations, a major task for management is gaining (or winning) a sense of legitimacy from those working in them, so that managerial power is not questioned. Questioned power is illegitimate and can result in managers having to enforce power, which can produce unintended consequences for management and organisations. Questioned power is also time-consuming, since management wants to get things done efficiently and effectively, without wasting time having its authority challenged and needing to respond to such challenges. The implication is that modern managements prefer to manage by consent, rather than through applying naked power.

The old-fashioned, traditional response of management to achieve legitimacy was by claiming the 'right to manage'. In today's business context, more sophisticated sources of managerial legitimacy are claimed. These include technical expertise, the importance of the role of trained professional managers, the necessity of a specialist division of labour within organisations, with management leading, formulating policy and organising resources, and managerial ideology. The knowledge and skills of professional managers and contemporary belief systems, in other words, supersede proprietary ownership and traditional business values as management's prime sources of legitimacy. The search for a means of managing by consent underpins this philosophy.

Building on the discussion in the previous section, the possible relationships between power resources, modes of influence, legitimacy and likely employee responses are illustrated in Figure 3.9. This indicates that if management seeks to manage by consent, rather than by coercion, then the least legitimacy is generated by physical power and the greatest by normative power. Although access to and control of economic resources are the typical basis of managerial power, they are only partially legitimised by employees. Managers also possess both administrative and technical knowledge power, acquired through education, training and experience and through personal technical knowledge. However, these too are only partially legitimate. Indeed, the research evidence suggests that normative and knowledge power are more likely to be regarded as legitimate than are physical and economic power. Further, managers themselves prefer using knowledge and normative power as bases of legitimacy (Kipnis et al 1984).

Figure 3.9 Power resources: modes of influence, legitimacy and likely employee responses

Power resources	Personal forms of power	Positional forms of power	Modes of influence	Legitimacy	Likely employee responses
Physical	Individual strength Possession of means for violence	Access to means of violence	Force	Not legitimate	Alienative compliance or withdrawal
Economic	Individual wealth and income	Access to and disposal of organisational resources	Reward	Partially legitimate	Economic calculation or instrumental compliance
Administrative knowledge	Individual experience	Access to and control over organisational information	Accepted rules or procedures	Partially legitimate	Instrumental compliance
Technical knowledge	Individual skill and expertise	Access to and control over technical information and technology	Accepted methods	Partially legitimate	Rational calculation or cognitive commitment
Normative	Individual beliefs, values, ideas and personal qualities	Access to and control over organisational values, ideas	Moral persuasion	Legitimate	Moral commitment

Adapted from Hales (2001).

The central managerial problem, then, appears to be not overcoming resistance and alienation by employees but finding ways of achieving positive employee commitment to certain kinds of managerial actions. The power resources typically available to managers for doing this are, first, positional economic power in the forms of access and control over organisational resources. Second, there is personal knowledge power in the forms of information and expertise acquired through training and experience. Third, there is positional knowledge in terms of access to organisational information, expertise and technology. It can be concluded, therefore, that management's ability to manage 'inheres predominantly in their capacity to reward, promote, dismiss, instruct, regulate or suggest' (Hales 2001, p32).

Historically, in seeking authority and legitimacy, managers did this, first, by looking for alternative sources of power likely to be perceived as legitimate. Second, they sought to depersonalise power and influence, thus downplaying their own personal power. A major role in the depersonalisation process was moral justifications for why work is organised as it is and management's role in this. These are known as ideologies of management, where work is portrayed as not being subject to the personal whims of managers but to broader societal, or more recently global, imperatives. Economic power is exercised through reward systems and is depersonalised by reference to the imperatives of the market and demands of consumers. It is economic efficiency and organisational effectiveness that justify the ways work is organised and people managed. Knowledge power is exercised through systems of rules and is depersonalised by reference to the imperatives of science and technology. Here technical efficiency justifies how work is managed, with the manager acting as the 'technician-scientist'.

Normative power is exercised through organisational rationales and is depersonalised by reference to the moral values of organisational goals and organisational missions, which transcend the interests of individuals. Here the manager has a quasi-evangelical role. Both the management consultancy industry and popular management literature have been instrumental in promoting these ideologies. However, unintended responses to institutional power and influence mean that new forms of managerial power, influence and legitimacy meet with only partial success.

According to Hales (2001, p36f), one solution to the problem of legitimacy 'may lie in a recognition that a different kind of power, power in the sense of "transformative capacity" or "power to", resides in the interdependence which is characteristic of work organization'. He argues that the future of managerial legitimacy may come from creating greater workplace consensus. This means power sharing: economic power through various forms of stakeholding, knowledge power by participative forms of decision-making and normative power through a wider culture of co-operation (Fox 1985). For him and some other writers, the focus for the search for managerial legitimacy has shifted 'from management as an interpersonal process to management as an organisational process.'

ACTIVITY 3.14

Describe, analyse and review how management in your organisation attempts to obtain legitimacy at (a) senior level, (b) middle level and (c) first-line level. If different sources of legitimacy are used at each level, what are these and why is this so?

MANAGERIAL POLITICS AND THE CHANGE AGENDA

The pervasiveness of power is the central aspect of organisational life. And managerial politics and the change agenda are the fifth 'M' within the managerial and business context. Control of the levers of power that authority confers gives those with power the means to determine policies and practices within organisations. This is most fundamentally expressed in terms of whom the organisation chooses to employ and whom it chooses not to employ. Organisational politics is the process of mobilising power within organisations, where authoritative power rests ultimately with management who are agents of the owners. Pettigrew (2002, p45) sees the mobilisation of power as what happens when either individuals or groups make a claim against an organisation's resource-sharing system. Pettigrew suggests power is central to the strategy process in organisations, because decisions about what strategy to determine is always political. Such decisions are 'likely to threaten the existing distribution of organisational resources as represented in salaries, in promoting opportunities and in control of tasks, people, information and new areas of business'. These organisational politics are generated by the following:

- **Structural cleavages:** these involve different components, elements and identities in the organisation, and the different values associated with each of them.

- **Complexity and degree of uncertainty:** these vary at different times and occasions.

- **Salience of the issues:** these are the differential impacts for different actors and identities of possible changes and decisions in the organisation.

- **External pressures from stakeholders:** these vary by group and their degrees of influence at the time decisions are made.

- **History of past politics:** this influences perceptions and the possibilities for change and the direction of decision-making.

Power and organisational politics, then, are central to much of what happens in organisations. The parties involved seek to legitimise the proposals, ideas, values and demands they espouse, whilst denying those they seek to oppose. Clegg et al (2008) claim that power ultimately is deployed in games of organisational symbolism, wrapped up in myths, beliefs, language and legend – the stuff of organisational culture. Whenever discussion switches to organisational culture, they claim, organisational politics are not far behind.

Mintzberg (2002) sees organisations as political arenas, where the system of politics comes into play whenever systems of authority, ideology or expertise are contested. This is done by political game-playing including:

- **Insurgency games**: played by lower-status participants against dominant elites.
- **Counter-insurgency games**: played by dominant elites against lower-status participants.
- **Sponsorship games**: played by patrons and clients.
- **Alliance-building games**: played by peers seeking reciprocal support.
- **Empire-building games**: where a political actor or subsystem seeks to capture others and enrol them to their interests.
- **Budgeting games**: with the objective of securing resources.
- **Expertise games**: games of strategic contingency.
- **Lording games**: where relatively powerless players seek to 'lord it', through using their power over those with lower status.
- **Line versus staff games**: where each side uses legitimate power in illegitimate ways in games of rivalry.
- **Rival-camp games**: where alliance or empire-building games develop into rival blocks facing each other in zero-sum games.
- **Strategic candidate games**: where those in power seek to ensure the succession of preferred candidates as vacancies arise.
- **Whistle-blowing games**: where lower status participants seek to expose unlawful or unethical acts outside the organisation to influence policy changes.
- **Young Turk games**: where a coup unseats present incumbents to institute regime change, whilst preserving organisational authority.

It follows that politics are normal within organisations and that they serve several orderly functions, such as providing sources of innovation or instruments of change. As a result, managers, like any other actors in micro-political systems, play political games that are neither aberrant nor deviant. Mintzberg (1984) specifies some types of political games that are not mutually exclusive and may overlap and link together. They typically find expression in four major forms in the political arena.

- **Confrontation**: characterised by intense, confined, unstable conflict, such as in a takeover or merger.
- **Shaky alliances**: characterised by conflict that is moderate, confined and relatively stable, such as in organisations subject to public accountability.
- **Politicised organisations**: characterised by conflict that is moderate, pervasive, and relatively stable, such in as large public sector bodies.
- **Complex political arenas**: characterised by intense, pervasive and brief unstable conflict, driven by major fault lines of factual and doctrinal division, both internally and in terms of external alliances and relationships.

Power in organisations rarely flows effortlessly as 'pure' authority and, because legitimacy is often contested, power is typically not friction-free. Where there is friction, there is resistance; resistance to change, for example, is a normal reaction by those affected. A central tension in organisations is between resistance and obedience. Analysis of power in organisations needs to focus on the subtle mechanisms through which obedience is produced. This is often done by 'soft domination', characterised by the administration of rules giving discretion to managers whilst reinforcing the strength of centralised authorities. Authorities create legitimised rules, reinforced by threats to career, rewards, status, employment and so on. What sustains senior management and limits organisational members from effective resistance is political concentration of the levers of control over the deployment of people in the hands of a minority, combined with constraints, incentives and clear rules. As Clegg *et al* (2008) put it, soft domination is based on the appearance of equality in the organisation among peers and the reality of a pervasive system of controls. Chief amongst these are 'instrumentally legitimate techniques used by the entire management community, such as human resource management, audit, and holding managers accountable to plans'. These forms of accountability often form the basis of the 'games' people play at work (Burawoy 1979).

To conclude, because power is a normal feature of organisations, managers must learn how to manage with it on a daily basis in positive ways. To be an effective manager means knowing how and when to use power wisely. Pfeffer (1992) suggests that there are seven steps to the effective use of power by every manager:

- **Goals**: what are your goals and what are you trying to achieve in consultation with the stakeholders in your organisation?

- **Individuals**: which individuals both inside and outside the organisation are influential to achieving these goals?

- **Points of view**: what are the points of view of the important people likely to be?

- **Others' power bases**: what are the power bases of the important people and which one is the most influential in the decision?

- **Your power bases**: what are your bases of power and influence?

- **Strategies and tactics**: which strategies and tactics for exercising power are the most appropriate?

- **Action**: choose an ethical course of action to get something done.

ACTIVITY 3.15

Reflect on any situation in your organisation where the chief executive has used power to initiate and set out a change management programme. How was power used to do this and what were (a) some of the *intended* consequences and (b) some of the *unintended* consequences? Was there any resistance to this change programme and was it successful or not?

MODELS OF THE HR FUNCTION AND RELATIONSHIPS WITH EMPLOYEES

As observed in Chapter 1, the managing people function in the UK has generally shifted from one focused on traditional personnel management to one driven by a business agenda generically called 'HRM'. The final and sixth 'M' to be considered is models of the HR function and relationships with employees. If organisations are imperatively co-ordinated institutions established for specific purposes, and management is the agency for directing, leading and controlling them, then incorporating and motivating the people employed in them to achieve these purposes is an essential managerial goal. Indeed, some observers would argue that this is the key task, since people as resources are not inanimate beings but have free wills and some choices in the way they behave in organisations, including the choice of quitting them.

In practice, what HR departments do, how they are structured, their role in strategy determination, their size, their relationships with senior management, line managers and employees, and their standing in organisations vary widely. These issues are contingent upon the organisation and its external and internal contexts. This is brought out forcibly in Crail's (2006) study of the HR function in 179 UK organisations. It concludes that a 'standard' HR department might typically have the following characteristics:

- It would have a team of 12 people serving a workforce of around 1,200.

- This team would consist of an HR director, three HR managers, one HR supervisor, three HR officers and four HR assistants.

- The department would spend a lot of its time on HR administration, despite some activity as a 'business partner' and strategic contributor.

- Attempts would have been made to shift some HR responsibilities to line managers, not always successfully.

- The department would enjoy some influence over the way the organisation was run and HRs standing in the organisation would be generally high, partly because the external contexts have changed and HR is seen as the source of knowledge and expertise on legal and regulatory requirements.

Given the diversity and range of activities in HR departments, it follows that 'models' or analyses of the roles of the HR function vary too. The basic characteristics of modern HRM include its business focus, its contribution to added value for an organisation, a unitary perspective of the employment relationship, and an underpinning belief that people make a difference to organisational performance. But there is no universal model of HRM or any consensus about its wider features. Many models co-exist and practices differ amongst organisations. As Boxall et al (2007) point out, HRM covers an array of activities and it shows a huge range of variations across occupations, organisations, levels, business units, firms, industries and societies. Above all, approaches to HR strategy determination, HRM modelling and what constitutes 'good' HRM practices are diverse and wide ranging. For the purposes of analysis, some of the main models identified in studies of HRM are summarised in Figure 3.10.

Figure 3.10 Some models of the HRM function

Writers	Classificatory roles of HR	Descriptors
Legge (1978)	Conformist innovator	• HR goes along with an organisation's ends, adjusts means to achieve them
	Deviant innovator	• HR attempts to change the means/ end and relationship by gaining acceptance of different set of criteria
Tyson and Fell (1986)	Problem solver	• HR acts as HR problem-solver
	Clerk of works	• HR policies reactive, all authority vested in line managers, HR activities largely routine
	Contracts manager	• HR policies well established, heavy emphasis on industrial relations, HR has interpretive role
	Architect	• HR policies explicit, HR power derived from contribution to the business and its professionalism
Monks (1992)	Traditional/administrative	• HR has a mainly supportive role, with focus on administration
	Traditional/industrial relations	• HR concentrates on industrial relations
	Innovative/professional	• HR aims to reform traditional practices and take more proactive approach to HRM
	Innovative/sophisticated	• HR is on the board, attempts to integrate HR and business strategies, deliver sophisticated HR services
Storey (1992)	Change makers	• HR interventionist and strategic, close to classic HRM role
	Advisers	• HR non-interventionist and strategic, acts as internal consultants
	Regulators	• HR interventionist and tactical, formulates and monitors employment rules
	Handmaidens	• HR non-interventionist and tactical, simply provides services to line managers
Wilkinson and Marchington (1994)	Service provider	• HR responds to routine problems of line managers
	Internal contractor	• HR is operational but with a high profile
Proctor and Currie (1999)	Adviser	• HR works to help shape HR policies and practices
	Change agent	• HR seeks to establish new HR cultures and initiatives

Reilly (2000)	Strategist/integrator	• HR makes long term strategic contribution to the organisation • HR has both short term and long term contributions
	Adviser/consultant	
	Administrator/controller	• HR makes a short term tactical contribution
Ulrich and Brockbank (2005)	Employee advocate	• HR focuses on immediate needs of employees
	Human capital developer	• HR focuses on preparing employees to be successful in the future
	Functional expert	• HR is concerned with HR practices central to HR value
	Strategic partner	• HR has multiple roles including business expert, change agent, strategic HR planner, knowledge manager, and consultant, with a view to aligning HR systems to achieve organisational vision and mission
	Leader	• HR leads the HR function, collaborating with other management functions

Adapted from Legge (1978), Tyson and Fell (1986), Monks (1992), Wilkinson and Marchington (1994), Proctor and Currie (1999), Reilly (2000), Ulrich and Brockbank (2005).

A number of common themes appear to emerge out of this analysis. First, the HR role in the UK has evolved over time, in response to the changing internal and external contexts impacting on it, and this evolution continues. Second, at the organisational level, the HR role is both eclectic and pragmatic and is structured and operates in line with the organisational contingencies facing it. Third, HR operates at both strategic and operational levels, with varying degrees of planning, advice, support and expertise being provided to line managers by HR specialists, although in small organisations HR is likely to be operational only. The scope and distribution of HR activities depends, in each organisation, largely on its business strategy, market and competitive position, managerial awareness, type of workforce employed, sector and size.

SHAPING THE HR AGENDA

To survive, organisations require resources, including people or human resources. Typically, in acquiring resources, organisations have to interact with their contexts, other organisations and the institutions controlling or influencing such resources. The organisations or stakeholders controlling these resources, in turn, have power over those demanding them. Organisations, then, are resource-dependent bodies and only survive by coping with these contextual uncertainties and negotiating exchanges to obtain the resources they need. This is the focus of much organisational activity and involves all management functions: strategic, finance, marketing, operations, risk, quality, performance and HR (Pfeffer and Salancik 1978). In their search for productive, skilled human resources, organisations have to respond to a number of external factors or contexts shaping the HR agenda. Knowledge and understanding of these enables organisations to respond appropriately to them.

Labour markets

There is no single labour market in the UK but thousands of small, specific labour markets delineated by geography, skill, occupation and organisation. Like all markets, labour markets are concerned with the interplay of demand and supply. Employers determine the nature and level of demand; labour supply is determined by geographic factors, educational attainment and the attributes and skills of individual workers. Labour markets are dynamic, with supply and demand never in equilibrium. Where labour supply exceeds demand, pay is likely to fall and unemployment rise, with employers finding it relatively easier to recruit new starters. Where labour demand exceeds supply, pay is likely to rise and employers experience skills shortages. Both situations generate responses from government, in the forms of short-term and long-term policy initiatives.

Employers have to respond to different labour market conditions. On the one hand, in tight labour markets where there are labour and skills shortages, employers have to compete to secure the services of the people they need. This necessitates offering attractive employment packages and good working conditions. Some labour markets, however, are always tight, whatever the prevailing macro-economic climate, because of specific skills shortages. In slack or loose labour markets, on the other hand, when people are in plentiful supply, employers are likely to find recruitment easier but are more likely to have to lay off workers as orders for their products or services decline or, in the public sector, spending is cut.

Flexibility

Flexibility at work is both demand-driven and supply-driven. Where employers want flexible work organisations, it is to enable them to respond to their market positions speedily and efficiently, and affects the ways in which they employ people, whether numerically, functionally, temporally or financially. Flexibility also improves organisational performance. Workers, in turn, want flexibility to enable them to achieve work–life balance, the benefits of family-friendly policies, and opportunities for flexible rewards and benefits. Matching these requires good will and mutuality on both sides. Further, flexible working has been promoted by successive governments since the 1990s, underpinned by the assertion that flexibility promotes growth, productivity and competitiveness in a globalised economy. Unsurprisingly, there is much debate about the desirability of flexible working and its use in practice (Davies and Freedland 2007).

Employment legislation

Since the 1970s, as shown in more detail in Chapter 10, employers have had to take account of a large number of statute laws, emanating from the UK

Parliament and the EU, in taking employment decisions. Kahn-Freund (1983) classifies these as auxiliary, restrictive and regulatory legislation. Auxiliary legislation provides a statutory framework for 'organised persuasion' in relation to employment rule-making. Restrictive legislation sets down legal rules relating to what is allowed and not allowed in the employment arena. Regulatory legislation, by far the largest area today, provides a floor of employment rights for individual employees. It covers individual job protection rights, equal pay, equality and discrimination issues, health and safety at work, working time and flexible working. Successive surveys of employers demonstrate that employers view the law as a major trigger for change (McCann 2008).

Public policy

All governments seek to influence, by legislation and other means, what they perceive to be good employment relations and employment practices at work. These include: relations between employers, employees and trade unions; individual relations between employers and employees; health and safety at work; fair terms and conditions employment; and other areas. The latter include labour market policy, the learning and development agenda, helping UK businesses increase productivity and making them successful exporters.

RELATIONSHIPS WITH EMPLOYEES

To get good performance out of employees, employers need to gain their commitment to their work and the organisation employing them. Two main approaches are recognised as means of achieving these goals, although the two are not necessarily incompatible or exclusive. One, the traditional approach, is rooted in collectivism and a pluralist frame of reference; the other, the HRM approach, is rooted in individualism and a unitary frame of reference. A third approach, which is less common than the other two, is rooted in partnership and mutuality between employer and union. These three approaches are summarised in Figure 3.11.

ACTIVITY 3.16

What of the three above approaches to managing employee relations has your employer adopted? Is it effective in managing employee relations and why?

THE HR EQUATION AND THE PSYCHOLOGICAL CONTRACT

As noted at several points throughout this text so far, much HR research seeks to demonstrate the links between effective people management practices and improved business performance, although the literature only partially demonstrates this link. As one study argues: 'They reveal wide variations in the extent to which HR practices are applied and rather low levels of HR

Figure 3.11 Managing employee relations: the traditional, HRM and partnership approaches

	The traditional approach	The HRM approach	The partnership approach
Frame of reference	• underpinned by a pluralist perspective of organisation, with a number of parties having interests in it • strong emphasis on the joint regulation of work • competing interests of management and employees recognised	• underpinned by a unitary perspective of organisation, with one system of managerial authority, one focus of loyalty • strong emphasis on management's right to manage • common interests of management and employees emphasised	• underpinned by partnership perspective of organisation, based on trust and mutual respect between management and union • strong emphasis on mutuality between management and workers • recognition of plurality of interests in the workplace
Methods of management	• management manage by consent • agreement between management and trade unions achieved by negotiation • based on collective agreements between employers and trade unions • based on collective methods of managing people	• managers manage unilaterally • managers lead, employees follow and generally no unions involved in the employment relationship • based on individual contracts of employment between employer and employee • based on individual methods of managing people	• managers manage by agreement • managerial and employee problem-solving and joint problem-solving through consensus • based on secure employment contracts, with built-in flexibility and training • based on consensual methods of managing people
Objectives	• to manage power in organisations by sharing it between management and unions	• to obtain individual employee commitment to organisational goals and business plans	• to facilitate management and unions working together and joint problem-solving and communication
Methods of communication	• joint consultation and representative methods of communicating	• employee involvement techniques, such as information and communication	• employee voice and employee involvement techniques and good communication
Working arrangements	• joint consultation and representative methods of communicating	• teamwork • increased flexible working • harmonisation of terms and conditions	• teamwork • flexible working • single status

effectiveness' (Guest et al 2000, p39). However, academic and professional interest in the 'HR equation', or between effective people management and high performing organisations, continues. This links with Pfeffer's (1998) analysis, based on the importance of the 'human equation' in firms, which argues that profits are built by putting people first in organisations. A key concept in this debate is the 'psychological contract'. Originating in the 1960s, the term has been adopted as a broad explanatory framework for understanding employee–organisation linkages (Rousseau 1995). It is a term now widely used when considering the employment relationship because, first, there has been a significant shift in the focus of the employment relationship from the collective to individual level, together with HRM as a means for managing employment relations. Second, there have been subsequent changes in the nature of the employment relationship, arising out of global, organisational and economic change.

There is no definitive explanation of the psychological contract. However, basically it refers to the sets of beliefs that individuals hold regarding promises made and accepted between themselves for their common interests (Rousseau and Wade-Benzoni 1994). In employment relations, the psychological contract is concerned with an individual employee's subjective beliefs, shaped by an organisation, in relation to its role as an employer. It is also concerned with the organisation's subjective beliefs in relation to the individual. Since psychological contracts represent differences in the ways people interpret promises and commitments, both parties in the same employment relationship can have different views regarding specific terms of this relationship. However, a major feature of the psychological contract is the concept of mutuality. This involves the common and agreed 'understandings' of promises and obligations made between the respective parties to each other, regarding work, pay, loyalty, trust, fairness, commitment, flexibility, security and career advancement.

Guest and Conway (2002) analyse the psychological contract in terms of inputs, content and outcomes. The extent to which individual employees and the employer consider their expectations are 'matched' determines whether the 'contract' is seen to be positive or negative by each party.

- **Inputs:** these are the background factors, relating to the individual (such as age, gender, education, type of work, marital status) and the organisation (such as size, location, sector), and the organisation's HR policy influences (such as HR practices and the promises made by the employer to employees).

- **Contents of the contract:** these include fairness, trust and 'delivery of the deal'.

- **The outcomes of the contract:** these are attitudinal consequences (such as commitment, satisfaction, motivation, job security) and behavioural consequences (such as intention to stay or quit).

It is generally recognised that there are two forms of psychological contract. One is 'relational'; the other is 'transactional', as shown in Figure 3.12. The first refers to long-term relationships based on trust and mutual respect between the parties. On the one hand, the employer supposedly offers security of employment, promotion prospects, training and development, and some flexibility about the demands to be made on employees. On the other hand, employees offer loyalty, conformity to requirements, commitment to the employer's goals, and trust in their employer not to abuse their goodwill.

The transactional contract, in contrast, is more short term, concerned with economic factors, and well defined. Some observers argue that old relational contracts have been violated and superseded by new, transactional ones. These are imposed by employers rather than negotiated and are based on short-term economic exchanges between the parties. The 'deal' is that the employer offers '(to some) high pay, rewards for high performance and simply a job' (Arnold *et al* 1998, p338). This is in return for the employee offering longer hours, broader skills and willingness to accept change.

Figure 3.12 Stereotypical relational and transactional psychological contracts for employers and employees

Relational		Transactional	
• concerned with people		• concerned with economic factors	
• long term		• short term	
• broad and pervasive		• narrow	
• very subjective		• well defined	
Employer offers	**Employee offers**	**Employer offers**	**Employee offers**
• job security	• loyalty	• pay	• long hours
• career prospects	• conformity	• pay for performance	• flexibility
• training and development	• commitment to goals	• having a job	• willingness to change

ACTIVITY 3.17

Write down what your employer expects from you in the employment relationship and what you expect from your employer. To what extent are these expectations matched?

ACTIVITY 3.18

Is the psychological contract between you and your employer a relational or transactional one and why?

CONCLUSION: MANAGEMENT, HR STRATEGY AND HR SOLUTIONS

Management is a key power resource in organisations. Those with managerial power and authority use their resources as part of a collective group to determine, implement and review organisational strategies and deliver them through appropriate business and HR practices. They also use power and authority at individual level to protect (and advance) their managerial positions and further their professional careers. As organisational stakeholders, therefore, managers are by definition key players in organisational politics. Within management structures, the finance function normally drives organisations, so finance is a major player in organisational politics. Managers at every level are often measured in terms of their financial contribution to organisational success, so they, including the HR function, need to demonstrate how their areas of responsibility keep within budget, operate efficiently and add value to the enterprise.

There are three consequences if HR specialists want to be strategic players in organisational politics. First, HR has to understand the internal political structures of organisations and how they influence the determination and effective implementation of policy and strategy. In doing this HR specialists need to build alliances with key managerial players in the organisation and demonstrate the added value of the HR contribution to organisational efficiency and performance. Second, of the three HR roles identified by Legge (1978), that of the conformist innovator is the one most likely to gain the support of senior and line managers in the cut-and-thrust of contemporary organisational life, driven as it is by economic imperatives and demands of the market. This requires HR specialists to accept the 'ends' of the organisations in which they work but to adjust their 'means' to achieve them.

Third, in adding value to organisational processes and outcomes, HR is increasingly using metrics to demonstrate its utility to the business. Such data typically emanate from a variety of organisational sources, including financial performance, customer service, HR performance and, in the market sector, sales and marketing data. The datasets, deriving from these, that are most common include business performance data, customer data and employee data. These types of metrics draw upon customer surveys, customer satisfaction indices, HR data and staff opinion surveys. Comparisons, correlations and inferences are drawn from such datasets, which are updated and reviewed regularly.

Drawing upon Ulrich (1997), the role of HR as business partner provides an important role for HR specialists to develop. This means working with senior and line managers in strategy determination and implementation and trying to promote vertical integration of HR and corporate strategies. In undertaking this role, HR has to identify the underlying ways the organisation does its 'business'. This involves understanding the organisational architecture, undertaking regular audits to identify needs for change in the light of adaptations in the external context, and building capability within the organisation. It also means playing a significant part in creating systems and processes that deliver organisational performance. For Ulrich (1997), HR's role as change agent is also important for organisations undergoing innovation and change and the challenges related to these. This implies building the capacity of an organisation to embrace and capitalise on the change management process. It also means shaping processes which help the organisation identify key success factors and assess their strengths and weaknesses. Ulrich argues that the HR function needs to help organisations benefit from change by transforming 'visions' into realities.

New ideas continually permeate organisational thinking. Miller and McCartney (2010), for example, indicate that successful organisations sustain their performance over time, not just in the short term or through periods of economic growth. The CIPD believes that sustainability in terms of an organisation's people, financial, environmental and societal contribution over time is critical in this, with HR having a vital role in facilitating it. It identifies three key enablers for gaining sustainable organisation performance: leadership, engagement and organisational development. It also identifies three emergent enablers: culture, communication, and assessment and evaluation.

KEY LEARNING POINTS

1. Management has a variety of meanings. Basically it is a power resource in organisations, comprising a hierarchy of those people, managers, who have responsibility, both collectively and individually, for enabling organisations to achieve their objectives and making them work. Managerial work is often organised by function and is fragmented, commonly fire-fighting in nature, and involves attending meetings and working with people. The higher managers rise in an organisation, the more concerned they are with integrating, co-ordinating and controlling the work of other managers.

2. Whether management is a profession, like other liberal professions, is doubtful. First, despite the growth of management education in the past 30 years, there is little evidence of there being an agreed body of substantive knowledge in the field of management which all managers need to know to be effective. Second, the study, theory and practice of management are not researched and examined by a single professional body claiming to advance standards of managerial performance and managerial practices in organisations, although there are specialist bodies in some areas such as HR and marketing. Third, any semblance of patronage control by managers within organisations seems to have been weakened by the changing balance of power in senior management teams, following the rise of the 'cult' of the chief executive. This has undermined the traditional culture of collegiate management.

3. Management in the UK is normally organised by function. A classic division of this functional work is finance, marketing, operations, strategy and HRM. More recent specialisms include risk management, quality management and customer care, and performance management. It is the central function of senior management to integrate and co-ordinate the various activities and managerial functions, in order to create internal coherence and added value. As managers move up managerial hierarchies, they tend to take on more generalist roles, rather than specialist ones.

4. Effective financial management plays a central role in the private, public and third sectors. This is partly because financial inputs, processes and

outputs, whether in the forms of profits or added value, are relatively easy to measure and quantify. Also in the UK, there are strong emphases on creating 'shareholder value' in the private sector and 'value for money' in the public and third sectors. Marketing, in turn, has become increasingly important in all sectors, resulting from the competition, choice and change agendas driving organisations. Operations management is increasingly linked with quality management, with effective strategy formation and implementation being critical for ensuring that organisations can adapt to rapid, externally generated challenges facing them.

5. Risk management, quality and customer care, and performance management are also key functions of contemporary management practice. With hyper-competition in many markets, more government or state regulation of the three sectors, and rising expectations from private customers and public clients, organisations have to incorporate these regulatory managerial functions in their internal systems. The main consequences of these developments are the increasingly short time spans for taking some organisational decisions, the problems involved in managing large, complex, sometimes multinational businesses, and making sense of changing organisational contexts.

6. Power, authority and influence in organisations are central to understanding the nature of management and how organisations are managed. They are the means through which management (or managers) manage and attempt to control organisations and their resources. A useful way of analysing organisational power is to consider it as a resource. Typical power resources in organisations are physical, economic, administrative, technical and normative, which are both personal and positional to managers at various levels. Power resources are the means through which the behaviour of others may be influenced and modified. Power is also a dependency relationship, because resources are unequally distributed and they create dependencies, as, for example, between managers and managers and managers and subordinates.

7. In their search for legitimacy, managers draw upon physical, economic, administrative, technical and normative resources. Their most important source of influence is through rewards, which are based on their economic power. However, rewards based on economic calculation or instrumental compliance are only partially legitimate. Managers' administrative and technical knowledge are only partially legitimate too. Only normative power, influenced by moral persuasion, is fundamentally legitimate.

8. Managerial politics play a central role in organisational life. Since managers control the levers of power that authority confers upon them, they use this power to determine key policies and practices, as well as to advance their own career interests. Consequently, managers use a variety of strategies, tactics and 'games' to protect their areas of managerial responsibility and their career pathways. This implies that managers must learn how to manage using power on a daily basis. Being an effective manager means knowing how and when to use power ethically.

9. There are a variety of models of the HR function, with research indicating that contemporary HRM operates at both strategic and operational levels.

In taking on these roles, HR specialists provide a wide variety of planning, advice, support and expertise to line managers. In practice, the scope and distribution of HR activities varies by organisation, depending largely on its business strategy, market and competitive position, managerial awareness, type of workforce employed, sector and size. In the context of the economic imperatives of contemporary organisational life, the role of conformist innovator, as identified by Legge (1978), appears to be the one most likely to gain the support of senior and line managers today.

10. Forces shaping the HR agenda include the labour market, patterns of employment, flexibility, employment legislation and public policy. Relationships with employees, in turn, are managed collectively through collective bargaining, individually through HRM policies and techniques; or, in some cases, partnership and mutuality between employer and union. In the search for an understanding of contemporary HR practices, the psychological contract is a useful analytical device to draw upon. In distinguishing between relational psychological contracts and transactional ones, the empirical evidence indicates that the transactional model has largely superseded the relational one and is based, mainly, on short-term instrumental relations between the parties.

REVIEW QUESTIONS

1. What are the cases for and against regarding management as a profession?

2. 'Of all the management functions in organisations, financial management is the most important.' Do you agree or not agree, and why?

3. A friend of yours has emailed you: 'I've just had a very bad experience with a retailer selling electrical goods. Their customer service standards are a joke and all the talk about "quality" is simply rhetoric.' Draft an email explaining, from your experience and knowledge of quality management, that it is neither a joke nor merely rhetoric but something with a strong theoretical underpinning and practical base.

4. One of your managerial colleagues has said to you: 'The more that I observe managerial behaviour in our organisation, the more I realise that it is about power and control.' Drawing upon research evidence and observation in your organisation, what is your view of this statement and why? What are the implications for the HR function?

5. Examine the view that the psychological contract at work between employer and employee is more important than the legal contract of employment between them. Justify your response.

CASE STUDY 3.1 NORTHERN CITY COUNCIL AND COMMUNITY INVOLVEMENT

Background

Northern City is one of England's largest cities, with metropolitan borough status. It has grown from largely industrial roots to encompass a wide economic base. It obtained worldwide recognition during the nineteenth century for its manufacturing industries and the many innovations that took place in these industries. This led to an almost 10-fold increase in its population during the Industrial Revolution. It gained its city charter in 1875 and officially became Northern City.

Northern City Council has big ambitions, seeking to be the most democratic council in the country. It also seeks to ensure that all its services are customer focused, by responding to individual needs and preferences. The Head of Organisational Change (HOC) oversees the implementation of the authority's strategies to achieve these ambitions. She has wide and extensive experience of culture change and organisational development programmes. She is also experienced in devolution and citizen and customer involvement, and has demonstrable commitment in all these areas. The HOC is part of Northern City Council's Modern Governance Department in the Deputy Chief Executive's team. This is a pivotal role in the Council and she works with a range of transformational programmes with senior colleagues. She is strongly committed to public services and social justice and is capable of driving change to realise the Council's corporate objectives. The authority spends £1.4 billion a year providing a range of services for the people of Northern City and employs about 10,000 staff.

Head of Organisational Change and Northern City's management structure

The role of the HOC is:

- to provide leadership and management of the organisational change strategy, key development programmes and communications campaigns that aim to promote 'One Council' and a positive culture within the Council and amongst its partnerships

- to lead the customer focus strategy ensuring all efforts and services focus on outcomes for local people, businesses and visitors and to provide excellent access to services and customer care

- to develop and oversee strategic policy and practice in relation to the above

- to consistently maintain excellent standards of delivery

- to innovate and ensure best practice in Northern City Council

- to act as the Council's principal adviser on the above areas, working closely with the Communications, HR and Customer Services departments

- to create and manage a dynamic and successful team which delivers the priorities of the administration and improves the quality of life for Northern City Council staff and citizens in the city

- to embody and promote the values of the Council

- to act as a key senior manager of Northern City Council by working to promote positive cultural change and a One Council approach.

The Council's Executive Management Team (EMT) provides strategic direction and deals with key corporate issues and strategic service issues. It makes decisions, formulates recommendations for the political leadership, and gives a steer on policy issues where this is necessary. EMT can make managerial decisions on how it operates or on the application of policy that has already been politically agreed. However, it cannot set new policy, which is the role of elected members. Issues going to EMT requiring a political decision then go on to a Cabinet Management Team/EMT meeting, then on to Cabinet and, where necessary, on to a meeting of the full Council. Members of EMT are responsible for a team or portfolio of responsibilities.

The Community Involvement Strategy (CIS) and Sustainable Communities Act

Northern City Council wants to make sure that everyone in the city has a voice and more control over the decisions affecting them. The CIS supports its aim of making sure that the Council listens to local people. That is why the initiative is called 'Putting Northern City People in the Driving Seat'. The strategy has been developed to enable the Council to involve local people and to make sure they can have a say and act upon how, where and why the Council delivers its services and the actions it takes. The Council also wants to encourage local communities to influence services provided by its partners.

The CIS sets out why extending citizen and community involvement in the Council's work and in the city generally is important to everyone. It also sets out what the Council will do to lead this work, support local people and communities to be involved and empowered to take action themselves, and how the Council will change and develop to expand and improve involvement and democracy in Northern City. There has already been a lot of good work and excellent practice that has already taken place with the Council, its partners and local people sharing ideas to make improvements. Now the Council wants to build on this and do more, because the strategy will help the Council to be more open and transparent in the way decisions are made and empower local people to be part of the process.

On 30 April this year, there was the first Northern City Sustainable Communities debate. This arose out of the Sustainable Communities Act 2007. This gives an opportunity for councils and communities

to put forward new thinking on how to meet the challenges of sustainability and local well-being. It starts from the principle that local people know best what needs to be done to promote the sustainability of their area. It also accepts that sometimes they need central government to act to enable them to do so. The Act provides a channel for local people, and the councils which represent them, to ask central government to take such action.

Earlier, the Secretary of State had invited proposals from communities and councils which will contribute to sustainability. These could advocate changes to the law, and changes to the body that provides particular public services. The Act also requires the Secretary of State to publish statements detailing the public spending in the area on the services provided. This is to enable proposals to be made to change the way public money is spent in the area.

The main provisions of the Sustainable Communities Act are:

- The Secretary of State should publish local spending reports, statements showing the scope of public spending by all bodies exercising public functions in the area.

- Local proposals from councils can be put forward to the Secretary of State, aimed at improving the economic, social and environmental well-being of the area including participation in civic and political activity.

- This can include proposals to transfer functions from one organisation to another.

- Councils should develop proposals through wider community consultation, using a panel or panels of local people.

- In developing proposals, councils should have regard to a range of sustainability issues such as local production of goods, local food, transport, energy use and others.

- Local proposals are submitted via local

authorities for short-listing by a 'selector' body, such as the Local Government Association, representing the interests of local government, before being put to the Secretary of State for a response.

- The Secretary of State publishes an action plan setting out decisions on proposals, and should report annually to parliament on progress made as a result of this Act.

Attended by over 150 people, the Northern City Sustainable Communities debate was a full day of activity around the Sustainable Communities Act including:

- introducing the Act

- identifying the issues members of the public think are most important for a sustainable Northern City

- developing potential ideas for addressing these issues.

Four ideas were identified by the local panel and these are now being submitted to the Council for further development:

- bringing empty shops into use through initiatives to encourage landlords to accept short-term leases

- improving bus services through re-municipalising them

- increasing the amount of affordable housing in Northern City through allowing the Council to keep more of the proceeds of 'right to buy' sales

- maximising the amount of land available

for local food growing, by allowing community groups to grow crops on vacant land that is not being developed in the near future.

Tasks

1. Justify the role of Head of Organisational Change within Northern City Council.

2. As Head of Organisational Change, you have been asked by the head of the Council's Modern Governance Department to prioritise the four ideas identified by the local panel. What criteria will you use to do this? Drawing on these criteria, what order of priority will you recommend to the Council and why?

3. Assume that the list you have prioritised is recommended to the Council to follow through. Critically examine the role of Head of Organisational Change in facilitating this change programme. In what ways will this leadership role help deliver this initiative within Northern City Council? What are likely to be the main implications for the HR function?

4. Identify and discuss up to three organisational political issues that will need managing if this planned change is to go ahead.

5. Which *three* management functions are going to be crucial in delivering this programme for change and why?

EXPLORE FURTHER

BARRY, D. and HANSEN, H. (eds). (2008) *The SAGE handbook of new approaches in management and organization.* London: Sage.

Provides an analysis and review of contemporary approaches to management and organisation, with new chapters allowing readers to stay one step ahead of the latest thinking. Contributors draw on research and practice and introduce ideas that are considered fringe and controversial. Some interesting insights into contemporary management theory and practice.

COLLEY, J., DOYLE, J., HARDIE, R., LOGAN, G. and STETTINIUS, W. (2007) *Principles of general management: the art and science of getting results across organisational boundaries.* New Haven, CT: Darden Graduate School of Business Administration.

Examines the theories and practices of general management, drawing on its origins, steps, analytical concepts, crucial activities of general managers, and the various activities to make general management work.

WILKINSON, A., BACON, N., REDMAN, T. and SNELL, S. (eds) (2009) *The SAGE handbook of human resource management.* London: Sage.

Focuses on familiarising readers with the fundamentals of applied human resource management, whilst contextualising practice within wider theoretical considerations; has international chapters combining a critical overview with discussion of key debates and research.

PART 2

Strategy formulation and implementation

CHAPTER 4

Developing corporate strategies

INTRODUCTION

This chapter examines some basic ideas about strategy, strategy-making, the strategic process and strategic management. Strategy has a long history and there are conflicting perspectives of the process, so the approach adopted here is a selective but demanding one. With organisations operating in increasingly complex, unstable external contexts, those leading them – in the private, public and third sectors – are using systems and techniques of strategic management in response to uncertainty, change and market competition. One major view of strategy, the *deterministic* view, is rationalist and assesses where an organisation is at the moment and how it got there, analyses the directions in which it might go to survive and prosper, determines how it can get there and subsequently evaluates whether it has achieved its objectives. Another major approach is the *emergent* view. This is where strategy is 'shaped', without predetermined objectives, and 'emerges' over time in response to changing organisational needs. In this case, the final objectives of strategy are unclear and its elements are developed as strategy unfolds. It is the tensions between these two approaches to strategy that are explored in this chapter, as well as some techniques of environmental analysis, constraints on strategy, and ways in which organisations help shape their strategic contexts.

LEARNING OUTCOMES

By the end of this chapter, readers should be able to understand, explain and critically evaluate:

- different approaches to strategy-making and the concepts of strategic search, choice, formulation and implementation

- the major constraints on an organisation's activities created by its business contexts

- tools and techniques of environmental analysis

- the internal and external constraints on strategy.

In addition, readers should be able to:

- understand how strategy is developed in their own organisation
- contribute to the process of strategy-making, strategy implementation and strategic review
- participate in strategy-making in response to contextual developments which affect HR.

DEBATES ABOUT STRATEGY

Strategy is a disputed concept, with different meanings for different people at different times. De Wit and Meyer (2004) say there are strongly differing opinions on most of the key issues within the field and the disagreements run so deep that even a common definition of the term 'strategy' is illusive. Originally strategy – from the ancient Greek *strategia*, 'generalship' – was associated with the planning and winning of wars. Nowadays strategy, such as business strategy, marketing strategy or HR strategy, is linked with the management function in organisations and with those people and groups responsible for planning organisational success in the marketplace. But the term strategy is also used in a personal sense. Someone might have 'a strategy for developing their career', another might claim to have a 'strategy for the good life', and someone else a 'strategy for self-development and personal growth'. More generally, however, strategy is used in the collective sense. Thus people might say that 'the team's strategy for beating its opponents is to base our position on past experience' or 'the company's strategy for recruiting the best staff is to provide career opportunities internally.'

In his classical study of strategies for change, Quinn (1980) distinguishes the words 'strategy', 'objectives', 'goals', 'policy' and 'programmes.' For him, a strategy is the pattern or plan that integrates an organisation's major goals, policies and actions into a coherent whole, whilst objectives or goals state what is to be achieved, when the results are to be achieved, but not how to achieve them. All organisations have multiple goals within a complex hierarchy of goals, so Quinn defines an enterprise's major goals as those affecting its overall direction and viability. These are its 'strategic goals'. Policies are rules or guidelines expressing the limits within which action takes place, with the major ones being 'strategic policies.' Programmes, in turn, specify the step-by-step sequence of actions required to achieve major objectives, with strategic decisions being those determining the overall direction of an enterprise and its viability. Quinn also accepts that strategies exist at different levels in large organisations.

In distinguishing between 'strategies' and 'tactics,' Quinn argues that the primary difference lies in the scale of action or the perspective of the leader. What appears to be a 'strategy' to a departmental head may seem to be a 'tactic' to the chief executive; tactics are of relatively short-term duration in their impact on the organisation; strategies are longer term.

Quinn goes on to argue that effective formal strategies contain four main elements. First, they incorporate the most important goals to be achieved, policy guidelines for action and programmes to accomplish defined goals. Second, effective strategies develop around a few key concepts and thrusts, giving them cohesion, balance and focus. Third, strategies deal with not only the unpredictable but also the unknowable, with organisations needing to build 'strong postures' so they can achieve their goals despite the external forces acting on them. Fourth, organisations have a number of hierarchic and mutually related supporting strategies. Effective strategies appear to encompass certain critical success factors such as: clear, decisive objectives; maintaining the initiative; concentration; and flexibility. They also require co-ordinated and committed leadership, surprise and security.

Mintzberg (1987a) sees the need for eclecticism in defining strategy. He provides five interpretations of strategy, arguing that a good deal of confusion stems from contradictory and ill-defined uses of the term. He examines various definitions of strategy to avoid this confusion and to enrich people's ability to understand and manage the processes by which strategies are formed. He believes that these different definitions of strategy interrelate and each one 'adds important elements to our understanding of strategy; indeed encourages us to address what is really intended.' These definitions are:

- **Strategy as plan**: defined as some kind of consciously intended course of action or set of guidelines to deal with a situation.

- **Strategy as ploy**: where a specific manoeuvre is developed which is intended to outwit opponents or competitors to bring their strategies into the open.

- **Strategy as a pattern**: involves patterns of actions where intended strategies are realised through resulting behaviours that emerge as substantive 'strategy' only in retrospect. Thus, as one business executive has said, 'Gradually the successful approaches merge into a pattern of action that becomes our strategy. We certainly don't have an overall strategy on this' (Mintzberg et al 1998, p15).

- **Strategy as position**: locates an organisation in its external contexts. By this definition, strategy becomes a mediating force between organisations and their external contexts. This definition is compatible with those obtained through a preselected plan or position, aspired to through a plan or ploy, or reached through a pattern of behaviour.

- **Strategy as perspective**: consists of not only a chosen position but also an ingrained way of seeing the world. This definition suggests that strategy is a 'concept' and an abstraction, existing only in the minds of interested parties. It is a shared perspective, in the 'collective mind', which unites individuals by common thinking and behaviour.

Another attempt to provide an understanding of the nature of strategy is suggested by Hax and Majluf (1996). Whilst agreeing that a simple definition of strategy is not easy, they argue that some elements have universal validity and can be applied to any organisation. They assume that strategy embraces all the critical activities of a firm or organisation and that, as a concept, it can be considered separately from the process of strategy formation. They identify six critical dimensions to be included in any unified definition of strategy:

- a coherent, unifying and integrative pattern of decisions
- a means of establishing an organisation's purpose in terms of its long-term objectives
- a definition of a firm's competitive domain
- a response to external opportunities and threats and to internal strengths and weaknesses as a means of achieving competitive advantage
- a logical system for differentiating managerial tasks at corporate, business and functional levels
- a definition of the economic and non-economic contribution the firm intends to make to its stakeholders.

Since the concept of strategy embraces the overall purpose of an organisation, Hax and Majluf (1996) believe that it is necessary to examine the many facets making up the whole strategic dimension. By combining these, a comprehensive definition is obtained. In this way, strategy becomes the fundamental framework through which organisations assert their continuity, whilst at the same time enabling them to adapt to their changing external contexts to gain competitive advantage. For Hax and Majluf, the ultimate objective of strategy is to address the needs of organisational stakeholders; this provides a base for establishing the host of transactions and social contracts linking a firm to its stakeholders.

Whittington (2001) provides an interesting typology of strategy, explaining its multi-dimensional and complex nature. He distinguishes between deliberate and emergent strategic *processes*, with either revenue-maximising or pluralist *outcomes*. As indicated in Figure 4.1, this classification results in four typologies of strategy:

- **Systemic** (deliberate process and pluralist outcome): strategy is shaped by the wider social system within which it is rooted, with strategic choices being influenced by the wider culture and institutions of society – HR strategy mirrors societal and institutional contexts.
- **Classic** (deliberate and revenue-maximising): adopts a rational approach to strategy, leaving little room for choice regarding HR planning since it is assumed that there is 'one best' way to manage people – choice in HR systems is limited.
- **Processual** (emergent and pluralist): strategy emerges out of disagreements within management, acknowledges that organisations have conflicting goals and accepts that strategy can never be perfect – HR choices reflect these ambiguities.
- **Evolutionary** (emergent and revenue-maximising): strategy is a response to market forces, where the promotion of flexible systems, including HR systems, provides an important component of competitive advantage.

Figure 4.1 Whittington's typology of strategy

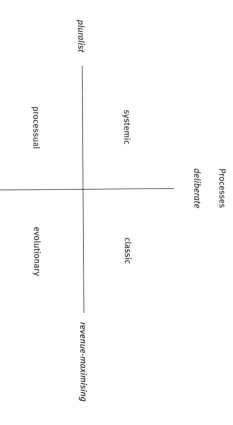

Processes

deliberate

Outcomes   *pluralist*   systemic   classic   *revenue-maximising*

processual   evolutionary

emergent

Adapted from Whittington (2001).

The concept of strategy, then, is a problematic one. To provide a precise definition is misleading, since there is widespread disagreement among practitioners, academics and researchers about the boundaries, methods and philosophical underpinnings of the strategy process. Determining and applying strategy processes is a contingent, complex activity, in part rational, in part humanistic, in part value driven. As de Wit and Meyer (2004, p4) conclude: 'the variety of partially conflicting views means that strategy cannot be reduced to a number of matrices or flow diagrams that one must learn to fill in.' There is, in short, no simple definition of what strategy is. A number of perspectives, conceptual tools and approaches may be identified, but no definitive answer is possible.

ACTIVITY 4.1

Examine the view that 'strategy is about beating your enemies'.

THE RATIONAL APPROACH TO STRATEGY

There are a number of approaches to conceptualising, analysing and describing the strategy process. A simple typology suggests a spectrum of models ranging from 'rational planning' approaches, on the one side, to 'natural selection' ones, on the other, with 'logical incrementalism,' the emergent approach', and other approaches (such as 'chaos theory' and 'institutional' approaches) in between. The basic dichotomy is between the 'planning' and 'incrementalist' perspectives. In the planning perspective, the emphasis is on deliberate strategy, where strategy is designed intentionally. Strategy is formally structured, implementation is focused on programming and strategic change is implemented from the top down. In the incrementalist perspective, emphasis is on 'emergent' strategy, where strategy is unstructured, fragmented, and shaped gradually. Implementation is focused on learning or organisational development, with strategic change requiring cultural and cognitive shifts.

The rational or planning approach to strategy provides 'textbook' models of the strategy process. It emphasises the rational, scientific nature of the strategic process which, if properly applied, can improve the effectiveness and growth of organisations in conditions of change. The underlying principle is that strategies are the outcome of objective analyses and planning. It is rooted in the assumption that analytical, logical methods of managing strategy can be prescribed, individuals can be trained to use these methods, and pay-offs can be demonstrated by using them effectively.

The rational approach is a prescriptive one, where strategies have objectives defined in advance, although they may be adjusted if circumstances change. The rational strategic process shown in Figure 4.2 includes: analysing the external contexts; analysing resources and identifying vision, mission and objectives; developing strategic options; choosing among these options; and implementing and evaluating the chosen strategy.

The advantages of the prescriptive approach include: the opportunity provided of giving an overview of the organisation; the possibility of making comparisons with defined objectives; and the ability to monitor what has been agreed, so that an evaluation of progress can be made. There are many versions of the rational, planning model of strategy; three are presented here: the 'hopper method', 'recipe view' and 'linear sequential' approaches.

THE HOPPER METHOD

Andrews (1987, p28) illustrates the hopper method. This approach 'feeds' or 'funnels' (like a hopper) a number of variables into the strategy process, such as organisational, informational and managerial variables, and integrates them to create organisational responses capable of facilitating corporate purpose.

In this method of strategy determination, interdependence of purposes, policies and action is seen to be crucial to any individual strategy, so as to achieve competitive advantage for the organisation. The essential elements of strategy for Andrews are 'formulation' and 'implementation'. Formulation is about deciding what to do and implementation is about achieving results. Formulation involves identifying 'opportunity and risk', determining the company's material, technical, financial, and managerial resources', taking account of 'the personal values and aspirations of senior management', and acknowledging the company's

Figure 4.2 The rational approach to strategy

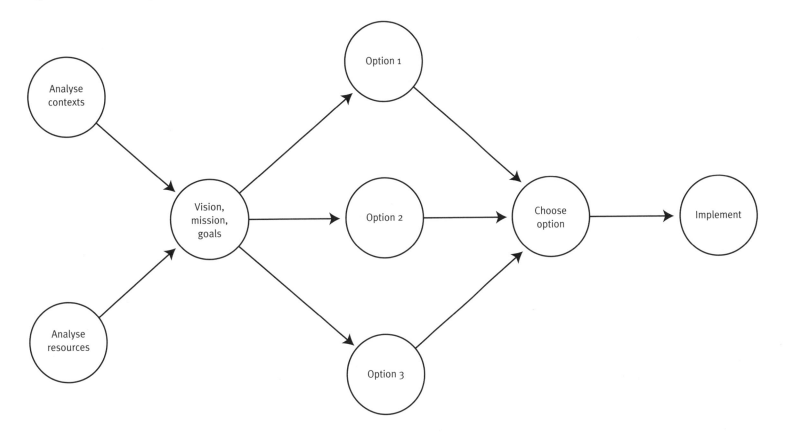

'non-economic responsibility to society'. Implementation, in turn, necessitates adopting appropriate 'organisational structures and relationships', designing necessary 'organisational processes and behaviour' and drawing on the strategic and personal skills of 'top leadership'.

This method of formulating and implementing suitable strategies for organisations begins by identifying 'opportunities and risks' in the external contexts and links these with the organisation's 'distinctive competence' and 'corporate resources'. The matching of opportunities and resources results in the schematic development of a viable economic strategy. In undertaking this to determine choice of products and markets, top managers are expected to take account of economic, technical, physical (eg locational), political, social and global factors, and match them with the company's competence and resources. The former might include the organisation's financial, managerial and organisational competence, as well as its reputation in the market. 'In each company, the way in which distinctive competence, organizational resources and organizational values are combined is or should be unique.'

THE RECIPE VIEW

The recipe view provides structured procedures for determining strategy and is illustrated in a major British text by Johnson et al (2008). For them, corporate strategy is concerned with the overall purpose and scope of the organisation to meet the expectations of owners or major stakeholders, and adding value to the different parts of the organisation. In arguing that strategic management is different from other aspects of management because of its ambiguity, complexity, organisational impact, fundamental nature and long-term implications, Johnson et al provide a three-dimensional model of strategic management. They analyse it in terms of 'strategic analysis', 'strategic choice' and 'strategic implementation'. Strategic analysis is concerned with the strategic position of the organisation in terms of its external contexts, internal resources and competences, and the expectations and influence of stakeholders. In language similar to that of Andrews (1987), strategic choice understands the underlying bases guiding future strategy, generating strategic options for evaluation and selecting from among them. Strategic implementation translates strategy into organisational action through organisational structure and design, resource planning and managing strategic change.

Johnson et al (2008) identify at least three different levels of organisational strategy: corporate, business unit and operational. The first is the organisation's overall purpose and scope; the second how to compete successfully in the market; and the third how resources, processes and people can effectively deliver corporate and business-level strategies. They also explore the vocabulary of strategy, defining key terms such as: 'mission', 'vision', 'goal', 'objective', 'core competencies', 'strategies', 'strategic architecture' and 'control'. In arguing that different organisations are likely to emphasise different aspects of the strategic management process, Johnson et al claim strategic priorities are understood in the particular contexts of organisations.

THE LINEAR SEQUENTIAL VIEW

The linear sequential view is a logical, rationalist approach to conceptualising corporate strategy, using a systems model of 'inputs', 'processes' and 'outputs'. It is epitomised in many basic American texts, such as those of Higgins and Vincze (1993) and David (2009). Higgins and Vincze, for example, define strategic management as the process of managing the organisation's mission and the relationship of the organisation to its internal and external contexts. They provide a five-stage model of strategic management for determining objectives and formulating strategy. These are:

- formulation of vision statement, mission statement and goals

- determination of strategic objectives

- formulation of strategies

- implementation of strategies

- evaluation and control of strategies.

The first three stages make up 'strategic policies', with the last two providing 'policies that aid implementation' and 'control policies'. In the determination of organisational objectives and strategy formulation, Higgins and Vincze argue that business leaders take account of organisational mission, internal and external environmental analyses and an assessment of the organisation's 'strengths, weaknesses, opportunities and threats'. This leads on to a set of 'strategic alternatives', 'evaluation of alternatives', 'decision-making and a 'hierarchy of strategies.'

David (2009) defines strategic management as the art and science of formulating, implementing and evaluating cross-functional decisions enabling an organisation to achieve its objectives. He sets out three main stages in the strategic management process: strategy formulation, strategy implementation and strategy evaluation.

- **Strategy formulation**: includes developing a business mission, identifying an organisation's external opportunities and threats, determining internal strengths and weaknesses, establishing long-term objectives, generating alternative strategies and choosing particular strategies to pursue. Strategy formulation also decides 'what new businesses to enter, what businesses to abandon, how to allocate resources, whether to expand operations or diversify, whether to enter international markets, whether to merge or form a joint venture and how to avoid a hostile takeover.'

- **Strategy implementation**: requires organisations to establish annual objectives, devise policies, motivate employees and allocate scarce resources so that formulated strategies can be executed.

- **Strategy evaluation**: is the primary means of determining whether or not particular strategies are working and involves reviewing external and internal factors that provide bases for current strategies, measuring performance and taking corrective actions.

In David's model, strategy implementation demands developing a strategy-supportive culture, creating an effective structure, directing marketing efforts, preparing budgets, utilising information systems and linking employee compensation to performance. This is often the most difficult stage in strategic management and hinges upon the abilities of managers to motivate employees and carry them with them to achieve organisational purpose. He sees interpersonal skills as being especially critical for successful strategic implementation. The challenge of implementation is to stimulate managers and employees throughout an organisation to work with pride and enthusiasm towards achieving stated objectives.

For David, strategy formulation, strategy implementation and strategy evaluation take place at three hierarchical levels in large organisations: corporate, divisional or strategic business unit, and functional levels. In his view, by fostering communication and interaction among managers and employees across hierarchical levels, strategic management helps firms and organisations work as teams. This model is based on the belief that organisations need continually to monitor internal and external events and trends so that timely changes can be made as required so as to adapt to change.

Lynch (2006) regards corporate strategy as important because it deals with the fundamental issues affecting the future of an organisation. It does this by integrating an organisation's functional areas and activities to ensure its survival and growth. In his view, strategy develops out of considering the resources of an organisation in relation to its contexts, with the prime purpose of adding value and then distributing the added value among stakeholders. He identifies five key elements of strategy, which are principally related to gaining advantage in the marketplace. These are sustainability, distinctiveness, competitive advantage, exploitation of linkages between the organisation and its external contexts, and vision. He identifies three 'core areas' of corporate strategy:

- **Strategic analysis:** this is concerned with the organisation's external contexts, its resources, and its vision, mission and objectives.

- **Strategic development**: this focuses on the strategic options available to the organisation, rational selection of the ways forward, finding the strategic route ahead and considering strategy, structure and style.

- **Strategy implementation:** this enables selected options to be put into operation, although there may be practical difficulties in motivating staff and from external pressures such as legislation, regulation and market forces.

Lynch identifies the major contextual factors impacting on corporate strategy as increased global competition, consolidation and development of trading areas, and cheap telecommunications and computer technology. Other factors include the collapse of the command economies of Eastern Europe, the emergence of Asian economies and better-educated workforces.

Corporate strategy becomes, as a result, international in scope and has moved out of being the preserve of North American and European countries. Markets have become more international, making it necessary to balance global interests with variations in local demand. The essential elements of a 'prescriptive corporate strategy' are: developing and defining the organisation's objectives, analysing the external contexts, reconsidering the organisation's objectives, developing strategy options, selecting the option against the likelihood of achieving the objectives, and implementing the chosen option. The advantages of the prescriptive approach are that it provides: an overview of the organisation, the possibility of comparing objectives, a summary of the demands on an organisation's resources, a picture of the choices that the organisation may need to make, and the possibility of monitoring agreed plans.

Mintzberg (1994), however, identifies some difficulties with the prescriptive strategic process. These include:

- The future may not be predicted accurately enough to make rational choices.
- It may not be possible to determine the long-term good of an organisation.
- The strategies proposed may not be capable of being managed in the ways expected.
- Top management may not be able to persuade others to follow their decisions.
- Strategy decisions may need to be altered because circumstances change.
- Implementation is not necessarily a separate and distinctive phase and comes only after a strategy has been agreed.

ACTIVITY 4.2

Identify and discuss the similarities and differences amongst rationalist models of strategy.

EMERGENT AND OTHER APPROACHES TO STRATEGY

In contrast to rational approaches, there are non-rational approaches to strategy, based around the 'emergent approach'. This is where final objectives are unclear and the elements are developed as strategy proceeds. It arises from the observation that human beings do not always react rationally and logically to situations and that strategy emerges over time in adaptation to human needs. Logical incrementalism, which derives from the emergent approach, is where strategic management is seen not as a formal planning process, but as a series of subprocesses by which strategies develop based on the experiences of managers and their sensitivity to changes in their external contexts. It is the process of developing strategy by small, incremental and reasonable steps rather than by macroscopic 'grand plans'. Incrementalists do not question the value of planning and control as means of managing organisational processes but claim that strategy formation is not one of them, since planning is less suitable for non-routine activities such as innovation and change.

THE EMERGENT APPROACH

According to de Wit and Meyer (2004), the distinction between deliberate and emergent strategy goes to the heart of the debate on strategy formation. While theorists disagree on many points, the crucial issue is whether strategy formation should be deliberate or emergent. The key principle of emergent strategy is that it does not have a single, definitive objective and that strategy develops over time. The test for emergent strategy is to examine how strategy has developed in practice over a defined period. The emergent approach draws on corporate vision, mission and objectives, analyses the external contexts and its resources and, out of these processes, strategy is developed, implemented and evaluated in response to the issues facing it. A systematic representation of the emergent approach to strategy is provided in Figure 4.3.

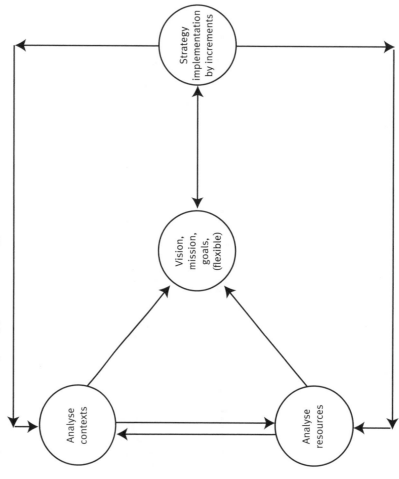

Figure 4.3 The emergent approach to strategy

According to Lynch (2006), the advantages of the emergent approach are that it:

- accords with organisational practice
- takes account of people issues, such as motivation, that make the rational approach unrealistic in some cases

- allows strategy to develop as more is learnt about the strategic situation
- redefines implementation so that it becomes an integral part of the strategy development process
- provides an opportunity for the culture and politics of an organisation to be included in the strategic process
- provides flexibility to respond to changes, especially in fast-moving markets.

Concerns about emergent strategy include:

- In multi-functional or multi-divisional organisations, resources need to be allocated between the demands of competing units and this requires some central strategic overview.
- In some industries where long-term issues are involved, decisions have to be taken and adhered to by direction from the centre.
- Management control is simpler where the basis of the actions to be taken has been planned in advance.

Emergent strategies develop, then, when strategies emerge from situations and issues rather than being planned and prescribed in advance. Such strategies came to the fore in the light of market turbulence in the 1970s, when some researchers argued that the basis of rational, prescriptive strategy was false. Three types of emergent strategic theory are distinguished: 'survival-based theories', 'uncertainty-based theories' and 'human resources-based theories'.

Survival-based theories

These are rooted in the belief that strategy is decided primarily in the marketplace, hence the optimal strategy for organisational survival is to be efficient. As Williamson (1991, p75) writes: 'economy is the best strategy.' If organisational survival is paramount, survival-based theorists argue, the most appropriate strategy is to pursue a number of strategic initiatives at any one time and let the market decide the best one (Whittington 2001).

Uncertainty-based theories

These use mathematical probability to show that development of corporate strategy is complex and uncertain, thus making accurate predictions of the future impossible. Because the external context is turbulent and uncertain, only limited strategies are possible. Miller and Frieson (1984) found that sudden shifts in strategy and in the organisational structures of companies occurred before they had reached a steady state. It is possible to provide mathematical models of such systems and show that they oscillate between stable and turbulent states. Stacey (1993) suggests that the external contexts of many businesses, such as computer firms, are inherently unstable, so business strategy has to emerge rather than aiming at the false certainties of the prescriptive approach.

Human resources-based strategies

These stress the importance of people in strategy development. They highlight the motivation of people, the politics and cultures of organisations, and the desires of individuals in developing strategy. The ways in which people act and interact in strategic development is vital, and a process of trial and error can be used to devise acceptable strategies. These theories emphasise the difficulties arising as new strategies are introduced which confront people with the need to change.

In the 1990s, there was some discussion on the learning aspects of strategic development. In his conceptualisation of the learning organisation, Senge (1990) suggests that there are five 'learning disciplines', crafted to enable individuals and organisations to learn, where learning is creative activity aimed at developing new strategies and opportunities. First, personal mastery creates an organisational context that encourages groups to develop goals and purposes. Second, mental models reflect upon the images that managers and workers have of the world, and how these influence actions and decisions. Third, shared vision builds commitment to achieve group aims by agreeing what these aims are. Fourth, team learning uses group skills to develop individual abilities and competencies. Fifth, systems thinking enables groups to understand the major forces influencing organisations.

LOGICAL INCREMENTALISM

A well-known pioneer of emergent strategy is Quinn (1978), who is widely credited with being influential in developing the logical incremental perspective. In his view, when well-managed major organisations make significant changes in strategy, the approaches they use frequently bear little resemblance to the rational-analytical systems so widely touted. The processes used to arrive at total strategy are typically fragmented, evolutionary and intuitive. He criticises both the formal systems planning approach, which underemphasises power-behavioural factors, and the power-behavioural approach, because studies of them have been conducted in settings far removed from the realities of strategy formation. His research into 10 major companies in the 1970s provided the following important findings:

- Neither the formal planning nor power-behavioural models adequately characterise the ways in which successful strategic processes operate.

- Effective strategies tend to emerge from a series of 'strategic subsystems', each of which attacks a specific strategic issue in a disciplined way but is blended incrementally and opportunistically into a cohesive pattern that becomes the company's strategy.

- The logic behind each subsystem is so powerful that it may serve as a normative approach for formulating these key elements of strategy in large companies.

- Because of cognitive and process limits, almost all these subsystems – and the formal planning activity itself – are managed and linked together by an approach best described as 'logical incrementalism'.

- Incrementalism is not muddling through: it is purposeful, effective, proactive management for improving and integrating both the analytical and behavioural aspects of strategy formulation.

According to Quinn, strategic decisions do not lend themselves to aggregation in a single massive decision. Successful managers link together and bring order to a *series* of strategic processes and decisions. They proceed incrementally to handle urgent issues. In his view, logic dictates that managers proceed flexibly and experimentally from broad concepts towards specific commitments. Managers make the latter concrete as late as possible in order to narrow the bands of uncertainty and to benefit from the best available information. This is the process of logical incrementalism. It is logical in the sense that it is reasonable and well considered. It is incremental in the sense that it is structured on a piecemeal basis. Properly managed, logical incrementalism allows executives to bind together the contributions of rational systematic analyses, political and power theories, and organisational behaviour concepts, thus allowing them to attain cohesion and focus.

Mintzberg's (1987b) 'crafting strategy' complements Quinn's analysis. The crafting image of strategy captures the actual process by which effective strategies are made. Using metaphor, Mintzberg argues that managers are craftworkers and strategy is their clay. Like the potter, they sit between the past of corporate capabilities and a future of market opportunities. To manage strategy is to craft it. This involves dedication, experience, involvement with the material, the personal touch, mastery of detail, a sense of harmony and integration by practitioners.

Ultimately, for Mintzberg, the crafting of strategy, like managing a craft, requires a natural synthesis of the future, present and past. This incorporates: managing stability, not change; programming a strategy which has already been created, not actually creating it; and detecting subtle discontinuities that might undermine a business in the future. It also requires: knowing the business on the basis of personal knowledge and understanding; managing emerging patterns of strategy and helping them take shape, which requires creating a climate within which a variety of strategies can grow; and reconciling both change and continuity.

ACTIVITY 4.3

Consider the view that logical incrementalism is the only approach to strategy appropriate for public sector organisations.

ACTIVITY 4.4

Your manager has come across the term 'logical incrementalism' when reading a book on strategy. She has asked you to define the term and explain its relevance for your organisation. What will you say and why?

TOOLS AND TECHNIQUES OF ENVIRONMENTAL ANALYSIS

A major task that strategists have to undertake in determining an organisation's strategic direction is assessing the external forces acting upon it. These forces vary in importance depending on the type of organisation and the impact of its political, economic and legal contexts. Increasingly, technological developments and social changes are impacting too, as well as issues of environmentalism and changing public attitudes. All have to be appraised, if an organisation is to respond effectively to these forces insofar as they influence corporate strategies. An analysis of these helps senior managers not only to understand the complexities and interrelationships to be taken into account in predicting future trends but also to be aware of the key factors affecting the success or otherwise of the organisations they manage. The relationship between organisations and their external contexts is a two-way one. Organisations have to respond to changes in the environment; the environment reacts, in turn, to organisational changes. Ultimately, if an organisation does not respond effectively to the external forces acting on it, it will fail regardless of how well its internal affairs are managed.

THE SCOPE OF ENVIRONMENTAL ANALYSIS

The main areas requiring strategic environmental analyses are socio-cultural, technological, economic, environmental, political, legal and ethical contexts.

Socio-cultural contexts

These include demographic trends and population projections. They require robust assessment, since they influence demand for goods and services and provide indicators of future labour supply. The size, distribution, age structure, ethnic mix, income levels and geographic distribution of the population are important indicators when undertaking environmental analyses. Such analyses need to give specific consideration to the impact of demographic change on the sector where the organisation is competing. To compete and survive, organisations have to ensure that their products or services are wanted and, to this end, consumer behaviour has to be examined and analysed. Consumer behaviour affects sales, or results in negative purchase decisions, and has to be assessed effectively if an organisation is to react appropriately to such forces.

Technological contexts

Technological change is one of the most visible and pervasive forms of change and it brings in its wake new products, processes and materials, so awareness of technological developments is essential for most organisations. Technology directly impacts on transportation, energy use, communications, entertainment, healthcare and so on. Organisations having knowledge of technological breakthroughs are likely to have distinct advantages in the marketplace over those that do not. If organisations affected by technological change only become aware of it through subsequent publicity, then it may be too late to respond. A further feature of technological change is reduction in time between scientific discovery and commercial application. Technological innovation also affects not only operational systems but also the finance, administrative and HR functions.

Economic contexts

These are of vital concern to organisations. The overall economic climate determines business opportunities, because an expanding economy stimulates demand for goods, services, investment and labour, whilst a declining economy (or one in recession) chokes off demand for production, consumption and resources. Top leaders have to be able to distinguish between short-term and long-term economic trends, since long-term trends relate to more fundamental changes in the economy, which need to be addressed proactively. In addition to the general economic situation, each organisation has to examine specific trends in the sector where it operates, including competitor behaviour. The areas requiring sector appraisal include: availability of materials, finance capital and labour, and research and development. Pricing policy, marketing and advertising, and the cost structure of the sector are also important.

Environmental contexts

A major issue in terms of the environment is global warming. A series of research reports have demonstrated the importance of moving to a low-carbon or no-carbon global economy. According to this research, the global economy's appetite for energy is large and rising. At the same time, Earth's ability to digest the waste products of energy consumption is decreasing. Much scientific evidence suggests that global warming is proceeding more rapidly than previously anticipated. The growth of carbon dioxide emissions is higher than previously thought. The capacity of oceans to act as natural carbon sinks has declined and there are likely to be further decreases, resulting from the cooling effect caused by aerosols and other factors. According to these proponents, dangerous climate change becomes ever more likely and its mitigation ever more pressing. The suggested responses all have HR implications in a 'low-carbon' world:

- setting mitigation targets and costs
- introducing mitigation technologies
- investing in low-carbon technologies
- decarbonising power generation
- initiating mitigation options in sectors such as agriculture
- introducing the pricing of carbon dioxide emissions
- promoting sustainable development on sector-wide bases.

Political contexts

This is important because decisions of the UK government, devolved assemblies and the EU affect the ways in which organisations are managed. Organisations have to respond continually to public policy and EU policy changes. Government and EU regulations cover a range of issues, including product competition, consumer interests and workers' rights. These demand actions from organisational leaders so that they can develop appropriate strategic responses. Recent political changes, such as the number of interest groups in the community, and the degree of activism amongst interest groups (such as consumer, animal welfare and ecological groups), need to be observed and acted upon by business leaders.

Legal contexts

Legal factors affect an organisation's reactions to its external context and can constrain an organisation's actions or facilitate them. Areas affected by legal regulation include: the type of products or services produced, how products or services are developed, and labelling of products. In HR, they cover how employees are hired, salaries and other payments, workplace design and health and safety.

Ethical contexts

One measure of the notional 'ethical organisation' is the US practice of corporate ethics programmes. These incorporate: ethics audits, advice and guidance for publicly stated expectations about employee behaviour, the need for organisational structures to support ethical behaviour, and ethical behaviour supported by the reward systems of organisations (Post et al 2002). Another measure to identify 'ethical' organisations is the use of corporate governance structures that reinforce the connections between ethical behaviour and governmental processes in firms. In 1992, for example, the Cadbury Report (1992) presented a voluntary code of practice, aimed at boards of listed companies based in the UK. Broadly, it argued for adequate disclosure of financial information and for checks and balances within the governance structures of companies. Following this code means that it 'is more likely than not to lead to a corporate governance regime with greater openness of information, less likelihood of domination by one or a few people and fewer excesses in the remuneration packages of senior executives' (Kitson and Campbell 1996, p115).

THE PROCESS OF ENVIRONMENTAL ANALYSIS

Environmental analysis is divided into four analytical stages: *scanning* the environment, *monitoring* specific environmental trends or patterns, *forecasting* the future direction of contextual changes, and *assessing* current and future contextual changes for their organisational implications. There are two approaches to environmental analysis. One is a 'macro' (outside–in) approach; the other is a 'micro' (inside–out) approach. Using the macro-approach, organisations engage in scanning, monitoring, forecasting and assessing to identify and examine plausible alternative future external contexts that might confront them. The driving force is to ensure organisations understand the dynamics of change within each context, before deriving organisationally specific implications. The micro-approach takes the organisation as the starting point – its products, markets, technologies and so on. This approach asks the question, given these contexts, what elements of the external context the organisation should scan, monitor, forecast and assess (Fahey and Narayanam 1986).

Scanning

Scanning involves general surveillance of all contextual segments (socio-cultural, technological, economic, environment, political, legal, ethical) and their interactions. This is done either to identify early signals of possible contextual change or to detect changes already under way. Environmental scanning is aimed at alerting organisations to potentially significant external developments before they are fully formed. The fundamental challenge is to make sense of vague, ambiguous and unconnected data, using judgement, observation and consulting experts inside and outside the organisation for their specialist views. Analysts have to make connections among diverse data, so that signals of future events are created. The outputs of scanning are, therefore, signals of potential change and detection of change under way; the organisational outcomes are greater awareness of the general external context.

Monitoring

Monitoring involves tracking the evolution of contextual trends, sequences of events or streams of activities. It involves following signals or indicators identified during environmental scanning. The purpose of monitoring is to assemble sufficient data to discern whether certain predicted trends or patterns are emerging. Data sources are focused reading, selective use of individual expertise and focus groups. The outputs of monitoring are specification of trends and identification of scanning needs. The organisational outcomes are consideration and detailing of specific developments and time for developing flexibility.

Forecasting

Scanning and monitoring provide data of what has already taken place in the external context and what is currently happening there. Strategic decision-making, however, requires a future orientation and the need to develop plausible projections of the future. The data sources are outputs of monitoring, with data being collected by means of forecasting techniques (see below). Outputs are alternative forecasts of the future and identification of scanning and monitoring needs. The organisational outcomes provide understanding of future contextual changes.

Assessment

Scanning, monitoring and forecasting are not ends in themselves. Assessment involves identifying and evaluating how and why current and projected changes are affecting or are likely to affect the strategic management of an organisation. The outputs are specific organisational implications and the organisational outcomes are specific actions. Assessment answers questions such as what are the key issues presented by the external context and what are the strategic implications of these for the organisation.

TECHNIQUES OF EXTERNAL ANALYSIS

There are a range of environmental analysis techniques. Some are data-gathering methods, others are forecasting techniques. Data-gathering methods specify data sources and methods of data collection. Sources of data are either primary or secondary and may be collected on ad hoc, periodic, real-time or continuous bases. Primary sources are organisational data, or specialist agencies may be hired to provide data. The sources are individuals, sampled populations or expert panels.

Secondary sources are gathered by various agencies for general purposes and are typically available to all organisations. The nature of the data may be quantitative, qualitative or inferential. Inferential data are arrived at as a result of drawing conclusions from various data sources. For example, social values may not be directly manifest or self-explanatory but they have 'meanings' for those internalising them that imply certain substantive behaviours.

Forecasting techniques

Forecasting techniques are procedures for transforming data to provide answers to questions posed by environmental analysts in manners consistent with the data available. Forecasting techniques serve three main purposes: they verify 'hunches' or intuitive judgements; they answer 'what if?' questions; and they facilitate the forecasting of trends, events and patterns.

Forecasting techniques may be deterministic, adaptive or inventive. Deterministic techniques assume that the future can be known from the past, provided that the analyst has a model of the underlying causes. Adaptive techniques do not assume that the future is knowable and are oriented to creating descriptions of how the future is unfolding and revealing the process of change that is taking place. Inventive techniques are directed towards 'open futures'. These emphasise how an organisation can 'redesign' its future and its external context. The analyst is guided by the intentions of the organisation and the analysis creates 'pathways' to the future.

Delphi forecasting

The Delphi technique brings a number of experts together to analyse specific aspects of the current and future context. It is intended as a technique to enable them to contribute to each other's understanding of the issues and to refine their opinions as a result of their interactions with one another. The Delphi technique involves the following steps.

1 Each expert is asked to make an initial prediction.

2 Predictions are tabulated and clarified by a neutral investigator.

3 The output of the above is fed back to the experts, who are asked to make a second round of predictions based on the information provided them. Making predictions and receiving feedback may go on for several rounds.

Cross-impact matrices

Cross-impact matrices provide a systematic approach to identifying and tracing chains of effects among several forecasts or elements in the external context that are believed to interact with one another. The matrix provides a means of identifying secondary and tertiary consequences. When one environmental phenomenon being forecast affects the likelihood or timing of another, cross-impact matrices allow assessment of the consequences to be made in an explicit manner. The raw material of a cross-impact matrix is a set of events that are forecast to happen within a specified time period (the horizontal axis). The analyst specifies the time period within which the event is likely to occur and its probability of occurrence (the vertical axis).

Scenarios

Scenarios represent hypothetical descriptions of sequences of future events and trends. They are plausible, alternative futures. They allow analysts to explore the possible consequences of a series of complex, interrelated possibilities about the future. A scenario typically includes some trends, patterns, events, assumptions pertaining to these, conditions in the current environment and the dynamics leading from the present state of the environment to some future state. They allow the analyst to lay out possible blueprints for the future and assess the risks and implications of environmental change, as follows:

- identifying the strategic decision context
- identifying key industry, competitive and organisational forces
- identifying key macro-environmental forces
- analysing the key forces
- developing scenario logics or explanations for how the elements in the scenario fit together
- elaborating the scenarios
- determining the implications for strategic decisions.

ACTIVITY 4.5

Why is environmental analysis so important to organisations today? How can the results of an environmental analysis assist the strategic management process?

ACTIVITY 4.6

Outline how you would carry out an environmental analysis of your organisation (or part of it). Indicate the data that you would collect and discuss how you would use them.

FORMULATING STRATEGY

In the private sector, it is generally recognised that the profit-maximising model of the firm has serious shortcomings when trying to explain strategic decision-making in practice. Firms have to make some level of profit to survive but they do not maximise profits and, in some cases, other managerial goals may be an important element in determining the strategic goals of organisations (Mintzberg 1989). In the public (and voluntary) sectors, or 'not-for-profit' bodies, organisations have different, more complex goals from those of private sector bodies.

There are many ways of describing and analysing the major stages in strategy-making. Johnson et al (2008, 2009), for example, provide a model of strategic management incorporating three main elements: 'strategic position', 'strategic choices' and 'strategy into action'. For Lynch (2006), the three core areas of strategy are 'strategic analysis', 'strategy development' and 'strategy implementation'. Basically, making strategy can be analysed in terms of *formulation* (ie searching and choosing strategy) and *implementation*.

VISION AND MISSION

Vision is the strategic intent or desired future state of an organisation, as defined by its leading strategists, normally the chief executive. Johnson et al (2008) state that there are a number of ways in which strategic vision may be determined. It might be formulated deliberately, as part of the planning process. It might be associated with the founder of a business. It might be derived from external forces, such as privatisation, market testing or compulsory competitive tendering in the public services. It might even be related to intuition. Vision encapsulates a view of a realistic, credible and successful future for the organisation.

For Bartlett and Ghoshal (1989), building a shared corporate vision gives context and meaning to every manager's roles and responsibilities and it helps individuals understand the company's stated goals and objectives. In their view, vision must be crafted and articulated with clarity, continuity and consistency because, first, clarity of expression makes corporate objectives understandable and meaningful. Second, continuity of purpose underscores those objectives' enduring importance. Third, consistency of application across business units ensures uniformity throughout the organisation. Hamal and Prahalad (1994) suggest five criteria for judging the relevance and appropriateness of an organisation's vision: foresight, breadth, uniqueness, consensus and actionability.

The mission of an organisation is a general expression of its overall purpose and the broad directions it seeks to follow. The mission derives out of its leaders' vision and takes account of the values and expectations of its leaders and major stakeholders. Some claim that corporate mission is an organisation's reason for existence. Others view corporate mission as encompassing the basic points of departure that direct an organisation in a particular direction. Corporate mission can be articulated in a 'mission statement', although there is disagreement over exactly what a mission statement is and what it should include. Some have questioned the lengthy nature and content of mission statements, whilst others have indicated that organisations should concentrate on short, concise statements of 'strategic intent' (Hamal and Prahalad 1989). The sorts of items included in mission statements, although the list is neither exclusive nor exhaustive, are:

- direction of the organisation
- organisational purpose
- values of the organisation
- points of departure for the strategy process
- nature of the business on which the company intends to focus
- competitive ambitions of the organisation.

The mission statement has a number of functions. First, it points the organisation along a stated pathway, by defining the boundaries within which strategic choices and actions take place. Second, it conveys to stakeholders that the organisation is pursuing valued activities affecting their interests. Third, by specifying the fundamental principles driving organisational actions, the mission statement can inspire individuals to work together co-operatively. In formulating mission statements, those responsible take account of factors such as the nature of the business of the organisation, the importance of customer interests, and the basic values and beliefs for which the organisation stands.

ACTIVITY 4.7

Write a mission statement for your organisation and outline its possible limitations.

STRATEGIC OBJECTIVES

These state more precisely than mission statements what is to be achieved and when the results are to be achieved, but are distinguished from functional and business unit objectives. The purpose of strategic objectives is to focus the tasks of management on specific outcomes and provide a means of assessing whether the outcomes have been attained. In the past, writers like Ansoff (1965) were keen to stress the importance of setting quantifiable objectives, but nowadays it is generally recognised that some strategic objectives cannot be easily quantified.

In developing corporate objectives, those responsible normally recognise that overall strategic objectives need subsequently to be translated into objectives for different functions and, in larger organisations, for different business units. In larger organisations, strategic objectives have to be adjusted to take account of the circumstances and business conditions of different parts of the organisation. They cover:

- **Financial targets:** relating to issues such as profitability, costs relative to key competitors, financial stability, earnings on capital invested, revenue growth, dividends, cash flow and share price.

- **Marketing targets:** including market share, products or service diversity, growth opportunities, ability to compete in international markets and quality issues.

- **Other strategic targets:** covering customer relations, customer service, product/service leadership, research and development, investment in human resources, training and development, and operational costs.

ACTIVITY 4.8

Specify some possible strategic objectives in your organisation. Discuss how they may be operationalised and measured. Explain how these targets might be blocked.

LEVELS OF STRATEGY, STRATEGIC OPTIONS AND PREFERRED STRATEGY

Strategy is the key link between what an organisation wants to achieve (its objectives) and the policies guiding its activities. However, organisations can have more than one strategy, since strategies can exist at:

- **Corporate level:** this is concerned with the type of business the firm is in and addresses issues such as the balance of the organisation's portfolio, markets, contribution to profits, growth and possible diversification.

- **Business level:** this is concerned with how operating units within the organisation can compete in particular markets, divisional plans and the strategies of strategic business units that are 'parts of the whole'.

- **Operational level:** this is concerned with how various functions (such as finance, marketing, operations, HR and research and development) contribute to corporate and business strategy.

Approaches to strategy formulation involve identifying strategic options and selecting a preferred strategy (or strategies). The generation of strategic options is not a random process but may be stimulated by shortfalls in current performance or business effectiveness. Hrebiniak and Joyce (1984) suggest five factors affect identification of strategic options: organisational learning, distinctive competencies, past performance and type of search activity, power differentials in organisations, and absorption of uncertainty.

Organisations approach the task of strategy formulation differently, depending on the type of markets they operate in, their culture, management style, external context and so on:

- **The top-down approach**: this is driven by corporate management; strategy is unified and coherent, and provides corporate direction and performance targets.

- **The bottom-up approach**: this takes place at business unit level and is passed upwards for approval and integration with the strategies of other business units; as a result corporate strategy may lack unity, coherence and consistency.

- **The interactive approach**: this is managed jointly by corporate and business unit managers, with the process being participative, negotiated and reflecting links between corporate centre and business units.

- **The semi-autonomous approach**: this is determined by relatively independent strategy formulation activities at corporate and business unit levels; at corporate level, formulation is virtually continuous; at business unit level, formulation is suited to each business unit's circumstances and objectives.

At corporate level, selecting a preferred strategy utilises techniques such as 'portfolio analysis' and 'horizontal strategy'. At business level, strategy selection draws upon techniques such as SWOT analyses, which examine the internal strengths and weaknesses and external threats and opportunities facing organisations. Such approaches have been described as normative, however, and addressed implicitly by organisational leaders as formulators of strategy (Leavy and Wilson 1994).

The Boston Consultancy Group (BCG) growth share matrix

One of the most publicised business portfolio techniques is the BCG growth share matrix. The matrix plots a firm's relative market share position in an industry (or market) on the horizontal axis against business growth rates of industry (or market) on the vertical axis.

- **Stars**: these are businesses with strong market share in a high-growth industry and represent the best profit and growth opportunities.

- **Cash cows**: these are businesses with high market share in a low-growth industry. They represent a valuable resource, because the cash they generate can develop new 'stars' and provide funds for corporate spending.

- **Dogs**: these are businesses with low market share in a low-growth industry because of their poor competitive position, and are not usually very profitable.

- **Question marks**: these are businesses with low market share in a high-growth industry. Their high growth rate makes them an attractive market position but their weak market share means their cash generation is low.

The weaknesses of the BCG model include its relative simplicity; business growth rate is not a sufficient description to describe industry attractiveness and business growth rate and relative market share are not the only factors determining the standing of a business in its portfolio.

Strategy formulation and implementation

ACTIVITY 4.9

Explain whether your organisation is a 'star', 'cash cow', 'dog' or 'question mark'. Justify your response.

The nine-cell General Electric (GE) matrix

The GE matrix relates a firm's competitive position on the horizontal axis (whether 'strong', 'average' or 'weak') to the industry's attractiveness on the vertical axis (whether 'low', 'medium' or 'high'). Measurement of a firm's competitive position includes indicators such as market share, competitive ability, knowledge of customers, understanding of markets, technological capability, and calibre of management. Industry attractiveness, in turn, is a function of a number of factors, including market growth rate, market size, profitability, market structure, competitive rivalry, seasonality, economies of scale, technological requirements, capital requirements, and social, legal and contextual issues. Unlike the BCG model, the GE matrix takes into account a wider range of strategic variables and it allows for intermediate rankings between 'high' and 'low', and between 'strong' and 'weak'.

Horizontal strategy

Porter (1998, pp318–19) describes horizontal strategy as 'a co-ordinated set of goals and policies across distinct but interrelated units', which he regards as 'the essence of corporate strategy'. In his view, without horizontal strategy, 'there is no convincing rationale for the existence of a diversified firm because it is little more than a mutual fund.' The main analytical steps in this approach are:

- identifying all interrelationships deriving from opportunities to share activities among related businesses

- tracing such interrelationships outside the boundaries of the firm

- identifying possible interrelationships involving the transfer of managers' knowledge between businesses

- identifying competitor interrelationships

- assessing the importance of interrelationships to competitive advantage

- developing a co-ordinated strategy to achieve and enhance the most important interrelationships

- creating horizontal organisational mechanisms to ensure implementation.

SWOT analyses

These focus on strategy-related strengths, weaknesses, opportunities and threats, as illustrated in Figures 4.4 and 4.5. SWOT analyses provide a useful way of screening strategic options, where options maximising 'strengths' or 'opportunities' are preferable to those that are not.

Figure 4.4 Example of a SWOT analysis for an organisation in the market sector

INTERNAL	
Strengths	**Weaknesses**
Market position	Management skills
Economies of scale	Lack of key skills/competencies
Cost advantages	Weak image in the market
Financial resources	Lack of strategic direction
Staff skills and competencies	Competitive disadvantage

EXTERNAL	
Opportunities	**Threats**
Potential new markets and products	Possible new competitors
Reputation	Potential substitute products
Vertical integration	Low market growth
Demographic changes	Government policies
Competitor complacency	Power of customers

Figure 4.5 Example of a SWOT analysis for an NHS hospital trust

INTERNAL	
Strengths	**Weaknesses**
Expertise of professional staff	Management skills
Range of medical provision	Lack of key skills/competencies
Up-to-date technology	Low 'star rating'
Financial resources	Lack of strategic direction
Good facilities and estate	Lack of resources

EXTERNAL	
Opportunities	**Threats**
Additional government funding possibilities	Possible new competitors
Potential new services	Demographic changes
Developing new partnerships locally	Loss of key staff
Private financial initiatives	Changing government policies
Generating new revenue sources	Power of patients

ACTIVITY 4.10

Undertake a business portfolio analysis of your organisation using the Boston Consultancy Group growth share matrix. Do a similar exercise using the nine-cell General Electric matrix. What do these indicate about selecting a business strategy for your organisation?

IMPLEMENTING STRATEGY

The budget is the common method used for strategic implementation and incorporates the communication of attainable goals and targets, whilst engaging the participation and support of all levels of management in the process. Budgeting is central to the planning and control process, because it converts all elements of organisational plans into financial numbers. The overall budget includes a number of elements, such as sales, production/operations and administration, each of which is broken down into smaller segments, although there are some problems in budgets:

- They are dependent upon predictions about future performance and a range of assumptions which are subject to error, so budgets are not exact tools.

- They can facilitate modification of plans and strategies in the light of the latest information.

- They are often misused, particularly during evaluation of the actual outcomes compared with the planned ones.

- They involve the use of resources, as with any management information system.

- They result in the production of elaborate reports that are not always easy to understand.

The function of budgeting in converting strategy into action plans has three main elements:

- **Planning:** this is not simply an estimate based on past performance. The budget is designed to articulate in greater detail the agreed strategic direction of the organisation. This includes preparing a projected income statement and balance sheet to ensure that the aggregate detailed action plans meet predetermined criteria such as return on investment and profit levels.

- **Co-ordination:** this requires dovetailing individual elements of the budget to ensure internal consistency. Co-ordination of budgets determines the iterative nature of the budgetary process.

- **Control:** this requires an effective communication system, including both formal and informal methods. Formal measures include written policy statements, procedural manuals, job descriptions and meetings. Informal measures include informal gatherings and interpersonal communications. Control is important because management control is the process guiding organisations to their objectives.

To implement strategy, organisations need to be committed to achieving the goals that have been stated by those responsible for the organisation. This requires employee motivation. Motivation can be best achieved by positive means such as higher pay, promotion and intrinsic reward. Once the budget is recognised to be an element that helps to motivate people, attention needs to be paid to individual needs, group needs and enterprise values. When these elements are incorporated in the overall planning and control process, the resulting budget is likely to fulfil its function as an aid to employee motivation.

Alexander (1985) identifies five main features for successful strategy implementation based on the assumption that successful implementation is intended to prevent problems occurring. This is followed by quick action to resolve any problems that occur. Successful implementation involves doing things that help promote success rather than just preventing problems. Alexander's features are:

- **Communicating**: clear communication on strategic decisions to all employees is required. Communication is two-way, permitting questions about formulated strategy, issues to be considered and potential problems to be raised.

- **Starting with a good idea**: this must be fundamentally sound, since nothing can rescue a poorly formulated strategic decision.

- **Gaining employee commitment and involvement**: this suggests that managers and employees should be involved right from the start in the formulation process. Where people are involved in the implementation process, commitment typically follows.

- **Providing sufficient resources**: these include money, time, technical expertise and people.

- **Developing an implementation plan**: likely problems and their contingent responses need to be addressed, and the plan needs to strike a balance between too much detail and too little.

INTERNAL CONSTRAINTS ON STRATEGY

Determining an organisation's current position and the way forward to the future also involves consideration of its internal resources. Unless these resources are adequate to the task, they act as internal constraints on developing an effective strategy. An internal analysis of these resources and appraising their utilisation involves, first, developing a profile of the organisation's principal skills and resources. Second, this resource profile has to be compared with the product and market requirements, so as to identify strengths and weaknesses. Third, the strengths and weaknesses need to be compared with those of major competitors to identify where competitive advantage exists.

Internal appraisal requires a review of the main functional areas of the organisation – human resources, finance, marketing, operations, and research and development – in terms of their added value to the business. The aim of assessing these functional areas is to determine their effects on the organisation's strategy and address any internal constraints on it.

HUMAN RESOURCES

The importance of analysing the HR of an organisation should not be understated, although it is problematic to form balanced judgements. Some of the key issues to be considered include:

- the relationship between individuals and the organisation
- the impact of informal groups and whether they are supportive of the formal organisation
- management sensitivity to human resources issues
- morale in the organisation and the 'health' of the organisational climate
- the qualifications and expertise of staff, given the present and projected activities of the organisation
- the organisation's policy in terms of recruitment, selection, placement, rewards, employee relations and training
- the organisation's relationship with trade unions (if they are recognised)
- the organisation's position in relation to its competitors regarding pay, promotion, fringe benefits and so on
- the extent to which HR is considered strategically within the organisation and its role in formulating and implementing strategic decisions.

FINANCE

A financial analysis is important to strategy because it evaluates the financial resources of the organisation and how well they are being utilised. Financial indicators also provide important pointers concerning the way that the organisation is managed and the systems used in the management process. This information is crucial in assessing the appropriateness of past, present and future strategies. Some of the main issues to be considered include:

- the financial results and financial status of the organisation
- links between financial budgets and overall strategic and operating plans
- consistency between divisional budgets and overall budgets
- the process of budget preparation and whether management across the organisation participates in this process
- utilisation of forecast profit and loss statements, balance sheets and cash flow projections
- the information provided for management control
- the attitude of managers to planning and control reports
- whether such documents are utilised as motivational elements in the organisation

- utilisation by management of control reports for evaluating performance and formulation of strategy; in particular whether the reports compare actual results with budgets or standards and whether corrective action is taken.

MARKETING

The marketing function encompasses market research, sales forecasting and promotions activity, and represents a vital communication link between the organisation (whether 'for-profit' or 'not-for-profit') and the outside world. Marketing does this by considering changes in the economic, technological, social and other external contexts and bringing such knowledge into the organisation, as well as making information about the organisation available to customers and potential customers. Two important internal relationships are between marketing and operations, and between marketing and research and development. The way in which marketing relates to and communicates with these two functions is vital, since this provides the information required by marketing staff for the strategic decisions they take.

The main issues to be considered include:

- the use made of market research and the extent to which it influences product or service development

- the relative position of each 'product group' in terms of sales and contribution to profits or organisational objectives

- the market share of each product group and its stage in the product life cycle

- the distribution channels used and the extent to which new distribution development indicates need for change

- the relationship between sales price and sales volumes

- the pricing policy pursued by the organisation

- the organisation's competitive features such as quality, price, service and delivery, as well as the extent to which such features are appropriate to the industry or sector

- the extent to which the marketing function is aware of competitor moves, technological change and external contextual aspects relevant to the organisation.

OPERATIONS

The operations function within an organisation, whether in manufacturing, service or public organisations, has responsibility for more physical, financial and human resources than any other function. The links between operations and research and development are fundamental to the successful development of products in terms of cost, quality and effectiveness. The main issues include:

- production planning and control and their interface with marketing and production

- information received from sales and marketing, accounting and quality control, with particular reference to its usefulness in managing the operations function

- production costs and their movement in relation to sales prices and identification of the causes of cost changes

- use of performance standards and the exercise of cost control

- control over key cost elements such as labour, materials and packaging

- stock levels in relation to output and sales and the relationship between levels of raw material stocks, work in progress and finished goods

- plant and equipment, their adequacy, age, state of repair and level of investment in relation to industry/sector norms

- the extent of computerisation of production facilities and the organisation's policy on replacement

- communications between all aspects of the operations function and other areas of the organisation

- the organisation of the function including purchasing and materials management

- the reputation of the organisation as a producer, coupled with the requirements of the industry and contextual conditions.

RESEARCH AND DEVELOPMENT

Research and development (R&D) is aimed at improving products, introducing new ones or enhancing the production process. For non-manufacturing organisations, R&D is unlikely to be of great importance. But for manufacturing, R&D is crucial to survival and future success. The effectiveness of the R&D function is dependent upon the past record of R&D in product and process innovation and upon future expectations for R&D-driven innovations. The main issues to be considered include:

- sector expenditure on R&D and the organisation's commitment to it

- the nature of the organisation's products and whether they require continual development

- whether the market requires such development

- the nature of the production process and whether it requires enhancement

- the return to the organisation for a product breakthrough

- the resources that the organisation can devote to R&D, analysed between projects and products

- the record of the organisation in terms of new or improved products and the present state of likely innovations for future exploitation

- the way in which R&D is organised, in particular its links with marketing and operations

- links between the organisation and other R&D organisations such as universities and hospitals
- whether the organisation has R&D joint ventures with other bodies.

EXTERNAL CONSTRAINTS ON STRATEGY AND SHAPING THE EXTERNAL CONTEXT

Porter (1998) identifies the immediate contexts in which business organisations operate. His study provides a framework for examining the industry or sector relevant to particular firms. It is these 'competitive forces' that are potential constraints on the success of each firm or organisation operating in a competitive market, and of its strategic responses to contextual changes. But they also provide potential opportunities for developing appropriate strategic responses to contextual change. Such forces affect all firms in a sector and each firm tries to respond to these forces by 'shaping' the external context.

Porter's five basic competitive forces – threat of new entrants, rivalry among existing firms, threat of substitutes, the bargaining power of buyers and the bargaining power of suppliers – determine the state of competition and its underlying structure. Firms have to identify the key structural features of their sector, so that the strength of the five competitive forces, and hence industry profitability, can be determined. The essence of such an analysis is to identify the sources of each force to enable the firm to develop a strategy that builds on the 'opportunities' provided and avoids the 'threats'. An important feature of Porter's model is recognition that competition in an industry goes beyond immediately competing firms. All five forces determine the intensity of competition and profitability; identifying the strongest force (or forces) is critical in effective strategy formulation.

The five forces influencing competition in an industry are explored in Chapter 6. Basically however, after a firm has identified how these forces are affecting it, it can consider its own position in relation to the underlying *causes* of each competitive force. Porter argues that an effective strategy has to be designed to establish a defendable position vis-à-vis the five competitive forces. There are three possible approaches:

- Positioning the organisation so that it has the best defence against these competitive forces (ie matching the organisation's strengths and weaknesses to the given industrial structure).
- Influencing the balance of forces by altering their causes in order to improve

the organisation's relative position. This requires structural analysis to identify key factors and assess where action influencing the balance yields the best pay-off.

- Forecasting changes in the factors underlying the five forces and responding to them, thus exploiting change by selecting an appropriate strategy before the organisation's competitors recognise the change.

Having analysed the nature of the external contest and an industry's structural features, business leaders can then identify the environmental/contextual issues most likely to have an impact on their organisation. This provides focus in strategy formulation. Two issues need to be addressed by top management in looking at possible opportunities and threats in the external contexts.

First, consideration needs to be given to the extent to which the strategy matches or fails to match the external context; an organisation's context may have changed but not its strategy. Alternatively, the structure of an organisation may not be suited to the conditions prevailing in the external context and different structures may be needed. In order to determine whether the change is permanent or just short term, as well as the speed and extent of the change, management has to assess those changes in the external context in relation to the nature of the organisation and its business. For example, change in the wider external context may significantly affect the structure of an industry. On the other hand, the balance in competitive forces may have altered because barriers to entry may have been reduced by technological innovation. Examining the external context and its constraints on an organisation is an important part of any systematic approach to strategy-making.

Second, consideration needs to be given to the strengths of the organisation relative to the contextual changes it faces. These strengths depend on a variety of factors, such as an organisation's record of product/service innovations that involve changes in working practices, new organisational structures, entry into new markets and so on. This could indicate that the organisation is well placed to deal with and respond to change effectively. Its key strength may be not product/ service development but its flexibility in response to change (Porter 2004).

In managing change in organisations in response to internal and external constraints on strategy, business leaders have five main strategies from which to choose:

- **Participative strategies:** these are particularly effective where management needs the active co-operation of staff, but participation can be regarded sceptically if it is used manipulatively.

- **Power strategies:** these are appropriate where change must be introduced rapidly and where commitment of those affected is not necessary for successful implementation.

- **Manipulation strategies:** this involves conscious restructuring of events so that others behave in the way that the manipulator wants. The manipulator can either restructure the situation or alter the subjects' perception of the existing situation.

- **Negotiation strategies:** this is useful where there are likely losers resulting from change and where losers can disrupt the implementation of change.

- **Contingency strategies:** this approach suggests that all relevant factors in the situation should be considered before selecting the appropriate change strategy.

CONCLUSION: STRATEGY, HR STRATEGY AND HR SOLUTIONS

Organisations now operate in a period of economic globalisation, open markets, hyper-competition, and public management reforms. Developing appropriate strategies to protect or expand an organisation's markets and client base in these circumstances is of central concern to business leaders. This chapter has attempted to outline the complexity of this process and to indicate some of the different approaches used for doing this. How strategy is converted into practice and how links are made between corporate and functional strategies (including HR strategy) in each case is contingent to the specific organisation concerned.

The search for an 'ideal' framework for analysing and determining strategy is both an ongoing and a challenging one. In making strategic choices, the following factors are generally apposite. Choices have to be made by generating options that are likely to achieve an organisation's goals and objectives, costing them and choosing the best or optimum solution. There are a variety of ways in which strategic options are determined within the strategic process, with strategic choice decisions being made at corporate and business unit levels. Two main ways are:

- **Resource-based strategic options:** these look for sources of added value in organisations and make use of core competencies within them. They utilise the concept of the 'value chain' (or supply chain) to link the value of the activities of an organisation with its functional parts and to assess the contribution each makes to the added value of the business and to the 'value' perceived by its customers. Such options examine the range of capabilities present in organisations, such as people, finance, patents, IT and core competencies. All are important in developing strategic options, because they deliver sustainable competitive advantage to firms.

- **Market-based options:** these arise from market opportunities and market constraints. They build on analyses of customers and the competition. Generic, industry-based strategies are a means of generating basic strategy options in the marketplace and are concerned with seeking competitive advantage for the firm.

Porter (1998) identifies three generic strategies that explain sources of competitive advantage and the competitive scope of targeted customers:

- **Low-cost leadership:** this aims to place the organisation among the lowest-cost producers in the market.

- **Differentiation:** this occurs when the products of an organisation meet the needs of some customers in the marketplace better than other producers. The concept underlying it is 'market segmentation' or identifying specific groups who respond differently from other groups to competitive strategies.

- **Focus (or a niche strategy)**: this involves targeting a small segment of the market, because particular groups of customers are likely to pay more for a differentiated product when it is targeted towards them.

Building appropriate organisational designs and structures is an important response to strategic implementation if organisations are to deliver their missions and objectives effectively. Where innovation is important, non-traditional structures have been noted. Kanter (1984) has examined the structures and processes most conducive to innovation. The sorts of criteria to be taken into account in developing appropriate organisational structures include: simplicity, least-cost solutions, motivating staff and adopting a pertinent culture. Change and complexity indicate the necessity for flexible, decentralised structures; standardisation and mass production require more centralised structures. Some writers assert that a strategic approach to managing people is largely, if not wholly, associated with the emergence of HRM (Guest 1987, Keenoy 1990), which assumes that no distinctive human resources strategies existed prior to HRM. It has been claimed that business strategies merely define the nature of competition in the marketplace, leaving the HR contribution to be secured pragmatically. Thomason (1991) rebuts this view by arguing that historically the acquisition and utilisation of human resources in organisations have been approached in a number of different ways at different times.

This point is repeated by Boxall and Purcell (2008), who argue that improving the process of strategic management has a lot to do with HRM, since making strategy decisions involves making key HR decisions. These include appointing, developing and promoting key individuals and engaging in astute teambuilding activities, within the senior management team and outside it. They identify some key links between business strategy and HR strategy; an issue that is explored more fully in Chapter 5.

KEY LEARNING POINTS

1. With organisations operating in unstable external contexts, those leading them use strategic management techniques in response to uncertainty and market competition. There are various definitions of strategy but effective strategies have four main elements: goals to be achieved, cohesion, taking account of the unpredictable, and hierarchic levels. Mintzberg provides five interpretations of strategy: as plan, as ploy, as a pattern, as position, and as perspective.

2. The deterministic view of strategy is rationalist and prescriptive and assesses where an organisation is, how it has got there, and how it can achieve its objectives. The rational planning approach adopts a 'scientific' methodology, underpinned by processes that are the outcome of objective analyses, rooted in logical methods of managing strategy. This process includes: analysing the external environment; analysing resources and identifying vision, mission and objectives; developing strategic options; choosing among these options; and implementing and evaluating the chosen strategy.

3. Another view of strategy is that it can be 'shaped', without predetermined objectives, and that it 'emerges' in response to changing organisational needs.

The emergent approach is where final objectives are unclear and its elements are developed as strategy proceeds. Its key principle is that it does not have a single, definitive objective but develops over time. Emergent strategy also provides flexibility in response to fast-moving, unpredicted external changes.

4. Logical incrementalism, as analysed by Quinn, derives out of the emergent approach. Here strategic management is seen not as a formal planning process but as a series of subprocesses by which strategies develop. These draw upon the experiences of managers and their sensitivity to changes in their external contexts. It is 'logical' because it is based on reason; it is 'incremental' because it is structured on a piecemeal basis. For Mintzberg, strategy is 'crafted', with a personal touch and mastery of detail, requiring a sense of the future, present and past.

5. A task for strategists in determining strategic direction is assessing the external contextual forces acting upon their organisations. These forces include socio-cultural, technological, economic, environmental, political, legal and ethical contexts. Organisations failing to acknowledge these external-contextual forces in decision-making are likely to fail.

6. Environmental analysis scans the environment, monitors specific environmental trends, forecasts the future direction of environmental changes, and assesses current and future environmental changes and their organisational implications. It takes account of the socio-cultural, technological, economic, environmental, political, legal and ethical contexts outlined above.

7. The techniques of environmental analysis include Delphi forecasting, cross-impact matrices and scenarios. They incorporate data-gathering methods and forecasting techniques, using primary and secondary forces. Data may be collected in a variety of ways.

8. The main stages in strategy-making are strategy formulation and strategy implementation. Formulating strategy includes setting strategic objectives covering corporate level, business level, and operational level. The techniques for doing this include the BCG growth share matrix, the nine-cell General Electric matrix, horizontal strategy (or a co-ordinated set of goals and policies across distinct but interrelated units), and SWOT analyses. Strategy implementation is the main means through which strategic objectives and policies are translated into specific, measurable, attainable goals and plans.

9. The major internal constraints on implementing and delivering strategy are the organisation's resources, as well as appraising their utilisation. The main resources are HR, finance, marketing, operations, and research and development. Weaknesses here are likely to weaken an organisation's strategy implementation.

10. Porter provides an analytical framework for examining the industry or sector relevant to particular firms. It is the 'competitive forces' that are external constraints on the success of each firm and its strategic responses to external contextual change. These forces provide opportunities for developing appropriate responses to such change. Porter's five competitive forces are: threat of new entrants, rivalry amongst existing firms, threat of substitutes, the bargaining power of buyers and the bargaining power of suppliers.

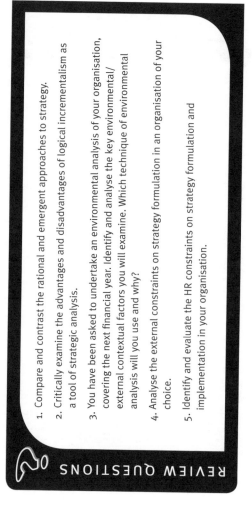

1. Compare and contrast the rational and emergent approaches to strategy.

2. Critically examine the advantages and disadvantages of logical incrementalism as a tool of strategic analysis.

3. You have been asked to undertake an environmental analysis of your organisation, covering the next financial year. Identify and analyse the key environmental/external contextual factors you will examine. Which technique of environmental analysis will you use and why?

4. Analyse the external constraints on strategy formulation in an organisation of your choice.

5. Identify and evaluate the HR constraints on strategy formulation and implementation in your organisation.

CASE STUDY 4.1 DEVELOPING STRATEGY IN A LEISURE INDUSTRY ORGANISATION

Background

NiceHols PLC is a leading self-catering holiday operator, formerly family owned but now owned and controlled by a well-known venture capital group. It has a wide variety of holiday accommodation throughout the UK, with an annual turnover of more than £100 million. The company provides self-catering apartments, cottages and houses, boating and boathouse canal facilities, accommodation in lodges and parks, a small selection of overseas villas, and sporting and leisure resources for its wide range of customers. Like many leisure organisations, NiceHols faces some very hard competitive pressures at present, both nationally and internationally.

The company employs some 500 employees, 250 of whom work within the company's call centre. The company has a relatively small head office establishment of some 30 staff. These are separated into five divisions, headed by a new chief executive. These are the operating, marketing, finance, business development and central services divisions; the latter includes a small HR department. Apart from call centre teams, who are centrally organised, all other operational and support staff are employed locally. These include office administrators, maintenance staff, cleaners, gardeners and local services facilitators. Staff turnover is low, as many company workplaces are within areas and locations where there are higher than average levels of unemployment. In general, the company's HR policies are reactive rather than proactive and it provides few training and development opportunities for its staff at all levels. 'Muddling through' summarises its business philosophy until recently.

The new chief executive is very concerned about the company's ad hoc approach to strategy formulation and implementation, as well as its reactive and unstructured approach to HR issues. She has therefore asked NiceHols to undertake robust SWOT and STEEPLE analyses to find a way forward for the organisation. She wants these 'soft' data to provide some reliable information for developing appropriate, planned responses to the company's challenging market situation. She is also aware that the contexts affecting the company's business plans and activities need critically examining, and she wants a discernible, strategic way forward for the company to ensure profitability and satisfactory customer service. Now completed, the SWOT and STEEPLE data are outlined below.

NiceHols' SWOT analysis

The results of this are summarised as follows.

INTERNAL	
Strengths	**Weaknesses**
Market leader in UK self-catering	Saturated market in the UK
Variety and diverse range of holiday products	Old-fashioned corporate image
Investor backing with high purchasing power	Perception that the company only provides boating holidays
Recent investment in latest technology	Traditionally older customer base.
Strong brand name and reputation	Difficulty of recruiting new staff in sector
Long-serving staff with vast experience and extensive knowledge of products	More government regulation

EXTERNAL	
Opportunities	**Threats**
Massive potential overseas market	Decline in high street travel agent sales
Internet advertising, booking and marketing	Shorter holiday breaks
Low-cost airlines for European products	Competitors selling own products through the Internet
Quality leisure products demanded by customers	Volume of competition entering the market

NiceHols' STEEPLE analysis

This has highlighted the following contexts, within which the company is currently operating.

Field	Factors
Socio-cultural	More holiday breaks, increase in short breaks; people want holidays with ethical companies; increasingly sophisticated holidaymakers with more specific expectations and demands; increasing level of independence when researching and booking holidays
Technological	Owners marketing own holidays online; increased ease of access to the Internet, making shopping around easier; text messaging; new methods of information gathering; no need for travel agents and brochures
Economic	Slower economic growth; economic and market uncertainty, resulting in late bookings and fewer multiple bookings; fuel tax; airline tax; road tax; rising fuel prices; limits on credit
Environmental	Natural disasters; global warning; environmental costs of flights; general increase in environmental awareness and pressure to 'go green'; increased pollution due to air flights; need to exploit greener modes of transport
Political	Political instability overseas; threats of terrorism; effect of government policies on leisure sector
Legal	Legal intervention on travel; duties on goods and services; EU regulation; planning restrictions; trading standards guidelines; advertising standards
Ethical	Balancing stakeholder interests; promoting employee welfare; human rights; corporate social responsibility

Tasks

1. Explain how the company might respond to the strengths, weaknesses, opportunities and threats facing it, as outlined above, in the short to medium term.

2. Given the external factors impacting on NiceHols' business opportunities, show how the firm might respond to the STEEPLE analysis, given its current market situation.

3. Using a rational methodology, outline a *corporate level* business strategy for NiceHols, taking account of the SWOT and STEEPLE analyses provided above.

4. Identify any HR issues that will need to be addressed by the company in developing an integrated HR strategy for NiceHols.

5. What areas might be included in an HR strategy for NiceHols and why?

BOXALL, P., PURCELL, J. and WRIGHT, P. (eds) (2007) *Oxford handbook of human resource management*. Oxford: Oxford University Press.

Covers a wide range of topics in HR, HR strategy and links with business strategy; provides keen insights into the contribution of HR to business performance and organisational effectiveness.

FRIEDMAN, A. and MILES, S. (2006) *Stakeholders: theory and practice*. Oxford: Oxford University Press.

Includes a discussion of the concept of the stakeholder in fields such as management, corporate governance, accounting and finance, strategy, politics and in public policy debate, with practical examples of a range of stakeholders.

JOHNSON, G., SCHOLES, K. and WHITTINGTON, R. (2008) *Exploring corporate strategy: texts and cases*. Harlow: Prentice Hall.

Provides a comprehensive insight into the nature of strategy and its basic components, covering four 'lenses' of strategy – design, experience, ideas and discourse – and strategic positioning, strategic choices and strategy in action. The text is supported by a selection of case studies and extended cases.

SALAMAN, G., STOREY, J. and BILLSBERRY, G. (2005), *Strategic human resource management: theory and practice*. London: Open University Press.

Brings together a variety of perspectives on HR strategy, covering strategic human resource management (SHRM) and knowledge, SHRM and business performance, the emergence of new organisational forms and relationships, and SHRM in practice.

Developing corporate strategies

CHAPTER 5

Developing human resource strategies

INTRODUCTION

A distinguishing feature of HRM is its strategic focus, as explained in Chapter 1. With the development of corporate strategy having been examined in the previous chapter, this core chapter focuses on HR strategies, their links with business strategy, and their role in improving organisational performance. It starts with the assumption that the key objective of any HR strategy is to guide the process by which firms recruit and deploy people and develop their capabilities so as to enhance organisational competitiveness. This chapter examines the emergence of HR strategy, its nature, the significance of HR strategies within organisations, how HR strategies are developed and delivered, possible links between HR and organisational strategy, and issues relating to effective strategic leadership. HR strategy is not something new in management practice. Ever since the Industrial Revolution, firms have always had HR strategies, even if they were not explicitly recognised or stated as such. What has changed over this period are the contexts within which organisations, managements and HR specialists operate and how they manage what was formerly called the 'labour problem' (Farnham 2008) and what is now often referred to as the search for talent, investment in human capital or 'next generation HR' (Sears 2010).

LEARNING OUTCOMES

By the end of this chapter, readers should be able to understand, explain and critically evaluate:

- the origins and nature of HR strategy

- the development of HR strategy and the nature of vertical and horizontal integration

- different approaches to HR strategy such as best practice HR, best fit HR and the resource-based view of the firm

- critiques of these approaches

- debates about effective strategic leadership.

In addition, readers should be able to:

- understand how HR strategy is developed in their own organisations
- identify and evaluate strategic HR responses in their own organisations
- advise on the choice of effective HR strategies in line with business goals
- review the effectiveness and limitations of HR strategic interventions.

THE EMERGENCE OF HR STRATEGY

It was assumed in the early management literature that business strategies merely defined the nature of competition in the marketplace, leaving the HR/personnel management contribution to be secured pragmatically. But the emergence of HR strategy was more complex than this. This section outlines the historical development of HR strategy, drawing upon Anglo-American literature, showing that HR strategy, even if it was not defined as such, has been a continuous thread running through the evolution of personnel management and HRM as a management function in the UK and North America. Underpinning HR strategy is the key objective of guiding the process by which firms develop and deploy people, relationships, and capabilities to enhance competitiveness (Snell *et al* 2001).

BUSINESS STRATEGY AND HR STRATEGY

Thomason (1991) was one of the first to rebut the view that historically business strategies merely defined the nature of competition in the marketplace. He argues that the acquisition and utilisation of human resources in organisations have been approached in different ways at different times. He concludes that at each stage in the history of HRM some relationship exists between business strategy and HR responses to external labour market conditions, even if the HR strategy is, or was, not always fully integrated with business strategy. He is not arguing that the surrounding market conditions solely determine the approach adopted but that they impose limits on available options, as well as predisposing enterprises to adopt one particular approach in preference to others.

All organisations need business strategies to survive in the competitive marketplace. Private firms are likely to express their business strategies in terms of how they can compete with their competitors. Public services do this in terms of how they can secure their revenues in the face of competing calls on the public purse. In any organisation, strategic responses in the marketplace have to take account of both the opportunities and threats offered by its product/service markets and the strengths and weaknesses of its own combination of resources, and not just the one. One set of decisions relating to opportunities and threats in product or service markets indicates that firms tend to select one of four main types of business strategy. Building on Porter's (1998) classification of generic strategies for gaining competitive advantage, Thomason identifies four possible choices for businesses to adopt.

- **Low-cost leadership**: this aims to supply mass production goods or services more cheaply than one's competitors.

- **Differentiation**: this emphasises a superior product or service commanding a premium price in the market.

- **Focus**: this relies upon *either* differentiation *or* low-cost leadership to supply a product or service to a niche market.

- **Asset parsimony**: this depends on high entry costs to a sector as protection against competitors, or flexible use of limited assets to generate high-output performance.

A second set of decisions for management takes account of whether the suppliers of the organisation's resources are capable of meeting the market's demands. This determines whether the preferred competitive strategy is facilitated or frustrated by availability of the resources needed. As Porter (1998) argues, competitive advantage depends not only on conditions in product or service markets but also on the availability of factors of production.

Thomason identifies at least three historical shifts in business strategy since the Industrial Revolution. Currently, businesses can be found following any one of these strategies. However, the strategy of asset parsimony is losing ground as a source of competitive advantage, largely because the cheapness of modern technologies allows freer entry by competitor firms into many markets.

- **Period 1**: this is associated with the onset of the Industrial Revolution, where the typical business strategy was one of differentiation or producing premium price products.

- **Period 2**: this is associated with industrial rationalisation, starting in the late nineteenth century, where the typical business strategy was low-cost leadership.

- **Period 3**: this is associated with 'new wave rationalisations' from the 1960s, where the typical business strategy was 'focus', or supplying niche products, with competitive advantage being secured by concentrating on customer needs and emphasising quality, reliability, delivery and teamwork.

As indicated in Figure 5.1, there are a number of components of business and HR strategies and their relationship to labour acquisition and utilisation. Figure 5.1 shows that the approaches to labour acquisition adopted by typical enterprises have varied, depending on what the business strategy requires of its workforce or on labour force capacity in the labour market. The differentiation strategy was dependent upon the availability of a core workforce of skilled labour, which, in industrialising Britain, was satisfied by its apprenticeship system and a flow of workers from the countryside to towns and cities. The low-cost strategy in the

Figure 5.1 The components of business and HR strategies

	Period 1 **Industrial revolution**	Period 2 **Mass production**	Period 3 **Niche production**
Main business strategy	Differentiation	Low cost leadership	Focus
Labour acquisition	External	External	Internal
Labour utilisation	Workshops/factories	Fragmented and reorganised	Flexible, multi-tasked
Emphasis	Labour acquisition	Labour utilisation	Learning and provision of learning opportunities *or* developing personality traits and ability to handle change
HR strategy	Selection	Supervision	Development *or* partnership
Purpose of HR strategy	Labour control	Labour control	Employee flexibility (based on low cost leadership) *or* employee commitment (based on differentiation)
Type of HR strategy	Pre-personnel management	Traditional personnel management	HRD or HRM

Adapted from Thomason (1991)

period of mass production needed a workforce capable of doing short-cycle tasks for relatively low wages. Recruiting workers from the external labour market and subjecting them to close supervision and linking their pay to output secured this.

When enterprises developed new customer relationships in the face of global competition in the late twentieth century, the strategic remedy lay in developing internal labour markets, because most skills were job-specific and non-transferable between firms and industries. Firms needed to train and develop their employees to assure the future supply of labour, and retain them until they had recouped their investment from the flexible performance of employees.

In terms of labour utilisation:

- Work during the first period was organised by putting it in workshops and factories, which imposed a new discipline on the workforce.

- In the second period, work was fragmented and reorganised to make jobs capable of being done by relatively unskilled, untrained employees.

- In the third period, work is characterised by being flexible, versatile and multiskilled, with workers being expected to achieve quality, reliability and commitment.

This analysis suggests that labour acquisition and utilisation vary with business strategy and the capacity of the external labour market to supply the necessary labour or human resources firms want. In the first historical period, labour acquisition of the core workforce was paramount. In the second period, labour acquisition was important but the emphasis switched to labour utilisation. In the latest, third period, two distinct developments associated with the creation of internal labour markets are discernible. In one case, the criteria to be satisfied in labour acquisition are related to trainability, with provision of learning opportunities becoming a salient feature of labour utilisation. In the other case, the criteria are extended to embrace broader personality traits related to capacity for handling change and personal learning opportunities generated by the creation of 'learning organisations' and ability to solve problems.

Thomason concludes that different HR strategies were necessary for different circumstances and serve different business strategies. These are summarised in Figure 5.2 and indicate four possible types of HR strategy to match the business demands of firms:

- **Pre-personnel management**: this still exists in parts of the small-firm sector and depends on the ability of firms to recruit skilled labour in external labour markets in response to business needs. A selection strategy is used as the main mechanism for labour control.

- **Traditional personnel management**: with mass production, firms depend on their ability to draw on the external labour market to supply the workers they need. A supervision strategy for labour control is adopted, where company rules are policed in order to secure targeted levels of performance.

- **A development strategy for employee flexibility**: in modern niche markets,

Figure 5.2 **Strategies for controlling the labour process: a summary**

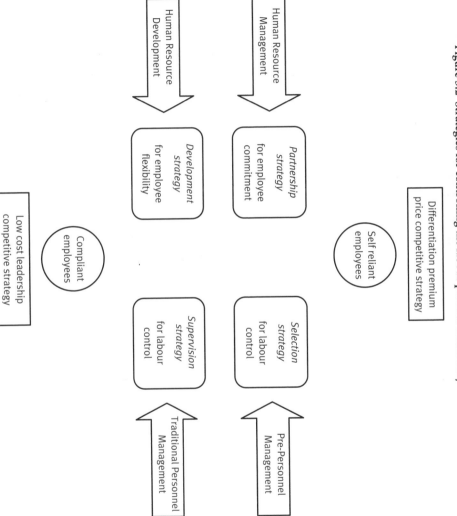

Adapted from Thomason (1991)

and where the business relies on low-cost leadership, labour supply is obtained by developing internal labour markets, using appropriate training and development strategies.

- **A partnership strategy for employee commitment**: in cases where business strategy relies on differentiation, labour supply is obtained by using a partnership strategy aimed at employee commitment. This requires problem-solving and creative skills in the workforce.

ACTIVITY 5.1

Drawing upon Thomason's analysis, identify and discuss the HR strategy adopted by your organisation in pursuing competitive advantage in the marketplace.

THE EVOLUTION OF HR STRATEGY

In the early development of HR strategy from the Industrial Revolution onwards, managing HR was seen as the most costly and uncontrollable activity of the firm. Morris and Snell (2009) identify three evolutionary stages in the development of HR strategy.

THE PERSON–JOB FIT STAGE

The first stage in the evolution of HR strategy, which Morris and Snell call the 'person–job fit' stage, began with the Industrial Revolution, continuing throughout the nineteenth century and most of the twentieth century. This first stage went through a number of subphases but it was largely concerned with the strategic goal of making sure that people 'fitted' their jobs. As a model of employment, it was oriented towards employment stability, efficiency and productivity through job specialisation and standardisation of work. As firms adjusted to the Industrial Revolution and mass production, the focus of HR strategy was an administrative role. Its prevailing logic focused on job analysis to make sure that the person's knowledge and skills directly matched the job requirements. If the firm was to achieve its business strategy of making profits for shareholders and holding its market position, workers were seen as commodities and labour as a cost that required minimising. This model of HR strategy continued for almost 200 years but had to adapt with the growth of free markets and greater global competition in the last two decades of the twentieth century.

THE SYSTEMIC FIT STAGE

The second stage in the evolution of HR strategy is described by Morris and Snell (2009) as one of 'systemic fit'. Driven by a shift in the external contexts arising out of increased global trade and market competition in the last decades of the twentieth century, firms developed internal diversification strategies and aspects of TQM. The concept of 'HR strategy' was first conceived in the United States and was identified as the pattern of planned HR deployments and activities adding value to the business (Wright and McMahon 1992). Baird and Meshoulam (1988) noted two key activities in HR deployment activities: 'internal' and 'external fit'. Internal or horizontal fit is how the components of HR support and complement each other. For example, firms need to ensure that recruitment and selection, pay and rewards, promotion and training strategies are compatible with one another and integrate horizontally. External or vertical fit is how HR strategies and practices are aligned with the overall strategic direction of the firm. For example, firms operating domestically need to align with local strategies but, as they diversify and internationalise, HR practices have to adapt to the changing demands of operating in different countries, national cultures and institutional contexts.

In examining the adaptive advantages of internal and external fit, researchers in the field identified the focus of HR strategy as strategy implementation, the prevailing logic as integration and the locus of value as organisational knowledge.

The key design parameters varied. One stream demonstrated how 'bundles' of HR practices were more important for understanding strategy than the practices themselves (MacDuffie 1995). Others focused on high-commitment HR (Arthur 1994), high-performance work systems (Huselid 1995), human capital enhancing systems (Youndt et al 1996) and the 'transformed workplace' (Kochan et al 1986). This shift in emphasis made HR practices more strategic in a globally complex marketplace, where, in large firms and MNCs at least, it was the overarching relationships that firms established with their employees which dominated the HR agenda.

Another stream of research examined how firms developed different business strategies depending on the sector and contexts in which they operated. Miles and Snow (1984), for example, adopted a contingency approach, showing a typology of competitive strategies and matching these strategies with specific HR strategies. There were also debates about 'best practice' HR and 'best fit' HR (Boxall and Purcell 2000). A proliferation of other strategic frameworks was also produced during this time. Emerging out of these debates was recognition of the importance of matching or aligning the internal activities of the firm, including HRM, with its external contexts. This meant that HR specialists needed to know not only how HR strategy could be aligned with or implement the firm's strategic purposes but also how the business was run, giving rise to the business partner model of HR.

By the end of the twentieth century, the external context was changing yet again. With continued globalisation, hyper-competition and new ICTs, business could be done online, reducing the need for face-to-face interactions. Driven by the World-Wide Web, knowledge-based competition and differentiated workforces, firms began to turn to creative human capital as a means for achieving competitive advantage. This meant that firms could rely on a much larger pool of talent to respond to the challenges facing them, drawn from around the world. For example, the pools of talent for international sportspeople such as footballers, or international scholars, became globally based and there were significant shifts of footballers, football coaches and academic 'stars' between elite football clubs and elite universities. Moreover, the very concept of the 'firm' was being questioned, as many companies consisted of shifting networks of suppliers, partners, outsourcers and contingent workers that came together when necessary to do so (Lepak and Snell 1999).

THE VALUE CREATION STAGE

These developments gave rise to a third stage in the evolution of HR strategy. Described by Morris and Snell (2009) as a period of 'value creation,' knowledge, skills and abilities were identified as the primary components of a firm's human capital. It is these that are seen increasingly as the most valuable and distinctive resources upon which a company can draw (Barney and Wright 1998). Hyper-competition places a premium on the knowledge-based assets of firms, such as human capital, and social capital relationships. It is these which underlie learning and innovation within businesses, whereas in the past HR strategy focused on the behaviours required by individuals to implement a given strategy. For example, a low-cost business strategy necessitated an HR strategy incorporating efficient behaviours. This meant routine job design, output-based incentives and low levels of training. In an age of value creation, the strategic drivers of HR strategy are innovation and change and outsourcing and alliances. Its prevailing logic is generative and its locus of value is individual knowledge and relationships. Underpinning individual heterogeneity, where a variety of employment relationships and a differentiated working environment typify the firm (Rousseau 1995), HR strategy began to centre on an architectural approach to managing talent. Just as finance or marketing focuses on how to acquire, allocate and make strategic decisions about money or clients, the role of HR evolves to make strategic decisions about talent.

In addition to an architectural approach to managing talent, other key design parameters in a period of value creation include understanding the strategic value of people and relationships, the uniqueness of resources (including human resources) in the firm, knowledge creation, knowledge transfer and integration. Measurement issues include knowledge, relationships, processes, systems and capabilities. The importance of relationships and learning has brought HR strategy firmly into the 'strategy mix', as knowledge within the firm is considered to be the main source of competitive advantage (Grant 1996). This means that it is important to manage pools of talent and relationships between these pools.

In a period when cutting-edge firms are increasingly relying on people to create new knowledge and integrate that knowledge in-house, this has led to a shift towards 'capabilities' rather than practices as the key source of competitive advantage. There are signs too that the fields of strategy and HR strategy are converging. Further, the models that have emerged in recent years are focusing increasingly on the value of human capital, social capital, capabilities and their underlying mechanisms for developing competitive advantage (Morris and Snell 2009).

ACTIVITY 5.2

Which of the person–job fit, systemic fit and value creation generic HR strategies apply to your organisation? Justify your response.

CURRENT APPROACHES AND THE DEVELOPMENT OF HR STRATEGY

The above discussion illustrates how the search for effective HR strategy has adapted to the dynamic contexts and contingencies facing senior managers and organisations over time. HR strategy has moved on from humble beginnings in the days of the Industrial Revolution to be a widely debated topic at board level today. The HR administrative role existing then, when employers sought efficiency and productivity from their workforces, has been superseded in the early twenty-first century by, first, debates about the internal and external 'fit' of HR strategy and practices, and, more recently, the search for talent, managing diversification and strategy formulation. With hyper-competition, the Internet and differentiated workforces, knowledge and knowledge management become the trigger for achieving sustained competitive advantage.

TALENT MANAGEMENT AND WORKFORCE PLANNING

In current debates about effective HR strategy, talent management is increasingly seen as a critical success factor in organisations, as firms strive to compete in the marketplace for both sales and people. Talent consists of those people in organisations that make a difference to organisational performance. In the UK, persistent skills shortages, the changing structure of the population and working population, its widening diversity and the work–life balance agenda mean that there is strong competition for talented individuals capable of making a difference to organisational performance. The ability to attract and retain high-performing, quality individuals is important for organisations. It is now widely recognised that planned strategies for managing these people's talents is crucial in attracting and retaining them. This is supported by processes to develop investment in human capital, retain the commitment of talented individuals and utilise their abilities.

Tansley *et al* (2007, p xii), drawing upon research based on nine case studies and over 100 interviews, conclude that a successful approach to talent management is based on an agreed, organisational definition of talent and talent management. These definitions provide the basis from which both talent strategy and talent management processes can be developed. The main findings of this research were:

- A proactive strategic approach to talent management offers benefits in terms of developing a pool of talent to meet identified needs.

- Support for talent management must flow from those at the top of an organisation and cascade downwards.

- Engaging line managers at an early stage is critical in order to get them committed to talent management and its processes.

- Talent management can be used to enhance an organisation's image and supports employer branding.

- Talent management activities should be joined up with other HR policies and practices.

- Developing talent is based on both formal and informal methods.

- Processes are needed to track the performance and progress of those identified as talented individuals.

- HR specialists have an important role to play in providing support and guidance in designing and developing approaches to talent management to fit the needs of the organisation.

It has also been noted that in a knowledge-based economy, where dependence of firms on talent is increasing, not having the right people at the right time in the right place presents risks to business success. Howes (2009) argues that this source of risk needs addressing, calling it 'human capital risk'. He claims that risk managers need to develop a comprehensive perspective of 'human capital risk' and he describes the way to address this issue as 'workforce planning'. His argument is two-fold. First, risk management is failing to monitor and manage human capital risk and a stronger understanding of risk associated with workforce capacity and capability is required. This is to manage enterprise risk. Second, HR and risk management professionals need to work together to develop joint strategies for managing human capital risk. This means increasing the awareness of human capital risk within organisations, by implementing workforce planning. The latter includes demand forecasting, supply forecasting and analysing the gap between demand and supply for each scenario.

ACTIVITY 5.3

Who makes talent management happen and how is talent management justified in strategic terms?

VERTICAL AND HORIZONTAL INTEGRATION

Vertical and horizontal integration are key concepts in the development and implementation of HR strategy and are explored in more detail in the following sections. Marchington and Wilkinson (2008, p28) argue that integration is at the heart of HRM and HR strategy. Integration takes two forms: vertical integration and horizontal integration. Vertical integration refers to the links between HR and wider business strategies and the external political, economic, social, legal and institutional forces helping to shape them. In other words, it relates to the degree of 'external fit' between HR activities and strategies, the management of an organisation as a whole, and the competitive contexts within which it operates. Horizontal integration is the 'fit' between different, internal HR strategies, policies and practices and the degrees to which they support or contradict one another. It is concerned with the degree of 'internal fit' between core HR activities within an organisation. These include organisation design, organisation development, resourcing and talent planning, learning and talent development, performance and reward, employee engagement, employee relations and service delivery and information. Marchington and Wilkinson assume that 'both vertical and horizontal integration need to be strengthened in order to maximise the HR contribution, as well as minimise the likelihood of conflicting messages.'

Examples of vertical integration in practice, however, indicate that there is little convincing empirical evidence supporting the integration of business and HR strategies in most organisations. Integrating HRM with business strategy appears to be a highly complex and iterative process, one which is very dependent upon the interplay and resources of different organisational stakeholders. Where business strategies are emergent and their coherence accrues through action, their integration with HRM is generally a similarly tentative and exploratory process. They are more likely to exist 'largely in retrospective rationalisations, couched in appropriate rhetoric' than in reality. In an evolutionary approach to strategy, in turn, conscious attempts to integrate strategy and HRM policy are 'at best a hit and miss affair'. The systemic model of strategy, however, is useful in explaining why integration of business strategy and HRM strategy is the exception rather than the rule. This is largely because in this strategic model, strategy-makers are embedded in social networks and their characteristic social values. In the UK, these are inherently short term and finance centred, not long term and people centred (Legge 1995, p135f).

In terms of horizontal integration, and the internal consistency of the soft HRM model in organisations, contradictions may be found between the hard and soft versions of the model itself. Thus conflicts may emerge between the goals of commitment, flexibility and quality (Guest 1987) and of 'strong' culture sought by the soft version of the model. First, there may be some confusion over the concept of commitment, which has multidirectional dimensions directed towards not only the employer but also career, job, group or union. Second, soft HRM appears torn between the virtues of individualism and collectivism. There are tensions, for example, between promoting teamwork, on the one hand, and delivering individual performance-related pay, on the other. Further, individuals socialised into a strong corporate culture are, at the same time, often subject to unobtrusive collective controls by the employer. Third, there is potential tension between developing a strong organisational culture and the ability of employees to respond flexibly and adaptively to organisational change (Legge 1995).

Issues of vertical and horizontal integration, and between vertical and horizontal integration, are therefore not unproblematic. They illustrate the complexity associated with developing coherent, integrative strategies promoting organisational performance and HR's difficult role in doing this. These issues are explored in more detail below.

ACTIVITY 5.4

Do vertical and horizontal integration work in your organisation? If they do not, or are not present, explain why.

THEORETICAL DEVELOPMENTS IN HR STRATEGY

There are also theoretical developments in the study and practice of HR strategy. Theory building, commonly based on empirical studies, has moved on significantly since the 'pre-personnel management' period, or even the 'traditional personnel management period', noted by Thomason (1991) and the 'person–job fit' stage observed by Morris and Snell (2009). More than two decades of research have accumulated a considerable body of knowledge, theories and evidence suggesting that HR practices which motivate employees, and impact on the knowledge, skills and behaviour of employees, lead to improved employee, organisational and financial outcomes (Huselid 1995, Batt 2002). All these studies start from the assumption that firms or businesses need strategies to survive. This is what strategic management is about. In their study of strategy and HRM, Boxall and Purcell (2008) distinguish between 'strategic problems' and 'strategy'. Strategic problems are what firms face in their external contexts; strategy is the characteristic way firms typically try to cope with them. For these writers, a firm needs an appropriate set of goals and a relevant set of human and other resources to be viable. A firm also needs a configuration, or system of ends and means, consistent with survival in the competitive marketplace and in the society in which it operates. Without certain human capabilities, firms are simply not viable. Developing appropriate HR strategies and HR practices within firms, in other words, matters.

To explain linkages between HR practices and organisational effectiveness, researchers have utilised concepts, theories and models drawn from a range of fields including economics, psychology, sociology and strategy. There is, however, no comprehensive agreement about what constitutes an 'ideal' HR strategy or what works in every case. Instead, there are a variety of theories and approaches to it. But there is no general agreement about the frameworks, and constituent parts defining the strategy, which promote sustained organisational performance. Empirical evidence, upon which these theories are built, supports, to varying degrees, different perspectives of HR strategy.

Colakoglu *et al* (2009), drawing upon Delery and Doty (1996), classify and categorise HR strategies into three alternative perspectives: the universalistic, the contingency and the configurational. This literature, much of which emanates from the United States, attempts to understand the ways and conditions under which HR practices contribute to improved organisational performance. Colakoglu *et al* also identify two main theoretical frameworks that have been influential in the field of strategic HR research (the resource-base view of the firm and the behavioural perspective), as well as some emerging perspectives:

- **The universalistic perspective:** this suggests that there is a set of HR practices that work in all organisations, regardless of context, and that all firms should use them (Pfeffer 1998). The assumption is that some HR practices are simply such 'good' or 'best' practices that all firms should adopt them to gain competitive advantage.

- **The contingency perspective:** this holds that the impact of HR practices on organisational performance depends on their 'fit' or alignment with a firm's internal and external contingencies. Organisations need to focus on designing HR systems that develop employee skills, knowledge and motivation, so that employees behave in ways aligned with these contingencies (Jackson *et al* 1989, Jackson and Schuler 1995).

- **The configurational perspective:** this perspective holds that it is not sufficient to address the vertical fit of HR practices with contingencies that are both internal and external to the organisation. The congruence of HR practices within the system is equally important. Within this perspective, there are two main approaches:

- One approach extends the universalistic perspective, suggesting that it is the combination of HR practices, rather than any single practice, that drives organisational performance (Baird and Meshoulam 1988).

- The other adopts a 'contingent' configurational approach. This examines whether or not the benefits of internally aligned systems, or bundles of HR practices, depend on contextual factors (Miles and Snow 1984).

- **The resource-based view of the firm**: this perspective claims to provide HR research with a clear strategic orientation. Studies in this area suggest that firms are heterogeneous in terms of the strategic resources (ie physical, organisational, human) they control and that these resources are imperfectly mobile in factor markets. Companies that control these resources, it is claimed, generate sustained competitive advantage (Barney 1991). Human capital and social capital have large roles to play here.

- **The behavioural perspective**: this argues that although human capital is essential in organisations, employees need to exhibit appropriate role behaviours to contribute to the achievement of organisational goals. The central tenet of the behavioural perspective is that HR practices affect organisational outcomes, through managing the displayed behaviour of employees (Schuler and Jackson 1987). The role of organisations is to determine which behaviours are appropriate, depending on organisational strategy and other contingencies.

- **Emerging perspectives**: Recent developments in HR strategy theorising, largely originating from the US literature, attempt to uncover the mediating mechanisms through which HR practices impact on organisational performance. Two examples are outlined below:

  - *The cognitive perspective*: this suggests that employees are not simply passive responders to events. They make active judgements about the causes of events to which they are exposed or which they observe. Bowen and Ostrof (2004), for example, argue that the HRM–performance link is best understood by analysing the psychological and collective climates that HR systems create as mediating mechanisms in this relationship. Other theories and constructs in this field include social exchange theory (Gouldner 1960), perceived organisational support (Shore and Wayne 1993) and psychological contracts (Rousseau 1995).

  - *Social capital*: this is defined as the sum of the actual and potential resources embedded within, and derived from, the network of relationships possessed by individuals or a social unit. Social capital research tries to demonstrate how these relationships affect employee and work outcomes in terms of HR strategy. These are claimed to affect, amongst other things, knowledge transfer and learning, the motives, expectations and norms of the actors in networks (Nahapiet and Ghoshal 1998), and the way groups are motivated to act in the interests of the collective entity, rather than private, individual interests (Coleman 1988). Trust, for example, is a key element in affective relations among networking parties.

Even where they draw upon US sources, most UK studies of HR strategy concentrate on three strategic models: 'best practice HR', 'best fit HR', and the resource-based view of the firm (Boxall and Purcell 2008, Marchington and Wilkinson 2008, and Torrington *et al* 2008). The basic elements of each of these three approaches to HR strategy are shown in Figure 5.3.

Figure 5.3 Main approaches to HR strategy: a summary of best practice, best fit and the resource-based view of the firm

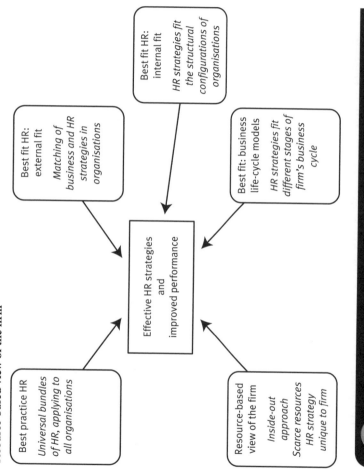

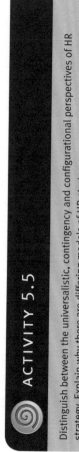

ACTIVITY 5.5

Distinguish between the universalistic, contingency and configurational perspectives of HR strategy. Explain why there are differing models of HR strategy.

BEST PRACTICE MODELS

In the last few years there has been much debate about the notion of 'best practice HR', which is sometimes called 'high-performance work systems' (Appelbaum *et al* 2000), 'high-commitment HR' (Guest 1997), or 'high-involvement HR' (Wood, 1999). The central idea of best practice models is the claim that a number of specific HR strategies and practices can bring about improved organisational performance in all organisations. Best practice is not a new notion. A number of individual 'best practices' were identified in the early days of personnel work in the UK, so they have a long tradition in this country. These covered selection, training and appraisal, for example, where the application of industrial psychological principles had a significant impact, as in the officer selection in the armed services in the Second World War (Crichton 1962).

More recently, ideas about best practice, whatever their differences in detail, suggest that the same basic 'bundles' of HR practices tend to enhance business performance in all organisations, irrespective of product markets, technology and other contingent factors affecting them. It is these bundles of HR practices, it is argued, which help organisations achieve competitive advantage in the marketplace. It is also claimed that these bundles contribute to improved employee attitudes and behaviours, lower levels of absenteeism and labour turnover, and higher levels of productivity, quality and customer service. They are also seen as generating higher levels of profitability.

Underpinning the argument of a positive link between HR strategy and business performance is the assertion that the effect is only optimised where the 'best' HR policies are used. All best practice models argue that the same (or similar) basic HR policies and practices universally enhance business performance, whatever the organisational circumstances. The variety of mechanisms through which this optimisation takes place includes enhancing the competence of employees, gaining their commitment, motivating them and adopting appropriate methods of job design. Given the divergent HR bundles put forward by best practice writers, Youndt et al (1996, p839) say that best practice approaches are concerned with:

enhancing the skill base of employees through HR activities such as selective staffing, comprehensive training, and broad developmental efforts like job rotation and cross-utilization. Further, [they] tend to promote empowerment, participant problem-solving, and teamwork with job re-design, group-based incentives, and a transition from hourly to salaried compensation for production workers.

Many of the policies and practices typically associated with best practice approaches, though not explicitly stated, are rooted in neo-human relations theory (Maslow 1943, Herzberg 1966, McGregor 1960). Some of their underlying beliefs and ideas include widespread use of the 'team' analogy in these models, assumptions about high levels of trust within enterprises, and perceptions of HRM being central to business strategy. Top managers are presumed to be highly visible and able to provide a 'vision' for the future of their organisations which employees can identify with and share. Middle managers, in turn, are seen as inspiring, encouraging and facilitating change by harnessing the commitment and co-operation of employees. Best practice models also generally assume federal, decentralised corporate structures, where job design is congruent with organisation structure, technology and HR policies, and where work teams enjoy large measures of autonomy involving a great deal of task flexibility.

In summary, best practice models typically emphasise three main elements in their prescriptions for high-commitment, high-performance HR strategies and practices. The first element is enhancing employee abilities or knowledge and skills through effective recruitment and selection and thorough training. The second is motivating desired behaviours in the workplace, through strong incentives. The third is opening up opportunities for better-trained and more motivated workers to contribute their ideas at work, through job redesign and indirect forms of employee participation.

THE HARVARD MODEL

An early, well-known, path-finding best practice approach is the Harvard model, proposed by Beer *et al* (1985). As outlined in Chapter 1, these writers suggest that managerial HR policy choices are influenced by stakeholder interests and the situational factors interacting on them. The strategic task of management is to take policy choices in the light of these circumstances. Such choices result in certain HR outcomes and long-term consequences for individuals, organisations and society at large. Its main elements are:

- Stakeholder interests include shareholders, management, employees, government, the community and trade unions.

- The situational factors impacting upon the organisation's stakeholders are workforce characteristics, business strategy, management philosophy, the labour market, task technology, laws and societal values.

- Four clusters of HRM policy choices are seen to be critical and relate to the degree and nature of influence that employees are likely to have. These are 'employee influence,' 'human resource flow', reward systems' and 'work systems'.

- The perceived HR outcomes are the four 'Cs': 'commitment,' 'competence,' 'congruence' and 'cost-effectiveness'. The long-term consequences are identified as individual well-being, organisational effectiveness and societal well-being.

The implicit HR policies incorporated within the Harvard, best practice approach comprise six key elements:

- **Flexibility**: includes numerical flexibility, temporal flexibility and single status.

- **Selection processes**: emphasise attitudes as well as skills.

- **Appraisal**: is open and participative, with two-way feedback between managers and employees.

- **Learning and development of core employees**: are central to the model, with lateral as well as upward career advancement and an emphasis on general as well as specific employability.

- **Reward systems**: utilise individual and group performance-related pay, skill-based pay, profit and gain sharing, share ownership and flexible benefits packages.

- **Participation and employee involvement**: is based on the extensive use of two-way communication and problem-solving groups, with trade union organisation, while not necessarily excluded from best practice models, not being central to this approach to HR strategy.

GUEST: STRATEGIC INTEGRATION, COMMITMENT, FLEXIBILITY AND QUALITY

According to Guest (2001), best practice borrows from expectancy theory. It implies that competence, commitment, motivation and effective job design are needed to ensure the best organisational outcomes. Positive employee behaviour should in turn impact upon establishment-level outcomes such as low absence, quit rates and wastage, as well as high quality and productivity. In an earlier paper Guest (1989) proposed four sets of HR policy goals: strategic integration, commitment, flexibility and quality. These relate to specific HRM policies, which are expected to result in desirable outcomes for organisations:

- Strategic integration means making sure that HRM is fully integrated into strategic planning (vertical integration), that HR policies are consistent with one another (horizontal integration) and that line managers use appropriate HR practices in their daily work.

- Commitment aims to ensure that employees feel bound to the organisation and are driven to high performance.

- Flexibility requires an adaptable organisational structure and functional flexibility based on multiskilling.

- Quality is expected to result in high-quality products or services delivered through high-quality flexible employees.

A number of HR policies are claimed to facilitate this. These are linked with organisational and job design, the management of change, recruitment and selection, internal socialisation, appraisal, training and development, rewards and communication. Expected organisational outcomes include high levels of job performance, problem-solving, innovation, and cost-effectiveness, matched by low levels of labour turnover, absence and grievances.

PFEFFER AND THE HUMAN EQUATION

A high-profile commentator on best practice HR is the American Jeffrey Pfeffer. In an early study, Pfeffer (1994) provides a list of 16 best HR practices for promoting competitive advantage through people. A few years later, he consolidated these into seven components of best practices, which have strongly influenced HR theory building and practice in the UK. His underpinning analysis is based on the importance of the 'human equation' in organisations, enabling profits to be built by putting people first. His seven components are:

- **Employment security and internal labour markets:** these underpin the other six practices. This is on the grounds that it is unrealistic to ask employees to work hard and with commitment without some expectation of job security and concern for their future careers.

- **Selective hiring and sophisticated selection:** recruiting and retaining outstanding people is seen as an effective way to achieve sustained competitive advantage and involves using psychometric tests, structured interviews and work sampling. Competencies sought include trainability, commitment, drive, persistence and initiative.

- **Extensive training, learning and development**: employers need to ensure that 'outstanding talent' remains at the forefront of their field. This includes product knowledge, working in teams and interpersonal relations, with employers needing to synergise the contributions of talented and exceptional employees in the organisation.

- **Employee involvement, information sharing and worker voice**: this rests on the view that open communications about financial matters, strategy and operational problems ensure employees are informed about organisational issues. Also, for teamworking to be successful, employees need information to provide a basis from which to make suggestions and contribute to organisational performance.

- **Self-managed teams/teamworking**: teamwork is seen as leading to better decision-making and the achievement of more creative solutions to operational problems.

- **High compensation contingent upon performance**: there are two elements to this: higher than average compensation and performance-related reward (PRR). PRR can be based on an individual, team, departmental or establishment-wide basis.

- **Reduction of status differentials/harmonisation**: this is seen as encouraging employees to offer ideas within an 'open' management culture. The principal point behind moves to single status and harmonisation is that they aim to break down artificial barriers among different groups of staff, thus encouraging teamworking and flexibility.

HIGH-PERFORMANCE WORK SYSTEMS

The term high-performance work systems (HPWS) was first coined by Appelbaum and Batt (1994) and Appelbaum *et al* (2000), followed by some UK studies (West *et al* 2002). Although the terminology used by researchers differs, their key theme is that HPWS are supposed to increase employee involvement in decision-making and improve motivation and commitment. These, in turn, result in improved business performance and improved employee outcomes. A key part of the HR dimension in this model is the conditions under which people perform well. This suggests that performance is a function of three key factors: employee ability, employee motivation, and employee opportunity to perform well. In these conditions, performance is likely to be improved where:

- Employees are able to do so, because they have the knowledge and skills for this.

- Employees have the motivation, because they want to perform well and are rewarded for it.

- Employees are provided with a working environment that gives them the necessary support and opportunity for achieving good performance.

The work systems seen as being supportive of high performance imply three things: rigorous selection and good training systems to raise ability levels; effective incentives such as employee bonuses and internal promotion to enhance motivation; and participative structures such as self-managed teams and employee involvement for improving the opportunity of employees to contribute to the business. A key argument running through the literature on HPWS is that supportive HR practices work much better when bundled together. Productivity appears to be best served by the interaction of a combination of practices, whereas single HR practices seem to have no effect on performance at all. In addition, it is necessary to have supportive contextual factors that promote good performance. These include the firm's business policies, the sector where it is located and the political-economic framework within which it operates. High performance is a feature of clusters of firms in certain industries in Italy, for example, where networking and social capital serves them well (Appelbaum and Batt 1994). Appelbaum and Batt also argue that it is difficult to transplant foreign models of HPWS to other countries, because of different social contexts such as levels of unionisation, economic policies and national institutions.

Other studies of high performance show the importance of teamwork in HPWS. The volume of communication exchanges between team members and management in the production process, in terms of operational, customer-related or work routines, is much higher in HPWS than in control-oriented work systems. This type of teamwork is associated with work satisfaction. It is

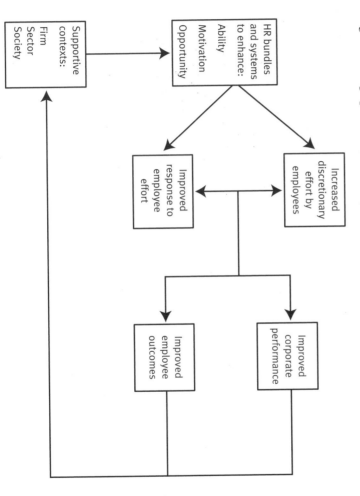

Figure 5.4: High performance work systems: some possible links

claimed that jobs allowing workers to use their knowledge and skills, providing some autonomy and giving opportunities for learning lead to high levels of job satisfaction (Berg 1999). Teamwork and task integration appear to be of fundamental importance to HR issues. The team becomes the focal point for learning and work is pressure exerted on the team by customers and by employees on each other. Further, Appelbaum et al (2000, p26) identify three crucial processes for managing people for high performance, based around the fundamental requirement to use discretionary effort effectively. Workers need appropriate motivation to use discretionary effort; they need the necessary skills to make their effort meaningful; and employers need to give them 'the opportunity to participate in substantive shop-floor decisions through the way work is organized'. Figure 5.4 provides a summary of some possible links within HPWS.

THE PARTNERSHIP MODEL

The partnership model is not a mainstream approach to best practice HR. However, its significance is that unions have some legitimacy within it. The partnership model has well-established roots in the HR literature and in practice. Its virtues have been long extolled by a variety of interests such as the Industrial Partnership Association (1992), the Department of Trade and Industry (1997), the Trades Union Congress (1999) and Dundon et al (2004). Even here, however, the union role is ambiguous. Indeed, as Sisson and Storey (2000) comment, it is controversial whether partnership is in essence about the relationship between the organisation and the union or the organisation and the individual. The partnership best practice model, in short, is strategic HRM, combined with some form of collective representation or employee voice, with or without trade unions. In most other best practice literature, employee voice or the union role is muted.

There is no agreed definition of partnership but six key principles appear to underpin it:

- shared commitment to the success of the organisation, including support for flexibility and replacement of adversarial employment relations by co-operative relations

- recognition that the interests of the partners (employer and union; employer and staff) may legitimately differ

- employment security, including measures to improve the employability of staff, as well as limiting compulsory redundancy

- focus on the quality of working life

- commitment to managerial transparency, openness to discussing future plans, genuine consultation, and willingness to listen to the business case for alternative strategies

- adding value by drawing on resources not previously accessed.

There are three main sources of the partnership model. First, there was the new industrial relations literature in the United States during the 1980s, which emphasised the common interests of employers and unions in the employment relationship, in contrast to the traditional adversarial approach (Kochan *et al* 1986). A second source was mainland Europe with its version of social partnership or 'concertation' amongst employers, unions and governments at national level in many EU countries, complemented by social dialogue at EU level. This involves employer and union confederations, public employers and EU institutions. Its purpose is two-fold: to promote social policy for citizens and support the modernisation of work organisations so as to advance competitive success (European Commission 1997). Third, in the UK, debates over the new realism during the 1990s suggested that unions should develop a joint approach with employers, thereby creating the conditions for both economic success and social cohesion (Farnham 1994).

There is some evidence to show that partnership works, although it is not widespread. Both survey and case study evidence point to there being some positive links between partnership and business performance. Both management and unions have had to adapt to the partnership model. Management has had to change its style from one of 'doing' to 'facilitating', to act more openly and change its approach to the unions by adopting a problem-solving methodology. Unions, in turn, have had to accept the need for joint communication and recognise that the long-term interests of their members are best served by helping organisations be successful and not by opposing change for its own sake. They have also had to give away some collective bargaining power.

CRITIQUES OF BEST PRACTICE

Not all best practice studies present positive links between HR bundles and organisational performance. Some have doubts about the precise sorts of HR practices that make up the high-commitment bundle, about their synergy with one another, and their universal applicability. Research by Purcell *et al* (2003) sought to open up this 'black box'. These studies were undertaken over a 30-month period in 10 organisations from different business sectors, comprising a wide range of employment contexts, with interviews being conducted with HR, line managers and non-managerial staff. The results were, first, that the research team used the 'AMO' model. This argues that in order to perform better, people must have the *ability* and skills to work with others, be *motivated* to work and want to do it well, and have the *opportunity* to deploy their skills in the job and contribute to workgroup and organisational success. Second, each organisation was recognised as operating with a 'big idea'. This was embedded within the organisation and served to glue it together and make it successful. Third, line managers were identified as being critical in achieving high-performance work. Finally, measures of performance were adapted to be relevant for each organisation. Indeed, it makes sense to vary measures of best practice bundles so as to adjust them to specific workplace conditions, since workers are likely to stress different practices due to their occupational status, age or gender.

Another criticism of best practice models is their claimed universality. Best practice works on the assumption that employers are able to take a long-term perspective of their businesses and HR strategies. But changes in a firm's external contexts, such as the economic business cycle or international currency movements, can impact on a firm's business strategy with unplanned effects. In economic downturns, for example, these can result in loss of sales, lower profits and redundancies. The prospect of continued, future growth is uncertain for most organisations. In these circumstances, expectations about employment security and extensive training, for example, are unrealistic (Marchington and Grugulis 2000). Further, institutional forces beyond the control of organisations may shape the HR agenda more significantly than is realised. Indeed, Boselie et al (2003) observe that, for institutional reasons, employers in some countries may take for granted certain HR best practices which in the UK apply only to relatively few, market-secure organisations.

It is also easier to adopt best practice HR when labour costs are a low proportion of a firm's total costs. Thus in capital intensive organisations, it makes little sense to cut back on highly skilled, professional staff, and a best practice 'contract' can be maintained within the company when it faces difficult market conditions. In labour-intensive organisations, in contrast, the dominance of the finance function means that it is difficult to persuade top managers to invest in human capital by adopting market-led pay, investment in learning and development, and other best practice policies. Best practice HR leads to higher labour costs too. This brings Godard (2004) to claim that supporters of best practice might both overestimate the positive effects of these practices and underestimate their costs. Indeed, MacDuffie (1995) argues that best practice HR may only work in certain, specific circumstances. Where there is a plentiful supply of labour for an employer and the time taken to train new staff is relatively short, the rationale for introducing best practice HR is limited.

Advocates of best practice also tend to fudge issues of 'goals' and 'interests' in these studies. Whose goals and interests are being served by best practices? Practices often seem to become ends in themselves, disconnected from the goals of an organisation in a specific context. For example, some practices may be good for the company but not for the workforce. Best practice models are typically silent on these tensions. Thus the limited empirical evidence available about partnership arrangements in the UK indicates that there are mutual gains for both management and employees in the process. However, the ultimate advantage appears to be skewed in the favour of management, which sets the partnership agenda and appears to try to protect its own prerogatives (Guest and Peccei 2001).

In a similar way, an examination of the Harvard model seems to allow for some variation in HR strategies and choices, thus appearing to contrast itself with situational determinism. But, in reality, its analysis of strategic choice has strong prescriptive overtones. For example, the specified desirable outcomes – the four Cs – are attempting to elevate one particular type of strategic approach over others. Indeed, the Harvard approach appears to suggest that there is one preferred set of HR policy choices which are superior to all others; those incorporated within its own framework.

Other critiques of best practice are methodological. For example, there is no consistency in the number of specific HR practices included in the described bundles. Wood (2003) argues it is more important to focus on the underlying orientation for integrated management that may be reflected in different types of practices, rather than spending time trying to identify a set of practices applicable across all organisations. Also there are variations in the proxies used to measure best practice by researchers and different types of performance measures, some of which are based on objective and others on subjective assessments. Finally, many HR specialists are respondents to the questionnaires and interviews used in best practice studies. They often lack expertise or detailed knowledge of some business areas covered in these investigations, so there could be dangers in relying on the self-report scores of HR managers. As Marchington and Wilkinson (2008) conclude, such anxieties mean that considerable caution is needed in interpreting data and conclusions from these studies.

ACTIVITY 5.6

Examine whether your organisation is a best practice employer. If it is not, explain why. If it is, what best practice model does it approximate to? Using this model, how can it improve its HR performance? If it is not a best practice organisation, would it be useful to adopt another type of strategy? Why?

BEST FIT MODELS

Best fit models, sometimes described as 'outside-in' theories, are based on the proposition that different types of HR strategy are suitable for different types of business conditions and organisational contexts. The best fit approach claims that there is a link between HR strategy and competitive advantage but that HR strategy is contingent upon the particular circumstances of each enterprise. This means that organisations have to identify those HR strategies which 'fit' their enterprises in terms of their product markets, labour markets, size, structures, strategies and other factors. What is 'right' for one organisation is not appropriate for others. In other words, best fit HR strategy is based on the idea that HR practices vary amongst organisations, depending on business strategy or product-market circumstances. There are three main types of best fit models.

- **The matching model:** this matches HR strategies to different business strategies.

- **The structural configuration model:** this relates HR strategic choices to the different strategic and structural configurations of organisations.

- **The business life-cycle model:** this links HR strategic choices to different stages in a firm's business cycle.

THE MATCHING MODEL

Sometimes called 'external fit' models, these best fit models try to match business strategy directly with HR strategy. An early example where HR strategy was linked with competitive strategy was developed by Miles and Snow (1984).

As shown in Figure 5.5, Miles and Snow identify three basic types of strategic behaviour. Defenders have a narrow product line and aim to succeed through efficiencies. Prospectors continually search for product and market opportunities, aiming to compete through innovation. Analysers have some stable operations but keep a lookout for market opportunities, aiming to compete through 'fast follower' strategies. In each case, the implied staffing and development, performance appraisal, and pay strategies differ. The basic recipe is to bring HR strategy into line with the firm's product markets.

Figure 5.5 Some HR implications of competitive strategy

Organisational characteristics	Defenders	Prospectors	Analysers
Competitive strategies	Stable product line Growth through penetration, with emphasis on efficiency	Changing product line Growth through innovation and market development	Stable and changing product lines Some focus on efficiency but also 'fast followship'
Staffing and development strategies	Emphasis on internal training and development ('make')	Emphasis on recruitment ('buy')	Mixed approaches ('make' and 'buy')
Performance appraisal	Process oriented, linked to training needs analysis	Results oriented, linked to rewards	Mostly process oriented
Pay policies	Focused on internal equity	Focused on external competitiveness	Concerned with both internal equity and external competitiveness

Adapted from Miles and Snow (1984)

Other matching models draw on Porter's distinction based on innovation, quality enhancement, and cost reduction strategies (Porter 2004). Typical of this group is the work of Schuler and Jackson (1987), who have attempted to link the competitive strategies of firms with HR strategies and practices. They have done this by conceiving HR strategy in terms of generating the desired employee 'role' behaviours required to fulfil given business strategies. They then identify the HR strategies and practices likely to achieve and reinforce such behaviours, as shown in Figure 5.6. Their indicative findings include:

- Where the strategic goal is innovation as a means for getting competitive advantage, this sets up certain predictable patterns of role behaviour. These include creativity, a capacity to focus on longer-term goals, and moderate concern for quality. The HR strategies to match these include rewards based on internal equity, low pay rates and broad career paths.

- Where the strategic goal is quality enhancement, in contrast, Schuler and Jackson (1987) argue that a long and medium-term focus and high concern for quality by employees can be generated by relatively egalitarian treatment of staff, with some guarantees of employment security. Quality enhancement also requires a moderate amount of co-operative, interdependent employee behaviour. The sorts of HR strategies encouraging this are likely to incorporate

Figure 5.6 Business strategy and HR strategy choices: some examples

Strategy	Employee role behaviour	HR strategies
Innovation	High degree of creative behaviour Long term focus High levels of co-operative behaviour Moderate concern for quality Greater degree of risk taking and high tolerance of ambiguity	Jobs requiring close interaction and co-ordination Performance appraisal longer term and focused on group-based achievements Rewards emphasising internal equity, not market-based pay Low pay rates Broad career paths to reinforce developing a broad range of skills
Quality enhancement	Repetitive job behaviours Long or medium focus Moderate amount of co-operative behaviour High concern for quality Modest concern for quantity of output	Fixed job descriptions High levels of employee participation Individual and group criteria for performance appraisal Egalitarian treatment of employees Extensive and continuous training of employees
Cost reduction	Relative repetitive and predictable behaviour Short term focus Autonomous or individual activity Moderate concern for quality High concern for quantity of output	Fixed job descriptions Narrowly defined jobs, encouraging specialisation Results-oriented performance appraisals Close monitoring of market pay levels Minimum levels of employee training

Adapted from Schuler and Jackson (1987)

mixes of individual and group criteria for performance appraisal, which is mainly short-term and results oriented.

- Where cost reduction is a strategic goal, desired employee behaviour demands moderate concern for quality of output but high concern for quantity. The HR strategies supporting these behaviours are close monitoring of market pay levels when making payment decisions and minimal levels of training and development. Whilst agreeing that the success or failure of firms does not turn entirely on their HR strategies, Schuler and Jackson (1987, p217) conclude that 'HRM practices are likely to be critical.'

THE STRUCTURAL CONFIGURATION MODEL

This best fit approach, sometimes called 'internal fit' models, links HR strategy to the strategy and structure of firms, exemplified by Fombrun *et al* (1984) in their basic model for analysing strategic HRM, which was outlined in Chapter 1. For these writers, effective systems for managing human resources lead to increased effectiveness within organisations, where HR systems are internally 'fitted' to business strategy. Their model provides a set of frameworks for conceptualising HR strategy and explores the link between HRM and the formulation and implementation of strategic and business objectives. Fombrun *et al* (1984) have elaborated the traditional view of how managers should think about strategic management by including HRM as an integral tool to be used in strategy determination. For Fombrun and his colleagues (1984, p37), 'the critical managerial task is to align the formal structure and human resource systems so that they drive the strategic objectives of the organisation.'

Known as the Michigan model, this best fit approach identifies a range of HR strategic choices, in terms of selection, appraisal, rewards and development that are dependent upon an organisation's strategic/structural configurations, as shown in Figure 5.7. These configurations range from single-product strategies with functional structures, through diversified-product strategies linked to multidivisional structures, to multiple-product strategies operating globally. Thus a business depending on a single-product strategy and a functional structure is likely to pursue basic HR strategies which are largely functional, subjective and unsystematic. Businesses following a diversification strategy within a multidivisional structure, in contrast, are likely to be characterised by an HR strategy driven by impersonal, systematic HR processes, adaptable to different parts of the organisation. Selection, for example, is likely to be functionally and generalist oriented, with systematic criteria being used. Appraisal will be impersonal and based on returns on investment and productivity, with subjective assessments of contribution to the business. Rewards, in turn, could incorporate large pay bonuses based on profitability, linked with subjective assessments of contribution to business performance. Finally, learning and development would be cross-functional, cross-divisional and cross-business. Other examples are provided in Figure 5.7.

Figure 5.7 HR links to strategy and structure

Strategy	Structure	Selection	Appraisal	Rewards	Development
Single product	Functional	Functionally oriented, subjective criteria used	Subjective measure, via personal contact	Unsystematic, allocated paternalistically	Unsystematic, largely job experiences
Single product (integrated vertically)	Functional	Functionally oriented, standardised criteria used	Impersonal, based on cost and productivity data	Related to performance and productivity	Functional specialists, with some generalists
Growth by acquisition of unrelated businesses	Separate, self contained businesses	Functionally oriented, but varies from business to business how systematic	Impersonal, based on return on investment and profitability	Formula based, includes return on investment and profitability	Cross-functional but not cross-business
Related diversification of product lines through internal growth and acquisition	Multi-divisional	Functionally and generalist oriented, systematic criteria used	Impersonal, based on return on investment and profitability and subjective assessment of contribution to firm	Large bonuses based on profitability and subjective assessment of contribution to overall company	Cross-functional, cross-divisional and cross-corporate
Multiple products in multiple countries	Global organisation, regional and worldwide	Functionally and generalist oriented, systematic criteria used	Impersonal, based on multiple goals such as return on investment, profit tailored to product and country	Bonuses, based on multiple planned goals, with moderate top management discretion	Cross-divisional and cross-subsidiary to corporate, formal and systematic

Adapted from Fombrun *et al* (1984)

Once management has articulated a philosophy about managing people, the Michigan model focuses on designing the HR system. Four generic functions performed by HR managers are identified in the model. These are the 'human resource cycle', where performance is a function of all HR components. The Michigan School argues that success in implementing strategic objectives depends on how well organisations carry out the human resource cycle. This requires four things: selecting the people best able to perform the jobs defined by the structure, appraising their performance to ensure equitable distribution of rewards, motivating employees by linking rewards to high-level performance, and developing employees to enhance their performance at work. The strength of this best fit approach is therefore that it provides a basic framework showing how selection, appraisal, rewards and development can be mutually linked to encourage appropriate employee behaviours.

THE BUSINESS LIFE-CYCLE MODEL

The business life-cycle model tries to link HR strategy choices with the varying needs of firms at different stages in their life-cycles from start-up, through growth, maturity and decline. At each stage, it is claimed, a firm has different business priorities which, in turn, demand different HR strategies. A number of these models have been proposed (Kochan and Barocci 1985, Baird and Meshoulam 1988, Lengnick Hall and Lengnick Hall 1988).

In Kochan and Barocci's (1985) business life-cycle model, four critical HR activities are identified. These require different HR responses at different stages of the business life-cycle, as illustrated in Figure 5.8. This shows the different HR responses organisations need at the start-up, growth, maturity and decline stages of a business. The four sets of HR functions needing to be addressed by management are: recruitment, selection and staffing; compensation and benefits; training and development; and employee relations. During a firm's start-up stage, for example, the compensation and benefits function needs to meet or exceed labour market rates. During periods of growth, the compensation and benefits function concentrates on meeting external market rates, whilst considering the internal equity effects and establishing formal compensation structures. In the maturity stage, it concentrates on controlling compensation. In the decline stage, it focuses on tighter cost control. Other examples are shown in Figure 5.8.

CRITIQUES OF BEST FIT MODELS

At a basic level, one critique of best fit models is their simplistic responses to organisational strategy. Indeed, the model has been criticised because of its dependence on a rational strategy formulation process rather than an emergent one. Another issue that is never addressed is the question of what happens if it is not possible to produce an HR response that enables required employee behaviours or performance to be achieved. Issues such as the time between present and future performance requirements, the strengths, weaknesses and potential of the workforce, the motivation of the workforce and employee relations are also not considered. Linked with this, best fit models, like best

Figure 5.8 Critical HR functions and the organisation business life-cycle

HR functions	Start-up stage	Growth stage	Maturity stage	Decline stage
Recruitment, selection and staffing	Attract best talent	Recruit adequate numbers Management succession Manage rapid internal labour market shifts	Encourage turnover to minimise lay-offs Encourage mobility as re-organisations change jobs	Plan and implement workforce reductions and reallocations
Compensation and benefits	Meet or exceed labour market rates to attract talent	Meet external labour market but consider internal effects Establish formal compensation structures	Control compensation	Tight cost control
Training and development	Define future skill requirements Establish career ladders	Focus on management and organisation development	Maintain flexibility and skills of an ageing workforce	Implement retraining and career counselling
Employee relations	Set basic employee relations philosophy and organisation	Maintain labour peace and employee motivation and morale	Control labour costs, maintain labour peace, and improve productivity	Maintain peace

Adapted from Kochan and Barocci (1985)

practice ones, whether the external fit or internal fit variety, in emphasising alignment of HR strategy with competitive strategy, overlook employee interests. They generally fail to recognise the need to match employee interests with those of the firm or comply with prevailing social norms and legal requirements. If motivation issues are central to HRM, the matching processes of HRM need to integrate business and employee needs, not simply fit HR strategy with competitive strategy. Best fit models typically ignore this issue.

External fit models are criticised on the grounds that linking HR strategy with competitive strategy lacks sophistication in describing what competitive strategy is. Miller (1992) argues, for example, that competitive strategy is multidimensional and that managing people is unlikely to be based on a single strategy as indicated by Porter. In Sanz-Valle et al's (1999, p666) study of 200 Spanish firms, the fit between HR strategy and competitive strategy was not always complete. Their results showed that some HR practices did not vary with strategy. Most firms in their study, with a range of competitive strategies, had internal recruitment policies and similar appraisal criteria. It was jobs that appeared to have more influence on some HR practices than corporate strategy. In some cases, firms with a quality strategy had a 'more, not less, hierarchical payment system than companies with an innovation strategy.' This was the opposite of Schuler and Jackson's (1987) assumptions.

Neither external fit nor internal fit models give sufficient attention to processes of change. They are static models. They relate only two variables together, such as strategy and structure or HRM and the business life-cycle. Nor do they take account of the behavioural processes involved. In business life-cycle models, for example, it is difficult to determine where one stage in the life-cycle ends and another begins. Indeed, there may be different life-cycles for different products or services within the same firm. As Boxall and Purcell (2008) observe, management is unwise to focus solely on 'fit' with any single variable at any one point in time. This is because the objectives of people management are plural and complex. They cannot be encapsulated in one goal or summarised in a single theme. Employees need to be motivated by having their needs met as far as possible.

Boxall and Purcell (2008) make similar observations about internal fit models. For them, the notion of internal fit is discussed in ways that oversimplifies the paradoxical elements involved in the management of people. This is because HR strategies and practices are linked with a range of internal tensions in firms, such as that between short-term focus and long-term flexibility (Boxall 1999). Pil and MacDuffie (1996) show how in automobile manufacturing there have been not only steady increases around the world in high-commitment HR but also periodic downsizing. The climate of insecurity arising out of short-term job losses has not prevented the long-term implementation of high-commitment practices for the remaining workforces. The notion of internal fit does not reinforce a single desirable theme in HRM but involves a process that balances tensions among competing objectives. As Boxall and Purcell (2008) argue, consistency is important but there is an element of paradox in the ways people are managed.

Also the Michigan 'internal fit' model, whilst useful, raises questions about the model's simplistic responses to organisational strategy. Further, the model has also been criticised because of its dependence on a rational, deliberate approach to strategy formulation, its unitary assumptions about the employment relationship, and its lack of recognition of employee interests in the HR equation.

Marchington and Wilkinson (2008) identify other shortcomings of best fit models. First, they are deterministic and top-down approaches to strategy determination. The models provided are normative ones, stressing what 'ought' to be done rather than what is done. Competitive strategies and HR strategies vary, even for organisations in similar product markets or competitive conditions. Second, managers do not have complete control over workers but each model follows traditional scientific management principles. There are strict limits to the extent to which managers are able to control the activities of their staff. Employer policies emerge through negotiation within organisations and are shaped by external political and institutional forces. Third, best fit models do not take account of institutional factors shaping HRM. Top managers are not free agents able to make corporate decisions simply on their own assessment of the situation.

Boxall and Purcell (2008) argue that firms are embedded in societies which regulate and influence them and the social capital of firms is of varying quality. Firms are never unilateral creators of their own HR strategies and practices. It is also problematic fitting outside-in theories to real organisations. Kelliher and Perrett (2001), for example, found it difficult to identify best fit principles in their study of links between strategy and HR in designer restaurants. These establishments stressed the importance of 'quality' and an innovation strategy but there was little evidence that any alignment occurred. The dominant HR practices were short term and hard-nosed, with only some key kitchen staff having employment packages in line with a contingency approach.

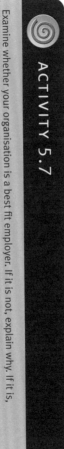

ACTIVITY 5.7

Examine whether your organisation is a best fit employer. If it is not, explain why. If it is, what best fit model does it approximate to? Using this model, how could it improve its HR performance? If it is not a best fit organisation, what measures need to be taken for it to adopt a best fit HR strategy?

THE RESOURCE-BASED VIEW OF THE FIRM

The origins of the resource-based model of HR strategy emerged out of the new business strategy literature. Linking the resource-based model of strategy with HRM has been influential in initiating developments in pay systems, learning and development, and other HR issues. The significance of resource-based theory is that it led to a change in strategic management thinking, by shifting from an emphasis on an 'outside–in' approach, focusing on external, industry-based competitive forces, to an 'inside–out' approach focusing on the firm.

THE FRAMEWORK OF RESOURCE-BASED THEORY

The inside–out approach views the firm's internal resources as the starting point for understanding successful organisational performance (Paauwe and Boselie 2003). The resource-based view of the firm (RBVF) provides therefore a critique of the dominant strategic models of the 1980s associated with Porter (revised editions 1998, 2004). Whereas the outside–in approach of Porter analyses the external contexts of firms in terms of opportunities and threats, the inside–out approach of Barney (1991) and others analyses their internal contexts in terms of strengths and weaknesses. It is this shift in strategic management thinking that has had major implications for HRM and HR strategy.

The essence of the resource-based argument is that organisations are made up of unique bundles of assets, including 'human assets', and that access to these, and the firm's ability to make effective use of them, provide the source of its competitive advantage in the marketplace. The RBVF is generally accepted as the main theoretical foundation explaining the linkages between HRM and organisational performance at the present time. The assumption underpinning the RBVF is that sustained competitive advantage derives from astute use of a firm's internal resources, where the contribution of a firm's human resources is to promote the development of its 'human capital' rather than just aligning human resources to the firm's strategic goals. The focus is not just on the behaviour of human resources but on the skills, knowledge, attitudes and competencies which people bring into an organisation, to promote sustained competitive advantage and business growth. As Sisson and Storey (2000, p34) argue: 'such an approach to understanding strategy places managers' role in identifying, utilizing and renewing such assets centre-stage.' The RBVF is useful because it focuses on an organisation's internal resources and the specific factors enabling organisations to remain viable in the market and achieve growth. Figure 5.9 outlines the main components of this model.

Figure 5.9 The resource-based view of the firm

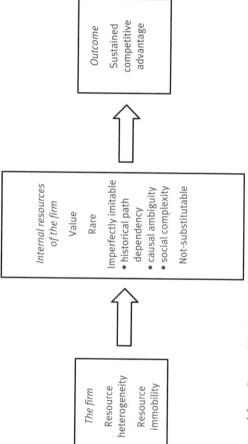

Adapted from Barney (1991)

THE INTERNAL RESOURCES OF THE FIRM

The theory of the RBVF is rooted in the business economics literature, where theories of profit and competition have identified the internal resources of the firm as the major determinants of competitive success (Penrose 1958). Proponents of this model, such as Barney (1991), define 'resources' as all the assets, capabilities, organisational processes, firm attributes, information, knowledge and other assets controlled by a firm that enable it to conceive of and implement strategies to improve its efficiency and effectiveness. He classifies them into three categories: physical capital, organisational capital and human capital, where 'human capital resources' include the experience, judgement and intelligence of individual managers and workers in the firm. In the RBVF, competitive advantage occurs when a firm implements a value-creating strategy that is not being simultaneously implemented by its competitors. This only occurs in situations of 'resource heterogeneity' (ie where resources vary across firms) and 'resource immobility' (ie where competing firms are unable to obtain resources from other firms). The main assumptions underpinning the RBVF are, first, firms are heterogeneous regarding the strategic resources they control. Second, these resources are imperfectly mobile within factor markets. Third, firms controlling valuable, rare, imperfectly imitable and non-substitutable resources are able to generate sustained competitive advantage.

Sustained competitive advantage, in turn, only exists when other firms are incapable of duplicating the benefits of competitive advantage. Hence a competitive advantage is not considered sustained until all efforts by competitors to duplicate the advantage have ceased. According to Barney (1991, p116), 'the resource-based model of strategic management suggests that organisation theory and organisational behavior may be a rich source of findings and theories concerning rare, non-imitable, and non-substitutable resources in firms.' It is the mix of resources, including human resources, that gives each firm its unique character and may lead to differences in performance (Rugman and Verbeke 2002). Barney identifies four criteria indicating whether the resource is gaining sustained advantage. The resource must:

- **Add positive value to the firm:** value means that the resource must be capable of making a difference to the firm, because it adds value in some way.

- **Be unique or rare among competitors:** rarity means that there must be a shortage of these particular resources in the market to the extent that they are insufficient to be shared amongst all organisations.

- **Be imperfectly inimitable:** this means that it is very difficult, if not impossible, for other employers to imitate or copy these valuable, rare resources, even if they are sufficiently available in the marketplace. There are three reasons for resources being imperfectly inimitable:

  - *Historical path dependency:* this makes it difficult for competitors to copy another firm's resources, because valuable resources are developed over time. Competitive success does not come from making choices in the present but has its origins in chains of events in the past.

  - *Causal ambiguity:* this makes it difficult for people to understand the precise nature and mix of resources providing competitive advantage, because people who are not involved in decision-making cannot assess specific cause–effect relationships in organisations.

– *Social complexity*: the complexity of a firm's resources means that it is beyond the ability of firms to systematically manage and influence them. Unique networks of internal and external connections are natural barriers for imitation by competitors.

● **Not be substituted with another resource by competing firms**: these resources must not be easily substitutable by other factors, so that they are rendered obsolete or unnecessary.

THE ROLE OF HUMAN RESOURCES IN SUSTAINED COMPETITIVE ADVANTAGE

Building on this analysis, Wright *et al* (1994, p308) discuss how human resources meet the above criteria for sustained competitive advantage:

● Drawing on 'utility analysis' literature, they conclude that human capital resources provide value to firms, as well as providing methods for estimating this value.

● Since cognitive ability is normally distributed in populations, human resources with high ability are rare. Thus 'it is safe to say that firms with high average levels of cognitive ability relative to their competitors possess more valuable human capital resources than those of their competitors.'

● They also argue that, since HR advantages are most frequently characterised by unique historical conditions, causal ambiguity and social complexity, human capital is almost always inimitable. A potential problem is the notion that human resources are highly mobile but Wright *et al* conclude this is not the case, because of high transaction costs in moving from one employer to another.

● Whilst accepting that it might be possible to substitute other resources in the short term, they suggest that it is very unlikely that such substitution could result in sustained competitive advantage. This is because, to the extent that the resource offsetting the advantage of human resources is itself rare, inimitable or non-substitutable, it will not be imitated and human resources will constitute a competitive advantage.

Turning to the role of human resources in sustained competitive advantage, Wright *et al* (1994) claim, first, that firms with high levels of human capital have relative productivity advantages over their competitors. This is because they develop more efficient means of accomplishing their tasks. Such firms also have greater capacity to respond to external changes, through sensing the need for change and developing strategies to adapt to it. Second, HR practices help develop human resources as a source of sustained competitive advantage by creating and developing a pool of high-quality human capital. Third, those firms in an industry developing effective mixes of selection and reward systems have strategic advantage because human resources are not perfectly mobile. Fourth, having the correct mix of HR practices is a necessary condition for maximising the effectiveness of the human resources capital pool. Thus, although HR practices are not themselves sources of sustained competitive advantage, they play an important role in developing sustained capital advantage, through developing the human capital pool. By affecting HR behaviour, HR practices moderate the relationship between this pool and sustained capital advantage.

The RBVF suggests the necessity of integrating human resources in the formulation stage of a firm's strategy. It also provides a framework for examining the potential for a given pool of human capital to carry out a given strategy. It is claimed that the resource-based view of HR strategy demonstrates that strategies are not universally applicable but are contingent on having an HR base necessary to implement them (Grant 1991). The view of human resources as a pool of capital implies a change in treating the costs incurred in HR interventions. If human resources are a source of sustained capital advantage, they are better viewed as an investment in a capital asset rather than an outgoing expense.

CRITIQUES OF THE RBVF

There are a number of critiques of the RBVF. For example, Boxall and Purcell (2000, p15) argue that there has been a tendency to focus in HRM almost exclusively on industry leadership and competitive advantage. They suggest that caution is necessary before being carried away with the notion of differentiation. In their view, the RBVF exaggerates differences between firms in the same sectors. All viable firms in the same sector need similar resources to establish their 'identify and secure some legitimacy'. A minimum set of human resource investments is necessary to play the competitive game in any industry. Boxall and Purcell (2008) also state that from the HRM perspective, the RBVF literature, like most strategy literature, can become too absorbed with the firm as the unit of analysis. Human resources vary in quality across countries and this variability affects the strengths that firms are capable of building.

Priem and Butler (2001) have other concerns with the RBVF. They claim that there are tautological problems with the RBVF model and question whether the RBVF can be regarded as a theory at all. For them, there appears to be an underlying problem in the statement that the value and rarity of resources lead to competitive advantage. This is because valuable and rare organisational resources and competitive advantage are themselves defined in terms of value and rarity. Further, they question what exactly is meant by performance and how sustained competitive advantage can be identified and measured. These writers also question the lack of clarity in the relationship between HRM and the performance link, the so-called 'black box' dilemma. Part of the problem is the multilevel nature of this link and the complex value chain involved. First, in the human value chain, there are top managers, HR professionals, middle managers, first-line managers and employees at different organisational levels. Second, in the organisational value chain, there are strategic alignments at different levels: business and HR strategy; HR design and policy development; HR implementation between HR professionals and line managers; employee reactions in terms of attitudes and behaviours to HR practices; and firm performance in terms of productivity, profitability, flexibility and legitimacy.

Priem and Butler also question the static nature of resource-based view statements, claiming that they do not fully take into account organisational dynamics and notions of change. In their analysis of strategic fit and internal fit, Boon *et al* (2007) identify the concept of 'adaptation fit' or the capability of an organisation to adapt to changes in its contexts and the extent to which HR practices support, or do not support, this adaptation process. This is missing in the RBVF model. Most importantly, and with few exceptions (Boxall and Steeneveld 1999), the RBVF model pays little attention to the external contexts of firms. This is because the RBVF is based exclusively on the internal contexts of firms in the search for the unique combinations of resources and internal organisational factors promoting competitive advantage. It does not fully take account of the impact of the external context, such as market and institutional mechanisms. Nor does it take account of the potential for unique combinations between internal resources and external mechanisms. An example of this is 'institutional entrepreneurship.' This reflects the opportunities organisations have to be fastest in adapting to new rules, agreements and legislation. It is a concept closely related to strategic choice (Child 1997) and is ignored in the RBVF literature.

In addition, the RBVF implicitly builds on the assumption of the economic rationality of the actors involved, which is unrealistic. Whenever decisions are taken, other rationalities are involved such as 'normative rationalities', or 'taken for granted' decisions, closely related to institutional mechanisms. Indeed, strategic decision-making can be affected by institutional mechanisms and their related rationalities. These include coercive mechanisms stemming from legislation, trade unions or employers' associations, and normative mechanisms stemming from professional bodies (DiMaggio and Powell 1983). Another limitation of the RBVF is its underestimation of critical incidents in the literature. Critical incidents where firms are rocked by financial scandals or unethical behaviours, for example, can impact adversely on firms and the people employed in them. They can result in job insecurity, employee dissatisfaction and labour turnover and destruction of the firm's human capital, social capital and organisational capital, thus undermining the firm's short- and long-term performance.

Marchington and Wilkinson (2008, p116f) identify some other issues regarding the RBVF model. First, they question whether the resource-based view relates to the entire human capital pool of an organisation or just senior managers. Wright *et al* (1994) are clear that it is to everyone, because the workforce is directly involved in making or doing things, less mobile and less able to claim excessive pay for its efforts. For Mueller (1996), value is dispersed throughout an organisation. A second issue is whether the RBVF relates to human resources/ human capital or to the HR practices employers use to manage people. They point out that perfectly executed HR practices cannot guarantee the appointment of staff who will perform at a high level, since 'high-quality and appropriate recruits may still be taken on with poorly executed HR practices.' Third, since the

RBVF recognises the importance of historical path dependency; it is important to recognise the role of trust amongst organisational actors and the informal styles used by first-line managers. These factors impact on the attitudes and behaviours of workers, which are heavily influenced by previous experiences (Marchington 2005).

Finally, as noted by Priem and Butler (2001) and others, the RBVF downplays the significance of institutional arrangements beyond the workplace. HRM choices are not shaped by managers alone and strong institutional mechanisms can decrease the impact of HRM on performance. Individual organisations have limited autonomy in determining their futures.

DEBATES ABOUT EFFECTIVE STRATEGIC LEADERSHIP

Just as 'strategy' is an elusive concept, so is 'leadership.' The essence of strategy is the direction and scope of an organisation over the long term, which achieves *advantage* for the organisation through its configuration of *resources* within a changing *environment*, to fulfil *stakeholder* expectations. The essence of leadership is the process of influencing an organisation (or group within an organisation) in efforts towards achieving an aim or a goal (Johnson *et al* 2009). In practice, however, a full understanding of these two concepts and their interrelationships is problematic, since there is a lack of theoretical integration between the strategy and leadership fields. The concept of 'strategy' has multiple meanings and interpretations, and so too has the concept of 'leadership.' As Bennis and Nanus (1985, p4) comment: in the field of leadership research, 'never have so many labored so long to say so little.'

The central issue is whether organisational leaders are in control of their destinies. Alternatively, is the external context of an organisation the controlling and determining factor? Where does the 'locus of influence' over leadership and strategy lie? The debate and research in these areas are polarised into competing views along the 'human agency–determinist' spectrum, as outlined below (Bennis and Nanus 1985, Mintzberg 1987b, Zaleznick 1992).

HUMAN AGENCY VIEWS OF LEADERSHIP AND STRATEGY

The assumption underlying much understanding of effective leadership starts with rational theories of the firm, workgroups or individuals. These theories try to get a 'best fit' between the functional demarcations of organisations and managerial performance. The same process is assumed where groups and individuals are concerned. Effective leaders are seen to be those who match their leadership styles to the needs of the organisation, group or individuals (Lickert 1967). The overriding theoretical framework linking such studies and approaches is one that ascribes primacy to the role of human agency (Gouldner 1980). This assumes that the leader makes an important contribution to the strategy of an organisation and that such actions are linked directly to its economic performance. Leadership is identified as the key factor in securing the assumed link between management and organisational performance.

Human agency theory runs through much of the literature on strategic management. Such studies support the view that patterns of organisational action *should be* based on the assumption (ie they are normative) that forming this pattern is a matter of a leader's will, intellect and administrative skills. Generic strategy models are addressed at organisational leaders as formulators of strategy, with linear-rational models of decision-making supporting such theories (Cyert and March 1992). Within this framework, the role of leaders is to reduce unwanted constraints on an otherwise 'optimal' managerial process. Development of the human agency perspective extends beyond the field of strategic management. Total quality management also takes a proactive, human agency view of leadership as achievable and desirable. Deming (1986) argues, for example, that effective leadership acts as a substitute for structure, hierarchy and organisational controls.

It is also argued that strategic objectives can best be met by leaders who know how they can be met, whilst emphasising quality and empowering others to perform to their highest ability. Ultimately, strategy and the performance of the organisation are seen to be in the hands of effective leaders.

DETERMINIST VIEWS OF LEADERSHIP AND STRATEGY

Determinist views of leadership and strategy, in contrast, focus on identifying the determinants of organisation structures within which leaders are constrained in taking strategic actions. In her pioneering studies, Woodward (1965, 1970), for example, saw structure as setting parameters around managerial processes, while Perrow (1970), drawing upon substantial empirical evidence, supported the thesis that structure was determined largely by the type and complexity of technology used. Three further observations can be made. First, Burns and Stalker (1961) demonstrated the importance of links between organisation structure and the nature of the task environment. Second, the 'open systems' model provided a unifying, integrated conceptual framework of the deterministic view of organisations (Katz and Kahn 1978). Third, building on earlier works, socio-technical systems theory viewed organisations as social and technical systems located within, and in constant interaction with, through permeable boundaries, a 'supra-system' or environment. Within these perspectives the role of the leader was to work within such constraints and take charge of what little autonomous discretion remained.

CONTINGENCY VIEWS OF LEADERSHIP AND STRATEGY

There are a number of contributions that have challenged the determinist paradigm. For example, Child (1972) argued that when the facts of organisational life are faced, and the contingencies spelled out, organisations have choices. Child reviewed the case for 'contingent' determinants such as organisation size, technology and environment, concluding that 'strategic choice' was a critical variable in the theory of organisations. Further, Astley (1985, p239) rejected the total determinism of the population ecology perspective, arguing for a 'community ecology' perspective. This was one in which 'chance, fortuity, opportunism and choice are the dominant factors determining the direction in which the evolution of populations of organisations progresses.'

The debate is ongoing. The field of industrial economics, for example, has traditionally seen the 'invisible hand' of the market as the prime regulator of organisation and strategy in the market economy. Chandler (1977), however, has shown that over time retained earnings within organisations have outstripped new capital as the primary source of funding for the expansion of American businesses. He concluded that the 'visible hand' of managerial capitalists has long since replaced the 'invisible hand' of capital markets as the basic mechanism for strategic resource allocation in western economies. Galbraith (1952, 1984), in turn, has argued that the tendency towards the concentration of economic power in business corporations has invoked a countervailing tendency in the organisational context. This suggests that the 'locus of influence' over leadership and strategy is contextually dynamic and historically shifting over cycles of time.

MODELS OF STRATEGIC LEADERSHIP

Johnson et al (2009) argue that strategic leadership is commonly directly linked with the managing of change, where leadership is the process of influencing an organisation (or a group) in its efforts towards achieving an aim or goal. Leaders are often categorised as 'charismatic' or 'instrumental' or 'transactional'. Charismatic leaders are characterised as building 'visions' of their organisations and energising people to achieve it. Instrumental or transactional leaders focus on designing systems and controlling the organisation's activities.

The leadership literature suggests that successful leaders have exceptional personal characteristics including: visionary capacity, being good team players, effective team builders, with a capacity for self-analysis and self-learning, mental agility, ability to cope with complexity, self-confidence and creating commitment (de Vries 1994). Peters and Waterman (1982) argue that effective strategic leaders need to be both charismatic and instrumental, and must have the ability to undertake detailed analysis in strategy creation and be visionary about the future, demonstrate insights about the future in achieving credibility for a strategy and make things happen, and maintain organisational performance in consolidating strategy.

Farcas and Wetlaufer (1996), however, provide evidence of different strategic leadership approaches in managing strategy and change in different circumstances. These depend upon the 'focus of attention' in managing strategy, resulting in different indicative behaviours, roles of other managers and implications for managing change. First, where the focus of attention is on strategic analysis and strategy formulation (the *strategy* approach), indicative behaviour is scanning markets and technological change, while managing of change is delegated. The role of other managers is to concentrate on day-to-day operations. Second, where the focus of attention is on developing people (the *human assets* approach), indicative behaviour is getting the right people and creating a coherent culture, while the implications for managing change are recruiting and developing people capable of managing strategy locally. The role of other managers is involvement in strategy development. Third, where the focus of attention is on disseminating expertise as a source of competitive advantage (the *expertise* approach), indicative behaviour is cultivating and improving areas of expertise, while the implications for managing change are doing this in line with the expertise available. The role of other managers is being immersed in and managing the area of expertise.

Farcas and Wetlaufer provide two other scenarios. Where the focus of attention is on setting procedures and measures of control (the *control box* approach), indicative behaviour is monitoring performance against controls to ensure uniform predictable performance, while the implications for managing change are to carefully monitor and control change. The role of other managers is to ensure uniform performance against control measures. Finally, where the focus of attention is on continual change (the *change* approach), indicative behaviour is communicating and motivating through speeches, meetings and so on, while the implications for managing change are to make change central to the approach. The role of other managers is to act as change agents and themselves be open to change.

LINKING STRATEGY AND LEADERSHIP

For Leavy and Wilson (1994), the leader is only one important element in strategy formation. The others are 'context' and 'history'. Their empirical study of 13 leaders in four Irish organisations – a state agency, public limited company, state-owned enterprise and producer co-operative – examined how leadership, context and history interacted in the formation of organisational strategy, which changed over time. They classified these leaders as 'builders', 're-vitalisers', 'turnarounders' and 'inheritors'. They identified and analysed the five most salient contextual factors influencing strategy formation in the four case study organisations: technology, industry structure, international trading environment, national public policy, and social and cultural transformation. But the 'key theme' to emerge from this study was the historical perspective. Long time frames of analysis lent a perspective to the potency and powerlessness of individual action. They also re-emphasised the role of strategic choice: leaders might be tenants of time and context but are rarely reduced to being purely passive agents.

Leavy and Wilson (1994, p187) conclude that leaders often could and did make the histories of their organisations, although not always in circumstances of their own choosing. Their findings reveal a variety of ways in which the 'leader–organisation–context' interaction fitted together but did not reveal any single best way to manage for long-term success. What their case studies demonstrated was four things. First, the strategies and development of their sample organisations never appeared at any stage to be wholly predetermined by managerial action or external events. Second, any patterns and predictability that emerged in both the strategies of organisations and the actions of leaders were 'significant only with regard to historical context'. Third, variations in context emerged as the dominant unit of analysis rather than individual or organisational strategies. Fourth, their data questioned the preoccupation with 'transformational leadership' as the sole route of organisational success or revival.

ACTIVITY 5.9

Which model of strategic leadership is the most effective one to achieve the business goals of your organisation? Justify your response.

CONCLUSION: HR STRATEGY AND HR SOLUTIONS

There have been some significant developments in the theory and practice of HR strategy in recent years. In whatever ways strategic HRM is examined and analysed today, whether in conceptual or practical terms, it is now firmly on the HR research and managerial agendas. The underpinning reason for this is clear: there is now widespread acceptance amongst senior HR and line managers that an appropriately designed and implemented HR strategy (with attendant solutions) is capable of making a managerially significant contribution to a firm's bottom line and its generic performance. Many senior HR professionals now want a strategic role in their organisations, if for no other reasons than senior line managers demand it. However, to be effective in strategic roles, HR professionals have to move away from demonstrating cost controls and efficiency gains in organisations, to demonstrate bottom-line success, towards strategy formulation and strategy implementation in partnership with senior managers.

This raises an important distinction between managing the workforce and managing the HR function. In this context, the concept of developing and implementing a 'workforce strategy' appears to be an emerging organising principle for strategic HRM. This is because of the involvement of line managers in it, and because it provides a clear line of HR delivery, emphasising strategy implementation. Indeed, the term 'workforce strategy' highlights a shared responsibility for *strategic* workforce performance between line managers and HR specialists. It is also apparent that concepts such as strategic alignment and strategic fit are more easily implemented when line managers and HR professionals focus jointly on strategic business processes, not on individual HR practices. This helps mitigate the common situation, where HR professionals find the organisation's strategic goals either unclear or inconsistent.

Becker and Huselid (2009) claim there is increased emphasis on differentiation in delivering HR strategy. Differentiation has at least two dimensions. One is structural. This means differentially focusing workforce strategy on strategic rather than non-strategic jobs. Where the phrase 'employees are our most valuable asset' is used, managers often interpret this to mean the need to invest in everyone in equal measure. But the notion of differential investment, based on a strategic logic, provides a contingent solution to the issue. The second dimension of differentiation relates to employee performance. For Becker and Huselid (2009), this means making meaningful distinctions amongst employees when reviewing their performance, particularly in strategic jobs. This is likely to result in greater rather than less variation in rewards, for example, as well as more effort to get rid of those employees who are not meeting high organisational performance standards. This necessitates, in turn, an increased role for line managers in delivering HR strategies. A major challenge in doing this is getting line managers to implement such HR systems, including a workforce strategy.

HR professionals face an additional challenge of providing meaningful measures of their performance, so as to demonstrate their strategic contribution. Traditional HR measures, such as the performance of the HR function, tend to rely on external benchmarks including turnover, absenteeism and sickness rates. These limit consideration of HR's performance to issues of administrative efficiency, while treating strategies as commodities with appropriate market benchmarks. A possible solution is making a distinction between the human capital aspect of strategy implementation and the HR function itself. For firms to deliver business strategy effectively, it is necessary to develop a better understanding of the causes and consequences of workforce performance. It also necessitates holding line managers accountable for their HR decisions and HR performance. HR specialists increasingly recognise the value of such measures, because line managers value them too (Huselid *et al* 2005).

In these conditions, it is likely that the HR's strategic role needs to focus on the workforce component of the firm's strategic capabilities. This has implications for how HR is managed and evaluated in organisations. A focus on strategic capabilities means, again, more emphasis on differentiation in relation to a firm's competitors and within the organisation. Managers need to align HR systems and workforce inputs at a strategic business process level. Nevertheless, there remain considerable variances in the capabilities of HR managers, who are generally more effective in the technical and operational levels of their roles than in strategic ones, including strategy implementation. In short, they need to be effective managers of workforce strategy.

Many writers note that the role of the HR manager is a complex one. Their multiple constituencies are likely to require multiple competencies from HR leaders as well (Ulrich and Brockbank 2005). When strategic HRM was originally HR-focused, it was broadly in the control of HR specialists. Some would argue that it is moving out of the hands of HR professionals into those of line managers and senior managers; HR professionals may not be taking the lead. The role of strategy implementation in the 'black box' between the HR architecture and business performance, reflects the importance of line managers and the broader focus on workforce management within contemporary HR strategy.

KEY LEARNING POINTS

1. HR strategy is not a new phenomenon. Starting in the Industrial Revolution, firms tried to find ways of managing their labour inputs as efficiently as possible. Although not explicitly stated, the main HR strategic goal of firms was to control their labour costs to gain competitive advantage. Labour was seen as a problem to be dealt with, controlled and encouraged to work co-operatively with the managers employing it. Thomason's observation of the three historical shifts in the development of HR strategy, from pre-personnel management to traditional personnel management to the HRD and HRM models of HR strategy, is useful for analysing HR strategy historically. His identification of the selection, supervision, or development and partnership strategies provides the core of his classificatory system.

2. The evolution of HR strategy developed in three main stages, in response to specific competitive market situations and contextual circumstances. These were the 'person-job fit', 'systemic fit' and 'value creation' stages. These were the dominant models of HR at particular times, but not all firms conformed to the dominant paradigm in each period. The first stage started with the Industrial Revolution, ending in the late twentieth century. The second stage emerged in response to increased global trade and increased market competition in last decades of the twentieth century. It was largely concentrated on the internal fit or external fit of HR strategies within organisations. The value creation stage identified human knowledge, skills and abilities as the primary drivers for sustained competitive advantage. Human capital, social capital, capabilities and their underlying mechanisms provide the foci of HR strategy.

3. Talent management and workforce planning have become increasingly important on the HR strategic agenda. Talent management is the task of building a pool of talent within organisations, without necessarily having a clear view of how it will be used in the future. Developing a talent pool is a dynamic approach and fits well with the RBVF. Developing talent at different leadership levels is important and current debates focus on definition of talent in terms of what it means and to whom it applies. Workforce planning, in turn, increases awareness of human capital risk within organisations. It includes demand forecasting, supply forecasting and analysing the gap between demand and supply for each scenario.

4. Vertical and horizontal integration are key concepts in understanding strategic HRM. Achieving vertical integration, or fit with business strategy, requires knowledge of the business strategy, knowledge of the skills and behaviours necessary to implement strategy, and knowledge of the HR practices necessary to elicit those skills and behaviours. It also requires the ability to develop and implement the desired HR system. Horizontal integration, or fit between HR strategies, is achieved where the HR 'bundles' are collectively coherent and mutually supporting. These bundles are achieved by: identifying appropriate HR practices; assessing how the bundle can be linked together and by mutually reinforcement; and drawing

up programmes for developing these practices, paying attention to links between them.

5. A number of current theoretical perspectives of HR strategy have been identified for describing and analysing HR policies and practices. This chapter concentrates on three main ones: best practice, best fit and the RBVF. The perspectives identified are the universalistic, contingency, configurational, RBVF, behavioural and emerging perspectives. The emerging perspectives, in turn, incorporate two sub-models, the cognitive and social capital categories.

6. Best practice HR involves identifying bundles of HR practices with the potential to enhance organisational performance when implemented. Best practice HR incorporates a number of submodels, including the Harvard model, Guest's analysis of strategic integration, commitment, flexibility and quality, Pfeffer's human equation model, and the partnership approach. A main criticism of these models is their claimed universality. Best practice is claimed to work on the assumption that employers are able to take a long-term perspective of their businesses and continual market growth. The reality of business life is different from this, bringing into doubt the universal application of these models.

7. Best fit (or outside-in) HR focuses on the alignment between HRM and business strategy and the external contexts of the firm. They tend to link or fit generic type business strategies to generic HR strategies. The three main types of best fit HR models are the matching (external fit), structural configuration (internal fit) and business life-cycle models. A main criticism of best fit models is that they are deterministic and top-down approaches to strategy determination. They stress what ought to be done and there are limits to the extent to which managers are able to control the activities of their staff. Employer policies are largely shaped by external political and institutional forces, rather than internal ones.

8. The RBVF is an inside-out theory of strategic HRM, originating in the strategic management literature on resource-based theory. This model is concerned with the relationships among the internal resources of a firm, including its human resources, strategy and organisation performance. Its focus is on promoting competitive advantage through the development of human capital, not simply aligning human resources to corporate strategy. The RBVF model argues that the people employed in an organisation provide competitive advantage for the firm, because they are valuable, rare, not imitable and not substitutable by competing firms. Its focus is on the behaviour, skills, knowledge, attitudes and competencies of these people.

9. Critiques of the RBVF include that it is a tautological concept, is static in nature and not dynamic, and is based on unrealistic assumptions of economic rationalities in organisations. Others observe built-in barriers to the language of the resource-based view. Some writers consider the term 'human capital' as being unduly instrumental. The focus on firms and competitive advantage raises questions about the relevance of the RBVF to public services. There is also the issue of what is being measured and who decides this. Measures often seem to be taken without drawing upon a coherent framework and different firms measure different things.

10. A central issue in effective strategic leadership is whether organisational leaders are in control of their destinies, through human agency, or whether the

...contexts within which they work are the main determinants. When considering the role of leadership in both business and HR strategy, the evidence suggests that there is no single best way of managing organisational success. Strategic effectiveness is contingent upon a range of personal, organisational and chance or circumstantial factors at the time.

REVIEW QUESTIONS

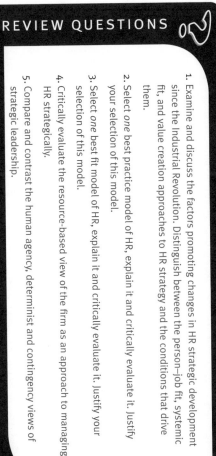

1. Examine and discuss the factors promoting changes in HR strategic development since the Industrial Revolution. Distinguish between the person–job fit, systemic fit, and value creation approaches to HR strategy and the conditions that drive them.

2. Select one best practice model of HR, explain it and critically evaluate it. Justify your selection of this model.

3. Select one best fit model of HR, explain it and critically evaluate it. Justify your selection of this model.

4. Critically evaluate the resource-based view of the firm as an approach to managing HR strategically.

5. Compare and contrast the human agency, determinist and contingency views of strategic leadership.

CASE STUDY

CASE STUDY 5.1 HARTLEY ELECTRONICS LTD: HR STRATEGIES FOR THE FUTURE

Background

Based on the south coast of England, Hartley Electronics Ltd was established in 1977 by Trevor Cook, a well-qualified and experienced electronics engineer, as a small business manufacturing micro-electronic components. Its early customers were in the defence and satellite sectors. Initially, sales were limited to the UK, especially to the Ministry of Defence, motor industry and other specialist manufacturers. Over the next few years, however, the business grew steadily by developing new products and new markets. By the late 1980s, Hartley was selling its products not only in the UK but also overseas in Europe, North America and Asia Pacific.

From employing some 50 workers when it started, Hartley expanded to 100 workers by 1989 and to about 180 by the mid-1990s. The nineties were an 'up and down' period for the company and there were redundancies in both 1995 and 1999. Another wave of redundancies took place recently following the financial crisis in 2008 and the subsequent economic downturn. Currently, the firm employs 125 staff. These consist of 25 managers and support staff, 40 technical and design staff, and 60 production workers. There is a 'personnel officer', with one assistant/secretary, who deals mainly with resourcing, pay, and health and safety issues in the company.

The company's products

In recent years, with its experienced, well-qualified workforce, an excellent technical sales team and an expanding market, Hartley has become a world leader in (a) specialist radio frequency and microwave (RF&M) systems, subsystems and components, and (b) both standard and custom power supplies (PS).

With over 30 years' designing and manufacturing for markets in Europe and the United States, the RF&M division has established Hartley as a quality supplier of reliable products. These include RF&M components in communications, air traffic control, and weather systems. Products are specifically designed for end users and are also an integral part of the supply chain for major programmes within each of the industries in which the company operates. These products are sold worldwide, with over 80 per cent of output now being exported.

Hartley's reputation in the PS market for reliability is very high. This has been achieved by producing the best possible solutions for all applications, with an option for custom-designed units to maximise overall lifetime value. The company's excellent in-house technical and production facilities enable it to respond quickly and effectively to customer needs. The company manufactures, for example, a wide range of customised power supplies to meet the exacting requirements for electronic equipment onboard aircraft.

The company's proven military custom design capabilities make it ideally placed to design and manufacture highly specified, reliable power supplies for critical aircraft systems. Applications include liquid crystal displays, mission and stores management computers, laser systems, infra-red guidance, and systems for ground mobile, air and seaborne environments.

HR issues

HR issues have never been a major interest or focus for Trevor Cook and

his management team. The technical, financial and marketing aspects of the business have been its strong points. HR has been based on short-term goals and 'muddling through'. For example, all staff are on annual salaries. However, the salary structure is distorted. Some staff are doing identical jobs but with pay differences between them amounting to some £2,000–£3,000 per year. An incentive bonus scheme exists for the company's 60 production workers, with *in lieu* payments for other staff. But targets have not been met and therefore no bonuses have been paid.

Two years ago the company sought Investors in People status but it was unsuccessful in achieving this. No trade union is recognised by the company but some production staff have recently joined 'Unite – the union'. There is a minimalist approach to learning and development at all levels within the company.

There are no formal consultative or information arrangements in the company. Managers tend to be friendly and helpful to their staff but do not generally act consistently, or always fairly, in HR matters. This causes tensions between management and the workforce at times.

HR issues have come to a head, following the recent round of redundancies. It would not be an exaggeration to say that employee morale has plummeted. Some staff are still feeling very vulnerable and fearing that their jobs are likely to disappear in the wake of the macro-economic situation. On the positive side, there is a prospect of some expected big orders coming into the company in the next few months.

What is bringing HR issues to head is the recent appointment of a new, dynamic and young, MBA-qualified chief executive, James Ryder, now that Trevor Cook has retired. James realises that something needs to be done if the company is to be turned round in the near future. He is very anxious to carry the remaining staff with the management team and to secure the firm's future. He sees the design and development of appropriate HR strategies and practices as the key for doing this. In his view, there are some immediate, short-term strategic HR issues to be addressed, and some longer-term ones too.

HR strategy in the short term

Having worked in Japan on earlier assignments, James has been strongly influenced by Japanese management thinking and is personally receptive to it. He believes it to be based on a number of underlying HR principles, which, if sensitively introduced, are transferable to Hartley. He has identified these principles as:

- People are a company's greatest asset.
- Competent, motivated people who are treated with respect will demonstrate commitment to the company's goals and objectives.
- People should be provided with opportunities for personal growth and stable employment.
- Effective teamworking and communication contribute to the bottom line.
- The above are best achieved by securing the long-term prosperity of the firm.

James realises that developing this short-term strategy is not within the competence of the present personnel officer. He has therefore appointed an external consultant to undertake this activity.

HR strategy in the longer term

If the above short-term aims can be achieved, James also wants to take a longer-term view of Hartley's prospects. Here, he believes, an appropriate HR strategy, linked and integrated with Hartley's business strategy, is necessary to take the company forward. He wants the consultant to plan and outline this too.

Tasks

1. Taking on the role of the external consultant, suggest ways in which the short-term HR strategy, based on the principles identified by the chief executive, might be introduced into Hartley.

2. How can issues of vertical and horizontal integration be built into this strategy?

3. What will be some of the implications for the HR function in doing this?

4. Demonstrate how these proposals can be made cost-effective and how the chief executive can gain support from line managers in implementing this strategy.

5. Again as the external consultant, make recommendations to the chief executive whether to adopt a best practice, best fit or resource-based view of the firm model of HR strategy to achieve a longer-term solution to the HR issues facing the company. Justify your response.

Strategy formulation and implementation

EXPLORE FURTHER

BOXALL, P. and PURCELL, J. (2008) *Strategy and human resource management*. 2nd ed. Basingstoke: Palgrave Macmillan.

Links strategic and HR concepts and theories to provide an innovative conceptual framework for exploring the growing field of strategic HRM; drawing upon a wide range of sources, this text seeks to demonstrate how HRM fulfils a strategic function in maintaining the firm's viability and provides a basis for sustained competitive advantage; also shows how managers can pursue goals of increased labour productivity and organisational flexibility in socially acceptable ways.

BOXALL, P., PURCELL, J. and WRIGHT, P. (eds) (2007) *Oxford handbook of human resource management*. Oxford: Oxford University Press.

Covers a wide range of topics in HR, HR strategy and links with business strategy; provides keen insights to the contribution of HR to business performance and organisational effectiveness. This handbook brings together leading scholars from around the world, and from a range of disciplines, to provide an authoritative account of current trends and developments; it is divided into four parts: foundations and frameworks, core processes and functions, patterns and dynamics, and measurement and outcomes.

SPARROW, P., BREWSTER, C. and HARRIS, H. (eds) (2004) *Globalising human resource management*. London: Routledge.

Is an edited volume that explores the growing influence of internationalisation on organisations, both large and small; the essential argument of this text is that with increasing numbers of internationally operating organisations, and internationally operating employees, international human resource management is becoming ever-more critical for more and more organisations in terms of HR strategies and practices.

WILKINSON, A., BACON, N., REDMAN, T. and SNELL, S. (eds) (2009) *The SAGE handbook of human resource management*. London: Sage.

Bringing together contributions from international scholars that examine the fundamentals of HRM, including HR strategy, it contextualises HR practices with wider theoretical considerations, combines a critical overview of topics with discussion of key debates, and reveals important emerging issues through the academic lens of psychology, sociology, politics and economics.

PART 3

The external contexts of human resource management

CHAPTER 6

Markets and the competitive context

INTRODUCTION

The central economic problem facing humankind is how to satisfy the infinite wants of an ever-growing population within the constraints of the finite resources available. With the economic demands of people virtually unlimited, and the supply of economic resources to satisfy those demands fixed in the short term, choices have to be made about economic priorities. Economic goods and services are those human-produced commodities requiring the use of scarce resources to create them. They include finished consumption goods and services, capital (or investment) goods, raw materials and public goods (produced by public authorities). More generally, economic goods are commodities for which people's demands exceed the availability of scarce resources to meet them. It is the task of any economy to solve the economic problems associated with this universal feature of resource scarcity. This chapter outlines some of the key issues in the UK market economy arising out of economic scarcity, competition and choice. It makes the traditional distinction between micro- and macro-economics. The chapter provides the setting for other parts of the book, by touching on economic policy, globalisation, strategy and labour market trends. After 30 years of economic liberalism, the UK is embedded in an open market economy driven by competition, choice and change management agendas, imbued with strong market values in a marketised society.

LEARNING OUTCOMES

By the end of this chapter, readers should be able to understand, explain and critically evaluate:

- the nature of the market economy, its structure and macro-economic policy choices
- the price mechanism
- capital markets and the roles played by major financial institutions

- developments in the labour market and their consequences for organisations
- the impact of marketisation, competition and change management agendas on public services
- the concept of competitive advantage and ways in which it is gained and retained in the contemporary business context.

In addition, readers should be able to:

- review major current trends in an organisation's employment markets and take appropriate action in response to their short- and long-term implications
- examine the competitive contexts of organisations through appropriate analytical techniques
- advise on the contribution of the HR function in situations of intensified competition.

MARKET ECONOMIES

In modern economies, the constituent economic actors are households, firms and government agencies. They consume goods and services produced in or imported into an economic system. Firms are agents in transforming and converting scarce resources into the goods and services demanded for consumption and investment purposes. Households supply key resources, such as labour and finance, to aid the production process. Investment is the flow of expenditure channelled into activities producing new resources not intended for immediate consumption, such as plant and machinery. Through planned investment, production capacity becomes possible. Government's economic role is a complex one. It provides services to taxpayers, collects taxes from households and firms, transfers income from individuals and households to other individuals and households, and manages the macro-economy.

The scarce resources used by firms and government in creating new economic goods and services for consumption and investment are 'the factors of production', usually defined as land, labour and capital. Land incorporates those natural resources such as oceans, forests, minerals and soil fertility used in production. Labour is the sum total of human resources skills, knowledge and competencies that are available, nationally and internationally, to contribute to the supply of goods and services. Capital is those human-made aids to production, such as machinery, advanced technology and communication systems, which raise economic productivity and real output per worker. Capital is also used to describe money (ie finance capital) as a commodity, available for investment. The total output of all the commodities produced by a country over a given period, normally a year, is its gross domestic product (GDP). With net property income included, the aggregate is gross national product (GNP).

Issues of scarcity and choice mean that all economic systems have a number of common problems to resolve:

- What goods and services are to be produced and in what quantities, including the balance between consumption and capital or investment goods?

- How are these goods and services to be produced, given current resources, technology and productive capacity?

- Who is to get the goods and services produced, or how is GNP to be divided among a country's economic and non-economic participants?

- How efficient are the methods used in the production and distribution processes?

- Are existing resources being fully utilised, or are some unemployed or underemployed?

- In monetary economies, are prices stable or are they rising out of line with productivity, which is described as 'inflation'?

- Is the economy growing and increasing its capacity over time?

Three types of economic system have provided institutional frameworks for solving these problems. These are planned (or command) economies, free market capitalist economies, and market (or mixed) capitalist economies. Planned or command economies, such as that of Cuba, are rare today. Economic processes within them are determined not by market forces but by planning agencies which determine and implement society's economic goals. The nearest approximations to such systems were the countries of Eastern Europe and the former Soviet Union until the breakdown of communism in the late 1980s and early 1990s. They have now been transformed into market economies and shifted towards private enterprise and market-based economic systems.

FREE MARKET ECONOMIES

In free market economies, economic decisions about resource allocation, and production of goods and services, are made through money prices, generated by economic exchanges among producers, consumers, workers and owners of the factors of production. Decision-making is largely decentralised, with private ownership of the means of production and limited forms of social ownership. The market mechanism (or the price system) allocates resources, adjusts production and consumption decisions, distributes incomes to those owning factors of production, and paves the way for economic growth. Its main features are:

- Individual economic units decide what, how, where and when to produce and consume, with reference to money prices.

- Prices respond to the forces of demand and supply for individual goods or factors of production.

- The outcome is a balance of demand and supply, with co-ordination of the economic activities of individual units and agents achieved through the price system.

MARKET ECONOMIES

Market economies, combining private enterprise with varying degrees of government intervention and regulation, dominate the world economy today. Resource allocation between alternative uses is determined largely by individual firms seeking profits and market share in the marketplace, which is increasingly globalised. Governments attempt to influence overall economic performance, distribution of incomes and welfare policies. Hutton (1995) identifies four principal types of market economy (or capitalist systems): the American, Japanese, European social market and UK economies. There are some similarities between the European social market and the Japanese market economy, and between the American and UK market economies. The greatest contrast is between the UK market economy and the European social market economies.

The main differences between the UK market economy and the European social market economies are summarised in Figure 6.1 below:

Figure 6.1 Main differences between UK market economy and European social market economies

	UK market economy	European social market economies
General		
Dominant economic factor	• finance	• partnership between capital and labour
Public spirit of business	• low	• high
Price-driven markets	• high	• medium
Supply relations	• arms' length	• bureaucratic
Privatisation	• high	• medium
Firms		
Goals	• profits	• market share
Management	• hierarchic	• consensual
Social overheads	• medium	• high
Financial system		
Main feature	• marketised	• bureaucratic
Banking	• marketised, advanced, centralised	• traditional, regulated, regional
Stock market	• very important	• less important
Returns on finance capital	• high, short term	• medium, long term
Labour market		
Job security	• low	• high
Labour mobility	• medium	• medium
Labour management	• often adversarial	• co-operative
Labour turnover	• medium	• medium
Level of skills	• poor	• high
Union organisation	• occupational	• industry-based
Union power	• weak	• strong

	• UK market economy	• European social market economies
Welfare system		
Universal provision	• medium and falling	• high
Means testing	• medium and rising	• low
Private welfare	• medium and rising	• low
Participation in higher education	• strongly related to social class	• weakly related to social class
Government policy		
Role of government	• strong, centralised	• wide ranging
Trade policy	• open	• fairly open
Industrial policy	• non-interventionist	• interventionist
Top tax rate	• relatively low	• relatively high

- **Basic principles:** in the UK, the dominant factor is (finance) capital, and the tradition of 'public spirit' in business is low. There is high reliance on price-driven markets, supply relations are at arms' length and price driven, and privatisation is high. In the European social market economy, the dominant relationship is partnership between capital and labour, and the degree of public spirit in business is high. There is medium reliance on price-driven markets, supply relations are bureaucratic and planned, and the extent of privatisation is in the middle range.

- **Firms:** in the UK, the main goal of firms is profits, managerial structures are hierarchic and social overheads are in the middle range. In the European social market economy, the main goal of firms is market share, managerial structures are consensual, and social insurance overheads high.

- **Financial systems:** in the UK, the financial system is marketised, banking is advanced, marketised and centralised, and the stock market is very important. Returns on finance capital are expected to be high and short term. In the European social market economy, the financial system is bureaucratic, the banking system traditional, regulated and regional, and the stock market less important. Returns on finance capital are expected to be in the middle range.

- **Labour markets:** in the UK, job security in the labour market is low, labour mobility is medium and labour management can be adversarial. Pay differentials are large (and rising), labour turnover is medium and the level of skills in the labour market is generally poor. Unions are organised on a general or occupational basis and their power is weak. In the European social market economy, job security in the labour market is high, labour mobility is in the middle range and managing labour is co-operative. Pay differentials and labour turnover are medium and the level of skills in the labour market is high. Unions are organised on an industrial basis and their power is strong.

- **Welfare systems:** in the UK, the basic principle of the welfare system is a mixed one, where universal provision is medium (and falling), means-testing is medium (and rising) and private welfare is medium (and rising). Participation in higher education is related to social class. In the European social market economy, the basic principle of the welfare system is a corporatist-social democratic one, where universal provision is high, means-testing is low and private welfare low. Participation in higher education is weakly related to social class.

- **Government policies:** in the UK, the role of government is strong and centralised. Government supports open trade and industrial policy is non-interventionist. The top rate of income tax is low. In the European social market economy, the role of government is wide. Government supports quite open trade and industrial policy is interventionist. The top rate of income tax is high.

A central feature of modern market economies is the institutional frameworks within which they operate (Basu 2000). There is, nevertheless, intensive competition for business between firms for customers, especially with increasingly globalised, relatively free markets. This leads to mergers and acquisitions of businesses so that they can gain competitive advantage through economies of scale. Within market economies, Kay (2003, p17) concludes: 'Economic differences persist because output and living standards are the complex product of the intersection of the economic environment with associated social, political and cultural institutions.'

THE UK MACRO-ECONOMY: POLICY AND ECONOMIC STRUCTURE

The UK's contemporary economy has emerged out of the historical legacies of the nineteenth and twentieth centuries, reflecting its historical path dependency. These legacies continue to influence the country's economic activities today. During the late twentieth and early twenty-first centuries, further developments took place, so that the UK is now often described as de-industrialised, 'post-industrial' economy within a globalised market.

LAISSEZ-FAIRE

Britain was the first country to industrialise, from the mid-eighteenth century onwards, and to shift from a predominantly agrarian economy to an industrial one. Changes in the techniques and organisation of production resulted in increases in investment, productivity and output, enabling Britain to feed a rapidly growing population and penetrate expanding overseas markets. By the mid-nineteenth century, Britain had become a largely urban and industrial economy, a net importer of food, the world's leading producer of manufactured goods, a major exporter of goods and services and a strong imperial power. Her staple industries were coal, textiles, cotton, engineering and iron and steel, with the benefits of the 'Industrial Revolution' beginning to 'trickle down' to the 'lower orders'. This prosperity was achieved in a free-market, *laissez-faire* economy, where the state's role was the limited one of providing national defence and a framework of law and order (Pollard 1969).

THE INTER-WAR YEARS

The late nineteenth century was an economic watershed for Britain. There was an economic depression, with rising unemployment, caused by increased competition in world markets from a newly unified Germany and the United States. Britain's policy of 'free trade' and no restrictions on imports and exports resulted in cheap agricultural products coming in from the New World, which led to a crisis in arable farming. This was followed by a brief period of rapid economic growth in the early twentieth century and renewed expansion in the staple trades, exports and employment. But rising prices and downturns in the economy followed (Landes 1998). During the First World War (1914–18), markets were lost, new international rivals emerged and national capital consumed. There was a decline in Britain's stock of capital and a significant decline in her holdings of overseas assets (Aldcroft 1993).

The inter-war years (1919–39) were generally a period of slump, depression and high unemployment although, because of falling prices, those in employment enjoyed rising living standards. Britain's staple industries, upon which the economy had traditionally relied, declined but new industries expanded such as chemicals, electrical goods, motor vehicle manufacture and the component industries supplying it. Following the Wall Street crash in the United States in 1929, free trade was abandoned and import controls introduced internationally. This triggered a worldwide slump between 1931 and 1934. It was not until the late 1930s, with military rearmament, that the UK, as well as other European economies, experienced renewed growth and falling unemployment. The Second World War (1939–45) led to further capital consumption and loss of international markets. During the war, production and 'manpower' were centrally directed, prices controlled by government and food and clothing rationed according to need. To maximise output and promote efficient use of scarce national resources, the UK had shifted to a closed, command economy.

THE POST-WAR SETTLEMENT

The period from 1945 to the mid-1970s has been described as the 'post-war settlement' or the 'social democratic consensus'. The UK economy was slowly freed from its wartime constraints, industry was rebuilt and pre-war private enterprise replaced by a mixed market economy, operating in an international economy of fixed exchange rates. The post-war Labour government (1945–51) nationalised the Bank of England, the coal, gas, electricity, telecommunications, and railway industries, and introduced the modern welfare state, which would ensure the basic social and economic necessities of its citizens. It did this by providing (from tax revenues) public goods and services. These included the National Health Service (NHS), provided 'free' at the point of use, tax-funded secondary, technical and university education, and other universal social services (Booth 1995).

For over 30 years, successive governments – both Conservative and Labour – intervened in the management of the economy through fiscal and monetary policies based on the economic theories of John Maynard Keynes (1936) or 'Keynesianism.' These aimed to maintain full employment, price stability, balance of payments equilibrium and economic growth, through a combination of fiscal, monetary and industrial policies to manage aggregate (or total) demand in the economy. It was assumed that raising aggregate demand stimulated economic activity. There were, however, both technical and practical problems in doing this. The outcome was a 'stop–go' cycle of economic expansion, near full employment and rising prices followed by economic contraction, rising unemployment and slower price rises. By the mid-1970s, 'stagflation' had taken root, with unemployment and prices rising together. This coincided with a breakdown of the fixed exchange rate mechanism, determined at the Bretton Woods conference in 1944, a quadrupling of oil prices and balance of payments crises in the UK. In 1976, the Labour government turned to the International Monetary Fund (IMF) for help. Government, in return for a loan to support sterling, adopted strict monetarist policies involving tight control over the money supply and tight fiscal policy to contain aggregate demand. The net result was a slowdown in price rises but rising unemployment (Owen 1999).

NEO-LIBERALISM AND NASCENT GLOBALISATION

The succeeding Conservative administrations (1979–97), led by Margaret Thatcher (1979–90) and John Major (1990–97), continued initially with a monetarist policy but also adopted what became known as supply-side economic policies (Oulton 1995). Monetarism, in contrast to Keynesianism, contends that controlling inflation is the most important policy goal for government. Demand management is self-defeating, because public spending crowds out private spending. Hence growth of money supply should be geared to the expected growth rate of real output in the economy or GNP, while the exchange rate is allowed to float, thus protecting the balance of payments. This means that public spending must balance tax revenues and be kept under tight control to prevent inflation.

Supply-side economics links with monetarism, since it rests on the assumption that market supply must be created before demand, if non-inflationary growth is to be sustained. It is the level of supply which ultimately determines the level of employment, not, as Keynes argued, the level of aggregate demand. Supply-side economics and monetarism, it is claimed, allow tax cuts, leave more income to be spent by households, provide incentives to work and generate real growth.

Growth, in turn, provides additional jobs in sectors where there is genuine private demand by households and consumers for new products or services. This 'genuine' demand is distinguished from the 'artificial' demand generated by government spending, which is often seen as keeping uncompetitive and technologically backward firms in business when they should go into liquidation. These theories reflected a resurgence of classical economic orthodoxy, which emphasises individual responsibility in the marketplace and denies government a major role in providing relief to the weak. Called neo-liberalism, these policies were associated with the ideas of the 'New Right' in politics, underpinned by the belief that market competition is the best way of promoting both economic growth and political freedoms. Under neo-liberalism, economic efficiency supersedes social equity as the guiding principle of public policy (Britton 1991).

During the Thatcher and Major administrations, control of inflation was the main policy goal and governments relied upon interest rates as their means of regulating demand. Exchange rate policy presented ambiguities, however, since rates were never permitted to float as freely as advocates of monetarism argued. There were testy debates about whether the UK should become a committed member of the European Exchange Rate Mechanism and whether she should sign up to European economic and monetary union (EMU). There were attempts to deregulate markets by removing constraints upon competition, especially in the banking sector, thus allowing the free interplay of supply and demand in the marketplace (Beatson 1995). Governments transferred important public assets, such as gas, electricity, telecommunications, water and railways, to the private sector through privatisation, and required the remaining public services to open their activities to the private sector through compulsory competitive tendering. Unemployment rose and continued at high levels throughout the period. The UK economy was transformed, as manufacturing declined rapidly and the service sector grew, especially financial services, to account for more 75 per cent of employment. For some observers, this was when a 'new' global capitalism emerged and political democracy was weakened (Hertz 2001) and where alternative economic policies were deemed to be both necessary and tenable (Ormerod 1998, Stiglitz 2002).

Promoting economic globalisation, examined more fully in Chapter 7, became a matter of public policy. The UK began weakening its restrictions designed to keep out overseas products and foreign investment, chiefly driven by cost changes caused by technological advances. New technology and lower transportation costs not only enhanced market size but also reduced managerial diseconomies of scale. It became easier to run large multinational companies globally. Global companies such as Microsoft, Shell, Nike and Nokia successfully transferred some operations in other countries, including the UK, with economies of scale enabling them to undercut domestic competition. Globalisation reflected, and continues to reflect, cheaper transport costs, better information technology, and a deliberate policy of reducing cross-country barriers to get efficiency gains from large-scale production and international specialisation.

THE ECONOMY UNDER 'NEW' LABOUR

The Blair administrations, from the election of 1997 until his resignation in 2007, claimed to have adopted a 'third way' in economic policy. In renewing 'social democracy', successive 'New' Labour governments argued that they had integrated the need for economic efficiency with social justice. The party claimed that it had also moved 'beyond an Old Left preoccupied by state control, high taxation and producer interests; and a New Right treating public investment, and often the very notion of "society" and collective endeavour, as evils to be undone' (Blair 1998, p1). According to Giddens (1998, p26), the third way transcended 'both social democracy and neoliberalism' and was presented as an alternative to state socialism, associated with the post-war Labour party, and market-liberalism advocated by the Conservatives in the 1980s and 1990s. Others argued that Labour governments simply adopted and adapted neo-liberal approaches through their support of a Third Way in politics (Budge *et al* 2007). Whatever the debates concerning the theoretical underpinning of the New Labour project, the economic record of these governments was remarkably successful during the years from 1997 until around 2007, when Gordon Brown was Chancellor of the Exchequer. He resigned as Chancellor in June 2007, on the retirement of Mr Blair, and became prime minister.

In historical terms, the period 1997–2007 was one of steady economic growth, low unemployment, low inflation and a stable currency. Income tax remained the same as under the Conservatives and interest rates were also low. Public spending began to rise in Labour's second administration 2001–05, as expenditure on health and education rose to nearer the levels in continental Europe. Serving as Chancellor of the Exchequer for just over 10 years meant that Gordon Brown, a fierce advocate of globalisation, was the UK's longest serving modern Chancellor. Some of the major measures he initiated included:

- making the Bank of England independent of government

- changing the measure of inflation from the retail price index to the consumer price index

- reducing the basic rate of income tax from 23 per cent to 20 per cent

- reducing corporation tax from 33 per cent to 28 per cent and from 24 per cent to 19 per cent for small businesses

- introducing working tax credits

- transferring responsibility for banking supervision to the Financial Services Agency

- supporting major expansions of government spending on healthcare and education

- selling off some 60 per cent of the UK's gold reserves

- raising UK tax revenue from 39.2 per cent in 1997 to 42.4 per cent in 2006.

LABOUR AND THE GLOBAL FINANCIAL CRISIS, 2007–08

In summer 2007, a financial crisis, starting in the United States, began spreading to the West, providing a timely reminder of one of the perennial truths of financial history: 'Sooner or later every bubble bursts. Sooner or later the bearish sellers outnumber the bullish buyers' (Ferguson 2009, p9). The cause was a spasm in the credit system precipitated by mounting defaults on a type of debt known as sub-prime mortgages. Relatively poor families in the United States had bought homes financed by complex loans that were packaged or 'bundled' together and sold by American banks to overseas banks. When the borrowers defaulted on their payments, US house prices fell, followed by falls in the value of various securities. A chain reaction followed, resulting in the banks taking over these securities and the ratio of bank assets to their capital resources leaping upwards. American and European banks suffered enormous losses and turned to their central banks (such as the Bank of England) for short-term assistance, and to Asian and Middle Eastern sovereign wealth funds to rebuild their capital bases. In the UK, matters came to a head, when long queues started forming outside the branches of Northern Rock, a demutualised former building society which had become a bank, wanting to withdraw their savings. The Bank of England announced that it was supporting the bank and, shortly afterwards, the new Chancellor, Alistair Darling, said that government would guarantee the bank's deposits. Northern Rock and the Royal Bank of Scotland were subsequently partially nationalised. The UK's financial establishment had been shaken to its core and, with the Treasury's injection of additional spending power into the national economy financed by public borrowing, Keynesian policy prescriptions had been rediscovered.

Ferguson (2009) argues that six interrelated financial phenomena go some way in explaining what happened:

- By using debt to finance investment, many US and European banks had highly leveraged balance sheets.

- A whole range of debts, both mortgages and credit cards, were re-bundled into bond-like securities and sold in the markets.

- The monetary policies of central banks focused on a narrow definition of inflation, ignoring potential 'bubbles' in stock and property prices.

- The insurance industry branched out of traditional risk coverage into the market for derivatives, effectively selling protection against highly uncertain financial risks.

- Politicians in both the United States and the UK sought to increase the percentage of households owning homes, using inducements to widen the mortgage market.

- Asian governments, especially the People's Republic of China, helped finance the US current account deficit by accumulating trillions of dollars in international reserves.

Cable (2009, p3) goes further and describes this financial crisis as 'The Storm,' since it combined 'a systemic crisis in the financial system, price shocks, cyclical downturn and painful structural adjustment'. The main focus of attention centred on the banking system but there was also a severe price shock, with sharp increases in the prices of energy, raw materials and food. The commodity price shock coincided in the UK, the United States, Spain and elsewhere with the creation of a bubble in the housing market and a new generation of home owners who had persuaded themselves that property prices could only go up. The bursting of the house price bubble was linked to the so-called 'credit crunch', since bank credit was drastically curtailed in the wake of a collapse of confidence in the financial system. In Cable's view, the painful economic transformation under Mrs Thatcher, and then the decade of sustained growth under New Labour, had produced national overconfidence. This arose out of having an economy that seemed to be working well and rested on three foundations: first, the success of the global financial services sector, centred on London; second, an openness to overseas investors as a source of technology, management and capital; and, third, a sense of personal prosperity and well-being derived from rising property prices and household consumption, financed by borrowing.

For Cable (2009, p154) and others, the so-called economic miracle was exposed as being fundamentally flawed. First, the housing bubble, and associated mortgage debt, had exposed a serious weakness in economic policy, because of the failure of the central bank to manage asset inflation, followed by deflation. Second, the property bubble was a symptom of a deeper problem and the spilling over into the banking system of an excess of liquidity, originating in cheap foreign money. For many, rising living standards had been financed by household borrowing, with household saving declining 'from 7 per cent of disposable income in 1998 to under 3 per cent in 2008'. Since the late 1980s, the UK had been running current account deficits financed by imported capital. Third, New Labour's servile reverence to the City and its exaggerated deference to their concerns had led to the UK having 'a seriously unbalanced economy, more exposed to major financial shocks than others.'

ACTIVITY 6.2

What are the major differences between monetarism and supply-side economics and Keynesianism? Why did governments adopt monetarism and supply-side economics and abandon Keynesianism? Have these economic policies been more successful in achieving their objectives? What has been their impact on the HR function?

STRUCTURE OF THE UK ECONOMY

The structure of the UK economy has changed significantly over the past 60 years. In 1950 manufacturing accounted for over a third of national GDP; now it has declined to around 10 per cent. There is some debate about the causes and consequences of the relative (but not absolute) decline of manufacturing output in the UK, since real output in manufacturing continues to rise slowly due to capital investment, rising productivity and improved production systems. One reason for the relative decline is that as households and individuals become richer, demand for manufactured goods declines and rising incomes are spent on services including leisure, financial products and healthcare. De-industrialisation or the post-industrial economy, however, is not limited to the UK; it is common to all developed economies (Griffiths and Wall 2004).

The UK is facing keen competition from other Organisation for Economic Co-operation and Development countries and is losing her share of world markets in manufactured goods to Germany, France, Sweden and Spain. She lacks competitive edge in terms of price and quality. The UK's exports of services such as finance, where growth is now located. The UK's exports of services such as finance, insurance and information technology continue to expand, compared with other economies, with some three-quarters of her workforce employed in the service sector. In this sense, the UK is in transformation from an industrial to a post-industrial, information or knowledge-based economy (Kahin and Foray 2006).

A main reason for the relative decline of UK manufacturing is competition from the newly industrialising economies of South-East Asia – the so-called 'Tiger Economies' of Malaysia, Thailand, Singapore, Korea and Taiwan, as well as the emergence of China and India as major economic forces. Because firms in these countries pay lower wages, have lower social security costs and invest heavily in new plant and machinery, they have a competitive advantage over manufacturers in developed countries. It is these socio-economic conditions and higher levels of productivity which encourage Western multinational corporations to locate in the Far East. This raises profits and gets higher returns on capital investments. While these countries export manufactured goods, they also import them and their share of exports into developed countries remains fairly low. Indeed, most trade of developed countries is with other developed countries.

Some take a less sanguine view of de-industrialisation. They argue not only that are there job losses, de-skilling and rising unemployment but also that a strong manufacturing base is crucial for economic growth, technological innovation and export potential (Blackaby 1979). Whether de-industrialisation can be accounted for by import penetration, low investment, low productivity or lack of competitiveness is the subject of debate. During the 1970s and 1980s, Keynesians argued that the UK's problem was that she could not get economic growth without suffering import penetration. What was needed was reflation and economic protectionism to prevent import penetration. Writers like Bacon and Eltis (1976), in contrast, attributed manufacturing decline to growth of the non-market sector. They argued that public sector spending was crowding out the private sector, which was unable to expand for lack of sufficient resources. Further, such spending is seen as 'taxing' the private sector, which has less money to spend in the marketplace.

Another important economic sector is energy and water supply, which are now largely privately owned by overseas investors. The share of output provided by this sector to GDP has remained fairly constant over the past 50 years at around 5 per cent, although it went up to over 10 per cent during the mid-1980s. Energy and water supply cover capital-intensive industries such as oil, gas and water. The importance of oil has grown, giving rise to debates about 'peak oil' and whether world supplies have reached their limits (Strachan 2007). Other sectors remaining fairly stable over the past 50 years are: construction, public administration and defence, the wholesale and retail trades, hotels and restaurants, and transport and communications. The sectors demonstrating the most significant rises in their shares in GDP over the last 50 years, as indicated above, have been services. The share of financial and business services has increased from some 3 per cent to about a fifth, while that of education, health and social work has increased from about 3 per cent to 12 per cent.

The largest relative decline to UK GDP has been agriculture, forestry and fishing. They accounted for about 5 per cent of GDP 50 years ago but now constitute only 2 per cent. The differential decline of agriculture can be explained in terms of more intensive farming methods, greater competitiveness, and the impact of the Common Agricultural Policy on the supply of agricultural products in the marketplace, resulting in overproduction (European Commission 2008).

ACTIVITY 6.3

Examine the cases for and against the service-based, post-industrial economy. What possible impacts does de-industrialisation have on the HR function?

THE MICRO-ECONOMY: DETERMINANTS OF SUPPLY AND DEMAND IN THE MARKETPLACE

A market is where the buying and selling of goods or services takes place, although it does not need a physical presence. Markets may be local, regional, national or global. Although most economists regard markets as primarily economic phenomena, they are social constructs too that enable buying and selling to take place within certain rules and conventions. In Far Eastern cultures, for example, there is often no 'fixed' market price for particular goods (say a suit) or a service (say a haircut), since it is expected that the parties will bargain over the price at which the commodity is actually bought and sold.

Markets consist of producers and consumers or sellers and buyers, who may be individuals, households, businesses or government agencies. In modern advanced market economies, business corporations and government agencies dominate the supply side of markets, with households, firms, public agencies and individuals buying commodities. A free market is one in which the forces of supply and demand are allowed to operate without the interference of third parties or institutions. In free markets, it is the pressure produced by the interplay of market forces, or supply and demand, which induce adjustments in market prices and/or the quantities traded in the marketplace. Prices are normally measured in monetary values, with equilibrium being reached where the quantity that consumers are prepared to buy equals the quantity that producers are prepared to sell at that price. Prices act as signals which co-ordinate the economic actions of individual decision-making units and provide a mechanism whereby changes in supply and demand affect the allocative efficiency of resources in the economy as a whole (Begg *et al* 2008). A basic analysis of market supply and market demand is provided below.

MARKET SUPPLY

The quantity of a commodity supplied by a producer (including labour, for example) is the amount the producer is prepared to sell at a particular price at a particular time. It is influenced by four main factors:

- market price of the commodity
- costs of the factors of production
- goals of the producer
- current state of technology.

It can be hypothesised that the higher the market price of a commodity, the greater the quantity that the producer is willing to supply, because more profit is made in doing this. Conversely, the lower the market price, the smaller the quantity that the producer is willing to supply. Similarly, the lower the costs of factors of production, the greater is the quantity the producer is willing to supply, while the higher the costs of the factors of production, the smaller is the quantity that the producer is willing to supply. Quantity supplied also changes according to the producer's goals – whether it is aiming to maximise profits, maximise sales, enter a new market or maintain an existing market position. Technological developments affect quantity supplied, because they lower unit costs of production and ensure higher output at lower cost.

Market supply increases when there is a rise in the quantity supplied at each price. It decreases when there is a fall in the quantity supplied at each price. Factors causing an increase in market supply include:

- falls in the prices of other commodities
- falls in the costs of factors of production
- changes in the goals of producers
- technological improvements.

The causes of a decrease in market supply are rises in the costs of factors of production and changes in the goals of producers.

MARKET DEMAND

The quantity of a commodity demanded by a consumer is the amount the consumer wishes to buy at a particular price at a particular time. It is influenced by a number of factors. These include:

- market price of the commodity

- prices of other commodities
- size of consumer income
- consumer tastes
- social factors.

It can be hypothesised that the lower the price of the commodity, the greater the quantity the consumer is willing to buy. Conversely, the higher the price, the smaller the quantity the consumer is willing to buy. Where commodities are substitutes for one another – butter and margarine, for example – a fall in the price of one causes a fall in the quantity demanded of the other. Conversely, a rise in the price of one causes a rise in the quantity demanded of the other. Where commodities are complementary, such as pipes and tobacco, a fall in the price of one results in a rise in the quantity demanded of the other, while a rise in the price of one causes a fall in the quantity demanded of the other. Where commodities are unrelated, a change in the price of one does not directly affect the quantity demanded of the other.

Normally a rise in consumer income results in a rise in the quantity demanded of a commodity. Similarly, a fall in consumer income results in a fall in demand. This is usually the case with consumer goods. In other cases, a rise in consumer demand results in a rise in the quantity demanded up to a certain level; then it falls away. Consumer demand for basic foods, for example, is not infinite. Quantity demanded may decline above a certain level of income, as consumers transfer income to more expensive foods. In other cases, quantity demanded rises to a certain level of income and then remains unaffected. Social factors such as sex, age, social class, educational attainment and occupation affect quantity demanded, while changes in consumer tastes have similar effects.

Market demand increases when there is a rise in quantity demanded at each price, and decreases when there is a fall in quantity demanded at each price. The factors causing an increase in market demand include:

- rises in the prices of substitutes
- falls in the prices of complements
- rises in consumer income
- changes in consumer taste.

Decreases in market demand are the reverse of the above and are caused by: falls in prices of substitutes, rises in prices of complements, falls in consumer income, and changes in taste.

MARKET CLEARANCE

In economic theory, a market clears, or is in equilibrium, when the price balances the quantity supplied with the quantity demanded in the marketplace. At prices below the equilibrium price, there is excess demand in the market, which tends to raise the price of the product. At prices above the equilibrium price, there is excess supply, which tends to reduce the price of the product. In a free market, deviations from the equilibrium price tend to be self-correcting.

Any factor increasing supply increases equilibrium quantity but reduces equilibrium price, whilst reductions in supply reduce equilibrium quantity but increase equilibrium price. Similarly, any factor increasing demand increases equilibrium price and equilibrium quantity, whilst decreases in demand reduce both equilibrium price and quantity.

MARKET STRUCTURES AND MARKET REGULATION

In free or 'perfect' markets (with many small producers selling homogeneous or identical products, for example), prices are determined by the interplay of supply and demand, and market equilibrium is reached where, in aggregate, consumers and producers are satisfied with the current combination of price and quantity of units bought and sold per period of time. However, there are few 'perfect' or 'free' markets in the real world and competition among producers or suppliers of goods and services is a normal part of economic behaviour, although the intensity of competition varies (Office of Fair Trading 2007). These market structures, together with lack of full knowledge of markets by consumers, lead to market imperfections, as shown in Figure 6.2.

Figure 6.2 Types of market competition

Type of competition	Main features of the market
Perfect competition	• There are many producers in an industry or sector (such as fruit or vegetable markets) • The typical firm is small in size • Products are homogeneous. • There are no barriers to entry to the market • The degree of market concentration in the market
Monopolistic competition	• There are many producers in an industry or sector (such as clothes retailing) • The typical firm is small in size • Products are differentiated • There are few barriers of entry to the market • The degree of market concentration in the sector is very low
Oligopoly	• There are few producers in an industry or sector (such as car manufacturing) • The typical firm is large in size • Products are either differentiated or homogeneous • There are many barriers of entry to these markets • The degree of market concentration is high
Monopoly	• There is one producer in an industry or sector, with no close substitutes, such as water supply • The typical firm is large in size • Only one product is sold • There are high barriers of entry to the market • The degree of market concentration in the sector is very high

Since markets are based on demand, backed by ability to pay, not on need, they can operate at below optimum use of available resources. Governments find it necessary to intervene in markets for various economic, social and moral reasons. One form of intervention is regulation of markets. Since the 1960s, there have been many examples of market regulation. These include: employment protection (such as the statutory minimum wage); equal opportunities; health and safety at work; controls on prices, wages and profits; regulation of financial markets; and competition policy through control of monopolies and mergers. Since the 1980s, new forms of regulation have been introduced, including industry-specific regulatory bodies linked to the privatisation of gas, water, electricity, railways and telecommunications (Corry 2003). At the same time, extensive deregulation has occurred, allowing markets such as bus transport and financial services to expand.

ACTIVITY 6.4

Identify three local businesses in the area where you live. What kind of market structure does each one of them operate in? In each case, on what basis do their products or services compete with other businesses in the same sector?

ACTIVITY 6.5

Identify and analyse the factors affecting property prices in the UK over the last 15 years. Are house prices likely to rise or fall over the next five years and why?

CAPITAL MARKETS

In the market economy, the capital or financial markets are among the most important elements. These are interrelated markets where money is bought and sold and finance capital is raised, lent and borrowed on varying terms for varying periods of time. They incorporate sub-markets such as the credit market, stock market and foreign exchange market. There are strong forces causing conditions in one set of financial markets to affect the others, nationally and internationally.

THE BANK OF ENGLAND

The Bank of England is the central bank of the UK. The Bank, founded in 1694, was nationalised in 1946 and gained operational independence in 1997. Standing at the centre of the UK's financial system, the Bank is committed to promoting and maintaining a stable and efficient monetary and financial framework as its contribution to a healthy economy. The Bank's roles and functions have evolved and changed over its 300-year history. Since its foundation it has been the government's banker, and since the late eighteenth century it has been banker to the banking system more generally or the bankers' bank. As well as providing banking services to its customers, the Bank manages the UK's foreign exchange and gold reserves and the government's stock register. The Bank is most visible to the general public through issuing banknotes and, more recently, its interest rate decisions. The Bank has had a monopoly on the issue of banknotes in England and Wales since the early twentieth century. It is only since 1997 that the Bank has had statutory responsibility for setting the UK's official interest rate.

Monetary policy

One of the Bank's core purposes is maintaining the integrity and value of sterling as the national currency. It pursues this core purpose primarily through the conduct of monetary policy. This involves, above all, maintaining price stability, as defined by the inflation target set by government, as a precondition for achieving a wider economic goal of sustainable growth and employment. High inflation can be damaging to the functioning of the economy. Low inflation or price stability can help foster sustainable long-term economic growth. In 1997, the Chancellor of the Exchequer announced that government was giving the Bank operational responsibility for setting interest rates, and this was achieved through The Bank of England Act 1998.

The Bank's monetary policy objective is to deliver price stability, as defined by the government's inflation target, and support the government's economic policy, including its objectives for growth and employment. The government's inflation target is confirmed in each Budget statement. The Bank's inflation forecast is published in the form of a probability distribution and is presented in what is now known as the 'fan chart'. The price stability objective is to normally achieve an inflation target of, say, 2 per cent as measured by the 12-month increase in the Consumer Prices Index, which is the retail prices index excluding mortgage interest payments.

The Bank aims to meet the government's inflation target by setting short-term interest rates through its Monetary Policy Committee (MPC). Monetary policy operates by influencing the cost of money. The Bank sets an interest rate for its own dealings with the market, and that rate then affects the whole pattern of rates set by the commercial banks for their savers and borrowers. This, in turn, affects spending and output in the economy, and eventually costs and prices. Broadly speaking, interest rates are set at a level to ensure demand in the economy is in line with its productive capacity. If interest rates are set too low, demand may exceed supply and lead to the emergence of inflationary pressures. If they are set too high, output is likely to be unnecessarily low and inflation is likely to decelerate.

The MPC takes interest rate decisions and implements them through its financial market operations by setting the interest rate at which the Bank lends to banks and other financial institutions. The Bank has close links with financial markets and institutions. This contact informs a great deal of its work, including collating and publishing monetary and banking statistics. The MPC meets monthly and takes decisions by majority vote, with the Governor having the casting vote if necessary. The Treasury has the right to be represented in a non-voting capacity and legislation provides that in extreme circumstances, and if the national interest demands it, the government has power to give instructions to the Bank on interest rates for a limited period.

A stable financial system

The Bank is also responsible for maintaining stability in the financial system, since a healthy financial system is vital to the proper functioning of the economy. The Bank analyses and promotes initiatives to strengthen the financial system and monitors financial developments to identify potential threats to financial stability. It also undertakes work for handling financial crises should they occur and, in exceptional circumstances, is the financial system's 'lender of last resort'. In this work, the Bank co-operates closely with Her Majesty's Treasury and the Financial Services Authority, the regulator of banks and other financial institutions in the UK. In March 2009, for example, the Monetary Policy Committee announced that, in addition to setting the Bank Rate at 0.5 per cent, it would start to inject money directly into the economy ('quantitative easing') in order to meet the inflation target. The instrument of monetary policy shifted towards the quantity of money provided rather than its price (Bank Rate). But the objective of policy remained unchanged – to meet the inflation target of 2 per cent on the CPI measure of consumer prices. Influencing the quantity of money directly is essentially a different means of reaching the same end.

The Bank also works to ensure that the UK financial system provides effective support to the rest of the UK economy and that the UK remains an attractive location for the conduct of international financial business. This involves working on issues such as firms' access to finance and, over recent years, the evolution of the Euro financial markets and infrastructure.

THE LONDON STOCK EXCHANGE

The London Stock Exchange (LSE) is one of the world's oldest stock exchanges and its origins can be traced back more than 300 years. Starting life in the coffee houses of seventeenth-century London, the Exchange quickly grew to become the City's most important financial institution. Today, the LSE is at the heart of global financial markets and is home to some of the best companies in the world. It grows its business through business development initiatives, acquisitions, joint ventures and alliances where appropriate. To implement this strategy, the LSE has three objectives (London Stock Exchange Group 2009). The first is to reinforce and extend its position as the premier source of equity market liquidity, benchmark prices and market data in the European time zone. The second is to operate a diversified business that capitalises on the emergence of an increasingly innovative environment, through leadership in technology and market services. The third is to deliver superior value to its customers and shareholders.

The LSE has three 'core businesses.'

- **Equity markets:** the LSE enables companies from around the world to raise the capital they need, by listing securities on its highly efficient, transparent and well-regulated markets. Through its main market, the LSE gives companies access to one of the world's deepest and most liquid pools of investment capital. Once companies have been admitted to trading, it uses its staff expertise in the global financial markets to help them maximise the value of their listing in London.

- **Trading services:** the LSE provides the trading platforms used by broking firms around the world to buy and sell securities. Its systems provide fast and efficient access to trading, allowing investors and institutions to tap quickly into equity, bond and derivative markets. Internationally recognised standards of regulation and market practice make its markets some of the most attractive and liquid in the world. Over 300 worldwide firms trade as members of the LSE.

- **Information:** the LSE supplies high-quality, real-time prices, news and other information to the global financial community. Strong relationships with data vendors help ensure the markets receive the information they depend upon. It invests heavily in the best technology to create new applications for its data and works closely with its world-class partners to constantly upgrade its products and services.

COMMERCIAL BANKS AND RELATED INSTITUTIONS

Commercial banks and related financial institutions, such as savings banks, building societies, insurance companies and credit organisations, are financial intermediaries. All these institutions are now networked and interconnected, using the latest information technologies to manage their businesses. This means that their commercial responses are speedy and efficient. The large, major banks take in funds principally as deposits repayable on demand or at short notice, which they use to make advances by overdrafts and loans to their customers. They hold financial stocks and maintain a money transaction mechanism by accepting deposits on current accounts and operate a system of transferring funds between banks by cheques (which are becoming less common nowadays) and credit transfers. Other important banking functions include providing credit to businesses, providing foreign exchange services for customers, financing foreign trade, operating in money markets and providing advisory services to customers. Banks have a central position in the financial system and financial markets. They control the money payments mechanism, form a major element in the money stock and have an important role as short-term lenders.

With deregulation of financial markets since the late 1970s, the lines of division between banks and other financial institutions are increasingly blurred and overlapping. For example, the retail banks engage not only in normal retailing activities but also in more risky investment banking. However, with the renewed dominance of these reformed institutions in the financial marketplace, Augar (2000) describes the period as 'the death of gentlemanly capitalism', while Soros

(2000), in turn, argues for further reforms as necessary to manage and stabilise the new 'global capitalism'.

Soros's warning was not heeded, however, and there was a profound financial crisis in the banking system in UK, and other parts of the world, in 2007–08. This financial and economic crisis caused intense pain, with lots of people losing their jobs, pensions, homes and businesses. Further, it provoked questioning among some commentators not only of international economic integration or globalisation (see Chapter 7) but also of the private enterprise system generally. Many prudent, socially responsible people in the UK were suffering because of the crisis while reckless, incompetent people, such as senior bankers and financial speculators, were not. On the one hand, the commercial banks were rescued by government action and therefore by taxpayers' money. On the other hand, banks were generally reluctant to stop paying bonuses to staff, on the grounds of their claimed worth internationally, and were withdrawing their credit facilities from businesses. To stop the national banking system collapsing completely, and to revitalise it, some short-term measures were adopted by the UK government and some possible longer-term solutions proposed, as indicated in Figure 6.3.

Figure 6.3   UK government's economic measures following the financial crisis post-2008

Short-term measures
<ul><li>The UK government injected some £37 billion into the banks in 2008 to provide fresh capital and to try to get them lending again</li><li>The UK government guaranteed inter-bank lending</li><li>The UK government part-nationalised some banks such as the Royal Bank of Scotland and Lloyds-TSB</li><li>The UK government continued trying to keep the banks transforming short-term assets into long-term loans, until a more fundamental reform of the banking system could be introduced</li></ul>
Longer-term solutions
<ul><li>Further recapitalisation of the banks</li><li>Forcing banks to lend to their customers</li><li>Providing lending guarantees for banks</li><li>Enforcing a much increased role for the state in the banking system</li><li>Creating a new regulatory regime providing better protection against systemic risk within the banks</li></ul>

ACTIVITY 6.6

Identify as many as possible of the different organisations that supply money to customers, and consider the effects this has on government's ability to control money supply.

ACTIVITY 6.7

The late Professor James Tobin proposed a global tax, collected by national governments, on foreign exchange transactions to reduce speculation in international currency markets. The proceeds of this tax could then be used to fund Third World projects or support the United Nations. In reaction to the global financial crisis 2007–08, some influential supporters of a 'Tobin' tax have argued for a 0.05 per cent tax on speculative bank trading of every £1,000 traded to help the urgent needs of the world's poorest peoples. What are the cases for and against a Tobin tax?

LABOUR MARKETS

The national labour market consists of the working population, or all those men and women available for and capable of work in the economy as a whole. It includes those in paid employment or self-employment, as well as those who are unemployed (ie those seeking work). Over the last 40 years, unemployment has fluctuated widely, as a result not only of industrial restructuring and recessions but also of the ways governments have recorded the numbers who are unemployed. Table 6.1 shows the incremental growth of the UK working population for selected years from 1971 until 2008.

Table 6.1 Estimated UK working population 1971–2008 (for selected years)

Millions

Year	Employed	Economically active
1971	24.6	25.6
1976	24.8	26.1
1981	24.7	27.0
1986	24.7	27.8
1991	26.7	28.9
1996	26.0	28.4
2001	27.6	29.1
2006	28.7	30.3
2008	29.0	31.5

Adapted from Economic and Labour Review (2010)

A major determinant of pay rates and numbers of workers employed nationally, and by organisations, is the demand for labour relative to its supply in the labour market. Where labour demand exceeds supply, pay rates rise. Where labour supply exceeds demand, pay rates fall. The determinants of an employer's demand for labour are complex. It depends partly on the structure of the external labour market (which may be international for some types of labour), the firm's internal labour market and the local labour market. The total supply of labour available to an economy is determined by the size of the population of working age, the availability of labour globally, and the number of hours that workers are prepared to work. From an employer's point of view, labour supply is affected by its quality, mobility and potential productivity.

A firm's external labour market (ELM) is the number of workers available to work for it. Within the ELM, pricing and allocation decisions are controlled largely by economic variables, but employer decisions are crucial. In practice the ELM is highly segmented by occupation, industry, geography, gender, ethnicity and age (Rubery 1989). The dual labour market hypothesis claims that the ELM is dichotomised into primary and secondary sectors. The primary sector is characterised by 'good' jobs and the secondary sector by 'bad' ones. Good jobs have high pay, high status, promotion prospects, fringe benefits and job security. Bad jobs, with contrary characteristics, are allocated to those excluded from the primary sector because of lack of investment in 'human capital' or because they are discriminated against. In the secondary sector, pay rates are established largely by competition and market supply and demand. Work in the secondary sector is generally low paid, unattractive and unstable.

Internal labour markets (ILMs), which are used by some 'best practice' employers (see Chapter 5), are arrangements where labour is supplied and demanded within a firm, without direct access to the ELM. Employment policies are directed towards those employed in the firm, with most jobs being filled by the promotion or transfer of workers who are already working for the company. ILMs therefore are sets of employment relationships, embodying formal and informal rules governing each job and the relationships between them.

Local labour markets (LLMs) are largely the consequences of the financial and psychological costs and disadvantages to workers of extensive time spent travelling to work. These costs further segment a labour force which is already stratified by the characteristics outlined above. LLMs tend to restrict a firm's labour market to that which is accessible from a defined geographical area, for less skilled occupational groups at least.

THE UK WORKFORCE

In November 2009, there were some 38 million people of working age in the UK. Some 29 million of these were in full-time or part-time employment, with around two million unemployed and actively seeking work. Within the total labour force, 22.8 million were employed in the private sector and 6.2 million in the public sector. A further estimated seven million people of working age were defined as being economically inactive, or about 18 per cent of the total. The economically inactive category consists of full-time students, people who have taken early retirement, people who are disabled or suffering from a long-term medical condition, and people looking after a family or home. The percentage of people of working age classified as economically inactive has not changed dramatically over the past 40 years. It was at its lowest in the late 1980s and early 1990s but has increased since 1991. Table 6.1 above shows estimates of the UK working population for selected years.

One of the most significant workforce and labour market trends in recent years has been the growth of female participation in the workforce. In 1979, 59 per cent of women were classed as being economically active. By 1981 the proportion had risen to 65 per cent, and by 1991 to 72 per cent. It now stands at around 73.3 per cent, compared with 83.5 per cent of economically active men of working age. It is the increase in the female participation rate which is the main reason for the long-term increase of people in paid work in the UK over the past 40 years (Office for National Statistics 2008b).

Patterns of work and employment have changed significantly since the end of the Second World War, in both the UK and elsewhere. General occupational and industry trends in UK employment are summarised in Figure 6.4 (Office for National Statistics 2008b). Further details of the distribution of workforce jobs by industry in 2009 are indicated in Table 6.2.

Figure 6.4 Occupational and industry trends in UK employment 2008

Expanding occupations	**Expanding sectors**
• managerial and senior official occupations (15.2 per cent)	• distribution, hotels and restaurants employ some 6.5 million, compared with 4.8 million in 1978
• professional occupations (12.9 per cent)	• transport and communications employ some 1.4 million, compared with 1.5 million in 1978
• associate professional and technical occupations (14.6 per cent)	• finance and business services employ some 5.2 million, compared with 2.5 million in 1978
• administrative and secretarial occupations (12.6 per cent)	• public administration, education and health employ some 7 million, compared with 5 million in 1978
• personal services (8.6 per cent)	• other services employ 1.4 million, compared with 800,000 in 1978
Occupations in decline	**Sectors in decline**
• skilled occupations or trades (8.2 per cent)	• agriculture and fishing employ some 200,000, compared with 500,000 in 1978
• sales and customer services (8.5 per cent)	• energy and water employ some 100,000, compared with 750,000 in 1978
• process, plant and machine operatives (6.9 per cent)	• manufacturing employs some 3 million, compared with 7 million in 1978
• elementary occupations (12.5 per cent)	• construction employs some 1.2 million, compared with 1.3 million in 1978

Adapted from Office for National Statistics (2008b)

Table 6.2 Workforce jobs by industry and sex 2009

	All jobs	Agriculture & fishing	Energy & water	Manufacturing	Construction	Distribution & hotels	Transport & communications	Finance & other services	Public administration
	30,861	487	195	2,840	2,095	6,830	1,836	8,342	8,237
Males	16,315	388	143	2,128	1,855	3,382	1,385	4,546	2,488
Females	14,546	99	52	712	240	3,448	451	3,796	5,749

Adapted from Economic and Labour Review (2010)

ACTIVITY 6.8

Explain the changes in the occupational and sector structures of the working population in the UK since the late 1970s.

WORKING PATTERNS

The growth and widespread use of computing technology and the World-Wide Web, and the shift from a manufacturing-based economy to a service-based one, have encouraged changes in the ways people work. The standard pattern of work, from nine to five, Monday to Friday, is less common than in the past. This move towards non-standard work is fuelled by 'employer-pull' for more employment flexibility and 'worker-push' for a balanced approach between working time and the needs of families and individuals. Changes have been taking place in part-time working; temporary work and shift work. These changes in working patterns over time indicate attempts by individuals and employers to develop a more flexible approach to work. As McOrmond (2004, p24) concludes: 'Employers may be using non-standard working arrangements to create a labour force that is more flexible and thus suited to meet market demand, and employees may be attempting to create a more effective work–life balance.'

Part-time working

In November 2009, there were 21.3 million people in full-time work and 7.7 million part-timers. Of these, 13.6 million men were in full-time employment and 7.8 million women. In terms of part-time employment, there were 5.8 million women working part time, compared with 1.8 million men.

The reasons why people work part time have changed since the late 1990s. There has been a slight increase in the proportion of people not wanting full-time jobs and those who cannot find them. The largest increase in those taking part-time work is among students. Women make up a larger proportion of part-time workers than men, who are likely to work part time voluntarily, because they do not need to work full time. Women working part time are most likely to want to spend more time at home with their families. Doogan (2001) has shown that part-time work provides long-term employment options. Indeed, a majority of women who have been in full-time employment before taking maternity leave are likely to switch to part-time work on their return. This has contributed to long-term employment among women. There is also a trend for people past the default retirement age, or who have been made redundant from full-time jobs but not yet reached retirement age, to take part-time employment.

People aged 16 to 19 are the most likely age group to be working part time in the UK. About a half of men and two-thirds of women in this group work part time. Women aged 25 to 29 are the least likely to be in part-time employment. However, in all age groups, women are more likely to work part time than men.

The proportion of employees working part time is greatest in distribution, where women are more likely to work part time than men. This is also the case in other services, public administration and agriculture.

Temporary working

Temporary employment ranges from seasonal, casual work in sectors such as agriculture to independent consultants taking on a series of contracts for a single employer. It is work of limited duration. Temporary employment is most common amongst those aged under 25, irrespective of gender. Prime-age people are least likely to do temporary work, although women are almost twice as likely to do so as men. The reasons for working temporarily include not being able to find permanent work or not wanting it.

Shift work

The proportion of people doing shift work (ie working non-standard hours) has hardly changed over the years. It is men who predominantly work shifts, and this is related to the higher proportion of men employed in manufacturing, where shift work remains common. Shift work is also common in transport but is least common in construction. There is a strong history of shift work in health-related occupations, personal services and emergency services, where there is a need for 24-hour, seven-day coverage. A high proportion of women work shifts in healthcare, although emergency services such as police, fire and prison services are populated largely by male workers. For men, shift work is common among those aged 16–19. Men aged 60–64 are the group least likely to work shifts. Among women, those aged 16–19 are the highest proportion doing shift work. These trends are possibly linked to the growing need to finance their post-secondary education.

Working time

In terms of working time, managers are most likely to work more than 45 hours per week, with the greatest proportion being men. Long working hours are also common among skilled trades, plant/machine operatives and professional occupations. Those least likely to work more than 45 hours are administrative workers. In nearly all occupations, over half of those employed are likely to work between 31 and up to 45 hours per week. The exceptions are normally personal services, sales and elementary occupations (Office for National Statistics 2009a).

ACTIVITY 6.9

Critically examine the reasons given for increased employment flexibility. Identify and evaluate the different types of flexibility that enable an organisation to meet both its organisational needs and those of its employees.

ACTIVITY 6.10

Identify and describe the types of labour market that your organisation recruits from.

THE 'HOUR-GLASS' DEBATE

According to a number of commentators, an 'hour-glass' occupational structure could be emerging in the UK. This is one in which half of the new jobs being created are 'high skill/high pay' ones and the other half 'low skill/low pay' ones. The debate has been popularised by Goos and Manning (2003), who argue the following is happening:

• Increasing numbers of people are employed in relatively high paid, secure, professional and managerial occupations in finance, private services and parts of the public sector.

• Jobs in manufacturing, along with many clerical and administrative roles, are being exported to Eastern Europe, the People's Republic of China, India and other developing countries, where wages are lower.

• At the same time, growing numbers of higher-paid people in the UK are using their disposable incomes to buy services not provided from overseas. Thus there is growing domestic demand for hairdressers, beauticians, restaurant workers, and people working in the tourist and entertainment sectors.

• There is also a demand for, and shortage of, some groups of skilled workers, such as plumbers, electricians and builders, whose jobs cannot be easily exported.

Fitzner (2006) challenges this analysis by arguing, first, that the Goos and Manning paper relies on old data collected from 1976 to 1999. Second, he claims, more recent data demonstrate that the 'disappearing middle' is no longer disappearing. Third, polarisation between Apple 'Macjobs' and McDonald's 'Mcjobs', in his view, has already halted. Notably, the period covered by Fitzner's analysis was when around half of all new jobs created were in the public sector, such as hospitals, education, the police and public administration. Most of these are middle-income professional occupations. Expansion of the public sector had ceased by 2008 and was unlikely to resume after the financial crisis of 2007–08, in view of the increases in public borrowing incurred at this time, and subsequent cutbacks in public spending by the Coalition Government.

ACTIVITY 6.11

Do you agree (or not agree) with the hour-glass thesis and why?

MARKETISATION, COMPETITION AND CHANGE MANAGEMENT IN PUBLIC SERVICES

Central and local government are an important part of the economy. They provide public services, funded largely from taxes, although there is a trend for some charging to individual users to be introduced. This is known as 'co-payment'. However, public services are generally provided collectively for individual consumption as citizen rights, not according to ability to pay. A series of reforms in the way public services are managed, reviewed and assessed has taken place since the late 1970s. Traditionally, public services were insulated from the pressures of the market, competition and change management. They were relatively stable organisations administered by civil or public servants for the 'public good'. Today market forces, competition, choice and change management are as commonplace within public services as they are in the private sector.

THE SCOPE OF PUBLIC SERVICES

Public services include national defence, law enforcement, fire protection, environmental health, healthcare, personal social services, education, roads, recreational facilities and consumer protection. Central government has overall responsibility for public services and for deciding what services are to be provided, funded and administered. But there is no rational explanation for the current distribution of responsibilities between central and local government, which has evolved in a pragmatic fashion (Windrum and Koch 2008). Public organisations are involved in a wide range of activities and encompass all those public bodies involved in making, implementing and applying public policy throughout the UK. There are separate, devolved governmental systems for Scotland, Wales and Northern Ireland, which have their own law-making bodies for some delegated matters. All countries of the UK have common defence, foreign affairs and economic policies, but there are significant differences in domestic policies, policing and legal systems between Scotland, Northern Ireland and England and Wales. The major administrative organisations in England and Wales include central government departments, departmental agencies, non-departmental agencies (sometimes called QUANGOs or quasi-autonomous non-government organisations), the NHS and local authorities.

The criteria of success by which business organisations have traditionally been judged are primarily market and economic ones (Horton and Farnham 1999). How performance in public organisations is assessed is less easy to define and measure than for private organisations, since they include social and political measures as well as market ones. The provision of central and local public services was transformed during the 1980s and 1990s, as some were privatised (such as energy, telecommunications, bus services, while there was also the widespread sale of council houses) and others were deregulated and exposed to market competition. The remaining services were subjected to internal market structures and requirements to operate as if they were commercial businesses, with reforms continuing today (Painter and Isaac-Henry 1999).

PUBLIC MANAGEMENT REFORM

Public management reform, sometimes described as administrative reform or 'new public management', has been an issue of intense scrutiny and review for almost three decades and has been central to the public sector agenda during this period (Pollitt and Bouckaert 2004). The reforms that have taken place, at central government, local government and government agency levels, have had a number of purposes. These have included economies in public expenditure, improving the quality of public service provision, making government operations more efficient, and making public policies more effective (Flynn 2007). The impact of these reforms has resulted in changes in the way public services are organised, structured, managed and delivered and public officials are employed. Several generic studies have traced the origins of public management reform programmes, classified and analysed them (Kickert 1997, Pollitt 1993). Others have concentrated on specific areas such as financial management, organisational change, performance management and performance measurement (Pollitt 1998). Specialist studies have analysed and reviewed how public officials are recruited, deployed, rewarded, appraised, trained, promoted, disciplined and made redundant within public services (Farnham et al 1996, Farnham and Horton 2000, Farnham et al 2005).

In the UK, public management reforms were not the product of a master plan and their long-term effects are unclear. Indeed, they arouse some controversy. Three issues stand out. First, the UK state has always been fragmented but reforms since the 1980s have made the problem worse. Public services and the quasi-public sector are even more fragmented today than they were earlier, with possibly over 8,000 public bodies (or QUANGOs) adding to this fragmentation. Second, fragmentation undermines political accountability. This is partly because it is difficult to find out who is responsible for what, and partly because these bodies often work and take decisions in secret. Many QUANGOs are not accessible to the public and not subject to full audit. Third, there are questions about the efficiency of some of these bodies, with many of them being run inefficiently. Further, small independent agencies involve additional administrative costs and inefficiencies. One response to issues of fragmentation, lack of accountability and inefficiency has been new layers of regulation and inspection (see Chapter 10), resulting in some 150 auditing organisations being created, spending close to one billion pounds sterling per year to do this (Budge et al 2007).

In analytical terms, Horton (2005) categorises public management reform in the UK in terms of five possible trajectories:

- **Privatisation and marketisation:** the fundamental problem to be addressed here is the role and size of government and the need to shrink it. It is assumed that markets are better than state provision as co-ordinating mechanisms and in providing choice. They are deemed to be more flexible, more responsive to public demand and more innovative. An entrepreneurial culture, it is argued, is needed to stimulate economic activity and growth. Privatising state activities means that consumers benefit from better services and more accountability.

- **Structural reorganisation and re-engineering:** this is based upon the perception that public organisations need to be 'right for the job'. Old bureaucratic multifunctional bureaucratic structures, with long hierarchies and over-centralised communication and control systems, are seen as being inefficient and ineffective and need to be replaced by uni-functional agencies with flexible matrix structures. Co-ordination through rules, regulations and supply-based financial systems is replaced by contracts, specifying desired outputs and performance indicators, which chief executives and managers are responsible for delivering.

- **Enhancing the three Es:** in this case, the problem is seen to be the inefficient and wasteful use of public money. Emphasis is on economy, efficiency and effectiveness. Management reforms are an opportunity to introduce private sector management skills into public organisations so as to address failures to deliver on policy outcomes. There is a need to eliminate obvious waste and introduce tight financial controls and pinpoint responsibility at every level of public organisations (Farnham and Horton 1996).

- **In search of excellence:** this sees the problem of reform as one of a bureaucratic culture and excessive emphasis on standardisation, uniformity, regularity and risk avoidance. Reform means replacing bureaucracy with a culture committed to change and continuous improvement, which incorporates responsiveness to public needs and client expectations. Total quality management (TQM) is introduced from the private sector, with its emphasis on getting things right first time, avoiding mistakes and waste, and developing learning organisations.

- **Reinventing democracy and public service orientation:** this approach emphasises decentralisation and democratisation of the policy and management processes. Services are provided at the lowest level and are accountable to their communities, through traditional channels of local authorities and functional boards and by democratising the process and involving the public through subsystems of governance. Neighbourhood forums, community groups and joined-up government are used to meet public needs.

In their detailed international comparative study, Pollitt and Bouckaert (2004) provide an alternative framework for analysing public management reform. They suggest that public management reform can be analysed in terms of maintaining, modernising, marketising or minimising the administrative system:

- **Maintaining the administrative system:** this results in tightening up traditional controls, restricting spending and freezing recruitment. It also involves running campaigns against waste and corruption and generally squeezing the public sector.

- **Modernising the administrative system:** this brings in faster, more flexible ways of budgeting, managing, accounting and delivering services to users.

- **Marketising the administrative system:** this creates as many market-type mechanisms as possible within the public administration system, so that public organisations are made to compete with one another to increase efficiency and

Figure 6.5 Public management reforms in the UK since 1979: some HR implications

Policy initiative	Objective	Implications for HR
Accountability	Provides clear lines of responsibility and accountability; in the civil service, for example, ministers 'steer', agencies 'row'	Needs managers, rather than public administrators to implement policy
Competition	Reduces costs	Leads to possible redundancies and redeployments of public employees
Customers, not clients	Treats public service consumers in the same ways as markets treat private customers	Requires training and development for all grades of staff
Decentralisation	Creates more flexible organisations, using modern methods of management	Increases numbers of managers, HR professionals and diversifies HR policies; recruitment and selection strategies required, arising from an increased size of workforce
Deregulation	Removes red tape and sets service providers free to do their jobs efficiently	Means more autonomy for managers, working within performance guidelines; trickles down to the workforce
Efficiency	Results in fewer employees and lower costs, thus making public service costs lower and public service provision more efficient	Leads to possible redundancies and redeployments of public employees and possible conflicts with staff unions
Markets	Improve provision of services through market reforms	Has training and development implications for all staff
Quality	Raises service standards	Has training and development implications for all staff
Responsiveness	Uses charters to make public services more responsive to citizen expectations	Has training and development implications for all staff
Separating 'steering' from 'rowing'	In the civil service, leaves ministers and senior civil servants free to get on with policy making	Results in performance targets and reviews of performance standards
Specialised skills	Develops specialist skills to perform particular jobs	Need to recruit, select and train suitable staff
Sweeping away bureaucracy	Replaces bureaucracy with more efficient market or quasi-market mechanism – public service ethos weakened	Requires 'new' forms of skill sets from staff and the workforce

user responsiveness. This 'represents a penetration of the administrative system by the culture and practices of the market sector' (Pollitt and Bouckaert 2004, p176).

• **Minimising the administrative system:** this involves handing over as many tasks as possible to the market sector, through privatisation and contracting out, resulting in what some have called the 'hollowing out' of the state. Clearly, since the 1980s, those responsible for driving public management reform in the UK have adopted all these approaches at various times.

Public management reforms have had major impacts on the structure and activities of UK public services. The impacts of markets and competition on public services, since the late 1970s, and their implications for HR practice are summarised in Figure 6.5

ACTIVITY 6.12

What do you understand by the term 'public management reform'? What are its key characteristics? Identify and discuss the major effects of adopting public management reforms in UK public services since 1979 for (a) users, (b) taxpayers and (c) public sector workers.

SOURCES OF COMPETITIVE ADVANTAGE AND RESPONSES BY FIRMS TO COMPETITION AND HYPER-COMPETITION

In competitive market economies, firms are always looking for sources of competitive advantage, with several factors generating a long-term tendency for competitiveness to increase in market economies. These include increases in the quantity of business information, improvements in the quality and comparability of business data, the development of the accounting profession, the adoption of recognised standards of reporting, improvement in communications and the progressive professionalising of the management function. The universality of modern business and management practices and the emergence of multinational corporations are central to the expansion of the geographical domain of economic activity and of competition on a worldwide scale (Auerbach 1988).

One of the most influential scholars to get competitive strategy recognised as an accepted part of management practice is Porter (1998). His book, *Competitive strategy: techniques for analyzing industries and competitors* (originally published in 1980) provides a framework for understanding the forces of competition in industries, tools for capturing the heterogeneity of industries and companies and the concept of competitive advantage. Drawing on rich data from a number of case studies, Porter offers a 'sophisticated view of industry competition', brings 'some structure to the question of how a firm could outperform its rivals' and shows how 'competitive costs could be thought of in terms of cost, differentiation and scope' (Porter 1998, p xi).

According to Porter (1998, p3f), the essence of competitive strategy is relating a company to its business context. For him, the essence of competition in an industry depends on five basic competitive forces, as shown in Figure 6.6. These are 'threat of entry to the industry', 'intensity of rivalry among existing competitors', 'pressure from substitute products', 'bargaining power of buyers' and 'bargaining power of suppliers'. The goal of competitive strategy for a business unit in an industry is to find a position in the industry where the company can best defend itself against these competitive forces or can influence them in its favour. Competitive strategy, in essence, is the ability to take 'offensive or defensive action to create a defendable position in an industry, to cope successfully with the five competitive forces and thereby yield a superior return on investment for the firm'.

Figure 6.6 Porter's five forces analysis

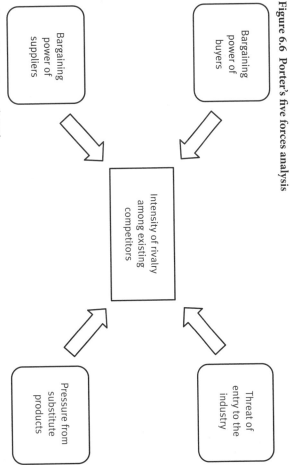

Adapted from Porter (1998)

The basic elements of Porter's analysis can be examined in terms of the contexts within which competitive strategy is formulated, his 'five forces' that drive industry competition, generic competitive strategies and analysis of the competitive context.

THE CONTEXTS OF COMPETITIVE STRATEGY

For Porter, formulation of competitive strategy involves four key factors that determine the limits of what a company can successfully accomplish: two are internal to the organisation and two are external. All four factors – organisational strengths and weaknesses, the personal values of key executives, industry opportunities and threats, and societal expectations – have to be considered before a business can develop a realistic and implementable set of goals and policies.

- **Internal factors**: there are, first, the organisation's strengths and weaknesses in terms of its profile of assets and skills relative to its competitors, including financial resources, technologies and brand identification. Second, there are the personal values and motivations of the key executives responsible for implementing the chosen strategy. These strengths and weaknesses combined with these values determine the 'internal' limits to the competitive strategy that an organisation can effectively adopt.

- **External factors**: the limits of an organisation's competitive strategy are determined by the industry in which it operates and the broader expectations of society. The third factor, industry opportunities and threats, defines the competitive context with its attendant risks and potential rewards. The fourth factor, societal expectations, reflects the impact on the organisation of government policy, social concerns, public mores and similar issues.

The appropriateness of a competitive strategy is determined by testing its proposed goals and policies for consistency in terms of 'internal consistency', contextual 'fit', 'resource fit' and 'communication and implementation'. Developing an optimal competitive strategy requires three sets of questions to be addressed. First, what is the business doing now? For example, what assumptions need to be made about the organisation's relative position, strengths and weaknesses, competitors and industry/sector? Second, what is happening in the external context? This requires an industry analysis, competitor analysis, societal analysis and an examination of the organisation's strengths and weaknesses relative to present and future competitors. Third, what should the business be doing? This involves testing underlying assumptions in the strategy, strategic alternatives and strategic choice.

THE FIVE FORCES MODEL

Porter argues that the five competitive forces that he identifies 'jointly determine the intensity of industry competition and profitability, and the strongest force or forces are governing and become crucial from the point of view of strategy formulation.' (Porter 1998, p6).

Threat of entry to the industry

There are several barriers to entry into an industry. A major one is economies of scale (ie unit costs of production decline as the volume of the product/service per period increases). This barrier can deter new entrants by forcing them to either come in at a large scale and risk strong reaction from existing firms or come in at a small scale and accept a cost disadvantage. Another barrier is product differentiation. This is where established firms have brand identification and customer loyalties stemming from past advertising or being first in the industry. Differentiation creates a barrier to entry by forcing entrants to spend heavily to overcome existing customer loyalties. Another barrier to entry is 'switching costs.' These are created by the one-off cost facing buyers of switching from one supplier's product to another, such as costs of employee retraining or of new equipment. A barrier to entry can also be created by the new entrant's need to secure effective distribution of its product or service.

The potential entrant's expectations about the reaction of existing competitors to its presence also influence threat of entry. If existing competitors are expected to react forcibly to make the entrant's position in the industry a difficult one, then entry may be deterred. This is most likely where there are histories of vigorous retaliation to new entrants, established firms with high commitment to the industry (with illiquid assets) or slow industry growth rates that limit the ability to absorb a new firm without pressure on sales and financial performance of existing firms.

Intensity of rivalry among existing competitors

This is the central focus of Porter's model, since increased rivalry among existing competitors leads to increased competition and a possible reduction in profits for firms within an industry. A number of factors operate here, including the relative number and size of competitors in an industry, its growth rate, high fixed costs relative to value added, lack of differentiation of products or services, and high exit barriers.

The number and relative size of competitors in an industry are important factors, since under monopolistic competition, for example, rivalry is intense, although under oligopoly it tends to be less. The growth rate of an industry affects competition, since with slow growth competition is intense, but where growth is rapid it is less so. In industries with high fixed costs (or storage costs), there is strong pressure for all firms to fill productive capacity and this often leads to price cutting when excess capacity is present. Where there is a lack of differentiation of product or service, pressures for intense price and service competition are likely to follow. When exit barriers are high, excess capacity does not leave the industry. Firms losing the competitive battle do not give up the struggle but remain in the sector and, as a result, profitability in the entire industry can be persistently low.

Pressure from substitute products

All firms in an industry are competing with industries producing substitute products. Substitutes limit the potential returns in an industry by placing a ceiling on the prices that firms can charge. Where there are few (or no) substitutes for a product or service, producers face little competition, whereas with substitutes, competition is stronger.

Bargaining power of buyers

Buyers compete within an industry by forcing down prices, bargaining for higher quality or more services and playing competitors against one another – all at the expense of industry profitability. The power of each of the industry's important buyer groups depends on a number of characteristics of its market situation. It also depends on the relative importance of the group's purchases from the industry, compared with its overall business. A buyer group is powerful where:

- The products it purchases from the industry represent a significant fraction of the buyer's costs or purchases.

- The products it purchases from the industry are standard or undifferentiated.

- It earns low profits.

- The industry's product is unimportant to the quality of the buyer's products or services.

- The buyer has full information about the market.

Bargaining power of suppliers

Suppliers can exert bargaining power over participants in an industry by threatening to raise prices or reduce the quality of purchased goods and service. Powerful suppliers can squeeze profitability out of an industry that is unable to recover cost increases in its prices. A supplier group is powerful where:

- It is dominated by a few companies and is more concentrated than the industry to which it sells.

- It is not obliged to contend with other substitute products for sale to the industry.

- The industry is not an important customer of the supplier group.

- The supplier's product is an important input to the buyer's business.

- The products of the supplier group are differentiated.

GENERIC COMPETITIVE STRATEGIES

To cope with these five competitive forces, Porter (1998) identifies three potentially successful generic strategic approaches to outperforming other firms in the industry: overall cost leadership, differentiation and focus. Porter (1998, pp41–2) concludes that these three generic strategies are alternative but viable approaches for dealing with competitive forces. Firms failing to develop their strategy in at least one of these directions are 'stuck in the middle' and are placed in an extremely vulnerable strategic situation. A firm of this sort lacks the market share, capital investment, and resolve to play the low-cost game, the industry-wide differentiation necessary to obviate the need for a low-cost position, 'or the focus to create differentiation or a low-cost position in a more limited sphere.' Such firms are almost guaranteed low profitability and are likely to suffer from 'blurred corporate culture and a conflicting set of organizational arrangements and motivation system.'

Overall cost leadership

A low-cost generic strategy provides the firm with above-average returns in its industry, despite the presence of strong competitive forces, which gives it distinct market advantages. Its cost position provides substantial entry barriers to others in terms of economies of scale or cost advantages. It also defends the firm against rivalry from competitors, places the firm in a favourable position regarding substitutes relative to its competitors in the industry, defends it against powerful buyers and defends it against powerful suppliers. 'Thus a low-cost position protects the firm against all five competitive forces because bargaining can only continue to erode profits until those of the next most efficient competitor are eliminated.' Also 'the less efficient competitors will suffer first in the face of competitive pressures' (Porter 1998, p36).

Achieving a low overall cost position often requires a high relative market share or other market advantages. It may well require having a wide line of related products or services to spread costs and serving all major customer groups to build sales volume. Implementing a low-cost strategy may require heavy capital investment, aggressive pricing and start-up losses to build market share. Once achieved, the low-cost position provides high profit margins that can be re-invested in new facilities so as to maintain the cost leadership position, as in the case of Tesco.

Differentiation

The differentiation strategy is 'one of differentiating the product or service offering of the firm, creating something that is perceived *industrywide* as being unique' (Porter 1998, p37, his emphasis). Differentiation takes many forms: design or brand image, technology, customer service or other dimensions. Differentiation is a viable strategy for earning above average returns in an industry, because it creates a defensible position for coping with the five competitive forces, although it does so in different ways from the cost leadership strategy. Customer loyalty and the need for competitors to overcome uniqueness provide entry barriers. Because of brand loyalty among customers and resulting lower sensitivity to price, differentiation provides insulation against competitive rivalry. It also increases profit margins, which avoids the need for a low-cost position. Also the firm that is differentiated to achieve customer loyalty is in a better position vis-à-vis substitutes than are its competitors. Finally, differentiation yields higher margins for dealing with supplier power and it mitigates buyer power.

Achieving differentiation may preclude gaining a high market share. It often requires a perception of exclusivity which is incompatible with high market share. More commonly, it implies 'a trade-off with cost position if the activities required in creating it are intensely costly' (Porter 1998, p38). This might include extensive research, product design, high-quality inputs or intensive customer support, as in the cases of cars manufactured by BMW and Mercedes.

Focus

The focus generic strategy targets 'a particular buyer group, segment of the product line, or geographic market'. The low-cost and differentiation strategies are directed at industry-wide objectives, whereas the focus strategy 'is built round serving a particular target well, and each functional policy is developed with this in mind'. The firm achieves either differentiation from better meeting the needs of the particular target or lower costs in serving this target or both, as in the case of the newspaper the *Financial Times*. Even though the focus strategy does not achieve low cost or differentiation from the perspective of the market as a whole, 'it does achieve one or both of these positions vis-à-vis its narrow market target' (Porter 1998, p38f).

ACTIVITY 6.13

Identify and explain your organisation's (main) generic competitive strategy. Justify whether it is appropriate or inappropriate for your organisation. How might its generic competitive strategy be improved?

ACTIVITY 6.14

Explain Porter's five forces model and comment on its usefulness as a tool of competitive analysis. Apply this model to your organisation.

ANALYSING THE COMPETITIVE CONTEXT

The external contexts of organisations are complex, because they are concerned with everything outside an organisation that affects its prospects and activities. This includes the industry and markets in which it operates, its competitors, the customers it aims to satisfy and the general social, technological, economic, environmental, political, legal, ethical and global contexts over which it has little control. Analysing the external context is therefore a difficult and challenging task for strategists. First, there is fundamental disagreement about the nature of the strategic management process (see Chapter 4). Prescriptive strategic theorists, for example, argue that uncertainties in the external context can be predicted. Emergent strategic theorists, on the other hand, argue that the external context is so turbulent and unstable that prediction serves little purpose. Second, because the external context is dynamic, strategies have to be developed against a backdrop of continual change. Third, since the external context contains so many outside influences affecting the strategic direction of organisations, only selected ones can be explored.

STEEPLE analysis provides a useful starting point for analysing the general external contexts of an organisation. As outlined in Chapter 1, STEEPLE stands for the 'socio-cultural', 'technological', 'economic', 'environmental', 'political', 'legal', and 'ethical' contexts impinging on an organisation. STEEPLE provides a useful checklist for examining the factors most likely to influence an organisation's market and business prospects:

- The sorts of socio-cultural issues affecting demand for an organisation's goods or services and its labour supply include education, health, demographic change, attitudes to work and leisure, and general social developments.

- Technological factors include the impact of computers and information technology on working life, rates of technological change and levels of spending on research and development in an organisation.

- The economic ones include market competition, energy and communication costs, consumer spending, government spending, interest rates, currency fluctuations, exchange rate policy, inflation and investment spending.

- The main environmental factors affecting an organisation cover pollution, resource conservation, the 'social costs' of given policies and other 'green' issues.

- The political ones include public policies and legislation at local, national and European levels and the distributions of political power at each level.

- Ethical factors are concerned with the impact of business decisions on organisational stakeholders.

A SWOT analysis is useful in bringing together the environmental analysis of an organisation, its resource/competence analysis and its strategic capacity for dealing with them. SWOT stands for the *internal* strengths and weaknesses and *external* opportunities and threats relating to an organisation.

- **Strengths:** the internal, positive attributes of organisations that help them to gain advantage in order to achieve their strategic objectives. Some organisations define their strengths by benchmarking them through comparing their own processes, products, service or activities with those of 'good practice' organisations.

- **Weaknesses:** the internal negative attributes of organisations that may result in them failing to achieve their strategic objectives. Weaknesses, too, can be identified and possibly remedied by benchmarking and following 'good practice'.

- **Opportunities:** the external factors that substantially assist organisations in their efforts to achieve their strategic objectives.

- **Threats:** the external factors that may result in organisations failing to achieve their strategic objectives.

HYPER-COMPETITION

The conditions under which many firms operate today are called hyper-competition (D'Aveni 1994). Hyper-competition is characterised by uncertain markets, diverse global players, rapid technological change, price wars and continual internal reorganisations. It is exacerbated by the shifting age structures of populations, urbanisation and social change. For some organisations, these forces are seen as reshaping the competitive landscape across the world. Under these conditions, a firm's survival is no longer assured by selecting a high-margin industry and defending it against new competitors. The speed at which competitive conditions are changing is so rapid that it does not always make sense to define an attractive market. Firms need to develop and exploit new capabilities to generate their attractiveness to the market, requiring a more aggressive, proactive strategy to attack their competitors' existing strengths. This places a premium on organisational spontaneity and adaptability. Hyper-competition places special demands on the way organisations organise to survive. The key appears to be flexibility, so that strategies, deployment of competencies and activities can be reformulated in anticipation of new competitive opportunities and threats in the marketplace (Volberda 1996). Some implications of these increased competitive tendencies in product markets on the HR function are summarised in Figure 6.7.

Figure 6.7 Some implications of the impact of product market competition on the HR function

Area of activity	Implications
Organisation of HR	• Function needs to be run as efficiently as possible • Results in HR shared services and HR outsourcing • Increased emphasis on measuring HR outcomes
Management of change	• Now on HR agenda, along with development of capacity for flexibility • Re-organisations and re-structuring commonplace • Skills needed to manage the HR aspects of mergers and acquisitions
Knowledge management	• Becomes more important as the external contexts change rapidly • Becomes more complex as technological innovation accelerates
Core HR functions	• The more competitive an industry, so the capacity to recruit, retain and motivate high performers is increasingly significant • Firms with the best performers gain competitive edge
Pay and conditions	• Competitive conditions can restrict pay demands and rewards • Firms have to motivate and engage staff to retain them through increased focus on the relational aspects of employment, and reduced focus on transactional ones
Quality and customer service	• Is more necessary to maintain high standards of quality and customer service • Means meeting customer expectations and surpassing them, treating them as individuals • HR and line managers have to elicit discretionary effort from staff

 **ACTIVITY 6.15**

Undertake either a SWOT analysis or a STEEPLE analysis of your organisation. What are the advantages and disadvantages of using SWOT or PESTLE analyses for your organisation?

CONCLUSION: MARKETS, HR STRATEGY AND HR SOLUTIONS

Managing scarcity is a challenge for managements in all organisations. There are never sufficient resources available for businesses, public services and third sector bodies to satisfy all their economic wants. To fulfil their goals, private and public organisations require skilled human resources, finance capital and access to intermediate goods and services and raw materials in managing operations. Since resources are limited in supply, organisations compete in factor of production and commodity markets for them. Prices act as signals and indicators to firms and public enterprises in their continuous search for resource sufficiency, organisational effectiveness and improved performance.

Managements also have to decide what resources to use, in what quantities, how to use them and how to maximise efficiency. In carrying out these activities, managements are constantly confronted with the problem of making choices about combinations of resources, work methods and the products or services to supply. These tasks continually face managements and there are both financial and opportunity costs in taking these decisions.

This raises the question of the extent to which managers react to market forces or control them. In product markets, given the relative imperfections of most market structures in the modern world, businesses are generally price-makers rather than price-takers. Anecdotal and research evidence suggests that 'big business' is able, to varying degrees, to influence market prices, their returns on capital and profitability. With vast amounts of finance capital at stake, managers' ability to work market forces in their favour and facilitate corporate viability is not without its benefits. Whether this benefits business firms or their clients is debated. As Galbraith (1967, p204f) argues, the control or management of demand by big business is 'a vast rapidly growing industry itself'. In everyday language, this great machine and the varied talents it employs claim 'to be engaged in selling goods.'

In money and financial markets, management influence is less apparent. Indeed, some commentators argue that there is increasing divergence between City of London interests and those of the manufacturing and service sectors. Money markets are internationalised and demonstrate more approximation to free markets than other markets do. With advances in computer technology, and interdependent international money markets, there is great volatility in global money markets, as shown in the financial crisis 2007–08. The major actors in international equity and security markets are themselves corporate bodies, not individual investors. They include hedge funds and private equity firms. Those supporting this interpretation of modern capitalism argue that real economic power has passed out of the hands of the managerial elite running companies to the relatively small group of entrepreneurial capitalists working money markets, and controlling financial resources.

Marris (1964) argues that 'managerial capitalism' better describes the power structure of modern market economies. These are dominated by large business corporations, where power and resources are located within a definable managerial class distinctly separate from the property-owning class, as well as being independent of its control. This managerial class, it is argued, pursues goals and aims that are independent of workers, shareholders and the state. Theories of managerial capitalism are closely linked with managerial theories of the firm. Given imperfect capital markets and uncompetitive product markets, managers have scope to pursue business goals other than profit maximisation, such as growth and market security.

In making economic choices in conditions of scarcity and globalisation, top managements are believed to act rationally and decisively, but some decisions are more normative than rational. Some organisations adopt business practices not because they are efficient but because they provide legitimacy to outside stakeholders. Other managements, on the other hand, draw upon sophisticated cost–benefit analyses in both the private and public sectors. Understanding the nature of economic scarcity and the principles underpinning markets and price determination is an important skill for managerial decision-makers, including HR professionals. Managers need to know the types of products, capital and labour markets in which their organisations operate. They need to be sensitive to the sorts of market changes likely to affect these markets.

Top managers also try to anticipate the actions of their competitors, thus maintaining or improving the market positions of their organisations wherever possible. In public services, in turn, the introduction of market testing and internal markets has brought significant changes in organisational culture, managerial values, HR strategies and HR practices within them. In these circumstances, recruiting, rewarding, retaining and reviewing talented, resourceful, committed people are seen to be key factors for improving organisational and corporate performance.

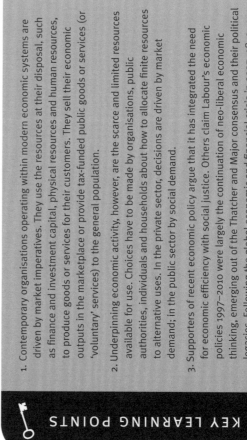

KEY LEARNING POINTS

1. Contemporary organisations operating within modern economic systems are driven by market imperatives. They use the resources at their disposal, such as finance and investment capital, physical resources and human resources, to produce goods or services for their customers. They sell their economic outputs in the marketplace or provide tax-funded public goods or services (or 'voluntary' services) to the general population.

2. Underpinning economic activity, however, are the scarce and limited resources available for use. Choices have to be made by organisations, public authorities, individuals and households about how to allocate finite resources to alternative uses. In the private sector, decisions are driven by market demand; in the public sector by social demand.

3. Supporters of recent economic policy argue that it has integrated the need for economic efficiency with social justice. Others claim Labour's economic policies 1997–2010 were largely the continuation of neo-liberal economic thinking, emerging out of the Thatcher and Major consensus and their political legacies. Following the global economic and financial crisis in 2007–08, a

series of emergency economic packages were initiated by the UK government to salvage the banking system from collapse, stop the economy falling further into recession and create conditions to fight inflation. There was a large cost to the Exchequer in terms of public borrowing as well as rising unemployment.

4. The structure of the UK economy has changed significantly in the last 30 years, shifting from an industrial base to a post-industrial one. The current structure shows it is now based on service and knowledge provision rather than old 'staple' industries. This has occurred under pressures from globalisation, technological innovation and changing consumer tastes. The political drive underpinning this project has been the creation of a competition, choice and change management agenda in UK society, supported by government policy.

5. Micro-economic analysis provides a framework for understanding the forces of supply and demand and the role of prices in allocating scarce resources. Few if any markets in the contemporary world are perfect free markets, since modern market structures are in their nature 'imperfect', because consumers lack full knowledge or information about them. Markets range from perfect competition to monopoly provision. This necessitates the introduction of a variety of regulatory mechanisms, such as a statutory minimum wage, to protect weaker parties from being exploited in market transactions by stronger parties.

6. The market for capital and the financial system is made up of interrelated markets where money is bought and sold and finance capital is raised, lent and borrowed on varying terms for varying periods of time, for various clients and customers. The prime agencies in this system are the Bank of England (the UK's central bank), the stock exchange (with its financial trading activities), and the commercial banks and related institutions (such as insurance firms and building societies).

7. The independent Monetary Policy Committee of the Bank of England sets interest rates in the UK. These affect credit, mortgages and all other transactions where money is borrowed. After the financial and credit crisis of 2007–08, the Bank of England adopted a number of short-term measures, such as recapitalising the banks, to prevent the financial system crashing.

8. UK labour markets have changed significantly in the past three decades, with major changes in the occupational structure and industrial distribution. The UK is now frequently described as a post-industrial or service economy. Working patterns have changed, with more part-time, temporary and shift workers compared with 30 years ago. Working time is generally longer in the UK than in mainland Europe. Supporters of the 'hour-glass' debate argue that the labour market is polarising into 'high skill/high pay' jobs and 'low skill/low pay' ones, although the evidence is mixed.

9. Public services are created for purposes different from those of private businesses. They have multiple objectives, including political and social ones, since they have a range of stakeholders to satisfy. Ultimately, however, public organisations are accountable to politicians and third sector bodies to their trustees and the Charity Commission. In public services, successive waves of reform have been implemented for some 30 years, through maintaining, modernising, marketising and minimising them; all have implications for HR strategy and practices.

10. Competition in product and service markets is intense, demonstrating, in some cases, hyper-competition. Hyper-competition arises from a variety of external factors, such globalisation and technology and necessitates organisational flexibility. Porter (1998) provides an analytical framework for understanding the forces of competition in industries, tools for capturing the heterogeneity of industries and companies, and the concept of competitive advantage. He presents a 'five forces' model of competitive advantage, where the state of competition in an industry depends on five basic competitive forces: threat of entry, intensity of rivalry among existing competitors, pressure from substitute products, bargaining power of buyers and bargaining power of suppliers.

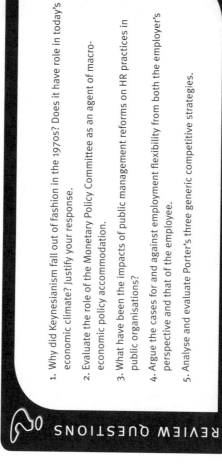

REVIEW QUESTIONS

1. Why did Keynesianism fall out of fashion in the 1970s? Does it have role in today's economic climate? Justify your response.

2. Evaluate the role of the Monetary Policy Committee as an agent of macro-economic policy accommodation.

3. What have been the impacts of public management reforms on HR practices in public organisations?

4. Argue the cases for and against employment flexibility from both the employer's perspective and that of the employee.

5. Analyse and evaluate Porter's three generic competitive strategies.

CASE STUDY

CASE STUDY 6.1 THE ECONOMICS OF SUSTAINABLE DEVELOPMENT: WORKING TIME AND PROSPERITY WITHOUT GROWTH

Background

An important debate is emerging in the UK, and elsewhere, about the economics of a finite planet. The basic argument is that the amount of primary energy needed to produce each unit of the world's economic output has fallen more or less continuously over most of the last half-century. This sounds promising but, it is argued, is counteracted by population growth and economic growth.

Professor Tim Jackson and others claim that

to stabilise climate change on relatively optimistic assumptions will require global carbon emissions of below 4 billion tonnes per annum by 2050 – a global reduction of some 5 per cent every year from now until then. By 2050 the average carbon content of economic output would need to be less than 40 kg per thousand dollars, a 20-fold improvement on the current global average. The growing consensus is that a level of 350 parts per million, not 450 per million, will be required to avoid dangerous climate change, which only worsens the arithmetic. Even if this were accomplished, it would allow for no greater catch-up by the developing world, leaving inequalities to widen.

To achieve social justice globally, alongside continuing growth in high-income countries, with the entire population enjoying an income comparable with EU citizens today, the world economy would need to grow six times between now and 2050, implying a technical shift of still higher orders of magnitude to avoid climatic disaster. There is thus no credible, socially just, ecologically sustainable scenario of continually growing incomes for a world of 9 billion people. If the market economy cannot grow, there will be no expansion of tax revenues to invest in health, education, social care, and other essential services. On this basis, the potential for growth lies in the human resources of the 'core' economy.

The case for the 21-hour working week

In 1930, John Maynard Keynes imagined that by the beginning of the twenty-first century, the working week could be cut dramatically – not just to 21 hours but to 15 hours. He anticipated that people would no longer need to work long hours to earn enough to satisfy their material needs and their attention would turn instead to how to use freedom from pressing economic cares. Keynes was wrong in his forecast, but not wrong, it seems to some observers, to envisage a very different way of using time.

Sustainable economic development pressure groups, such as the New Economics Foundation, argue that moving towards much shorter hours of paid work offers a way out of the multiple crises facing countries such as the UK today. In their views, people are consuming well beyond the country's economic means and well beyond the limits of the natural environment but in ways that fail to improve people's well-being. Besides, continuing economic growth in high-income countries will make it impossible to achieve carbon reduction targets. Widening inequalities, a

failing global economy, critically depleted natural resources and accelerating climate change pose grave threats to the future of humankind.

The New Economics Foundation proposal is to promote a 'normal' working week of 21 hours. This could help to address a range of urgent, interlinked problems including overwork, unemployment, over-consumption, high carbon emissions, low well-being, entrenched inequalities, and lack of time to live sustainably and care for each other, and simply to enjoy life.

Why select the 21 hours per week norm?

- Twenty-one hours is close to the average that people of working age in the UK spend in paid work and just a little more than the average spent in unpaid work. Experiments with shorter working hours suggest that they can be popular, where conditions are stable and pay is favourable.

- A new standard of 21 hours could be consistent with the dynamics of a decarbonised economy.

- There is nothing natural or inevitable about what is considered 'normal' working hours. Time, like work, has become commodified, which is a legacy of the market economy.

- The logic of industrial time is out of step with today's conditions, where instant communications and mobile technologies bring new risks and pressures, as well as opportunities.

- The challenge for reformers is to break the power of the old industrial clock, without adding new pressures, and free up time to live sustainable lives.

- To meet the challenge, the way paid and unpaid work is valued could change. For example, if the average time devoted to unpaid housework and childcare in Britain in 2005 were valued in terms of the minimum wage, it is estimated to be worth the equivalent of 21 per cent of the UK's GDP.

Planet, people, and markets: reasons for change

For reformists such as the New Economics Foundation, there are three interdependent economies or sources of wealth: (a) the natural resources of the planet, (b) human resources assets and relationships inherent in everyone's everyday lives, and (c) markets. All three economies could work together for sustainable social justice:

- **Safeguarding the natural resources of the planet:** a much shorter working week would help break the habit of living to work, working to earn, and earning to consume. People could become more attached to relationships, pastimes, and places that absorb less money and more time. It would help society to manage without carbon-intensive growth and reduce greenhouse gas emissions.

- **Social justice and well-being for all:** a 21-hour 'normal' working week could help distribute paid work more evenly across the population, reducing the ill-health associated with unemployment, long working hours and little control over time. It would make it possible for paid and unpaid work to be distributed more equally between women and men. Critically, it would enable the 'core'

economy to flourish by making more and better use of uncommodified human resources in defining and meeting individual and shared needs.

- **A robust and prosperous economy:** shorter working hours could help to adapt the economy to the needs of society and the environment, rather than subjugating society and environment to the needs of the economy. It could also help to end credit-fuelled growth, develop a more resilient and adaptable economy, and safeguard public resources for investment in a low-carbon industrial strategy and other measures to support a sustainable economy.

Tasks

1. What are the advantages and disadvantages of a 21-hour working week to individuals, organisations and society?

2. Identify some of the barriers to achieving a sustainable 21-hour working week at individual, organisational and governmental levels in the short term.

3. What are some of the transitional political, economic and social issues arising from a public policy shifted towards establishing a 21-hour working week norm?

EXPLORE FURTHER

BEGG, D., FISCHER, S. and DORNBUSCH, R. (2008) *Economics*. 9th ed. Maidenhead: McGraw-Hill.

Provides a wide-ranging introduction to economic theory, by examining micro-economic principles, welfare economics and macro-economics; the book has an interesting section covering the world economy, international trade and economic development.

GRIFFITHS, A. and WALL, S. (eds) (2008) *Economics for business and management*. 2nd ed. Harlow: Financial Times Prentice Hall.

Is an introductory text, emphasising the perspectives needed for understanding the various functional areas of business and management, by covering a wide range of issues relevant to business practice.

JACKSON, T. (2009) *Prosperity without growth: economics for a finite planet.* London: Earthscan.

Gives a radical critique of the 'economic growth' orthodoxy that ever-increasing consumption adds to human happiness; the underpinning argument is that more economic growth is not sustainable as a policy and that humankind needs to lower the environmental impact of economic activity to promote the common good.

OATLEY, T. (2004) *International political economy: interests and institutions in the global economy.* New York: Pearson Longman.

Examines the relationship between economic and political processes in the history and development of the international economic system; the author does this by demonstrating how economic interests and political processes interact to shape government policies.

CHAPTER 7

Globalisation and international factors

INTRODUCTION

National economies in the developed world have become increasingly deregulated and opened up to international competition from other countries, including those of the developing world, in both their manufacturing and service sectors over the past three decades. As a result, global markets are playing an increasingly significant part in today's business relationships, capital movements and labour mobility. Some UK businesses, for example, are competing not only with one another in the EU and globally, but also with their mainland European counterparts, which are sometimes parts of the same multinational corporations (MNCs). Globalisation, which incorporates the internationalisation of economic activity as well as its social, cultural and political dimensions, has implications for organisations in all three sectors. It also impacts on those managing them, their workers and other corporate stakeholders, such as customers, suppliers and local communities.

This chapter examines the phenomenon of contemporary globalisation, the responses of market economies to globalisation and the role of MNCs, major international organisations and the EU in the global economy. The essence of contemporary economic globalisation is its links with the international spread of production and new ICTs, promoted by the mobility of finance capital and changing patterns of international trade in what some have controversially called the 'borderless world' (Ohmae 1995). The key features of contemporary globalisation are the expansion of cross-border trade, exponential growth of ICT systems, internationalisation of finance and production, and downsizing of governments and the public sector (Cerny 1995). However, this increasingly international economic integration is complemented by mass communication systems and popular culture that promote individualism, consumerism and materialist cultures.

LEARNING OUTCOMES

By the end of this chapter, readers should be able to understand, explain and critically evaluate:

- the complex nature of globalisation, contemporary debates in the field and its consequences for organisations and the HR function

- the roles and nature of MNCs

- the importance of other international bodies in the global economy

- the evolution and development of the EU.

In addition, readers should be able to:

- assess the likely impact of globalisation on particular business sectors and organisations

- advise on the role played by international institutions in shaping the business context

- understand the cultural and institutional factors affecting the global context.

THE NATURE AND ORIGINS OF GLOBALISATION

Globalisation is a complex, controversial phenomenon. Petrella (1996) argues that a new competitive era emerged in the 1970s, especially in connection with the globalisation of economic processes. In his view, competition no longer describes a particular type of market configuration but has acquired the status of a universal credo or ideology. For industrialists, bankers and financiers, competitiveness has become the short-term primary goal of businesses, with profitability remaining their long-term *raison d'être*. In the UK, for example, Hutton (1995, pp13 and 170ff) argues that the financial system, already biased to thinking only in the short term, has been further deregulated, which has intensified its greed for high, quick returns. In his view, 'the more market-based the financial system, the less effectively it mobilises resources for investment.' The reduced powers of trade unions and the abolition of institutional mechanisms such as wages councils, in turn, have contributed to the deregulation of the UK labour market, making it more flexible. These changes have allowed employers to bid down wages and working conditions for the unskilled and poorly organised, with the impact particularly marked in high-labour-content domestic services industries such as hotels, catering and cleaning. For governments, too, national competitiveness is a major concern, because they want to attract and retain capital within their own territories 'to secure a maximum level of employment, access of local capital to global technology, and revenue needed to maintain a minimum of social peace' (Petrella 1996, p62ff).

Economic globalisation is associated with international trading between business corporations operating in relatively free, unregulated markets, uninhibited by tariff barriers and protectionist, national economic policies. Polanyi (1944, p69) describes the idea of the 'free market' as follows:

Nothing must be allowed to inhibit the formation of markets ... Neither must there be any interference with the adjustment of prices to changed market conditions – whether the prices are those of goods, labour, land, or money. Hence there must not only be markets for all elements of industry, but no measure or policy must be countenanced that would influence the action of these markets. Neither price, nor supply, nor demand must be fixed or regulated; only such policies and measures are in order which help to ensure the self-regulation of the market by creating conditions which make the market the only organizing power in the economic sphere.

Seldon (1990, p1ff) contrasts the free market with an 'imperfect capitalism' and an 'imperfect socialism'. For him, the market is a capitalist instrument that rewards the risks and penalties of individual ownership and judgement. It is 'not a socialist instrument' subject to the irresponsible mercurial collective decisions of "public" men or women' who control other people's resources, but are ultimately compelled, like the rest of fallible humankind, to put their personal interests first.

One implication of voracious global free markets is that sovereign national states are set against one another in geo-political struggles for dwindling natural resources. What makes the 'new globalisation' different from earlier periods of global trading is that ICTs throw the economic and social division of labour into turmoil, as traditional Keynesian full-employment policies become unworkable within independent nation states.

Gray (2009) defines economic globalisation as the worldwide spread of industrial production promoted by unrestricted mobility of capital and unfettered freedom of trade, while Giddens (1990, p64) sees it as the displacement of local activities by networks of relationships whose reach is worldwide. He defines globalisation as the intensification of worldwide social relations linking 'distant realities in such a way that local happenings are shaped by events occurring many miles away and vice versa'. For Ruigrok and van Tulder (1995), globalisation encompasses a more complex set of features:

- globalisation of financial markets

- internationalisation of corporate strategies, in particular their commitment to competition as a source of wealth creation

- diffusion of technology and related research and development and knowledge on a worldwide basis

- transformation of consumption patterns into cultural products with worldwide consumer markets

- internationalisation of the regulatory capabilities of national societies into a global political economic system

- the diminished role of national governments in designing the rules for global governance.

The essence of the globalisation phenomenon is that national economies become networked with other economies around the world through international trading, ICTs, especially email, electronic commerce and the World-Wide Web, and a common consumerism. This consumerism is fuelled by sophisticated marketing techniques, a continual search for new products and services, and large-scale MNCs claiming to be 'customer-centred' or 'quality-focused' enterprises, such as Hewlett Packard, Volkswagen-Audi, Sony, Nokia and News International.

IS GLOBALISATION A NEW PHENOMENON?

Some writers view globalisation as a new phenomenon; others see it as something that has been around, in one form or another, ever since the discovery of the 'new worlds' by European explorers in the sixteenth century. Those supporting the novelty of current global markets argue that the 'new' globalisation has rendered the nation state irrelevant and that it is powerless countries and homeless big business corporations that now inhabit the 'global economy' and 'global marketplace'. For Ohmae (1995, p20), 'in a borderless economy, the nation-focused maps we typically use to make sense of economic activity are woefully misleading.' In his view, people must face up at last to the awkward and uncomfortable truth: 'the old cartography no longer works. It has become no more than an illusion.' Others, such as Negroponte (1995, p1), have written: 'Like a mothball, which goes from solid to gas directly, I expect the nation-state to evaporate. ... Without question, the role of the nation-state will change dramatically and there will be no more room for nationalism than there is for smallpox.' For 'new globalisers', global markets are the unique creations of late twentieth-century and early twenty-first-century ascendant capitalism. Its markets are seen as orderly and stable institutions, operating under conditions of near-perfect or perfect competition, where the nation state is perceived as an increasingly anachronistic and redundant entity (Mann 1997).

Those claiming globalisation is not new argue that prior to 1914 the world already resembled a global market. Their view is that from about 1880 till 1914, money, goods and people flowed freely, and an international financial system based on the gold standard came into existence, which effectively limited the economic autonomy of national governments. Hirst and Thompson (1996, p6) argue, for example, that present-day globalisation 'is a myth for a world without illusions', where it is held that Western social democracy and socialism of the Soviet bloc are finished. 'One can only call the political impact of "globalization" the pathology of overdiminished expectations.' In their view, international trade and capital flows were much more important relative to GDP before 1914 than they are today, both among the industrialising economies themselves and between these and their colonial territories. For them, the present period is not unprecedented.

Boyer and Drache (1996, p13) accept that globalisation is an important contemporary phenomenon, though it is neither totally new nor completely overwhelming. Their analysis provides quantitative evidence demonstrating that globalisation is not novel when measured by national indicators such as share of exports as a percentage of GDP or share of foreign investment in total investment flows. In their estimation, the internationalisation of economic activity has not changed dramatically from the time when Britain was the leading global power; many features of the contemporary world were present then. They claim that the internationalisation of trade, production and finance has fluctuated widely over time, collapsing at the end of the 1930s and recovering only in the 1950s. Nevertheless, they see today's globalisation as quantitatively and qualitatively different from that of previous periods. 'State activity has been internationalized to an unprecedented degree in all industrialized countries.'

Even countries such as France, Japan and Sweden, which were not initially advocates of economic *laissez-faire*, have accepted the need to open up their national markets to international competition. Further, with recurrent financial crises and slowdowns in economic growth, governments have not changed their basic policy frameworks. They continue to support the orthodoxy that external markets must be kept open, unlike state policy in the 1930s when protectionism was in the ascendant. Boyer and Drache suggest, therefore, that it would be wrong to conclude that capitalism has become global, since production methods, employment relations, taxation and economic policy styles remain very specific to each national state. They reject the contention that the nation state is *passé* or an accident of history.

APOLOGISTS FOR GLOBALISATION

Apologists of globalisation and the free market, such as the international financier and speculator George Soros (1995, p194), argue that 'the collapse of the global marketplace would be a traumatic event with unimaginable consequences' and that reform of global capitalism is a necessary condition for continued prosperity and social peace (Soros 2000). Support for globalisation, and the transformation of social markets into free markets, is the overriding objective of trans-national organisations such as the World Trade Organisation (WTO), International Monetary Fund (IMF), Organisation for Economic Co-operation and Development (OECD) and the World Bank. In advancing the 'globalisation' project, they are following the lead of the United States, where progress today is seen as another step towards a universal civilisation – one based on a global free market. Gray (2009), a fierce critic of globalisation, argues that this model of a single worldwide civilisation, supported by the 'Washington consensus', expects democratic capitalism to be accepted throughout a world in which a global free market becomes a final reality. He attributes this to the neo-conservative ascendancy in the United States, where free markets are seen as not only a way of organising a market economy but also a prerequisite for human freedom everywhere.

Supporters of economic globalisation view it as being commercially and socially benevolent, adding to the total sum of human happiness, whilst its critics see it as potentially challenging, with a range of harmful effects. Thus, for the WTO, the economic case for an open, international trading system, based on multilaterally agreed rules, rests largely on common sense, since economic protectionism leads to bloated inefficient companies, business closures and job losses. Writers such as Fukuyama (1992), with his vision of the 'end of history', claim that the inevitability of 'democratic capitalism' constitutes the final form of human government and its global reach is the triumph of the Western idea. Those arguing for a global free market, then, see its growth as a period inaugurating a universal civilisation, replicating Western societies throughout the world.

FACTORS INFLUENCING GLOBALISATION

There is no definitive agreement about the factors influencing globalisation, since there are competing interpretations of the globalisation phenomenon. Four main interpretations have been proposed: the 'Utopian' scenario, the 'modernist' one, globalisation as 'diversity' and the 'sceptical' interpretation. Each emphasises different factors that influence globalisation, such as the changing role of the state, the spread of 'new' ideas in human societies, and the role of ICTs in promoting globalisation. Each interpretation weighs each factor differently.

UTOPIANS

Those supporting the utopian image of globalisation emphasise the role of ideas or ideology in promoting it. They argue that globalisation is associated with the establishment of a single global market, which benefits all the parties concerned – suppliers, consumers, workers and societies. The aim is to establish a global free market, free from politics, where the manifold economic cultures and economic systems that the world has always contained will die out and become redundant. Most international agencies and many MNCs support this agenda, because they want to impose free markets on societies throughout the world. The ultimate objective is to incorporate the world's diverse economies into a universal global market, benefiting the corporate sector. It is MNCs overseeing the world economy that are the vehicles of this post-Keynesian orthodoxy. With the demise of Communist regimes in Eastern Europe and the former Soviet Union, utopians believe that the advance of a singular, universal type of Western capitalism – the American free market model, where government is a bystander – will eventually emerge triumphant throughout the world. As Ohmae (1995, pp7 and 15) argues:

with the ending of the Cold War, the long familiar pattern of alliances and oppositions among industrialized nations has fractured beyond repair. Less visibly, but arguably far more important, the modern nation-state itself – that artifact of the eighteenth and nineteenth centuries – has begun to crumble. … For more than a decade, some of us have been talking about the progressive globalization of markets for consumer goods, like Levi jeans, Nike athletic shoes and Hermes scarves. … Today, however, the process of convergence goes faster and deeper. It reaches well beyond taste to much more fundamental dimensions of worldview, mind-set, and even thought-process.

GLOBALISATION AS MODERNISATION OR MODERNITY

Modernists interpret globalisation more pluralistically, stressing the role of the nation state in enabling globalisation. They observe globalisation being driven by the forces of modernity. Noting the economic successes of 'First World' countries, developing countries seek to achieve the higher standards of living and quality of life of the Western world. The end of colonialism and the emergence of newly independent states with their modernising elites mean that they welcome overseas investment and copy Western ways of working, living and thinking. This results in a process of economic systemisation, an emerging global culture and global consciousness, and a global economy with a diverse cosmopolitan culture. For modernists, globalisation is a multifaceted, uneven process but an inexorable one.

Giddens (1985) and Robertson (1992) challenge the capitalist interpretation of globalisation as too simplistic, but see globalisation as a modernist phenomenon. Both perceive it as a multicausal phenomenon and emphasise the importance of international relations in creating globalisation, which, in their view, has occurred independently of the dynamics of individual societies. For them, globalisation has its roots in the emergence of the culturally homogeneous nation state. Nation states, competing for resources, markets and territory, develop political, economic, military, administrative and diplomatic systems for exchanges with other states, which incorporate elements of both co-operation and conflict. As nation states multiply and the nation state becomes universal, so international relations have to accommodate this development. The world comes to be conceptualised as a whole and new systems emerge to make it more unified. But this does not mean that it becomes more integrated or less conflictual, only more conscious of its singularity.

Giddens (1985) explains the process as one in which the first European nation states successfully married industrial production to military action and succeeded in colonising tribal societies and destroying earlier empires. Their rational-bureaucratic systems enabled them to harness resources to industrial development and modernisation to manage relations with other states (Hardt and Negri 2000). The destabilisation of international relations caused by two world wars in the twentieth century led subsequently to the blossoming of international organisations, offering more security and providing a setting within which new nations states emerged. Giddens (1990) argues that globalisation has been driven by four, interrelated dimensions of 'modernism' or 'modernity':

- **Capitalism**: the world that is emerging is a universal capitalist, market system.

- **Surveillance**: the nation state provides the institutional framework for internal surveillance and control. This is enhanced by the development of international information systems and the sharing of knowledge and data across national boundaries.

- **Military order**: war has been globalised and a system of alliances, centring on the present hegemony of the United States, means that only local and peripheral conflicts occur, but this depends on the stability of international alliances.

- **Industrialism:** industrialisation has eroded Western economic dominance but has resulted in commodification of services and information, with a globalised culture underpinning the whole process.

DIVERSE PATHWAYS TO GLOBALISATION

Those who see globalisation as representing diverse systems of economic production and exchange argue that it is a complex phenomenon, taking different forms in different societies. It is not homogeneous, following a sequential pathway to uniformity, but heterogeneous with diverse impacts on different countries. Its roots lie in the complexities of the modern world.

For observers such as Held *et al* (1997, p257ff), globalisation is not a singular condition, 'a linear process or a final end-point of social change'. This means, first, since different countries are developing along different pathways to the market economy, globalisation impacts on them differentially. Second, globalisation does not mean that world markets affect all aspects of economic life. Some economic activity, such as local, labour-intensive services or local public services, continues to be largely unaffected by world markets. Third, globalisation is not homogeneous, since global markets, where capital and production systems move freely across national frontiers, depend on differences among localities, regions and nation states to operate effectively. Fourth, the growth of global markets does not mean that North American business culture is being copied throughout the world, since the spread of globalisation and ICTs does not result in convergence of national cultures. In fact, globalisation helps retain cultural differences among national economies. Fifth, globalisation does not lead irrevocably to the withering away of the nation state. This remains the decisive mediating structure that MNCs compete to control, whether in Europe, North America or the Asia-Pacific.

GLOBALISATION SCEPTICS

Globalisation sceptics explore what is different about globalisation during a period of increased capital mobility, internationalisation of production and the introduction of ICTs into business processes. They see globalisation largely as the result of changes in the roles of the state. They argue that even if Keynes, Beveridge and Fordist employment relations structures were once the pillars of state policy, they no longer are (Hutton 1995, 2002). The emergence of a 'lean and mean' state, dedicated to providing lower levels of public services, is symptomatic of the new economic order. For many countries grappling with new competitive pressures, home markets remain where the best jobs are, where investment takes place and where indigenous firms make the difference. Petrella (1996) argues that globalisation is partial and unstable and creates cleavages between social classes in advanced countries and between developed and developing countries. Sceptics also view markets as complex social institutions that are not self-organising and do not respond to universal laws of supply and demand. To be efficient, markets have to be embedded in national institutions, including money, labour and their contextual circumstances.

ACTIVITY 7.1

What factors have led to globalisation? Explain the following interpretations of globalisation: (a) globalisation as Americanisation, (b) globalisation as the restructuring of state power, (c) globalisation as imperialism, and (d) globalisation as transformation.

GLOBALISATION: SOME CONSEQUENCES AND RESPONSES

The consequences of globalisation, and responses to it by organisations, governments and international governmental bodies, are far reaching. Globalisation affects businesses, public services, governments, workers and other organisational stakeholders. However, despite the claims of free market utopians, a universal model of contemporary market capitalism does not exist and the consequences of globalisation vary in different market economies and different business sectors.

THE CULTURES OF CAPITALISM

Hampden-Turner and Trompenaars (1993, pp6–10), for example, examine seven cultures of capitalism, focusing on the United States, the UK, Sweden, France, Japan, the Netherlands and Germany. They identify 'seven fundamental valuing processes', without which wealth-creating organisations could not exist, although each value has a tension within it. These are:

- **Making rules and discovering exceptions:** here the integrity of enterprises depends upon how well 'universalism' or rules of wide generality are reconciled with 'particularism' or special exceptions to rules.

- **Constructing and deconstructing:** here the mental and physical processes of 'analysing' and 'integrating' keep enterprises in a constant state of renewal or refinement.

- **Managing communities of individuals:** here the integrity of enterprises depends on how well the 'individualism' of employees, shareholders and customers is reconciled with the 'communitarianism' of the larger system.

- **Internalising the outside world:** here enterprises have to reconcile their 'inner-directions' and 'outer-directions' so that they can internalise the outer world to act decisively and competently.

- **Synchronising fast processes:** here the task is reconciling 'sequential time' with 'synchronised time' (ie how time is organised).

- **Choosing amongst achievers:** here the capacity to create wealth depends upon balancing 'achieved' with 'ascribed status.'

- **Sponsoring equal opportunities:** here the integrity of enterprises depends on how they balance the need for 'equality' of inputs with 'hierarchy' in judging the merits of these inputs.

The typology outlined in Figure 7.1 suggests that there are at least five types of market economy around the world. Each varies according to how its markets are regulated, the prime accountability of the market, the nature of the labour market, and its underpinning value system. Using this typology (although there are others), Anglo-Saxon systems of market economy, such as those found in the English-speaking world in the UK, United States, Canada and Australasia, are typified by free markets, the centrality of contract law, dominance of shareholder interests, deregulated labour markets and an individualistic value system. In contrast, Central European economic systems are typified by social markets, public law, stakeholder interests, regulated labour markets and social cohesion.

Figure 7.1 Types of market economy

System	Market	Regulation	Prime accountability	Labour market	Value system
Anglo-Saxon	free	contract	shareholder	deregulated	individualist
Central-European	social	public law	stakeholders	regulated	social cohesion
Russian	anarchic	power	managers–workers	local	mutual-aid
Japanese	managed	trust	networks of firms	internal	collectivist
Chinese	interpersonal	trust	families	parochial	paternalist

In the Far East, two types of market system stand out – the Japanese and Chinese. In Japan, businesses work within a framework of managed markets, market regulation is based on trust, and market accountability is through networks of firms working together. Japanese businesses favour internal labour markets and a collectivist value system. In China, including Hong Kong, Taiwan and other parts of the world with Chinese businesses, markets are largely interpersonal and, as in Japan, are based on trust, with primary market accountability centred on family networks. Labour markets are anarchic, regulated by naked power, and primary market accountability is to managers and workers. Russia has largely local labour markets and a 'mutual aid' value system based on extended families.

In the Far East, two types of market system stand out – the Japanese and Chinese. In China, including Hong Kong, Taiwan and other parts of the world with Chinese businesses, markets are largely interpersonal and, as in Japan, are based on trust, with primary market accountability centred on the recruitment and employment of ethnic Chinese workers, in a system incorporating strongly paternalist values. In the emergent economy of the Russian Federation, markets are anarchic, regulated by naked power, and primary market accountability is to managers and workers. Russia has largely local labour markets and a 'mutual aid' value system based on extended families.

In Anglo-Saxon market economies like the UK, global forces impact on companies, national government, local government, customers, workers and other organisational and societal stakeholders in a variety of ways. Many private businesses, including MNCs, have to respond to increasing competition in their markets for goods, services, capital, labour and other resources by changes in their policies, structures and management systems. In order to gain 'competitive edge', and some control over indeterminate market forces, firms adopt and develop a variety of business strategies to manage change, competition and uncertainty under globalisation.

ORGANISATIONAL RESPONSES TO GLOBALISATION

The typical responses of private sector businesses to globalisation include:

- addressing competitive pressures in the marketplace
- seeking to retain and expand their market share of products or services, domestically and internationally
- searching for new markets, products and methods of providing them
- investing in information and communication technologies
- taking over and merging with other businesses
- investing and relocating operations overseas in transnational groupings
- responding to pressures on productivity, quality and performance
- seeking to improve profits and profitability.

In terms of HR policies and strategies, leading-edge companies are likely to seek greater commitment and motivation of their workforces. This is in the expectation that committed and motivated people contribute to improved performance and higher profitability and that 'people make a difference'. Linkages are claimed to exist between supportive corporate contexts and specific HR practices, on the one hand, and improved company performance and better worker outcomes in 'high-performance work systems', on the other (see Chapter 5). A key assumption is that 'performance is a function of employee ability, motivation and "opportunity"'. In other words, people perform well when they have the necessary knowledge and skills, and the motivation to do so because they are incentivised for it. The work environment has to provide the necessary support and avenues for bringing out this performance (Boxall and Purcell 2008).

Other consequences of globalisation for managing people include less job security, widening pay differentials, more job flexibility, changing job structures and higher unemployment in flexible labour markets. To meet the demands of increased product market competition and high customer expectations about quality, employers try to respond by drawing upon HR strategies and practices that recruit, motivate, retain and engage committed workers.

GOVERNMENTAL RESPONSES TO GLOBALISATION

In some respects, the impact of globalisation on governments at both national and local levels in Anglo-Saxon market economies is one of its most distinctive features. The main responses to globalisation by governments in such cases include:

- weakening the redistributive dimensions of the welfare state
- moving from the welfare state to the provision of public services

- emphasising market solutions to resolving economic and social welfare problems as the preferred approach to making resource decisions

- emphasising the importance of flexible labour, product and capital markets

- viewing regulation of the economy no longer as a managerial task but as a steering one for government

- recognising and accepting the central role of the private sector in creating wealth

- managing expectations arising from a 'low taxation' culture, where personal and corporate taxpayers have expectations of tax reductions or at least a low tax regime

- dealing with a more limited concept of citizenship, where the boundaries of the public domain become narrower and more circumscribed

- accepting that financing public goods becomes harder to achieve and that government has to draw on the private sector as a major source of 'public investment'

- delivering a more limited range of 'public services' by replacing birth-to-death welfare state regimes.

The ways that those managing public services respond to globalisation, in turn, include emphasising 'good' management practices and the effective managing of their limited sector resources, and addressing governmental demands for more efficiency, greater effectiveness and better value for money. Governments also split public services into 'purchaser' and 'provider' units through the creation of internal markets or quasi-markets, and redraw the boundaries between the public and private sectors through subcontracting, market testing and creation of public agencies. Governments use private sector benchmarks to guide best management practices to respond more directly to client needs and engage in continual public management reforms (see Chapter 6). All these developments push the HR function to being more business focused.

INDIVIDUAL RESPONSES TO GLOBALISATION

It is also argued that globalisation provides greater consumer choice and benefits to customers in the marketplace. It is asserted that the 'consumer' once again becomes 'king' and that one of the main drivers of corporate and public service performance is 'customer satisfaction'. Consumer sovereignty replaces producer sovereignty, as increasingly competitive markets propel the economic system to satisfy the economic wants of consumers. However, there are possible dangers in consumer sovereignty. First, consumers may be ill informed or persuaded by advertisers to make bad choices. Second, consumer preferences may be frustrated by monopoly or imperfect competition. Third, consumers can be considered the best judges of their needs and preference, and as making rational choices, only if they can learn by trial and error what to avoid and how to choose better. This is difficult to do in complex consumer markets, where consumer choice can often be too wide and confusing. Consumers may also make decisions which have high social costs resulting in the consumption of illness-inducing products that lead to health costs, absenteeism from work and high dependency.

ACTIVITY 7.2

Drawing on Figure 7.1 above, discuss and review the major differences between these types of market economy. What are the major effects, both positive and negative, of the growth of MNCs locating in the UK for (a) the UK economy, (b) government and (c) people?

CRITIQUES OF GLOBALISATION

For critics of globalisation like Hirst and Thompson (1996, p10), today's world economy shows many features that bring it closer to a disorderly global market, rather than an orderly one. For them, the international system becomes socially disembedded as markets become truly global. 'Domestic policies, whether of private corporations or public regulators, now have routinely to take account of the predominantly international determinants of their sphere of operations.' Other critics, such as Gray (2009), argue that this is a US-centric perspective, purveying a view of the world that is unrecognisable to most Europeans and Asians. Indigenous varieties of capitalism emerging in Eastern Europe and the Far East cannot be contained within a single framework designed to reproduce the 'American dream' with its 'ideal type' of corporate, shareholder capitalism.

Cohen (1996), in turn, addresses the way in which the nation state is being challenged and changed by new international trade agreements, such as the North American Free Trade Agreement. She concludes that free trade agreements adversely affect equality-seeking groups by disenfranchising and excluding them from power. Such analyses lead Bienefeld (1996) and others to conclude that the nation state remains a necessary and feasible response to the pressures driven by increasing global disorder. In Bienefeld's view, the nation state is the only entity capable of restoring some congruence between the economic, social and political dimensions of modern life.

In Gray's analysis (2009), the global economy that has emerged is a result of the worldwide spread of new technologies, not the spread of free markets. For him, the outcome is not a universal free market but the anarchy of sovereign states, rival capitalisms and stateless zones. He argues that global free markets fracture societies and weaken states. Where there are weak governments, states have collapsed or ceased to be effective and market forces, over which governments have no control, have desolated societies, as was the case in Iceland in 2010. His prognosis is that only a framework of global regulation, involving currencies, capital movements, trade and environmental conservation, can enable the creativity of the world economy to be harnessed in the service of human needs.

There is also an 'anti-globalisation' movement, which is the umbrella term for a group of different protest causes, including environmentalism, Third World debt, animal rights, child labour, anarchism, anti-capitalism and opposition to MNCs. It includes increasing numbers of cross-border social, cultural and technological links (Hertz 2001, Stiglitz 2002, Monbiot 2001). The targets of anti-globalisation protests have been meetings of the WTO, which promotes free trade between countries, the IMF, which gives countries loans when their economies are in crisis, and the World Bank, which gives longer-term loans to countries for development. Other events that have been consistently hit are meetings of national leaders and businesses, such as the World Economic Forum, climate change summits and other international meetings supporting global free trade. May Day, originally a pagan festival but now the day of workers and international socialism, is often a focus for these protests, some of which have resulted in violence. But most protesters are supporters of non-violent direct action and use tactics such as 'guerrilla gardening' by giving pigeons food when authorities try to remove them.

Some of the specific objections of critics within the anti-globalisation movements are outlined below. These objections are underpinned by the ideas, as ICTs and cheaper transportation bring the world closer together, that the power of money or finance capital and the ideas of market fundamentalism are subverting the principles of inalienable human rights, to which every person is entitled.

- **Market failure:** the roles of MNCs are typically quoted here, because of their immense power in using scarce resources and undertaking activities across national boundaries, enabling them to buy physical and labour resources in the cheapest markets, and sell their products in the most expensive ones, to increase their profits. With capital being highly mobile and labour being largely immobile, this gives many advantages to large MNCs in comparison with indigenous companies and peoples. Where competition ends and market power begins, MNCs have the power to make national economies less governable.

- **Market creep:** this is the idea that democracy (one person, one vote) is being replaced by the primacy of the market (one dollar, one vote). Hertz (2001) argues that MNCs have become huge global giants, wielding immense political power. In their evolution, justice, equity, rights, the environment and even national security fall by the wayside. Issues such as democracy and human rights are moral issues and are areas where global corporations are morally ambivalent. Sen (2001), in turn, argues that democracy and human rights should be the primary measure of development, rather than being seen as distinct from it. Another area where markets are invading and becoming all pervasive is the media. With global magnates like Rupert Murdoch and Silvio Berlusconi acquiring ever more of the total global media market, it is argued, freedom of expression and ideas are becoming more and more subject to economic decisions. Beyond this, Altman (2001) argues that with globalisation and economic development, hundreds of thousands are forced into sex work to survive.

- **Intellectual property:** the argument here is that more intellectual property is being protected; or, alternatively, less intellectual property, or intellectual capital, remains free. Many things that are now becoming intellectual property were formerly owned collectively. An example is governments that sell data which were previously free to users. In this case, public assets and revenue streams are privatised, with only fractional benefits accruing to the public in return. Another example is public universities becoming corporations, patenting what is discovered within them and generating revenue from the licensing. Another negative element of intellectual property rights for some disciples of anti-globalisation is that they grant a monopoly on the items they purport to protect, thus giving market power to the proprietary organisation. Most anti-globalisation writers cite intellectual property as an area in need of reform.

- **Labour**: a main concern of anti-globalisation supporters is increases in unemployment arising from corporate activity, which becomes more mobile, unrestricted, opaque and unaccountable. As Stiglitz (2002) argues, privatisation more often destroys jobs than creates them and this is viewed as gaining efficiency. Further, there are social costs associated with unemployment that private firms do not take into account in decision-making. There is also evidence of the use of child labour in developing economies and sweatshop conditions in some countries. Where there have been massive population shifts from rural to urban areas, this has often resulted in poverty, famine, poor infrastructures, bad housing, and ethnic friction. These are often accompanied by evidence of degradation of living and working conditions and human rights abuses. Even in countries with minimum wages and labour standards, these are not always enforced rigorously and robustly by public authorities.

- **The environment**: a major aspect of this concern is the 'race to the bottom' argument. This posits that as MNCs select and negotiate terms of trade with countries they wish to invest in, one item most likely to be sacrificed is the environment. Firms may arrange to be exempted from local laws on the environment, or they will simply move to countries where laws are unenforced. Also as trade increases, the transportation infrastructure expands to keep pace, leading to increased pollution and rises in greenhouse emissions. In agriculture, chemically intensive farms are also said to pollute considerably more than single-owner farms.

ACTIVITY 7.3

How persuasive are the arguments of the anti-globalisation movement(s)?

MULTINATIONAL CORPORATIONS (MNCS)

MNCs are global businesses operating on a transnational basis across regions and continents. They are drivers of and driven by globalisation. Sometimes called transnational companies or multinational enterprises, MNCs have been around for a long time. The former Dutch East India Company, created in 1602, is sometimes quoted as being the first modern MNC. Today, MNCs with national headquarters and branches and plants around the world are commonplace. They play important roles in local economies, the world economy, international relations and promoting globalisation. As powerful players in the world and local economies, MNCs employ large quantities of physical resources, engage multinational workforces, invest vast amounts of finance capital in their businesses and provide wide ranges of goods and services to their customers. Unsurprisingly, with their immense power and little local accountability, they are not without their critics and groups opposing them.

MNCs represent important conduits for international flows of HR strategies, practices and ideas. Edwards and Rees (2006), for example, argue that notions of 'good practices' in MNCs are likely to flow from their countries of origin to other countries. Thus MNCs from economically successful countries have incentives to diffuse those practices that are deemed to have contributed to this success to their foreign subsidiaries. This 'dominance' effect is apparent as MNCs originating from successful global regions, such as the United States, Europe and Japan disperse their home-centred HR practices across their global operations – such as HRM, Japanese MNCs, for instance, frequently transpose systems of lean production, just-in-time manufacturing and quality standards to their North American and European subsidiaries. US companies, in turn, transfer their HR 'good practices' to their subsidiaries around the world such as selective recruitment, individualised employment packages, performance-related pay and anti-union policies.

THE GROWTH OF MNCS

According to Rugman and Collinson (2009), in the late 1980s the largest 500 MNCs conducted over half of all world trade. By the late 1990s, of the world's largest 500 MNCs, 88 per cent came from the United States, EU and Japan. Of these, 32 per cent were American owned, 31 per cent from the EU and 25 per cent from Japan. The remaining 12 per cent were from Switzerland, South Korea, Canada, Brazil, Australia and China.

In 2009, one estimate suggests that there were over 35,000 MNCs globally, controlling many foreign subsidiaries and accounting for about one-third of entire world trade. Much of this investment has gone into developing countries with the highest growth potential. These included China, Singapore, Malaysia, Thailand, Mexico, Brazil and Argentina. According to this source, the 10 biggest recipients of foreign direct investment received almost 95 per cent of the total, with all African countries receiving less than 4 per cent and the poorest 50 countries in the world only 2 per cent (Bossman Baafi 2009).

Lazar (2005) says that MNCs are created to leverage their ownership-specific advantages, and they do this by combining this advantage with country-specific and location advantages under a common governance structure. He makes three main points. First, the ownership (or firm) advantage relies on the ability to create a competitive advantage. Second, country-specific advantages include: market access, the market's size and potential growth; availability of low-cost resources, whether labour, capital or materials; a favourable policy environment;

Table 7.1 Comparative percentage global growth rates, 2007–10

Region	2007	2008	2009 (projected)	2010 (projected)
World output	5.1	3.1	-1.4	2.5
Advanced economies	2.7	0.8	-3.8	0.6
United States	2.0	1.1	-2.6	0.8
Euro area	2.7	0.8	-4.8	-0.3
Germany	2.5	1.3	-6.2	-0.6
France	2.3	0.3	-3.0	0.4
Italy	1.6	-1.0	-5.1	-0.1
Spain	3.7	1.2	-4.0	-0.8
United Kingdom	2.6	0.7	-4.2	0.2
Japan	2.3	-0.7	-6.0	1.7
Canada	2.5	0.4	-2.3	1.6
Other advanced economies	4.7	1.6	-3.9	1.0
Newly industrialised Asian economies	5.7	1.5	-5.2	1.4
Emerging and developing economies	8.3	6.0	1.5	4.7
Africa	6.2	5.2	1.8	4.1
Sub-Sahara	6.9	5.5	1.5	4.1
Central & east Europe	5.4	3.0	-5.0	1.0
Russia	8.1	5.6	-6.5	1.5
Developing Asia	10.6	7.6	5.5	7.0
China	13.0	9.0	7.5	8.5
India	9.4	7.3	5.4	6.5
ASEAN-5	6.3	4.8	-0.3	3.7
Middle East	6.3	5.2	2.0	3.7
Others	–	–	–	–
Brazil	5.7	5.1	-1.3	2.5
Mexico	3.3	1.3	-7.3	3.0

Adapted from IMF (2009).

and proximity and access to other large markets. Third, location advantage provides several options for benefiting, including foreign direct investment, licensing, joint ventures and subcontracting.

For Gray (2009), the direct investment route with a common governance structure is selected if it minimises transaction costs and taxes and protects proprietary rights. In his view, MNCs emerged with the development of European colonialism, but the role of modern MNCs is on a different scale. They are able to divide the production process into discrete operations and locate them in different countries around the world. In this way, they can choose the countries whose labour markets, tax and regulatory regimes and infrastructures are the most congenial to them. For him, it is the promise of direct inward investment, and the threat of its withdrawal, which have the most significant leverage on the policy options of national governments.

There are a number of factors driving the growth and increasing importance of global companies in the world economy. The globalisation of business corporations has emerged out of growing economic interdependence among countries, reflected in increasing border flows of goods, services, capital and knowledge. The factors promoting this include:

- An increasing number of countries have embraced the free-market ideology, including Eastern Europe, Russia and the Far East, for example China, Taiwan and Malaysia.

- The economic centre of gravity is shifting from developed countries to developing ones, as indicated in Table 7.1. This shows higher economic growth rates in newly industrialised Asian economies, emerging and developing economies, developing Asian economies, the Middle East and parts of Latin America than in advanced economies.

- Technological advances, and their declining real costs, are continuously improving business communications.

- The opening up of borders to trade, investment and technology transfers not only creates new market opportunities for MNCs but also enables competitors from abroad to enter domestic markets.

- Declining trans-continental transportation costs facilitate the transfer of goods across the world economy.

- As market competition intensifies, MNCs seek wider markets for their goods and services, want to exploit the cost-reducing (or quality-enhancing) potential of optimal locations, and expect to tap technological advances to serve their global customers.

- And, very importantly, since the 1990s, the major international organisations responsible for the world economic order, such as the GATT, OECD and World Bank, have aggressively supported the reorganisation of MNCs on a worldwide basis.

LOCAL AND GLOBAL MARKETS

MNCs dominate international production in automobiles, consumer electronics, chemicals, pharmaceuticals and petroleum, because of their economies of scale, extensive production networks, and their products and services selling across national borders, often through well-developed networks of subsidiaries, partner firms or corporate alliances. It is also estimated that as much as two-thirds of trade and investment in these sectors is on an intra-firm basis. Of that trade and investment, the largest MNCs are involved in over three-quarters of the world's stock of foreign direct investment and over half its total trade. What is intensifying the concentration of economic power in the hands of MNCs are cheap ICTs, which enable companies to improve their manufacturing and distribution processes, raise productivity, increase efficiency and expand profits.

To what extent MNCs are fully global, however, is a matter of debate. Free market utopians, such as Ohmae (1995), have no doubts about the hegemony of MNCs and their pivotal role in the world economy, compared with national governments, hence his 'homeless big business', 'powerless countries' and 'borderless world' visions. However, as Bryan and Farrell (1996, p1) write, 'increasingly, millions of global investors, operating out of their own economic self-interest, are determining interest rates, exchange rates, and the allocation of capital, irrespective of the wishes or political objectives of national political leaders.' Reich (1991), in turn, speaks of the growing irrelevance of corporate nationality. In his view, as corporations of all nations become 'transformable global webs', it is not what citizens own that matters from the standpoint of national wealth; it is 'which citizens learn how to do what counts'. This makes a country's human resources capable of adding value to the world economy, therefore increasing its own potential worth.

Writers such as Rugman and Doh (2008), while seeing MNCs as vehicles of increasing global interdependence, argue that most of them remain firmly rooted in their native economic regions. One reason for this is the presence of non-tariff barriers to trade and investment. These are designed to limit access to internal markets in the regions where they apply, or give preferential access to certain partners in return for reciprocal advantages. The barriers include rules of origin, health and safety codes, exemptions from trade agreements for certain sectors, poorly administered anti-dumping laws, and so on. Many US restrictions are aimed at European and Japanese competitors, and vice versa. This is why this strong triad of regional trading and investment blocks in North America, Europe and the Far East arose in the first place. The situation is advantageous for triad-based MNCs but makes life difficult for non-triad ones, since they have to gain access to triad markets to pursue a full global strategy.

The prominent role that MNCs appear to play in globalisation is by acting as 'flagship firms'. Rugman and Collinson (2009) describe flagship firms as those operating at the hub of an extensive business network or cluster of firms. They identify four kinds of long-term partners that MNCs nurture: suppliers, customers, competitors and non-business infrastructure. The latter includes network partners in research and education, transport, financial services and branches of government. MNCs, therefore, help build bridges for big business with the public and services sectors. Some of the key partners of MNCs are other MNCs, driven into alliances by costs of research and development and difficulties in accessing new markets. These alliances tend to be less stable than relationships with key suppliers and customers. Key suppliers and flagship MNCs are mutually dependent, and therefore invest more trust in their long-term managerial relationships than is normally the case between MNCs and other suppliers. However, MNCs need government support to compete and survive in local and international marketplaces, as indicated in Figure 7.2.

Figure 7.2 Government support for MNCs

Policy area	Actions taken
Infrastructure	covering the costs of basic infrastructure, such as funding high-risk research, universities and vocational training systems, promoting dissemination of scientific information and facilitating technology transfers
Tax	providing tax incentives needed for investment in industrial research and development, and in technological innovation
Local markets	guaranteeing that national MNCs have a sufficiently stable home base by providing privileged access to the internal market via public contracts, for example in defence, telecommunications and transport
Science and technology	guaranteeing basic scientific and technical competence, as well as protecting designated sectors of the internal market upon which national businesses may depend
State support	providing the necessary support and assistance – regulatory, commercial, political and diplomatic – to national businesses in their objective of surviving in international markets
Reducing labour standards	pressing states to introduce policies favouring their freedom of action in labour market regulation, so that MNCs can reduce labour standards to improve their competitiveness

Economies of scale or other advantages of globalisation often co-exist with needs for some degree of localism. Globalisation refers to features such as the production of standard goods or services for worldwide markets. Localism concerns features such as the provision of products tailored specifically for regional or national markets or the adoption of local management practices. It is the interaction of the tensions between global or local integration that determine an MNC's strategic preferences for global expansion in relation to standardisation of products, differentiation and cost in each case. This is demonstrated in Figure 7.3, which identifies four possible strategies for MNCs: multi-domestic, transnational, international and global. In practice, however, the situation is complicated because companies might combine these strategies according to the circumstances of their different product or service divisions. This illustrates the complex variants of the multinational approach in doing global, and local, business.

Figure 7.3 MNC strategies for global expansion

PRESSURES FOR GLOBAL INTEGRATION

	LOW Value creation activities co-ordinated on country-by-country basis	HIGH Value-creation activities co-ordinated on both a global and country basis
HIGH Products and approaches customised for each local market	*Multi-domestic strategy*, with goal of local differentiation advantage	*Transnational strategy*, with goal of both differentiation and low-cost advantage
LOW Same standardised products offered to customers in all countries	*International strategy*, with goal of global differentiation advantage	*Global strategy*, with goal of low-cost advantage

PRESSURES FOR LOCAL RESPONSIVENESS

Adapted from Jones (2001).

ACTIVITY 7.4

Examine the cases for and against MNCs in national and international economies.

CULTURAL AND INSTITUTIONAL INFLUENCES ON MNCS

MNCs are complex, many-layered organisations. Some internal characteristics derive from their countries of origin. Others derive from where their subsidiary bodies are located, the people employed in them and the contexts within which they operate. It is unsurprising that managerial and employee behaviour within MNCs varies across countries and is influenced by both cultural and institutional factors around the world. Hollinshead (2010) defines the cultural determinants as the 'software', or the psychological determinants of behaviour. Institutions are recurrent patterned forms of activities that fulfil basic functions in societies, such as their economic, political or educational institutions. Hollinshead describes the institutional determinants of behaviour as the 'hardware' underpinning organisational systems.

Cultural variables

The concept of culture has been touched upon many times throughout this text. The term is used at the individual level (personal culture), group level (group culture), organisational level (corporate culture) or societal level (national culture). Thus culture has many levels and layers of impact (Spencer-Oatey 2000).

Basically, however, culture is the pattern of shared meanings and understandings passed down through language, symbols and artefacts amongst humankind. At a more sophisticated level, Hodgetts and Luthan (2003) provide six characteristics of culture that define it at any level. For them, culture is:

- **Learned**: it is not biologically determined but acquired through personal learning and experience.

- **Shared**: people share culture as members of groups, organisations and societies.

- **Trans-generational**: culture transcends generations because it is cumulative and is passed on among generations.

- **Symbolic**: culture arises from the human capacity to symbolise. People symbolise by using 'things' to represent other things.

- **Patterned**: because culture is structured, it is integrated so that a change in one aspect of culture results in changes in another aspect.

- **Adaptive**: culture is rooted in the human capacity to change or adapt. It evolves over time.

Figure 7.4 Insights into cultural diversity

Relationship orientations	Main features
Universalism versus Particularism	Individual inclination to universal rules or principles according to circumstances
Individualism versus Communitarianism	Individual orientation to self or common goals
Achievement versus Ascription	Whether social status is achieved by merit or by position
Neutral versus Affective	Whether feelings are expressed impersonally or emotionally
Specificity versus Diffuseness	Separation of work and private life or the integration of work and private life
Sequential versus Synchronic	Whether time is linear and sequential or multiple and diffuse
Inner versus Outer directedness	Whether individuals and groups control their own destiny or are controlled by external forces beyond personal control

Adapted from Trompenaars and Hampden-Turner (1997)

Various studies provide useful insights into cultural predispositions across national boundaries, starting with Hofstede's (2001) influential works in the 1960s and 1970s. More recently, Trompenaars and Hampden-Turner (1997) have built on Hofstede's pioneering studies by focusing on 'meanings' or human interpretations of the world around them. They identify the relationship orientations indicated in Figure 7.4. Ingelhart and Welzel (2005) analyse contemporary global cultural values in terms of two major dimensions, each of which has contrasting orientations. On the one hand, there are 'traditional values' and 'secular-rational values' and, on the other, 'survival values' and 'self-expression values'. In their study, each was measured on a scale ranging from 'very weak', 'weak', 'moderate', 'strong' to 'very strong', with some examples of these values provided below.

- **Traditional values:** emphasise parent-child ties, family values and deference to authority.

- **Secular-rational values:** tolerate divorce, abortion and suicide.

Figure 7.5   The Inglehart Values Map

Protestant Europe • secular-rational values: ranging from *very weak* to *very strong* • self-expression values: ranging from *very weak* to *very strong*
Catholic Europe • secular-rational values: ranging from *very weak* to *moderate* • traditional values: ranging from *very weak* to *weak* • self-expression values: ranging from *very weak* to *very strong* • survival values: ranging from *very weak* to *strong*
The English-speaking world • secular-rational values: ranging from *very weak* to *weak* • traditional values: ranging from *very weak* to *moderate* • self-expression values: ranging from *weak* to *very strong*
Former Communist Europe • traditional values: ranging from *very weak* to *weak* • secular rational values: ranging from *very weak* to *strong* • survival values: ranging from *weak* to *very strong*
South Asia • traditional values: ranging from *very weak* to *very strong* • survival values: ranging from *very weak* to *very strong*
Latin America • traditional values: ranging from *weak* to *very strong* • self-expression values: ranging from *very weak* to *moderate*
Africa • traditional values: ranging from *moderate* to *very strong* • survival values: ranging from *weak* to *very strong*
The Confucian world (China, Japan, South Korea, Taiwan) • secular-rational values: ranging from *weak* to *very strong* • survival values: ranging from *very weak* to *moderate* • self-expression values: ranging from *very weak* to *strong*.

Adapted from Ingelhart and Welzel (2005)

- **Survival values:** prioritised in pre-industrial and industrial societies.
- **Self-expression values:** prioritised in knowledge-based societies.

Drawing upon this framework, Ingelhart and Welzel identify in the 'Inglehart Values Map' eight clusters of countries around the world and their contemporary cultural values. No cluster was homogeneous in its values, which varied; Protestant Europe, for example, contained countries as diverse as Denmark, Finland, East Germany, West Germany, Iceland, the Netherlands, Norway, Sweden and Switzerland. Apart from Israel, Middle Eastern countries were not in the survey. However, some general trends are observable and are summarised in Figure 7.5.

Institutional variables

A common set of institutions is found in all societies, rooted in ideological assumptions about the nature of the socio-economic world. Two dominant theoretical frameworks that have influenced Western societies in terms of the institutional arrangements for conducting business are 'corporatism' and 'neo-liberalism'.

Corporatism, or the UK version 'tri-partism,' dominated political and economic thinking in the post-war period from 1945 till 1979. Basically, corporatism is a system of policy-making where the major economic interests within the state – employers, unions and government – work together within formal structures of government to formulate and implement public policies. This meant that both Labour and Conservative governments sought co-operation with business and labour organisations to solve national economic problems. The most visible expression of this consensus style of policy formulation was the National Economic Development Council, created in 1961 to take joint action on economic policy. A number of similar bodies were created subsequently, and the practice of officially bringing insider groups into the consultative and decision-making processes spread widely in central and local government. An underpinning assumption of corporatist ideology is that the unbridled flow of market forces leads to unpredictable outcomes and is linked to high levels of material inequality in society, which is detrimental to the public good. In corporatist thinking, markets – whether for goods, labour or capital – need to be regulated and tempered by social awareness of market outcomes.

Neo-liberalism derives from the ideas of the 'New Right' in UK politics, influenced by some American thinkers, since the 1980s. The ideology underpinning neo-liberalism is that free markets and market competition are the best means of protecting economic growth and political freedom. Individual rights should be protected by maximising freedom of choice, limiting the powers of government and promoting market economics. Apologists for neo-liberalism such as Hayek (1944) argue that socialism and the welfare state inevitably lead to loss of individual freedom. The Chicago school of economics, led by Milton Friedman, in the 1970s and 1980s, rejected Keynesian economic theory in favour of classical economics. This strongly favours competitive markets and low public expenditure. The main function of government is to regulate money supply to control inflation. Such ideas strongly influenced the Thatcher and Major administrations from 1979 to 1997, with 'New' Labour not subsequently challenging this 'new' political, economic consensus.

ACTIVITY 7.5

Examine and discuss the implications of (a) cultural variables and (b) neo-liberalism for HRM in MNCs.

MAJOR INTERNATIONAL ORGANISATIONS

There is a range of international institutions seeking to influence patterns of international trading, national economic policies and economic development. Most were created at the end of the Second World War. The activities of four are outlined below. One critique by some observers is that these bodies are strongly identified with free market and global principles in their economic approaches. These encourage neo-liberal policies, privatisation and tax-cutting initiatives, rather than Keynesian, interventionist policies. At a lecture given at the Warsaw School of Economics, the Secretary-General of the OECD made it quite clear that that the organisation he headed: 'has a key role to play in managing globalisation – understanding it, explaining it, analysing its effects, and making policy recommendations to maximise its benefits and to tackle its challenges' (Gurria 2006).

THE ORGANISATION FOR ECONOMIC CO-OPERATION AND DEVELOPMENT (OECD)

The OECD is made up of 30 member countries sharing a common commitment to democratic government and the market economy. The OECD consists of like-minded countries and provides a setting for reflection and discussion based on policy research and analysis that helps governments shape policy that may lead to a formal agreement among member governments or be acted on in domestic or other international forums. With active relationships involving many other countries, non-governmental organisations, the OECD has global reach. It grew out of the Organisation for European Economic Co-operation, formed to administer American and Canadian aid under the Marshall Plan for reconstructing Europe at the end of the Second World War. Since 1961, the OECD's task has been to build strong economies in member countries, improve efficiency, hone market systems, expand free trade and contribute to developments in industrialised and developing countries.

In recent years, the OECD has moved beyond focusing on its member countries to offer its analytical expertise and accumulated experience to developing and emerging market economies. As it opens itself to new contacts around the world, the OECD is broadening its scope, looking ahead to a post-industrial age in which it aims to weave OECD economies into a prosperous and increasingly knowledge-based world economy. Its member countries are shown in Figure 7.6.

Figure 7.6 OECD member countries

Australia	Hungary	Norway
Austria	Iceland	Poland
Belgium	Ireland	Portugal
Canada	Italy	Slovak Republic
Czech Republic	Japan	Spain
Denmark	Korea	Sweden
Finland	Luxembourg	Switzerland
France	Mexico	Turkey
Germany	Netherlands	United Kingdom
Greece	New Zealand	United States

The OECD has around 2,500 staff in its Secretariat in Paris, who work directly or indirectly to support the activities of its many committees, working groups and expert groups. Senior officials from national administrations come to OECD committee meetings each year to request, review and contribute to work undertaken by the OECD secretariat. They have access to OECD documents and can exchange information through the OECD online data network. Teams of economists, lawyers, scientists and other professional staff, based mainly in substantive directorates, provide research and analysis (Organisation for Economic Co-operation and Development 2009).

The emergence of globalisation has seen the scope of OECD work move from examination of each policy area within each member country to analysis of how various policy areas interact with each other, between countries and beyond OECD countries. This is reflected in work on sustainable development, bringing together environmental, economic and social concerns across national frontiers for better understanding of the problems and the best way to tackle them together.

Best known for its publications and statistics, its work covers economic and social issues from macro-economics to trade, education and development, and science and innovation. The OECD also plays a prominent role in fostering good governance in public services and corporate activity. It helps governments ensure the responsiveness of key economic areas with sector monitoring. It is well known for its individual country surveys and reviews.

The OECD has been called a think tank, a monitoring agency, a 'rich man's club' and a 'non-academic' university. It has elements of all of these but none captures its essence. It gathers together its 30 member countries in a unique forum for discussing, developing and refining economic and social policies. They compare experiences, seek answers to common problems and work to co-ordinate domestic and international policies to help members and non-members deal with a globalised world. Their exchanges may lead to agreements to act in a formal way by, for example, establishing legally binding agreements to crack down on bribery or by drawing up codes for free flow of capital and services.

THE INTERNATIONAL MONETARY FUND (IMF)

The IMF is a specialised, long-established agency of the United Nations, set up by treaty in 1945 to promote the world economy. With headquarters in Washington DC in the United States, it is governed by its global membership of more than 180 countries. Since the IMF was established, its purposes have remained unchanged but its operations, involving surveillance, financial assistance and technical assistance, have developed in response to the changing needs of member countries in an evolving world economy. Again, there is hard evidence of the IMF's promotion of the globalisation agenda. The acting managing director was reported as saying in an address to an economics round table discussion at the University of California at San Diego: 'The Fund … is a facilitator of globalization. By promoting international financial stability, and by encouraging our 184 members to pursue sound macroeconomic policies we aim to enable everybody to enjoy the benefits that globalization brings' (Krueger 2003).

The IMF is the central institution of the international monetary system, or system of international payments and exchange rates among national currencies, that enables business and trading to take place between countries. The IMF's purposes have become more important, partly because of the expansion of its membership and the increasing complexity of the global economy. The expansion of IMF membership, together with changes in the world economy, has required the IMF to adapt in a variety of ways to continue serving its purposes effectively.

Figure 7.7 IMF policy areas

Policy areas	Actions
Global crisis	The IMF is working on several fronts to help members combat worldwide economic and financial crisis
	• It is tracking economic and financial developments globally, so that it can help policy-makers with the latest forecasts and analyses of developments in financial markets
	• It is giving policy advice to countries and regions, and money, to assist emerging-market and low-income economies that have been hit by the crisis
	• It is assisting the Group of 20 industrial and emerging economies with recommendations to reshape the system of international regulation and governance

Policy areas	Actions
The IMF in the global economy	In the wake of the financial crisis, policy-makers around the world are looking for ways to fix the international financial system, including how to better regulate banks and other financial institutions and how to address risk • The IMF is working with national governments, international financial organisations and groups of countries, such as the Group of 20 leading economies and the EU in this area • It is trying to strengthen international economic co-operation
A global fire-fighter	This is part of The IMF's efforts to support countries during the global economic crisis • The IMF is raising its lending capacity and approved a major overhaul of how it lends money • It is offering higher amounts and tailoring loan terms to countries' varying strengths and circumstances
Advanced economies	Advanced economies are experiencing a serious downturn in the face of the most severe shock in mature financial markets since the 1930s • The IMF wants to contribute to this debate and wants more to be done in this area • Leaders of advanced economies have undertaken an unprecedented and concerted fiscal expansion to create jobs • Central banks in many advanced economies have also taken exceptional action, aggressively cutting interest rates in many cases and pledging to maintain expansionary policies for as long as needed
Reducing poverty	The IMF is working to prevent millions of people in low-income countries from slipping into poverty • Low-income countries have sought the IMF's help in coping with the effects of the global financial crisis • Low-income countries are experiencing sharply lower exports and shrinking foreign direct investment • The IMF is taking measures to help low-income countries protect spending on health, education and other services
Transferring policy knowledge	The IMF shares its expertise with member countries by providing training in a wide range of areas • These include central banking, monetary and exchange rate policy, tax policy and administration, and official statistics • The IMF does this by strengthening skills in institutions such as finance ministries, central banks, and statistical agencies • The IMF has also given advice to countries that have had to re-establish government institutions following severe civil unrest or war
Fiscal issues	Fiscal policy affects macro-economic stability, growth, and income distribution. Citizens expect their governments to ensure value-for-money for public spending, a fair and efficient tax system, and transparent and accountable management of public sector resources • The IMF has been a leading source of fiscal policy and management expertise worldwide • The IMF monitors and analyses global fiscal trends and advises IMF member countries on fiscal issues directly

The IMF's general purposes are to foster global monetary co-operation, secure financial stability, facilitate international trade, promote high employment, advance sustainable economic growth and reduce poverty around the world. Its range of activities is shown in Figure 7.7. The IMF's fundamental mission is to help ensure stability in the international system. It does this in three ways: keeping track of the global economy and the economies of member countries, lending to countries with balance of payments difficulties, and giving practical help to members.

- **Surveillance:** the IMF oversees the international monetary system and monitors the financial and economic policies of its members. It does this by keeping track of economic developments on a national, regional and global basis, consulting regularly with member countries and providing them with macro-economic and financial policy advice.

- **Lending:** the IMF provides loans to countries that have trouble meeting their international payments and cannot otherwise find sufficient financing on affordable terms. This financial assistance is designed to help countries restore macro-economic stability by rebuilding their international reserves, stabilising their currencies, and paying for imports – all necessary conditions for re-launching growth. The IMF also provides concessional loans to low-income countries to help them develop their economies and reduce poverty.

- **Technical assistance:** to assist mainly low- and middle-income countries in effectively managing their economies, the IMF provides practical guidance and training on how to upgrade institutions and design appropriate macro-economic, financial, and structural policies.

THE WORLD BANK

The World Bank, established in 1944, has its headquarters in Washington DC. It has more than 10,000 employees in more than 100 offices worldwide. The Bank is a vital source of financial and technical assistance to developing countries around the world. Its mission is to fight poverty for lasting results and help people help themselves and their environment by providing resources, sharing knowledge, building capacity and forging partnerships in the public and private sectors.

The World Bank is not a bank in the common sense of the phrase but consists of five closely associated institutions, all owned by member countries. Each institution plays a distinctive part in its mission to fight poverty and improve living standards in the developing world. Collectively, these bodies provide low-interest loans, interest-free credits and grants to developing countries for a wide array of purposes. These include investments in education, health, public administration, infrastructure, financial and private sector development, agriculture, and environmental and natural resources management. The component parts of the World Bank 'Group' and their basic financial approaches are:

- **International Bank for Reconstruction and Development (IBRD):** provides loans and development assistance to middle-income countries and credit-

Figure 7.8 The Millennium Development Goals

Goals	Targets
Goal 1. Eradicate extreme poverty and hunger	• Halve, between 1990 and 2015, the proportion of people whose income is less than $1 a day • Halve, between 1990 and 2015, the proportion of people who suffer from hunger
Goal 2. Achieve universal primary education	• Ensure that, by 2015, children everywhere, boys and girls alike, will be able to complete a full course of primary schooling
Goal 3. Promote gender equality and empower women	• Eliminate gender disparity in primary and secondary education, preferably by 2005, and in all levels of education no later than 2015
Goal 4. Reduce child mortality	• Reduce by two-thirds, between 1990 and 2015, the under-five mortality rate
Goal 5. Improve maternal health	• Reduce by three-quarters, between 1990 and 2015, the maternal mortality ratio
Goal 6. Combat HIV/AIDS, malaria and other diseases	• Have halted by 2015 and begun to reverse the spread of HIV/AIDS • Have halted by 2015 and begun to reverse the incidence of malaria and other major diseases
Goal 7. Ensure environmental sustainability	• Integrate the principles of sustainable development into country policies and programmes and reverse the losses of environmental resources • Halve by 2015 the proportion of people without sustainable access to safe drinking water • By 2020 to have achieved a significant improvement in the lives of at least 100 million slum dwellers
Goal 8. Develop a Global Partnership for Development	• Develop further an open, rule-based, predictable, non-discriminatory trading and financial system • Address the special needs of the least-developed countries • Address the special needs of landlocked countries and small island developing states • Deal comprehensively with the debt problems of developing countries through national and international measures in order to make debt sustainable in the long term • In co-operation with developing countries, develop and implement strategies for decent and productive work for youth • In co-operation with pharmaceutical companies, provide access to affordable essential drugs in developing countries • In co-operation with the private sector, make available the benefits of new technologies, especially ICTs

Adapted from United Nations (2000)

worthy poorer countries. The IRBD obtains most of its funds through selling bonds in international capital markets.

- **International Development Association (IDA):** provides interest-free loans to the poorest countries, funded by contributions from its wealthier members.

- **International Finance Corporation (IFC):** promotes growth in developing countries, by providing support to the private sector. In collaboration with other investors, the IFC invests in commercial enterprises through loans and equity financing.

- **Multilateral Investment Guarantee Agency (MIGA):** encourages foreign investment in developing countries by providing guarantees to foreign investors against losses caused by non-commercial risks. The MIGA also provides advisory services to help governments attract private investments.

- **International Centre for Settlement of Investment Disputes (ICSID):** promotes international investment through conciliation and arbitration of disputes between foreign investors and host countries.

In September 2000, the United Nations Millennium Summit brought together the largest gathering of world leaders in history. In the summit's final declaration, signed by 189 countries, the international community committed to a specific agenda for reducing global poverty. This agenda listed eight Millennium Development Goals (MDG). These not only identified the gains needed but also quantified them and established yardsticks for measuring improvements in people's lives. The goals, indicated in Figure 7.8, guide the efforts of virtually all organisations working in development, including the World Bank, and are commonly accepted as a framework for measuring development progress. A World Bank report (2010) found that uneven progress was being made in terms of meeting the MDGs. The report says that if current trends in growth and poverty reduction continue, the goal for eradicating extreme income poverty is within reach. But it may well be the only goal to be attained; for many other non-income goals, such as universal primary education, promoting gender equality and reducing child mortality, current rates of progress are too slow.

ACTIVITY 7.6

Do you agree with the view expressed in World Bank report above? What other factors are likely to inhibit the achievement of the MDGs listed in Figure 7.8? Identify the roles that MNCs might have in achieving the MDGs.

THE WORLD TRADE ORGANISATION (WTO)

The WTO's overriding objective is to promote globalisation and help international trade flow smoothly, freely, fairly and predictably. The WTO does this by administering WTO trade agreements, acting as a forum for trade negotiations and settling trade disputes. The WTO also monitors national trade policies, assists developing countries in trade policy issues, and co-operates with other international organisations.

The WTO has over 150 member countries, which account for over 97 per cent of world trade. Decisions are made by its entire membership, typically by consensus. A majority vote is possible but has never been used in the WTO and was extremely rare under its predecessor, the General Agreement on Tariffs and Trade (GATT). WTO agreements are ratified in the parliaments of its Member States. The WTO Secretariat, based in Geneva, has over 500 staff and is headed by a director general. It does not have branch offices outside Geneva. Since members themselves take decisions, the Secretariat does not have the decision-making role of other international bureaucracies (Peet 2009).

The WTO was established in 1995 as one of the newest international organisations. As successor to GATT, which was established after the Second World War, the WTO has built upon the multilateral trading system that was originally set up under GATT over half a century ago. In dealing with global rules of trade between nations and ensuring that trade flows as smoothly and freely as possible, the WTO claims that consumers and producers know that they can enjoy secure supplies and have greater choice of the finished products, components, raw materials and services that they use.

The core of the WTO is the multilateral trading system, made up of WTO agreements negotiated and signed by a large majority of the world's trading nations. These agreements are the legal ground rules for international commerce. Essentially, they are contracts, guaranteeing member countries important trade rights. They also bind governments to keep their trade policies within agreed limits to everybody's benefit. Agreements are negotiated and signed by governments, but their purpose is to help producers of goods and services, exporters and importers conduct their business, with the goal of improving the welfare of the peoples of member countries.

The system was developed through a series of trade negotiations, or rounds, held under GATT. The first rounds dealt mainly with tariff reductions, but later negotiations included other areas such as anti-dumping and non-tariff measures. The Uruguay Round 1986–94 led to the creation of the WTO. However, negotiations did not end there. Some continued after the end of the Uruguay Round. The current set of agreements was the outcome of the 1986–94 Uruguay Round negotiations, which included a major revision of GATT. GATT is now the WTO's principal rulebook on trade in goods. The Uruguay Round also created new rules for dealing with trade in services, relevant aspects of intellectual property, dispute settlement and trade policy reviews. Through these agreements, WTO members operate a non-discriminatory trading system that spells out their rights and their obligations. Each country receives guarantees that its exports will be treated fairly and consistently in other countries' markets. Each promises to do the same for imports into its own market. The system also gives developing countries some flexibility in implementing their commitments.

Any disputes over trade are channelled into the WTO's dispute settlement process, where the focus is on interpreting agreements and commitments and how to ensure that the trade policies of countries conform to them. In this way, the risk of disputes spilling over into political or military conflict is reduced. By lowering trade barriers, it is argued, the WTO's system also breaks down other barriers between peoples and nations.

The 2001 Ministerial Conference in Doha set out tasks, including negotiations, for a wide range of issues concerning developing countries. Before that, in 1997, a high-level meeting on trade initiatives and technical assistance for least-developed countries resulted in an 'integrated framework' involving six intergovernmental agencies, to help those countries increase their ability to trade and some additional preferential market access agreements.

ACTIVITY 7.7

Outline the functions of the WTO, IMF and OECD. What evidence is there to support the view that major international organisations are furthering the Americanisation of the global economy?

THE EUROPEAN UNION

Politically, the EU is a unique political system combining elements of a supra-national and intergovernmental body. Its origins lie in the aftermath of the Second World War, when there was a need for rapid reconstruction and reintegration of Germany into the community of western European states. Anxious to assist Europe in becoming a strong buffer against the threat of Communist expansion from the Soviet bloc, the United States provided Marshall Aid and encouraged international co-operation within Europe. Proposals for a united states of Europe with a federal structure met with little support from post-war states. But six countries – Belgium, France, Italy, Luxembourg, the Netherlands, and West Germany – agreed to co-operate in restructuring their coal and steel communities, signing the Treaty of Paris 1951. Six years later, they signed the Treaty of Rome 1957, which created the European Economic Community (EEC) and the European Atomic Energy Community. The EEC committed its members to creating a 'common market' by removing internal tariff barriers and adopting common external tariffs.

Economically, the EU, as the world's biggest trader, accounting for 20 per cent of global imports and exports, is both a promoter of and a player in globalisation. Free trade amongst Member States underpinned the launch of the EU 50 years ago. The Union wishes to liberalise world trade for the benefit of rich and poor countries alike, claiming that international trade boosts world growth to everybody's advantage and brings consumers a wider range of products to choose from. The EU also believes that competition between imports and local products lowers prices and raises quality. Liberalised trade enables the most efficient EU firms to compete fairly with rivals in other countries. In its view, the disappearance of trade barriers within the EU has made a significant contribution to its prosperity and has reinforced its commitment to global liberalisation.

THE EXPANSION OF THE EU

The benefits of economic co-operation led other countries to seek entry. The UK joined after years of procrastination, as did Denmark and the Republic of Ireland in 1973, and Greece in 1981, followed by Portugal and Spain in 1986. The EU was further enlarged in 1995, when Austria, Finland and Sweden became members. In 2004, the biggest enlargement took place with 10 new countries joining: Cyprus, the Czech Republic, Estonia, Hungary, Latvia, Lithuania, Malta, Poland, Slovakia and Slovenia (Nugent 2004). They were followed by Bulgaria and Romania in 2007, making a total of 27 Member States with a population of some 486 million in 2010 and 23 official languages.

The founding members of the EU always had a vision of a politically united Europe but saw economic integration as the best means of achieving it. There was always ambivalence about political union amongst political leaders, because power was – and is – based on the nation state, not Europe. Their strategies have been essentially pragmatic and founded upon national interest. Between 1956 and 1986 there was some progress but integration was impeded by the need to get unanimous agreement on every issue. The 1980s and 1990s saw greater political will for further integration, prompted partly by the reunification of Germany and the end of the Cold War. The ground rules of the EU are set out in a series of treaties, which have forged strong legal ties amongst EU Member States, with EU laws directly affecting EU citizens and giving them specific rights. The five main treaties are: the Single European Act 1986, Treaty of Maastricht 1992, Treaty of Amsterdam 1997, Treaty of Nice 2000, and the Treaty establishing an EU constitution 2004.

THE TREATY OF LISBON

The Treaty of Lisbon 2009 ended several years of negotiation about institutional and constitutional issues in the EU. It amends earlier EC and EU treaties, without replacing them. It claims to provide the EU with the legal framework and tools to meet current challenges facing the EU and to respond to citizens' demands. This Treaty incorporates the following underlying principles:

- **A more democratic and transparent Europe**: with a strengthened role for the European Parliament and national parliaments, and more opportunities for citizens to have their voices heard.

- **A more efficient Europe**: with simplified working methods and voting rules, and streamlined institutions.

- **A Europe of rights and values, freedoms, solidarity and security**: promoting EU values, and introducing the Charter of Fundamental Rights into European primary law.

- **Europe as an actor on the global stage**: by bringing together Europe's external policy tools, and harnessing Europe's economic, humanitarian, political and diplomatic strengths.

As the world moved into the twenty-first century, it was increasingly recognised that Europe collectively needed to face the challenges of globalisation. With revolutionary new technologies and the World-Wide Web transforming the world economy, these profound economic changes were bringing with them social disruption and culture change. Meeting in Lisbon in March 2000, the European Council of the EU adopted a comprehensive strategy for modernising the EU's economy, enabling it to compete on the world market with other major players such as the United States and newly industrialised countries. The 'Lisbon strategy' included opening up all sectors of the economy to competition, encouraging innovation and business investment and modernising Europe's education systems to meet the needs of the information society (Kontrakou 2004).

The EU has created a single currency, the euro, within 16 of its 27 Member States, and a dynamic single market in which people, goods and capital move freely. It strives to ensure, through social progress and fair competition, that as many people as possible enjoy the benefits of this single market (Dinan 2004).

ACTIVITY 7.8

A visiting manager from the United States has asked you to explain what the European single market is. What would you say?

THE UNDERPINNING PRINCIPLES OF THE EU

A number of fundamental principles underpin the EU. One is 'social peace', arising out of the two wars that ravaged the continent of Europe during the first half of the twentieth century. Politicians who had resisted totalitarianism during the Second World War were determined to put an end to international hatred and rivalry in Europe and build a lasting peace between former enemies. There was the desire for a new order in Western Europe, based on the interests that its peoples and nations shared. It was founded upon treaties guaranteeing the rule of law and equality amongst all countries. It was the start of more than half a century of peaceful co-operation between Member States of the European Communities. With the Treaty of Maastricht, 1992, Community institutions were strengthened and given broader responsibilities, and the EU was born (Warleigh 2009).

A second principle is 'security and safety', especially as twenty-first-century Europe has to deal with safety and security beyond its borders in North Africa, the Balkans, the Caucasus and the Middle East. One of Europe's challenges is to make the EU an area of freedom, security and justice, where everyone has equal access to justice and is equally protected by the law. By the 1990s, European integration had reached a point where the EU began to go beyond its economic goals to acknowledge common problems of security and defence and to move slowly towards greater integration in those areas. The Treaty of Maastricht established two new pillars, foreign and security policy and justice and home affairs, but these remain areas of interstate co-operation. The war in Iraq exposed divisions within the EU, with each Member State taking independent decisions on its position. More co-operation is being achieved on cross-border policing and there have been attempts to get a common policy on immigration.

A third principle is 'economic and social solidarity'. The EU has been built to achieve political goals but its dynamism and success spring from its economic foundations: the 'single market' formed by all Member States and the single currency (the euro), which is now used by 16 Member States. With EU countries accounting for an ever-smaller percentage of the world's population, they have to pull together to ensure economic growth and be able to compete on the world stage with other major economies. No individual EU country is strong enough to act alone in world trade. To achieve economies of scale and find new customers, European businesses have to operate in a bigger market than just their home countries. But Europe-wide free competition has to be counterbalanced by Europe-wide solidarity, expressed in practical help for ordinary people and communities in terms of assistance from the EU budget, 'structural funds' managed by the European Commission, the Common Agricultural Policy and the European Investment Bank to improve Europe's transport infrastructure and boost trans-European trade.

The fourth principle is 'Working more closely together to promote the European model of society'. This reflects the increasingly complex nature of Europe's post-industrial societies. Standards of living have risen steadily but there are still gaps between rich and poor and they will widen as other post-Communist countries join the EU. That is why EU Member States work closely together on tackling social problems. The EU is based on the 'European social model', which is integrationist and collectivist in its philosophy. This is transmitted through legislation promoting workers and union rights in the workplace, such as European works councils and employment protection laws. In periods of transition, continental Member States in the EU traditionally give support to workers, who pay the price of economic reconstruction, with high welfare benefits and support with retraining. Social rights are rooted in many of the constitutions of the Member States, which have sought to develop and protect these rights. The EU Charter of Fundamental Rights, proclaimed in Nice in December 2000, sets out all the rights recognised today by EU Member States and their citizens. The UK has always been the reluctant partner in accepting this model and has worked, along with Spain, to change it (Warleigh 2009).

Fifth, the EU also wants to promote human values and social progress. Europeans see globalisation and technological change revolutionising the world, and they want people everywhere to be in control – not victims – of these changes. People's needs cannot be met simply by market forces or by the unilateral action of one country. So the EU stands for a view of humanity and a model of society that the vast majority of its citizens support. Europeans value their rich heritage, including belief in human rights, social solidarity, free enterprise, a fair sharing of the fruits of economic growth, the right to a protected environment, respect for cultural, linguistic and religious diversity and a harmonious conjugation of tradition and progress. Europeans have a wealth of national and local cultures distinguishing them from one another but are united by their common heritage of values, distinguishing them from the rest of the world (Cowles and Dinan 2004).

ACTIVITY 7.9

The UK has sometimes been described as the 'awkward partner' or 'reluctant member' in the EU. Why do you think this is so?

THE MAIN INSTITUTIONS OF THE EU

Under the treaties in the constitution of the EU, Member States delegate some of their national sovereignty to the Union's institutions. These political institutions represent not only their national but also their collective interests. The main institutions are shown in Figure 7.9. The treaties themselves constitute what is known as 'primary' legislation, and this juridical base enables the institutions to formulate 'secondary' legislation which takes the form of directives, regulations and recommendations. European legislation takes precedence over national legislation in areas to which it relates. These laws, along with EU policies in general, are the result of decisions taken by its three main institutions: the Council of the European Union (representing Member States), the European Parliament (representing citizens) and the European Commission (the civil service or permanent bureaucracy of the EU that upholds the collective European interest). This institutional triangle can only function effectively if the three institutions work closely together and trust one another (Warleigh 2009).

THE COUNCIL OF THE EUROPEAN UNION

The Council of the European Union is the main decision-making institution of the EU. Formerly known as the 'Council of Ministers', it is now called 'the Council'. Each EU country in turn presides over the Council for a six-month period. Every Council meeting is attended by a minister from each Member State. Which ministers attend depends on the agenda. If foreign policy, it is the Foreign Affairs Minister from each country. If agriculture, it is the Minister for Agriculture. There are nine different Council 'configurations', covering all policy areas including industry, transport, the environment and so on.

The Union Treaty groups the EU's activities into three separate areas: community activities, common foreign and security policy, and justice and home affairs. In the Community context, the Council has to ensure that the objectives laid down by the Treaty are attained by co-ordinating the general economic policies of Member States and by adopting, on proposals from the Commission, the

Figure 7.9 The main political institutions of the European Union

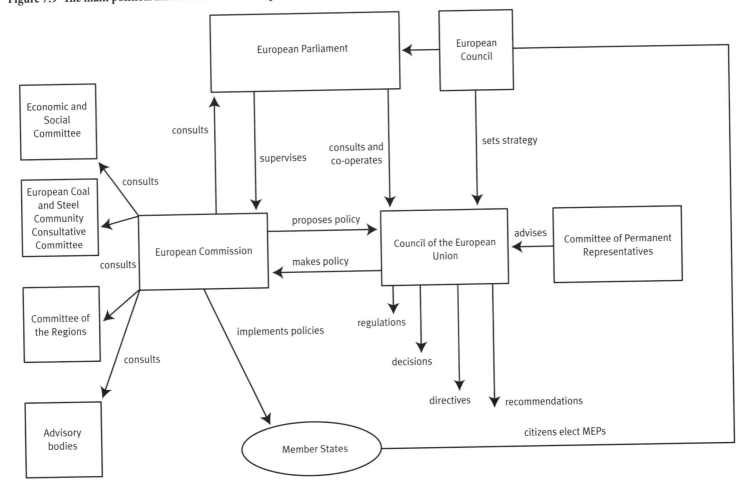

main decisions relating to the common policies in accordance with procedures involving Parliament to varying degrees.

The Council plays a predominant part in the two other areas based on intergovernmental co-operation. Under the common foreign and security policy, it defines common positions and adopts joint actions. In the case of justice and home affairs, the Council acts mainly through joint positions and by drawing up conventions which it recommends that the Member States adopt.

In Community activities, developments have provided for wider use of qualified majority voting in some cases; in other cases unanimity is required. A qualified majority constitutes 255 out of 347 votes. Where the vote is taken by qualified majority, the number of votes cast for each country is shown in Table 7.2. Unanimity is still required:

- where the Council wishes to deviate from the Commission's proposals or to reject amendments by Parliament that have been accepted by the Commission

- for action under the common foreign and security policy or in justice and home affairs co-operation, except where the Treaty authorises the Council to decide otherwise

- for taxation decisions (European Commission 2010c).

Table 7.2 Qualified majority voting by Member States in the Council of the European Union

Member States	Number of votes per country
Germany, France, Italy and the UK	29
Spain and Poland	27
Romania	14
Netherlands	13
Belgium, Bulgaria, Czech Republic, Greece, Hungary and Portugal	12
Austria and Sweden	10
Denmark, Ireland, Lithuania, Slovak Republic and Finland	7
Estonia, Cyprus, Latvia, Luxembourg and Slovenia	4
Malta	3

THE EUROPEAN COUNCIL

Established in 1974, the European Council is made up of the Heads of State or Government and the President, assisted by the Foreign Ministers and a Member of the Commission. It meets twice a year, providing the impetus and setting the broad guidelines for future action.

THE EUROPEAN PARLIAMENT

The European Parliament has been elected by direct universal suffrage since 1979. Parliament normally sits in Strasbourg, where plenary meetings are held for one week each month. Some part-sessions and committee meetings are held in Brussels to facilitate contacts with the Commission and the Council. Its Secretariat is based in Luxembourg.

The European Parliament is made up of political groups organised at Union level. Representing 486 million people, Parliament has 785 members (MEPs), as shown in Table 7.3. Its main role is a political driving force, generating various initiatives for the development of Community policies. It is also a supervisory body with the power to approve the appointment of the European Commission and dismiss it on a censure motion carried by a two-thirds majority. Parliament votes on the Commission's programmes and monitors day-to-day management of European policies, especially by putting oral and written questions to the Commission and Council. Parliament can set up committees of inquiry and examines petitions addressed to it by Union citizens. The Union Treaty empowers it to appoint an ombudsman to deal with complaints concerning instances of maladministration in Union institutions. Together, Parliament and the Council form the budgetary authority, with Parliament voting on the adoption of the annual budget and overseeing its implementation.

Table 7.3 Elected members of the European Parliament, 2010

Member States	Number of seats
Germany	99
France, Italy, UK (each)	78
Spain, Poland (each)	54
Romania	35
Netherlands	27
Belgium, Czech Republic, Greece, Hungary, Portugal (each)	24
Sweden	19
Austria, Bulgaria	18
Denmark, Finland, Slovak Republic (each)	14
Ireland, Lithuania	13
Latvia	9
Slovenia	7
Estonia, Cyprus, Luxembourg (each)	6
Malta	5

Union legislation is formulated by a three-way process: the Commission proposes legislative instruments, while the Parliament and Council share power to enact them. The Single European Act 1986 increased Parliament's legislative powers by introducing a co-operation procedure. This calls for two readings of legislative proposals by the Parliament and Council, with the active participation of the Commission. The Union Treaty took a further step towards conferring greater legislative powers on Parliament. It introduced a new co-decision procedure in a number of important areas, which gives Parliament the power to adopt regulations and Directives on an equal footing with the Council.

THE EUROPEAN COMMISSION

The European Commission has one member from each Member State. The Commission's term of office is five years, the same as the European Parliament. The full Commission has to be approved by Parliament before it is formally appointed. In carrying out their duties, members of the Commission are obliged to be completely independent of their national governments and act only in the interests of the EU. Each member of the Commission has special responsibility for one or more policy areas but decisions are taken on the basis of collective responsibility.

The Commission has three main roles:

- It is guardian of the treaties. As an impartial body, it sees that treaty provisions and decisions based on the treaties are correctly applied. It can initiate infringement proceedings against any Member State and may, if necessary, refer matters to the Court of Justice. It can also impose fines on individuals or companies, notably when they act in breach of the Union's competition rules.

- It has the sole right to initiate legislation. It can exert its influence at every stage of the process leading up to the adoption of a new European law. In the area of intergovernmental co-operation, the Commission has the same rights as individual Member States in making proposals.

- It is the EU's executive body. This involves issuing rules for the implementation of certain treaty articles and administering budget appropriations earmarked for Union operations. The bulk fall within one or other of the major funds: the European Agricultural Guidance and Guarantee Fund, the European Social Fund, the European Regional Development Fund and the Cohesion Fund.

THE COURT OF JUSTICE

The Court of Justice of the European Communities, located in Luxembourg, is made up of one judge from each EU country, assisted by eight advocates-general. They are appointed by joint agreement of governments of Member States. Each is appointed for six years, after which they may be reappointed for one or two further periods of three years. The Court's job is to ensure that EU law is complied with and that the treaties are correctly interpreted and applied.

THE COURT OF AUDITORS

The Court of Auditors, set up in 1977, has one member from each EU country, appointed for a term of six years by agreement between Member States after consulting Parliament. The Court of Auditors checks that all EU revenue has been received and all its expenditures are incurred in a lawful and regular manner and that the EU budget has been managed soundly.

THE EUROPEAN ECONOMIC AND SOCIAL COMMITTEE

When taking decisions in policy areas covered by the treaties, the Council and Commission consult the European Economic and Social Committee (EESC). Its members represent the various interest groups that collectively make up organised civil society and are appointed by the Council for a four-year term. The EESC has to be consulted before decisions are taken in a great many fields such as employment, the European Social Fund and vocational training (see Chapter 10).

THE COMMITTEE OF THE REGIONS

The Committee of the regions, set up under the Treaty on European Union, consists of representatives of regional and local government, proposed by Member States and appointed by the Council for a four-year term. Under the Treaty, the Council and Commission must consult the Committee on matters of relevance to the regions, and the Committee may also adopt opinions on its own initiative.

THE EUROPEAN INVESTMENT BANK

The European Investment Bank, based in Luxembourg, finances projects to support the EU's less developed regions and help small businesses to become more competitive.

THE EUROPEAN CENTRAL BANK

The European Central Bank, based in Frankfurt, is responsible for managing the euro and the EU's monetary policy (Eusepi and Schneider 2004).

ACTIVITY 7.10

You have been asked to brief a visiting manager from Canada about the processes through which European law is made and enforced. What will you say to her? She is also interested to know how European law impacts on your organisation and how it affects organisational policy and practice. Give her examples of this and the impact on the organisation.

CONCLUSION: GLOBALISATION, HR STRATEGY AND HR SOLUTIONS

Globalisation and complex networks of international trade have dominated the world economy for three decades. The result has been significant movements of capital, people and physical resources around the world, seeking financial returns, jobs and added value, in open global, national and local markets. There have been some winners and some losers. The winners include MNCs and big businesses. These are able to exploit their market positions and power to achieve greater economies of scale in the production process, cheaper resource inputs into their operational methods, and greater competitiveness in the marketplace, as demonstrated by rising sales, profits and customer satisfaction. Other winners include big governments. These are able to create employment opportunities in partnership with big businesses and raise taxes to redistribute resources to those deemed to be justified beneficiaries, whether organisations, communities, households or individuals. Losers falling behind in the global economic and technological revolutions include organisations, communities and people that are unable, or unwilling, to match the demands placed upon them in conditions of fast change and uncertainty. However, local, geographically discrete markets persist.

Whatever its impact on specific organisations, managers in both the private and public sectors cannot escape the logic and organisational consequences of economic globalisation. These include responding to competition from powerful MNCs, growth in international markets and migrations of people in developing countries seeking new lifestyles in the developed world. Every organisation, private, public or voluntary, has to deal with the business consequences arising from these forces. These create uncertainty and turbulence for organisations and managers leading them. Developing appropriate strategic, competitive and market responses, including within the HR domain, are necessary conditions for organisational success and stability.

In the private sector, globalisation encourages companies to search for new products and new markets so as to remain competitive. Faced with increased uncertainties and change in the marketplace, the corporate sector invests heavily in ICTs. Further, in seeking 'added value' for shareholders and investors, companies engage in takeovers, mergers and joint ventures and look for investment opportunities overseas. There are continuous pressures on managers and business organisations to raise productivity and performance, improve quality of products or services, increase profits, and engage and motivate staff. All these factors impinge on HR policies and organisational decision-making.

In a global age, the public sector becomes like the private sector in the ways in which it is organised and managed. It faces demands by politicians and taxpayers for increased efficiency, greater effectiveness and better value for money. The emphasis becomes one of seeking 'good practice' in management rather than adhering to standardised rules and procedures. Boundaries between the public and private sectors become blurred.

The implications of globalisation for governments are equally far-reaching. The redistributive functions of the welfare state are challenged and weakened. To promote business opportunities, governments deregulate labour, product and financial markets and encourage labour market flexibility. A more limited notion of citizenship emerges, rooted in what Galbraith (1993) calls a 'culture of contentment'. In Anglo-Saxon states, demands for lower taxation and recognition of their strong individualist cultures become normalised. Such forces affect the ways in which public and private organisations are structured and managed.

Decisions taken within EU institutions also affect business policies, HR strategies and HR practices. Managers have to be aware of EU regulations and Directives affecting their operations, especially when employing and managing people and managing competition. As the political power of the EU increases, the need for organisations to develop strategies in response to HR issues, consumer protection and environmental protection become paramount.

KEY LEARNING POINTS

1. Global markets have become an increasingly significant part of the business context over the past two decades. Globalisation is not an uncontested phenomenon. It is a problematic area, which is difficult to objectify, define and categorise precisely. Some commentators emphasise its benevolent consequences for people, organisations and societies; others highlight its dysfunctional aspects.

2. For some, globalisation is a neutral phenomenon rooted in the pragmatic behaviour of those engaged in mutually beneficial business exchanges in the marketplace. Others see it as an ideological construct, associated with the search for hegemony in the international economy by the developed world, led by the United States. Some observers view globalisation as a new phenomenon; others consider that is simply the continuation of a process of internationalisation of trade and exchange, which commenced when Europeans colonised North America in the early sixteenth century.

3. Parties and interests supporting globalisation argue that the liberalisation and expansion of international trade have restructured the world economy, increasing output, cross-national investment opportunities, job creation and quality products in the marketplace. Globalisation is also claimed to produce an international division of labour, enabling companies, countries and regions to specialise in producing those goods and services where they have a comparative advantage. Elimination of trade barriers has intensified international competition and reduced real prices to consumers.

4. Globalisation is not a homogeneous process. It takes different pathways in different countries. At least five different types of market economy have been identified around the world. Each varies according to how its markets are regulated, the prime accountability of the market, the nature of the labour market and its underpinning value system. The Anglo-Saxon model of capitalism is typified by free markets, contract law, primacy of shareholder interests, deregulated labour markets and an individualistic value system.

5. There is a wide range of critics of globalisation. But the core case against it is that capital is highly mobile and labour is distinctly immobile, which disadvantages working people to the advantage of big businesses. Globalisation is also seen to reflect the 'creep' of market values around the world, at the cost of the common good. Opponents claim that it commodifies intellectual property rights, damages the environment, is anti-union and causes unemployment. It is also believed to weaken the powers of national governments.

6. MNCs are central agents of globalisation, occupying a prominent and sometimes controversial role in the international economy. MNCs operate globally, nationally and locally. However, when a MNC based in one country creates a new production facility in a foreign state, or buys an existing one, it extends managerial control across national borders. This managerial control enables the firm to make decisions about how and where to employ the resources it uses, including people. These decisions have consequences for both the country where the firm is based and the country where the MNC invests. MNCs also promote cross-national HR policies and practices.

7. A number of international organisations facilitate global trade and the liberalisation of world trade. Four major bodies are the OECD, IMF, World Bank and WTO. All support globalisation, removal of trade barriers to free trade, and political democracy. Supporters defend the roles of these bodies in challenging economic protectionism, freeing international trade and spreading economic development around the world. Opponents argue against the unregulated political power of large MNCs and the powers exercised through trade agreements and deregulated financial markets.

8. The EU is a partnership of 27 democratic countries, working collectively for the benefit of their citizens. It aims to promote social and economic progress among its Member States, common positions in foreign and security policy, police and criminal matters, and European citizenship. The Treaty of Lisbon 2009 incorporates the principles of a more democratic Europe, a more efficient Europe, Europe as a global player, and a set of rights and values including freedom, solidarity and security.

9. The main three institutions of the EU, which work closely together, are: the Council of the European Union, which represents Member States; the European Parliament, which represents European citizens; and the European Commission or the permanent bureaucracy of the EU that upholds the collective European interest. The EU treaties constitute primary legislation. This legal base enables the institutions to formulate secondary legislation in the forms of Directives, regulations and recommendations.

10. The external forces of global markets, EU institutions and other international bodies are complex, and all organisations, private, public and third sector, have to deal with the business and HR consequences arising from each of these forces for themselves. These forces create uncertainty and turbulence for organisations and for the managers leading them. Developing appropriate strategic, competitive, market and HR responses to these forces is a necessary condition for organisational survival and growth in the contemporary world.

CASE STUDY 7.1 OUTWARD FOREIGN DIRECT INVESTMENT IN SMALL AND MEDIUM-SIZED ENTERPRISES (SMES) IN INDIA

Background

Indian enterprises have been investing abroad for a long time but it is only recently that Indian outward foreign direct investment (OFDI) has captured increasing international attention because of the magnitude of OFDI projects and the frequency of mergers and acquisitions (M&A) purchases by Indian enterprises. India is an emerging investor, with an OFDI stock of $6.6 billion and its OFDI flows are increasing.

Indian OFDI and SME competitiveness

OFDI has helped increase the export competitiveness of Indian manufacturing SMEs and their research and development (R&D) intensity, compared with SMEs that did not invest abroad. However, their profitability did not seem to change through the internationalisation process. Indian manufacturing SMEs are undertaking, in most cases, trade-supporting OFDI activities by establishing distribution and marketing centres in overseas markets and by enhancing their capability to ensure better sales and after-sales services. In

this way, the foreign affiliates of Indian manufacturing SMEs appear to have played a significant role in enhancing export performance.

Case studies of Indian SMEs reveal interesting insights into the nature and impact of their OFDI operations. OFDI undertaken by Indian SMEs has been primarily aimed at strengthening their export performance. Indian SMEs, unlike their MNC counterparts, do not possess the firm-specific competitive advantages to exploit value-adding activities abroad. For example:

- A-Manufacturing Ltd used OFDI as a strategy to enhance marketing and trade-supporting networks overseas.
- B-Manufacturing Ltd also used OFDI as a strategy to enhance marketing and trade-supporting networks overseas.
- C-Software also used OFDI as a strategy to enhance marketing and trade-supporting networks overseas.
- D-Manufacturing Ltd used OFDI to build marketing and warehouses overseas.

---

1. What is globalisation? What are its advantages and disadvantages, and to whom?
2. Account for the development and expansion of globalisation in the last 30 years.
3. Evaluate the main criticisms of globalisation by the anti-globalisation movement and its supporters.
4. Are MNCs an economic 'good' or an economic 'bad'? Justify your response.
5. Examine the cases for and against expanding membership of the EU.

- E-Retail, a subsidiary of an Indian MNC, used OFDI to establish retail outlets overseas.

F-Research Ltd demonstrated in the area of R&D that Indian SMEs are also internationalising their innovative activities and benefiting from them. This suggests that internationalisation of R&D is not entirely a strategy of developed country enterprises. Less technologically advanced firms from developing countries may also adopt the strategy to benefit from well-developed research infrastructures and the availability of skilled human resources in overseas markets.

G-Software showed that Indian SMEs are first movers in adopting an overseas acquisition strategy. G-Software used an M&A strategy to access the European market and technology overseas to improve its competitiveness.

Policy considerations supporting OFDI

India has a strong SME sector, which contributes about 50 per cent of industrial output and 42 per cent of India's overall exports. Indian SMEs are making a mark in internationalisation through OFDI. Their presence abroad is likely to be more significant than has been witnessed in the past decade. Liberalisation of OFDI policy alone is not enough to encourage more SMEs to go abroad to participate in internationalisation and benefit from it. OFDI activities by Indian SMEs are conditional upon both government policy initiatives and firm-specific endeavours.

A number of measures, fiscal and non-fiscal, which directly impinge upon the technological capabilities of SMEs, are crucial for helping them fully exploit their OFDI potential. The overseas expansion is held back by their low levels of technological capabilities, which are due to resource constraints, lack of technical and trained human resources, and lack of access to facilities of public-funded research institutions. Given that SMEs suffer from low levels of skills and have

limited capability to create their own brand names, the following are crucial for growth at home and in the global market:

- support in skills upgrading, such as training and management development
- assistance in gaining certification from international quality testing agencies
- help towards quality improvement
- access to finance.

Provision of market information and investment opportunities in host countries is another area where government can support SMEs in realising their full potential for OFDI. As government policies and the business context may differ sharply between the home and host countries, SMEs need assistance from home and host governments in dealing with:

- legal matters
- collecting information on overseas business opportunities and foreign market characteristics
- support for international M&As as a means of enhancing competitiveness.

A major constraint hindering research on the internationalisation of SMEs is the lack of accurate and reliable data. Hence, development of a readily available database on SMEs undertaking OFDI is an important precondition for assessing and examining the issues faced by Indian SMEs in internationalisation through OFDI.

A number of strategic lessons could be considered by enterprises that are exploring internationalisation strategies by OFDI:

- SMEs constrained by size and resources should not diversify production activities into a variety of products internationally. Specialising in a niche product is a good strategy for incremental internationalisation rather than spreading the limited resources thinly on too many products and too many places.
- SMEs operating in a particular product category could come together, collaborate and pool their resources

for creating their own respective niche market segment. There is a need for an interactive platform enabling enterprises, particularly SMEs, to share information and learning, and jointly develop differentiated products; this could go a long way in overcoming their size limitations.

- Indian enterprises could consciously invest in new technologies, particularly ICTs. This is critical, as it enables them to access information on global markets, regulations and finding business partners abroad.

- Indian enterprises could improve their capabilities and internationalisation capacity by upgrading their technology, product differentiation and management skills in collaboration with business schools and management.

- Indian enterprises with easy access to finance or in a strong financial position could consider internationalisation through using the M&A route.

- Indian enterprises could also observe good corporate governance and contribute to the host country's national development.

Conclusion

Indian OFDI activities have emerged as distinguishing features of the Indian economy since the 1990s. The number of OFDI approvals, as well as the size of OFDI flows, has increased significantly in the past decade. This new wave of OFDI has been accompanied by significant changes in their structure, characteristics and motivations, which differ from those of OFDI in the pre-1990s.

OFDI from India has not been entirely led by larger enterprises. Indian SMEs have also played a significant role in this growing OFDI phenomenon. Indian OFDI by SMEs has been growing since the 1990s, a trend that is conspicuous in both the manufacturing and software industries.

- OFDI by Indian manufacturing SMEs is visible in low-technology-intensive industries and in high-technology-intensive industries.

- Indian SMEs invest in both developed and developing countries but the software OFDI is more inclined to favour developed regions.

- There is also a growing tendency for Indian SMEs, as for MNCs, to pursue overseas acquisitions to expand markets and access to technology and other strategic assets.

Certain policy measures are needed to help Indian SMEs overcome the barriers to internationalising through OFDI, including access to finance and provision of market information. Facilitative measures such as institutional support and incentives can be considered. The OFDI promotion programme is another area where both the public and the private sector can work together in strengthening India's position as an emerging outward investor, with the Indian SMEs featuring prominently in the process. The need for capacity building and strengthening Indian technological capability deserves closer attention by government, the private sector and research institutions.

On the whole, the significant liberalisation of policies by the government and the growing competitiveness of Indian enterprises in such industries as software and pharmaceuticals have played significant roles in supporting the rapid growth of Indian OFDI in recent years. The need to secure natural resources abroad, such as oil, gas and minerals, to support the rapid growth of industrial development at home has led the government to actively encourage both public and private enterprises to venture abroad. Against this background, the prospect for Indian OFDI, including Indian SMEs, is promising.

Tasks

1. Identify the drivers and motivations of Indian OFDI in the era of globalisation since the 1990s.

2. Why have SMEs had such a major role in OFDI in India?

3. What competitive advantages do Indian SMEs have internationally regarding OFDI opportunities?

4. As managing director of a software SME, such as C-Software and G-Software above, what are some of the HR issues that you consider need to be addressed in enhancing your company's business objectives?

5. Explain why UK-based SMEs are less successful than Indian SMEs in exploiting OFDI initiatives.

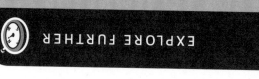

EXPLORE FURTHER

DICKEN, P. (2003) *Global shift: reshaping the global economic map in the 21st century*. London: Sage.

Summarises the various theories informing the globalisation debate and provides a comprehensive discussion of the complex interrelationships between national-level factors, multinational corporations and changing technologies.

HIRST, P. and THOMPSON, P. (1999) *Globalisation in question: the international economy and the possibilities of governance*. 2nd ed. Cambridge: Polity Press.

Discusses a wide range of issues concerning international political economy and presents a vast range of data and evidence to undermine the arguments of those who see globalisation as new and pervasive.

STIGLITZ, J. (2002) *Globalisation and its discontents*. New York: Norton

Provides a powerful critique of certain aspects of the strong globalisation thesis but focuses more on the controversial role of the International Monetary Fund and the World Bank in recent crises.

WHITLEY, R. (2000) *Divergent capitalisms: the social structuring and change of business systems*. Oxford: Oxford University Press.

Is a comprehensive and scholarly attempt to describe and explain the major differences in economic organisation between market economies in the late twentieth century, based on the notion of distinctive national business systems.

CHAPTER 8

Demographic and social trends

INTRODUCTION

Demography is the statistical study of populations and is concerned with the size, distribution and composition of the population of a country, region or area, or is studied on a worldwide basis. Data are obtained through census returns, records of births, deaths, marriages, divorce, immigration, emigration and labour force analyses. Demography charts changes and trends in population and seeks explanations and causes of these changes. The demographic structure of a country has implications for its economy. The size and age structure of the population, for example, affect the actual and potential availability of and demand for labour, and the demand for goods and services. They also affect public policy issues, such as healthcare, education, pension provision and social services. Governments at national and local levels need projections of future population statistics on which to base their policy decisions.

Social trends are reflected in the ways in which the major social institutions of society – such as family, social structure and work – change and evolve over time. Social trends are underpinned by values that fashion people's behaviour, how they relate to others, how they interpret and understand their own experiences, and how they make sense of and perceive the world and themselves within it. Societies are also continually evolving, although there is usually a cultural and time lag, since once acquired, attitudes and values are not easily replaced and institutional change is normally incremental. The UK, along with the rest of the advanced economies, has experienced rapid and constantly accelerating social change in the last 60 years. These social trends and changes are part of the contexts of organisations and the HR function.

LEARNING OUTCOMES

By the end of this chapter, readers should be able to understand, explain and critically evaluate:

- current and future demographic trends in the UK and internationally

- reasons for recent changing patterns of population

- the concept of an ageing population and its implications for organisations and HR

- changes in social attitudes, and their significance for organisations and managing people

- causes of key social trends in the UK and internationally.

In addition, readers should be able to:

- evaluate the short- and long-term implications of demographic developments for organisations and the HR function

- advise managers on the impact of demographic developments for HR and organisations

- report on social trends and their implications for HR and organisations.

POPULATION TRENDS

Table 8.1 shows the total UK population for selected years 1901–2021. There are now more people living in the UK than ever. In 2008, the population was 61.4 million, 5.5 million more than in 1971. The populations of England, Wales and Northern Ireland all grew between 1971 and 2008, while the population of Scotland remained fairly stable. Population projections suggest that the UK population will reach 67 million by 2021 and over 70 million by 2031. In 2008, there were 31.2 million females compared with 30.2 million males – or a million more females than males. In addition to sex, the composition of a population can be analysed by age, ethnicity, geographical distribution and occupation (Office for National Statistics 2009a).

Table 8.1 UK population, 1901–2021 (for selected years)

Millions

	1901	1981	2001	2011	2021
UK	38.2	56.4	59.1	62.6	67.0
England	30.5	46.9	49.4	52.6	56.5
Wales	2.0	2.8	2.9	3.0	3.2
Scotland	4.5	5.2	5.1	5.2	5.4
Northern Ireland	1.2	1.5	1.7	1.8	1.9

Adapted from Office for National Statistics (2009a)

AGE

The age structure of the population reflects past trends in births, deaths and migration. The number of people in any age group depends on how many people are born in a particular period and how long they survive. It is also affected by the numbers and ages of migrants moving into and out of the country. The UK has an ageing population. Historically, the ageing of the UK population was largely the result of a fall in birth rates, which began towards the end of the nineteenth century. Early in the twentieth century, lower infant mortality helped increase the number of people surviving into adulthood. Over the past four decades, lower fertility rates and decreases in mortality rates have resulted in the UK population being skewed towards older age groups.

In 2008, about a fifth of the UK population was under 16, about two-thirds were 16–64, and about another fifth was over retirement age (60 for women and 65 for men). Two per cent of the population was over 85. The gap between the sexes in the age structure increases markedly from the late 50s onwards and is most pronounced among those aged 75 and over. At younger ages, the increase in the proportion of females drives the sex ratio and is largely determined by differences in levels of net migration. At older ages, the longer life expectancy of women compared with that for men is the main determinant. However, male life expectancy is improving at a faster rate than female life expectancy, with the number of men in these older age groups being expected to increase, which is closing this gap.

ACTIVITY 8.1

How is pension provision affected by an ageing population (a) in terms of the state pension and (b) in terms of occupational or company pensions? Justify your response.

ETHNICITY

For statistical purposes, the British population is classified into 12 main ethnic groups and a residual 'other ethnic groups'. This diversity is illustrated in Table 8.2 by age. This shows that the British population consists predominantly of people from a 'white British' ethnic background. In 2008, around 83 per cent of the population belonged to this ethnic group. However, during the second half of the twentieth century, the pattern of migration into Britain produced a number of distinct ethnic minority groups within the general population. In 2008, the second largest ethnic group was 'other white' (5 per cent), those born overseas for example, followed by Indian (2 per cent) and Pakistani (2 per cent). The remaining ethnic minority groups accounted for around 8 per cent of the total population.

The age structure of the population varies across different ethnic groups. The 'mixed ethnic' group – for example, people who identify with both the differing ethnicities of their parents – had the youngest age profile in Britain. In 2008, more than half (51 per cent) of the people in this group were aged under 16. Only 2 per cent of people in the mixed ethnic group were aged 65 and over. The 'other black' group also had a young age profile, with 37 per cent of people in this group being under 16. Eighty-three per cent of people in the Chinese group in Britain in 2008 were aged between 16 and 64. Only 12 per cent in the Chinese group were under 16 and 5 per cent were aged 65 and over (Office for National Statistics 2009a).

Table 8.2 British population, ethnic groups by age, 2009

Percentages

Group	Under 16	16-64	65 and over
White British	18	65	17
White Irish	7	68	25
Other white	14	75	12
Mixed	51	47	2
Indian	20	72	8
Pakistani	34	62	4
Bangladeshi	36	61	4
Other Asian	23	73	5
Black Caribbean	20	66	13
Black African	33	64	2
Other black	37	57	6
Chinese	12	83	5
Other ethnic groups	20	75	4
All ethnic groups	19	65	16

Adapted from Office for National Statistics (2009a)

ACTIVITY 8.2

Access the last census data for your local area and identify and analyse its age and ethnic distributions of population.

GEOGRAPHICAL DISTRIBUTION

By the mid-1800s, the UK's large cities were already established, with London being the largest urban area. Large-scale movements into cities were not yet under way. This was partly because travel over large distances was still difficult and expensive. Also, industry providing employment was not yet centred on large towns but based around rural craft industries. It was not until the last quarter of the nineteenth century that there was a large increase in urbanisation. Improvements in transport, better education, large-scale industrialisation and agricultural depression were factors in this change.

Throughout the twentieth century, the UK population remained highly urbanised. The largest urban area was Greater London which, by 2008, had a resident population of 7.6 million. This was more than the populations of the next three largest metropolitan conurbations combined – the West Midlands, Greater Manchester and West Yorkshire. In 2008, the largest local authority area in terms of population was Birmingham, with a population of just over a million, followed by Leeds with around three-quarters of a million residents. The Isles of Scilly and the City of London had the smallest populations. The most densely populated area within the UK was the London borough of Kensington and Chelsea, with almost 14,900 people per square kilometre. The 10 most densely populated areas in the UK were all London boroughs.

OCCUPATION

The distribution of the working age population in the UK, by sex and occupation, for 2008 is shown in Table 8.3. The Labour Force Survey provides information on workforce classification, based on occupation for those of working age. These are men aged 16 to 64 and women aged 16 to 59. Students and those whose occupation was not stated, or who were not classifiable for other reasons, are excluded. The largest population group in 2008 was the lower managerial and professional category at 22 per cent, made up of 20 per cent of men and 24 per cent of women. This was followed by those who had never worked and the unemployed. This group made up 19 per cent, representing 17 per cent of men

Table 8.3   The working age population in the UK, by sex and occupation, 2008

Percentages

	Men	Women	All
Higher managerial and professional	16	7	12
Lower managerial and professional	20	24	22
Intermediate occupations	5	14	9
Small employers and own-account workers	11	4	8
Lower supervisory and technical	11	5	8
Semi-routine occupations	9	16	12
Routine occupations	11	7	9
Never worked, unemployed	17	22	19

Adapted from Labour Force Survey (2009a)

and 22 per cent of women. The smallest overall category was the small employers group and own-account workers. The smallest category for men was intermediate occupations. This includes clerical workers and those working in sales. For women, the smallest category was small employers and own-account workers (Office for National Statistics 2008a).

SOME INTERNATIONAL COMPARISONS

Table 8.4 shows a selection of demographic indicators based on United Nations estimates and projections averaged over the period 2005 to 2010. The more developed regions of the world, such as Europe and North America, have total fertility rates (TFRs) below the population replacement level; less developed regions have TFRs above the replacement level. In Africa, for example, the rate is 4.61 children per woman. These differences in TFRs partly reflect infant mortality rates. On average across Europe and North America, fewer than eight babies per 1,000 live births die during their first year: around 7.2 in Europe and 5.8 in North America. These compare with 82.6 deaths per 1,000 live births in Africa. This is a considerable improvement from the period 1965 to 1970, when the infant mortality rate in Africa averaged 143.5 deaths per 1,000 live births. In Europe and North America, the infant mortality rate has fallen from around 29.8 and 22.2 infant deaths per 1,000 live births respectively, since the late 1960s.

Table 8.4 Some world demographic indicators 2005–10

Region	Population (millions)	Population density (sq km)	Infant mortality per 1,000 births	Total fertility rate	Life expectancy males	Life expectancy females
Asia	4,167	131	41.5	2.35	67.1	70.8
Africa	1,033	34	82.6	4.61	52.9	55.3
Europe	732	32	7.2	1.50	71.1	79.1
Latin America and Caribbean	587	29	21.8	2.26	70.2	76.7
North America	352	16	5.8	2.04	77.0	81.5
Oceania	36	4	22.8	2.44	74.1	78.9
World	6,907	51	47.3	2.56	65.4	69.8

Adapted from Office for National Statistics (2009b)

Estimates and projections show that average worldwide life expectancy at birth for males and females is less than 70 years: 65.4 for males and 69.8 for females. For Africa, life expectancy is much lower at 52.9 for males and 55.3 for females. The world population reached nearly 6.1 billion in 2000, which was more than three and a half times the size 100 years earlier. The UN estimate the world population will be 6.9 billion people in 2010. China was the country with the largest population in 2005 with 1.31 billion people, representing 20 per cent of the world's population, followed by India with 1.13 billion people (17 per cent) (Office for National Statistics 2009b).

DETERMINANTS OF POPULATION CHANGE

Historically, the net natural change of the population – the difference between births and deaths – was the main driver behind population increase, accounting for 98 per cent of population growth in the UK between 1951 and 1961. Since 1971, the influence of net natural change has been much lower and net inflows of immigrants (ie people moving into the UK) have had a larger impact on its population growth. These net inflows accounted for 62 per cent of population growth between 2001 and 2008. In 2008, net immigration accounted for 46 per cent of population growth in the UK, compared with 52 per cent in 2007 and 71 per cent in 2002.

BIRTHS

The two World Wars had major impacts on births. There was a substantial fall in the number of births during the First World War, followed by a post-war 'baby boom' with the number of births reaching 1.1 million in 1920. This was the highest number of births in any single year during the twentieth century. Births then decreased in number and remained low during the depression of the 1930s and during the Second World War. A second 'baby boom' occurred after the war, followed by a further boom during the 'affluent' 1960s.

During the 1990s the number of births fell gradually, to a low of 668,800 in 2002, but it has increased each year since then. In 2008, there were 794,400 births in the UK, which was the sixth consecutive annual increase. Projections suggest that the number of births will decline over the next few years but then increase gradually to around 804,000 in 2041.

The TFR is the average number of live children per woman that a group of women would have if they experience the age-specific fertility rates for a particular calendar year in their childbearing lifespan. This is generally considered to be from the ages of 15 to 44. The number of births in the UK depends on both the fertility rates of women living in the UK and the size and age structure of the UK childbearing population. Replacement-level fertility is the level of fertility needed for a population to replace itself in size in the long term, in the absence of migration. To replace themselves, each woman needs to have, on average, one daughter who survives long enough to have a daughter herself. In developed countries replacement fertility is usually measured at 2.1 children per woman. This is slightly higher than two children per woman to take account of female mortality and the fact that slightly more boys are born than girls. Indicators of TFRs in the UK are shown in Figure 8.1.

Figure 8.1 The UK total fertility rate

• The TFR reached 1.96 children per woman in 2008, the highest level since 1973 when it was 2.05
• This is the seventh consecutive rise, since a low of 1.63 in 2001
• Fertility rates remain much lower than the rates seen during the 'baby boom' of the 1960s
• The TFR peaked in the 1960s at a little fewer than three children per woman
• The TFR fell below the replacement level of 2.1 children per woman in 1974
• It has remained below this level ever since

Adapted from Office for National Statistics (2009b)

Over the period 2011–21, natural change is expected to become more important in influencing population change than other population movements. It is estimated that natural change will account for around 58 per cent of the increase in population. The remaining 42 per cent of the projected population increase over this period is expected to be directly attributable to the assumed level of net inward migration.

DEATHS

Despite considerable population growth since 1901, the annual number of deaths remained relatively constant during the twentieth century. In 2008, there were almost 580,000 deaths in the UK, compared with 632,000 in 1901. However, this masks large declines in mortality rates. In 2008, mortality rates in England and Wales were the lowest on record at 6,860 deaths per million of the male population and 4,910 per million for females.

MIGRATION

Since the beginning of the twentieth century, the pattern of people entering and leaving the UK has varied. In the first 30 years of that century, there was a net loss of people each year. However, in the 1930s there was an overall net inflow of people, mainly refugees from other European countries. After a period of net outflow during the 1960s and 1970s, the direction of the trend reversed again and, in most years since 1990, more people have entered the UK as migrants than have left the UK, reflecting the effects of globalisation.

In 2007–08, an estimated 554,000 people came to live in the UK for at least a year. This was equivalent to around 1,500 people per day. Around 371,000 people were estimated to have left the UK to live abroad for at least one year in 2007–08. Thus the UK experienced a net gain of around 184,000 people.

An estimated 14 per cent of long-term migrants into the UK in 2007–08 were British citizens, compared with 45 per cent of those moving abroad. Of those coming to live in the UK, 32 per cent were EU citizens, 23 per cent were citizens of the New Commonwealth and around 8 per cent were citizens of the Old

Commonwealth (Australia, Canada, New Zealand and South Africa) (Office for National Statistics 2009a).

REVIEW

Unlike that of most other European countries the UK population is currently growing, because birth rates exceed death rates and because of net immigration. This is a reversal of the situation in the 1970s and early 1980s. But fertility rates generally remain below replacement levels. As a result the UK has an ageing population. There are many more people in their 40s and 50s than in their 20s and 30s. The reasons for continuing low fertility rates are disputed, as are likely developments in the population structure. However, two current trends are readily identifiable. First, women are generally having babies later in life than they used to. Since the 1970s, the average age at which women give birth to their first child has steadily increased. It is now 29 and women aged 30–34 now have more babies than women in the 25–29 age group. This results in fewer babies per woman on average. Second, there has been a reduction in the number of children that women say they intend having, whilst an increasing number of women do not wish to be mothers at all.

The main reasons for this are that more women are going into higher education and modern contraception methods provide more effective means of birth control than in the past. Increased educational levels and economic independence among women gives them real choices of life style, which influences their decisions about family size. Other factors include greater emphasis on quality of life and leisure preferences, a retreat from permanent commitment in some relationships, and changes in social norms about relationships and family formation. The cost and availability of suitable housing stock may also be an issue.

The UK population is not only ageing but also ethnically diverse and largely urbanised. Eighty per cent of people live in urban areas, with over a third concentrated in the UK's 10 largest conurbations. Density of population varies widely, as does the age structure, with the highest concentrations of older people being in coastal resorts along the south and east coasts. There is also a growing migrant population in the UK. Migrants are generally younger than the indigenous population, and almost half of them settle in London and the south-east of England. But Manchester and the north-west also have net inflows of new immigrants each year, many of whom are students.

It is estimated that over 9 million people in the UK are over 65 years of age. By 2025 around 27 per cent of the population will be over 60, rising to 38 per cent by 2050. A major implication is the increase in the 'dependency ratio' or proportion of people of working age in relation to the proportion above retirement age. One consequence is the amount of public spending needed to provide pensions, benefits, healthcare and long-term nursing care, since demand for these will increase substantially. Another is the larger proportion of the population that will be out of the labour market, thus reducing national output and productivity. There is also likely to be increased demand for suitable housing for an ageing population, much of which will be in single-person households. Third, there are product market implications of an ageing population, which tends to spend less on entertainment and consumer goods and more on healthcare products, heating and energy, and certain types of holidays.

ACTIVITY 8.3

Why have birth rates declined across much of Western Europe since the 1970s?

ACTIVITY 8.4

Government forecasts estimate that the UK population will increase to 71 million by 2031, with most growth being concentrated in the south-east. What factors are contributing to this increase? Examine and discuss the main implications of this projection for (a) employing organisations and (b) government.

THE WORKING POPULATION

The working population, known as the labour force or economically active population, consists of those people aged 16 and over who are employees, self-employed or unemployed and looking for work. The labour force participation rate (or activity rate) is the percentage of the population in a given group that is economically active. Most people spend a large part of their lives in the labour force, so their experience of work has an important impact on their lives and attitudes. The proportion of time spent in the labour force, however, has been falling. Young people are remaining longer in education and older people, due to increases in longevity, are spending more years in retirement. A counter-trend is that more women than ever are in paid employment and tend to spend longer in work than in the past. Employment is increasingly in the service industries, whilst employment in manufacturing continues to fall.

A PROFILE OF THE UK LABOUR MARKET

Among those of working age, the number of economically active people in the UK increased by 5.1 million from 24.8 million to 30.0 million from 1971 to 2009. The working-age economic activity rate has remained relatively stable, at 78 per cent in 1971 and 79 per cent in 2009, with a high of 81 per cent in 1990 and a low of 77 per cent in 1983.

Working-age population

The proportion of the working-age population in the UK who were in employment (the recorded employment rate) decreased from 76 per cent in the mid-1970s to a low of 68 per cent in 1983. Since then, employment rates have generally risen, although they fell following the recession in the early 1990s, and fell again in the 12 months to 2009, when the rate was 73 per cent following another recession. This was the lowest employment rate since 1996. The fall in the employment rate in the 12 months to 2009 was mirrored by a rise in the recorded unemployment rate from 5 to 8 per cent.

Men

Working-age men and women have different patterns of labour market participation at most ages. In 2009, 15 per cent of men aged 16 to 19 worked full-time, the equivalent of 250,000 men of this age. Men in this age group were least likely of all working-age men to be in full-time employment, since participation in post-compulsory education is a factor in the proportion of young people of this age who are economically inactive. Men in their 30s and 40s were most likely to be in full-time employment (around 82 per cent in each case); they were the least likely of all working-age men to be economically inactive.

From age around 50, men begin to withdraw from full-time employment and there is an increase in both part-time employment and economic inactivity. However, after state pension age, around one in five men (21 per cent) aged 65 to 69 continue to work either full or part time.

Women

For women the picture is different. At 53 per cent, full-time employment was highest for women aged 25 to 29 in 2009. After this, the proportion fell to 45 per cent of 30- to 34-year-olds and 42 per cent of 35- to 39-year-olds, which could reflect family formation. The proportion of women in full-time employment then rose to 46 per cent for 45- to 49-year-olds. Part-time employment and economic inactivity were generally more common among women of working age than among men, particularly in younger age groups. In the 10 years before state pension age, similar proportions of men and women were economically inactive (18 per cent of 55- to 59-year-old men and 22 per cent of 50- to 54-year-old women).

In the five years immediately before state pension age, a lower proportion of women than men were economically inactive (33 per cent of 55- to 59-year-old women compared with 41 per cent of 60- to 64-year-old men). A contributory factor to this may be that working-age women are less likely than working-age men to have an occupational or personal pension. Men can therefore afford to retire earlier.

EMPLOYMENT

From 1971 to 2009, employment rates for men and women converged but did not equalise. This convergence largely took place in the 1970s and 1980s. Between 1971 and 1993, the gap in employment rates between men and women fell from 35 percentage points to 10 percentage points, with the rate for men falling to 75 per cent and for women rising to 65 per cent. Since then, the trend towards convergence has slowed. The gap in employment rates between men and women was between 8 and 11 percentage points in the period 1992 to 2008, but narrowest in 2009 at 7 percentage points.

In 2008, the overall EU-27 working-age employment rate was 66 per cent. The UK had the fifth highest employment rate (72 per cent) after Denmark (78 per cent), the Netherlands (77 per cent), Sweden (74 per cent) and Austria (72 per cent). The UK was also one of eight member states with a rate above the 2010 target of 70 per cent, set at the meeting of the EU heads of state and ministers at the European Council in Lisbon in 2000. Since that meeting employment rates have increased in most member states, the exceptions being Portugal and Romania. The largest increase was in Bulgaria (13.6 percentage points).

For working-age men, the average employment rate in the EU-27 was 73 per cent in 2008. The UK had the fifth highest male rate (77 per cent) across member states. Employment rates for men ranged from 63 per cent in Hungary to 83 per cent in the Netherlands.

For working-age women, the average employment rate across the EU-27 in 2008 was 59 per cent, close to the 2010 target of 60 per cent. This target was set at the Stockholm Council in 2001. By 2008, 10 member states had still not reached the intermediate target set for 2005 of 57 per cent. The UK, along with Austria, had the sixth highest female rate (66 per cent) in 2008. The lowest employment rates for women were in south Europe in Malta, Italy and Greece. They all had female employment rates below 50 per cent. In contrast, the northern European countries of Denmark (74 per cent), Sweden (72 per cent), and the Netherlands (71 per cent) had employment rates for women above 70 per cent.

A range of factors underlies these differences. As well as economic cycle effects, which vary across countries, employment rates are also affected by population structures and differing cultures, retirement ages and participation in post-compulsory full-time education across the EU.

PATTERNS OF EMPLOYMENT

Employment by occupation

In 2009, 16 per cent of those in employment in the UK were employed as managers or senior officials – the largest occupational group – compared with 7 per cent employed in each of sales and customer service, and process, plant and machine operation occupations. The pattern of occupations followed by men and women is quite different. In 2009, men were most likely to be employed as managers or senior officials (19 per cent), while women were most likely to be employed in administrative and secretarial work (19 per cent). Around one in six women (16 per cent) worked in personal services (such as hairdressers and child care assistants) and more than one in 10 (11 per cent) worked in sales and customer service. These occupations were less common among men. Only professional occupations, associate professional and technical occupations (such as nurses, financial advisers and IT technicians), and elementary occupations (such as catering assistants, bar staff and shelf fillers) were almost equally likely to be followed by both men and women.

Employment by industry

Table 8.5 shows changes in numbers of jobs by industry for selected years over the period 1978 to 2008. In 1978, manufacturing accounted for the highest proportion of jobs at 28.5 per cent. This has fallen steadily over these years to reach just over 10 per cent in 2008, the lowest proportion since records began. This represents a fall of around two-thirds since 1978. Conversely, the finance and business services sector has shown an increase of around 10 percentage points over the same period, from 10.5 per cent in 1978 to 20.8 per cent in 2008. In 2008, public administration, education and health had the largest proportion of jobs at 26.9 per cent. This compares with 21.1 per cent in 1978, an increase of 5.8 percentage points.

Table 8.5   Employee jobs by industry, 1978–2008 (for selected years)

Millions

Sector	1978	1988	1998	2008	Change 1978 to 2008
Agriculture and fishing	1.7	1.4	1.3	1.0	–0.7
Energy and water	2.8	1.8	0.8	0.7	–2.1
Manufacturing	28.5	20.7	17.0	10.5	–18.0
Construction	5.7	5.1	4.4	4.8	–0.8
Distribution, hotels and restaurants	19.5	21.3	23.8	23.6	4.1
Transport and communications	6.5	5.9	5.7	5.9	–0.6
Finance and business services	10.5	14.8	18.1	21.4	10.9
Public admin, education and health	21.1	24.5	24.2	26.9	5.8
Other services	3.8	4.5	4.7	5.3	1.5
All industries	24.3	23.7	24.7	27.2	2.9

Adapted from Office for National Statistics (2009b)

Employment by sector

Another important distinction in the analysis of employment is between private and public sector employment. In 2009, over six million people aged 16 and over in employment in the UK worked in the public sector. The public sector estimate in 2009 was the largest annual change in the sector since 1993. This recent increase is because the 2009 estimate included employment in Royal Bank of Scotland Group and Lloyds Banking Group, following their classifications as public corporations, with effect from October 2008 (Office for National Statistics 2009a).

Working hours

People work either full time or part time. In 2009, 1.9 million men and 5.7 million women worked part time. The Working Time Regulations 1998 implemented the EU Working Time Directive on working time in the UK, and apply to full-time, part-time and temporary workers. Employers must limit working time to 48 hours a week (averaged over a 17-week period), unless they offer individuals the right to opt out of this maximum working week. In 2009, 17 per cent of full-time employees in the UK normally worked more than 48 hours a week, including regular paid and unpaid overtime.

Data from the Labour Force Survey show that the longest average week among full-time employees was reported by managers and senior officials (45 hours) and the shortest by those in administrative and secretarial occupations, personal services, and sales and customer services (each 39 hours). For male employees, managers and senior officials had the longest average working week (46 hours); female employees with the longest average working week were in professional occupations (44 hours).

The opportunity to work flexible hours helps people to balance home and work responsibilities. Legislation in the UK provides parents and carers (under certain criteria) with the right to request a flexible work pattern. Almost a quarter (23 per cent) of full-time employees, and over a quarter (27 per cent) of part-time employees, had some form of flexible working arrangement in 2009. Female employees were more likely than male employees to have flexible working arrangements and the most common form for full-time employees of both sexes was flexible working hours. Figure 8.2 outlines the attitudes of working women in the EU to work–life balance, drawn from the Eurobarometer survey by the European Commission (2010a).

Figure 8.2   Attitudes of working women in the EU to work–life balance

- In 2009, 66 per cent of women in employment in the UK said they managed to balance their personal and working lives
- In EU-27, the average was 70 per cent
- Women managing to achieve a work–life balance ranged from 57 per cent in Greece, and 61 per cent in France and the Czech Republic, through 83 per cent in Hungary and Romania, to 84 per cent in the Netherlands
- Women were more likely to say that their personal life was hindered by the demands of their working life than that their working life was hindered by their personal life in all member states, with the exceptions of Slovenia and Denmark

Adapted from European Commission (2010d)

UNEMPLOYMENT

The unemployment rate fluctuates through the economic cycle. During periods of economic growth the number of jobs generally grows and unemployment falls, although mismatches between the skills needs of new jobs and the skills of those available for work may slow this down. Conversely, as the economy slows, particularly if it goes into recession, unemployment tends to rise, although a rise in unemployment tends to lag behind an economic slowdown. Since 1971, total recorded unemployment for people aged 16 and over peaked in 1984 (11.9 per cent) and again in 1993 (10.4 per cent). Although still lower than in 1993, there was another increase to 7.8 per cent during the recession in 2009. Unemployment rates for men aged 16 and over increased to 12.2 per cent in 1983, equivalent to 1.9 million unemployed men. The unemployment peak for women over this period was in 1984, when the rate was 11.8 per cent, equivalent to 1.3 million unemployed women aged 16 and over.

Recession in the early 1990s had a much greater effect on unemployment among men than women, and the unemployment rate for men peaked at 12.3 per cent in 1993. The female unemployment rate also rose but to a lower level of 8 per cent. Rates for both men and women increased in the 12 months to 2009, from 5.8 per cent to 8.8 per cent for men (equivalent to 1.5 million men aged 16 and over) and from 4.9 per cent to 6.6 per cent for women (equivalent to 0.9 million women of the same age). Figure 8.3 outlines changes in employment in response to the economic cycle.

Figure 8.3 Employment in the UK and the economic cycle

- In periods of economic growth between the recessions of the 1980s and the early 1990s, male and female employment rates both increased

- The recession of the early 1990s caused the employment rate to fall more for men than for women

- The employment rate for men reached 82 per cent in 1990 and fell by 7 percentage points to a low of 75 per cent in 1993

- The employment rate then picked up again as the economy recovered

- In contrast, the female employment rate fell from 67 per cent in 1990 to 65 per cent in 1993

- This pattern seemed to occur again during the recession that began in 2008

- Between 2008 and 2009 employment rates for men fell from 79 per cent to 76 per cent, while falling for women from 70 per cent to 69 per cent.

Adapted from Office for National Statistics (2008a)

REVIEW

One of the most significant labour market trends in recent years has been the growth of the female participation rate, which is now in the region of 75 per cent. Indeed, female participation in the labour market is the main reason for the long-term increase in the total number of people in paid work in the UK. The UK labour market is also highly segmented, and one of the major differentiators is educational qualifications. Thus people with degrees or equivalent qualifications are heavily concentrated in the professions; 70 per cent of professional people have university degrees. In contrast, people without qualifications, or who left school without advanced levels, are concentrated in manual and elementary occupations or in lower-paid jobs in service industries. Indeed, the chances of being unemployed in the UK diminish substantially as people gain higher qualifications. Analysts have long criticised the UK's poor record in levels of educational and training attainment compared with other countries. The Leitch report (2006) identified the UK's relatively weak position in terms of skills levels and the consequences for long-term economic performance. In its view, the UK's skill base was mediocre by international standards, with over a third of the working population having no qualifications at all.

According to research carried out for the Leitch committee, it was reported that until 2020 there will be continued increases in the number of employees within the UK, by around 2.3 million. Four major labour market trends were noted. First, there would be continued growth in demand for people working in the service sectors, with the highest growth being in financial and business services. Second, there would be reductions in demand for people working in construction, manufacturing, primary and utility industries. Third, there would be increases in demand for managers, professionals, associate professionals, sales and customer services, and personal services. Finally, there would be decreases in demand for administrative and secretarial roles, skilled trades, machine and transport operatives, and people working in elementary occupations (Beaven et al 2005).

According to these and other analyses, future growth in the labour market is going to be for people with either 'soft' skills such as customer services, technical skills or higher skills requiring degree-level education. Unless things change radically, the UK is facing a growing skills gap, because of her low standards of education and training. The situation is likely to be made worse by the ageing population and the retirement, over this period, of the 'baby boomer' generation.

The aims and objectives of the late Labour government's policy were clearly stated: these were promoting employability and labour market flexibility. Employability was promoted by education policy (see Chapter 10). This was done by providing training incentives and assistance to employers and by encouraging people who were not economically active to become so. Flexibility was promoted by deregulating the labour market, or at least by making sure it is less regulated than in other EU member states. Flexibility was also promoted by encouraging flexible working practices. This was done, first, by statutory measures such as working time regulations and family-friendly policies. Second, government imposed flexible working practices across many public service organisations by subcontracting, public–private partnerships, and introducing variable payment schemes. The Conservative–Liberal Democrat coalition government is unlikely to diverge from these broad policy objectives. However, it has stated that it will concentrate on providing pre-employment training, new training schemes and additional training places (Conservative Party and Liberal Democrats 2010).

ACTIVITY 8.5

What have been the most significant changes in patterns of employment over the last 25 years? Discuss the factors explaining these patterns.

ACTIVITY 8.6

What are the main features of the labour markets where your organisation recruits staff? What is their likely impact on the organisation in the short term?

IMMIGRATION, EMPLOYMENT OF MIGRANT WORKERS AND WORK PERMITS

Immigration and employment of migrant workers are products of globalisation and economic conditions in less developed countries. Both are complex and contested issues in the UK, especially in the light of the recent economic recession. They are complex partly because getting reliable statistics on exactly how many immigrant workers are working in the UK is a difficult task; consider for example the lack of hard data on illegal immigration. They are also complex because the drivers and reasons behind large-scale immigration into the UK over the last decade are not always transparent or consistent. Immigration and the employment of migrant workers are contested, because while government and certain employers are strongly committed to this process, some people and bodies such as Migration Watch question the legitimacy of what has happened and its possible detrimental impacts on the UK economic and political structures.

THE CASES FOR AND AGAINST IMMIGRATION

Coyle (2005) supports the economic case for immigration by arguing that immigration into the UK has increased in response to high labour demand. In her view, this additional supply of labour has helped keep interest rates lower and growth higher than might otherwise have been the case. Indeed, in her analysis, the longer-term impact of immigration may increase productivity. Although the evidence on such long-term economic effects is incomplete, she concludes that there is no reason to believe market principles are any less relevant when it comes to flows of people than for goods or capital in the economy.

The former Labour government's case for immigration was that it supports the wider economic policy objectives of economic growth and increased productivity. Migration policy, in this perspective, is designed to bring in those migrants who can best contribute to these objectives. In particular, these are claimed to be highly skilled workers who, through their knowledge, skills and earnings, can raise economic growth, increase productivity and, through their taxes, add to the welfare of the population as a whole. For government, migration policy is also judged as being useful to fill important skills gaps in the labour market and ensure that the UK economy remains as dynamic and flexible as possible. The late Labour government's position is supported too on the grounds that immigration may help to address the problems of an ageing population and that immigration will help contribute to funding the 'pension gap' in the UK. The position of the Coalition government, elected in May 2010, is broadly supportive of immigration, whilst accepting that it is currently too high, needs reducing and must be closely regulated.

A high-powered House of Lords Select Committee on Economic Affairs (2008) argues that immigration has become highly significant to the UK economy, with immigrants comprising some 12 per cent of the total workforce, and a much higher proportion in London. Yet it found no evidence supporting the argument, made by the Labour government, business and others, that net immigration generates significant economic benefits for the UK population. In its review of the evidence, it concluded that increasing overall GDP, which the government has persistently emphasised as being important, is an irrelevant and misleading criterion for assessing the economic impacts of immigration on the UK. The Committee did not believe that the total size of an economy is an index of

Figure 8.4 House of Lords Select Committee's recommendations to government on immigration to the UK

Areas for action	Recommendations
Migration statistics	Improve radically the present inadequate migration statistics
Immigration policies	Review government's immigration policies and explain the economic and other impacts, the reasons for and objectives of the policies, and how they relate to other policy objectives such as improving the skills of the domestic workforce
Minimum wage	Enforce the minimum wage and other statutory employment conditions, taking effective action taken against employers who illegally employ immigrants
Points-based system	Clarify the objectives and implications of the new, partially points-based immigration system
Monitoring	Monitor immigration by publishing periodic 'immigration reports' giving details of the numbers and characteristics of non-European nationals entering the UK under each tier of the new system
Citizenship	Give further consideration to which channels of immigration should lead to settlement and citizenship and which ones should be strictly temporary

Adapted from *House of Lords Select Committee* (2008)

national prosperity. Rather, the focus of analysis should be on the effects of immigration on income per head of the resident population. Both theory and the available empirical evidence indicate that these effects are small, especially in the long run when the economy fully adjusts to the increased supply of labour. In the long term, the main economic effect of immigration is to enlarge the economy, with relatively small benefits for the incomes of the resident population. The Select Committee's overall conclusion was that the economic benefits to the resident population of net immigration are small, especially in the long run. Many immigrants make a valuable contribution to the UK but the real issue is how much net immigration is desirable. The Committee's recommendations to government are summarised in Figure 8.4.

Figure 8.5 Types of immigration into the UK

Type of immigration	Characteristics
Economic migrants	• Come to the UK to work and improve their life chances • Is estimated that government trebled the number of work permits issued, from 43,000 in 1997 to 129,000 in 2007, with dependants being additional to this
Family reunion	• Dependants, such as spouses and children, come to the UK to join their families • The government changed the rules in 1997 to permit marriage as a justification for immigration • Is too early to assess the impact of the points-based system on work permits, introduced in 2008, but there is no sign of a significant reduction in the number being issued
Asylum seekers	• Claim residence in the UK on the grounds of persecution in their countries of origin • The government has sought to tighten the system and made a number of improvements • It is still not removing as many asylum seekers as are rejected each year and it is claimed that the pool of illegal immigrants continues to grow • Applications are currently running at about 30,000 a year • It is estimated that numbers have since risen by about 50 per cent to about 42,000 people per year
Illegal immigrants	• Three main sources of illegal immigration: those who enter illegally concealed in vehicles; visitors and students who overstay their visas; and rejected asylum seekers whom the authorities fail to remove • In autumn 2009, the press reported extensive exploitation of the student visa system, notably on the Indian subcontinent • In March 2009 a study by the London School of Economics suggested an estimate of 725,000 'illegals,' of whom 518,000 were in London

Migration Watch also challenges the impact of relatively large flows of immigrants into the UK. As an independent body whose objective is to monitor developments, conduct research and provide the public with the facts of immigration, its central claim is that governments have lost control over UK borders since the early 1990s. In its view, this has resulted in immigration on a scale that is placing huge strains on public services, housing, the environment, society and quality of life. In recent years, the focus of attention has been on migrants from the new Eastern European members of the EU. Migration Watch argues that there has been a massive inflow of nearly a million people from Eastern Europe, about half a million of whom are still believed to be in the UK. In its view, it is not clear how the economic crisis in Eastern Europe will affect these flows. Migration Watch also believes that asylum is back in the news, with hundreds of mainly young men seeking to cross the channel from Calais, although the number of asylum claims is small compared to immigration as a whole. In Migration Watch's analysis, recession is likely to reduce immigration but previous experience suggests that this will be only a temporary phenomenon, since after the last three recessions immigration numbers resumed their strong upward trend (Migration Watch 2010). Types of immigration into the UK are summarised in Figure 8.5.

ASYLUM SEEKERS

There were around 25,900 applications for asylum to the UK (excluding dependants) in 2008, an increase of 11 per cent on the previous year. This was the first time there had been an annual increase in applications since 2002, when applications peaked at 84,100. Including those with dependants, there were around 31,300 applications for asylum in 2008. Around one in 10 applications, excluding dependants, were made at the point of entry into the UK. The majority were made after the applicant had entered the country.

Around 40 per cent of asylum applications in 2008 were made by African nationals. Thirty-seven per cent were nationals from Asia and Oceania, 19 per cent from the Middle East, 3 per cent from Europe and 2 per cent from the Americas. This compares with 241,300 applications for asylum received by member states of the EU in 2008, including dependants. France received the most applications (15 per cent) followed by the UK and Italy (13 per cent each).

About 19,400 initial decisions were made on asylum applications to the UK in 2008, excluding dependants, with just over 13,500 of these applications (70 per cent) being refused. In 19 per cent of cases, the applicant was granted asylum. The remaining initial decisions were either to grant discretionary leave to stay in the UK or, in less than 1 per cent of cases, to grant humanitarian protection. At the end of 2008, there were 10,600 cases awaiting initial decision.

In 2008, 156,000 applications were received for British citizenship. With the exception of a sharp rise in applications in 2005, when there were 211,900 applications, the number of applications has remained fairly stable since 2003. This was just before requirements for applicants to demonstrate knowledge of life in the

UK and ability in the English language came into force. The most common basis for granting British citizenship was residence of five or more years in the UK.

- Around 129,400 people were granted British citizenship in 2008, 21 per cent fewer than in 2007.

- Around 9,000 applications were refused or withdrawn, or the applicant was found to be British already.

The nationalities with the largest number of British citizenship grants awarded in 2008 were: Indian (11,825), Pakistani (9,440) and Iraqi (8,895). In total, 14,830 European nationals were granted British citizenship. Around a quarter (27 per cent) of these were nationals of the European Economic Area, which comprises all 27 EU member states plus Iceland and Norway (Office for National Statistics 2009a).

WORK PERMITS

Following recent concerns about immigration into the UK, it is now regulated under a points-based system. Issued by the Home Office UK Border Agency, the points-based system is the biggest shake-up of the UK immigration system for over 40 years. It consists of five tiers, which have replaced more than 80 routes to work and study in the UK. Its aims are, first, to allow businesses to recruit the skills they need from abroad and, second, to provide rules for immigrants wanting to study in the UK. The points-based system also seeks to reassure the public that only those immigrants that are needed can gain entry into the UK. The five tiers are listed below in Figure 8.6, although only Tiers 1, 2, 4 and 5 were open to applications in 2010.

Figure 8.6 The points-based immigration system into the UK

Tier	Covers	Sponsors
Tier 1	Highly skilled workers, such as scientists and entrepreneurs	No sponsors required
Tier 2	Skilled workers with a job offer, such as teachers and nurses	Sponsor must be an employer
Tier 3	Low-skilled workers filling specific temporary labour shortages, such as construction workers for a particular project	Sponsor must be an employer
Tier 4	Students	Sponsor must be an education provider based in the UK
Tier 5	Temporary workers, such as musicians coming to play in a concert, and participants in the youth mobility scheme	Sponsor must be an employer for temporary workers No sponsor needed for youth mobility scheme

Adapted from www.ukba.homeoffice.gov.uk, accessed 26 February 2010

The points-based system covers only immigrants from outside the EU, Norway, Iceland and Switzerland. If organisations want to employ or teach EU, Norwegian, Icelandic or Swiss nationals, they can do so without needing permission from the UK Border Agency, although there are restrictions on the nationals of countries that have recently joined the EU. Under the points-based system, migrants must pass a 'points' assessment before they can get permission to enter or remain in the UK. Each of the five tiers has different points requirements. The number of points immigrants need, and the way points are awarded, depends on the tier. Points are awarded to reflect the migrant's ability, experience and age and, when appropriate, the level of need in the migrant's chosen industry (www.ukba. homeoffice.gov.uk, accessed 26 February 2010).

ACTIVITY 8.7

Examine the cases for and against employing migrant workers (a) generally and (b) in your organisation.

FAMILY STRUCTURES

A family is a social group, within which there are many different structures including nuclear families, extended families, single-parent families, same-sex families and multicentric families. Although historically the family seems to be an enduring feature of society, it is a constantly evolving and changing institution. Attitudes to and perceptions of the family also vary. There are idealised views of the family, which see it as a source of sustenance, nurturing, security and focus of loyalty for individuals. It is also seen as the cornerstone of society and the basis for the stability, order, continuity and evolution of our culture. In contrast, some feminists see the family as an artificial institution, a social construction, which imposes collective goals on free personalities, particularly women, and interferes with the full development of the autonomous individual. In a similar vein, earlier philosophers such as Hobbes (1947) and John Stuart Mill (1972) saw it as an oppressive institution. For Hobbes, family relations were merely another exercise in power, involving male dominance over women and children, while Mill thought the family was a seedbed of despotism and source of human misery. Berger and Carlson (1993) go as far as to suggest that the family is the spawning ground for imperialism, racism, violence, homophobia and religious intolerance. Family structures are important because they affect people's demand for work, the supply of labour and the proportion of time spent working by individuals.

THE DIVERSITY OF CONTEMPORARY FAMILIES

The concept of the contemporary family is both a complex and debated one. For some in the late twentieth century, a family was a social group characterised by common residence, economic co-operation and reproduction, 'with adults of both sexes, at least two of whom maintain(ed) a socially approved sexual relationship, and one or more children, own or adopted, of the sexually co-habiting adults' (Gittins 1993, p60). Abercrombie and Warde (2000, p265), in contrast, define family as 'a kinship grouping of adults or adults and children, who may not necessarily have a common residence'. When examining current trends in family composition, it is clear that between 1961 and 2009 the proportion of people living in the 'traditional' family household of a couple with dependent children fell from just over a half (52 per cent) to just over a third (36 per cent) of the UK population (Office for National Statistics 2009a).

Neither of the above definitions seems able to encompass the variety of social groups referred to as families in today's world. The nuclear family of a married couple with children, all living in the same household, and the extended family with a married couple living with children and grandparents and aunts or uncles still exist, especially amongst Asian communities. So too do kinship groups which live separately but are bound by birth and marriage. These families, although not having physical contact as frequently as in the past, do keep in constant or regular contact through telephone and ICTs such as email. But, in addition, there are many one-parent families. Some 20 per cent of children live in one-parent families, headed mostly by women. There are also increasing numbers of childless families and same-sex families. The latter are now recognised in law and have recently acquired rights to adoption, whilst *in vitro* fertilisation, with sperm donors or surrogate mothers, makes it possible for them to have their own children. These families are likely to increase in number in the future.

The decline of traditional same-residence extended families can be attributed to greater social and geographical mobility, while the relaxation of divorce laws has resulted in not only more one-parent families but also multicentric, extended families. One in two marriages ends in divorce, with the percentage rising. People continue to remarry, however, and have children with more than one partner. This suggests that marriage is still seen as an important social relationship. The reasons for marital breakdown are complex and multicausal but appear to be linked to unrealistic expectations about marriage, increased individualism, hedonism and the opportunities for developing new relationships, as both partners work and are more affluent than people in earlier generations. Also the importance of the family as an economic unit has declined, as more women are now employed and are economically independent of men. The family has emotional importance and is the locus for love, affection and belonging. If those feelings change, then the reasons for being in the relationship cease and the search for these needs to be met elsewhere resume (Smart and Shipman 2004, Welstead and Edwards 2008). However, as one piece of research concludes, the centrality of the formally married couple has diminished since the mid-twentieth century. 'A majority see unmarried cohabitation as more or less equal to marriage' in everyday life. People want to maintain good relationships and functional family lives, 'not cling to their own self-projects in isolation' (Duncan and Phillips 2008, p26).

MULTIPLE FAMILIES

During a lifetime, an individual may become a member of several families and households. This may include living in a family with natural or adoptive parents, involve a stepfamily, or result from divorce and remarriage by one or both original parents. During adulthood, people may marry or cohabit with a partner or several partners sequentially. This may be interspersed with periods of living alone. Women may have a child without a partner and live with the child or children, while the father may continue to support them or decline any responsibility. Many people live alone again, after divorce or the death of a former partner. Social attitudes towards contraception, abortion, women working, cohabitation and divorce have changed remarkably among both sexes over the last 60 years. Thus traditional social constraints supporting 'conventional' family patterns have been removed or weakened (Giddens 1992, Whitmarsh 1995). However, some negative attitudes towards same-sex relationships, civil partnerships and same-sex parents remain, although the law has changed to prohibit discrimination against gay men and lesbians.

One of the consequences of divorce, and of the increase in the number of women choosing to have children without a permanent partner, is the fatherless family (Dennis and Erdos 1993). This is often seen as a social problem, partly because of the dependency of these families on the state and partly because they are seen as the cause of anti-social behaviour, particularly amongst youths, resulting in juvenile delinquency, truancy from school and low academic performance (Berger and Carlson 1993). Parenting problems arising after divorce have been well researched and suggest that it is the social position of the fatherless family, including income, occupation and education, which are important explanatory variables rather than the status itself (Silva and Smart 1999).

THE STATE AND FAMILY LIFE

The state increasingly intervenes in family life, whether by providing income support, helping dysfunctional families or protecting vulnerable children. This is an area in which state intervention has increased in recent years. Government has continually viewed the family with two parents as the most stable environment for children to grow up in. Therefore its policy has been to help keep the family together. It has advocated better services and support for parents including 'Sure Start', mediation services for couples contemplating divorce, better support services for families with serious problems and help for those experiencing family violence (Romito 2008). Government has also promoted better financial support for families and helped them balance work and home by introducing more family-friendly employment rights. There was also a new deal for single parents and help with finding them employment. This was clearly intended to reduce the cost on the state, provide working 'models' for the children and assist women in becoming more independent. Most of these policies have been implemented in the past few years.

The approach of the Labour government to the family in the years 1997–2010 recognised that the family is the meeting point of many current social trends.

These include increased equality between the sexes, more women in the labour force for longer periods of their lives, changes in sexual behaviour and a changing relationship between work and home (Giddens 2009).

ACTIVITY 8.8

What are some of the implications of single-parent families for (a) employers, (b) your organisation and (c) government?

GENDER, ETHNICITY AND DIVERSITY IN ORGANISATIONS AND SOCIETY

The contemporary workplace is now recognised as one embracing individuals with a range of identities and legal and human rights, which in the past were barely accepted and even less understood by those in power and authority in organisations and the wider society. What was historically blatant, irrational prejudice against certain individuals or groups who were perceived as being 'different' from others became eventually legally condemned as discriminatory behaviour by employers. Examples included women employees who had to resign from their employment on marriage (for example, in banks or insurance companies) or women who were paid on different pay scales from men (as in the civil service or school teaching).

THE EQUAL OPPORTUNITIES AND MANAGING DIVERSITY AGENDA

The first stage of public enlightenment in favour of 'rights' at work was promoting equal opportunities; this was done through the agency of the law. This legislation covered areas such as terms and conditions of employment, promotion and pension rights, with equal opportunities becoming part of a wider societal shift towards social inclusion and human rights. Equal opportunities have been on the employment agenda in the UK since the 1970s. For governments, the remedy was through legal, social and fiscal policy, and for organisations, through the introduction of equal opportunities policies and practices. Equal opportunities were based on the recognition that certain groups experienced disadvantage and inequality in the workplace and wider labour market which needed to be rejected and eliminated. The primary vehicle for achieving equality in the workplace, and outside it, is anti-discrimination legislation. This currently covers age, disability, gender, race, human rights, religion and belief, sexual orientation and transgender equality. In a liberal society, the generic arguments for promoting equal opportunities are those of social justice, penalty avoidance and human capital optimisation, linked with the business case (Gatrell and Swan 2008).

At the organisational level, equal opportunities are about eliminating unlawful discrimination at work and introducing measures aimed at removing the effects of earlier disadvantages experienced by individuals. A good-practice model suggests a systematic process of strategy formulation, audit of the existing situation, action planning and implementation, monitoring and policy review. The HR specialist plays a key role in promoting and implementing equal opportunities, although the balance of power within organisations either facilitates or inhibits this. Guidance on both legal compliance and development of good practice is available from the Equality and Human Rights Commission.

As time has passed, the main avenue for addressing equal opportunities in organisations is increasingly focused on the management of diversity. Gatrell and Swan (2008) argue the term 'diversity' is used in two ways. One is the notion of diversity as being more inclusive than the idea of equal opportunities. The second is in relation to managerial practices for dealing with the changing demographics of employees and customers, and inequalities in the workplace. So in some cases, equal opportunities policies have been superseded by notions of diversity and diversity management. From a managerial perspective, this typically means making the business case for equal opportunities in terms of the benefits accruing to the organisation as a whole, rather than any assessment of how this might enhance the lives of individual workers. Industrial Relations Services (2003) argue that the business benefits of organisational diversity include: improved customer satisfaction and market penetration by employing a diverse workforce whose composition is similar to that of the local population, enhanced worker motivation and drawing on the skills of a diverse workforce, and improved supply of labour because the employer is seen as a good employer. Diversity policies also avoid costly discrimination cases, because action has been taken to ensure the use of systematic, professional HR practices in selection, reward and promotion.

The concept of diversity in the workplace is thought to have originated in the United States, with the publication of the report *Workforce 2000* (Litvin 2002). In the UK, the concept emerged in the 1990s and organisations shifted from an initial focus on social justice through to equal opportunities, thence to a managing-diversity approach. The business case for managing diversity is related to improving service delivery and economic productivity, and depoliticising models of social relations (Kandola and Fullerton 1994), but Kirton and Greene (2004) claim that it is possible to have a sociological model of diversity. This moves diversity away from the business case model, and associated ideas of individual differences, which posits that all differences matter equally. Kirton and Greene argue that it is feasible to have a view of diversity management that favours a structural account of inequality based on a notion of social justice. By this view, the sociological model can lead to better equality outcomes for individuals and groups, because diversity management emphasises the heterogeneity of differences within social groups. It is a model of managing diversity which acknowledges that some differences matter more than others. However, despite these debates, Gatrell and Swan (2008, p63) conclude that 'the jury is out on the political efficacy of diversity as a concept in the workplace,' since the workplace 'is still a space of discrimination, violence and oppression'.

PROMOTING EQUALITY THROUGH THE LAW

The Equality Act 2010 has two main aims: to introduce a streamlined, single legal framework for tackling disadvantage and discrimination in the UK, and to strengthen the law to support progress on equality. First, the Act brings together all current equality laws and a number of other related provisions by seeking to harmonise existing provisions to give a single approach, where appropriate. Second, the Act strengthens the law in a number of areas. Its main provisions are summarised in Figure 8.7

Figure 8.7 Main provisions of the Equality Act 2010

Aims

The Act harmonises and in some cases extends existing discrimination law covering the protected characteristics of age, disability, gender reassignment, marriage and civil partnership, pregnancy and maternity, race, religion or belief, sex, and sexual orientation. It seeks to address the impact of recent case law, which is generally seen as having weakened discrimination protection, and harmonise provisions defining indirect discrimination.

Key areas

- Provides powers to extend age-discrimination protection outside the workplace
- Clarifies protection against discrimination by association, for example in relation to a mother who cares for her disabled child
- Extends protection from discrimination on the grounds of gender reassignment to school pupils
- Extends discrimination protection in the terms of membership and benefits for private clubs and associations
- Creates a unified public sector duty, intended to promote equality in public policy and decision-making, existing provisions being extended to the protected characteristics of sexual orientation, age, and religion or belief, and proposes a new public sector duty related to socio-economic inequalities
- Provides for legislation requiring that employers review gender pay differences within their organisations and publish the results
- Provides for changes to the way that individual claims are enforced, and gives employment tribunals wider powers to make recommendations for the collective benefit of employees
- Allows a minister to amend UK equality legislation to comply with European law without the need for primary legislation
- Extends the period for which all-women shortlists may be used for parliamentary and other elections until 2030 and allows parties to reserve places on shortlists of candidates for people on the grounds of race or disability

⟳ **ACTIVITY 8.9**

Distinguish between equal opportunities and managing diversity.

ACTIVITY 8.10

What are the differences between (a) equality of opportunity, (b) equality of outcome, (c) equality of redistribution, and (d) equality of recognition?

ACTIVITY 8.11

Examine the possible impacts of the Equality Act 2010 on your organisation.

SOCIAL STRATIFICATION

All modern societies are socially stratified and hierarchical, reflecting degrees of inequality amongst individuals, families, households and social groups in wealth, status and power. Those at the top of the hierarchy tend to have more of all these three resources than those at the bottom. Social divisions within the UK reflect differing occupations, lifestyles, patterns of social behaviour and life opportunities. The major social divisions are traditionally seen as class, gender and ethnicity, although age, religion and regional cleavages are also important. This diversity, however, is overlaid and held together by systems of beliefs, language, law, symbols and institutions. All societies consist of elements of heterogeneity and homogeneity. It is the integration of these elements that produces social stability, whilst at the same time enabling societies to change (Giddens 2009).

DEFINING SOCIAL CLASS

The term 'social class' rather than 'social strata' has traditionally been used by social scientists within the UK. Class is sometimes described as the 'British obsession' and Britain is perceived as the most class-conscious society in the world. Even so, the concept of class has been disputed amongst social scientists. The classical view, associated with Weber (1968, 1971), is that social position is a complex phenomenon with economic, social, political and cultural dimensions, linked to occupation, status and power.

- **Class situation**: Weber recognised three types of class situation: property classes, commercial classes and social classes. Property classes are determined by property differences and may be positively or negatively privileged. Commercial classes are determined by their ability to sell their skills or goods in the market. Social classes are wider groups, including property and commercial classes, between which there is some mobility. These groups include the working class, intelligentsia, propertied classes, educated classes and small businesses. Weber identified a significant 'middle class' composed of the self-employed, public officials and those in liberal professions.

- **Group solidarity:** classes can be identified in terms of their possessions and skills, but it is status not class that is the root of group solidarity. Status refers to the way that society regards individuals or groups. It is conferred externally and reflects the positive or negative values attached to knowledge, skill, circumstances of birth, social position or patterns of behaviour. It has its origins in the ability of groups to claim privileges denied to others. For Weber, conflicts between classes and status groups, and between status groups, cause social change.

- **Power and party:** power is the ability to influence decisions, either positively or negatively, and to make things happen, reflecting one's own interest or collective interests. Parties are social groups established to influence or change the *status quo*. Their focus may be broad or narrow, national or local, but they try to influence particular communal outcomes and may or may not be related to class or status.

The Marxist materialist view emphasises that class is fundamental and determined by the relationship of people to the means of production:

- All those selling their labour constitute a 'working' class. In contrast, those owning the means of production constitute a ruling or 'capitalist' class, described as the 'bourgeoisie'.

- The relationship between the two major classes is inherently exploitative, as the capitalist extracts part of the value of the social production of the workers as profit and pays wages to the workers, which are less than the value of what they have produced.

- This exploitation causes class conflict, which is the engine of social change.

- Other classes, consisting of the self-employed, professionals and small businesses such as shopkeepers and artisans, are the 'petite bourgeoisie'.

- Neo-Marxists have refined this by acknowledging a more complex class structure, consisting of lower, middle and upper classes. Each of these has differential economic rewards, affecting lifestyles and giving access to other resources such as property, wealth, social position and political power (Poulantzas 1975, McLellan 2007).

Debates about class today revolve around whether social class is any longer a meaningful concept that describes 'reality' and whether the meta-narratives of Marx and Weber can accommodate the complexity of modern classes that are increasingly fragmented. There is also debate about how to describe the new systems of social stratification that are emerging, which seem to confuse the traditional divisions of working, middle and upper class. There are debates about how to integrate the structural and behavioural elements of Marx and Weber into an analysis of class structures in modern societies (Giddens 1981).

This debate identifies what Bradley (1996) has described as a set of interrelationships arising out of the social organisation of production, distribution, exchange and consumption. These include the allocation of tasks in the division of labour (occupation, employment hierarchies), control and ownership relationships within production, the unequal distribution of surplus (wealth, income, state benefits), relationships linked to the circulation of money (markets, shareholding and investment), patterns of consumption (lifestyle, living arrangements), and distinctive cultures that arise from all these (behavioural practices and community relations). Class is a much broader concept, then, than occupational structure, though the latter is often taken as a measure of it.

Recent social changes have led to the claim that the class system in the UK is coming to an end and that the UK is moving to a classless society. Observers point to a 'new' working class, more skilled, educated and affluent than the old working class, with similar lifestyles and consumption patterns to the middle classes. Members of the 'new' working class are more likely to be homeowners, have holidays abroad, enjoy eating out and have a wide range of material possessions. In addition, increased social mobility within working class families, and the higher status attached to new occupations, are also seen as blurring boundaries between the working and middle classes.

Another perspective is that class is a function of not only market position but also work situation. Market position is reflected in income, job security and opportunity for upward mobility, while work situation is reflected in the degree of autonomy, independence and control individuals have over work. The working class is distinguishable not only by the type of work they do and their market position but also by their lack of control or autonomy over the work process (Lockwood 1958). Rather than 'embourgeoisification' of the working class, Lockwood and others (Wood 1989, Crompton et al 2000) point to the 'proletarianisation' of the middle classes. Changes in the work process affecting white-collar and lower professional groups (traditionally seen as middle class) are leading to loss of job autonomy, which is blurring the distinction between the classes, with negative effects. Further, the shift to flexible employment patterns is seen as reducing job security for manual, white-collar and professional workers. Thus the middle classes are being more exposed to risk and insecurity in employment, as job flexibility crosses the traditional manual/mental divisions of labour.

Underpinning analyses of social class is inequality. There have been many studies of the relationship between class and inequality. A recent, authoritative study of inequality argues that more equal societies normally do better than unequal ones (Wilkinson and Pickett 2009). These authors point out that the life-diminishing results of valuing growth above equality in rich societies can be seen all around us. Inequality causes shorter, unhealthier and unhappier lives. It increases teenage pregnancy, violence, obesity, imprisonment and addiction, and destroys relationships between individuals born in the same society but into different classes. Further, the function of inequality as a driver of consumption depletes the planet's finite resources. On almost every index of quality of life or wellness or deprivation, there is evidence showing a strong correlation between a country's level of economic inequality and its social outcomes. Almost always, the UK, the United States and Portugal are at the unfavourable 'high' end. And almost always, Japan and the Scandinavian countries are at the favourable 'low' end, with Canada, Australasia and continental European countries in between. Dorling (2010) complements this evidence. He argues that five new sets of beliefs (elitism, exclusion, prejudice, greed and despair) are replacing Beveridge's five social evils (ignorance, want, idleness, squalor and disease), identified at the dawn of the welfare state, as society's dominant values. These new values, he claims, have become entrenched in the UK and some other affluent countries.

THE CHANGING SOCIAL STRUCTURE

The period between 1945 and the late 1970s was one of relative prosperity, full employment and a growing working population. New occupations and professions emerged within the continuously expanding welfare state, and wages rose along with productivity. High levels of consumption led to a general rise in living standards and there was a high 'social wage' (ie 'free' public services and transfer payments by the state to individuals and households), resulting in some narrowing of the inequalities between social classes. There was also increased social mobility, and distinctions and boundaries between classes became blurred as general affluence resulted in converging consumption patterns and lifestyles across old class divisions.

A large working class of manual workers, a smaller middle class of white-collar workers, the professions, self-employed and a small upper class distinguished the old class structure. In 1951, about two-thirds of the working population and their families were in manual occupations and identified themselves as working class. Their shared economic or material position was the basis for a group identity. Their identity was expressed similarity of outlook and sense of common condition. This identity was expressed in terms of shared interests that provided a basis for political organisation and action, as well as trade union organisation (Abercrombie and Warde 2000). Between 1971 and 1981, the proportion of employed people in manual work fell from 62 per cent to 56 per cent for men and 43 per cent to 36 per cent for women (Halsey 2000). By 2000, less than 30 per cent of the labour force had manual jobs and an increasing proportion of those were women and minority ethnic groups.

Explanations of these changes were to be found, first, in the decline of manufacturing and extractive industries where manual workers were employed, such as mining, shipbuilding, iron and steel, docks, textiles and transport. Second, jobs have been lost to automation and new technology in industries such as printing and car assembly. Third, jobs have disappeared as corporations have transferred production to low-labour-cost countries and UK plants have closed. This process of globalisation is creating a new international division of labour, so that the working class has not declined globally.

The social structure of the UK changed significantly in the second half of the twentieth century (Halsey 2000), with new patterns of social stratification emerging as it was transformed from an industrial to a post-industrial society. The major differences between industrial and post-industrial societies lie in their economic systems, types of commodities produced, the distribution of the labour force and the dominant technology. For Bell (1973), this involved the change from a goods-producing to a service economy, the emergence of new professions and technical classes, the central role of knowledge as the key resource and source of innovation, and the dominance of new information-based technologies.

By the early twenty-first century, in contrast to the declining working class, the middle class had grown, as white-collar occupations had expanded, new professions had been created and technology had transformed working processes. The middle class has become numerically and socially the most significant social stratum and is predicted to grow between 10 and 14 per cent over the next decade. The middle class, however, is very heterogeneous and has been described by Dahrendorf (1982) as consisting of an 'upper', middle, 'middle' middle and 'lower' middle class. The upper-middle class includes the higher professions, senior managers and those holding senior technical posts. The middle-middle class consists of the lower professions, middle managers and technical grades, small business owners and farmers. The lower-middle class are those in clerical and supervisory positions, shop workers and para-professionals.

The upper class remains the smallest class, but it has also changed. It consists of interconnected families owning a disproportionate amount of property and wealth. In 2001, it was estimated that the top 1 per cent of people owned 23 per cent of marketable wealth and 33 per cent of marketable wealth less the value of dwellings (Summerfield and Babb 2004). The upper class also controls and owns large parts of industry, land and commerce, and holds top posts in major institutions of the state, commerce and the arts. In addition to the royal family and the traditional landowning aristocracy, it includes chief executives and directors of large national and multinational corporations; those at the top of the major financial institutions in the City, including banks, finance houses and law firms; senior judges; military leaders and some top politicians and civil servants. This class is economically dominant, operates through national and international networks and is often referred to as 'the Establishment'.

Dahrendorf (1982) distinguishes between the 'old' and 'new' upper class. The latter are 'entryists' or *nouveaux riches* that have acquired property and wealth but generally lack the personal advantages deriving from birth and ascribed social status. Examples include Sir Richard Branson, Sir Paul McCartney, Lord Alan Sugar, Lord David Sainsbury and Dame Shirley Porter, all of whom appear in the top 200 wealthiest people in the UK, along with the Queen and the Duke of Westminster. The *nouveaux riches* themselves are becoming increasingly heterogeneous, as the number of multi-millionaires and billionaires continues to increase. In 2010, for example, the five richest (or super-rich) people resident in the UK owned some £47.9 billion in assets between them, with four of them having been born outside the UK. This compared with £33.3 billion in assets owned by the richest five residents in the previous year. This was an increase of some 44 per cent during the year. The assets of these five families are summarised in Figure 8.8 (Beresford 2010).

As a further example of globalisation, only one of these five families was a member of the old upper class (the Duke of Westminster). Clearly, the importance of inherited wealth is declining and the UK is fast becoming a plutocracy. This is seen in the growing power and control exercised by a trans-national capitalist elite, which is a crucial feature of the new globalisation. According to Sampson (2004, p354), the new elite is held together by a desire

Figure 8.8 The five wealthiest (super-rich) families in the UK 2010

Family	Assets and estimated wealth	Country of origin
Lakshmi Mittal and family	Investments in steel, with assets valued at £22.4 billion – *increased by 108 per cent over the previous year*	India
Roman Abramovich	Investments in oil, finance and football, with assets valued at £7.4billion – *increased by 6 per cent over the previous year*	Russia
The Duke of Westminster	Investments in property, with assets valued at £6.7 billion – *increased by 4 per cent over the previous year*	UK
Ernesto and Kirsty Bertarelli	Investments in pharmaceuticals, with assets valued at £5.9 billion – *increased by 19 per cent over the previous year*	Switzerland
David and Simon Reuben	Property and Internet, with assets valued at £5.5 billion – *increased by 121 per cent over the previous year*	Iraq

Adapted from Beresford (2010)

for personal enrichment, their acceptance of fast capitalism and the need for the profit motive, 'while the resistance to money values is much weaker.' Today the circles of Britain's power-centres look very different from the pattern 40 years ago.

The palace, the universities and the diplomats have drifted towards the edge. Many institutions – including parliament, the cabinet, trades unions and industry – look smaller. The prime minister, the Treasury and defence loom larger at the centre. The bankers are more dominant, overlapping with corporations and pensions funds, while the nationalised industries have almost disappeared as separate entities. The media are more pervasive, seeping everywhere into the vacuum left by the shrinking of the old powers. (Sampson 2004, p354)

In spite of changes in social mobility, if class is an indicator of access to resources and therefore of life chances, the UK remains a highly stratified society. In 2009, it was still the case that the distribution of income was more unequal in the UK than in most other European countries, with the gap between the highest and lowest incomes widening. The skewed distribution of wealth was even greater.

ACTIVITY 8.12

A visiting manager from China is fascinated by the continued significance of social class in UK society. He asks you to explain the main characteristics of the middle class and why its numbers are rising, whilst those of other classes appear to be falling. What would you say?

PUBLIC SERVICES AND CHANGING SOCIAL VALUES

The UK's welfare state was established by post-war Labour governments between 1945 and 1951. Broadly, their aims were to meet the basic social and economic needs of its citizens by providing collectively, through its revenues raised from taxes and other sources, goods and services such as education, health, housing and social security to individual citizens and their families. Based on the Beveridge report (1942), which was initially resisted by the Conservatives, the welfare state became incorporated in the post-war political consensus and was subsequently supported by all political parties and the electorate for many years.

FROM WELFARE STATE TO PUBLIC SERVICE REFORM

The first overt challenge to the welfare state came when the Conservative party won power in 1979. Arguing that high public spending was at the root of the UK's economic difficulties at that time, and that levels of taxation needed to support the welfare state were unsustainable in the future, the Conservatives set about privatising public industries, reforming the remaining public sector and reducing public spending. They also sought to destroy the 'dependency culture', which they claimed the welfare state had reinforced, by reforming support systems. They favoured selectivity rather than universal services and targeting spending more effectively on those most in need. They also promoted more choice and a 'consumerist' attitude towards what were increasingly being called 'public services' rather than the welfare state. They also wanted to encourage greater use of privately funded welfare services, emphasising personal responsibility in areas such as private healthcare and private pensions.

In many ways, Labour governments in the period 1997–2010 adapted rather than reversed the broad thrust of Conservative policies, although they made attempts to improve the level of support for children, low-income families and pensioners and to assist people getting into work. Social demands, however, continue to increase and make it difficult for governments to reduce public spending. As incomes rise, people want better education and improved healthcare services and an ageing population makes greater demands on healthcare, social care and pensions.

There is general agreement that there have been significant changes in the provision of public services over the past 40 years, although there is less agreement about whether this amounts to a new or modified form of 'welfarism' (Powell 1999). The major changes have included:

- until recently, and now once more, generally tighter controls on public spending
- decline in social housing, with transfer of properties to registered social landlords
- growth in private pensions
- increased involvement of private providers in public services
- increased private funding of public services

- more 'co-payments' for public services such as university 'top-up' fees
- greater means-testing of benefits.

Today, there is, at one and the same time, some resistance at attempts to reduce or redefine public services, support for modernising them, and a growing divide between these two positions, depending on which aspect of public services is the focus of attention. First, there has been public resistance to attempts by successive governments to restrict spending on public services, especially healthcare and education. The evidence suggests that support for higher spending has been driven by general dissatisfaction with public services. Periods when support for higher spending increased have followed growing dissatisfaction with the National Health Service and state schools. Using student top-up fees to finance spending in higher education, for example, does not so far appear to have dampened public enthusiasm for public higher education provision.

Second, some studies have shown that the public appear to be in sympathy with government's attempts to modernise public services. Decline in support for spending on state benefits for the poor and redistribution, especially among Labour supporters, has occurred at the time when Labour governments have shifted policy away from income redistribution towards a more preventative approach of tackling poverty. People have continued to favour higher spending on benefits to vulnerable groups and the retired, but they have become more selective about who should benefit from increased spending.

Third, and surprisingly, the increase in support for higher spending on public services has been concentrated among Conservative supporters, whereas the hardening of attitudes towards benefit claimants has been concentrated among Labour supporters. Further, increased use of private health and education services does not appear to have undermined support for core public services. However, younger people have become less disposed towards increases in public spending and harder in their attitudes to the benefit system, relative to older generations.

CHANGING SOCIAL VALUES

People's personal value systems reflect their enduring beliefs or philosophies about what is 'good' or desirable. These, in turn, underpin a person's attitudes towards a range of issues such as religion, politics, social matters and morals (Alwin and Scott 1996). Two sets of value systems are especially relevant: 'left–right' values and 'libertarian–authoritarian' values.

Left and right values are associated with economic issues such as the desirability of government intervention in the economy, income and wealth distribution, and relations between workers and managers. Left-wing values emphasise redistribution and the unequal relationship between workers and those employing them in the labour market. Right-wing values emphasise individualism, the value of competition and impersonal allocation of resources in markets. This value dimension is closely related with political attitudes and opinion and support for left or right parties.

Libertarian and authoritarian values are concerned with authority. Libertarians stress the importance of individualism and freedom of personal action. Authoritarians stress conformity and obedience to authority. This value dimension is closely related to the ways in which people live their lives and their tolerance or intolerance of deviance from social norms.

These two sets of value system do not always go together. The four dimensions tend to be cross-cutting, adding 'to the complexity of the ways in which they influence social and political attitudes in Britain and interact with the political party system' (Park and Surridge 2003). Three observations stand out. First, traditionally, the notion of 'left' and 'right' has been closely connected with class, so that left-wing approaches have tended to favour working-class interests and right-wing ones the interests of the middle classes. Second, those who have been through higher education tend to be more libertarian than authoritarian. Third, there has been a tendency for people with left-wing values to support the Labour party and people with right-wing values to support the Conservatives (Sanders 1999).

British social attitudes surveys in the early twenty-first century examined the different values held by certain social groups and the ways in which they had changed over time. They were particularly interested in the impact that higher education had had on libertarian and authoritarian values, the extent to which social changes had affected the left–right values of different classes, and how the values of different party supporters had changed over the past two decades. In terms of left-wing and right-wing groups, the evidence showed that there appeared to be a strong relationship between class and left–right values. Those in the working class and manual employment were especially likely to hold left-wing values and very unlikely to hold right-wing ones. Professional and managerial workers, in contrast, were more likely to have right-wing ones. There were also links between household income, house tenure, education and left–right values, with those in more advantageous socio-economic circumstances being more likely to have right-wing values than those who were less advantaged.

For authoritarian and libertarian groups, the evidence indicated that more highly educated people, especially graduates, were substantially more libertarian than those with lower levels of education. But if education remained the most important influence on these values, social class was important too. The most libertarian group was professional and managerial staff; the most authoritarian was manual supervisors and technicians. The relationship with household income followed a similar pathway, with those on very high incomes being the most likely to be libertarians and those on very low incomes most likely to be authoritarians.

The evidence also demonstrated that when a range of socio-economic characteristics were taken into account, a person's left–right values were still the most important predictor of their being identified with the Conservatives or Labour. There were also marked differences in the libertarian–authoritarian values of party supporters. Conservatives were most likely to be authoritarians, Liberal Democrats were most likely to be libertarians, and Labour supporters were towards the libertarian end of the spectrum. The overall analysis was that there had been 'very small changes in left/right and libertarian/authoritarian values since 1986'. There was a small shift towards the middle of the scale of left–right values and a small shift away from the most authoritarian position of the libertarian–authoritarian scale (Park and Surridge 2003, p143).

INDIVIDUALISM, CONSUMERISM AND SECULARISM

Globalisation, new technology and socio-demographic change are important contexts of the post-industrial economies of the contemporary Western world. As shown in other chapters, business leaders, politicians and individuals have no direct influence on these mega-trends and can only respond to them incrementally and reactively. However, there are other social forces at work within societies, and globally, which are affecting and changing individual behaviours and individual perceptions of the world. These forces are rooted in the renewal and reinforcement of individualist values, consumerism and secularism, resulting in increased social segmentation, consumerism and changing self-images.

THE PRIMACY OF INDIVIDUALISM

Individualism is not a new concept of human behaviour and its origins lie in three movements: liberalism, the Reformation and the Enlightenment. Liberal theorists such as Locke (1947) and Hobbes (1947) saw individuals as endowed with natural, inalienable human rights by virtue of their humanity, including rights to life, property and happiness. For Hobbes, individuals were selfish, acquisitive and aggressive by nature, whereas Locke saw them as moral, reasonable and capable of self-government. These ideas were translated into the perception that individuals were the best judges of their own welfare and that pursuit of individual interests in society was likely to result in maximum happiness. This utilitarian view of the world underpins the argument today for neo-liberalism, free markets and business competition. It also underpins the contemporary human rights movement, liberal democracy and the basic tenets of market economics. These include property rights, the rights of individuals to produce and consume, enter into contracts, buy and sell artefacts, satisfy their wants in their own way and dispose of their property and labour as they themselves decide. Thus economic individualism underpins free enterprise, market economies and contemporary capitalism.

Individualism was also the child of the Reformation and religious Protestantism. Weber (1930) argues that the Protestant ethic of hard work had a major impact on post-reformation capitalism. Protestants, particularly the puritan sects, saw salvation as being made manifest through hard work and discipline in their daily lives. These led to capitalistic conduct based upon individualistic profit making and a moral responsibility towards using resources to increase wealth by effort, moderate consumption and saving for investment (Hopper and Hopper 2009). The third strand of individualism can be traced to the Enlightenment with its rejection of superstition, religious faith, tradition and custom, and its turning to the use of reason to explain the 'modern' world. Through science, with its emphasis on empiricism and positivism, and reason, humankind could ultimately control nature in the interests of humanity. It was the Enlightenment that gave birth to modernism.

In the English-speaking world especially, individualism became the catchword for free enterprise, limited government, personal freedom and minimum state intervention in economic affairs. This was in contrast to the collectivist values of socialism (Lukes 2005). It reasserted itself from the 1980s onwards with the political and economic reform movements discussed above, and justified attacks on the 'big state', over-regulation and lack of personal choice.

Individualism today is also used to describe social 'atomism', where individuals pursue primarily individualistic, personal ends rather than collectivist, altruistic ones. Social atomism gives priority to individuals and their rights, which are seen as existing prior to any particular form of social life. This is neatly summarised by Macpherson (1962, p3), who states that 'possessive individualism' is based on 'a conception of the individual as essentially the proprietor of his [sic] own person or capacities, owing nothing to society for them'. The reassertion of individualist values has been reinforced by the decline of social democratic politics in Western societies over the past 40 years and in changes within post-communist societies since the 1990s. It is reflected in the workplace with the increasing individualisation of the employment relationship and the ways people are managed.

CONSUMERISM

Individualism in economic and social affairs is further reinforced by mass 'consumption', which is the driving imperative of contemporary capitalism, and with which it is closely related. Continually rising levels of affluence and money incomes enable people to consume, with individual consumption of personal goods and services becoming the ultimate goal or 'good' for those in gainful employment and an expectation of those who are retired or unable to work. Sophisticated shopping malls, targeted marketing campaigns and readily available 'credit' are the agents of mass consumerism by individual consumers that takes the forms of demands for niche products, luxury goods and customised services. Such patterns of economic consumption reinforce individualist values in Western societies and they, in turn, reinforce personal consumption. The consumption culture spills over into the public sector, where users are increasingly seen as consumers, and satisfying their needs and expectations becomes the driving force of public managers and service providers.

SECULARISM

The shift towards market individualism based on consumerism and personal choice based on personal freedom is, in turn, reinforced by another trend – secularism. There was a long-term trend in the decline of organised religion during the nineteenth and twentieth centuries. Religious attendance has continued to fall consistently across all Western religions, as individuals have become their own arbiters of morality, choice and social action, in response to rising economic prosperity, wider accessibility to education and the 'consumer society.' Some social scientists observing these changes in the dominant values and norms within society claim that there is a transformation of Western cultures taking place which they call the movement from 'modernism' to 'postmodernism'. Postmodernism rejects the belief that reason and the scientific method can 'discover' the reality of the physical and social worlds. It rejects objectivism and claims there are no facts, only interpretation, and no objective truths, only the constructs of individuals and groups. One person's reality is as real as any other's and reason gives way to intuition, sentiment and imagination. Postmodern culture rejects the Protestant work ethic, order and discipline for nihilism, hedonism and experientialism (Smart 1993). Postmodernism is also associated with a new language which plays a key role in our understanding of postmodernist complexity and 'reality.' The words used in the contemporary world are never neutral but value-laden, contingent and tied to periods of time, location, situations and conflicts. They are closely associated with particular modes of knowledge and understanding, which is clearly illustrated in this book.

UK society has changed significantly over the past 60 years. The population is growing, ageing and becoming more multicultural. Family structures are more diverse and single-person and single-parent households are common features of the country today. The working population is increasingly feminised, as more women have entered the labour market and more women are becoming financially independent of men. Also new patterns of flexible employment reflect the transition from an industrial to a post-industrial, knowledge-based economy. These changes are reflected in the system of social stratification, as household incomes rise, social mobility increases and differences between social classes and statuses simultaneously become both more blurred and more distinctive, with people working to consume and accumulate personal wealth rather than just 'survive', although globalisation results in both winners and losers.

Each of the factors outlined in this chapter has implications for HR strategy and HR solutions in organisations, all of which are driven by a competition, choice and change agenda. In the private sector, organisations are responding to the diverse needs of their customers in segmented and competitive product markets. More social diversity, changing family structures, rising affluence and assertive individualism are putting pressures on businesses to diversify their products and increase choice to meet the rising expectations of customers in the marketplace. Both households and business customers want quality products at competitive prices, with choice and good service. These developments have implications for how people are selected, managed and motivated.

371

in younger age groups. Employers have to manage more diverse workforces. Working age employment rates vary around Europe, and the UK has the fifth highest employment rate in the 27 member states of the EU. These different rates of employment participation are affected by population structures and differing cultures, retirement ages and participation in post-compulsory full-time education across the EU.

4. Employment by occupation has shifted to managerial and administrative work and employment by sector to private services and the public sector. More people are working flexible hours. Unemployment fluctuates through the economic cycle. During periods of growth, the number of jobs generally grows and unemployment falls, although mismatches between the skills needs of new jobs and the skills of those available for work may slow this process down. Conversely, as the economy slows, unemployment tends to rise.

5. There has been an increase in the number of migrant workers in the UK since the 1990s. Those supporting immigration do so largely on economic grounds. Those against it highlight the knock-on effects on housing provision, public services and quality of people's lives. Different types of immigration have been identified: economic migrants, migrants reuniting with their families, asylum seekers and illegal immigrants. Following recent concerns about immigration into the UK, work permits are now regulated under a points-based system, where employers play a sponsoring role. Issued by the Home Office UK Border Agency, the points-based system is the biggest shake-up of the UK immigration system for over 40 years.

6. Family structures are diverse and many are 'non-traditional'. Indicators are fewer marriages, more divorces, more living in partnerships without marrying, generally fewer children being born per family, more single-parent families, and greater acceptance of relationships such as those based on homosexual partnerships, compared with more traditional family lives and family values in the past. At the same time, government increasingly intervenes in family life. It does this by providing income support, helping dysfunctional families or protecting vulnerable children.

7. Promoting diversity in the workplace is the aim of both good practice employers and government. The equal opportunities agenda of minimum compliance with the law has been superseded in many instances by managing diversity. This is based on equity and fairness to people, being good for business and on moral grounds. Diversity covers a range of personal issues including age, disability, gender, race, human rights, religion and belief, sexual orientation and transgender equality. It is a controversial and complex area of managerial and public policy.

8. Issues of social stratification continue to run deep in British society. Different tools of analysis are used to examine social stratification. All societies are stratified but some more than others. However, underpinning social stratification are degrees of inequality of resources, power and opportunity. Evidence indicates that the UK exhibits much stronger degrees of inequality than other comparable countries. Inequality is embedded in families, education, jobs and throughout most of the country's major social institutions. The social structure of the UK was transformed in the second part of the twentieth century. This coincided with the decline of the traditional working

class and the rise of an assertive new middle class, which was well educated, ambitious and had new job roles in the knowledge-based, post-industrial economy.

9. The late twentieth century and early twenty-first century witnessed the transformation of the welfare state into a smaller group of modernised public services, with generally more limited and restrictive provision than 40 years ago. They are also more costly and employ a wide range of the new professional middle classes. There are indicators that the UK adult population is more liberal in its social values than in the past. This is partly the result of more people having access to higher education, even if, in addition to tax support, university graduates have to co-pay for it.

10. The UK of the early twenty-first century is predominantly an individualised, secular, consumerist society. People's identities as workers, consumers and citizens are increasingly rooted in the self, values of instant gratification and economic materialism. Some would argue that this epitomises a postmodern culture, where there are no objective truths only the constructs of individuals and groups in interpreting what is perceived to be their own reality and truth.

REVIEW QUESTIONS

1. Analyse recent population trends in the UK. What are the main implications of these changes for (a) organisations and (b) government?

2. Evaluate the economic and social cases for promoting immigration of foreign workers into the UK.

3. Discuss some of the issues in your organisation for managing diversity.

4. How have changing social values influenced the demand for and delivery of public services in the UK?

5. Examine the implications for managing people in your organisation arising out of the primacy of individualism, consumerism and secular values in the UK.

CASE STUDY

⊙ CASE STUDY 8.1 MANAGING DIVERSITY, EQUALITY AND SOCIAL INCLUSION IN METRO-CITY COUNCIL

Background

Metro-City is a large, district local authority located in the Midlands. It provides the usual range of local authority services for this type of authority. These include: housing; waste and recycling; leisure and tourism; planning and the environment; education, learning and libraries; community and living; streets, transport and parking; and health and social care.

Metro-City has a good reputation in the community where it is located and is regarded as a good employer in its area. The Council also provides a comprehensive public business-information service for starting, growing and developing local businesses, learning new skills, and safeguarding people's intellectual property.

The current administration has identified diversity and equality issues as priority areas to be addressed by the authority. As a result of this initiative, Metro-City Council has a strong commitment to promoting diversity, equality and social inclusion within its boundaries.

The Council's written policy on diversity, equality and social inclusion states:

Metro-City Council is committed to the values of diversity and social inclusion in all its dealings with staff, service users, customers and our communities.

The Council will strive to ensure that there will be no discrimination or unfair treatment on the grounds of gender, gender reassignment status, social background (such as gypsies and travellers, asylum seekers), race, colour, ethnic or national origin, faith, sexual orientation, marital/civil partnership status, age, disability, social position, politics, union membership or social disadvantage.

The Council aims to ensure that everybody is treated equally and has equal opportunity to receive the services and employment opportunities offered by the Authority.

The Council recognises that there are many barriers to equality of opportunity, ranging from overt prejudice in favour of, or against, particular individuals or groups, to unwitting ignorance of different lifestyles and personal needs. At whatever level discrimination exists, it is neither acceptable nor tolerable.

The Council's commitment therefore is to ensure that no individual or group is less likely than another to be provided with a service or recruited by the authority. It also confirms that all services provided are to be carried out fairly and in accordance with the law, good practice and what it is morally justified to do.

The Council is also developing a 'positive action' culture. Through this, the achievement of equality is a 'golden thread' underpinning everything that the Council does. To achieve this, the Council will set clear objectives for its services, regularly measure its performance, and take positive action to deal with any imbalances found within its areas of responsibility.

The Council is working to ensure that appreciation of issues relating to equality, diversity and inclusion are embedded throughout the organisation.

The case for diversity, equality and social inclusion

The Council has identified three reasons why diversity, equality and social inclusion are important to its agenda of provision. These are summarised below.

- **The moral case:** In some instances, Metro-City Council is still dealing with hidden disadvantages amongst its communities. So the moral principles underpinning the origins of the authority remain applicable in exactly the same way in today's campaign against inequality and social and economic disadvantage as they were in the past.

- **The legal case:** Discrimination is unlawful, whether it is direct or indirect. The law requires the Council to demonstrate its commitment to equality of opportunity in all of its dealings with the people with whom it engages. The authority is working towards the elimination of discrimination through promoting good relations with all sectors of the community within its remit.

- **The business case:** The authority deals with increasingly diverse customers and staff. Thus its service delivery plans have to respond to a range of different physical, cultural and religious needs, which impact significantly upon lifestyle preferences. For example, the Council's employment practices must be flexible enough to attract staff with the right skills and experience to perform well in their job roles.

The need for positive action

The Council has also identified the need for taking positive action in some areas. The problem stated by the Council is that there is a difference between 'equal treatment' and 'equal outcome'. Most people take the view that, if they work to rules and procedures which are fair and treat people in the same way, fair and equal outcomes follow. In a lot of cases this is true but, in reality, it cannot be relied upon, because it does not take account of the barriers to fairness – barriers that people are often unaware of and do not realise exist.

Positive action is a process designed

to address the disadvantage of people affected by these issues. Measures range from legislative action taken by the government to enforce equal pay and combat discrimination against the disabled, to 'good practice' guidance for improving access both to the Council's services by its customers and to job applicants from minority groups.

Examples of the latter may involve, for example, setting targets for black, minority and ethnic representation among the Council's housing residents relative to the balance in the community overall. Similarly, offering interviews to all disabled people who meet the basic job criteria may be a means of redressing imbalances in this area. This is different from positive discrimination. That is unlawful and favours an individual (or individuals) based on reasons which have no relevance to their actual needs or abilities, by comparison with others in the same position.

Accordingly, Metro-City has:

1. Agreed objectives in relation to the achievement of fair and equal treatment of:

   – all customers in the areas of lettings, sales, customer satisfaction, dealing with harassment and hate-crime, governing body membership, staffing, representation in residents' associations (and other bodies) and the employment performance of suppliers, contractors and consultants

   – all staff and applicants in the areas of recruitment, employment, remuneration and promotion.

2. Identified the need for:

   – the development of suitable performance metrics for this area of the Council's work

   – an annual review of the impact of the Council's actions and compliance with this policy

   – the creation of an annual action plan to address areas for improvement and enhancement.

Implementation

There is an Equality, Diversity and Inclusion Group (EDIG), chaired by the Council's chief executive officer, and consisting of nominees from within the Council and client groups. Its task is to liaise with relevant parties as necessary. The EDIG meets at least quarterly to review performance against the policy, progress against action plans and objectives, and consider any new compliance issues arising from changes in legislation, policy and organisational best practice.

Further, Metro-City Council has responsibility for ensuring that its positive action policy is reflected in all aspects of its work. It has to ensure, in particular, that:

- Performance is monitored in the authority.
- Action is taken to address areas of weakness or improvement.
- Each department is given responsibility for ensuring that the policy's objectives are properly reflected in operational plans and there is adequate monitoring of compliance against objectives and targets.

In particular departments have responsibility to ensure that:

- An annual impact assessment is undertaken.
- Action plans are appropriate and are delivered.
- All new and revised policies are assessed for their equality, diversity and social inclusion impact.

Tasks

1. Good governance is a precondition for consistent action to promote equality in all aspects of the local authority's work. Identify and discuss some of the governance issues for Metro-City Council arising from its diversity and equality agenda.

2. What are the implications for the Council regarding recruitment and selection of council officers in terms of its equality, diversity and social inclusion policy?

3. The Council's housing objectives include providing housing for local people that meets their needs, and ensuring all its customers and prospective customers can access the services and homes it provides. How is the equality and diversity policy likely to affect provision and delivery of these services?

4. The Council is committed to dealing promptly and effectively with all aspects of hate-related crime, harassment, whether racial or on other grounds, anti-social behaviour and domestic violence as it impacts on customers and communities as well as staff. Explain the consequences of this policy for (a) Council–staff relations and (b) Council–customer relations.

5. Identify some suitable performance metrics for the authority's response to its positive action policy.

EXPLORE FURTHER

EUROPEAN COMMISSION. (2009c) *Demography report 2008: meeting social needs in an ageing society.* Luxembourg: Office for Official Publications of the European Communities.

Examines on a European-wide basis the statistics of an ageing population and the policy implications of this social, demographic fact; covers issues such as the implications of an ageing population in Europe, the social and economic costs of this, and how the EU and national governments can address the issues involved.

GIDDENS, A. (2009) *Sociology.* 6th ed. Cambridge: Polity Press.

Provides a wide-ranging, up-to-date introduction to its field, with every area of study covered, including theoretical issues; is packed with student-friendly features such as boxes on thinking critically, using your sociological imagination, classic studies and global society.

KANDOLA, P. (2009) *Managing diversity.* 2nd ed. London: CIPD.

Argues that managing diversity is not just socially desirable but is a driver of competitiveness; provides a comprehensive set of tools showing how diversity can gain organisational acceptance and form part of the overall strategic framework supporting long-term business goals.

PARK, A., PHILLIPS, M. and THOMSON, K. (2010) *British social attitudes survey: 26th report.* London: Sage.

Is an annual survey which covers a wide range of public attitudes to current social, economic and political issues including in this volume religion, politics and voting, extended working and lone parents – published every year since 1983, the *British social attitudes report* examines what people in Britain think about today's issues and debates.

CHAPTER 9

The technological context

INTRODUCTION

Technology is the application of scientific knowledge to help humans produce goods and services more efficiently. It also makes work processes more effective and less labour-intensive. There are many types of technology, and advances in technology have generally accompanied major waves of economic change, wealth creation and social transformation. Toffler (1970, 1981) points out that in all societies the energy, production and distribution systems are interrelated parts of a 'techno-sphere', which takes specific forms at each stage of socio-economic development. Fossil fuels provided the energy for industrial societies, while new technology spawned, first, steam-driven and, later, electro-mechanically-driven machines. These were brought together into interconnected systems to create factories, mass production and Fordist, bureaucratic organisational structures.

Today's new technologies, which are energising post-industrial societies, are rooted in information and communication technologies (ICTs), which in their strictest sense are the science of collecting, storing, processing and transmitting information, that facilitate globalisation (Forester 1987, Standage 2005). ICTs are the result of a convergence of three separate technologies – electronics, computing and communications – and the invention of the silicon chip. Discoveries of the transistor (1947), integrated circuit (1957), planar process (1959) and microprocessor (1971) converged to constitute a new scientific paradigm, with ICTs now playing a central role in contemporary technological and economic change. This chapter largely examines ICTs. These are important technologies, because they have emerged as among the key technological developments over the past 30 years. They take a variety of forms including the World-Wide Web, intranets, interorganisational networks, computer-aided design, computer-aided manufacture, automated production systems, automated teller machines, biotechnology, telecommunications, robotics and many other systems (Frickel and Moore 2006).

LEARNING OUTCOMES

By the end of this chapter, readers should be able to understand, explain and critically evaluate:

- technological developments and their impacts on organisations and their stakeholders
- the evolution of a knowledge economy and its implications for organisations and the HR function
- some applications of evolving technologies
- debates about technological developments in relation to people, organisations and society.

In addition, readers should be able to:

- identify ways in which technological developments affect the HR function
- contribute to the formation of organisational responses to technological change in their own organisations
- understand how new technologies affect their own organisations.

DEVELOPMENTS IN TECHNOLOGY

Grübler (1998, p117) summarises the technological changes that have taken place in the world since the Industrial Revolution in the eighteenth century. For him, technological change is driven by a series of 'technology clusters'. A technology cluster is 'a set of interrelated technological and organizational innovations whose pervasive adoption drives a particular period of economic growth, productivity increases, industrialization, trade, and associated structural changes'. These clusters do not follow sequentially, one after another in a rigid temporal sequence. 'Various clusters coexist in any given period, although the relative importance of each keeps shifting.' In his view, elements of an emerging cluster develop initially within specialised applications or specific market niches. Eventually, they emerge as a new dominant technology, after an intensive period of experimentation and cumulative improvements. As the dominant technology structure expands, other technological innovations are developed through subsequent scientific discoveries, experimentation and small-scale applications.

Grübler (1998, p119) argues that there is no simple 'cause–effect relationship' between technological, institutional, organisational and global change. The appropriate model is one of co-evolutionary processes, 'rather than one of linear cause–effect relationship'. He identifies a series of technological, economic and organisational changes distinguishing particular technology clusters. These are:

- New products and markets emerge.
- Transportation infrastructures widen existing markets.
- New process technologies, forms of organisation, and systems of management make it possible to raise productivity.

- Macro-economic and social policies help distribute productivity gains.
- Rising incomes create a powerful demand-induced stimulus for output growth.
- Energy, transportation and communication infrastructures facilitate changes and adjustments in agriculture, industry and consumer markets.

Grübler goes on to identify four historical technological clusters and an emerging one, each with important implications for economic growth and development. He classifies the industrial and economic developments that have taken place since 1750 into five overlapping periods: (i) 1750–1820, (ii) 1800–1870, (iii) 1850–1940, (iv) 1920–c2000 and (v) post-1980. Some of these clusters are summarised in Figure 9.1. Each is characterised by dominant organisational styles and distinctive economic and social institutions. Between 1920 and c2000, for example, the dominant organisational style of the technological cluster was Fordism and Taylorism, multinational corporations (MNCs) and vertical integration of businesses. Post-1980, the dominant organisational style was just-in-time management, total quality control and horizontal integration between businesses. Between 1920 and c2000, economy and society were linked with the welfare state, Keynesian economic policies and open societies. Post-1980, economy and society were linked with economic deregulation, environmental regulation and networks of actors. The core countries experiencing technology clusters associated with the industrialisation of agriculture, mass production and mass consumption during 1920 and c2000 were the United States, Canada, Japan, Australia, New Zealand, the UK and West European countries.

Figure 9.1 Technology clusters by sector in the UK, 1750 to the present day

Sector	Technology clusters	Period
Agriculture	Agricultural innovations	1750–1820
	Mercantilist agriculture	1800–1879
	Industrialisation of agriculture	1850–1940
		Since 1920
Industry	Textiles	1750–1820
	Steam power	1800–1870
	Heavy engineering	1850–1940
	Mass production	1920–c2000
	Total quality	Since 1980
Services	Mass consumption	Since 1920

Adapted from Grübler (1998)

Post-1980, the core countries experiencing a total quality cluster are OECD members. ICTs have been central to this period, where the products of new IT industries are information processing devices or information processing itself. As Castells (2010) argues, a networked, deeply interdependent economy emerges that becomes increasingly able to apply its progress in technology, knowledge and management to technology, and management itself.

ACTIVITY 9.1

Compare and contrast Toffler's and Grübler's analyses of technological change.

INFORMATION AND COMMUNICATION TECHNOLOGIES

The scientific and industrial predecessors of ICTs were rooted in the years before 1940, and included the invention of the telephone by Bell in 1876, the radio by Marconi in 1898 and the vacuum tube by Forest in 1906. However, it was during the Second World War and its aftermath that major technological breakthroughs in electronics took place. The transistor, invented in 1947, made possible the fast processing of electrical impulses in a binary mode of interruption and amplification. This enabled the coding of logic and communication between machines. These processing devices were semi-conductors and were eventually developed into 'micro-chips', now made up of millions of transistors. The shift to silicon manufacture of semi-conductors achieved by Texas Instruments in 1954, and the invention of the planar process in 1959, opened up possibilities of integrating miniaturised components with precision manufacturing (Hall and Preston 1988).

By the early twenty-first century, ICTs comprised a set of converging technologies in microelectronics, computers, computing software, telecommunications, broadcasting and optoelectronics. In addition, they included developments in biotechnology, because genetic engineering is focused on decoding, manipulating and reprogramming information codes of living matter (see below). Around this nucleus of ICTs, a constellation of major breakthroughs took place in the last two decades of the twentieth century in advanced materials, energy sources, medical applications, manufacturing techniques and transportation technology. This process of technological transformation expands exponentially, because of its ability to create interfaces between diverse technological fields through a common digital language in which information is generated, stored, retrieved, processed and transmitted. In these ways, the advanced world has become 'digitalised' in the 'information age' (Negroponte 1995, Loos *et al* 2008).

Microelectronics

The decisive step in microelectronics was the invention of the integrated circuit by Kilby and Noyce in 1957. It triggered a technological explosion as prices of semi-conductors fell and production increased. Developments in new microelectronic technology accelerated in the 1960s, as manufacturing technology improved and computers, using faster and more powerful microelectronic devices, helped improve chip design. The average price of an integrated circuit fell from US$50 in 1962 to US$1 in 1971. However, according to Castells (2010), only in the 1970s did new information technologies diffuse widely, accelerating their synergistic development and converging into a new paradigm.

A major breakthrough in the diffusion of microelectronics took place in 1971, when Intel invented the microprocessor (ie a computer on a chip). Information processing power could now be installed everywhere. The race was on for an ever-greater integration capacity of circuits on a single chip, with the technology of design and manufacturing constantly exceeding the limits of integration previously thought to be physically possible, without abandoning the use of silicon material. Even today, technical evaluations still predict more years of silicon-based integrated circuits, although research in alternative materials has been stepped up. Combined with developments in 'parallel processing' using multiple microprocessors, the power of microelectronics is relentlessly increasing computing capacity. Greater miniaturisation, further specialisation and the decreasing price of increasingly powerful chips have made it possible to put them in every machine in everyday life. These include dishwashers, microwave ovens, motorcars, electronic tracking systems and many others. Speed, cheapness and reliability have become the hallmarks of new microelectronic technology.

Computing

Computers were created in 1946, when researchers at the University of Pennsylvania, under US army sponsorship, produced the first general purpose machine – the Electronic Numerical Integrator and Calculator. According to Forester (1987), this first electronic computer weighed 30 tons, was built on metal modules nine feet tall, and consisted of 70,000 resistors and 18,000 vacuum tubes. It occupied the area of a gymnasium and, when turned on, its electricity consumption was so high that Philadelphia's lighting dimmed.

In 1958, Sperry Rand produced a second-generation mainframe computer, followed immediately by International Business Machines (IBM) with its 7090 model. In 1964, IBM with its 360/370 mainframe machine came to dominate the computer industry, which was populated at this time by both 'new' and 'old' business machine companies. By the 1990s, most of these firms were ailing or had vanished from the market. In these 30 or so years, the computer industry had organised itself into a well-defined hierarchy of mainframes, minicomputers, terminals and supercomputers. Microelectronics changed all that, inducing a 'revolution within a revolution'. The advent of the microprocessor in 1971, with its capacity to put a computer on a chip, turned the electronics industry upside down. By 1982, Apple Computers had ushered in the age of diffusion of computer power with its microcomputer. IBM reacted by producing its own version of the 'personal computer' (PC) that soon became the generic name for all micro-computers. However, because IBM's PC was based on technology developed for IBM by other sources, it was vulnerable to cloning. This eventually doomed IBM's dominance in PCs but also spread use of IBM clones around the world. It also diffused a common standard in microcomputing, in spite of the superiority of Apple machines.

A fundamental condition for diffusing microcomputers was fulfilled by the development of new software adapted to their operation. In the 1970s, two young Harvard dropouts, Bill Gates and Paul Allen, created Microsoft, today's software giant. The creation of this business translated dominance in operating software into dominance in software for the exponentially growing microcomputer market as a whole.

Over the last 40 years, increasing chip power has resulted in a dramatic enhancement of microcomputing power, thus shrinking the function of large computers. Networked microprocessor-based systems, composed of smaller desktop machines (clients), served by more powerful, more dedicated machines (servers), have supplanted specialised information processing computers, such as traditional mainframe machines and supercomputers. Since the mid-1980s, microcomputers cannot be perceived in isolation. They perform in networks, with increasing mobility based on portable computers. This extraordinary versatility, and the capacity to add memory and processing capacity by sharing computer power in an electronic network, decisively shifted the computer age from this time onwards. It shifted from one based on networked, interactive computer power sharing. The whole technology has changed but so has its social and organisational interactions, with the cost of processing information falling dramatically. This networking capacity became possible because of major developments in computer technologies and telecommunications in the 1970s. The changes had been driven by new microelectronic devices and enhanced computer capacity, and were striking illustrations of synergistic relationships in the ICT revolution (Stalling 2004, Standage 2005).

Telecommunications

Telecommunications, in turn, have been revolutionised by the combination of 'node' technologies (such as electronic switches and routers) and new linkages or transmission technologies. By the mid-1970s, progress in integrated circuit technologies made the digital switch possible. This increased speed, power and flexibility also saved space, energy and labour. Major advances in optoelectronics such as fibre optics and laser transmission technology dramatically broadened the capacity of transmission lines, enabling the introduction of integrated broadband networks. This optoelectronics-based transmission capacity, together with advanced switching and routing architectures, provided the basis for the so-called information superhighway.

Different forms of using the radio spectrum, such as traditional broadcasting, satellite broadcasting, microwaves and digital cellular telephony, as well as coaxial cable and fibre optics, offer a diversity and versatility of transmission technologies. These are being applied to a range of uses, making possible ubiquitous communication between mobile users. Each development in a specific technology amplifies the effects of related ICTs. Thus mobile telephony, relying on computer power to route messages, also provides the basis for ubiquitous computing and real-time, interactive electronic communication.

ACTIVITY 9.2

Identify up to five applications of ICTs in your organisation and assess their impact on HR practice.

BIOTECHNOLOGY

The revolution in biomedical sciences can be traced to the discovery of the basic structure of life – the 'double helix' of deoxyribonucleic acid (DNA) – by Watson, Crick and Wilkinson in 1953. DNA is a nucleic acid found in all living cells which carries the organism's hereditary information. However, it was not until the early 1970s that gene splicing and related developments made possible the application of cumulative knowledge in this field. Gene cloning was discovered in 1973, the first mammalian gene was identified in 1975 and the first human gene was cloned in 1977. What followed was a rush to start up commercial firms to exploit these developments. These were driven by the possibilities opened up by the potential ability to engineer human life. Agro-business followed, with the decision to develop genetically modified foods. Yet scientific difficulties, technical problems and legal, social and ethical obstacles slowed down the so-called biotechnological revolution during the 1980s.

Since the 1990s, a new generation of scientist-entrepreneurs has revitalised biotechnology, focusing on genetic engineering and gene therapy. A major international collaborative programme, co-ordinated by James Watson, brought together some of the most advanced microbiological research teams to map the 'human genome' or the thousands of genes making up the 'alphabet' of the human species. This project was completed, ahead of time, in 2003. The Human Genome Project (HGP) was a 13-year project co-ordinated by the US Department of Energy and the National Institutes of Health (www.genome.gov). During the early years of the HGP, the Wellcome Trust (UK) became a major partner, with additional contributions from Japan, France, Germany, China and others. Although the HGP is completed, analyses of the data will continue for many years. The project goals are to:

- identify all the approximately 20,000–25,000 genes in human DNA

- determine the sequences of the three billion chemical base pairs that make up human DNA

- store this information in databases

- improve tools for data analysis

- transfer related technologies to the private sector

- address the ethical, legal, and social issues arising from the project.

This study has opened up possibilities of acting on such genes, and those identified in the future, thus enabling humankind to not only control some diseases but also identify biological dispositions and intervene in them, potentially altering genetic conditions. However, Lyon and Gorner (1995, p567) warn of the potential dangers of genetic engineering: 'Emotionally ... we are still apes, with all the behavioral baggage that the issue brings. Perhaps the ultimate form of gene therapy would be for our species to rise above its baser heritage and learn to apply its new knowledge wisely and benignly.'

Genetic engineering techniques now allow scientists to insert specific genes into plants or animals without having to go through the trial-and-error process of selective breeding. Genetic engineering is therefore extremely rapid compared to selective breeding. With genetic engineering, zoological and botanical species can be crossed very easily. A variety of techniques can be used to modify plants and animals through genetic engineering. For example, there is a widely used herbicide that kills any plant it touches. Genetically modified soybeans and other crop plants have been created that are not affected by it. By planting genetically modified seeds, farmers can control weeds by spraying this herbicide over their crops. The crop ignores the herbicide but weeds are eliminated. Genetically modified seeds like these reduce production costs and increase yields, so other things being equal food becomes less expensive. Other scientists have inserted genes that produce a natural insecticide into corn plants to eliminate damage from 'corn borers', and a variety of anti-fungal genes can be inserted too (Ratledge and Kristiansen 2001).

With scientists, regulators and philosophers debating the humanistic implications of genetic engineering, some researchers and entrepreneurs have tried to gain legal and financial control of the human genome. In 1994, however, Merck, the global pharmaceutical and chemical corporation, provided substantial funding to Washington University to make such data public, so that there would be no private control of this knowledge which might block development of products based on systematic understanding of the human genome. Since that time, with more open markets, expanded educational opportunities and greater research capabilities globally, the biotechnological revolution has accelerated, thus triggering an on-going debate about the blurred frontier between nature and human society (Gibbon and Novas 2008).

TRANSPORTATION

In the digital age, road transport, passenger transport (such as high-speed trains), sea and air transport provide one of the institutional underpinnings supporting economic and social changes taking place locally, regionally, nationally and globally. For example, real benefits accrue from using chips and computers in transport systems. This began with variations in classic information networks such as improving traffic flows by controlling city traffic lights, helping airport flight handling, organising railway signalling and taking pressure off the routine work of airline pilots and ships' officers.

The impetus to using computer technology in motor vehicles was to improve the efficiency of motor transport through control of ignition and fuel timing and throttle and gear selection. Motor vehicles used for both domestic and commercial purposes are now provided with wider dashboard information such as digital speedometers, clocks and radios, electronic control of air conditioning, calculations of distances on particular journeys and warnings about fuel consumption. Today, matters have gone further, with chip technology being used for navigating journeys by satellite, road charging by transport authorities and monitoring traffic density and flows. In public transport, computer-driven driverless trains have been introduced at some airports and parts of cities. In Germany, a computer-based system taking over the main line driver's function – observing signals, controlling speed and responding to radio instructions – was tested as early as the 1980s. That system, and others like it, had triple security procedures, with a third computer taking over if one of the others failed.

Dial-a-bus schemes have been tried, again in Germany, to give public transport the flexibility that people gain from using private taxis. These offer door-to-door services for disadvantaged people. With no fixed schedules and booking by phone-call or email, drivers are in radio contact with the computer control centre. This selects the best bus to go to each call, bills the customer for the journey provided and produces operational statistics for management to use. In more sophisticated cases, buses can be called from computer terminals at bus stops. These terminals give customers tickets, state the fares required, when the bus will arrive, how long the journey will be, where customers need to change for other services and details of that journey. In sea transport too, advanced computers provide navigation technology, safety protection during sailing and computerised operational and information systems.

Modern airbuses using ICT systems can 'fly-by-wire', with computers programmed to override the instructions of pilots. Silicon chip technology is used for controlling engines, flaps and slats. Each of the microchips controlling these movements has back-up technology. Both 'front-line' and 'reserve' chips have to agree. If they do not, they inform the plane's captain who can take manual action to override them. If flight crews order the computers to do something against the rules, computers are able to reject the order and inform the captain of the aircraft why. However, where the crew wants deliberately to try the unorthodox, in an emergency for example, the chips do as requested when the order is repeated. This automation goes still further in military aviation. Fast, low-flying aircraft carry computers responding to touch. With the lightest of touches by the pilot, they can act faster on split-second decisions than computers taking instructions from buttons or voice commands. Computer technology has even brought the 'pilotless' aircraft to reality in frightening fashion, with laser-guided missiles speeding at low level across the landscape, fitting their flight to the contours of the land and direction of their target (Hester and Harrison 2004).

ENERGY SUPPLY

Gas, electricity and oil remain the main sources of energy supply in the global economy but some use is made of solar power and wind power. Related developments include use of clean technologies and recovery, re-cycling and control systems for energy production. ICTs can be applied in a variety of ways in energy supply. At macro-level, using integrated computer technology to control the production of gas, electricity and oil supplies results in greater efficiency, lower costs and conservation of resources. At micro-level, computers used in offices and factories save greatly on power and its usage. For many years, computers have been used to run heating, lighting, air conditioning, burglar alarms and fire alarms within organisations. They can be programmed for a year in advance, with details about the days and hours when buildings are in use and what temperatures are required. They then 'learn' from the data provided to fine-tune the programming to deal with seasonal irregularities and unseasonable changes in weather conditions. Although these systems were very costly till microchips became cheaper, they are now cost-effective not only for large enterprises but also for smaller ones and household buildings, which can save unnecessary expenditure on heating bills.

Microelectronics is also a key to a new source of power: solar energy. The basic case for solar power is that the sun's energy is readily available, does not pollute the atmosphere and is relatively cheap to produce. Basically, the earth gets more energy from the sun in one hour than the world uses in a whole year. Indeed, on a bright summer day, the UK receives almost as much energy from the sun as does Africa. It is estimated that a solar array mounted on a south-facing roof in the UK produces around 700 kilowatt hours for every kilowatt of panels installed. The technology providing energy from the sun uses photovoltaic systems. This semi-conductor-based technology, similar to the microchip, converts light energy directly into electric current that can be either used immediately or stored for use later. Anything requiring electricity can potentially be powered by solar energy. The benefit of solar power is its reliability and low maintenance costs. Photovoltaic systems do not release carbon dioxide, sulphur dioxide or nitrous oxide, unlike conventional electricity generating systems (European Commission 2009b).

MEDICINE

The applications and potential applications of digital technology to medicine are immense. Indeed, ICTs are increasingly taking centre-stage in the provision of healthcare, in both hospitals and general practice in the UK and elsewhere. Selective examples are provided here. With ICTs making a massive move into medical practice, both in high-technology ('hi-tech') medicine and throughout the medical field generally, research in information technologies is taking place in areas such as medical imaging, tele-consultation, education and training. Medical images are produced in such number and richness of detail that they can only be analysed with the help of computers. Computers not only improve the quality of images but also help in reconstructing structures, detecting anomalies and measuring sources. In particular, computers help with appropriate visualisation to make the image contents understandable to clinicians. Three-dimensional images are used more and more. Mechanisms exist that highlight the relevant detail of images, whilst hiding other structures that are not relevant for a particular situation. The selection and composition of mathematical modelling depend on the medical goals of a particular analysis and can only be determined together with medical experts. With images needed to plan and control micro-invasive surgical procedures, it is necessary to design systems that support medical practitioners with appropriate visualisations throughout the whole process from image acquisition, diagnosis, treatment planning, and surgery to final control (Semmlow 2009).

As medical professionals become more specialised, diagnosis and treatment occur in co-operation between different specialists who may be geographically separated. They use computers to exchange their medical data in particular images. However, data transfer alone is not sufficient. They must also be able to communicate about their patients, talk freely about medical data and refer to that data during their discussions. Merging these two communication channels (verbal and data communication) is challenging and needs addressing before effective tele-consultations become the norm.

Another example of the application of ICTs to medicine is medical information systems. This applies IT to healthcare and provides tools that enable the sharing and use of information to deliver healthcare solutions and promote the health of people and patients generally. Medical information systems include using computers in medical consultations (as outlined above), email and the World-Wide Web, and more advanced technologies, such as texting reminders for patients and using remote, palm-held devices by healthcare professionals.

Other applications of medical information systems include:

- architectures for electronic medical records and other health information systems for scheduling or research

- decision-support systems

- messaging standards for exchange of information between healthcare information systems

- controlled medical vocabularies allowing standard, accurate information exchange

- using hand-held or portable devices to assist providers with data entry or retrieval and with medical decision-making

- expert systems enabling both medical practitioners and patients to access information on treatments and drug therapies.

E-health uses ICTs that provide interactions between medical information systems, public health and the private sector. E-health enables health services and information to be delivered and enhanced through the World-Wide Web and related technologies. Such systems can provide long-distance health service delivery, which has become even more viable with broadband web connections. Other requirements of this approach to medical care include the availability of expert advice and of adequate time to assess requests of this type (Latifi 2008).

Clearly, medical knowledge is increasing at an accelerating pace and medical practitioners have to keep up to date with new knowledge during their professional lives. To ensure quality of diagnosis and treatment, special emphasis on continuous education is needed. Computer-based techniques help with this task, by providing training on the job and assisting in the analysis of images and tele-consultations.

ROBOTICS

A robot is an automatic device that performs functions normally done by humans or machines. The first industrial modern robots were 'Unimates', developed in the late 1950s and early 1960s. Since then, industrial robots have increased in their capability and performance through controller and language development, improved mechanisms, sensing and drive systems. In the early to mid-1980s, the robotic industry grew very fast, due primarily to large investments in the car manufacturing industry in the United States. This quick leap into the 'factory of the future' subsequently failed, when the integration and economic viability of these efforts at robotisation were demonstrated as being neither cost-effective nor able to deliver quality outputs. More recently, robotics has been linked with ICTs, resulting in more reliable, cost-competitive and effective systems of automation (Castells 2010).

Basically, a robot consists of three elements: a mechanical device, sensors and systems. The mechanical device, such as a wheeled platform, arm or other instrument, is capable of interacting with its environment. Sensors on or around the device are able to sense the environment and give feedback to it. Systems process the sensory input in the device's current situation and instruct it to perform actions in response to it.

Robotic automation has many applications. It enables organisations to improve safety and quality, reduce costs, increase productivity and achieve good returns on investments. Integrated robotic systems are used in a variety of industries, including aerospace, agriculture, construction, consumer products, electronic and telecommunication products, fabricated metals, furniture, marine and shipping, and motorcar assembly. Robotic systems are used in a number of job activities, including arc welding, spot welding, gas metal arc welding, gas tungsten welding, gluing, grinding, material handling, machine tending, packaging, plasma cutting, part loading and unloading, plasma spraying, rooter cutting and thermal spraying (Craig 2005, Ghosal 2006).

In manufacturing, robotic development has focused on robotic arms that perform manufacturing processes. In the space industry, for example, robotics have been applied to making highly specialised 'planetary rovers.' Unlike in a highly automated manufacturing unit, a planetary rover operating on the dark side of the moon, without radio communications, might run into unexpected situations. At a minimum, a planetary rover needs some source of sensory input, some way of interpreting that input and a way of modifying its actions in response to a changing world. Further, the need to sense and adapt to a partially unknown environment requires 'artificial intelligence' by the robotic device (Jones 2008).

From military technology and space exploration to the healthcare sector and commerce, the advantages of using modern robots (incorporating electronic control, sensory systems and micro-controller systems) are so widely accepted that they are now part of people's collective experience and everyday lives. Using them relieves people from both danger and tedium.

- **Safety**: robotics have been developed to handle nuclear and radioactive chemicals for many different uses, including nuclear weapons, power plants, environmental clean-ups and processing certain drugs.

- **Unpleasantness**: robots perform many tasks that are very tedious and unpleasant but necessary, such as welding, lifting and cleaning work.

- **Repetition and precision**: assembly line work has been one of the mainstays of the robotics industry. Robots are used extensively in manufacturing and space exploration, where minimum maintenance requirements are emphasised.

In medicine, there are many applications where the precision of robots is better than that of a skilled surgeon. Precision is obviously critical in neuro-surgery but also in orthopaedics, when drilling out bone for hip replacements. The higher level of accuracy of robots can lead to a lower number of implants needing revision after a few years. Minimal-access surgery, often called keyhole surgery, requires the surgeon and other human operators to hold and manipulate a number of tools, as well as an endoscope for viewing the operation. The endoscope can be held and manipulated by a robot, able to move under the precise control of the surgeon. In all these surgical applications the robot is not replacing human operators but enhancing their abilities.

Medical robots are used during operations in hospitals. There are 'passive tool holders,' 'autonomous active robots,' 'synergistic systems' and 'master–slave' systems. Master–slave robotic systems are those in which the 'master manipulator' (often a kind of joystick) is controlled by the surgeon, while the 'slave manipulator' performs the operation on the patient. A computer interface provides the connection between 'master' and 'slave', enabling the surgeon to perform an operation at a distance and, more importantly, in an ergonomically better fashion.

The slave manipulator consists of a mechanism that follows the motions of the master manipulator and performs the operation with the help of surgical tools, while the surgeon gets visual feedback on a screen from a small camera in the operative area. This permits use of scaled motions so that large movements of the master result in accurate micro-motions, with small forces and without tremor, applied by the slave. In this way, soft tissues in the body can also be handled appropriately. Currently, master–slave systems are being clinically used mainly for minimally invasive 'closed' heart surgery (ie the robot performs the operation through small incisions in the body, as keyhole surgery). One manipulator arm normally carries a small camera, while two other arms carry interchangeable tools, such as scissors and grippers. One of the key problems is that the systems are large and very expensive. Furthermore, there is no sense of 'feel feedback' from the slave to the master (ie no so-called 'tactile feedback'). During the operation, the surgeon relies solely upon high-quality endoscopic vision for monitoring the process. New designs of microsurgical instruments enable new surgical procedures with better outcomes for patients. Safety demands are very important, because the systems need to work in a complex and changing environment, with no harm being done to patients (Bozovic 2008).

NANOTECHNOLOGY

Put simply, nanotechnology is engineering functional systems at molecular level. Other terms used in this field include 'molecular manufacturing' and 'molecular nanotechnology'. Nanotechnology describes those types of research where the characteristic dimensions involved are less than about 1,000 nanometres, where one nanometre is one millionth of a metre or the length of 10 hydrogen atoms; hence the term 'molecular'. All manufactured products are made from atoms and the properties of these products depend on how those atoms are arranged within them. For example, if the atoms in coal are re-arranged, diamonds are made. By today's standards, manufacturing methods are very crude at molecular level. For example, casting, grinding, milling and lithography move atoms around laboriously. In the future, it is claimed, nanotechnology will create new manufacturing systems. These will integrate the fundamental building blocks of nature easily, inexpensively and in most ways permitted by the laws of physics (Jackson 2007). However, these possible systems are not without their potential dangers. The Committee on Implications of Emerging Microtechnologies and Nanotechnologies of the US Air Force (2002, p1), for example, concluded that: 'from an applications perspective, microtechnologies and nanotechnologies offer a particularly powerful combination for future Air Force missions and thus deserve careful consideration.'

Using more advanced computer hardware in the next decade and beyond will facilitate the manufacture of entirely new generations of products that are cleaner, stronger, lighter and more precise than those existing today. Many improving trends in computer hardware capability have remained steady for the last 50 years. It is generally held that these trends are likely to continue for at least several more years. If this is the case, it will be necessary to develop a new manufacturing technology enabling inexpensive computer systems to be built, using 'mole' logical elements that are molecular in size and precision, interconnected in complex and highly idiosyncratic patterns. Nanotechnology will enable this to be done (Pradeep 2008). The aims of nanotechnology are to get essentially every atom in the right place, make almost any structure consistent with the laws of physics that can be specified in molecular detail, and have manufacturing costs not greatly exceeding the cost of the required raw materials and energy.

Nanotechnology has a range of possible applications. One area is energy, through more efficient use and ways of generating electricity. Nanotechnology could bring energy savings from more streamlined manufacturing and bring energy technologies such as fuel cells to the market. Cheap and efficient solar cells appear to be within reach too, using new types of material to replace the fragile, expensive, silicon-based wafers currently being used. Although nanotechnology is still in its infancy, in the next few years an increasing number of products and applications are likely to incorporate it in some way (Standage 2005).

ACTIVITY 9.3

Identify any *one* of the above technological developments and its implications for people, organisations and society.

ACTIVITY 9.4

What are some of the HR implications of these technological developments?

IMPACT OF TECHNOLOGY ON PEOPLE AT WORK

In the information age, work is plentiful and more complex, the occupational structure is changing and demand for labour is generally high. There are more jobs and a higher proportion of people of working age are employed in developed countries. People have been absorbed into the labour market, without major disruptions. The diffusion of ICTs, though displacing some workers and eliminating some jobs, has not, on balance, resulted in mass unemployment. Work becomes disaggregated in performance and fragmented in organisation. Those who work are diverse in their experience and divided in their collective action. Workers lose their collective identity, with work becoming increasingly individualised in its conditions, interests and projects. Owners, producers, managers and managed become increasingly blurred through systems of networking, outsourcing, subcontracting and teamworking.

Because of ICTs, the dominant model of labour in the information-based economy is that of a core labour force and a disposable one. The core labour force consists of information-based managers and by those described by Reich (1991) as 'symbiotic analysts' or collaborating professionals. The disposable labour force can be automated, hired, fired, outsourced or off-shored, depending on market demand and labour costs. Traditional forms of work based on full-time employment, clear occupational boundaries and a career pattern over a lifetime become eroded, and flexible modes of working increase. In general, firms are able to adopt a variety of strategies in managing labour, such as downsizing, subcontracting, employing temporary and flexible labour, automating or relocating some tasks and functions, and tightening labour control through more stringent working arrangements. Another feature of labour and labour markets in knowledge-driven economies is their changing employment structures. These main structural changes are shown in simplified form in Figure 9.2.

The changing occupational structure emerging in the information age, as outlined above, results in two main types of employment structures in information, knowledge-based economies:

- **The service economy model**: epitomised by the UK, the United States and

Figure 9.2 The changing employment structure in knowledge-based economies

Emerging sectors and occupations
A rise in business service and social services, especially health and social care
A rise in managerial, professional and technical jobs
A simultaneous increase of the upper and lower levels of the occupational structure
The relative upgrading of the occupational structure over time, with an increasing share of occupations needing higher skills and advanced education than those in lower-level occupational categories
A continued substantial share of employment in the retail sector
Increasing diversification of service activities as sources of jobs
The emergence of a 'white-collar' working class made up of clerical and sales staff

Declining sectors and occupations
Continued decline in agricultural employment
Steady decline in manufacturing employment

Canada. This is characterised by a rapid phasing-out of manufacturing employment after 1970, as the pace of informatisation has accelerated. Having witnessed the elimination of almost all agricultural employment, this model emphasises a new employment structure, where differentiation among service activities becomes the key element for analysing and structuring working arrangements. This model emphasises 'capital management' services over 'producer services' and keeps expanding the social service sector, largely because of dramatic rises in healthcare jobs. There is to a lesser extent an increase in educational employment. This model of the economy is characterised by expansion of managerial work, including a considerable number of middle managers. This model arose following the neo-liberal, non-interventionist economic policies of the Thatcher and Reagan administrations in the 1980s, when in the midst of world turmoil, the manufacturing and trade bases of the UK and American economies were radically changed.

- **An advanced manufacturing model**: epitomised by the German and Japanese economies. While reducing the share of manufacturing employment, it keeps it at a relatively high level. This allows for the restructuring of manufacturing activities drawing upon socio-technical systems. It reduces manufacturing jobs but reinforces manufacturing activity. Producer services are more important than financial services. Financial services remain important but the bulk of service growth is in services to companies and social services. In between these two models, France seems to be leaning towards a service economy but maintaining a strong manufacturing base.

In knowledge-based work especially, there are potential tensions between the competing loyalties or identities of teams, organisations, professions and clients.

Some problems can only be solved in interdisciplinary teams. Open-minded specialist professionals are needed to think about new computer-based approaches and applications to their work. Computer scientists, in turn, need to listen to the problems facing professional colleagues. Psychologists may well have to look at human-to-human and human-to-computer interactions. Engineers and administrators may be necessary to make things work in practice. Very often, a single profession can no longer deal with all aspects of the complex problems associated with knowledge-based work. New systems have to be designed iteratively, with users in mind, and they have to be addressed to real user problems. However, it is not possible to assess completely the value of a new development before it is taken into daily practice with users. Developers of systems need to be ready to change their systems radically, until these meet user needs. Users, in turn, must be involved in these processes and a constructive dialogue between users and developers, involving a sequence of prototypical systems, is needed to satisfy user needs.

Because of labour immobility and differences in language and culture, there is not a unified global labour force. However, there is global interdependence in the information economy, characterised by segmentation across borders, not between countries. Global interdependence operates, first, through global employment in MNCs and their associated cross-border networks and, second, through the effects of global competition and the impact of flexible employment practices. In each case, ICTs link different segments of the labour force across national boundaries.

There is also a dichotomy in the work process. Work is unified through complex global networks but there is differentiation of work, segmentation of workers and disaggregation of labour on a global scale. Capitalist production relationships still persist but capital and labour exist in different times and spaces as, for example, the instant time of computerised networks (capital) and the clock time of everyday work (labour). It would appear that the life of global capital depends less on specific labour and more on generic labour, driven by the demands of networked businesses. Working life goes on, with recruitment, promotions, training, negotiations, conflicts, dismissals and retirements. But the interests of capital are mobilised and insulated in flows of global capital. Labour, in contrast, loses its collective identity, which dissolves into infinite variations of employment and work. In the digital age, capital is co-ordinated globally; labour is individualised locally. Moreover, as Schiller (2000, p209) concludes: we may be confident 'that digital capitalism has strengthened, rather than banished, the age-old scourges of the market system: inequality and domination.'

ACTIVITY 9.5

In what ways are labour markets likely to be affected by technological developments in the next five years? Analyse how labour markets are likely to change within your own organisation over this period.

IMPACT OF TECHNOLOGY ON ORGANISATIONS

One main implication of ICTs for organisations is the centrality of knowledge creation and knowledge management within them. For Nonaka and Takeuchi (1995), the knowledge-creating firm is based on organisational interaction between explicit (open) knowledge and tacit (unspoken) knowledge as the source of innovation. They argue that knowledge accumulated in the firm comes out of experience and cannot be communicated by workers in formalised management procedures. Where innovation is critical to organisational success, organisational ability to increase sources of information from all forms of knowledge becomes the basis for innovation. This requires full participation of workers in the innovation process, so that they do not keep their tacit knowledge solely for their own benefit. Online communication and computerised storage capacity are powerful tools in developing the complexity of organisational links between tacit and explicit knowledge. What makes 'knowledge intensive firms' (KIFs) different is the nature and quality of their intellectual capital, work processes that create market value through knowledge, and deployment of knowledge involving innovation, initiative and competence building (Swart et al 2003).

Technologies, including ICTs, impact on organisations in a variety of complex, interrelated and sometimes disputed ways. The economic restructuring of the 1980s induced a number of reorganising strategies in both the private and public sectors in advanced market economies. There were some common features arising out of these changes:

- Whatever the causes and development of these organisational transformations, there was from the mid-1970s a major divide in the organisation of production and markets in the global economy.

- Organisational changes interacted with the diffusion of ICTs but changes were largely independent and generally preceded the diffusion of ICTs within firms.

- The fundamental goal of these organisational changes was to deal with the uncertainty caused by the fast pace of change in the economy, institutions and technology in firms. This was done by enhancing flexibility in production, management and marketing.

- Many organisational changes were aimed at redefining employment practices. These were done by 'lean-production' systems to save labour through automating jobs, eliminating certain tasks and de-layering management structures.

FLEXIBLE PRODUCTION

Coriat (1994) and others claim that the long-term evolution from Fordism (based on mass production and mass consumption) to post-Fordism (based on flexible specialisation and fragmented consumption) represents a historical transformation of relationships between production and productivity, on the one hand, and consumption and competition, on the other. The mass production model was based on productivity gains obtained from economies of scale. This involved assembly-line, mechanised production of standard products, sold in mass markets dominated by big businesses. These businesses were structured by vertical integration and had institutionalised social and technical divisions of labour. They used rationalist, scientific management methods for organising work and their workforces. However, as demand for goods (and services) became more unpredictable, technological change has made mass production systems too rigid and costly, resulting in flexible production methods.

One form is flexible specialisation, where production (or operations) accommodates to continuous change, without attempting to control it. Another is dynamic flexibility or high-volume flexible production. High-volume production systems combine high-volume production (permitting economies of scale) and customised, reprogrammable production systems (providing 'economies of scope') where a range of products reduces unit costs. New technologies, including robotics, automation and integrated computer networks, enable the transformation of assembly lines, characteristic of large corporations, into easily programmable production units sensitive to variations in the market (product flexibility) and changes of technological inputs (process flexibility).

NEW ORGANISATIONAL FORMS

Writers such as Piore and Sabel (1984) argue that the economic crisis of the 1970s resulted in the exhaustion of the mass production system, constituting a further stage in the development of industrial capitalism. For others, the diffusion of new organisational forms, some of which had been practised in certain countries and firms for many years, was a response to a crisis of profitability and capital accumulation in businesses (Harrison 1994). For Piore and Sabel (1984), there has been a relative decline of the large vertically integrated firm as an organisational model. To survive in the increasingly competitive, open marketplace, large organisations had to respond to growing demand in the developing world. To do this, they changed their organisational structures. ICTs, such as computer networks, email, teleworking and mobile telephony, enable large firms to both centralise and decentralise their structures, reorganise spans of control, and stretch their internal communication systems (Jackson and Van der Wielen 1998). The traditional corporate model of organisation, based on vertical integration and hierarchic, functional management, with its staff and line structure of technical and social division of labour, has become increasingly untenable for some businesses. The vertical disintegration of production is replaced by networks of external firms, which substitute for the vertical integration of departments within a corporate structure. These networks allow for greater differentiation of the labour and capital components of production units.

NEW METHODS OF MANAGEMENT

In facilitating new production and operations systems, technology has also impacted on organisations by facilitating new methods of management, some originating in Japan. These are assumed to result in productivity gains and competitive advantage. This new model of management – sometimes called 'Toyotism' (Wilkinson et al 1992) – has been widely imitated, partially or wholly, by corporations around the world, leading to substantially improved performance, compared with firms using more traditional production and management systems. The elements of this management model include:

- **Just-in-time management**: this is where inventories are eliminated or reduced substantially through delivery of supplies to the production site at exactly the required time, with the characteristics specified for the production line.

- **Total quality control**: this aims at near-zero defects of products on the production line and best use of resources facilitating this.

- **Employee involvement**: this enables workers to be involved in the work process, by using teamwork, decentralised workplace initiatives, greater autonomy on the shop floor, rewards for team performance, and a flat management hierarchy with few status symbols in the daily life of the firm.

THE ORGANISATION OF WORK

Another impact of technology on organisations has been in the ways in which work is organised. Since the 1990s, several factors have accelerated changes in work processes:

- Computer technology and its applications are cheaper, better and affordable.
- Global competition has triggered a technology/management race between MNCs.
- Organisations have evolved and adopted new shapes, generally based on flexibility and networking.
- Managers and consultants understand the potential of new technology and how to use it.
- The massive diffusion of ICTs causes similar effects in factories, offices and service organisations.
- The role of direct work has increased, because IT empowers direct workers on the shop floor. What disappears, through integral automation, are routine, repetitive tasks that can be pre-coded and programmed for execution by machines.
- IT enhances work that earlier required analysis, decision and reprogramming activities which only human brains could achieve.

Increasingly, the organisation of work is determined by the characteristics of the information production process. First, value added is mainly generated by innovation of process and products. Innovation is itself dependent upon research potential, applied to specific purposes in given organisational contexts. Second, executive tasks are more efficient when they are able to adapt higher-level instructions to their specific application and when they generate feedback. Most production activities take place in organisations, where ability to generate flexible strategic decision-making and capacity to achieve organisational integration between all elements of the production process are key features of the work process. Third, IT becomes critical in the organisation of work, because it largely determines innovation capacity and makes possible corrections of errors and generation of feedback effects at executive level. IT also provides the infrastructure for flexibility and adaptability throughout the managing of the production process and capacity to increase and centralise control and direction.

Tasks in the organisation of work create a new division of labour within organisations. In production and operations systems organised around IT, the following tasks are distinguished:

- **Senior managers:** strategic decision-making and planning are performed by senior managers.

- **Researchers:** innovation in products and process is performed by researchers.

- **Executives:** managing relationships between decision, innovation, design and execution is performed by executives.

- **Operators:** executing tasks under their own initiative is performed by operators.

- **Implementers:** executing ancillary, pre-programmed tasks that have not been automated is performed by implementers.

Technology has also impacted on political organisations and the political system. ICTs are transforming the structures and delivery systems of government, with one-stop shops and e-government. Governments have e-government policies, and all public organisations have websites and are accessible to the general public through the World-Wide Web and email. ICTs not only are radically changing the way that politicians interact with the public and vice versa but also have the potential to transform the system of representative democracy into direct democracy by using interactive television, referendums via electronic voting and transmission of text messages from politicians to the electorate (Nixon and Koutrakou 2007).

TELEWORKING

In the digital age, teleworking becomes an increasingly important way of structuring work. In the 1980s, Toffler (1981) suggested that the information age would enable work to be relocated out of offices and factories, where the Industrial Revolution had put them, back into the home. Widespread interest in teleworking started in the 1970s, when interest began to be shown by organisations, workers, transportation planners, communities and the telecommunications industry. Developments in ICTs make it easier and enable more occupations to be performed from locations other than the employer base. Apart from homeworking, there are 'telecommuting cottages', other work centres and mobile work, where the 'office' can be in the car or suitcase, creating a results-oriented, trust-based mode of work.

Baruch and Nicholson (1997) argue that four factors need to be considered before teleworking becomes feasible and effective: the job, organisation, home-to-work interface and the individual. In terms of the job, the nature of the work and fit of technology for the specific work role need to be examined. For the organisation, the way the business culture supports homeworking arrangements, including the willingness and ability of management to trust teleworkers, needs to be determined. In the home–work interface, this covers a diverse range of factors from the quality of family relations to the kind of physical space and facilities available to the worker. For the individual, it is necessary to determine the extent to which there is a fit between teleworking and the individual's personal attitudes, values, norms and needs. Most of the early writing on teleworking focused on its innovative and positive influence. Other views are more balanced and raise questions about the idea of a 'best way' or the suitability of teleworking to all types of work (Davenport and Pearlson 1998).

For individuals, the possible benefits of teleworking include less time spent on commuting, improved quality of working life and more time for family and non-working activities. The possible disadvantages include fewer opportunities for group affiliation and detachment from social interaction, less influence over people and events at work, and fewer career development possibilities. For organisations, the possible advantages of teleworking include higher productivity and work performance, savings on space and overheads, and less absenteeism. The possible disadvantages for organisations include less committed workers, how to control and monitor teleworkers' activities, and the need for alternative motivational mechanisms. The possible benefits of teleworking for national economies include less pollution, congestion and traffic accidents, support for local communities and more work opportunities for people. The possible disadvantages of teleworking for society include individuals becoming atomised and isolated from social institutions and the need to adapt the legal system (Jackson and Van der Wielen 1998).

ACTIVITY 9.6

Describe and evaluate the impact of technology on your organisation in the last 10 years. What has been the impact of technology on your personal lifestyle in the last 10 years?

ACTIVITY 9.7

Describe and evaluate the impact of technology on the culture of society in the last 10 years.

IMPACT OF TECHNOLOGY ON MARKETS

The major impact of technology, especially ICTs, on markets has been to open up new markets (see also Chapter 7). With deregulation from the 1980s, finance capital required great mobility and firms needed enhanced communication capabilities, linking valuable market segments of each country into a global network through ICTs. The earliest, most direct beneficiaries were high-technology firms and financial corporations. Indeed, the global integration of financial markets since the early 1980s, made possible by ICTs, has had a dramatic impact on the growing disassociation of capital flows from national economies. Chesnais (1994) measured movements of international capital in the 1980s and 1990s by calculating the percentage of cross-border operations in shares and other financial obligations over GDP. In 1980, this percentage was less than 10 per cent in any major country. But by the early 1990s, it varied between 72.2 per cent of GDP in Japan and 109.3 per cent in the United States and 122.2 per cent in France.

ICTs have extended the global reach of businesses and integrated certain markets, such as consumer durables and financial services. They have also maximised comparative advantages of location and finance capital. Since the 1990s, firms in electronics, telecommunications and financial services have increased their profitability, restoring the precondition for investment upon which market economies depend. Earlier, throughout the 1980s, there was massive technological investment in ICT infrastructures. This made possible the twin shifts towards the deregulation of markets and globalised capital markets. Around this core of new, dynamic, entrepreneurial firms, successive layers of industries, firms and workplaces were either integrated into the new market system or shifted out of it.

There are, however, limitations to globalised markets. There is not, nor is there likely to be, a fully integrated, open world market for goods, services, technology or labour. As long as nation states exist, or associations of nation states such as the EU develop, governments foster the interests of their citizens and firms within their own jurisdictions. Further, corporate ownership is not necessarily irrelevant to corporate behaviour. Carnoy et al (1993) show that American MNCs have followed the instructions of their governments, European MNCs have been the objects of systematic support by their own governments (as well as by the EU), and Japanese companies have been supported by their governments. In all these cases, the objectives have been to support the technologies, products or services, markets and labour forces of nationally owned firms. Nor is market penetration always reciprocal. While the North American and to a lesser extent the European economies are relatively open markets, economies in the eastern world, such as Japan and Korea, remain more protective.

However, the overall trend is towards increasing interpenetration of markets, particularly after the creation of the World Trade Organisation in 1995 and with the steady development of the European single market. Other indicators of market integration include the signing of the North American Free Trade Agreement in 1994, the intensification of economic exchanges within Asia, and the gradual incorporation of Eastern Europe and the Russian Federation into the global economy. There is also a growing role played by trade and foreign investment in economic growth, while the almost total integration of finance capital markets makes all economies globally interdependent.

Greater integration of markets leads to more competition for resources and customers. Four main processes appear to be instrumental in determining the forms and outcomes of this competition: technological capacity; access to a large, integrated affluent market; the differential between production costs and market prices; and the political capacity of national or supra-national institutions, as shown in Figure 9.3. Product markets may be increasingly global but labour markets remain predominantly local. As a rule, capital is mobile geographically, because digitalisation leads to the concentration and globalisation of capital; labour is immobile, largely for social and cultural reasons.

Figure 9.3 Critical influences on forms and outcomes of competition

Critical success factors	Critical influences
Technological capacity	• the science base in the production and management process • the strength of research and development (R&D) • the human resources necessary for technological innovation • adequate utilisation of new technologies and their diffusion into networks of economic activity
Access to large, integrated affluent markets	• the North American trading zone and EU • the best competitive position enables firms to operate unchallenged in these markets, whilst having access to other markets with few restrictions • the dynamics of trade and foreign investment between countries and regions affecting the performance of individual firms
The differential between production costs and market prices	• the differential between production costs and prices at the market of destination • the winning formula is the addition of technological and managerial excellence and having production costs lower than those of competitors
The political capacity of national/supra-national institutions	• the ability of political institutions to steer growth strategies of their countries or areas under their jurisdiction • creation of competitive advantage in the world market for firms serving the interests of populations in their territories by generating jobs and income • government markets for defence, ICTs and telecommunications • government subsidies for R&D and training in positioning firms in global competition • government support for technological development and HR training

Adapted from Reich 1991, Evans 1995, Weil 2009

RESISTANCE TO TECHNOLOGY

Life has always been organised around and in response to technology, which is central to human existence. But technology is not neutral and resistance to it is commonplace among those most affected by it. Sometimes resistance appears to be rational, when, for example, jobs are threatened by technological change. Sometimes resistance appears to be irrational to those with other interests, for example when groups who oppose technologies – birth control for example – do so not on scientific grounds but on ethical or religious ones. Resistance to technology may be by individuals or organised groups. Individual resistance is direct and immediate; collective resistance is indirect and planned. In either case, the objective is to prevent or obstruct the introduction or application of new technology to a particular system.

The Luddite machine breakers in early nineteenth century England provide a classic case study of resistance to technological change, although machine breaking has a long history in England that predates and post-dates the Luddite rebellion (Hobsbawn 1964). The Luddites, or machine breakers, were workers opposed to mechanisation of the woollen industry, where hand-spinning was being replaced by mechanised spinning jennies and by 'gig mills' for raising the nap of wool before shearing. The wool trade was crucial to the economy of eighteenth- and nineteenth-century England and the centres of the industry were the west of England and West Riding of Yorkshire. Lancashire was also involved in Luddite protests, as was Nottinghamshire's lace industry. The west of England trade used a 'putting out' or 'outworking' system of production; Yorkshire used a 'domestic system' where large numbers of masters undertook all work processes in their own homes with their families (Randall 1991).

Luddite campaigns against the new mechanisation varied. In Yorkshire, for example, the Luddites were violent, aiming their attacks at machinery as much as the masters. They sought to stop certain technological developments rather than gain advantage from them. It was not just a form of bargaining with the masters but war against the new machinery. In Nottinghamshire, Luddites focused their attacks on the machines that threatened quality of work, singling out individual masters who rejected traditional working methods. Their aim was to secure economic advantage, through bargaining by riot. Following these and other physical attacks on the masters and their machinery, a number of trials took place, over 90 rioters were executed and the revolts gradually suppressed (Hobsbawn and Rudé 1969).

Grint and Woolgar (1997, p37) argue that the Luddism presents alternative explanations of why social resistance to technology occurs, where the boundary between the social and technical is part of the problem to be investigated. In their analysis: 'The nature and characteristics of technical capacity, what the machine can and cannot do, what it is for, how it can be enrolled and controlled and so on are crucial matters for the sociologist.' Five interpretations of Luddism are summarised in Figure 9.4.

Luddite resistance to change – to the mechanising of work and putting it into factories – during the early nineteenth century only slowed the rate of change but did not prevent it. The new machinery was only one of a series of potential threats facing the Luddites and its potential impact was largely unknown. Geographical, temporal and gender differences all played significant parts in the fragmented, differentiated and diffused responses to mechanisation. The

Figure 9.4 Interpretations of Luddism

Classification	Main features
Rational technology: irrational Luddites	• Establishment perspective viewing the Luddites as either anarchists or ignorant of the machine technology • In both cases, Luddites were seen as irrational • No concern on the part of the establishment that the new machinery and its associated factory employment could be anything other than self-evidently beneficial for both masters and workers • For the establishment, the combination of laissez-faire and new technology would ensure the hegemony of British trade throughout the world
Rational technology: irrational capitalism	• This traditional anti-establishment perspective of Luddism, epitomised by Marxist analyses, interpreted Luddism as not so much as against machinery as against the power behind the machinery • The real conflict was the struggle of the various classes, some working in factories, some in their homes, to maintain their standards of living • To the machine breakers, the technology presented threats to their employment, customary working methods and the established social relations between masters and workers
The machine as metaphor	• This symbolic perspective suggests that the machine was merely a metaphor for a cultural revolution that the Luddites recognised as being inherently destructive of all that they held dear • The pre-industrial 'moral' economy was about to be destroyed by laissez-faire capitalism • This interpretation of Luddite resistance to technical change implied that the technology was insignificant in itself, except as a trigger to the process of uncertain change
The actor–network perspective	• This view of the new machinery views its arrival as tantamount to introducing a new set of actors into existing networks of masters and workers. The arrival of the new machinery presented a potential disruption to a relatively stable balance of power between them. With the social organisation of work well established in the woollen trades, organised around established social networks, the introduction of new actors into the production system presented potentially new power relationships in working arrangements
Machinery as a Trojan horse	• For entrepreneurs of the time, the new mechanised machinery, incorporated within factories, could be interpreted as a solution to the problems of labour recalcitrance facing them and a means of securing compliance of the working population to laissez-faire economics and a new form of society • For the authorities, mechanisation was a 'Trojan horse'. If the new working class could be coerced or persuaded to accept the new technology, this would enable difficult questions about moral responsibility for unemployment and poverty to be 'transferred' to the new machinery

Adapted from Grint and Woolgar (1997)

government suppressed the revolt of the machine breakers but the crucial part was played by entrepreneurial masters who were intent on forcing through technological change and, at the same time, breaking the resistance of the most strategically placed groups of hand workers. By taking on these groups, the new breed of masters forced the government into repressive and coercive action against them. The Luddites failed not because they misrecognised the machine but 'because the alliance of the forces arrayed against them was too great for their interpretation to prevail' (Grint and Woolgar 1997, p64).

More generally, one reason why people resist technological change is that it breaks the continuity of the working context, creating a climate of uncertainty and ambiguity. In these conditions, it is not uncommon for established structures to be redefined and modified. Some workers may try to maintain the *status quo* and resist such changes. According to Dawson (2003), resistance has been identified as resulting from one or more, or a combination, of the following: substantive change in jobs (changes in skill requirements), reduction in economic security or job displacement (threat to employment), and psychological threat (whether perceived or actual). Other factors include disruption of social arrangements (new working arrangements) and lower status.

In a case study reported by Dawson (2003, p82), a bakery company developed a strategy to meet changing market needs, only to experience unanticipated market conditions that threatened the viability of its operations. Heavy investment in technology to produce large quantities of standard loaves was met by an unforeseen shift in demand for different types of bread that was not determined solely by price. Demand for greater customer choice was reinforced by the purchasing policies of powerful supermarkets. These acted to limit the strategic options available to the company. Dawson shows that employee innovations were instrumental in making the technology work. They were both creative and accommodating in finding new ways of doing things that were able to circumvent the limitations imposed by the design and implementation of new technology. 'During the course of employee engagement in using the technology, elements of the technology previously viewed as hard technical or structural constraints gradually became open to change.' This case illustrated 'the temporal process of company transition and the complex interplay between politics, context and substance in the social shaping and use of technology'.

ACTIVITY 9.8

Describe a situation known to you where people resisted technological changes affecting their interests. How did they do this? Were they successful in their resistance? How did management respond to this resistance?

ACTIVITY 9.9

Prepare a brief for your senior management team explaining the factors preventing the faster growth of e-business globally. How do you think that these barriers might be overcome?

KNOWLEDGE AND LEARNING IN ORGANISATIONAL AND ECONOMIC LIFE

In the post-industrial world, knowledge creation and knowledge management become important functions within the firm. Aoki (1988, p16) says American firms emphasise efficiency through specialisation and job demarcation. Japanese firms, in contrast, emphasise 'the capability of workers' groups to cope with local emergencies autonomously', developed through learning by doing and sharing knowledge on the shop floor.

KNOWLEDGE MANAGEMENT

Knowledge is now recognised as an important resource and product of the information age. It is increasingly accepted that both explicit and implicit knowledge are major resources contributing to the competency of organisations, regions and countries. The central issues are how such knowledge can be discovered, applied and managed. Initially, ideas and theories linked IT and the potential of computers with storing, interpreting, creating and communicating knowledge. It has now moved beyond that by capturing knowledge and applying it through social and behavioural strategies. Knowledge plays a major role in creating competitive advantage for organisations and for countries in a global economy where R&D is heavily concentrated in certain locations and companies. Communication of knowledge in global networks is both the condition to keep up with the rapid advancement of knowledge and the obstacle to its proprietary control.

Information and knowledge have always been critical components of economic growth and the evolution of technology has largely determined the productive capacity of societies and living standards. The emergence of the current technological paradigm organised around powerful ICTs makes it possible for information itself to become the product of the production process. For countries and organisations, knowledge in the information age is the key to increased productivity and profitability, which in turn drive the search for new knowledge. Nelson (1994) argues that agendas for economic growth need to be built around the relationships between technical change, firm capabilities and national institutions. He does not view firms and nations as agents of economic growth. In his analysis, these parties do not seek technology for its own sake, nor productivity enhancement for bettering humankind; they behave in given historical contexts within the rules of an economic system that rewards or penalises their conduct. Firms in market societies are not motivated by productivity but by profit. Productivity and technology may be important means for achieving this but they are not the only ones. Political institutions, shaped by broader values and interests, are oriented towards maximising the competitiveness of their economies. By this analysis, profitability and competitiveness are the determinants of productivity growth and technological innovation.

At organisational level, knowledge management seeks to make the best use of the knowledge available to an organisation, thus creating 'new knowledge'. Knowledge management is particularly associated with KIFs. These are organisations within the knowledge economy employing highly skilled individuals who create market value through the application of knowledge to satisfy complex client demands. These firms may work on their own or in collaboration with others (Drucker 1993). An important characteristic of KIFs is that a high proportion of their employees are knowledge workers, compared with the number of support staff who are not. They want to work on interesting projects where they can make good use of their knowledge and skills, involving the latest technology where possible. As Swart et al (2003, pp69 and 72) comment: 'Consequently, importance is attached to the creation and development of knowledge at the individual level,' sometimes referred to as 'learning-by-doing.' Whilst it is important for KIFs to satisfy the needs of individual knowledge workers for interesting work, they must also facilitate transfer of knowledge between separate project teams. Further, as noted by Swart et al, successful KIFs 'were better able to convert human capital into intellectual capital because they had people management practices and processes that supported and enhanced this conversion process'.

Knowledge management is concerned with issues of organisational adaptation, survival and competence in the face of continuous external change. Knowledge management embodies organisational processes that synergise the data and information processing capacities of ICTs with the creative capacity of human beings. Data, information and knowledge are distinguished as follows:

- Data are items of information that are structured but have not been interpreted.

- Information is 'messages' between senders and receivers that can be saved on computers.

- Knowledge is information that has a use or purpose, to which intent has been attached.

Knowledge management is rooted in the use of technology and sees it as an issue of information storage and retrieval. It derives from systems analysis and management theory and is linked to the development of so-called 'knowledge technologies.' This branch of knowledge management develops sophisticated data analysis and retrieval systems, with little thought of how the information contained is developed or used. Its failure to provide any theoretical understanding of how organisations learn 'new things' and how they act on this information means that this knowledge is incapable of managing knowledge creation (Scarbrough 2008).

Few doubt that better knowledge management within firms leads to improved innovation and competitive advantage. Most agree on better utilisation of internal and external knowledge, but how to achieve this goal is debated. Some identify with a technology-driven approach, using state-of-the-art storage systems; others emphasise the soft side of knowledge management and the need to create a learning culture approach, so that knowledge management takes care of itself. It is possible however that effective utilisation of knowledge and learning requires both technology and culture to be synergised. Explicit information and data can be codified, written down and stored. Yet collecting basic data is not where competitive advantage is found. An organisation's real edge in the market is located in complex, context-sensitive knowledge which is difficult if not impossible to codify in binary form. This knowledge is found in individuals and groups, usually referred to as tacit knowledge.

ORGANISATIONAL LEARNING

Another branch of knowledge management is based on the belief that organisations are capable of learning and that there is a link between learning theory and management. Hierarchical models of organisational structure are replaced by more organic models. This is based on the view that organisations are capable of structural change in response to their external contexts. This branch of knowledge management gives priority to the way that people construct and use knowledge. It derives ideas from complex systems, making use of organic metaphors to describe 'knowledge growth'. It is closely related to organisational learning, which recognises that learning and doing are more important to organisational success than dissemination and imitation (Nonaka and Takeuchi 1995).

From an organisational perspective, the purpose of knowledge management is to capture an organisation's collective expertise and allocate it where it can achieve its greatest payoff. In line with thinking on the resource-based view of the firm, knowledge management suggests that sources of competitive advantage lie within the firm, its people and its knowledge. Knowledge management thus allows organisations to capture, apply and generate value from the creativity and expertise of their workforce (Mecklenberg et al 1999). Knowledge management strategies may be driven by a strategy of either codification or personalisation. In the former, knowledge is codified and stored in databases, where it can be used and accessed by anyone in an organisation. In the latter, knowledge is closely linked to the people developing it and is shared through person-to-person contacts. It is not the knowledge itself but how it is applied to business strategy that is the critical factor in competitiveness. Technology may be central to companies adopting a codification strategy but for those following a personalisation strategy, it has a supportive role (Hansen et al 1999).

Organisational learning is concerned with developing 'new' knowledge or insights into how to influence people's behaviour in organisations. As Harrison (2009) argues, organisational learning is not just the sum of individual or group learning across an organisation, it requires processes and systems that link individual and organisational learning together. For Argyris and Schon (1996), organisational learning takes place within wider institutional contexts and relationships and refers to an organisation's acquisition of understanding, know-how, techniques and practices by any means available. It requires strategic thinking at all levels. Organisational learning is typically characterised as a three-stage process: knowledge acquisition, dissemination and shared implementation. Such learning has been classified in a number of ways, with Argyris (2004), distinguishing between single-loop and double-loop learning.

- **Single-loop or adaptive learning**: is incremental learning that corrects deviations from the norm by making small changes and improvements without challenging underpinning assumptions, beliefs or decisions. Learning is defined in terms of targets and standards, is monitored and reviewed, and corrective action is taken to complete the loop.

- **Double-loop or generative learning**: involves challenging assumptions, beliefs, norms and decisions, rather than accepting them. Learning takes place through examining the causes of problems, so that a new learning loop is established. This penetrates deeper than the traditional learning loop. It occurs when the monitoring process initiates actions to meet new situations imposed by changing contexts. In this way, the organisation has learned something in the light of changed circumstances.

Methods of organisational learning vary. For example, event-triggered learning is undertaken in response to specific organisational stimuli. The most common of these follow or precede the introduction of new technology. Another model is the 'learning organisation', however rare it is in practice. This is based on continuous learning within organisations as an integral part of business strategy. The commitment to learning is normally formalised and related to learning needs analysis, career development and benchmarking. Emphasis is placed on creating a stimulating environment where self-directed learning and interaction among colleagues is encouraged. Within such businesses, learning is integral to the dominant culture. The consistent factor promoting the learning organisation is a strongly held commitment by senior managers to the long-run competitive payoffs of investing in people's learning so as to promote personal and organisational benefits. There also needs to be an explicit process for assessing learning needs arising out of succession planning for employers and the career development plans of employees (Argyris 1999, Pedler et al 1997).

Organisational learning, then, is about processes of individual and collective learning. Its outcomes contribute to the development of a firm's resource capabilities. For Pettigrew and Whipp (1991), the focus of organisational learning is developing organisational capabilities. This means paying attention to 'hidden' learning within organisations, acquired in the course of work by individuals and groups.

ACTIVITY 9.10

What do you understand by knowledge? How can knowledge be managed in organisations?

CONCLUSION: TECHNOLOGY, HR STRATEGY AND HR SOLUTIONS

Technology is continually developing in response to new needs, the latest discoveries and advancing applications of them in everyday life. The emergence of new technology means, first, that businesses can remain competitive, find fresh markets, improve the quality of production and select appropriate technologies conducive to these ends. Second, governments encourage the development and dissemination of responsible innovatory technologies for further uses, as well as adopting them for their own activities, monitoring them and regulating them. But, third, there is also the need of humans to have some control over their working and private lives. While technology saves lives and enables humans to increasingly control the natural world, it also poses potential threats to civil and personal liberties. Technology can never be accepted unreservedly, without asking relevant questions about its human consequences and ethical implications.

If the unplanned and unintended consequences of technological innovation become dominant, this creates new problems for society, organisations and individuals. The Doomsday scenario argues that humans apply technology to destructive and amoral ends, while the positive scenario is that humans have reason, choice and opportunity to take moral and just decisions about the use and application of technology. The future is always uncertain, and those with power to make decisions about technological innovation and its applications need to be discriminating and informed about which technologies are adopted and which are not. This is the contrast between technological determinism, on the one hand, and political choice on the other. The ethics of new technologies and how they are used are particularly relevant to HR professionals.

In the digital age, HR professionals are increasingly incorporating ICTs into their professional work, through the use of computers, software, email, the World-Wide Web, teleworking and other systems. First, certain HR practices seem to be important in managing knowledge workers. They are associated with developing client management skills to gain business and ensure that the relationship is maintained, with implications for selection and promotion criteria and for developing knowledge workers. There are also skills associated with collaborating and sharing information with partners in the network. As Swart *et al* (2003, p71) put it: 'sharing the explicit knowledge is not likely to be the problem as much as communication skills that allow the transfer of tacit knowledge.' Such HR practices would seem to be more effective when developed inductively, from the bottom up rather than from the top down.

A second use of ICTs is in recruiting staff. The World-Wide Web is now a common medium for advertising job vacancies, with the advantage of reaching a global audience for high-level jobs. Similarly, job applicants are using the World-Wide Web to submit their *curricula vitae* (CVs), thus potentially speeding up the application process. References can be requested and returned by email. A key advantage of using such electronic applications is that CVs can be coded in terms of candidates' competencies and stored electronically, so that they can be more easily searched, both for current job vacancies and future jobs (Batram 2000).

A third use of ICTs in HR work is computer-based learning, especially for jobs that are heavily dependent on technology. The shift towards self-managed learning offers the prospect of better-focused and greater personal and professional development. Computer firms and publishers are expanding the range of materials available for this and are offering learning and development facilities. Use of ICTs to support efficiency and effectiveness in science-based pedagogy and instruction-based learning is expanding. Computer-based training includes computer-assisted learning, language laboratories and computer-based role plays. With increased access to electronic data, and a new generation of computers for interacting with learners, opportunities for this are considerable. In an era when knowledge management and intellectual capital are increasingly important, these become the focus for reviewing organisational effectiveness. The structure, design and culture of organisations have to be built around managing knowledge. This suggests that cognition is more important than ever in working life. The implication is that possession and use of knowledge permeates all productive activity, at all levels in organisations, and developing human potential forms a greater part of ensuring organisational effectiveness than in the past. ICTs play a key role in doing this.

A fourth use of ICTs in HR is databases for HR information. ICTs are used in payroll systems, career development, succession planning, forecasting HR supply and demand, and monitoring productivity, efficiency and performance. In some cases, databases are developed to match staff competencies with those for specific jobs. The range of applications of computers in HR goes beyond these applications. These include monitoring equal opportunity policies, absence and labour turnover data, learning and development profiles, and staff appraisal. Clearly, ICTs are impressively flexible in applications to HR activities.

A fifth use of ICTs in HR activities is creating direct communication channels between managers and employees within organisations, in both the private and public sectors. These systems take various forms, including staff surveys using email distribution and response systems, organisational intranets providing briefings to staff, electronic information bulletins from managements to staff, and video-conferencing facilities for interactive communications between managers and staff. Managers using these processes claim that they deliver improved results, productivity and performance in their organisations. By developing and utilising the human capital of their organisations, and enlisting support for agreed organisational changes, managers can ensure that change is managed effectively.

1. Western societies have undergone a series of fundamental technological revolutions since the early sixteenth century. In the past 30 years, advanced market economies have been dealing with the consequences of the latest: the digital revolution. The information technology revolution is profound, continuous and rooted in ICTs. A networked global economy has emerged out of the informatics revolution, based on new technologies, computers, micro-electronics and telecommunications. These are changing the ways in which goods and services are produced and distributed, how people work and how organisations are managed. They are also changing how businesses, governments and people interact and communicate with one another.

2. Grübler's review of technological change in terms of 'technology clusters' is a useful analytical tool. He shows that elements of an emerging technology cluster develop initially within specialised applications or specific markets. These emerge later as a new dominant technology, after a period of experimentation and cumulative improvements. As the dominant technology structure expands, further technological developments are developed through subsequent scientific discoveries, innovation and applications. According to Grübler, between 1920 and c2000, the dominant technological cluster was linked with Fordism and Taylorism. Since 1980, it has been linked with just-in-time management, total quality control and horizontal integration between businesses. The economy and society, in turn, have been linked with economic deregulation, environmental regulation and networks of actors.

3. By the early twenty-first century, ICTs comprised a set of converging technologies in microelectronics, computers, computing software, telecommunications, broadcasting and optoelectronics. Around this nucleus of ICTs, a range of major breakthroughs took place in the last decades of the twentieth century in advanced materials, energy sources, medical applications, manufacturing techniques and transportation technology. The developed world has become digitalised and technological transformation has expanded exponentially. This has arisen from the ability of technology to create interfaces between diverse technological fields through a common digital language, where information is generated, stored, retrieved, processed and transmitted.

4. The applications of ICTs are wide ranging. They include inter-organisational, intra-organisational and interpersonal communications, through intranets, the World-Wide Web, email, telecommunications, satellites and ICT networks. ICTs are now widely used in biotechnology, transportation, energy supply, medicine, robotics, nanotechnology and other applications. Biotechnology, for example, promises better drugs, medical treatment tailored to individual needs and new agricultural processes. Robotic systems do tasks (within the household, for instance), which previously were done by human power, including scanning groceries, washing dishes and making bread. Nanotechnology promises to provide humans with greater control of matter at molecular level, as well as creating new materials.

5. Innovatory information technologies are significant because flexibility, teamwork, teleworking, networks, and distributed and virtual organisations point to new ways of working and organising work, based on new technologies. In the era of the 'automation of automation', or 'cybernation', the totality of an organisation's automated operations are electronically integrated and linked

together. In the past, technology transformed processes rather than produced goods or services. Today ICTs are not only transforming processes but also producing information as an output. Information has itself become a commodity.

6. In the digital age, capital is largely global and mobile, whereas labour tends to be local and relatively immobile. Demand for jobs is high but the structure of the workforce changes. The dominant model of labour management in the information-based economy is through a core labour force and a disposable one. The core labour force consists of information-based managers and collaborating professionals. The disposable labour force can be automated, hired, fired, outsourced or off-shored, depending on market demand and labour costs. Traditional forms of work based on full-time employment, clear occupational boundaries and a career pattern over a lifetime become eroded and flexible modes of working increase.

7. ICTs are pervasive. They are not confined to the economic sphere but they are also changing the social, cultural and political spheres of society at an accelerating rate, through a fundamental technological revolution. ICTs have enabled production systems to shift from mass production to flexible production. They have enabled large organisations to centralise and decentralise their structures, reorganise spans of control and stretch their internal communication systems. There have been changes in management methods, such as just-in-time management, total quality control and employee involvement. Many organisations have redefined employment practices, by introducing 'lean production systems' to save labour through automating jobs, eliminating certain tasks and de-layering management.

8. A major impact of ICTs has been to open up new markets for new products and new services in wider regional and geographical areas. ICTs have created ever-larger markets in geographic and regional terms. There are now fewer local product and consumer markets than previously, because transportation technology enables goods and services to be supplied to larger markets, covering wider areas. International trade in products, services and financial services grows and globalisation becomes embedded through ICTs and the knowledge economy.

9. Technological change is often resisted but resistance weakens following appropriate responses to it. From a managerial perspective, it is important to reflect critically on the need and reasons for change, taking account of the concerns of others in the change process. This is preferable to assuming – since resistance is often inevitable – that the reasons why people resist change should be ignored. To overcome resistance to technological change, a number of strategies have been identified. They range from participation, communication and support at one end of the spectrum to negotiation, manipulation and coercion at the other.

10. Knowledge creation, knowledge transfer and knowledge management are facilitated by ICTs. Where innovation is critical to organisational performance, the ability to increase information from all forms of knowledge becomes the basis for innovation and change. Knowledge is an important resource and product of the information age and becomes a major resource contributing to the competencies of people, organisations, regions and countries. Leading-edge organisations that use and manage knowledge tend to promote organisational learning as a source of competitive advantage. This aims to integrate the processes of individual and collective learning to contribute to a firm's resource capabilities.

REVIEW QUESTIONS

1. Technological determinism argues that technology evolves according to its own internally derived logic and needs, independent of the social environment and social culture. It holds that to use technology effectively and secure its benefits for society, its development and application must not be inhibited by considerations other than those of its developers – engineers and technologists. What are the cases for and against this argument?

2. Identify *three* developments in technology that have impacted significantly on organisations and society over the last 10 years. Evaluate their consequences for people, organisations and the political system.

3. Examine and review the impact that technology has had on patterns of work and the organisation of work over the last decade. What have been the implications for the HR function?

4. Explain and discuss why some people resist the introduction of new technology. What methods do they use to do this? How can resistance be surmounted?

5. How important are knowledge and knowledge management in the digital, global economy and why?

CASE STUDY

CASE STUDY 9.1 VANDERWALLER ET CIE: HIGH-TECH INNOVATION, GLOBAL REACH AND ORGANISATIONAL CHANGE

Background

Vanderwaller *et Cie* (VEC) is based in Brussels. It is a multinational, hi-tech pharmaceutical company with 20,000 employees globally, specialising in prescription drugs especially, where it has unique expertise and an established reputation. Building on its specialist strengths from research and development (R&D) through to sales and marketing, VEC's basic strategy is to try gaining competitive advantage at every stage of its business processes. As a global player in pharmaceuticals, the company is a technological front-runner in therapeutic areas such as infectious diseases, neuroscience, diabetes, metabolic diseases and oncology. The key to its strategic position is the firm's ability to discover, develop and market new drugs, using leading-edge technology and a skilled

workforce recruited internationally to do this. Because of competitive labour market pressures, however, VEC is not always able to retain the well-qualified people it employs. Nevertheless, as a result of recent mergers with other biotechnology and pharmaceutical companies, the company now has strengths in the three basic technologies needed to generate new drugs. These are antibody technology, chemical synthesis and fermentation.

The challenges facing major drug companies like VEC are both daunting and pressing. They include:

- the introduction of revolutionary new technologies such as genomics and antibodies

- fierce competition from generic drugs

- slowing growth in developed markets

- downward pressures on prices from governments
- the rising costs of R&D
- product markets that are becoming increasingly complex and diverse
- recruiting and retaining key staff, especially in R&D and product development.

Building technological innovation

Last fiscal year, VEC spent about 20 per cent of its revenues on R&D. The most visible symbol of the company's commitment to the discovery of new drugs is the Vanderwaller Research Observatory (VRO). The observatory is located in the Science and Technology Park in Leuven, about half an hour's train journey from Brussels. Opened only three years ago, the VRO is a centre of international research excellence in the field.

An interesting feature of the centre is the architecture of the building. This consciously exploits common areas and open walkways to funnel people together, so as to spark the cross-disciplinary insights that lead to innovation and new discoveries in pharmaceutical products. The design is based on the assumption that researchers can sometimes get too wrapped up in their own projects, with the result that they fail to interact and share ideas with other researchers in cognate fields. By engineering encounters and interactions among people, the layout of the Observatory promotes new technical and scientific discoveries which otherwise might have been missed.

In terms of technological innovation, the company's approach to diversity and global partnering is as important as cross-disciplinary thinking. This is why the VRO is linked into a global network of other research centres. These include well-established research institutes in Chicago, Santa Monica and New Haven in the United States. The Chicago research institute specialises in urology;

Santa Monica in antibody-based cancer therapies; and New Haven in chemical synthesis. Clinical development, run from a headquarters in Santa Clara, and with bases in Japan and the Netherlands, follows the same cross-border approach.

A platform for growth

Geographical spread of the sort outlined above is claimed to come easily to VEC. The company now generates almost 60 per cent of its revenues from outside its domestic and European markets, with the United States and Asia-Pacific accounting for 20 per cent each. The company's focus now is on growing its sales internationally.

The company is proud of its track record in establishing successful businesses in every territory it has moved into. In Europe, for example, VEC is the leading drug company in terms of both its geographical coverage and sales. Meanwhile in the United States, thanks to a number of unique and specialised pharmaceutical products, the firm has built up a strong business platform extending from primary care physicians to hospitals and specialists.

But for VEC, as for so many other firms today, it is in the emerging economies that the greatest promise of growth lies. VEC has bases in most developing countries and its recorded sales in China are expected to grow by some 20–30 per cent next fiscal year, making the company one of the top players in that market too. A powerful presence has been established in the Russian Federation and the firm is currently recruiting medical representatives for new sales offices in India and Brazil, so that operations there can get off to a smooth start.

A changing tomorrow

While developments in emerging economies are encouraging for VEC, the outlook in developed markets is less promising. A main reason is that important patents for an immune-suppressant drug to prevent organ rejection and an advanced treatment for benign prostate enlargement are coming to the end, with generic competitors also entering the market. So a three-pronged response is planned by the company:

- The company is maximising ongoing sales of its unique products that are under patent, by emphasising the differential strengths of its specialist products.

- It is creating new products tailored to local needs, especially ones it licenses from third parties.

- It is generating a range of 'new' products, including:

  – a new compound for bladder control

  – a bronchial asthma drug

  – a migraine drug

  – a pain-relieving product

  – new antibody treatments

  – a prostate cancer therapy.

VEC claims that ultimately its key perspective is always the patient. Its mission is to contribute to improving people's health globally, through providing innovative, reliable pharmaceutical products. Through its range of drug products, VEC aims to help patients fight their illnesses and recover to good health and personal well-being. Engaging in a process of continuous change, the company believes that it has to respond internally, at both individual and organisational levels, to ensure it remains competitive so as to satisfy customer needs.

Tasks

1. Why is it likely that VEC will find it difficult to recruit and retain key staff in R&D and product development? How might it respond to this?

2. Identify and discuss some of the issues arising from employing a global workforce in this company.

3. How important is the Vanderwaller Research Observatory in promoting technological innovation within the company and why? How might its performance be improved?

4. Explain how the company can respond to the challenge of engaging in continuous change at both individual and organisational levels to remain competitive.

5. What is likely to be the impact of a global economic recession on a company like VEC?

EXPLORE FURTHER

CASTELLS, M. (2010) *The rise of the network society*. 2nd ed. Oxford: Blackwell.

Provides an authoritative account of the economic and social dynamics of the new age of information; this book formulates a theory of the information society that takes account of the fundamental effects of information technology on the contemporary world.

GIBBON, S. and NOVAS, C. (eds) (2008) *Biosocialities, genetics and the social sciences: making biologies and identities*. Abingdon: Rutledge.

Examines how the genetic make-up of humankind has transformed ways of thinking about humans and the world they live in; this affects not only ways of thinking about health and disease but also ideas about what it is to be human. This text explores the social, cultural and economic transformations resulting from innovations in genomic knowledge and technology.

LAUDON, K. and J. (eds) (2010) *Management information systems: managing the digital firm*. 11th ed. Upper Saddle River, NJ: Pearson.

Demonstrates how knowledge of information systems is essential for creating competitive firms, managing global corporations and providing valued, useful products and services to their customers. A central theme in this text focuses on helping managers make better decisions about technology to achieve maximum value for the business.

SCARBROUGH, H. (2008) *The evolution of business knowledge*. Oxford: Oxford University Press.

Challenges much of the rhetoric about the role of knowledge in business; although top managers claim to welcome knowledge and learning as the source of their firms' competitive edge, the rich empirical studies presented in the book question this top-down perspective.

CHAPTER 10

Government policy and legal regulation

INTRODUCTION

Government policies are decisions taken by the political executive on taxation, public spending, the economy, health, education and other issues affecting citizens, families and organisations as taxpayers, consumers and public service users. Policy decisions derive out of party manifesto commitments, the government's agenda, the resources available to government and the circumstances of the time. When discussing government policy, it is customary to distinguish the institutional context and style of policy-making from its substantive content. The most notable institutional characteristic of government policy in the UK is its centralised nature. The UK has a parliamentary system, with a dominant executive and relatively weak regional and local government. This contrasts with federal systems in Germany and the United States, where power is shared between federal or national government and *Länder* and states respectively. *Länder* and states derive powers from written constitutions, with their own legislative spheres of influence and tax raising powers.

A key issue in public policy is how the interface between state and market is managed. This is the role of state regulation. At one level, regulation sets the rules within which market activity takes place in relation to, for example, competition, employment, health and safety, and the environment. At another, regulation is used to achieve policy objectives set by government. The alternative to regulated markets is 'free' markets, where there is little or no social and political control, as in mid-nineteenth century England. In previous centuries, economic life had been constrained by the need to maintain social cohesion and had been conducted in interconnected 'social markets', subject to many kinds of regulation and constraint. But the goal of leading politicians and some political theorists in mid-Victorian Britain was to demolish social markets and replace them with 'deregulated' ones.

Subsequently, recent governments, provoked by different aspects of the free market in action, have tried re-regulating some markets, so that their impact on other social institutions and human needs is tempered.

LEARNING OUTCOMES

By the end of the chapter, readers should be able to understand, explain and critically evaluate:

- objectives of government and the EU on economic, industrial and social policy
- critiques of government policy and rival opposition platforms
- the impacts of government and EU policy on organisations and HR strategies and practices
- the evolution of governmental and European regulation of business
- the objectives of regulation, including employment legislation
- debates about the desirability of regulation from an organisational perspective.

In addition, readers should be able to:

- advise on the impacts of government policy on organisations
- analyse the significance of regulation for sectors and organisations, especially in the field of employment
- contribute to debates about organisational responses to regulatory measures.

POLITICAL INSTITUTIONS, DEMOCRATIC INCREMENTALISM AND COMPARATIVE PARTY POLICIES

Public policies affect all businesses and organisations and are strongly influenced by their historical development. The dominant executive institutions in UK public policy are the Prime Minister's Office, Treasury, Cabinet Office and government departments. Parliament, more particularly the House of Commons, is the legislature and can veto or amend legislation, but the major role of the Commons is to support government policy. This is because of the party and electoral systems, which normally result in single party majorities. The House of Lords is largely a legislative debating chamber, although it can delay government legislation for a year. The select committees of both houses of Parliament perform a useful scrutiny role, especially the Public Accounts Committee of the House of Commons. The EU is also a major source of policy, which is binding on the UK, with many Directives being incorporated into UK law. The primary actors taking policy decisions include the prime minister, Chancellor of the Exchequer, treasury officials, cabinet ministers, spending department officials, some pressure groups, local government and EU officials.

The style and substance of how policy is made depends upon the policy area. Economic policy, for example, is generally less open than social policy. The major feature of policy-making for much of the post-war period was 'tripartism', where governments consulted the peak associations of business and labour, namely the Confederation of British Industry (CBI) and Trades Union Congress (TUC). Constellations or networks of interest groups surrounded each major area, including agriculture, education, health, defence and local government. Policy emerged from departments and was discussed in advisory and consultative committees. Politicians and senior civil servants tended to initiate policy, which was then presented and defended, sometimes modified and changed after consultation, but the approach was top down. In some areas, it appeared to be characterised by 'crisis management', as governments pursued 'stop–go' policies. Because of the post-war political consensus, however, policy was characterised by incremental change. Political change, in other words, operated, and continues to do so, by 'democratic incrementalism.' This is a process of cumulative change which, to a large extent, is path-dependent on what has happened historically.

The election of the Conservatives in 1979 was followed by a period of transformational change where the policy style was quite different. Policy emanated from politicians, their advisers and external think tanks. Senior civil servants were relied upon less as policy advisers and more as policy implementers. Tripartism was abandoned and the unions marginalised. Although policy networks continued to be consulted, it was on a much reduced scale, except in areas where government needed key stakeholder co-operation, as in the case of police services. Governments were able to push through their radical policies without much resistance, because of large majorities in the House of Commons and the built-in Conservative majority in the House of Lords. During the John Major administration, when the Conservative party was more divided, there were more constraints on government but most policies were accepted.

When the Labour party came to office under Tony Blair, who was prime minister from 1997 till 2007, winning general elections in 1997, 2001 and 2006, there was initially some attempt to return to a more pluralist approach to policy-making. But this was not consistent. Between 1997 and mid-2005, Labour governments generally had an easy time getting their policies accepted in Parliament. The prime minister was broadly supported by both the cabinet and parliamentary party in his administration's policy initiatives, enjoying an unusual degree of support on policy fundamentals. Although there were some problematic policy areas such as foreign affairs, social security cuts, 'top-up' fees in higher education, identity cards, and immigration and asylum seekers, support for government held up. One factor was acceptance of the primacy of economic policy, with the aim of controlling inflation so as to maintain economic growth and low unemployment. After the Iraqi war in 2003, however, the parliamentary party became more divided and support for the prime minister fell among both Labour supporters and the country at large. There were smaller majorities in the House of Commons in the 2006 election, and coalitions of Labour rebels in the House of Commons and cross-bench opposition in the Lords frustrated some policies but could not stop them.

Tony Blair retired from office in June 2007, partly because of growing public hostility to the aftermath of war in Iraq and partly because of falling approval ratings. Gordon Brown, then Chancellor of the Exchequer, became party leader and prime minister. The Brown administration held office from 2007 till 2010. During his premiership, sandwiched between the legacy of the Blair years and the prospect of a general election within three years of taking office, the Brown administration 'muddled through', largely in fire-fighting mode. As a result policy stagnated. In the aftermath of the Iraqi war, the banking crisis of 2007–08 and the fiscal challenges of 2009–10, because of economic recession the issue of public borrowing and public debt came to the forefront. Much policy was focused on responding to economic and financial issues. Combined with the so-called 'expenses scandal' involving many MPs and the economic recession, the Brown administration struggled on in office till May 2010, putting off the general election to the latest possible moment. The general election resulted in a hung parliament, and the Conservatives and Liberal Democrats formed the first Coalition government since the Second World War, with David Cameron as prime minister and Liberal leader Nick Clegg as deputy prime minister. Shortly after taking office, the Coalition published its detailed, compromise policy programme covering 31 policy areas from 'Banking' to 'Universities and further education'. It promised 'a strong progressive coalition inspired by the values of freedom, fairness and responsibility' so as to deliver 'radical, reforming government, a stronger society, a smaller state, and power and responsibility in the hands of every citizen' (*The Coalition* 2010, p7).

In the new post-Thatcher, neo-liberal consensus, all three major political parties – Labour, Conservatives and Liberal Democrats – are generally agreed about the ends of public policy. What divides them is the means to achieve these ends. Figure 10.1 provides some comparisons of the main policies of the three major political parties, drawing from their manifestos during the 2010 general election. Policy differences among the parties are now often more ones of emphasis rather than principle. In general, Labour favours investment in public services and partnership in their delivery. The Conservatives favour a more market-based approach and the Liberal Democrats a more devolved, community-led approach. There is, however, a cross-party consensus among the three major political parties that the UK should support the basic political principles summed up in Figure 10.2.

Figure 10.1 Indicative policies of the main political parties in the 2010 general election

Policy area	Liberal Democrats	Labour	Conservatives
The economy	• Break up banks • Introduce banking levy • Set pay cap for public service workers	• Secure the economic recovery • Halve the budget deficit by 2014 • Realise stakes in public banks • Build hi-tech economy • Support creation of 1m skilled jobs • Raise national minimum wage in line with average earnings	• Set one-year public pay freeze • Start state pension at 66 in 2016 • Stop tax credits of families with incomes over £50,000 per year • Cap public sector pensions above £50,000 • Cut ministerial pay and make a 10 per cent reduction in number of MPs
Health care	• Prioritise illness prevention • Give patient right to register with GP of choice • Cut Department of Health in half • Provide respite care for 1m carers • Prioritise dementia research • Improve access to mental health counselling • Reform payments to GPs	• Provide legally binding guarantees for cancer treatments • Establish preventative healthcare check-ups for over-40s • Create major expansion of diagnostic testing • Give right to choose GP, open in evenings and weekends	• Scrap 'political' targets in NHS • Put NHS performance data online • Improve cancer and stroke survival rates • Enable patients to rate hospitals and doctors • Give power to patients to choose any healthcare providers meeting NHS standards • Open up NHS to independent and voluntary providers • Link GP pay to quality of results
Education	• Cut class sizes • Scrap university tuition fees • Invest £2bn in schools • Axe national curriculum • Scale back tests for 11-year-olds • Bring A-levels and vocational qualifications together • Reform league tables • Improve teacher training • Increase energy efficiency in school buildings	• Expand free nursery places • Ensure every child in primary schools has the 'basics' • Give parents power to bring in new school leadership teams • Provide every young person with guaranteed education or training until 18 • Increase spending on free child care, schools and 16-19 learning	• Raise entry requirement for primary teacher training • Pay student loan repayments for maths and science graduates • Establish simple reading test at age 6 • Reform National Curriculum • Overhaul school tests and league tables • Allow schools to offer international examinations • Give extra funding for disadvantaged children

Policy area	Liberal Democrats	Labour	Conservatives
Taxation	• Raise threshold at which people pay tax to £10,000 • Restrict tax credits • Restore link between state pension and earnings • Introduce 'mansion tax' for properties over £2m • Give tax relief on pensions at basic rate only • Tax capital gains the same as income • Replace air passenger duty • Close loopholes unfairly benefiting the wealthy • Reform local taxation	• Provide new 'toddler' tax credit from 2012 • Remove stamp duty for first-time buyers on houses under £250,000 • Help parents to balance work–life choices • Restore link with state pension and earnings from 2012 • Help people build savings through new Personal Pensions Accounts	• Raise inheritance tax threshold to £1m • Raise stamp duty to £250,000 for first-time buyers • Cut employers' national insurance contributions for first 10 employees of new businesses • Place a floor under landfill tax until 2020
Europe	• Work with European states to create new jobs • Work for stricter international regulation of financial services • Campaign for EU budget reform • Push for co-ordinated EU asylum system • Promote transition to low-carbon Euro-economy • Boost investment in clean energy	• Strengthen the EU's emission reduction • Co-operate in Europe to tackle climate change • Lead the agenda for an outward-looking EU • Support enlargement of the EU • Support reform of EU budget	• Obtain full opt-out from the Charter of Fundamental Rights • Give greater protection against EU encroachment • Restore national control over social and employment legislation
Defence	• Cancel Euro-fighter • Hold strategic defence review • No like-for-like replacement for Trident • Give pay rise to lower ranks • Reduce number of MoD staff	• Conduct a strategic defence review • Reform defence procurement • Support European defence	• Double bonus for troops serving in Afghanistan • Ensure forces' families and veterans are cared for • Monitor veterans' mental health • Launch a strategic defence review • Maximise efficiency in MoD • Streamline procurement process

Policy area	Liberal Democrats	Labour	Conservatives
Environment	• Insulate all homes in 10 years • Set target for 40 per cent of electricity from renewable sources by 2020 • Invest in manufacturing offshore turbines • Invest in bus-scrappage scheme • Reject new generation of nuclear power stations	• Achieve 40 per cent low-carbon electricity by 2020 • Create 400,000 new 'green' jobs • Make greener living easier • Provide energy bill discounts for pensioners • Ban recyclable and biodegradable materials from landfill	• Work towards zero waste • Provide incentives to recycle • Encourage sustainable water management • Work for reform of Common Fisheries Policy • Offer every household a green deal • Expand offshore and marine power
Foreign affairs	• Increase UK's aid budget • Work with other countries to establish new sources of development funding • Support reform of global financial institutions • Support establishment of international arms sales treaty	• Co-operate with Europe in foreign policy • Put human rights and democracy at the heart of foreign policy	• Create a National Security Council • Commit to the transatlantic alliance • Deepen alliances beyond Europe and North America
Transport	• Cut rail fares • Switch traffic from road to local rail improvements • Cancel plans for third runway at Heathrow • Prepare for road pricing • Introduce rural fuel discount scheme	• Build high-speed north–south link • Improve commuter services • Complete east–west rail link • Target motorway widening • Do not support road pricing • Support third runway at Heathrow • Ensure 10,000 electric vehicle charging points by 2014	• Build high speed north–south rail links • Block moves for third runway at Heathrow • Improve UK's railways • Cut congestion, make roads safer • Make local transport greener
Business	• Cut red tape • Reform business rates • Overhaul competition powers	• Build a high-tech economy • Modernise UK's infrastructure	• Cut corporation tax • Simplify tax system • Start Local Enterprise Partnerships • Provide loans to entrepreneurs

Adapted from the manifestos of Liberal Democrats, Labour and the Conservatives (2010)

Figure 10.2   The basic principles of the UK's political system

Area	Basic principles
The economy	Should be privately owned, with government's role limited to ensuring fair competition and protecting consumers
Economic policy	Should have an underlying aim of keeping inflation low
Welfare provision	Should be limits on welfare and public service expenditure
Plural democracy	Should support organised pressure groups and legitimate political interest groups
Foreign policy	Should support the North Atlantic Treaty Organisation and US leadership in the 'world order'

ACTIVITY 10.1

What do you understand by the term 'democratic incrementalism'? What are its implications for business organisations?

ACTIVITY 10.2

Identify and discuss the main party policies that determined the outcome of the 2010 general election. What are some of the implication of these policies for your organisation under the present government?

ECONOMIC POLICY

A distinction is made in economic policy between macro-policy and micro-policy. Macro-policy is concerned with total or aggregate economic performance and includes monetary policy, covering interest rates, money supply, exchange rates and inflation, and fiscal policy covering taxation, government spending and borrowing. Micro-policy is concerned with the performance and behaviour of individual units within the economy such as firms, unions, regional and local government, and consumers. Clearly, the two areas are interrelated, since the way firms, unions and consumers behave influences the macro-economy, overall demand for goods and services, and the savings ratio. These micro-activities, in turn, inform macro-economic management by government. The main institutions and actors in UK economic policy are summarised in Figure 10.3.

Figure 10.3 Main institutions and actors in UK economic policy

Policy area	Institutions	Actors
Interest rates, money supply, exchange rates (monetary policy)	Bank of England Treasury International financial markets	Monetary Policy Committee Chancellor of the Exchequer Prime minister Treasury Investors Speculators Pressure groups
Taxation and public spending (fiscal policy)	Treasury Cabinet Departments Public Accounts Committee EU International financial markets	Prime minister Chancellor of the Exchequer Treasury officials Cabinet ministers Officials of spending departments MPs Local government Pressure groups EU officials Investors Speculators
Labour market, industrial, regional, competition, environmental policy (micro-policy)	Cabinet Departments EU Parliament Local authorities Pressure groups	Prime minister Cabinet Departmental officials EU officials MPs, local councillors Pressure groups

THE POST-WAR SETTLEMENT

British economic policy has been dominated historically by free market and free trade principles. Britain was a leader of free market thinking and principles during the nineteenth century and early twentieth century. In contrast to France, Germany, Japan and Russia, industrialisation in Britain took place with little direct intervention by government. By the third quarter of the nineteenth century, the British economy was the largest in the world, where private capital and free markets had been the driving forces behind the construction of the institutional infrastructure and development of manufacturing and extractive industries. Britain was also a champion of international free trade. By the early 1930s, the system of world free trade was breaking down, which was one of the effects of the First World War. This led to major ideological and policy shifts in the UK, involving the abandonment of free trade and support for government intervention in the economy and society.

The interventionist macro-economic reforms initiated by national governments in the 1930s included some nationalisation, public works to stimulate employment and low interest rates to encourage investment. These were extended by the Labour government of 1945–51 and supported by both Conservative and Labour governments during the so-called 'post-war settlement', sometimes called the 'social democratic consensus', from 1945 until 1979. Keynesian economic policies, which gave a central place to government action in smoothing out the economic cycle, underpinned the consensus. This consensus advocated government intervention in the economy to achieve economic stability, steady growth and in particular full employment. The consensus was an implicit agreement amongst all political parties, up till 1979, that the fundamental economic and social policies of the reforming post-war Labour governments should remain unchallenged (Crowley 2008).

Both Conservative and Labour governments adopted Keynesian economic policies, free health provision, improved social benefits and state ownership of major public utilities. Keynesianism was its bedrock and aimed at avoiding unemployment by drawing upon 'counter-cyclical' fiscal and monetary policies. This meant that public spending was raised and taxes cut during recessions, and public spending was cut and taxes were raised when the economy overheated. At other times, attempts were made to control prices and incomes (Brittan 1964, Budd 1978).

NEO-LIBERALISM

As outlined in Chapter 6, the end of the post-war economic boom in the early 1970s revealed limits within the bipartisan social democratic consensus. Chronic balance of payments crises, the abandonment of fixed exchange rates, rises in commodity prices, poor economic performance and low productivity in the UK were symptomatic of an under-performing economy. Under governments led by Margaret Thatcher and John Major between 1979 and 1997, support for free trade and free markets was reasserted, replacing the former consensus with a 'neo-liberal' one. Neo-liberalism incorporated ideas associated with the 'New Right' of the 1980s. This argued that market competition was the best means of guaranteeing economic growth and political freedoms. Substantive policies included privatising key public services, promoting free markets, supporting market deregulation and introducing supply-side economic policies (Gamble 1994).

The underlying assumption was that the economy was best left to 'run itself', with a minimum of government regulation. Regulation should be undertaken on financial grounds alone, thus favouring City interests, to reduce inflation. Public services were run on the 'market model', with efficiency incentives, and the welfare state was more selective in the ways it distributed benefits. Supply-side economics comprised a range of measures aimed at unleashing market forces, raising productivity and encouraging greater market competitiveness (Grant 2002). These measures are summarised in Figure 10.4.

Figure 10.4 Supply-side economic measures

Policy area	Policy objectives
Public spending	Cut back public spending to release more resources for the private sector
Taxation	Lower direct taxes to increase economic incentives
Trade unions	Weaken the bargaining power of trade unions
Unions and the Labour party	Challenge the political power of trade unions and their links with the Labour party
Flexible employment	Encourage flexibility of pay and working practices
State benefits	Reduce entitlement to certain welfare benefits
Enterprise	Encourage investment and enterprise
Competition	Promote competition through deregulation and privatisation
Capital movements	Remove barriers to the free movement of finance capital

FROM 'BLAIRISM' TO 'BROWNISM' TO THE COALITION

When the Labour party returned to power in 1997 as 'New' Labour, after 18 years in opposition, it retained much of the Conservative economic policy agenda, including a commitment not to raise direct taxes and to keep to projected public expenditure targets for its first two years in office. Commonly associated with 'Blairism,' with Gordon Brown at the Exchequer, there were three strands to 'New' Labour's economic policy. The first was a strategy for delivering economic stability and economic growth through fiscal probity and a strong financial system. The second was to remove barriers to economic growth by tackling supply-side barriers, including lack of skills and employability of the labour force. Third, both strategies were linked to improving public services, since sustainable growth would generate the revenues needed to increase expenditure on public services without raising income tax (Thomas 2001). The economic policy of New Labour evolved over the next 10 years, as outlined in Figure 10.5

Labour's initial policy commitment was to keep within the Conservative spending plans, not to raise direct taxes, to reduce public debt and only to increase public expenditure when prudent to do so. To increase public investment in public services without borrowing, New Labour used the Conservative device of Private Finance Initiatives. These introduced private investment in building schools, hospitals and other public infrastructure, which were then leased back to public agencies for a specified period of 30 to 40 years. Although this involved higher government spending, it was spread over a longer period of time and did not appear on public expenditure accounts. There are similarities between the Conservative and New Labour approaches to economic policy but there are

Figure 10.5 Labour's economic policy objectives, 1997–2010

Policy objective	Rationale
Low inflation	• Low inflation was the prime economic policy objective • The globalisation of finance meant most governments viewed low inflation as the basis for economic prosperity and growth
Fiscal discipline	• Labour was convinced they should spend responsibly and finance expenditure largely through taxation • Government borrowing was permitted but not to rise to more than 3 per cent of GDP; in periods of sustained growth it was less • Public spending was designated as 'investment in public services', with government borrowing being limited to supporting public investment spending • After 2007–08, government borrowing escalated, rising to about 11 per cent of GDP; this was due to the banking crisis, credit crunch and economic recession
Low direct taxation	• Labour argued that high income taxes were disincentives to work and undermined economic efficiency • Indirect taxes provided consumers with the choice to save or spend
Market provision of goods and services rather than state provision	• All political parties, not just Labour, accepted the advantages of privatisation • Labour wanted more regulation of companies previously in public ownership but not to re-nationalise them
Supporting free trade	• Labour supported open international markets, with free and open competition at home and abroad • Labour saw only a minimal role for the state in protecting UK industry or firms

Adapted from Budge *et al* (2007)

also differences. There was a major recasting of public expenditure, and implicit in Labour's comprehensive spending reviews was an element of Keynesian counter-cyclical thinking. New Labour's economic policy can best be described as 'eclectic', with blends of monetarism, macro-economic pragmatism and Keynesian activism. Furthermore, their supply-side approach involved spending on training and removing the skills bottleneck, as well as introducing more regulation of the privatised public services to encourage investment and control price increases which had a big impact on the rest of industry.

In summary, Labour's post-1997 economic policy was effectively driven by the need to increase the size of the national economic cake, so that employment, standards of living and tax revenues would rise. Increased purchasing power would stimulate industry, which would also benefit from low inflation, low interest rates and money supply in line with GNP. Government's policies appeared to be initially successful, as after two terms in office inflation rates were the lowest for 40 years and the lowest in the EU; growth was consistent at between 2 and 3 per cent per annum and the highest in the EU. This supported business and promoted employment, recruitment and training.

However, following Gordon Brown's shift from the chancellorship to prime minister (and the marginalising of Labour's Blairite parliamentary supporters), the banking crisis of 2007–08 and large increases in public borrowing to deal with bank recapitalisation and offset economic recession in 2008–09, there was increasing criticism of Labour's economic record by its political opponents and pro-market economists. A *Financial Times* (2010, p20) editorial after the Chancellor of the Exchequer's pre-election budget in 2010 summed this up, when it stated: 'Mr Darling has a good story to tell on state activity through the crisis and the downturn ... government is entitled to claim credit for having generally been on the right side of the argument ... But the state of public finances is dire.'

For the Coalition, reducing the government's structural budget deficit was the prime economic policy objective, while continuing to ensure economic recovery. The Coalition stated that it would significantly accelerate the reduction of the structural deficit over the course of a parliament, with the main burden of deficit reduction being borne by reduced spending rather than by increased taxes. At the same time, it said that it would introduce arrangements that would protect those on low incomes from the effects of public sector pay constraint and other spending constraints, as well as protecting jobs by 'stopping the proposed jobs tax.' It planned to set out its deficit reduction in an emergency budget, as well as creating an independent Office for Budget Responsibility to make new forecasts of growth and borrowing for this emergency budget. Finally, it proposed holding a full spending review, following a fully consultative process involving all tiers of government and the private sector (Coalition 2010, p15).

ACTIVITY 10.3

Identify and explain how recent government economic policies have affected your organisation.

SOCIAL, EDUCATION AND TRAINING POLICY

Social policy relates to personal welfare, covering healthcare, income maintenance, housing and education. Government's role is providing public services and state benefits to individuals and households, not through the market. In many modern economies, such as the United States, most state benefits are provided selectively. The criteria normally used to determine eligibility include income, wealth, age and disability. In some countries, state benefits are provided universally, as in the case of the NHS in the UK, although elements of selectivity and 'co-payment' have been introduced. All social groups are eligible for such benefits on the basis of personal need. In this section, the NHS, income maintenance, social housing, and education are outlined (Powell 2008). Partly funded by National Insurance payments from employers and employees, social policy provisions are of course a direct employment cost for employers.

THE WELFARE STATE AND PUBLIC SERVICE REFORM

A 'welfare state' takes responsibility for providing at least minimum levels of economic and social security for all its citizens. These include healthcare, social housing, sickness and unemployment benefits, education and pensions, and state organisations employ large numbers of people. The reforming Labour governments of 1945–51 created the UK welfare state, although the Liberals had established a rudimentary unemployment insurance scheme and a low state pension in 1908. The modern welfare state was the product of the inter-war depression of the 1930s and the Second World War, which had shown how high levels of government spending could eliminate mass unemployment and address large-scale poverty. Its intellectual basis was rooted in Keynesian economics (Keynes 1936) and Beveridge's report on full employment and social welfare (Cutler et al 1986).

Beveridge argued that the new tools of economic management would enable mass unemployment to be eliminated and 'full employment in a free society' to become the norm, with government providing a system of social protection for those unable to work or provide for themselves. Based on the principle of universalism, a comprehensive welfare state would ensure that everybody was secure – 'from the cradle to the grave' – from the five great 'evils' of 'want', 'ignorance', 'disease', 'squalor' and 'idleness'. The social benefits included healthcare and education 'free at the point of use', subsidised public housing and flat-rate social security benefits, including a state pension. The new welfare system was in place by 1950.

By the 1970s, welfare spending had grown and become the largest item in the national budget. Right-wing commentators were arguing that unless public spending was reduced, the system would be unsustainable (Bacon and Eltis 1976). With the election to office of neo-liberal Conservative administrations during the 1980s and 1990s, ministers began rolling back the frontiers of the welfare state, although public support for welfare spending especially on healthcare and education remained high. Reforms saw the transfer of some services from the public to the private or voluntary sectors, or to private businesses delivering public services under contract.

With the return to office of Labour in 1997, 'modernisation' of what are now referred to as 'public services' rather than 'the welfare state' continued unremittingly, with successive waves of public management reforms (Farnham et al 2005). Some services are now selective, targeted and subject to 'co-payment'. This means that they are paid for mainly by taxes but involve 'top-up' payments by users when they receive the service, as in the case of dental and prescription charges. Government also encourages people to take responsibility for their own needs through private health insurance, pensions and hospitals.

ACTIVITY 10.4

What have been the objectives of public management reform or modernisation of the welfare state in the UK? Discuss some of their impacts on HRM strategies, procedures and practices.

THE NATIONAL HEALTH SERVICE

When the NHS was created in 1948, its administrative structure was a compromise between existing and new institutions. Its fundamental principle was that comprehensive healthcare should be provided to patients 'free at the point of use'. General practitioners (GPs) worked as independent contractors, hospitals were run by the central government and local authorities ran the remaining mental health and community health services. Structural changes were introduced in the 1970s, 1980s and 1990s. Supporters of reforms claimed had resulted in large increases in the number of managers employed while some improvements in performance took place, whilst critics argued that reform the quantity and quality of healthcare had not improved. During the 1990s, the rationing element in NHS provision was made more explicit, with some politicians and members of the public believing the internal market to be a backdoor to privatisation (Allsop 1995).

Reform did not cease with the Conservatives. After coming to power in 1997, the Labour government published a white paper *The new NHS: modern, dependable* (Ministry of Health 1997) identifying three themes for further reform: partially abolishing the internal market and replacing it with integrated care, mandating GPs to form primary care trusts (PCTs), and improving clinical care. Labour's reforms went in the same direction as those of the Conservatives, with large PCTs setting up long-term service agreements with NHS trusts. The reforms were ambitious, but incorporated within them were plans to increase spending on the NHS to reach European average expenditure on health and retain the principle of 'free healthcare' at the point of use. As North (2001, p138) comments: 'this is certainly a "rolling forward" rather than a "rolling back" of the state, but it is an engagement which is predicated on the citizen's involvement'.

Reform continues and new regulatory bodies have been set up to monitor improvements, such as the National Institute for Clinical Excellence to ensure cost-effective drugs and medical practices. Increasingly tight targets have been set for all health trusts. The Department of Health sets these and rewards or punishes trusts depending on their performance. There have been improvements in waiting times, patients have more choice and there have been significant changes in the contracts and roles of medical practitioners. However, there are clearly perverse effects and ever-closer links between public and private sectors.

INCOME MAINTENANCE

Following the Beveridge report and election of the reforming Labour government of 1945–51, a basic income-maintenance system was established within the UK. This comprised a flat-rate state pension, National Assistance payments for those past school-leaving age not in receipt of 'unemployment' benefit, and a flat-rate family allowance paid for second and subsequent children. These universal benefits were relatively modest, compared with those in mainland Europe and the Nordic states.

In 1998, the New Labour government stressed the need to help the poor and remove their dependency on state benefits. Subsequent Labour policy emphasised the need to 'empower' the poor and remove benefit dependency. A series of 'new deals' were introduced. The government also provided a minimum-income guarantee for working families with children, with tax credits and income tax reductions. This 'new deal', 'welfare-to-work strategy' or 'workfare' system, obliging parents to work rather than to depend on state benefits, was a sea change from the universalist welfare policies of the 1960s and 1970s.

The flat-rate element in the family allowance (now called child benefit) remains, although family allowances became taxable in 1968. The allowance was paid for all children in 1975, with one-parent families receiving a higher level of benefit. As a result of the changes outlined above, and a buoyant economy, expenditure on public income maintenance schemes levelled off during the late 1990s and early 2000s.

SOCIAL HOUSING

It was the Labour government that provided a new system of housing subsidies through local authorities at the end of the Second World War. Most new housing at this time was to be provided by local councils, and so was called 'council housing', with the private sector being relegated to a secondary status. As housing was in short supply, waiting lists were created, where family size, income and job status were the determining criteria for allocating the public housing stock. Generally, Labour governments supported local authority public housing and the Conservatives the private sector. But council house building decreased from the mid-1970s and the Conservatives applied a system of means tests from 1972, whereby rent rebates were given to needy tenants in both the public and private sectors (Lund 1996).

The Thatcher administrations from 1979 to 1990 were fundamentally opposed to council housing and a series of housing reforms took place. As a result, it is housing associations (supported by housing benefits) that largely provide 'social housing' in the early twenty-first century.

- Tenants were given a 'right to buy' their council houses in 1980.
- The government provided further incentives for council house sales in the late 1980s.
- The Conservatives attempted to increase the role of private landlords in housing provision.

- Many local authorities transferred their housing stock to housing associations.
- Local authorities were limited to building mainly sheltered accommodation and prevented from using the funds accumulated from the sale of their housing stock.

ACTIVITY 10.5.

Why is there continued high support for public provision of healthcare in the UK?

ACTIVITY 10.6

About two-thirds of housing is now owner-occupied, whereas 40 years ago most people rented their housing. To what extent has public policy produced this change in housing arrangements? Are there any implications for employers?

EDUCATION AND TRAINING POLICY

In post-war Britain, developing an effective and socially just education policy was a major concern of the Labour party. From the 1940s until the 1970s, Labour policy was aimed at facilitating social and occupational mobility in a meritocratic society. For Labour reformers, education was the means of promoting individual merit and promoting greater social equality. Educational opportunity would enable people with intelligence and personal application to develop into 'tomorrow's leaders' and promote a 'meritocracy' (Young 1958). The Education Act 1944 provided the basis for the new meritocracy, followed by the extension of university and higher education opportunities in the 1960s and 1990s.

A generation-and-a-half after the 1944 Act, education was central to the 'New Labour project' and was seen as pivotal to reform in a number of key economic and social policy areas. Underpinning New Labour policies were the beliefs that education enables individuals to obtain employment and stable incomes in a competitive global market. For Labour, education was crucial to overcoming the low-skill equilibrium of the UK economy – low productivity and supply-side constraints to sustained growth. Education had become, in short, a vehicle less for individual advancement and personal growth than for satisfying national and employer needs in a flexible labour market. Education and training policy were inextricably linked throughout the education system, including higher education and promotion of the knowledge economy.

In Labour's view, the key to securing efficiency and fairness at work were employability and flexibility. Employability meant ensuring that people were well prepared, trained and supported, both initially as they entered the labour market and throughout their working lives. Flexibility meant business was able to adapt quickly to changing market demand, competition and technology. For Labour, flexibility promoted employment and prosperity, by enabling business success (Board of Trade 1998). Underpinning the policy on employability was the idea that government needed to provide more assistance to the economically inactive, such as disability claimants, to find work. In return, they would be expected to take up the opportunities provided for them, with the implication that benefits would be withdrawn from those failing to co-operate with the policy.

Primary and secondary education

Under the reforming 1944 Act, central government assumed responsibility for universal free primary and compulsory secondary education up to the age of 15, raised to 16 in 1972. It was to be a national system, administered locally by local education authorities (LEAs). The task was a difficult one, largely because in the UK, unlike in other countries such as the United States and France, the private rather than the public sector had traditionally provided elite education, especially at secondary level. The Conservatives were always strongly supportive of private education and this has been a distinguishing feature of their policy on education from that of the Labour party. The 1944 Act was the defining piece of legislation in that policy dichotomy, since the Labour government could have abolished private schools or incorporated them into that new settlement but did neither. With rising household incomes and parental dissatisfaction with state secondary education in the intervening years, parents in the professional classes were increasingly able and willing to send their children to private schools during the 1990s and 2000s. This was to optimise their children's chances of gaining entry to elite universities and higher-paid jobs in the labour market.

The Conservatives had introduced a national curriculum in the 1980s and appointed the Office of Educational Standards to monitor standards of performance and produce league tables. Once again, it was thought that this would encourage competition between schools and raise their levels of performance and efficiency. These policies have not been abandoned but reinforced under Labour, with schools having to conform to central performance indicators and central financial directives. The national curriculum is being continually revised but still requires pupils to study English, mathematics, science and IT, along with foundation subjects. League tables on examination performance are widely published at both primary and secondary levels and classroom teachers are formally assessed and graded.

The School Standards and Framework Act 1998 created education action zones, consisting of two or three secondary schools together with feeder primary schools. Action forums of parents and representatives from business and LEAs were given the job of raising standards. However, selective schools remain, local government has not been given back its management function and performance indicators persist. So in most areas of education policy, Labour governments have followed Conservative policies. If anything, they have been tougher on failing schools than their predecessors and given support to 'specialist' schools (Ball 2008).

Further education

In post-war Britain, further or post-compulsory education provided largely part-time education in further education colleges to people working in commerce, skilled trades (such as construction and engineering), as technicians and supervisors in industry and the public sector. The courses provided were on a day-release, block or evening basis. From 1979 till 1997, however, following critical reports regarding performance in the sector, successive Conservative governments changed the structure, governance and curriculum of the sector. New Labour's approach was characterised by a range of policy initiatives and legislation. These indicated that while Labour had a stronger commitment to the sector than its Conservative predecessors, it was profoundly influenced by the legacy of marketisation, privatisation and the funding methodology of earlier Conservative administrations.

With the coming to office of the Coalition government, its policy is that both colleges and universities are essential for building a strong and innovative economy. Accordingly, it proposes to take action to create more college and university places, as well as helping to foster stronger links between colleges, universities and industries. It also seeks ways to support the creation of apprenticeships, internships, work pairings, and college and workplace training places as part of a wider programme to 'get Britain working'.

Higher education (HE)

After the Second World War, all HE was university education and was free to those able to gain entry to university, with a system of means-tested maintenance grants for those needing them. With only some 5 per cent of 18-year-olds going to university, the system did not drain the public purse. However, expansion of universities in the 1960s was not accompanied by financial reform, so the system became more expensive to administer. Following further expansion of a more diverse HE system from the late 1980s, a financial crisis occurred and government instituted tighter financial controls through, first, the University Funding Council and, then, the Higher Education Funding Councils of England, Wales and Scotland.

After Labour had been elected in 1997, it continued to implement the Conservative policy of annual tuition fees of £1,000 for all HE students and abolished what remained of the student grant system. Students were offered loans in place of maintenance grants. Loans were to be repaid after graduation, when a certain income threshold had been reached. In 2001, government set an HE participation target of 50 per cent for school leavers by 2010 and subsequently proposed a limited form of maintenance grant for those on very low incomes. More importantly, following legislation in 2004, universities were given the freedom to charge 'top-up' fees of up to £3,000 per year in England and Wales with effect from 2006, although the Scottish Parliament decided not to legislate. In general, by 2010, HE had become increasingly marketised and privatised, providing students with a range of choices in a mass marketplace, paid for by themselves, and geared towards the labour market and 'UK PLC'. HE was increasingly market-driven, commodified and instrumental in its purposes.

ACTIVITY 10.7

What is the difference between 'education' and 'training'?

ACTIVITY 10.8

To what extent is education policy geared towards training a skilled workforce and educating informed citizens?

ACTIVITY 10.9

What are the implications of university 'top-up' fees for potential students, universities and employers? Is a 50 per cent participation rate for 18–30-year-olds in universities justified and why?

EU ECONOMIC AND SOCIAL POLICY

Substantive areas of Euro-policy cover economics, social issues such as the Community Charter of Fundamental Social Rights, employment policy, regional policy, the Common Agriculture Policy, sustainable development, and technological innovation (Cowles and Dinan 2004). These policies affect employers, workers and the citizens of member states. Thus the European Commission published targets in 2010, known as Europe 2020. This followed a meeting of EU leaders in March 2010, which set a goal of driving the European economy firmly onto a path of smart, sustainable and inclusive growth. The leaders endorsed five headline targets, which became shared objectives guiding the actions of member states and the EU. They cover employment, education, research and development (R&D) investment, the environment and social inclusion. The education target, however, is being set by heads of state and government, who will also decide the most appropriate way to measure the promotion of social inclusion. The targets were (European Commission 2010b):

- 75 per cent of the European population aged 20–64 should be employed.

- Three per cent of the EU's GDP should be invested in R&D.

- The '20/20/20' climate/energy targets should be met.

- Education levels should be improved, in particular by reducing school drop-out rates and increasing the share of the population having completed tertiary or equivalent education.

- Social inclusion should be promoted, in particular through reducing poverty.

THE EUROPEAN ECONOMIC AND SOCIAL COMMITTEE

The European Economic and Social Committee (EESC) is a key institution in the EU. It represents various economic and social components of the EU's 'civil society'. It is an institutional consultative body established by the 1957 Treaty of Rome, whose main task is to advise the three major institutions – the European Parliament, Council of the European Union and European Commission. It is mandatory for the EESC to be consulted on those issues stipulated in the Treaties and in all cases where the institutions deem it appropriate. It can also be consulted on an exploratory basis by any of these institutions. It takes its own initiative to issue opinions, with around 15 per cent of these coming from itself.

The EESC's consultative role enables its members, and hence the organisations they represent, to participate in Community decision-making. With the wide variety of views and interests represented, the EESC's discussions often require complex negotiations involving not only the social partners (employers and employees) but also other socio-occupational interests. The expertise, discussions, negotiations and search for convergence help improve the quality and credibility of European decision-making, by ensuring that the views of different organisations and interest groups are taken into account, thus making the processes more open and transparent to Europe's citizens and civil organisations. As a debating and consultative chamber, the EESC helps strengthen the democratic credentials of EU-building. This includes promoting relations between the EU and socio-economic groupings in third countries. In doing this, it helps promote a genuine identification with Europe. For illustrative purposes, the range of policy issues debated within the EESC in 2009 is summarised in Figure 10.6

Figure 10.6 Policy issues discussed by the EESC 2009

- Communicating in partnership within Europe
- The Lisbon Treaty and civil society
- The renewed Lisbon Treaty
- Economic and monetary union and social cohesion
- The single market, production and consumption
- Employment and social policy
- Citizenship, immigration and integration
- Agriculture, rural development, the environment and sustainable development
- Transport, energy, infrastructure and the information society
- Industrial change
- Europe in the world

RECENT PRIORITIES OF THE EESC

Jobs, growth and competitiveness

Efforts are being made to co-ordinate the financial stimulus package, following banking difficulties within EU member states. A large sum of money has already been injected into the European economy, where positive effects are being felt.

This has also influenced the budget situation of member states, where debt has risen fast. The EESC has agreed that there is a need for an exit strategy for the EU from this situation, so as to create sustainable public finances. In its view, the stability and growth pact needs to be applied and sustainable growth achieved. In terms of unemployment, most measures to counteract high unemployment are taken at Member State level but some measures are addressed at EU level, including competitiveness and growth, within the review of the Lisbon strategy. In response to the financial crisis, a surveillance mechanism has been put in place to protect the EU from another '2008' crisis.

Climate change, environment and energy

The EU wants to act in multilateral forums to combat climate change. The EESC supports the EU programme for reduction of greenhouse gas emissions by 20 per cent up to 2020. It believes that this could be increased to 30 per cent, if agreed internationally. But the EU wants to ensure that other states do the same. This means inspiring developing countries to contribute to the process, with the EU helping those countries already affected by the costs of doing this.

EU institutions

It falls within the scope of the EESC to ensure that the Lisbon Treaty is functional and that relevant institutional changes are made. This includes a new institutional structure in the Council, establishing the External Action Service, linking budgeting procedures and altering the decision-making process used for justice and home affairs. Apart from these areas, a number of other matters have been of concern to the Committee. These include the Stockholm Programme on improved co-operation in the areas of justice, liberty and security, including criminal law. This replaces the Hague Programme and deals with a common asylum policy, improved facilities to combat crime, and a road map for the next few years.

The EU as a global actor

The EESC is promoting a micro-regional approach in the Baltic, to show how to use EU policies in the best way. This encompasses policy areas such as the environment, energy, competitiveness, innovation and research. The strategy has already triggered interest from Member States other than those directly involved. This may inspire more regional integration. There are expectations on renewed EU–US relations in many areas, including Afghanistan and Pakistan, other foreign policy relations, justice and security, as well as development policy. Summits take place internationally involving the United States, South Africa, Brazil, Ukraine, India, China and Russia, together with negotiations on a strategic partnership with the Russian Federation.

Enlargement of the EU

The EESC believes that the principles followed so far should continue to be applied. This means that when candidate countries deliver on their commitments,

EU institutions must deliver on theirs. Croatia, for example, has to solve its bilateral problems with Slovenia and Turkey before being considered for EU membership. Work with the countries of the Western Balkans continues on the same basis. If and when Iceland applies for membership, the usual procedures will be followed. The Commission would then be mandated to prepare an opinion. The Presidency of the EESC would get this done as speedily as possible, while taking into account application of the *acquis*. This is the total body of accumulated European law, such as the Schengen agreement on cross-border freedom (European Economic and Social Committee 2009).

ACTIVITY 10.10

Identify any three areas of EU policy affecting your organisation and explain how your organisation is addressing these policies.

HOW ORGANISATIONS INFLUENCE PUBLIC AND INTERGOVERNMENTAL POLICY

In modern society, formal participation in politics extends beyond voting in elections; it is also about influencing government policy through secondary political groupings. When individuals or organisations (including employers or professional bodies of managers) become involved politically, they join and participate in organised groups that reflect their political interests and opinions. Organised political groups are of two kinds, political parties and pressure groups, although their memberships can overlap.

NATURE AND SCOPE

UK political parties seek to influence policy decisions directly by getting their leading members into formal positions of political authority in the House of Commons, devolved Scottish and Welsh Assemblies, local authorities and the European Parliament. Parties try to win political control so as to use political power. What distinguishes pressure groups from political parties is they seek to influence policy decisions, not get representatives into positions of formal political authority. Some pressure groups, such as Shelter, Age UK or the Institute of Directors (IoD), are politically independent; others have links with parties or a single political party and help them fight elections, such as TUC-affiliated unions that generally support the Labour party.

Political parties and pressure groups are concerned with power. The power of political parties depends on electoral success and support at the ballot box; the power of pressure groups depends on their membership base, resources, appeal and effectiveness. Since political parties need to have relatively wide appeal to win votes for their candidates, their political programmes tend to be broadly based. Pressure groups have much narrower political objectives, sometimes based on a single issue, such as the Society for the Protection of Unborn Children or

Figure 10.7 A classification of pressure groups

Type	Main features
Interest groups	• National or central organisations, created because of their members' common socio-economic goals • Members of employers' organisations such as the Engineering Employers' Federation, for example, combine to protect the common interests of federated engineering firms, which may be large or small, multi-plant or single-plant, and geographically concentrated or geographically spread • What brings these enterprises together is their common commercial interest as organisations, not the organisational characteristics or personal aspirations of their representatives • The Institute of Directors performs similar functions, as do the British Medical Association (BMA), National Union of Students and trade unions
Attitude groups	• Based on the commonly held beliefs and values of their members • Motivating force behind joining the Royal Society for the Protection of Birds is not economic self-interest but concern for the protection and well-being of birds • Other examples are the Consumers' Association and Amnesty International • What draws their supporters together are the attitudes they share as individuals and their wish to organise collectively to protect the rights of the interests they represent
Peak associations	• Umbrella organisations that co-ordinate the activities of other pressure groups • Examples include the CBI and TUC • A European-wide, private sector employer association is the Union of Industrial and Employers' Confederations of Europe • International peak associations include the Red Cross and International Labour Organisation
Insider groups	• Have access to government officials and decision-making bodies and usually speak on behalf of legitimate mainstream interests in society, such as the National Farmers Union (NFU), which is an employers' organisation • Play by 'the rules of the game' • Have expertise which the government needs or whose co-operation is necessary if government policies are to be seen as legitimate and are to be implemented (eg BMA, Association of Chief Police Officers)
Outsider groups	• Do not normally have access to key officials or decision-makers and are kept at arm's length by the establishment because of who or what they represent • Examples include the Campaign for Nuclear Disarmament (CND) and animal liberation groups
Crossbench groups	• Maintain party neutrality, knowing that they must deal with whatever party is in power
Fire brigade groups	• Formed to fight specific issues and dissolve when the issue is settled, such as the Anti-Poll Tax Federation during the Thatcher administration or anti-fuel tax protestors
New Social Movements	• 'Political' groups, such as Greenpeace, with broader concerns than interest and attitude groups but more loosely knit than political parties

Abortion Law Reform Association. These lead to differences in organisation between political parties and pressure groups. Political parties contest elections, so they are organised nationally and locally. Pressure groups are much more varied and may be international, national or local and can be classified in a number of ways, as indicated in Figure 10.7.

ACTIVITIES, INFLUENCE AND POWER

In attempting to influence policy decisions, pressure groups try to gain access to those taking decisions and do this by lobbying key individuals at different power levels. This means trying to influence the prime minister, cabinet, ministers, government officials, local councillors or MEPs and European officials. They also seek to influence public opinion. The methods and levels each pressure group uses to communicate its opinions and demands vary widely, according to its power and circumstances. The most powerful pressure groups have almost instant access to the important parts of the political system, such as leading employers' and workers' organisations, but weak organisations have to improvise to make their views heard (Grant 2000). Figure 10.8 illustrates the factors affecting pressure group influence and power.

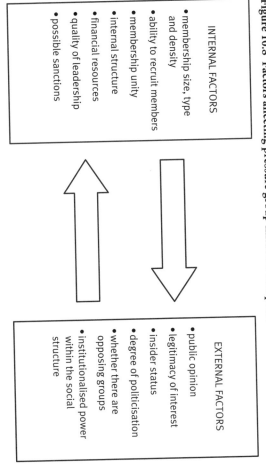

INTERNAL FACTORS

- membership size, type and density
- ability to recruit members
- membership unity
- internal structure
- financial resources
- quality of leadership
- possible sanctions

EXTERNAL FACTORS

- public opinion
- legitimacy of interest
- insider status
- degree of politicisation
- whether there are opposing groups
- institutionalised power within the social structure

Figure 10.8 Factors affecting pressure group influence and power

Some powerful groups have well-established relations with government, on a permanent or semi-permanent basis, sometimes channelled through advisory or standing committees staffed by civil servants and pressure-group representatives. As indicated above, the NFU has close links with the Ministry of Agriculture, Fisheries and Food and ministers. Relatively few pressure groups have the power to gain access to policy-making machinery but use representatives to pursue their objectives. If pressure groups cannot influence the main decision-makers directly, they lobby MPs, members of the Lords, or MEPs. If pressure groups cannot influence Parliament, or if parliamentary supporters do not carry enough political weight, they are forced to operate outside Parliament. They may try to influence political parties by building up support for their policies within them.

Where it is not possible for pressure groups to influence national political parties, even outside Parliament, or if they are unsuccessful in doing so, they are forced to use the mass media and influence public opinion. The objective of campaigning locally is to try to create shifts in public opinion in the hope that those in political power and influence respond to these pressures. Tactics used include rallies, marches, petitions and media campaigns to get their message across. These can lead to media coverage, television documentaries and in-depth analyses, thus putting pressure on government to modify policy. Recent examples have been related to concern for the environment. Some pressure groups, such as Friends of the Earth and Greenpeace, have mounted strong grass-roots campaigns to influence public opinion and government policies on lead-free petrol and organic farming.

Pressure groups vary widely in their power bases and in the ways in which they operate. Sometimes the more visible a pressure group is, the less is its influence, and the more likely it is to operate at media and grass-roots levels. The most powerful pressure groups rarely use such tactics. The most important determinant of a pressure group's power is its position in the economic system and its potential sanctions to back its demands. These may be positive, such as co-operating with the authorities, or negative, including withdrawal of financial resources or taking punitive actions against those in power. Large employer pressure groups, such as those representing banks, finance and insurance, are crucial to the economy and most governments listen to their views with some degree of deference.

Financial resources and effective leadership of pressure groups are also important determinants of group power and influence, since they affect the types of campaigns and activities that pressure groups pursue. Size of membership is another factor, especially in interest groups, as it determines their representativeness. The NFU, for example, is an employer's body and represents most farmers. Hence government channels all its agricultural communications through that body. If there were several farmers' unions, each would be much weaker than the NFU is collectively. Public support is particularly important for attitude groups, since they have few sanctions to use against the public authorities. Powerful groups with aims generally acceptable to the political system, such as the business community, find it easier to influence policy decisions than those whose views clash with dominant opinion such as fuel protest organisers. The most significant business organisation in Europe is the Union of Industrial and Employers' Confederations of Europe, which describes itself as the 'voice of Business in Europe' (UNICE).

ACTIVITY 10.10

Specify a named pressure group to which your organisation (or one known to you) belongs. Report and discuss how the pressure group operates. What benefits does the organisation get from being a member of this pressure group?

LEGAL REGULATION AND THE REGULATORY STATE

The law plays a central role in regulating individual and corporate behaviour in society. In recent years, however, new forms of legal regulation have grown in the UK, giving rise to the concept of 'regulatory agencies' and the 'regulatory' state. The latter is loosely defined, where the state acts as 'a kind of pilot for society, not actually supplying the motive power but providing overall guidance about direction' (Moran 2005, p528).

THE RULE OF LAW

The law or legal regulation is that body of rules, formally enacted or customary, which the state recognises as binding on its citizens. Law has been described by Kahn-Freund (1983, p3) as 'a technique for the regulation of social power', where power is the ability to direct and affect the behaviour of others, ultimately by sanctions. Sanctions that are positive reward people; those that are negative threaten them. In any liberal society, naked power to determine rules and decisions and enforce them by individuals, organisations or government is insufficient to maintain legitimacy, social stability and social order. The power to act needs to be accepted as authoritative by those affected by such decisions, whether employers, property owners, workers, consumers or citizens. To be acceptable in democratic societies, the right of those with power to take decisions has to be recognised by those lacking positional or resource power, irrespective of any sanctions the powerful may possess. In an orderly society, ultimate power, and the right to enforce it, rests with those controlling the machinery and agencies of the state. These are the legislative, executive and judicial organs of government.

In liberal democratic states, the concept of the 'rule of law' is a fundamental one and has three meanings. First, it reflects the preference of citizens for 'law and order' rather than anarchy or civil strife. It implies that conflicts and disputes between parties should be settled by peaceful and constitutional means rather than by force, physical coercion, armed force or terrorism. If the state is identified with force and coercive might, the rule of law lacks moral authority or legitimacy.

Second, the rule of law means that government itself must be conducted in accordance with the law and that the machinery of government must always operate through the law. This helps explain much of the public reaction following the scandal involving MPs' expenses in 2009. Thus the law acts as a buttress of democratic principles, since only the law-making assembly (ie Parliament) can confer new powers on the executive and administrative authorities.

Third, and very importantly, as law develops it results in the rule of law reflecting changing social values, because the legal system exists in a wider social and economic context. Harris (1997) argues that understanding of the law cannot be acquired unless it is examined in close relationship to the social, economic and political contexts in which it is created and implemented. Law is part of the overall social structure and has links and dependencies with other social elements and forces. Within society, some institutions and social groups are more important than others, some have more power than others, and some enjoy considerable prestige, such as Parliament, political parties and pressure groups. Law, in short, plays an important part in defining and regulating all kinds of social relationships, including relations between individuals, organisations, individuals and organisations – including employment relationships – and citizens and the state.

SOCIETY AND THE LAW

Viewpoints about the relationship between law and society are dichotomous. On the one hand, society and the legal system are seen as reflecting a prevailing social consensus. On the other, they are seen as reflecting fundamental social conflicts between competing interest groups and social ideologies. The former perspective perceives the law to be protecting social values to which all subscribe, while the latter holds that the law is less than neutral, protecting some values and interests at the expense of others. Developments in the law also reflect the historical, political and social contexts in which society evolves and changes. The emergence of a free labour market, for example, was a product of the Industrial Revolution. Given the early predominance of ideas about 'freedom' and 'equality of contract' between consenting parties, it took many years before the state began to intervene to provide basic legal protections for individual employees in their contractual relations with employers. It was the infinite variability of the terms of employment contracts and the fact that employees could neither negotiate their terms, nor readily ascertain the terms dictated by the employer, which led, over the years, to growing state intervention in regulating the employment relationship. This was done through a series of statutes, beginning effectively in the 1960s.

The basic legal rules governing contract stem almost wholly from cases determined by superior courts in the nineteenth century. The insistence of nineteenth-century judges on deciding cases, and creating legal contractual rules, using the juristic equivalent of *laissez-faire* economics – notions of freedom and equality of contract – eventually led to legislative intervention in the twentieth century, especially in the areas of employment and consumer protection. This was done to redress imbalances in power between employers and employees and businesses and customers (Harvey and Parry 2000). The nineteenth century also saw the development of legal rules relating to the form that business enterprises might take and of the legal protections that particular types of enterprise enjoyed. The most common form of business enterprise was and remains the limited company, its most striking legal feature being its 'corporate personality'.

The legal and regulatory systems of contemporary market economies exhibit comprehensive sets of legal rules and rights, especially on private property, because property is of fundamental importance to these societies. Yet the law does not treat property as a homogeneous category. Because it has taken different forms at different times, each type of property has particular legal rules attached to it. The legal rules dealing with land, for instance, can be traced back to feudalism, while those relating to manufactured goods, plant and machinery emerged during the development of early capitalism. Since capitalist market economies, such as those in Europe, depend upon the creation and acquisition of private personal wealth, legal systems concern themselves, to a large extent, with protection of that wealth, how it can be invested and consolidated, and how it can be transferred. Although the law purports to afford equality of treatment to everyone in society, regardless of social class, wealth or position, in practice it is used primarily for protecting and transferring various forms of property within market societies.

REGULATORY AGENCIES AND THE REGULATORY STATE

Since the 1980s, the UK government and its organs of state have become more fragmented and dispersed, for a number of reasons. Three trends are notable. First, the dominant form of government, the civil service department, controlled by a minister in Parliament, has in many cases been superseded by new kinds of executive agencies, although some departments remain. There are now over 100 executive agencies of various sizes which are responsible for delivering certain government or public services. A second development was the privatisation of key public services such as telecommunications, water, electricity, gas and railways in the 1980s and 1990s. As a result, the re-categorising of these bodies into 'public utilities' was accompanied by the creation of 'specialist' regulatory agencies with legal powers, responsible for regulating these industries in the public interest. Third, alongside the creation of specialist regulatory agencies covering privatised industries, a number of other 'general' regulatory agencies were also created. These now regulate a wide range of markets and other social spheres. Examples of both types of regulatory bodies are provided in Figure 10.9.

The specialist regulatory agencies outlined in Figure 10.9 (ORR, OFCOM, OFGEM and OFTEL) were largely created after the large-scale privatisations that took place in the UK during the 1980s and 1990s, mainly through flotation on the stock market. In contracting the state's role of owning and managing these sectors, government expanded its public authority by creating new agencies to regulate them as private enterprises (Moran 2003). The main features of such agencies are:

- They are new bodies and innovatory ones in the system of government.
- They regulate how these goods and services are produced and delivered.
- They are independent bodies, governed by director-generals whose powers are specified by statute.
- They are vital forms of economic management and were created for specific reasons under conditions where state invention is needed in a market economy. Their roles include: to control monopolies, regulate franchises delivering public goods through private enterprises, ensure the supply of essential services and make economic power accountable.

General regulatory agencies, in turn, are charged with controlling important domains of economic and social life where the state asserts a 'public interest'. These bodies have the following characteristics:

- They emerged out of the re-organisation of traditional 'inspectorates'

Figure 10.9 Some regulatory agencies in the UK

Name	Date established	Responsibilities
Tenants Services Authority (TSA)	2008	Watchdog for social tenants, regulates social landlords
Office for Standards in Education (OFSTED)	2007	Reformed in 2007, inspects education and training for learners of all ages, except higher education
Office of Rail Regulation (ORR)	2004	Regulates train and track operators, replacing Office of the Rail Regulator established in 1993
Office of Communication (OFCOM)	2003	Responsible for all broadcasting regulation, hitherto carried out by separate bodies
Office for Gas and Electricity Markets (OFGEM)	2000	Fused separate former separate authorities regulating these markets
Office of Telecommunications (OFTEL)	1984	Regulates telecommunication markets
Information Commissioners Office (ICO)	2001	Originated in 1984, responsible for data protection and data protection
Food Standards Agency	2000	Regulates food production in interests of public health
Competition Commission	1999	Replaced Monopolies and Merger Commission, responsible for merger, markets and other inquiries related to other industries
Financial Services Agency (FSA)	1997	Regulates financial institutions regarding honesty and stability
National Lottery Commission (NLC)	1999	Regulates all aspects of the national lottery
Human Fertilisation and Embryology Authority (HFEA)	1991	Regulates scientific research into interventions in human fertility
Office for Fair Trading (OFT)	1973	Promotes and protects consumer interests and ensures businesses are fair and competitive

- They transformed self-regulation by transforming what were once independent domains into domains now regulated by public agencies.
- They demonstrate growing regulation inside government itself.
- They regulate new social domains in response to governmental concerns about the problems of controlling everyday economic and social life. When 'new' social problems emerge, new regulatory agencies are created.

Three main factors explain the 'rise' of regulatory agencies. First, some regulatory bodies have resulted from large-scale breakdowns of traditional control which led to public scandal and crises, such as those in the Financial Services Agency and the Food Standards Agency in the 1990s. Second, with the UK's greater integration within the EU, a very different regulatory regime was encountered. In the EU, public law has traditionally has a much more influential role in regulating economic and social life. As a result, normally non-legal systems of self-regulation in the UK have been replaced and superseded by more legalistic systems, rooted in the law and legal language. These forces have been important in reshaping regulation in professions such as medicine, the law and accountancy. Third, the retreat of the UK state from many fields of intervention over the past three decades has resulted in new regulatory forms of public control.

The rise of a new 'regulatory state' is marked by three key features. First, new executive agencies within government are now contracted to deliver policy and are regulated to measure how effectively they deliver it. Second, the 'new' privatised sector is subject to specialised regulatory agencies. Third, government uses generalised regulatory agencies to control large areas of economic and social life, which were traditionally self-regulated. The benefits of this new regulatory regime are claimed to be greater transparency and a focus on performance by government. Whether it leads to more accountability and effectiveness in the public domain has been questioned by some observers (Moran 2005).

THE REGULATION OF EMPLOYMENT

Regulation of the employment relationship between employers and employees in the first three quarters of the twentieth century was rooted, first, in the contract of employment and, second, in collective bargaining between organised employers and organised bodies of workers (ie trade unions). The first was a legal relationship between employer and employee, that had evolved over centuries by the application of common law rules on contract, tort and crime in various employment situations. However, as the complex and special needs of employers and employees were not always adequately met by the application of broad common law principles, a series of statutory provisions were incrementally established in the UK to create a detailed framework of legal rules regulating the parties. These were aimed at regulating and controlling the conflicting demands of employers and employees in the labour market and the place of work. During the last quarter of the twentieth century, these parliamentary Acts, starting with the Equal Pay Act 1970, began to supersede collective bargaining arrangements and they now provide important legal sources for regulating the contract of employment.

The second relationship, outlined above, between employer and union, was a voluntary one, where the collective agreements determined between them were not legally enforceable but their terms were incorporated into the individual contracts of employment of the employees covered by them. This was the case whether or not they were union members. With the decline of trade unionism and collective bargaining during the last quarter of the twentieth century, and the increasing influence of European law on employment issues following UK entry into the 'Common Market' in 1973, legal regulation of the employment contract, rather than voluntary collective bargaining, became the major influence regulating relations between employers and employees. As Taylor and Emir (2009, p10) comment, in 40 years there has been a total transformation in the extent to which the employment relationship in the UK is regulated. In the vast majority of workplaces, terms and conditions of employment and employment policies and practices now owe far more to the requirements of law than they do to any trade union negotiation.

INDIVIDUAL LEGAL RIGHTS IN EMPLOYMENT

By the early twenty-first century, with the decline of collective employment relations, there is a rich range of legal sources of employment regulation affecting the individual relationship between employer and employee. Some collective legal issues continue to be important, such as statutory trade union recognition, information and consultation between employers and employees, European works councils and industrial action. However, most legal regulation is concerned with the individual employment relationship, not collective relationships. The sources of these law are: employment legislation passed in Parliament, including codes of practice and judicial interpretation; the common law developed by judges, using the doctrine of legal precedent, contract law and the law of tort; European law or law passed by the EU in the forms of Directives and regulations; the European Convention on Human Rights from the Council of Europe in relation to fundamental human rights; the UK Courts; and the European Court of Justice (ECJ). The ECJ can overrule decisions of the supreme courts of member states, where these concern EU treaties articles, directives or regulations.

The main legal rights of people in employment, deriving from the legal sources outlined above, are summarised in Figure 10.10 and employers are expected to comply with these regulatory requirements. The law distinguishes between legal rights for 'employees', 'independent contractors' and 'workers'. Normally employees are employed under contracts of employment (or contracts of services) and independent contractors under contracts for services. Some employment laws originate in Europe, so for definitional purposes a 'worker' category is used. The term 'worker' includes employees and *some* independent contractors. Some of the above statutory rights apply to all employed and self-employed persons, others to employees only, and others to workers but not to independent contractors. These legal distinctions are not made in Figure 10.10. In this commentary, the term 'employee' is used throughout.

Figure 10.10 Summary of the main legal rights of people in employment

Area of law	Legal rights
Contracts of employment	• Written particulars of employment • Minimum requirements for giving notice • Time off for public duties • Main trade union rights (eg the right to join a union and take part in its activities) • Transfer of undertakings (ie workers to be informed/consulted over transfers, contracts honoured and protection against unfair dismissal) • Not to be wrongfully dismissed (ie where dismissal is in breach of contract) • Not to be constructively dismissed (ie where resignation occurs because of the unacceptable conduct of the employer) • Not to be unfairly dismissed (ie where dismissal is in breach of statute law; this involves automatically fair reasons, automatically unfair reasons and potentially fair reasons) • Redundancy payment when dismissed because the job has disappeared
Wages and benefits	• Statutory minimum wage • Statutory sick pay • Itemised pay statement • Limitations on unauthorised deductions from pay • Regulation of occupational pensions
Working time	• 48 hours' a week limit • Four weeks' paid annual leave • Rest periods • Health checks
Family-friendly policy	• 26 weeks' maternity leave • Additional maternity leave (after one year) • Statutory maternity pay (after six months) • Paternity leave (after six months) • Adoption leave • Time off to case for dependants • Request for flexible working arrangements • Time off for study or training
Health and safety at work	• Civil law provisions • Criminal law provisions • Risk assessments • Policy statements • Health and safety representatives
Discrimination	• Equal pay for equal work • Not to be discriminated against on grounds of sex • Not to be discriminated against on grounds of race • Not to be discriminated against on grounds of disability • Not to be discriminated against on grounds of sexual orientation • Not to be discriminated against on grounds of religion or belief • Not to be discriminated against on grounds of age (but it is not unlawful to refuse to employ persons after they have reached the default retirement age) • Part-time workers not to be treated less favourably than full-time workers • Fixed-term workers not to be treated less favourably than full-time workers • Agency workers not to be treated less favourably than full-time workers
Other	• Data protection • Privacy and confidentiality • Whistle-blowing

These regulations can be categorised into six main areas of law: contracts of employment; wages and benefits; working time; family-friendly policies; health and safety at work; and discrimination in employment (Taylor and Emir 2009, Willey 2003, Smith and Baker 2010). Some of these legal employment rights apply as soon as an employee starts employment. These include, for example, rights to a written statement of employment, an itemised pay statement and the statutory minimum wage. Other rights accrue over time, such as unfair dismissal, statutory maternity pay and paternity leave. Legal remedies are available to employees when an employer fails to comply with any of these legal regulations. Most cases are heard in employment tribunals (ETs), comprising a legal chair and two 'lay' members. Possible appeals go to higher courts such as the Employment Appeals Tribunal through to the Court of Appeal, House of Lords and, finally, the ECJ on matters of EU law.

When claimants bring a case to an ET, they seek remedies for an employer's infringement of their legal rights. In the case of unfair dismissal, for example, where an ET finds in favour of the claimant, there are three possible remedies. First, a reinstatement order allows the employee to return to his/her previous job, where there has been no break in employment, with pay, conditions and length of service remaining the same. Second, the tribunal may make an order for re-engagement, instructing the former employer to re-employ the claimant. In making orders for either reinstatement or re-engagement, ETs only do this where the successful claimant has requested it. ETs also take account of whether it is reasonable and practical for an employer to comply with such an order and whether the claimant caused or contributed to the dismissal. Third, a tribunal can award compensation to the claimant, consisting of a basic and compensatory award. In discrimination cases, the award is less easy to quantify than in cases of unfair dismissal. This is because there are no set procedures and no maximum amount can be awarded. Issues such as financial loss, injury to feelings and aggravated damages are taken into account.

REASONS FOR THE GROWTH OF EMPLOYMENT REGULATION

One reason for increased employment regulation over the past 40 years has been economic policy. Both Labour and Conservative governments have wanted to boost productivity in the private sector where, in retrospect, unions were seen to be a barrier to national economic performance. Labour governments adopted a conciliatory approach to the unions; the Conservatives a confrontational one. Thus, Labour governments introduced employment legislation in the 1970s to protect groups of workers not covered by collective bargaining and to provide a 'floor' of minimum employment standards (or rights) that could be raised by collective bargaining. In contrast, Conservative governments, in the 1980s and 1990s, sought to reduce union bargaining power by using the law to remove closed shops, narrow the use of legitimate industrial action and make unions more accountable to their members. In the 1990s and early 2000s, New Labour governments, in turn, faced by falling unemployment and more women being employed in the labour market, used employment law, such as the statutory national minimum wage, to try to reduce the numbers of people living on state benefits. They also wanted to make working more attractive than being unemployed, and make concessions to part-time workers requesting part-time working and family-friendly policies in the workplace.

Second, there has been the impact of UK membership of Europe from 1973, particularly since signing the Social Chapter of the Treaty of Maastricht in 1997. As a result, an increasing proportion of UK employment law originates from Brussels. This includes: transfers of undertakings; consultation and information; protection from discrimination on grounds of fixed-term and part-time contracts, sexual orientation and religious belief; parental leave; working time; and data protection. This is despite continual attempts by UK governments to try to water down some of these provisions. It is inconceivable that such measures would have been agreed in the UK, driven as she is by ideas and values associated with free markets and protecting the right to manage, without membership of the EU.

A third factor has been the decline of trade unionism and collective bargaining. This is the case not only in the UK but also in Europe. With union density in the UK of around 58 per cent of the workforce in 1979 falling to under a quarter in 2005, the proportion of the workforce covered by collective agreements is now about a third of all workers. The underpinning rationale of voluntary collective bargaining, as a means for regulating employment conditions, has disappeared. Without employment regulation by the law, employers would be free to flout basic employment standards and act unfairly at will. Legal regulation of employment also guarantees a set of minimum employment standards applicable to all employees, including those working in small businesses where employers might be tempted to treat their employees badly. Interestingly, unions have recently campaigned to extend employment regulation, or what the Webbs (1897) called 'legal enactment', as they can no longer protect employees without support from the law (Farnham 2008).

Finally, there is the issue of political expediency. In other words, governments undertake measures such as regulation of employment, because these are popular with the electorate and help secure re-election. Thus the Conservatives promoted 'anti-union' legislation in the 1980s because unions were not generally popular with the electorate. Also early anti-discrimination legislation was enacted not only for its compelling case but also because of powerful pressure groups lobbying on behalf of women and ethnic minorities at the time (Davies and Freedland 1993). The Blair administrations used employment law too to gain support from their key constituencies. They advanced the regulatory agenda 'in a step-by-step fashion, consulting at length before legislating and not being afraid to reduce the radicalism of some original proposals' (Taylor and Emir 2009). The right to be represented by union officials in certain disciplinary and grievance hearings is a good example of this type of policy and political practice.

CONCLUSION: POLITICS, REGULATION, HR STRATEGY AND HR SOLUTIONS

The working of the macro-economy is complex and not fully explained by the most advanced economic theory, whilst public policy is often intuitive. Nevertheless, changes and developments in the national economy, single European market, global economy and public policy have had significant impacts on businesses, public services and third sector organisations. One of management's prime tasks is to plan for, or respond to, macro-economic changes driven by government policy that are likely to impact on the organisations they manage.

Projected growth of the national economy is a starting point for any business forecasting. The direction and expected rate of growth in aggregate demand and national output indicate the likely demand for an organisation's goods or services. They also have implications for the HR skills required, demand for labour and future staffing needs. Too rapid a rate of national growth can result in skills and labour shortages in the short term, with pressures to raise pay rates, since getting extra staff tends to lag behind rising sales. Where economic growth is sluggish, with national output falling, organisations want less capacity. This makes it more difficult to maintain productivity and keep labour costs down, thus affecting competitiveness and a company's ability to maintain its market position.

The components of national growth are important when examining their possible effects on product and labour markets. Strong consumer spending is good for producers of consumer commodities, retail outlets and service-related industries selling direct to consumers. Weak consumer spending has the opposite effect. Investment spending trends are particularly important in industries producing capital goods for domestic markets. When interest rates fall, rises in investment expenditure can be expected, but when interest rates rise, falls in investment spending are likely, although this depends on the state of the economy and business expectations of future trends. Changes in public spending, in turn, affect not only provision of public services but also demand for human resources and for intermediate goods within public organisations. Cutbacks in public spending result in lower demand for private sector goods, services and resources and vice versa.

Capital-intensive industries tend to borrow more heavily than other sectors and are much influenced by movements in interest rates. The relative proportion of debt capital to equity capital in a company does not necessarily indicate the impact of high interest rates on it, since one company may have raised its debt at a low rate of interest, whilst another may have to cope with a much higher rate of interest. High rates of interest help attract overseas money into the economy, which is needed to finance any balance of payments current account deficit, but they also push up the exchange rate. In the EU this is an important consideration, as the UK is not (yet) in the single European currency.

Politics make a difference to businesses too. Once in office, cabinet reshuffles and changes in political office holders can result in changes in economic, social or education policy, as demonstrated after the general election in 2010. These can affect an organisation's marketing, operations and financial strategies, as well as its business opportunities in the marketplace. Subsequent changes in legislation affecting businesses, consumers, workers or competition require relevant responses from senior managers. Changes in economic or social policy, in turn, influence managerial decisions on resource demand, use of resources and their allocation, as well as affecting social demand for welfare services.

The impact of EU decisions on management policies, planning and business practices is increasingly important. EU policies, implemented through Directives and regulations, cover employment, competition, consumer protection and social policy. All affect organisational and business policies, with EU rules having to be taken into account by corporate policy-makers. Within the large single European market, and more integration of the European economy, large companies have their own research departments and task forces to evaluate their strategies, marketing plans and transnational investments.

Few organisations are overtly party political, although some business leaders intervened in public debates about rises in national insurance and the business consequences of a 'hung Parliament' during the election campaign in 2010. Some organisations need to act politically, however, to defend or extend their economic interests and protect their markets and minimise business risks. Sometimes this is done on a one-off basis. At other times, it is done collectively through trade or business associations. Given the nature of public and European policy-making, managements often build working relations with the political authorities at various levels to influence policy decisions. This is done on a company-by-company basis, by membership of relevant employers' or trade associations and, at national level, through the CBI. Organisations can also be represented on permanent advisory or consultative committees of government departments or be invited to join ad hoc bodies of inquiry. Trade and business associations may also use full-time lobbyists or contact MPs to protect their members' commercial interests, when these arise in Parliament.

Increasingly, large organisations and pressure groups are opening offices in Brussels so that they can keep close to policy-making in the EU. In the UK, local authorities take decisions on the local environment, exercise regulatory powers over planning controls and facilitate business development. In seeking to influence these decisions, managements lobby council members, contact council officers or operate through local chambers of commerce.

Given the wide range of consumer, competition, employment and other regulatory legal provisions with which organisations have to comply, top managements have to ensure their organisations are regulatory compliant. One area of regulatory concern to employers is employment law. Employees now have a wide range of employment protection rights which, if infringed, enable applicants to take their claims to an ET for determination. A major implication is that managements need to know their obligations under legislation and ensure that subordinate managers do not flout the legal rights of employees. By developing effective HR policies and procedures, embodying at least the minimum standards required by law, employers are able to protect themselves from unreasonable tribunal claims. With properly designed and administered disciplinary and dismissal procedures, employers can avoid vexatious claims. In general, investing in learning and development opportunities for their managers and workforces is an obvious strategy for employers in dealing with the provisions of an ever-expanding regulatory state.

KEY LEARNING POINTS

1. The UK is a parliamentary democracy, with a centralised government where power is rooted in the political executive, especially the prime minister. There are some 'core' policy areas where there is cross-party support: a market economy, low inflation, limits on welfare expenditure, pressure group politics and NATO membership. However, in a competitive political system, policy differences remain among the main parties which come to the fore during general election campaigns. Public policy relates to those issues where the elected government implements its manifesto commitments. It covers the economy, social issues including the NHS and pensions, education, the environment, transport, law and order, and foreign affairs. The policies of the Coalition government, following the election of 2010, are set out in its programme for government.

2. Although there is some 'cross-party dressing' among the main political parties in the UK, politics today is less ideological than in most of the twentieth century. During that period, the Conservative party tended to support the business community and argue for less state intervention in the economy. The Labour party, with its constitutional links with leading trade unions, tended to support working people and work for more state intervention in the economy. In the last two decades of the twentieth century, both Conservative and Labour party ideologies were transformed. The Conservative version was changed by the rise of Thatcherism and Labour by the need to respond to it, with the Liberal Democrats a centrist party sandwiched between Conservatives and Labour ideologically. The Coalition government reinforces the shift towards pragmatic, rather than ideological, politics and policies.

3. A key issue in public policy in a market economy is how the interface between state and market is managed. In the nineteenth century, long-established social markets were deregulated and replaced by free markets. Much of the first half of twentieth century politics was about the relative merits of market freedoms versus state regulation. During the third quarter of the century, regulationists won the debate. In the last quarter century, bolstered by globalisation and entry into the European Economic Community, supporters of free markets dominated again, introducing regulatory innovations. By the early years of this century, a new regulatory state was in place.

4. Economic policy is the cornerstone of public policy. It affects businesses, individuals as workers, taxpayers and consumers, and what government does with its tax revenues. During the third quarter of the twentieth century, the social democratic consensus based on Keynesian and Beveridge prescriptions dominated policy decisions. In the last quarter of the century, there was a renaissance of neo-classical economic thinking, described as 'neo-liberalism', linked with globalisation. This resulted in a 'hollowing out' of the state by

privatisations, public management reforms and targeted spending priorities. Built upon and modified by New Labour, the neo-liberal-globalisation consensus, rooted in competition, choice and change agendas, became and remains the new economic orthodoxy. Within the new consensus, the market is seen as the prime driver of economic performance, with the state promoting market solutions within a regulatory framework established partly in Parliament, partly in the EU.

5. Social policy covers healthcare, education, housing, income maintenance and state pensions. Funded out of taxation and National Insurance contributions by employers and employees, social policy provides benefits for individual citizens and their families but is a cost to employers. This was highlighted in the debate during the general election campaign in 2010 between some employers and the Labour government over proposed rises in National Insurance contributions. The record shows on balance, however, that while broadly accepting the neo-liberal legacy of the Thatcher-Major administrations, New Labour significantly strengthened public services, compared with preceding governments, in the period 1997–2007. After this, first, the credit crunch and, then, economic recession resulted in higher levels of public borrowing by Labour, which now faced different policy objectives.

6. Education policy is an area of some agreement between the two UK major parties. In most areas, Labour governments have simply modified Conservative policies. Both main parties are market oriented in their approaches. Labour appears to be more committed to nursery education than the Conservatives. In terms of schools, both parties stress the importance of standards, robust inspection and working towards a society where everyone is educated and participating in social and community life. All three main parties view school and post-school education as the means for training and preparing young people for work in a knowledge-based economy.

7. The UK is now a committed member of the EU, although some political groupings, such as the United Kingdom Independence Party, remain sceptical about the European project. Also the UK is not in the Single European Currency and has not signed the Schengen agreement on 'open' cross-border movements. However, the EU plays an increasingly important role in micro-economic policy and in some areas of social policy affecting member states, employers and workers. The EU seeks to improve the contribution of EU policy to growth and competitiveness, promote social cohesion, extend working life and foster social inclusion, issues that do not conflict with the UK's national interests. Within the EU, the EESC plays a key role in Euro-decision-making and is consulted as a representative body on economic and social policy issues.

8. A variety of pressure groups exist within the UK's political democracy, where they try to influence policy at local, national, EU and global levels through democratic incrementalism. Pressure groups are classified as interest, attitude, peak association, insider, outsider, crossbench, fire-brigade and new social movement groups. Each varies in its political influence, depending on its networks, resources and membership base. The main business groups are the CBI, chambers of commerce, employers' associations, IoD, trade associations and, in Europe, UNICE. Trade associations operate in specific sectors. Pressure

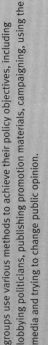

groups use various methods to achieve their policy objectives, including lobbying politicians, publishing promotion materials, campaigning, using the media and trying to change public opinion.

9. The emergence of the regulatory state is one of the dominant features of recent political and constitutional history in the UK. It has parallelled the decline of traditional state control, where the Whitehall department was the central institution. Regulation is epitomised by the rise of a new system of 'rule' where institutions contract, more explicitly than in the past, to deliver effective public services. Further, the spread of the regulatory agency model beyond the privatised sector is now a characteristic institution of the new UK regulatory state. With the retreat of the state from many fields of economic intervention in recent decades, the regulatory agency has become the primary means for public control to be exercised.

10. In employment, voluntary regulation of the contract of employment through the method of collective bargaining has now been largely superseded by legal regulation. A series of legal provisions have been established creating a detailed framework of legal rules, aimed at regulating and controlling the conflicting demands of employers and employees in the labour market and place of work. These cover the contract of employment, wages and benefits, working time, family-friendly issues, health and safety work and discrimination in employment, much of which has originated from the EU.

1. What was the nature of the social democratic consensus? To what extent did New Labour's 'third way' break this consensus? Explain some of the consequences of the current policy consensus on employers and employees.

2. Why did the Labour government introduce tuition fees for university students? What have been the consequences of this change in social policy?

3. 'Much public policy, especially in economic, social and environmental matters is now made in Brussels, rather than in London.' Do you agree or disagree with this statement? Justify your answer.

4. Discuss, with examples, how business pressure groups try to influence policy-making (a) locally, (b) nationally and (c) at European level.

5. Examine the impact of the regulatory state on (a) the public sector and (b) the private sector. How has the regulatory state affected the development of HR strategy?

CASE STUDY 10.1 UK FISCAL POLICY

Background

During the period 2008–10, the UK economy went into economic recession, after many years of steady economic growth and business expansion. Recession is typified by:

- declining demand for goods and services, leading to higher levels of spare productive capacity

- rising unemployment as firms lay off workers to control their costs

- sharp falls in business confidence and company profits

- decreases in capital investment spending, because of insufficient demand

- increases in personal and corporate savings as people and businesses seek to reduce their debts

- running down stocks of goods or rationalising of services; price discounting, possibly leading to lower inflation

- reduced inflationary pressure in the labour market, as unemployment rises

- falling demand for imports, unless exchange rates change

- increased government borrowing to boost aggregate demand and offset falls in government tax revenues.

At this time, there was growing public criticism of the public sector's 'structural deficit' from some quarters. This is where there is an excess of government spending over its revenues, even when economy is at maximum potential. Government had increased its borrowing not only to finance its current spending and maintain aggregated demand but also to help 'bail out' some of the UK's banks, following the so-called 'credit crunch'. At this time, annual net government borrowing was approximately 11 per cent of GDP, rising from 3 per cent in 2006.

The ways of addressing public debt are by:

- raising taxes

- cutting spending

- paying off government debts

- promoting economic growth.

Government must then decide time frames for determining its fiscal responses.

Professional reactions to the UK's structural deficit

In response to the UK's structural deficit in a period of economic recession, a number of professional economists wrote letters to national newspapers, pressing for credible medium-term fiscal consolidation plan is now necessary to promote a sustainable economic recovery. Without this, there could be loss of confidence in UK economic policy, as well as contributing to higher long-term interest rates and undermining economic recovery.

Letter 1

Sir

The UK's budget deficit is now its largest in size during peacetime and one of the largest in the developed world. A credible, medium-term fiscal consolidation plan is now necessary to promote a sustainable economic recovery. Without this, there could be loss of confidence in UK economic policy, as well as contributing to higher long-term interest rates and undermining economic recovery.

We propose:

1. Government should set out a detailed plan to reduce the structural budget deficit as quickly as possible, whilst being sensitive to the fragility of a recovery.

2. Government's goal should be to eliminate the structural deficit over the course of a single parliament, with the first measures being taken next fiscal year.

3. The bulk of this fiscal consolidation should be implemented by reductions in government spending, whilst being

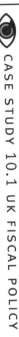

mindful of its impact on society's most vulnerable groups.

4. Tax increases should be broad-based and minimise damaging increases in marginal tax rates on employment and investment.

5. Government should also introduce more independence in generating fiscal forecasts and scrutiny of its economic performance.

Letter 2

Sir

We strongly disagree with the proposal to reduce government's budget deficit so rapidly, starting next fiscal year.

1. It would be dangerous to reduce government's contribution to aggregate demand beyond those planned for next fiscal year, when unemployment is still high. Immediate cuts would not offset an increase in private sector aggregate demand; it might even reduce it.

2. The UK's level of government debt is not out of control. Its net debt relative to GDP is lower than the average of the Group of Seven industrialised countries and it will peak at 78 per cent of annual GDP in four years' time. It will then fall. Current interest rates on government debt are low by recent standards.

3. Since the economic crisis started, private households and businesses have had to increase their savings to reduce their debts. These savings are financing the government deficit. Public spending has offset reduced spending in the private sector; without this the recession would be deeper.

4. There needs to be a plan for reducing government's deficit but the present one is sufficient.

5. A sharp shock to the economy now would not remove the need for a sustained programme of deficit reduction but it could be positively dangerous to do so.

Letter 3

Sir

We believe that an accelerated programme of fiscal consolidation is wrong.

1. What some commentators have omitted to say is that the current deficit reflects the deepest and longest global recession since the Second World War. They fail to acknowledge that recent output has fallen by more than 6 per cent and unemployment has risen by 2 per cent.

2. The timing of fiscal consolidation should depend on the strength of economic recovery. In urging a swifter pace of deficit reduction, these commentators implicitly accept as binding the views of the financial markets, whose mistakes precipitated the crisis in the first place.

3. These commentators do not mention that an automatic reduction in the deficit will be achieved as soon as growth resumes.

4. Nor do they take account of the effect of future growth on investor confidence.

5. The first priority must be to restore robust economic growth; the wealth of the nation lies in what its citizens produce.

Letter 4

Sir

I wish to make three brief points about the state of our public finances.

1. The public debt is owed to ourselves.

2. The greatest threat to economic well-being arising from the size of the public debt is not posed by the debt itself but by how we might react to it. In other words, excessive early tax rises could prolong the recession.

3. A good deal of what has gone on in financial markets in recent years has been at best useless and at worst harmful. Release of resources from financial services and their redeployment elsewhere is likely to bring no net loss and even a net gain.

EXPLORE FURTHER

MANDL, U., DIERX, A. and ILZKOVITZ, F. (2008) *The effectiveness and efficiency of public spending*. Luxembourg: European Commission.

Shows that efficiency in public services, more generally, and in public spending on education and research and development, in particular, varies significantly between countries; also demonstrates the difficulties of measuring efficiency and effectiveness and progress in developing the necessary measurement techniques.

MILLER, P. and ROSE, N. (2008) *Governing the present: administering economic, social and political life*. Cambridge: Polity Press.

Brings together studies of the government of economic, social and personal life and demonstrates the importance of analysing these as joint phenomena rather than separate domains; casts new light on some of the leading issues in contemporary social science, democracy and individualisation.

MORAN, M. (2003) *The British regulatory state: high modernism and hyper-innovation*. Oxford: Oxford University Press.

Explores why British government, which for the first two-thirds of the twentieth century was among the most stable in the world, has in the last three decades been a leader in innovation and its governing system has been in constant turmoil; explains this transformation and traces its consequences.

STIGLITZ, J., EDLIN, A., and DELONG, B. (2008) *The economists' voice: top economists take on today's problems*. New York: Columbia University Press.

More than 30 of the world's top economists contribute informative essays on a range of contemporary topics, explaining to the general reader the economic implications of today's most pressing issues. These issues include global warming, government spending, social security, tax reform, property and welfare reform.

Tasks

1. Why do economic experts differ about issues such as government debt?

2. Which of the above scenarios, outlined in letters 1–4, would you favour as a means for repaying public debt and why?

3. Identify and discuss the party political implications of the 'government debt' issue.

4. Examine the policy choices available to government for reducing and repaying government debt in, say, the next five years.

5. How, in the short term, do government debt and fiscal consolidation affect (a) your organisation and (b) you personally?

Bibliography

ABERCROMBIE, N. and WARDE, A. (eds) (2000) *Contemporary British society*. Cambridge: Polity Press.

ALDCROFT, D. H. (1993) *The European economy 1914–1990*. London: Routledge.

ALDRICH, H. (1979) *Organizations and environments*. Englewood Cliffs, NJ: Prentice Hall.

ALEXANDER, L. (1985) Successfully implementing strategic decisions. *Long Range Planning*. Vol. 18, No. 3, 91–97.

ALLSOP, J. (1995) *Health policy and the NHS*. Harlow: Longman.

ALTMAN, D. (2001) *Global sex*. London: Allen & Unwin.

ALWIN, D. and SCOTT, J. (1996) Attitude change: its measurement and interpretation using longitudinal surveys. In B. Taylor and K. Thomson (eds) *Understanding change in social attitudes*. Aldershot: Dartmouth.

ANDREWS, K. (1987) *The concept of corporate strategy*. Homewood, IL: Irwin.

ANSOFF, I. (1965) *Corporate strategy*. Harmondsworth: Penguin.

AOKI, M. (1988) *Information, incentives and bargaining in the Japanese economy*. Cambridge: Cambridge University Press.

APPELBAUM, E., BAILEY, T., BERG, P. and KALLEBERG, A. (2000) *Manufacturing advantage: why high performance systems pay off*. New York: Cornell University Press.

APPELBAUM, E. and BATT, R. (1994) *The new American workplace*. Ithaca, NY: ILR Press.

ARGYRIS, C. (1960) *Understanding Organizational Behavior*. London: Tavistock.

ARGYRIS, C. (1999) *On Organizational learning*. 2nd ed. Oxford: Oxford University Press.

ARGYRIS, C. (2004) *Reasons and rationalizations: the limits to organisational knowledge*. Oxford: Oxford University Press.

ARGYRIS, C. and SCHON, D. (1996) *Organisational learning: a theory of action perspective*. Reading, MA: Addison Wesley.

ARMSTRONG, M. (2009) *Armstrong's handbook of human resource management practice*. 11th ed. London: Kogan Page.

ARMSTRONG, M. and BARON, A. (2005) *Managing performance: performance management in action*. London: CIPD.

ARNOLD, J. (1996) The psychological contract: a concept in need of further scrutiny? *European Journal of Work and Organizational Psychology*. Vol. 5, No. 4, 11–20.

ARNOLD, J., COOPER, C. and ROBERTSON, I. (1998) *Work psychology*. 3rd ed. Harlow: Financial Times Pitman Publishing.

ARTHUR, J. (1994) Effects of human resource systems on manufacturing performance and turnover. *Academy of Management Journal*. Vol. 37, No. 3, 670–87.

ASTLEY, W. (1985) The two ecologies: population and community perspectives on organisation theory. *Administrative Science Quarterly*. Vol. 30, 245–73.

AUERBACH, P. (1988) *Competition: the economics of industrial change*. Oxford: Blackwell.

AUGAR, P. (2000) *The death of gentlemanly capitalism: the rise and fall of London's investment banks*. Harmondsworth: Penguin.

BACH, S. (ed) (2005) *Managing human resources: personnel management in transition*. Oxford: Blackwell.

BACON, R. and ELTIS, W. (1976) *Britain's economic problem*. London: Macmillan.

BAIRD, L. and MESHOULAM, I. (1988) Managing two fits of strategic human resources management. *Academy of Management Review*. Vol. 13, No.1, 116–28.

BALL, S. (2008) *The education debate*. Bristol: Policy.

BARBER, B. (1963) Some problems in the society of professions. *Daedalus*. Fall issue.

BARLEY, S. and KUNDA, G. (2001) Bringing work back in. *Organization Science*. Vol. 12, No. 1, 76–95.

BARNEY, J. (1991) Firm resources and sustainable competitive advantage. *Journal of Management*. Vol. 17, 99–129.

BARNEY, J. and WRIGHT, P. (1998) On becoming a strategic partner: the role of human resources in gaining competitive advantage. *Human Resource Management*. Vol. 37, No. 1, 31–47.

BARRY, D. and HANSEN, H. (eds) (2008) *The SAGE handbook of new approaches in management and organization*. London: Sage.

BARTLETT, C. and GHOSHAL, S. (1989) *Managing across borders*. Boston, MA: Harvard Business School Press.

BARUCH, Y. and NICHOLSON, N. (1997) Home, sweet work. *Journal of General Management*. Vol. 23, No. 2, 15–30.

BASU, K. (2000) *Prelude to political economy: a study of the social and political foundations of economics.* Oxford: Oxford University Press.

BATRAM, D. (2000) Internet recruitment and selection: kissing frogs to princes. *International Journal of Selection and Assessment.* Vol. 8, No. 4, 261–74.

BATT, R. (2002) Managing customer services: human resources practices, quit rates, and sales growth. *Academy of Management Journal.* Vol. 45, No. 3, 587–97.

BEARDWELL, J. and CLARK, I. (2007) An introduction to human resource management. In J. Beardwell and T. Claydon (eds) *Human resource management: a contemporary approach.* Harlow: Financial Times Prentice Hall.

BEARDWELL, J. and CLAYDON, T. (eds) (2007) *Human resource management: a contemporary approach.* Harlow: Financial Times Prentice Hall.

BEATSON, M. (1995) *Labour market flexibility.* London: Employment Department.

BEAVEN, R., BOSWORTH, D., LEWNEY, R. and WILSON, R. (2005) *Alternative skills scenario to 2020 for the UK economy: a report for the skills sector development agency as a contribution to the Leitch review of skills.* Cambridge: Cambridge Econometrics.

BECKER, B. and HUSELID, M. (2009) Strategic human resources management: where do we go from here? In A. Wilkinson, N. Bacon, T. Redman and S. Snell (eds) (2009) *The SAGE Handbook of Human Resource Management.* London: Sage.

BEER, M., SPECTOR, B., LAWRENCE, P., QUINN MILLS, D. and WALTON, R. (1985) *Human resource management: a general manager's perspective.* Glencoe, IL: Free Press.

BEGG, D. and WARD, D. (2009) *Economics for business.* 3rd ed. Maidenhead: McGraw-Hill.

BEGG, D., FISCHER, S. and DORNBUSCH, R. (2008) *Economics.* 9th ed. Maidenhead: McGraw-Hill Higher Education.

BELL, D. (1973) *The coming of post-industrial society.* New York: Basic Books.

BENNIS, W. (1966) *Changing organizations: essays on the development and evolution of organizations.* New York: McGraw-Hill.

BENNIS, W. and NANUS, B. (1985) *Leaders: the strategies for taking charge.* New York: Harper & Row.

BERESFORD, P. (2010) *The Sunday Times rich list.* London: Times Newspapers.

BERG, P. (1999) The effects of high performance work practices on job satisfaction in the United States steel industry. *Industrial Relations.* Vol. 54, 111–35.

BERGER, B. and CARLSON, A. (1993) Liberty, order and the family. In

J. Davies (ed) *The family: is it just another life style?* London: Institute of Economic Affairs.

BERGER, P. and LUCKMAN, T. (1967) *The social construction of reality: a treatise in the sociology of knowledge.* New York: Free Press.

BEVAN, S. and THOMPSON, M. (1992) *Personnel management in the UK: an analysis of the issues.* London: Institute of Personnel Management.

BEVERIDGE, W. (1942) *Social insurance and allied services.* London: HMSO.

BENYON, H. (1973) *Working for Ford.* London: Penguin.

BIENEFELD, M. (1996) Is a strong national economy a Utopian goal at the end of the twentieth-century? In R. Boyer and D. Drache (eds) *States against markets.* London: Routledge.

BLACKABY, F. (ed) (1979) *De-industrialisation.* London: Heinemann.

BLAIR, T. (1998) *The third way.* London: Fabian Society.

BLAU, P. and SCOTT, W. (1963) *Formal organisations.* London: Routledge.

BLAUNER, R. (1964) *Alienation and freedom.* Chicago: University of Chicago Press.

BOARD OF TRADE. (1998) *Fairness at work.* London: HMSO (Cm 3968)

BOON, C., BOSELIE, P., PAAUWE, J. and DEN HARTOG, D. (2007) Measuring strategic and internal fit in HRM: an alternative approach. In Proceedings of the Academy of Management Annual Meeting, Philadelphia, PA.

BOOTH, A. (1995) *British economic developments since 1945.* Manchester: Manchester University Press.

BOSANQUET, N. (1986) Interim report: public spending and the welfare state. In R. Jowell, S. Witherspoon and L. Brook (eds) *British social attitudes: the 1986 report.* Aldershot: Gower.

BOSELIE, P., PAAUWE, J. and RICHARDSON, R. (2003) Human resource management, institutional and organisational performance: a comparison of hospitals, hotels and local government. *Journal of Human Resource Management.* Vol. 14, No. 8, 1407–29.

BOSSMAN BAAFI, A. (2009) Multinational corporations and the developing world. www.ghanaweb.com 15 November, accessed 18 February 2010.

BOWEN, D. and OSTROFF, C. (2004) Understanding HRM-firm performance linkages: the role of 'strength' of the HRM system. *Academy of Management Review.* Vol. 29, 203–21.

BOXALL, P. (1999) Human resource management and industry-based competition: a conceptual framework and agenda for theoretical development. In P. Wright, L. Dyer, J. Boudreau and G. Milkovich (eds) *Research in personnel and human resource management.* London: JAI Press.

BOXALL, P. and PURCELL, J. (2000) Strategic human resources management: where have we come from and where are we going? *International Journal of Management Reviews*. Vol. 2, No. 2, 265–88.

BOXALL, P. and PURCELL, J. (2008) *Strategy and human resource management*. 2nd ed. Basingstoke: Palgrave Macmillan.

BOXALL, P., PURCELL, J. and WRIGHT, P. (eds) (2007) *Oxford handbook of human resource management*. Oxford: Oxford University Press.

BOXALL, P. and STEENEVELD, M. (1999) Human resource strategy and competitive advantage: a longitudinal study of engineering consultancies. *Journal of Management Studies*. Vol. 34, No. 4, 443–63.

BOYER, R. and DRACHE, D. (1996) (eds) *States against markets*. London: Routledge.

BOZOVIC, V. (2008) (ed). *Medical robotics*. Vienna: I-Tech Education and Publishing.

BRADLEY, H. (1996) *Fractured identities: changing patterns of inequality*. Oxford: Blackwell.

BRAVERMAN, H. (1974) *Labor and monopoly capital*. New York: Monthly Review Press.

BREARLEY, R., MYERS, S. and ALLEN, A. (2006), *Corporate finance*. 6th ed. Boston, MA: McGraw-Hill Irwin.

BREDRUP, H. (1995) Background for performance management. In A. Rolstadås (ed) *Performance management: a business process benchmarking approach*. London: Chapman & Hall.

BREWSTER, C., MAYRHOFER, W. and MORLEY, M. (2004) *HRM in Europe: evidence of convergence*. Oxford: Butterworth-Heinemann.

BRITTAN, S. (1964) *The treasury under the Tories 1951–64*. Harmondsworth: Penguin.

BRITTON, A. (1991) *Macro-economic policy in Britain 1974–1987*. Cambridge: Cambridge University Press.

BRYAN, L. and FARRELL, D. (1996) *Market unbound*. New York: Wiley.

BUCKS CONSULTANTS (2009) The Greening of HR Survey. www.buckssurvey. com, accessed 28 September.

BUDD, A. (1978) *The politics of economic planning*. Manchester: Fontana.

BUDGE, I., McKAY, D., NEWTON, K. and BARTLE, J. (2007) *The new British politics*. 4th ed. Harlow: Pearson Education.

BURAWOY, M. (1979) *Manufacturing consent: changes in the labor process under monopoly capitalism*: Chicago: University of Chicago Press.

BURNS, T. and STALKER, G. (1961) *The management of innovation*. London: Tavistock.

CABLE, V. (2009) *The storm: the world economic crisis and what it means*. London: Atlantic Books.

CADBURY, A. (1992) *Report of the Committee on the Financial Aspects of Corporate Governance*. London: Professional Publishing.

CANNON, T. (1994) *Corporate responsibility*. London: Pitman.

CAREY, A. (2002) The Hawthorne studies: a radical criticism. In S. Clegg (ed) *Central studies in organisation studies: Volume 1*. London: Sage.

CARNOY, M. (1993) *The new global economy in the information age*. University Park, Pennsylvania: Penn State University Press.

CASTELLS, M. (2010) *The rise of the network society*. 2nd ed. Oxford: Blackwell.

CERNY, P. (1995) Globalisation and the changing logic of collective action. *International Organisation*, No. 49, 595–625.

CHANDLER, A. (1977) *The visible hand: the managerial revolution in American business*. Cambridge, MA: Harvard University Press.

CHARTERED INSTITUTE OF PERSONNEL AND DEVELOPMENT (CIPD). (2007) *The changing HR function: survey report*. London: CIPD.

CIPD (2008) *The changing HR function*. London: CIPD.

CIPD (2009) *HR profession map*. London: CIPD.

CHESNAIS, F. (1994) *La Mondialisation du capital*. Paris: Syros.

CHILD, J. (1972) Organisational structure, environment and performance: the role of strategic choice. *Sociology*. Vol. 6, 1–22.

CHILD, J. (1997) Strategic choice in the analysis of action, structure, organisations and the environment. *Organisation Studies*. Vol. 18, No. 1, 43–76.

CHILD, J. (2005) *Organisation: contemporary principles and practice*. Oxford: Blackwell.

CHRYSSIDES, G. and KALER, J. (1993) *An introduction to business ethics*. London: Chapman & Hall.

CLEGG, S., KORNBERGER, M. and PITSIS, T. (2008) *Managing and organizations: an introduction to theory and practice*. 2nd ed. London: Sage.

COALITION, THE (2010) *Our programme for government*. London: HM Government.

COHEN, M. (1996) Democracy and the future of nations. In R. Boyer and D. Drache (eds) *States against markets*. London: Routledge.

COHEN, R. and KENNEDY, P. (2007) *Global sociology.* Basingstoke: Palgrave Macmillan.

COLAKOGLU, S., HONG, Y. and LEPAK, D. (2009) Models of strategic human resource management. In A. Wilkinson, N. Bacon, T. Redman and S. Snell (eds) (2009) *The SAGE handbook of human resource management.* London: Sage.

COLEMAN, J. (1988) Social capital in the creation of human capital. *American Journal of Sociology.* Vol. 94, 95–120.

COLLEY, J., DOYLE, J., HARDIE, R., LOGAN, G. and STETTINIUS, W. (2007) *Principles of general management: the art and science of getting results across organisational boundaries.* New Haven, CT: Darden Graduate School of Business Administration.

COMMITTEE ON IMPLICATIONS OF EMERGING MICROTECHNOLOGIES AND NANOTECHNOLOGIES. (2002) *Implications of emerging microelectronic and nanotechnologies.* Washington, DC: The National Academies Press.

CONFEDERATION OF BRITISH INDUSTRY. (2000) *Employment trends survey: measuring flexibility in the labour market.* London: CBI and William Mercer.

CONNOCK, S. and JOHNS, T. (1995) *Ethical leadership.* London: Institute of Personnel and Development.

CONSERVATIVE PARTY (2010) *Invitation to join the government of Britain: the Conservative manifesto.* London: Conservative Party.

COOKE, F, EARNSHAW, J., MARCHINGTON, M. and RUBERY, J. (2004) For better and for worse: transfer of undertaking and the reshaping of employment relations. *International Journal of Human Resource Management.* Vol. 15, No. 2, 276–94.

CORIAT, B. (1994) Neither pre- nor post-fordism: an original and new way of managing the labour process. In K. Tetsuro and R. Steven (eds) *Is Japanese Management post-Fordism?* Tokyo: Mado-sha.

CORRY, B. (2003) *The regulatory state.* London: Institute of Public Policy Research.

COSER, L. (1956) *The functions of social conflict.* London: Routledge & Kegan Paul.

COWLES, M. and DINAN, D. (eds) (2004) *Developments in the European Union.* Basingstoke: Palgrave.

COYLE, D. (2005) The economic case for immigration. *Economic Affairs.* Vol, 25, No.1, March, 53–55.

CRAIG, J. (2005) *Introduction to robotics: mechanics and control.* Upper Saddle River, NJ: Pearson Education.

CRAIL, M. (2006) HR roles and responsibilities 2006: benchmarking the HR function. *IRS Employment Review* 839, 20 January, 9–15.

CRICHTON, A. (1962) *Personnel management and working groups*. London: Institute of Personnel Management.

CROMPTON, R., DEVINE, F., SAVAGE, M. and SCOTT, J. (2000) *Renewing class analysis*. Oxford: Blackwell.

CROWLEY, P. (ed) (2008) *EU economic policy at the dawn of the century*. New York: Nova Science.

CROWTHER, D. and GREEN, M. (2004) *Organisational theory*. London: CIPD.

CROZIER, M. (1964) *The bureaucratic phenomenon*. Chicago: Chicago University Press.

CUNNINGHAM, I. and HYMAN, J. (1999) Devolving human resource responsibilities to the line: beginning of the end or a new beginning for personnel. *Personnel Review*. Vol. 28, No. 1/2, 9–27.

CUTLER T., WILLIAMS, K. and WILLIAMS J. (1986) *Keynes, Beveridge and Beyond*. London: Routledge & Kegan Paul.

CYERT, R. and MARCH, J. (1992) *A behavioral theory of the firm*. Englewood Cliffs, NJ: Prentice Hall.

D'AVENI, R. (1994) *Hypercompetition*. New York: Free Press.

DAFT, R. (2008) *The new era of management*. 9th ed. Mason, OH: South-Western.

DAHRENDORF, R. (1982) *On Britain*. London: BBC.

DALE, B. and PLUNKETT, J. (1999) *Quality costing*. 3rd ed. Aldershot: Gower.

DALE, B., VAN DER WIELE, T. and VAN IWAARDEN, J. (2007) *Managing quality*. 5th ed. Oxford: Blackwell.

DALE, M. (2008) *Developing people, delivering results: new approaches to managing and developing performance*. London: Educational Competencies Consortium.

DALTON, M. (1959) *Men who manage*. New York: Wiley.

DAVENPORT, T. and PEARLSON, K. (1998) Two cheers for the virtual office. *Sloan Management Review*. Vol. 39, No. 4, 51–65.

DAVID, F. (2009) *Strategic management: concepts*. 12th ed. Upper Saddle River, NJ: Pearson Education.

DAVIES, P. and FREEDLAND, M. (1993) *Labour legislation and public policy*. Oxford: Oxford University Press.

DAVIES, P. and FREEDLAND, M. (2007) *Towards a flexible labour market: labour legislation and regulation since the 1990s*. Oxford: Oxford University Press.

DAWSON, P. (2003) *Understanding organisational change: the contemporary experience of people at work*. London: Sage.

DE VRIES, M. (1994) The leadership mystique. *Academy of Management Executive*. Vol. 8, No. 3, 73–89.

DE WIT, B. and MEYER, R. (2004) *Strategy: process, content, context – an international perspective*. 3rd ed. London: Thomson Learning.

DEAL, T. and KENNEDY, A. (1982) *Corporate cultures: the rites and rituals of corporate life*. Reading, MA: Addison-Wesley.

DELDRIDGE, R. (1998) *Life on the line in contemporary manufacturing*. Oxford: Oxford University Press.

DELERY, J. and DOTY, D. (1996) Modes of theorizing in strategic human resource management: test of universalistic, contingency and configurational performance predictions. *Academy of Management Journal*. Vol. 39, No.4, 802–35.

DEMING, W. (1986) *Out of crisis*. Cambridge, MA: MIT Center for Advanced Engineering Study.

DENNIS, N. and ERDOS, G. (1993) *Families without fatherhood*. London: Institute of Economic Affairs.

DENT, J. (2008) *Distribution channels: understanding and managing channels to market*. London: McGraw-Hill Higher Education.

DEPARTMENT OF TRADE AND INDUSTRY (1997) *Partnerships with people*. London: DTI.

DESJARDINS, J. (2007) *Business, ethics and the environment: imagining a sustainable future*. Upper Saddle River, NJ: Pearson/Prentice-Hall.

DICKEN, P. (2003) *Global shift: reshaping the global economic map in the 21st century*. London: Sage.

DIMAGGIO, P. and POWELL, W. (1983) The iron cage revisited: institutional isomorphism and collective rationality in organizational fields. *American Sociological Review*. Vol. 48, No. 2, 147–60.

DINAN, D. (2004) *Europe recast: a history of the European Union*. Basingstoke: Palgrave.

DONALDSON, T. and PRESTON, L. (1995) The stakeholder theory of the firm: concepts, evidence and implications. *Academy of Management Review*. Vol. 20, 65–91.

DOOGAN, K. (2001) Insecurity and long-term employment. *Work, Employment and Society*. Vol. 15, No. 3.

DORLING, D. (2010) *Injustice: why inequality persists.* Bristol: Policy Press.

DOYLE, P. (2008) *Value-based marketing: marketing strategies for corporate growth and shareholder value.* 2nd ed. Chichester: Wiley.

DREWRY, G. (1989) *The new select committees.* Oxford: Clarendon.

DRUCKER, P. (1993) *Post-capitalist society.* Oxford: Butterworth-Heinemann.

DU GAY, P. (2003) *In praise of bureaucracy: Weber, organization and ethics.* London: Sage.

DUNCAN, S. and PHILLIPS, M. (2008) New families: tradition and change in modern relationships. In A. Park, J. Curtis, K. Thomson, *et al. British social attitudes: the 24th report.* London: Sage.

DUNDON, T., WILKINSON, A., MARCHINGTON, M. and ACKERS, P. (2004) The meaning and purpose of employee voice. *International Journal of Human Resource Management.* Vol. 15, No. 6, 1149–70.

DUNSIRE, A. and HOOD, C. (1989) *Cutback management in public bureaucracies: popular theories and observed outcomes in Whitehall.* Cambridge: Cambridge University Press.

DWYER, R. and TANNER, J. (2009) *Business marketing: connecting strategy, relationships, and learning.* New York: McGraw-Hill.

EDWARDS, T. and REES, C. (2006) *International HRM.* Harlow: Financial Times Prentice Hall.

ELDRIDGE, J. and CROMBIE, A. (1974) *A sociology of organisations.* London: Allen & Unwin.

ETZIONI, A. (1975) *A comparative analysis of complex organizations: on power, involvement, and their correlates.* Revised edition. London: Free Press.

EUROPEAN COMMISSION (1997) *Green paper: partnership for a new organisation of work.* Luxembourg: Office for Official Publications of the European Communities.

EUROPEAN COMMISSION (2001) *Promoting a European framework of corporate social responsibility.* Luxembourg: Office for Official Publications of the European Communities.

EUROPEAN COMMISSION (2002) *Corporate social responsibility: a business contribution to sustainable development.* Luxembourg: Office for Official Publications of the European Communities.

EUROPEAN COMMISSION (2008) *Agriculture and rural development.* Luxembourg: Office for Official Publications of the European Communities.

EUROPEAN COMMISSION (2009a) *Jobs and growth in the European Union.* Luxembourg: Office for Official Publications of the European Communities.

EUROPEAN COMMISSION (2009b) *Photovoltaic solar energy: development and current research.* Luxembourg: Office for Official Publications of the European Communities.

EUROPEAN COMMISSION (2009c) *Demography report 2008: meeting social needs in an ageing society.* Luxembourg: Office for Official Publications of the European Communities.

EUROPEAN COMMISSION (2010a) *Eurobarometer survey.* Luxembourg: Office for Official Publications of the European Communities.

EUROPEAN COMMISSION (2010b) *Europe 2020.* Luxembourg: Office for Official Publications of the European Communities.

EUROPEAN COMMISSION (2010c) *Your guide to the Lisbon Treaty.* Luxembourg: Office for Official Publications of the European Communities.

EUROPEAN COMMISSION (2010d) *Report on equality between women and men.* Luxembourg: Office for Official Publications of the European Communities.

EUROPEAN ECONOMIC AND SOCIAL COMMITTEE (2009) *The priorities of the European and Economic Social Committee during the Presidency of Sweden.* Luxembourg: Office for Official Publications of the European Communities.

EUSEPI, G. and SCHNEIDER, F. (2004) *Changing institutions in the European Union: a public choice perspective.* Cheltenham: Elgar.

EVANS, P. (1995) *Embedded autonomy: states and industrial transformation.* Princeton, NJ: Princeton University Press.

FAHEY, L. and NARAYANAM, V. (1986) *Macroenvironmental analysis for strategic management.* St Paul, MN: West Publishing.

FARCAS, C. and WETLAUFER, S. (1996) The ways chief executive officers lead. *Harvard Business Review.* May–June, 110–12.

FARNHAM, D. (1994) *Employment relations and the rebirth of history.* University of Portsmouth Lectures.

FARNHAM, D. (2008) Beatrice and Sidney Webb and the intellectual origins of British industrial relations. *Employee Relations.* Vol. 30, No. 5, 534–52.

FARNHAM, D., BARLOW, J., HORTON, S. and HONDEGHEM, A. (eds) (1996) *New public managers in Europe: public servants in transition.* Basingstoke, Macmillan.

FARNHAM, D., HONDEGHEM, A. and HORTON, S. (2005) *Staff participation and public management reform: some international comparisons.* Basingstoke: Palgrave.

FARNHAM, D. and HORTON, S. (eds) (1996) *Managing the new public services.* London: Macmillan.

FARNHAM, D. and HORTON, S. (eds) (2000) *Human resources flexibilities in the public services: international perspectives.* London: Macmillan.

FAYOL, H. (1916, reissued in English 1949) *General and industrial management.* London: Pitman.

FERGUSON, N. (2009) *The ascent of money: a financial history of the world.* London: Penguin.

FERGUSON, P. and FERGUSON, G. (2000) *Organisations: a strategic perspective.* Basingstoke: Macmillan.

FERNER, A. and QUINTANILLA, J. (1998) Multinationals, national business systems and HRM: the enduring influence of national identity or a process of 'Anglo-Saxonisation'. *International Journal of Human Resource Management.* Vol. 9, No. 4, 710–31.

FINANCIAL TIMES. (2010) Editorial: Fine if you forget the public finances, 25 March, 20.

FITZNER, G. (2006) *How have employees fared? Recent UK trends.* London: DTI.

FLYNN, N. (2007) *Public sector management.* 5th ed. London: Sage.

FOMBRUN, C., TICHY, N., and DEVANNA, M. (1984) *Strategic human resource management.* New York: Wiley.

FORESTER, T. (1987) *High-tech society.* Oxford: Blackwell.

FOUCAULT, M. (1991) *Discipline and punish: the birth of the prison.* London: Penguin.

FOX, A. (1985) *History and heritage: the social origins of the British industrial relations system.* London: Allen & Unwin.

FRENCH, J. and RAVEN, B. (1959) The bases of social power. In D. Cartwright and A. Zander (eds) *Group dynamics.* New York: Harper & Row.

FRICKEL, S. and MOORE, K. (eds) (2006) *The new political sociology of science: institutions, networks and power.* Madison, WI: University of Wisconsin Press.

FRIEDMAN, A. and MILES, S. (2006) *Stakeholders: theory and practice.* Oxford: Oxford University Press.

FRIESEN, D., HERON, R., HOLDAWAY, E., KELSEY, J. and SACKNEY, L. (1978) *Organizational structures: the educational sector.* Edmonton: University of Alberta.

FUKUYAMA, F. (1992) *The end of history and the last man.* London: Hamish Hamilton.

GALBRAITH, J. (1952) *American capitalism.* Boston, MA: Houghton Mifflin.

GALBRAITH, J. (1967) *The new industrial state.* Harmondsworth: Penguin.

GALBRAITH, J. (1984) *Anatomy of power*. London: Hamish Hamilton.

GALBRAITH, J. (1993) *The culture of contentment*. Harmondsworth: Penguin.

GALLIE, D. (1978) *In search of the new working class*. Cambridge: Cambridge University Press.

GAMBLE, A. (1994) *The free economy and strong state*. London: Macmillan.

GATRELL, C. and SWAN, E. (2008) *Gender diversity in management: a concise introduction*. London: Sage.

GENNARD, J. and KELLY, J. (1997) The unimportance of labels: the diffusion of the personnel/HRM function. *Industrial Relations Journal*. Vol. 28, No. 4, 27–42.

GEPPERT, M. and MAYER, M. (2006) *Global, national and local practices in multinational companies*. Basingstoke: Palgrave Macmillan.

GHOSAL, A. (2006) *Robotics: fundamental concepts and analysis*. Oxford: Oxford University Press.

GIBBON, S. and NOVAS, C. (eds) (2008) *Biosocialities, genetics and the social sciences*. Abingdon: Rutledge.

GIDDENS, A. (1981) *The class structure of advanced societies*. London: Hutchinson.

GIDDENS, A. (1985) *A contemporary critique of historical materialism*. Vol. 2: *The nation state and violence*. Cambridge: Polity Press.

GIDDENS, A. (1990) *The consequences of modernity*. Cambridge: Polity Press.

GIDDENS, A. (1992) *The transformation of intimacy: sexuality, love and eroticism in modern societies*. Cambridge: Polity Press.

GIDDENS, A. (1998) *The third way: the renewal of social democracy*. Cambridge: Polity Press.

GIDDENS, A. (2009) *Sociology*. 6th ed. Cambridge: Polity Press.

GITTINS, D. (1993) *The family in question*. London: Macmillan.

GODARD, J. (2004) A critical assessment of the high performance paradigm. *British Journal of Industrial Relations*. Vol. 42, No. 2, 349–78.

GOLDEN, K. and RAMANUJAM, V. (1985) Between a dream and a nightmare: on the integration of the human resource management and strategic planning processes. *Human Resource Management*. Vol. 24, No. 4, 429–52.

GOLDTHORPE, J., LOCKWOOD, D., BECHOFER, F. and PLATT, J. (1968) *The affluent worker: industrial attitudes and behaviour*. Cambridge: Cambridge University Press.

GOODERMAN, P. and BREWSTER, C. (2003) Convergence, statis or divergence? The case of personnel management in Europe. *Beta*, Vol. 17, No. 1, 6–18.

GOOS, M. and MANNING, A. (2003) McJobs and Macjobs: the growing polarisation of jobs in the UK. In R. Dickens, P. Gregg and J. Wadsworth (eds) *The labour market under new labour*. Basingstoke: Palgrave.

GOULDNER, A. (1954) *Patterns of industrial bureaucracy*. New York: Free Press.

GOULDNER, A. (1960) The norm of reciprocity. *American Sociological Review*. Vol. 25, 161–78.

GOULDNER, A. (1980) *The two Marxisms*. London: Macmillan.

GRANT, R. (1996) Toward a knowledge-based theory of the firm. *Strategic Management Journal*. Vol. 17, No. 2, 109–22.

GRANT, R. (1991) The resource-based theory of competitive advantage: implications for competitive advantage. *California Management Review*. Summer, 114–35.

GRANT, R. (2008) *Contemporary strategy analysis*. 6th ed. Oxford: Blackwell.

GRANT, W. (2000) *Pressure groups and british politics*. Basingstoke: Palgrave.

GRANT, W. (2002) *Economic policy in Britain*. Basingstoke: Palgrave.

GRAY, J. (2009) *False dawn: the delusions of global capitalism*. 2nd ed. London: Routledge.

GREY, C. (2009) *A very short, fairly interesting and reasonable cheap book about studying organizations*. 2nd ed. London: Sage.

GRIFFITHS, A. and WALL, S. (eds) (2004) *Applied economics*. Harlow: Financial Times Prentice Hall.

GRINT, K. and WOOLGAR, S. (1997) *The machine at work: technology, work and organisation*. Cambridge: Polity Press.

GRÜBLER, A. (1998) *Technology and global change*. Cambridge: Cambridge University Press.

GUEST, D. (1987) Human resource management and industrial relations. *Journal of Management Studies*. Vol. 24, No. 5, 503–21.

GUEST, D. (1989) Personnel and HRM: can you tell the difference? *Personnel Management*. January, 48–51.

GUEST, D. (1997) Human resource management and performance: a review and research agenda. *International Journal of Human Resource Management*. Vol. 8, No. 3, 263–76.

GUEST, D. (2001) Human resource management: when research confronts theory. *International Journal of Human Resource Management*. Vol. 12, No. 7, 1092–1106.

GUEST, D. and CONWAY, N. (2002) *Pressure at work and the psychological contract: research report*. London: CIPD.

GUEST, D., MICHIE, J., CONWAY, N. and SHEEHAN, M. (2003) Human resource management and performance. British Journal of Industrial Relations. Vol. 41, No. 2, 291–314.

GUEST, D., MICHIE, J., SHEEHAN, M., CONWAY, N. and METOCHI, M. (2000) Effective people management. London: CIPD.

GUEST, D. and PECCEI, R. (2001) Partnership at work: mutuality and the balance of advantage. British Journal of Industrial Relations. Vol. 39, No. 2, 207–36.

GUMMESSON, E. (2008) Total relationship marketing. 3rd ed. Amsterdam: Butterworth-Heinemann.

GURRIA, A. (2006) Address given to the Warsaw School of Economics by the Secretary-General, OECD. Challenges of globalisation: role of the OECD. 24 November.

HAGE, J. and AIKEN, M. (1969) Routine technology, social structure and organizational goals. Administrative Science Quarterly. Vol. 14, 366–76.

HALES, C. (2001) Managing through organization: the management process, forms of organization and the work of managers. 2nd ed. London: Thomson Learning.

HALL, P. and PRESTON, P. (1988) The carrier wave: new information technology and the geography of innovation. London: Unwin Hyman.

HALSEY, A. (2000) A hundred years of social change. In Social Trends No. 30. London: Office for National Statistics.

HAMEL, G. and PRAHALAD, C. (1989) Strategic intent. Harvard Business Review. May–June, 63–76.

HAMEL, G. and PRAHALAD, C. (1994) Competing for the future. Boston, MA: Harvard Business School Press.

HAMPDEN-TURNER, C. and TROMPENAARS, F. (1993) The seven cultures of capitalism. New York: Piatkus.

HANSEN, M., NOHRIA, N. and TIERNEY, T. (1999) What's your strategy for managing knowledge? Harvard Business Review. March–April. 106–16.

HARBISON, F. and MYERS, C. (1959) Management in the industrial world. New York: McGraw-Hill.

HARDT, M. and NEGRI, A. (2000) Empire. Cambridge, MA: Harvard University Press.

HARRIS, P. (1997) An introduction to law. London: Butterworth.

HARRIS, P. and BUCKLE, J. (1976) Philosophies of the law and the law teacher. The Law Teacher.

HARRISON, B. (1994) *Lean and mean: the changing landscape of corporate power in the age of flexibility.* New York: Basic Books.

HARRISON, R. (2009) *Learning and development.* 5th ed. London: CIPD.

HARVEY, B. and PARRY, D. (2000) *The law of consumer protection and fair trading.* London: Butterworth.

HATCH, M. and CUNLIFFE, A. (2006) *Organization theory: modern, symbolic and postmodern perspectives.* 2nd ed. Oxford: Oxford University Press.

HAX, A. and MAJLUF, N. (1996) *The strategy concept and process: a pragmatic approach.* London: Prentice Hall.

HAYEK, F. (1944) *The road to serfdom.* London: Routledge.

HECKSCHER, C. (1994) Defining the post-bureaucratic type. In C. Heckscher and A. Donnellon (eds) *The post-bureaucratic organization: new perspectives on organizational change.* Thousand Oaks, CA: Sage.

HEDING, T., KNUDTZEN, C. and BJERRE, M. (2009) *Brand management: research, theory and practice.* London: Routledge.

HELD, D., GOLDBLATT, D. and PARRATON, J. (1997) *Global transformations.* Cambridge: Polity Press.

HERTZ, N. (2001) *The silent takeover: global capitalism and the death of democracy.* London: Heinemann.

HERZBERG, F. (1966) *Work and the nature of man.* Cleveland: World Publishing.

HESTER, R. and HARRISON, R. (eds) (2004) *Transportation and the environment.* Cambridge: Royal Society of Chemistry.

HEYWOOD, A. (2008) *Essentials of UK politics.* Basingstoke: Palgrave Macmillan.

HICKSON, D., PUGH, D. and PHEYSEY, D. (1969) Operations technology and organizational structure: an empirical study. *Administrative Science Quarterly.* Vol. 14, 378–97.

HIGGINS, J. and VINCZE, J. (1993) *Strategic management: text and cases.* Fort Worth: The Dryden Press.

HILL, A. and HILL, T. (2009) *Manufacturing operations strategy.* Basingstoke: Palgrave Macmillan.

HIRST, P. and THOMPSON, G. (1996) *Globalisation in question.* Cambridge: Polity Press.

HOBBES, T. (1947) *Leviathian.* Oxford: Blackwell.

HOBSBAWN, E. (1964) The machine breakers. In E. Hobsbawn, *Labouring Men.* London: Weidenfeld & Nicolson.

HOBSBAWN, E. and RUDÉ, G. (1969) *Captain Swing*. London: Lawrence & Wishart.

HODGETTS, R. and LUTHANS, F. (2003) *International management: culture, strategy and behavior*. New York: McGraw-Hill.

HOFSTEDE, G. (2001) *Culture's consequences: comparing values, behaviors, institutions and organizations across nations*. Thousand Oaks, CA: Sage.

HOLLINSHEAD, G. (2010) *International and comparative human resource management*. Maidenhead: McGraw-Hill Higher Education.

HOME OFFICE. (2010) www.ukba.homeoffice.gov.uk, accessed 26 February.

HOPPER, K. and HOPPER, W. (2009) *The Puritan gift: reclaiming the American dream amidst global financial chaos*. London: Tauris.

HORTON, S. (2005) Trajectories, institutions and stakeholders in public management reform. In D. Farnham, A. Hondegehem and S. Horton, *Staff participation in public management reform: some international comparisons*. London: Palgrave.

HORTON, S. and FARNHAM, D. (eds) (1999) *Public management in Britain*. London: Macmillan.

HOUSE OF LORDS SELECT COMMITTEE ON ECONOMIC AFFAIRS (2008) *The economic impact of immigration: Vol. 1 report*. London: The Stationery Office.

HOWES, P. (2009) Strategic Workforce Planning: seminar 14 – CIPD Annual Conference. September.

HOYLE, D. (2006) *ISO 9000 Quality systems handbook*. Oxford: Butterworth-Heinemann.

HREBINIAK, L. and JOYCE, W. (1984) *Implementing strategy*. New York: Macmillan.

HUGHES, O. (2003) *Public management and administration*. 3rd ed. New York: Palgrave.

HUSELID, M. (1995) The impact of human resource management practices on turnover, productivity and corporate financial performance. *Academy of Management Journal*. Vol. 38, No.3, 635–70.

HUSELID, M., BEATTY, R., and BECKER, B. (2005) 'A players' or 'A positions'? The strategic logic of workforce management. *Harvard Business Review*. December, 110–17.

HUTCHINSON, S. and PURCELL, J. (2003) *Bringing policies to life: the vital role of front line managers in people management*. London: CIPD.

HUTTON, W. (1995). *The state we're in*. London: Cape.

HUTTON, W. (2002). *The world we're in*. London: Little Brown.

INDUSTRIAL PARTNERSHIP ASSOCIATION. (1992) *Towards industrial partnership*. London: IPA.

INDUSTRIAL RELATIONS SERVICES. (2003) IRS employment review 785: employers beg to differ. 3 October, 42–48.

INDUSTRIAL RELATIONS SERVICES. (2004) HR roles and responsibilities: climbing the admin mountain. *Employment. Review*. No. 795, 9–15.

INGELHART, R. and WELZEL, C. (2005) *Modernisation, cultural change and democracy*. Cambridge: Cambridge University Press.

JACKSON, M. (2007) *Micro and nanomanufacturing*. West Lafayette, IN: Springer Science.

JACKSON, P. and VAN DER WIELEN, J. (eds) (1998) *Teleworking: international perspectives, from telecommuting to the virtual organisation*. London: Routledge.

JACKSON, S. and SCHULER, R. (1995) Understanding human resource management in the context of organizations and their environment. *Annual Review of Psychology*. Vol. 46, 237–64.

JACKSON, S. SCHULER, R. and RIVERO, J. (1989) Organizational characteristics as predictors of personnel practices. *Personnel Psychology*. Vol. 42, 727–86.

JACKSON, T. (2009) *Prosperity without growth: economics for a finite planet*. London: Earthscan.

JAMES, O. (2007) *Affluenza*. London: Random House.

JOHNSON, G. and SCHOLES, K. (eds) (2001) *Exploring public sector strategy*. Harlow: Prentice Hall.

JOHNSON, G. SCHOLES, K. and WHITTINGTON, R. (2008) *Exploring corporate strategy*. 8th ed. Hemel Hempstead: Prentice Hall Europe.

JOHNSON, G. SCHOLES, K. and WHITTINGTON, R. (2009) *Fundamentals of strategy*. Harlow: Financial Times.

JOHNSON, T. (1972) *Professions and power*. London: Macmillan.

JONES, T. (2001) *Artificial intelligence: a systems approach*. Hingham, MA: Infinity Science.

JOYCE, P. (1999) *Strategic management for the public services*. Buckingham: Open University Press.

KAHIN, B. and FORAY, D. (eds) (2006) *Advancing knowledge and the knowledge economy*. Cambridge, MA: MIT.

KAHN-FREUND, O. (1983) *Labour and the law*. 3rd ed. London: Stevens.

KANDOLA, B. (2009) *The value of difference: eliminating bias in organisations*. Oxford: Pearn Kandola.

KANDOLA, P. (2009) *Managing diversity*. 2nd ed. London: CIPD.

KANDOLA, R. and FULLERTON, J. (1994) *Managing the mosaic: diversity in action*. London: Institute of Personnel and Development.

KANTER, R. (1984) *The change masters*. London: Allen & Unwin.

KAPTEIN, M. and WEMPE, J. (2002) *The balanced company: a theory of corporate integrity*. Oxford: Oxford University Press.

KATZ, D. and KAHN, R. (1978) *The social psychology of organizations*. New York: Wiley.

KAY, J. (2003) *The truth about markets: their genius, their limits, their follies*. London: Allen Lane.

KEENOY, T. (1990) Human resource management: rhetoric, reality and contradiction. *International Journal of Human Resource Management*. Vol. 1, No. 3, 363–84.

KELLIHER, C. and PERRETT, G. (2001) Business strategy and approaches to HRM: a case study of new developments in the UK restaurant industry. *Personnel Review*. Vol. 30, No. 4, 421–37.

KERR, C., DUNLOP, J., HARBISON, F. and MYERS, C. (1960) *Industrialism and industrial man: the problems of labor and management in economic growth*. Boston, MA: Harvard University Press.

KEYNES, J.M. (1936) *The general theory of employment, interest and money*. London: Macmillan.

KICKERT, W. (ed) (1997) *Public management and administrative reform in Western Europe*. Cheltenham: Edward Elgar.

KIPNIS, D., SCHMIDT, C. and WILKINSON, I. (1984) Patterns of managerial influence: shotgun managers, tacticians and politicians. *Organizational Dynamics*. Winter, 58–67.

KIRTON, G. and GREENE, A.-M. (2004) *The dynamics of managing diversity: a critical approach*. 2nd ed. Oxford: Elsevier-Butterworth-Heinemann.

KITSON, A. and CAMPBELL, R. (1996) *The ethical organisation: ethical theory and corporate behaviour*. Basingstoke: Macmillan.

KLASS, B., McCLENDON, J. and GAINEY, T. (2001) Outsourcing HR: the impact of organisational characteristics. *Human Resource Management Journal*. Vol. 40, No. 2, 125–38.

KOCHAN, T. and BAROCCI, T. (1985) (1985) *Human resource management and industrial relations*. Boston, MA: Little Brown.

KOCHAN, T., KATZ, H. and CAPELLI, R. (1986) *The transformation of American industrial relations*. New York: Basic Books.

KONTRAKOU, V. (ed) (2004) *Contemporary issues and debates in EU policy.* Manchester: Manchester University Press.

KORNBERGER, M., CLEGG, S. and PITSIS, T. (2008) *Managing and organizations: an introduction to theory and practice.* 2nd ed. London: Sage.

KOTTER, J. (1982) *The general managers.* New York: Free Press.

KRUEGER, A. (2003) Address given to the University of California at San Diego, by the Acting Managing Director IMF: Promoting international financial stability: the IMF at 60. 3 June.

LABOUR PARTY. (2010) *Labour Party manifesto: a fair future for all.* London: Labour Party.

LAL, H. (2008) *Organizational excellence through total quality management: a practical approach.* New Delhi: New Age International Publishers.

LANDES, D. (2003) *The unbound Prometheus: technological change and industrial development in Western Europe from 1750 to the present.* 2nd ed. Cambridge: Cambridge University Press.

LASH, S. and URRY, J. (1994) *Economies of signs and space.* London: Sage.

LATIFI, R. (ed) (2008) *Current practices and principles of telemedicine and e-health.* Oxford: IOS Press.

LAUDON, K. and LAUDON, J. (eds) (2010) *Management information systems: managing the digital firm.* 11th ed. Upper Saddle River, NJ: Pearson.

LAWTON, A. (1998) *Ethical management for the public services.* Buckingham: Open University Press.

LAYARD, R. (2005) *Happiness: lessons from a new science.* London: Penguin.

LAZAR, O. (2006) Examining existing concepts of power: multinational corporations and influence in world politics. Paper presented at the annual meeting of the International Studies Association, Montreal, Quebec, Canada, 17 March.

LEAVY, D. and WILSON, D. (1994) *Strategy and leadership.* London: Routledge.

LEGGE, K. (1978) *Power, innovation and problem-solving in personnel management.* London: McGraw-Hill.

LEGGE, K. (1995) *Human resource management: rhetoric and realities.* London: Macmillan.

LEITCH, Lord. (2006) *Leitch review of skills final report: prosperity for all in the global economy – world class skills.* London: HM Treasury.

LENGNICK HALL, C. and LENGNICK HALL, M. (1988) Strategic human resource management: a review of the literature and a proposed typology. *Academy of Management Review.* Vol. 13, No. 3, 454–70.

LEPAK, D. and SNELL, S. (1999) The human resource architecture: toward a theory of human capital allocation and development. *Academy of Management Review*. Vol. 38, 599–612.

LEPAK, D. and SNELL, S. (2007) Employment sub-systems and the HR architecture. In P. Boxall, J. Purcell and P. Wright (eds) *Oxford handbook of human resource management*. Oxford: Oxford University Press.

LIBERAL DEMOCRATS (2010) *Manifesto: change that works – building a fairer Britain*. London: Liberal Democrats.

LICKERT, R. (1967) *The human organization*. New York: McGraw-Hill.

LITTLER, C. and SALAMAN, G. (1982) Bravermania and beyond. *Sociology*. Vol. 16, 251–69.

LITVIN, D. (2002) The business case for diversity and the 'Iron Case'. In B. Czarniawska and H. Hopfl (eds) *Casting the other: the production and maintenance of inequalities in work organizations*. London: Routledge.

LOCKE, J. (1947) *An essay concerning the true original, extent and end of civil government*. Oxford: Oxford University Press.

LOCKE, R., KOCHAN, T. and PIORE, M. (eds) (1995) *Employment relations in a changing world economy*. Cambridge, MA: MIT Press.

LOCKWOOD, D. (1958) *The blackcoated worker*. London: Allen & Unwin.

LONDON SCHOOL OF ECONOMICS AND POLITICAL SCIENCE (2010) www.lse.ac.uk, accessed 26 February.

LONDON STOCK EXCHANGE GROUP (2009) *Interim Report*. London: LSE.

LOOS, E., HADDON, L. and MANTE-MEIJER, E. (eds) (2008) *The social dynamics of information and communication technology*. Aldershot: Ashgate.

LUKES, S. (2005) *Power: a radical view*. 2nd ed. London: Macmillan.

LUND, B. (1996) *Housing problems and housing policy*. Harlow: Longman.

LUTHANS, F., SCHONBERGER, R. and MOREY, R. (1976) *Introduction to management: a contingency approach*. New York: McGraw-Hill.

LYNCH, R. (2006) *Corporate strategy*. Harlow: Pearson Education.

LYNN, L. (2006), *Public management: old and new*. London: Routledge.

LYON, J. and GORNER P. (1995) *Altered fates: gene therapy and the retooling of human life*. New York: Norton.

MACDUFFIE, J. (1995) Human resource bundles and manufacturing performance: organizational logic and flexible production systems in the world autoindustry. *Industrial and Labor Relations Review*. Vol. 48, No. 2, 197–221.

MACPHERSON, C. (1962) *The political theory of possessive individualism.* Oxford: Oxford University Press.

MANDL, U., DIERX, A. and ILZKOVITZ, F. (2008) *The effectiveness and efficiency of public spending.* Luxembourg: European Commission.

MANN, M. (1997) Has globalisation ended the rise and rise of the nation state? *Review of International Political Economy.* Vol. 2, No. 4, 472–96.

MANT, A. (1979) *The rise and fall of the British manager.* Revised edition. London: Pan Books.

MARCHINGTON, M. (2005) Employee involvement: patterns and explanations. In B. Harley, J. Hyman and P. Thompson (eds) *Participation and Democracy at Work.* Basingstoke: Palgrave.

MARCHINGTON, M., CARROLL, M., GRIMSHAW, D., PASS, S. and RUBERY, J. (2009) *Managing people across networks.* London: CIPD.

MARCHINGTON, M., GRIMSHAW, D., RUBERY, J. and WARD, K. (2004) *Fragmenting work: blurring organizational boundaries and disordering hierarchies.* Oxford: Oxford University Press.

MARCHINGTON, M. and GRUGULIS, I. (2000) 'Best practice' human resource management: perfect opportunity or dangerous illusion? *International Journal of Human Resource Management.* Vol. 11, No. 4, 905–25.

MARCHINGTON, M. and WILKINSON, A. (2008) *Human resource management at work: people management and development.* 4th ed. London: CIPD.

MARRIS, R. (1964) *The economic theory of managerial capitalism.* Basingstoke: Macmillan.

MASLOW, A. (1943) A human theory of motivation. *Psychological Review.* Vol. 50, 370–96.

MASSEY, A. and PYPER, R. (2005), *Public management and modernisation in Britain,* Basingstoke: Palgrave Macmillan.

MAURICE, M., SELLIER, F. and SILVERSTRE, J. (1986) *The social foundations of industrial power.* Cambridge, MA: MIT Press.

MAY, S., CHENEY, G. and ROPER, J. (eds) (2007) *The debate over corporate responsibility.* Oxford: Oxford University Press.

MAYO, E. (1933) *The human problems of an industrial civilization.* New York: Macmillan.

McCANN, D. (2008) *Regulating flexible work.* Oxford: Oxford University Press.

McGREGOR, D. (1960) *The human side of enterprise.* London: McGraw-Hill.

McLELLAN, D. (2007) *Marxism after Marx.* 4th ed. Basingstoke: Palgrave Macmillan.

McORMOND, T. (2004) Changes in working trends over the past decade. *Labour Market Trends*. January, Vol. 112, No. 8, 25–35.

MECKLENBERG, S., DEERING, A. and SHARP, D. (1999) Knowledge management: a secret engine of corporate growth. *Executive Agenda*. Vol. 2, No. 2, 5–15.

MELLAHI, K. and WOOD, G. (2003) *The ethical business: challenges and controversies*. Basingstoke: Palgrave.

MERKLE, J. (1980) *Management and ideology*. Berkeley, CA: University of California Press.

MIGRATION WATCH (2010) What is the problem? Press Release, January.

MILES, R. and SNOW, C. (1984) *Organisational strategy, structure and process*. New York: McGraw-Hill.

MILL, J. S. (1972) *Utilitarianism, liberty and representative government*. London: Dent.

MILLER, D. (1992) Generic strategies: classification, combination and context. *Advances in Strategic Management*. Vol. 8, 391–408.

MILLER, D. and FRIESON, P. (1984) *Organisations: a quantum view*. New York: Harper.

MILLER, J. and McCARTNEY, C. (2010) *Sustainable organisational performance: what really makes the difference?* London: CIPD.

MILLER, P. and ROSE, N. (2008) *Governing the present: administering economic, social and political life*. Cambridge: Polity Press.

MILLERSON, G. (1964) *The qualifying associations*. London: Routledge & Kegan Paul.

MINISTRY OF HEALTH (1997) *The new NHS: modern, dependable*. London: Ministry of Health.

MINTZBERG, H. (1980) *The nature of managerial work*. London: Prentice Hall.

MINTZBERG, H. (1983) *Power in and around organizations*. Englewood Cliffs, NJ: Prentice Hall.

MINTZBERG, H. (1984) Power and organizational life cycles. *Academy of Management Review*. Vol. 9, No. 2, 207–24.

MINTZBERG, H. (1987a) The strategy concept: the five P's for strategy. *California Management Review*, Fall.

MINTZBERG, H. (1987b) Crafting strategy. *Harvard Business Review*. Vol. 65, No. 4, 65–75.

MINTZBERG, H. (1989) Strategy formation: schools of thought. In J. Fredrickson (ed) *Perspectives on strategic management*. California: Ballinger.

MINTZBERG, H. (1994) *The rise and fall of strategic planning*. London: Prentice Hall.

MINTZBERG, H. (2002) The organization as a political arena. In S. Clegg (ed) *Current trends in organization studies II*. London: Sage.

MINTZBERG, H., QUINN, J. and GHOSAL, S. (1998) *The strategy process*. London: Prentice Hall.

MOHRMAN, S., COHEN, S. and MOHRMAN, A. (1995) *Designing team-based organizations*. San Francisco, CA: Jossey-Bass.

MITCHELL, R., AGLE, B. and WOOD, D. (1997) Towards a theory of stakeholder identification and salience: defining the principle of who and what really counts. *Academy of Management Review*. Vol. 22, No. 4, 853–86.

MONBIOT, G. (2001) *The captive state: the corporate takeover of Britain*. London: Pan Books.

MONKS, K. (1992) Models of personnel management: a means of understanding the diversity of personnel practices? *Human Resource Management Journal*. Vol. 3, No. 2, 29–41.

MONKS, R. and MINOW, N. (2008) *Corporate governance*. 4th ed. Chichester: Wiley.

MORAN, M. (2003) *The British regulatory state: high modernism and hyper-innovation*. Oxford: Oxford University Press.

MORAN, M. (2005) *Politics and governance in the UK*. Basingstoke: Palgrave Macmillan.

MORRIS, S. and SNELL, S. (2009) The evolution of HR strategy: adaptations in increasing global complexity. In A. Wilkinson, N. Bacon, T. Redman and S. Snell (eds) *The SAGE handbook of human resource management*. London: Sage.

MUELLER, F. (1996) Human resources as strategic assets: an evolutionary resource-based theory. *Journal of Management Studies*. Vol. 33, No. 6, 757–85.

MUMFORD, L. (1967) *The myth of the machine. Volume 1: technics and human development*. San Diego, CA: Harcourt, Brace Jovanovich.

NAHAPIET, J. and GHOSHAL, S. (1998) Social capital, intellectual capital, and organizational advantage. *Academy of Management Review*. Vol. 23, No. 2, 242–66.

NATIONAL HUB OF EXPERTISE IN GOVERNANCE (2005) *Good governance: a code for the voluntary and community sector*. London: NCVO.

NEGROPONTE, N. (1995) *Being digital*. New York: Alfred A. Knopf.

NELSON, R. (1994) An agenda formal growth theory. Unpublished paper, Columbia University, Department of Economics.

NIXON, P. and KOUTRAKOU, V. (2007) (eds) *E-government in Euro: re-booting the state*. London: Routledge.

NOBES, C. and PARKER, R. (2008) *Comparative international accounting*. 10th ed. Harlow: Financial Times Prentice Hall.

NOBLE, D. (1984) *Forces of production: a social history of industrial automation*. New York: Knopf.

NOLAN, Lord. (1997) *First report of the Committee on Public Life*. London: HMSO.

NONAKA, I. and TAKEUCHI, H. (1995) *The knowledge-creating company: how Japanese companies create the dynamics of innovation*. Oxford: Oxford University Press.

NORTH, N. (2001) Health policy. In S. Savage and R. Atkinson (eds) *Public policy under Blair*. Basingstoke: Palgrave.

NUGENT, N. (ed) (2004) *European Union enlargement*. Basingstoke: Palgrave.

OATLEY, T. (2004) *International political economy: interests and institutions in the global economy*. New York: Pearson Longman.

OFFICE FOR NATIONAL STATISTICS (OFNS) (2008a) *Labour force survey: April–June*. London: OFNS.

OFNS (2008b) *Economic and labour market review: December*. London: OFNS.

OFNS (2009a) *Economic and labour market trends: December*. London: OFNS.

OFNS (2009b) *Social trends*. London: OFNS.

OFFICE FOR NATIONAL STATISTICS (2010) *Economic and Labour Review*. London: OFNS.

OFFICE OF FAIR TRADING (2007) *Annual report*. London: OFT.

OHMAE, K. (1995) *The end of the nation-state*. London: HarperCollins.

ORGANISATION FOR ECONOMIC CO-OPERATION AND DEVELOPMENT (2009) *Annual report*. Paris: OECD.

ORMEROD, P. (1998) *Butterfly economics: a new general theory of social and economic behaviour*. London: Faber & Faber.

OULTON, N. (1995) Supply side reform and UK economic growth: what happened to the miracle? *National Institute Economic Review*. Vol. 154, No. 1, 53–70.

OWEN, G. (1999) *From empire to Europe: the decline and revival of British industry since the Second World War*. London: HarperCollins.

PAAUWE, J. and BOSELIE, P. (2003) Challenging 'strategic HRM' and the relevance of the institutional setting. *Human Resource Management Journal*. Vol. 13, No. 3, 56–70.

PAINTER, C. and ISAAC-HENRY, K. (1999) Local government. In S. Horton and D. Farnham (eds) *Public Management in Britain*. Basingstoke: Macmillan.

PARK, A. and SURRIDGE, P. (2003) Charting change in British values. In A. Park, J. Curtice, K. Thomson, L. Jarvis and C. Bromley (eds) *British social attitudes: the 20th report*. London: Sage.

PARK, A., PHILLIPS, M. and THOMSON, K. (2010) *British social attitudes survey: 26th report*. London: Sage.

PARKER, M. (2002) *Against management: organization in the age of managerialism*. Cambridge: Polity Press.

PEARCE, J. (2009) *Formulation, implementation, and control of competitive strategy*. 11th ed. Boston, MA: Irwin.

PEDLER, M., BURGOYNE, J. and BOYDELL, T. (1997) *The learning company: a strategy for sustainable development*. 2nd ed. London: McGraw-Hill.

PEET, R. (2009) *Unholy trinity: the IMF, World Bank, and WTO*. 2nd ed. London: Zed.

PELTIER, T. (2009) *How to complete a risk assessment in 5 days or less*. Boca Raton: CRC Press.

PENROSE, E. (1959) *The theory of the growth of the firm*. Oxford: Blackwell.

PERROW, C. (1970) *Organisational analysis: a sociological view*. London: Tavistock.

PERROW, C. (1979) *Complex organizations: a critical essay*. Dallas: Scott Foresman.

PETERS, T. and WATERMAN, R. (1982) *In search of excellence*. New York: Harper & Row.

PETRELLA, R. (1996) Globalisation and internationalisation. In R. Boyer and D. Drache (eds) *States against states*. London: Routledge.

PETTIGREW, A. (2002) Strategy formulation as a political process. In S.Clegg (ed) *Current trends in organization studies II*. London: Sage.

PETTIGREW, A. and WHIPP, R. (1991) *Managing change for competitive success*. Oxford: Blackwell.

PFEFFER, J. (1994) *Competitive advantage through people*. Boston, MA: Harvard Business School Press.

PFEFFER, J. (1998) *The human equation: building profits by putting people first*. Boston, MA: Harvard Business School Press.

PFEFFER, J. (1992) Understanding power in organizations. *California Management Review*. Vol. 35, 29–50.

PFEFFER, J. and SALANCIK, G. (1978) *The external control of organisations: a resource dependence perspective.* New York: Harper & Row.

PIL, F. and MACDUFFIE, J. (1996) The adoption of high involvement work practices. *Industrial Relations.* Vol. 35, No. 3, 423–55.

PILBEAM, S. and CORBRIDGE, M. (2010) *People resourcing and talent management.* 4th ed. Harlow: Financial Times Prentice Hall.

PIORE, M. and SABEL, C. (1984) *The second industrial divide: possibilities for prosperity.* New York: Basic Books.

POLANYI, K. (1944) *The great transformation.* Boston, MA: Beacon Press.

POLLARD, S. (1969) *The development of the British economy 1914–1967.* London: Allen & Unwin.

POLLITT, C. (1993) *Managerialism and the public services.* Oxford: Blackwell.

POLLITT, C. (1998) Evaluation and the new public management: an international perspective. *Evaluation Journal of Australasia,* Vol. 9, No. 1, 7–15.

POLLITT, C. and BOUCKAERT, G. (2004) *Public management reform: a comparative analysis.* 2nd ed. Oxford: Oxford University Press.

PORTER, M. (1998) *Competitive strategy: creating and sustaining superior performance.* New York: Free Press.

PORTER, M. (2004) *Competitive strategy: creating and sustaining superior performance.* 2nd ed. New York: Free Press.

POST, J, LAWRENCE, A. and WEBER, J. (2002) *Business and society: corporate strategy, public policy, ethics.* Boston, MA: Irwin/McGraw-Hill.

POULANTZAS, N. (1975) *Classes in contemporary capitalism.* London: New Left Books.

POWELL, M. (1999) (ed) *New Labour, new welfare state? The third way in British social policy.* Bristol: Policy Press.

POWELL, M. (ed) (2008) *Modernising the welfare state: the Blair legacy.* Bristol: Policy Press.

PRADEEP, T. (2008) *Nano: the essentials – understanding nanoscience and nanotechnology.* New Delhi: McGraw-Hill.

PRIEM, R. and BUTLER, J. (2001) Is the resource-based 'view' a useful perspective for strategic management research? *Academy of Management Research.* Vol. 26, No. 1, 22–40.

PROCTOR, S. and CURRIE, G. (1999) The role of the personnel function: roles, perceptions and processes in an NHS trust. *International Journal of Human Resource Management.* Vol. 10, No. 6, 1077–91.

PURCELL, J., KINNIE, N., HUTCHINSON, S., RAYTON, B. and SWART, J. (2003) *Understanding the people performance link: unlocking the black box.* London: CIPD.

QUINN, J. B. (1978) Strategic change: logical incrementalism. *Sloan Management Review.* Fall.

QUINN, J. B. (1980) *Strategies for change.* Homewood, IL: Irwin.

RANDALL, A. (1991) *Before the Luddites: custom, community and machinery in the English woollen industry, 1776–1809.* Cambridge: Cambridge University Press.

RANDLESOME, C. (1993) *Business cultures in Europe.* Oxford: Butterworth-Heinemann.

RATLEDGE, C. and KRISTIANSEN, B. (2001) *Basic biotechnology.* Cambridge: Cambridge University Press.

REICH, R. (1991) *The work of nations.* New York: Alfred A. Knopf.

REILLY, P. (2000) *HR shared service and the realignment of HR: report 368.* London: Institute of Employment Studies.

RENWICK, D. (2003) Line manager involvement in HRM: an inside view. *Employee Relations.* Vol. 25, No. 4, 262–80.

RICE, A. (1963) *The enterprise and the environment.* London: Tavistock.

ROBERTS, K. (1996) Viewpoint: customer value and market-driven quality management. *Strategic Insights into Quality.* December, 16–20.

ROBERTSON, R. (1992) *Globalisation: social theory and global culture.* London: Sage.

ROETHLISBERGER, F. and DICKSON, W. (1939) *Management and the worker.* Cambridge, MA: Harvard University Press.

ROLLINSON, D. (2008) *Organisational behaviour and analysis: an integrated approach.* Harlow: Financial Times Prentice Hall.

ROMITO, P. (2008) *A deafening silence: hidden violence against women and children.* Bristol: Policy Press.

ROSE, A. and LAWTON, A. (eds) (1999) *Public services management.* Harlow: Prentice Hall.

ROUSSEAU, D. (1995) *Psychological contracts in organizations: understanding written and unwritten agreements.* Thousand Oaks, CA: Sage.

ROUSSEAU, D. and WADE-BENZONI, K. (1994) Linking strategy and human resource practices: how employee and customer contracts are created. *Human Resource Management.* Vol. 33, 463–89.

RUBERY, J. (1989) Employers and the labour market. In D. Gallie (ed) *Employment in Britain.* Oxford: Blackwell.

RUGMAN, A. and COLLINSON, S. (2009) *International business.* 5th ed. Harlow: Financial Times Prentice Hall.

RUGMAN, A. and DOH, J. (2008) *Multinationals and development.* London: Yale University Press.

RUGMAN, A. and VERBEKE, A. (2002) Edith Penrose's contribution to the resource-based view of the firm. *Strategic Management Journal.* Vol. 23, No. 8, 769–35.

RUIGROK, W. and VAN TULDER, R. (1995) *The logic of international restructuring.* London: Routledge.

RUSSELL, R. and TAYLOR, B. (2008) *Operations management: along the supply chain.* Hoboken, NJ: Wiley.

SALAMAN, G., STOREY, J. and BILLSBERRY, G. (2005), *Strategic human resource management: theory and practice.* London: Open University Press.

SAMPSON, A. (2004) *Who runs this place? The anatomy of Britain in the 21st Century.* London: Murray.

SANDERS, D. (1999) The impact of left/right ideology. In G. Evans and P. Norris (eds) *Critical elections.* London: Sage.

SANZ-VALLE, R., SABATER-SANCHEZ, R. and ARAGON-SANCHEZ, A. (1999) Human resource management and business strategy links: an empirical study. *International Journal of Human Resource Management.* Vol. 10, No. 4, 655–71.

SAVAGE, M., BARLOW, J., DICKENS, P. and FIELDING, T. (1995) *Property, Bureaucracy and Culture: middle class formation in contemporary Britain.* London: Routledge.

SCARBROUGH, H. (2008) *The evolution of business knowledge.* Oxford: Oxford University Press.

SCHEIN, E. (1980) *Organizational psychology.* 3rd ed. London: Prentice Hall.

SCHEIN, E. (1997) *Organizational culture and leadership.* San Francisco, CA: Jossey-Bass.

SCHILLER, D. (2000) *Digital capitalism: networking the global markets system.* Cambridge, MA: MIT Press.

SCHULER, R. and JACKSON, S. (1987) Linking competitive strategies with human resource management. *Academy of Management Executive.* Vol. 1, No. 3, 207–19.

SCHULTZ, T. (1971) *Investment in human capital: the role of education and of research.* New York: Free Press.

SEARS, L. (2010) *Time for change: towards next generation HR.* London: CIPD.

SELDON, A. (1990) *Capitalism.* Oxford: Blackwell.

SEMMLOW, J. (2009) *Biosignal and medical image processing.* London: CRC Press.

SEN, A. (2001) *Development as freedom.* Oxford: Oxford University Press.

SENGE, P. (1990) The leader's new work: building learning organisations. *Sloan Management Review.* Fall, 7–22.

SENNETT, R. (1998) *The corrosion of character: the personal consequences of work in the new capitalism.* New York: Norton.

SHORE, L. and WAYNE, S. (1993) Commitment and employee behaviour: comparison of affective commitment and continuance commitment with perceived human organizational support. *Journal of Applied Psychology.* Vol. 78, 774–80.

SILVA, E. and SMART, C. (1999) *The new family.* London: Sage.

SISSON, K. and STOREY, J. (2000a) *Managing human resources and industrial relations.* 2nd ed. Buckingham: Open University Press.

SISSON, K. and STOREY, J. (2000b) *Realities of human resource management: managing the employment relationship.* Buckingham: Open University Press

SLACK, N. (2009) *Operations and process management: principles and practice for strategic impact.* 2nd ed. Harlow: Financial Times Prentice Hall.

SMART, B. (1993) *Postmodernity.* London: Routledge.

SMART, C. and SHIPMAN, B. (2004) Visions in monochrome: families, marriage and the individualisation thesis. *British Journal of Sociology.* Vol. 55, No. 4, 291–309.

SMITH, I. and BAKER, A. (2010) *Smith's and Wood's employment law.* 10th ed. Oxford: Oxford University Press.

SNELL, S., SHADUR, M. and WRIGHT, P. (2001) Human resource strategy: the era of our ways. In M. Hitt, R. Freeman and J. Harrison (eds) *Handbook of strategic management.* Oxford: Blackwell.

SOETE, L. (2001) ICTs, knowledge, and employment: the challenges for Europe. *International Labour Review.* Vol. 140, No. 2, 143–62.

SOROS, G. (1995) *Soros on Soros.* New York: Wiley.

SOROS, G. (2000) *Reforming global capitalism.* New York: Little Brown.

SPANGENBERG, H. (1994) *Understanding and implementing performance management.* Cape Town: Juda.

SPARROW, P., BREWSTER, C. and HARRIS, H. (2004) (eds) *Globalising human resource management.* London: Routledge.

SPENCER-OATEY, H. (2000) *Culturally speaking: managing rapport through talk across cultures*. London: Continuum.

STACEY, R. (1993) *Strategic management and organisational dynamics*. London: Pitman.

STALLING, W. (2004) *Data and computer communications*. Upper Saddle River, NJ: Pearson Education.

STANDAGE, T. (ed) (2005) *The future of technology*. London: Profile Books.

STERN, E. and SOMMERLAD, E. (1999) *Workplace learning, culture and performance*. London: Institute of Personnel and Development.

STERNBERG, E. (2004) *Corporate governance: accountability in the marketplace*. London: Institute of Economic Affairs.

STEWART, R. (1967) *Managers and their jobs: a study of the similarities and differences in the ways managers spend their time*. Basingstoke: Macmillan.

STEWART, R. (1976) *Contrasts in management: a study of different types of managers' jobs: their demands and choices*. London: McGraw-Hill.

STIGLITZ, J. (2002) *Globalisation and its discontents*. New York: Norton.

STIGLITZ, J., EDLIN, A. and DELONG, B. (2008) *The economists' voice: top economists take on today's problems*. New York: Columbia University Press.

STOREY, J. (1992) *Developments in the management of human resources*. Oxford: Blackwell.

STOREY, J. and SISSON, K. (1993) *Managing human resources and industrial relations*. Buckingham: Open University Press.

STRACHAN, D. (2007) *The last oil shock*. London: Murray.

SUCHMAN, M. (1995) Managing legitimacy: strategic and institutional approaches. *Academy of Management Review*. Vol. 20, 571–610.

SUMMERFIELD, C. and BABB, B. (eds) (2004) *Social trends 2004*. London: National Statistics.

SWART, J., KINNIE, N. and PURCELL, J. (2003) *People and performance in knowledge-intensive firms*. London: CIPD.

TANNENBAUM, A. (1966) *Social psychology of the work organization*. London: Tavistock.

TANSLEY, C., TURNER, P., FOSTER, C. *et al*. (2007) *Talent: strategy, management, measurement*. London: CIPD.

TAYLOR, F.W. (1911, reissued 1947) *The principles of scientific management*. New York: Harper.

TAYLOR, S. (2008) *People resourcing*. 4th ed. London: CIPD.

TAYLOR, S. and EMIR, A. (2009) *Employment law: an introduction.* 2nd ed. Oxford: Oxford University Press.

THOMAS, R. (2001) UK economic policy: the Conservative legacy and New Labour's third way. In S. Savage and R. Atkinson (eds) *Public Policy under Blair.* Basingstoke: Palgrave.

THOMASON, G. (1991) The management of personnel. *Personnel Review.* Vol. 20, No. 2, 3–10.

THOMPSON, J. (1967) *Organizations in action.* New York: McGraw-Hill.

THOMPSON, P. and McHUGH, D. (2002) *Work organisations.* 3rd ed. Basingstoke: Palgrave Macmillan.

THURLEY, K. and WIRDENIUS, H. (1989) *Towards European management.* London: Pitman.

TIERNAN, S., MORLEY, M. and FOLEY, E. (2001) *Modern management.* Dublin: Gill & Macmillan.

TOFFLER, A. (1970) *Future shock.* New York: Random House.

TOFFLER, A. (1981) *The third wave.* New York: Bantam Books.

TOMKINS, C. (1987) *Achieving economy, efficiency and effectiveness in the public sector.* London: Routledge.

TORRINGTON, D., HALL, L. and TAYLOR, S. (2008) *Human resource management.* 7th ed. Harlow: Financial Times Prentice Hall.

TORRINGTON, D., HALL, L., TAYLOR, S. and ATKINSON, C. (2009) *Fundamentals of human resource management.* Harlow: Pearson Education.

TRADES UNION CONGRESS. (1999) *Partnerships for progress.* London: TUC.

TRIST, E., HIGGIN, G., MURRAY, H. and POLLOCK, A. (1963) *Organisational choice.* London: Tavistock.

TROMPENNAARS, F. (1985) The organization of meaning and the meaning of organization. *American Journal of Sociology.* Vol. 56, No. 5, 395–406.

TROMPENAARS, F. and HAMPDEN-TURNER, C. (1997) *Riding the waves of culture: understanding cultural diversity in business.* 2nd ed. London: Nicholas Brealey.

TYSON, S. (1995) *Human resource strategy.* London: Pitman.

TYSON, S. and FELL, A. (1986) *Evaluating the personnel function.* London: Hutchinson.

ULRICH, D. (1997) *Human resource champions: the next agenda for adding value and delivering results.* Boston, MA: Harvard Business School Press.

ULRICH, D. and BROCKBANK, W. (2005) *The HR value proposition*. Boston, MA: Harvard Business School Press.

ULRICH, K. and EPPINGER, S. (2008) *Product design and development*. 4th ed. London: McGraw-Hill Higher Education.

UNITED NATIONS. (2000) *Millennium development goals*. New York: United Nations.

VOLBERDA, H. (1996) Toward the flexible firm: how to remain vital in hypercompetitive environments. *Organizational Science*. Vol. 7, 359–74.

VOSE, D. (2008) *Risk analysis: a quantitative guide*. 3rd ed. Chichester: Wiley.

WALTON, R. (1985) From control to commitment in the workplace. *Harvard Business Review*. Vol. 63, March–April, 76–84.

WARLEIGH, A. (2009) *European Union: the basics*. 2nd ed. London: Routledge.

WEBB, S. and WEBB, B. (1897) *Industrial democracy*. London: Trade Unionists of the United Kingdom.

WEBER, M. (1930) *The Protestant ethic and the spirit of capitalism*. London: Allen & Unwin.

WEBER, M. (1947, reissued 1964) *A theory of social and economic organization*. New York: Free Press.

WEBER, M. (1968) Status groups and classes. In G. Roth and C. Wittlich (eds) *Economy and society*. New York: Bedminster Press.

WEBER, M. (1971) Class, status and party. In K. Thompson and J. Tunstall (eds) *Sociological perspectives*. Harmondsworth: Penguin.

WEIL, D. (2009) *Economic growth*. Boston, MA: Pearson Addison-Wesley.

WELLINS, R., BYHAM, W. and DIXON, G. (1994) *Inside teams: how 20 world-class organizations are winning through teamwork*. San Francisco, CA: Jossey-Bass.

WELSTEAD, M. and EDWARDS, S. (2008) *Family law*. 2nd ed. Oxford: Oxford University Press.

WEST, M., BORRILL, C., DAWSON, J. et al. (2002) The link between the management of employees and patient mortality in acute hospitals. *International Journal of Human Resource Management*. Vol. 13, No. 8, 1299–1310.

WHITLEY, R. (2000) *Divergent capitalisms: the social structuring and change of business systems*. Oxford: Oxford University Press.

WHITMARSH, A. (1995) *Social focus on women*. London: HMSO.

WHITTINGTON, R. (2001) *What is strategy and does it matter?* 2nd ed. London: Thomson Learning.

WILKINSON, A., BACON, N., REDMAN, T. and SNELL, S. (2009) (eds) *The SAGE handbook of human resource management*. London: Sage.

WILKINSON, A. and MARCHINGTON, M. (1994) TQM: instant pudding for the personnel function? *Human Resource Management Journal*. Vol. 5, No. 1, 33–49.

WILKINSON, B., MORRIS, J. and NICH, O. (1992) Japanising the world: the case of Toyota. In J. Marceau (ed) *Reworking the world: organisations, technologies and cultures in comparative perspective*. Berlin: de Gruyter.

WILKINSON, R. and PICKETT, K. (2009) *The spirit level: why more equal societies almost always do better*. London: Allen Lane.

WILLEY, B. (2003) *Employment law in context: an introduction for HR professionals*. 2nd ed. Harlow: Pearson Education.

WILLIAMSON, O. (1991) Strategising, economising and economic organisation. *Strategic Management Journal*. Vol. 12, 75–94.

WINDRUM, P. and KOCH, P. (eds) (2008) *Innovation in public services: entrepreneurship, creativity and management*. Cheltenham: Edward Elgar.

WINSTANLEY, D. and STUART-SMITH, K. (1996) Policing performance: the ethics of performance management. *Personnel Review*. Vol. 12, No. 6, 66–84.

WINSTANLEY, D., WOODHALL, J. and HEERY, E. (1996) Business ethics and human resource management. *Personnel Review*. Vol. 25, No. 6, 5–12.

WOLF, M. (2004) *Why globalization works*. London: Yale University Press.

WOOD, F. and SANGSTER, A. (2008) *Frank Wood's business accounting 1*. 11th ed. Harlow: Financial Times Prentice Hall.

WOOD, S. (1989) (ed) *The transformation of work*. London: Allen & Unwin.

WOOD, S. (1995) The four pillars of human resource management: are they connected? *Human Resource Management Journal*. Vol. 5, No. 5, 49–59.

WOOD, S. (1999) Human resource management and performance. *International Journal of Management Reviews*. Vol. 1, No. 4, 368–413.

WOOD, S. (2003) Organisational performance and manufacturing practices. In D. Holman, T. Wall, C. Clegg, P. Sparrow and A. Howard (eds) *The new workplace: a guide to the human impact of modern working practices*. Chichester: Wiley.

WOODWARD, J. (1958) *Management and technology*. London: HMSO.

WOODWARD, J. (1965) *Industrial organisation: theory and practice*. Oxford: Oxford University Press.

WOODWARD, J. (1970) (ed) *Industrial organisation: behaviour and control*. Oxford: Oxford University Press.

WORLD BANK (2010) *World development report 2010: development and climate change.* Washington, DC: World Bank.

WRIGHT, P. and McMAHON, G. (1992) Theoretical perspectives for strategic human resource management. *Journal of Management.* Vol. 18, No. 2, 295–320.

WRIGHT, P., McMAHON, G. and McWILLIAMS, A. (1994) Human resources management and sustained competitive advantage: a resource-based perspective. *International Journal of Human Resource Management.* Vol. 5, No. 2, 301–26.

YOUNDT, M., SNELL, S., DEAN, J. Jr. and LEPAK, D. (1996) Human resource management, manufacturing strategy, and firm performance. *Academy of Management Journal.* Vol. 39, No. 4, 836–66.

YOUNG, M. (1958) *The rise of the meritocracy 1879–2033.* Harmondsworth: Penguin.

ZALEZNICK, A. (1992) Managers and leaders: are they different? *Harvard Business Review.* Vol. 70, 126–35.

Index